WORKING AMERICANS

1880–2007

Volume VIII: Immigrants

WORKING AMERICANS

1880–2007

Volume VIII: Immigrants

by Scott Derks

A Universal Reference Book

Grey House
Publishing

PUBLISHER:	Leslie Mackenzie
EDITORIAL DIRECTOR:	Laura Mars-Proietti
EDITORIAL ASSISTANT:	Jael Bridgemahon
MARKETING DIRECTOR:	Jessica Moody
AUTHOR:	Scott Derks
CONTRIBUTORS:	Hudson Cargill, Emily Marturana, Michael Marturana, Tony Smith
COPYEDITOR:	Elaine Alibrandi
COMPOSITION & DESIGN:	ATLIS Graphics

A Universal Reference Book
Grey House Publishing, Inc.
185 Millerton Road
Millerton, NY 12546
518.789.8700
FAX 518.789.0545
www.greyhouse.com
e-mail: books @greyhouse.com

Publisher's Cataloging-In-Publication Data
(Prepared by the Donohue Group, Inc.)

Derks, Scott.
    Working Americans . . . / by Scott Derks.

    v. : ill. ; cm.

Title varies.
"A universal reference book."
Includes bibliographical references and indexes.
Contents: v.1. The working class—v. 2. The middle class—v. 3. The upper class—v. 4. Their children.—v. 5. At war.—v. 6. Women at work—v. 7. Social movements—v. 8. Immigrants.
    ISBN: 1-891482-81-5 (v. 1)
    ISBN: 1-891482-72-6 (v. 2)
    ISBN: 1-930956-38-X (v.3)
    ISBN: 1-59327-024-1 (v. 5)
    ISBN: 978-1-59237-101-3 (v. 7)
    ISBN: 1-59327-101-9 (v. 7)
    ISBN: 978-1-59237-197-6 (v. 8)

1. Working class—United States—History.   2. Labor—United States—History.   3. Occupations—United States—History.
4. Social classes—United States—History.   5. Immigrants—Employment—United States—History.   6. United States—Economic conditions.   I. Title.

HD8066   .D47 2000
305.5/0973/0904

Printed in the USA

ISBN 10: 1-59237-101-9
ISBN 13: 1-978-1-59237-101-3

PREFACE

This book is the eighth in a series examining the social and economic lives of working Americans. In this volume, the focus is on immigration—the men, women and children who abandoned everything they knew for a dream called America. Some were lured to the "Gold Mountain" by economic necessity, others found themselves persecuted and in serious need of a secure home. Their stories include a French Canadian boxer who tried to fight his way out of the Depression and a Haitian artist who was detained shortly after swimming ashore south of Miami. Some immigrants arrived by boat and landed with great expectation at Ellis Island. Others traveled from Costa Rica to Paterson, New Jersey, in the hidden panel of a cousin's pickup truck. Some were successful, some were not. Some stayed, some went back. All had a part to play in painting the rich mosaic known as the United States of America.

The first volume, *Working Americans: 1880-1999: The Working Class,* explores the struggles of the working class through the eyes and wallets of three dozen families. Employing pictures, stories, statistics and advertisements of the period, it studies their jobs, wages, family life, expenditures and hobbies throughout the decades. The second and third volumes, *The Middle Class* and *The Upper Class,* capture the struggles and joys of families possessing progressively greater wealth and their roles in transforming the economy of America from 1880 to 1999. The fourth volume, *Their Children,* builds upon the social and economic issues explored previously by examining the lives of children across the entire spectrum of economic status. The issues addressed include parents, child labor, education, peer pressure, food, fads and fun. *Volume V, Americans at War,* examines the life-changing elements of war and discusses how enlisted personnel, officers and civilians handled the stress, exhilaration, boredom and brutality of America's various wars, conflicts or incursions. *Volume VI: Women at Work* celebrates the contributions of women, chronicling both the progress and the roadblocks along the way. This volume highlights the critical role of women on the frontlines of change.

Working Americans VII: Social Movements explores the various ways America's men and women felt called upon to challenge accepted convention, whether the issue was cigarette smoking in 1901 or fighting the construction of a massive hydroelectric dam in 1956.

Working Americans VIII: Immigrants examines the lives of first- and second-generation immigrants with a focus on their journey to America, their search for identity and the emotions they experienced in a new land. Along the way, we experience the joy of a seven-year-old Swedish girl when greeted by her father for the first time and the struggles of a Chinese photography assistant in 1884 San Francisco. This study profiles both the coming-to-America experience of a Dutch resistance fighter from World War II and the adjustments required of a Hmong family who arrived following the Vietnam War. Along the way we meet an Irish woman employed as a maid surprised by her American employers' indulgence of house dogs and the difference in the intensity of light in Boston versus in her home in Ireland.

Some immigrants profiled came for freedom or to escape persecution, most came for economic opportunity, all came with the dream of a better life. Not all were successful and not all wanted to stay. The immigrant's experience is as unique as each individual. What does emerge is the universality of the immigrant's desires for a better life—no matter the decade—alongside the changing attitude of Americans concerning immigrants based on world events or economic downturns. From its earliest days, America offered more freedom and often more opportunity, yet perpetually fretted over the multitude of languages, customs and political beliefs entering the country. While embracing new immigrant workers as fundamental to its economic growth, America has always shown a vacillating reluctance to accept the inevitability of change imposed by the newcomers.

As in the previous volumes, each story is unique as each of us is unique: from the Kazakh man in 1916 who finds difficulty adjusting to canned food to the WWII British war bride who futilely seeks acceptance from her new husband's family. All the profiles are modeled on real people and events, although as in the previous books in this series, the names have been changed and some details added based on statistics, the then-current popularity of an idea, or writings of the time. Otherwise, every effort has been made to profile accurately the individuals' journey to America, work experiences and impressions of their new home. To ensure that each profile reflects the feelings of the subjects, diaries, letters, biographies, interviews and magazine articles were consulted and used. In some cases the people profiled represent national trends and feelings, but mostly, they represent themselves. Ultimately, it is the people, events and actions of working Americans—along with their investments, spending decisions, time commitments, jobs and passions—that shape society in our changing world.

Scott Derks

INTRODUCTION

Working Americans 1880–2007 Volume VIII: Immigrants, is the eighth volume in an open-ended series. Like its predecessors, *Immigrants* profiles the lives of Americans—how they lived, how they worked, how they thought—decade by decade. Previous volumes focused primarily on economic status. This volume focuses on individuals from all walks of life, who were born outside of the United States and voyaged to America in pursuit of a better life—more money, more freedom, more hope—for themselves and their family.

Immigrants takes you:

- Into the Newark, NJ home of 38-year-old cigar maker Bernard Schmidt from Germany who longed for his own tobacco farm in 1885;
- Onto crowded streets of New Bedford, MA, where Romanian Anzia Ravage watched her husband sell ice-cream from his Hokey Pokey Cart in 1909;
- On the train back to Mexico where American Maria Azuela was forced to return with her three small children after her husband's sudden death in 1932;
- To Benton Harbor, Michigan in 1957, where Polish teenager Kira Leszczow strove to be a typical American, and cared little about the life she left behind;
- Into war-ravaged Vietnam, from where prostitute Bian Le left with her American GI husband to a life almost as difficult in Westover, MA in 1969;
- Into the heavily Caribbean NYC neighborhood of 45-year-old Andrea Spencer, where she enjoyed traditional Jamaican food and customs in 1975;
- On a soul-searching journey of Gashwin Gomes, who shocked his Hindu family in 1998 by converting to Catholicism and pursuing the priesthood;
- To a small western Massachusetts town where Japanese teenager Stephen Teal found the freedom to pursue his artwork.

Arranged, as the previous seven volumes, in 11 decade-long chapters, this newest *Working Americans* volume averages three individual **Profiles** per chapter. The opening sections highlight the subject's journey from his or her native land, and details the transition into American culture. Personal information is followed by historical and economic data of the time. **Historical Snapshots** chronicle major milestones; **Timelines** outline the progress of immigration issues, often times by specific country; and a variety of **News Features** puts immigration in context. These common elements, as well as specialized data, such as **Selected Prices,** punctuate each chapter and act as statistical comparisons between decades. The 32 men, women, and children profiled in this volume represent 28 countries, from Armenia to Vietnam, and as many occupations, from floor scrubber to furrier. The Table of Contents following this Introduction provides a detailed list.

Like the other seven volumes in this series, *Working Americans 1880-2007 Volume VIII: Immigrants* is a compilation of original research—personal diaries and family histories—plus printed material—government statistics, commercial advertisements, and news features. The text, in easy-to-read bulleted format, is supported with hundreds of graphics, such as photos, advertisements, magazine covers, comic strips, political cartoons, letters, immigration documents, and buttons in support of political campaigns, labor strikes, and milk!

All eight *Working Americans* volumes are "point in time" books, designed to illustrate the reality of that particular time. Some immigrants portrayed in this 8th volume found the better life they were looking for and some did not. Many of their stories continue. As one immigrant realizes his or her dream, dozens more board ships, planes and trains to the American dream.

Praise for earlier volumes—

". . . the Working Americans approach to social history is interesting and each volume is worth exploring . . ."

"these interesting, unique compilations of economic and social facts, figures, and graphs . . . support multiple research needs [and] will engage and enlighten patrons in high school, public, and academic library collections."

Booklist

"the volume succeeds at presenting various cultural, regional, economic and age-related points of view . . . [it is] visually appealing [and] certainly a worthwhile purchase . . ."

Feminist Collections

". . . easy reading that will help younger students come to an understanding of the lives and situations of American women."

"The volume 'promises to enhance our understanding of the growth and development of the working class over more than a century.' It capably fulfills this promise . . . recommended for all types of libraries."

Stories from Social Movements . . . *"succeed in capturing the spirit of the issue and the times . . ."*

ARBA

"[the author] adds to the genre of social history known as 'history from the bottom up,' which examines the lives of ordinary people . . . Recommended for all colleges and university library collections."

Choice

"this volume engages and informs, contributing significantly and meaningfully to the historiography of the working class in America . . . a compelling and well-organized contribution for those interested in social history and the complexities of working Americans."

Library Journal

TABLE OF CONTENTS

This book is dedicated to my friend Jervey.

ACKNOWLEDGEMENTS

The exploration of immigration in America has been fascinating thanks to the intimacy of information and a great team that helped dig out the data integral to the writing this book. A generous round of applause must go to a team of researchers and writers who made this book possible: Tony Smith, Hudson Cargill, Lucia Derks, Jimmy Copening, Brian Stanley, Kenol Rock, Emily Marturana, Michael Marturana, Rosemary Gabriel, Donna Sanzone, and Tina Sell, who assisted with illustrations.

In addition, a generosity of spirit was displayed by Harry Allen, George Scouras, Holly H. Zimmer and Ellen Hanckel. Finally, at the risk of being redundant, thanks go to word-artist Elaine Alibrandi for her editing, Laura Mars-Proietti for her flexibility and patience, and publisher Leslie Mackenzie for supporting and promoting my eighth attempt to tell the fascinating stories of Americans at work.

1880–1899

The two decades leading to twentieth century were shaped by major change, especially the massive immigration of people from throughout the world, seeking freedom and opportunity. Historians believe it to be the largest worldwide population movement in human history, bringing more than 10 million people into the United States to fill the expanding need for workers. In the 1880s alone, 5.25 million immigrants arrived, more than the previous six decades of the nineteenth century. This early wave was dominated by Irish, German, and English workers. Scandinavia, Italy, and China sent scores of eager workers, normally men, to fill the expanding labor needs the U.S. To attract as much needed labor force, railroad and steamship companies advertised throughout Europe and Asia the glories of American life. In an economically depressed world, it was a welcome call.

Nearly everywhere the economic and social life of working Americans was changed, and not everyone agreed that the change was beneficial. After the courts gave the federal government jurisdiction over immigration policy in 1875, Congress passed its first laws concerning the flood of foreigners—the Chinese Exclusion Act of 1882 created to reduce Chinese immigration. By 1891 the U.S. Government assumed the task of selecting, admitting, rejecting, and processing all immigrants seeking admission to the United States. And by 1892, newcomers to

America experienced the excitement—mixed with fear—of reaching Ellis Island in New York Harbor and life in the land of promise.

Beneath the glitter and exuberant wealth of the Gilded Age swirled an ocean of discontent yearning for the gold-laden streets of America promised to millions of immigrants. Health for commoners was primitive, and infectious disease was rampant in crowded cities. Children of the working class routinely left school in their teens to work beside their parents, the middle class was small, and college was largely an institution reserved for the elite and wealthy men of America. Farmers, merchants and small-town artisans found themselves increasingly dependent on market forces and huge concentrations of power unprecedented in American history. The new emerging capitalistic order was quickly producing a continent where only a few were very rich and many were very poor. Child labor laws were largely non-existent, and on-the-job injuries were common, even expected. It was an economy on a roll with few rudders or regulations—an economy ripe for unrest, reform and new ideas.

The rapid expansion of railroads opened up the nation to new industries, new markets and the formation of monopolistic trusts that catapulted a handful of corporations into positions of unprecedented power and wealth. This expanding technology also triggered the movement of workers from farm to factory, the rapid expansion of wage labor, and the explosive growth of cities. The shift in the concentration of power was unprecedented in American history. At the same time, professionally trained workers were reshaping America's economy alongside business managers or entrepreneurs eager to capture their piece of the American pie.

Across America the economy—along with its workforce—was running away from the land. Before the Civil War, the United States was overwhelmingly an agricultural nation. By the end of the century, non-agricultural occupations employed nearly two-thirds of the workers. As important, two of every three Americans came to rely on wages instead of self-employment as farmers or artisans. At the same time, industrial growth began to center around cities, where wealth accumulated for a few who understood how to harness and use railroads, create new consumer markets, and manage a ready supply of cheap, trainable labor. Jobs, offering steady wages and the promise of a better life for workers' children, drew people from the farms into the cities, which grew at twice the rate of the nation as a whole. A modern, industrially based workforce emerged from the traditional farmlands, led by men skilled at managing others and the complicated flow of materials required to keep a factory operating. This led to an increasing demand for attorneys, bankers and physicians to handle the complexity of the emerging urban economy. In 1890, newspaper editor Horace Greeley remarked, "We cannot all live in cities, yet nearly all seem determined to do so."

Despite all the signs of economic growth and prosperity, America's late nineteenth-century economy was profoundly unstable. Industrial expansion was undercut by a depression from 1882 to 1885, followed in 1893 by a five-year-long economic collapse that devastated rural and urban communities across America. As a result, job security for workers just climbing onto the industrial stage was often fleeting. Few wage earners found full-time work for the entire year. The unevenness in the economy was caused both by the level of change under way and irresponsible speculation, but more generally to the stubborn adherence of the federal government to a highly inflexible gold standard as the basis of value for currency.

Between the very wealthy and the very poor emerged a new middle stratum, whose appearance was one of the distinctive features of late nineteenth-century America. The new middle class fueled the purchase of one million light bulbs a year by 1890, even though the first electric light was only 11 years old. It was the middle class, too, that flocked to buy Royal Baking Powder (which was easier to use and faster than yeast) and supported the emergence and spread of department stores that were sprouting up across the nation.

1884 PROFILE

Twenty-nine-year-old Liu Wang came to America on the promise of wealth and adventure, but found low wages and discrimination instead.

Life at Home

- Liu Wang's "coming to America" story always included being packed in a tiny wooden crate, a leaky ship, vicious dockworkers and severe dehydration.
- The story of his 61-day trip from China to San Francisco in 1872 always solicited cheers, tears and another round of drinks.
- Suffocating confinement in a tiny, wet box hidden in the well of a heaving ship made for a far better story than purchased, cramped space in steerage where everyone threw up on their neighbors and wondered why the trip to "Gold Mountain" started on such a rocky road.
- Besides, the spirit within Liu always quickened when he heard or told a fascinating tale of adventure and cunning.
- Since his first week in America, 29-year-old Liu continued to visit the docks and witness the excitement of fortune-seeking men as they clambered off clipper ships christened *Stag-Hound*, *Fleet Wing* or *Sea-witch*, all capable of traversing from New York, past the tip of South America and docking in San Francisco in just 100 days.
- Adventure hunters fresh from the boats were always eager to have their picture taken; some would even believe they cost $2 a pose—twice the normal price—after a few stiff drinks.
- Indeed, an American photographer with a lively Chinese assistant could make good money when the docks were full.
- Since Liu arrived in San Francisco 14 years ago from the desperately poor region of Suchow, China, he had panned for gold, lost a wife, picked strawberries and fallen in love with the life of a traveling photography wagon.
- Only starvation awaited Liu in China, where land ownership had become more concentrated in the hands of a wealthy few.
- Like most peasants, he could either revolt or leave.

Liu Wang was 29-years-old when he left Suchow, China.

Ships carrying fortune-seeking men arrived frequently in San Francisco.

- But he never seemed to be able to leave his love of water or the beauty of his homeland; homesickness always hovered nearby.
- Suchow was a city on the east bank of Tai Hu Lake.
- It was one of the oldest cities in China and prized for its delicate silk embroidery, magnificent palaces and soaring temples; its canals and ancient bridges had earned the city its Western name as the "Venice of China."
- As a boy, Liu learned to fish with cormorants on the lake.
- The birds were leashed at the boats and tossed into the water to fish.
- Once the cormorant caught a fish, the bird was hauled to the boat; a ring around its throat stopped it from swallowing its catch.
- It was a grand adventure, but a poor way to make a living.
- Like many in his village, Liu believed the stories told about America, where food was always plentiful.
- He told himself the journey would be only a few years until he made his fortune; repeatedly, he told the same story to his new wife.

Liu left his young wife in China when he traveled to America to make his fortune.

- China's closed-door policy to the rest of the world had ended in 1842 when England defeated China in the Opium Wars, which forced China to open itself to foreign trade and all ow its citizens to leave the country.
- The development of a passage system then allowed poor Chinese laborers to finance the journey by agreeing to work out their debt after arrival.
- This system quickly became popular among the emigrants to other parts of Southeast Asia, Australia, and North America.
- Arrangements were handled at the treaty ports by Chinese recruiters working for Western entrepreneurs; this kind of labor contracting was known as "pig selling."
- Liu's parents warned him repeatedly to be careful of the labor traders who roamed the docks looking for customers, but didn't ask him to stay, knowing they could never feed nine children adequately.
- To keep his young wife safe while he made his fortune, Liu made arrangements for her to stay behind.
- Chinese women did not go to strange places willingly.
- For two years she waited faithfully, mostly without complaint.
- When she decided to continue her life with another man, she regretted that she was never taught to write and explain the emptiness she felt.
- Liu would not know for another two years that his wife had run off, and then only through village gossip brought by new arrivals.
- Chinese men in America outnumbered Chinese women 20 to one.

Life at Work

- When Liu arrived in California in 1872, resentment toward immigrants was already well established.
- American feelings were deep-seated and often supported by public policy.
- The first Chinese entered California in 1848, and within a few years, thousands more came, lured by the promise of Gam Sann or "Gold Mountain."
- Quickly, discriminatory laws designed to protect American jobs forced the Chinese out of the gold fields and into low-paying, menial jobs.
- The Chinese immigrants laid tracks for the Central Pacific Railroad, reclaimed swampland in the Sacramento delta, developed shrimp and abalone fisheries, and provided cheap labor wherever there was work no other group wanted or needed.
- During the 1870s, an economic downturn resulted in serious unemployment problems, and more outcries against Asian immigrants who would work for low wages.
- In reaction to the states starting to pass immigration laws, in 1882 the federal government asserted its authority to control immigration and passed the first immigration law, barring lunatics and felons from entering the country.
- Later in 1882, the second immigration law barred Chinese, with a few narrow exceptions.
- Imperial China was too weak and impoverished to exert any influence against American policy.
- Through it all, Liu continued to work beside Edward Roberts, a traveling photographer, and move from place to place taking pictures of the newly wealthy, the soon to be wealthy and the newly arrived.

Liu worked in San Francisco as an assistant to a traveling photographer.

In the 1880s, Chinese men in America outnumbered Chinese women 20 to one.

- Liu liked to tell photography customers that the Chinese came to the United States before the arrival of most Jewish, Italian, Hungarian and Polish immigrants.
- Most ignored his comments, and a minority muttered, "They can go back now."
- In fact, Liu often wondered whether Thomas Jefferson had thought at all about the Chinese people when he wrote "all men are created equal" and that liberty was an "unalienable right."
- Many times, especially on the long buggy rides from town to town, Liu and his boss Edward talked about why the Chinese were so hated.
- "It's pretty simple," Edward declared. "The bosses know the Chinese workers will always stick together and will have too much power. They hate it when a bunch of Chinese gaggle together in a group to talk; they just know that they are being plotted against."
- Chinese workers were seen as being on the side of major corporations, railroads, and large landowners, and thus against workers and small farmers.
- "The workers resent the Chinese because they will work for less, even if it's a job they don't want," Edward remarked.
- Christian missionaries saw the Chinese immigrants as the chance of a lifetime; Liu believed he'd been baptized 12 times in 10 different cities by Christian performers eager for converts.
- Most of the time, he was rewarded with a nice dinner and new clothes.
- Often, the church people did not realize how well he spoke English and that he understood the slurs "yellow peril" and "heathen."
- Since 1872, groups such as the Anti-Coolie Association and the Supreme Order of the Caucasians had been staging boycotts of Chinese labor throughout the country.
- The boycotts cost Liu his job in the gold fields shoveling slurry, and later his job picking strawberries.
- The Panic of 1873 that followed, caused largely by the overcapitalization of the railroads, was blamed on the Chinese immigrants for the lost American jobs.
- Bloody riots erupted in Chinatowns from Denver to Los Angeles, where the Chinese were attacked by violent mobs.
- Anti-Chinese riots even occurred in Liu's home town of San Francisco, which had the largest and most well-established Chinatown.
- A community of only nine city blocks, it housed over 30,000 people.
- "The Chinese must go!" was the official slogan of Denis Kearney of the California Workingmen's party; politicians echoed this cry to win votes, and labor leaders exploited the issue to encourage unionization of real Americans.
- In 1876, anti-Chinese sentiment was so intense that Congress launched an investigation into Chinese immigration.
- During the hearings, held in San Francisco, the committee heard 1,200 pages of testimony.
- Industrialists like Leland Stanford and Charles Crocker testified that the Chinese were industrious and dependable, and that without them the Transcontinental Railroad would not have been built.
- Farmers, dependent on Chinese labor, defended the Chinese as well, praising them for their agricultural skill.
- Yet public officials referred to the Chinese as heathens who lived in filthy quarters.
- Labor leaders testified that the Chinese drove decent white men out of work, forcing their wives and children to starve.
- Before 1882, America had a free immigration policy without restrictions.
- Then, in the midst of the West Coast backlash against Chinese labor, Congress passed the Chinese Exclusion Act in 1882, temporarily suspending the immigration of skilled

and unskilled Chinese laborers for 10 years and prohibiting the naturalization of any Chinese.

- Only officials, teachers, students, merchants, and those who "traveled for curiosity" were exempted from the act in accordance with an 1880 treaty with China.
- The law also said resident Chinese must obtain a permit to re-enter if they left the country.
- It also stated that "hereafter no State court or court of the United States shall admit Chinese to citizenship; and all laws in conflict with this act are hereby repealed."
- Through it all, Liu continued learning English and traveling around California with the self-proclaimed "King of the Carte de Visite" in the back of his photography wagon.
- Packing, unpacking and setting up the camera was Liu's job, along with cooking, cleaning, fixing wagon wheels and scaring unhappy customers with his long sword.

Liu often fixed wagon wheels and helped pose subjects for his photographer boss.

- The heavy camera itself had four lenses designed to make four small photographs measuring 3.25 x 2.125 inches on a full-size plate of 6.5 x 8.5 inches.
- These photographs could be produced cheaply, selling for half the price charged by a portrait photographer.
- The pose was standardized; most often the subject stood next to a table piled high with books or sat in a fancy high-backed chair to display a favorite rifle or other weapon.
- The resulting photograph displayed the face small enough that slight movements by the subject would not cause the picture to be out of focus.
- Most of the men rarely smiled; instead, they stared grimly into the camera.

Life in the Community: San Francisco, California

- San Francisco was on its way to becoming a respectable town in 1848 when fate intervened in the form of gold.
- The result was a flood of gold seekers from the East Coast United States to the West Coast to China, all convinced they would become rich overnight.
- The discovery was a transforming event for California and the Chinese immigrants who responded to the lure of new wealth.
- Most immigrants were convinced they would return to the homeland someday.
- Many knew so little about the "new world," they were not even sure whether it rained in America.
- The Chinese were employed to build some intrastate railroads in California as early as 1858, but the first large-scale use of Chinese labor—some 12,000 to 14,000 workers—was in the construction of the Central Pacific portion of the transcontinental railroad, completed in 1869.
- They also constructed the western sections of the Southern Pacific and Northern Pacific, as well as a number of trunk and branch lines.
- Chinese labor and skill were essential to the construction of the Central Pacific, the western portion of the great Transcontinental Railroad, from 1865 to 1869.

- Ultimately, 12,000 Chinese carved tunnels and laid track across the Sierra Nevada; an estimated 1,200 of them were killed in the process, buried in avalanches during the severe winters or blown apart while handling explosives.
- The work required both skill and daring, including the ability to carve ledges from cliffs while hanging in baskets.
- Their speed was remarkable; when racing to meet the Union Pacific coming from the East, Chinese workers laid 10 miles of track in one day.
- By 1880, more than 105,000 Chinese were in the United States, most of them in California, where they converted the turtle swamps of the Sacramento-San Joaquin River Delta into rich farmland, cultivated and harvested vineyards, and raised sugar beets, citrus fruits and celery crops.
- Chinese farmers dominated the strawberry-growing industry in California and pioneered new methods of horticulture.
- In 1880, they amounted to more than a third of California's truck gardeners, and Chinese vegetable peddlers became a familiar sight in many towns.
- Chinese factory workers were also important in the California industries that had grown up during the Civil War, especially woolen mills and the cigar, shoe and garment industries of San Francisco.
- By the early 1870s they comprised 70 to 80 percent of woolen-mill workers and 90 percent of the cigar makers in the city.
- By the mid-1870s, they were a majority of the shoemakers and garment makers, producing almost all the undergarments on the market; they also manufactured brooms, slippers and cigar boxes.
- Although never more than a tenth of the California population, they formed about a quarter of the state's labor force because they were nearly all males of working age.
- In the 1880s, Chinese accounted for 86 percent of the work force in the salmon canneries of California and the Northwest, 80 percent of the shirt makers in San Francisco, 70-80 percent of the work force in the wool industry, 84 percent of the cigar industry, and 50 percent of the fishery workers.

Food peddlers were a common sight in many towns around the Sacramento/San Joaquin River Delta.

HISTORICAL SNAPSHOT
1884

- Theodore Roosevelt's wife died two days after giving birth to Alice Lee Roosevelt; his mother, Martha, had died just a few hours earlier
- Over 100 suffragists, led by Susan B. Anthony, demanded that President Chester A. Arthur support female suffrage
- Mississippi established the first state college for women in America
- Standard Time was adopted throughout the United States
- The first long-distance telephone call was made, between Boston and New York City
- Construction began on the first skyscraper, a 10-story structure in Chicago built by the Home Insurance Co. of New York
- The Institute for Electrical & Electronics Engineers (IEEE) was founded
- Civil War hero General William T. Sherman refused the Republican presidential nomination, saying, "I will not accept if nominated and will not serve if elected."
- A Chinese army defeated the French at Bacle, Indochina
- Congress declared Labor Day a legal holiday
- The Statue of Liberty was presented to the United States in ceremonies in Paris, France, to commemorate 100 years of American independence
- The first documented photograph of a tornado was taken near Howard, South Dakota
- The Equal Rights Party, formed during a convention of suffragists in San Francisco, nominated Belva Ann Bennett Lockwood of Washington, D.C., for president and Marietta Snow as her running mate
- The U.S. Naval War College was established in Newport, Rhode Island
- Greenwich was established as the universal time meridian of longitude
- Transparent paper-strip photographic film was patented by George Eastman
- Democrat Grover Cleveland was elected to his first term as president, defeating Republican James G. Blaine
- John B. Meyenberg of St. Louis patented evaporated milk
- Army engineers completed construction of the Washington monument

Chinese Immigration Timeline

1847–1850

A drought in Canton Province in China and the discovery of gold in California in 1848 ignited Chinese immigration to the United States.

1849

Three hundred twenty-five Chinese were recorded as residents of California; about 4,018 Chinese lived in the United States.

1850

Chinese were invited to march in President Zachery Taylor's funeral procession, and helped celebrate California's admission to the union later that year.

1852

California legislature reenacted the Foreign Miners' Tax law targeted at Chinese.

A monthly Alien Poll Tax charged each Chinese $2.50.

Twenty thousand Chinese arrived in America.

1854

The state of California barred any Chinese from testifying in court against a white; the courts also provided that "No Black, or Mulato person, or Indian, shall be allowed to give evidence in favor of, or against a White man."

1859

The California Superintendent of Education asked that state funds be withheld from schools that enrolled Chinese students.

1860

The census counted 34,933 Chinese.

1870

A San Francisco city ordinance prohibited the use of sidewalks against those carrying loads on a pole, aimed at the Chinese method of carrying heavy objects.

The census recorded 63,100 Chinese, an 81 percent increase from the previous decade.

1872

Chinese were forbidden to have business licenses or to own land.

1877

The California legislature appealed to Congress to limit Chinese immigration.

1879

The California legislature adopted a new constitution containing a section with punitive anti-Chinese provisions.

1880

President Hayes renegotiated the Burlingame Treaty with China, securing the right of the United States to regulate, limit, or suspend (but not prohibit) Chinese immigration.

Two years before the Chinese Exclusion Act was enacted, the census counted 105,465 Chinese, a 67 percent increase from 1870.

Selected Prices, 1894

Coffee, Pound	$0.25
Concert Ticket	$1.00
Cookie and Biscuit Cutter	$0.15
Dance Lessons, Waltz, Three Months	$10.00
Diapers, Six	$0.05
Fertilizer, Ton	$40.00
Parasol	$0.50
Photographs, President and Mrs. Harrison, Two	$0.15
Silk Walking Clothing	$16.84
Sleeve Buttons, Ivory and Pearl, Pair	$3.00

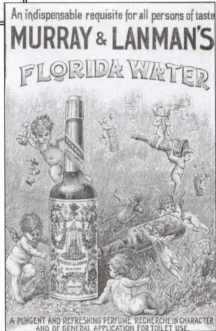

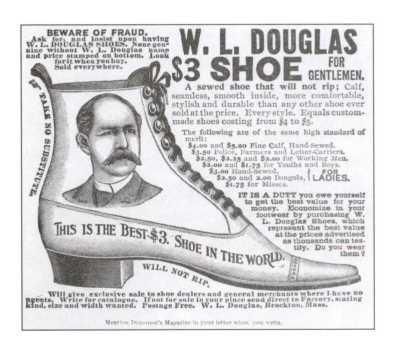

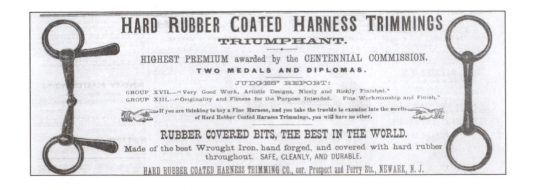

> ## Gen. James A. Garfield, in his letter accepting the Republican nomination for the presidency, 1880:
>
> The material interests of this country, the tradition of its settlement, and the sentiment of our people, have led the Government to offer the widest hospitality to emigrants who seek our shores for new and happier homes, willing to share the burdens as well as the benefits of our society, and intending that their posterity shall become an undistinguishable part of our population. The recent movement of the Chinese to our Pacific coast partakes but little of the qualifies of such an immigration, either in its purposes or result. It is too much like an importation to be welcomed without restriction; too much like an invasion to be looked upon without solicitude. We cannot consent to allow any form of servile labor to be introduced among us under the guise of immigration.

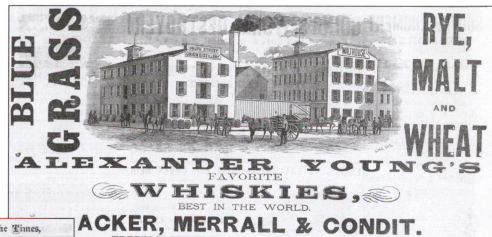

"Chinese Immigration, Meeting of Anti-Coolie Organizations in San Francisco—Incendiary Speeches and Threats of Violence—A Demand for the Abatement of the Chinese Evil," *The New York Times*, May 4, 1876:

San Francisco—The South San Francisco Anti-Coolie Club and the Young Men's Universal Reform Society held meetings last night, and passed resolutions approving the destruction of the Chinese quarters in the town of Antioch, and advocating a similar course in this city, unless the federal government should take immediate steps to abate the evil of Chinese immigration. Highly incendiary speeches were made, and letters read from societies in the interior of the state seeking the cooperation of the San Francisco anti-coolie organizations. The Sergeant at Arms of the Young Men's Universal Reform Society announced that he had a telegram from New York saying that 2,000 stand of arms could be delivered at 10 days' notice. . . .

C. P. O'Neil, a policeman, testified yesterday before the Senate commission appointed to investigate the Chinese question, now sitting in Sacramento, to have been a witness to the sale of a Chinese woman for $450. The woman soon after committed suicide, not liking the man to whom she had been sold. He also testified that he had been informed by Chinese that they attended mission schools solely to learn English, and laughed at the idea of becoming Christians.

Ah Dan, a Chinese interpreter, testified that two Chinese interpreters had been killed in Sacramento for their services in court in procuring convictions, and that an award was outstanding for his life. . . .

Charles T. Jones, District Attorney of Sacramento, gave his experience as to how the Chinese commit felonies, abduct females, etc. His testimony was in the main a recapitulation of similar evidence given before the commission when sitting in San Francisco.

Chinese Coolies in China.

"Talmage on the Chinese, He Takes Strong Ground in Defense of Them," *The New York Times*, September 20, 1880:

Mr. Talmage spoke yesterday morning in the Brooklyn Tabernacle on the Chinese question. The Tabernacle was crowded. His text contained these words, "Who is My Neighbor?" (Luke 10:29). The substance of the sermon will be found in the abstract which follows: "Is he brute or immortal? Will he help me or hurt me? Must he be welcomed or driven back? I am going to give the result of my summer observations in California. For many days I do not think there was a half hour in which I was not brought into the presence of the Chinese subject. The gentlemen who were my companions were, open and above-board, antagonistic to Chinese immigration. One of them was Dr. Moares, President of the Board of Health, than whom no greater enemy of Chinese immigration exists. So I saw the worst of it, and I tell you it is bad enough and filthy enough and dreadful enough, but I tell you also that the underground life of New York City is 50 percent worse. White wickedness is more brazen by far than yellow wickedness, and as for malodors, the only difference is between the malodors of whisky and opium, and the former is a thousand times worse than the latter. The crowded tenement-houses of New York are more abominable than the Chinese quarters of San Francisco. From what I saw on my recent visit and from my observations 10 years ago, of all the population that came to the United States during the past 40 years, none have been more industrious, more sober, more harmless, more honest, more genial, more courteous, more obliging than the Chinese.

"It is objected that the Chinese do not spend their money where they make it. This is false. They pay in the city of San Francisco yearly rentals amounting to $2.4 million. As a tax to the state government the Chinese pay over $4.0 million a year. All that stays in California. They pay in customs to the United States Government $9.4 million annually. All this stays in the country. It comes poorly from us to charge them with sending money out of the country when there are thousands of American and English merchants in China. Where do you suppose they send theirs to? Besides, we have been applauding for 25 or 30 years the German and Irish serving-maids for their self-denial in sending money home to the old folks, and I think what's good for one nation is good for another. It is again objected that the Chinese are pagans and wear a peculiar dress. What do the objectors refer to? To their cue? George Washington wore a cue. Benjamin Franklin wore a cue. John Hancock wore a cue. Your great-grandfathers wore cues. If this country stands it will be because the Joss house of the Chinaman, the cathedral of the Roman Catholic, the meeting-house of the pagan, and the church of the Presbyterian are protected alike. There are numerous Chinese missions in San Francisco, and I told the people of that city that the man who gives one penny toward those missions does more to settle the Chinese question than 10,000 orators speaking for 10,000 years. These Chinese make good Christians. How insignificant and contemptible will the Christians of the present day appear when it comes to be demonstrated that the Chinese were brought to this country, not by the Six Chinese Companies, but by God Almighty in order to Christianize them? Some of them are descendants of men who forgot more than we ever knew. Common school education is more widely spread in China than in America. You cannot find a Chinaman who is unable to read and write, while there are hundreds of thousands of Americans who, if called upon to sign a paper, would be obliged to affix their mark. The Chinese invented the art of printing, the mariner's compass, the manufacture of porcelain, paper-making, and many other things ages before any other nation thought them out. Five hundred years before Christ came Confucius, who anticipated the Golden Rule, and who, when asked to compress in one sentence a direction for human life, said: "Do not unto others what you would not have them do to you." I think the Chinese are God's favorite nation, from the fact that He made more of them than of any other nation on Earth.

"Talmage on the Chinese, He Takes Strong Ground in Defense of Them," . . . *(continued)*

People don't seem to understand that their right to come here implies our right to go there. It will not be many years before the cry in China may be, "Must the Americans go?" [Laughter.] The Chinese scare is the most unreasonable and unmitigated humbug ever invented. They have been coming over 25 years, and they do not number over 200,000, while other nationalities have been coming by millions. Compared with those they are as a drop of rain on a summer ocean. If they increase no faster for the next 100 years, they will be a most insignificant element in our population. Moreover, there are fewer Chinese in America today than last year, fewer than two years ago. The whole spirit of the Chinese Government is against any of its people leaving home. They are taxed for the privilege of landing on our shores, they are taxed for street-cleaning, yet not one cent is spent in the Chinese quarters. The United States Government broke its solemn treaty with them. When Americans were outraged in China, the Chinese Government cheerfully paid $500,000 compensation, but we refuse to pay a cent for the outrages on Chinamen. In the name of Almighty God, the maker of nations, He who made all of one blood, I impeach the United States Government for its perfidy against the Chinese. [Applause.] This question is a complicated and tremendous one. It is higher than your City Hall; higher than the heathen goddess on top of the Capitol at Washington; higher than your church steeples. It is so high as to be on a level with God's own throne."

Mr. Talmage said during the announcements previous to the sermon: "There is a delusion abroad that Mormonism is dying out, when it is growing hour by hour, and will overshadow the nation unless some means be taken to prevent it. Next Sunday I will discuss that question."

"On the Gold Mountain, a man eats enough meat at one meal to feed a family for a month," said Great Grandfather. "Yes, slabs of meat." The hungrier the family got, the bigger the stories, the more real the meat and the gold.

—*China Men* by Maxine Hong Kingston, 1977

Most of the men had already been to the Gold Mountain and did not ask as at the beginning of going-out-on-the-world, "Does it rain, then, on the other side of the world?"

—*China Men* by Maxine Hong Kingston, 1977

The White freeman with his wife and children cannot live in the same atmosphere as the Coolie slave. One or the other must leave the State, and it must be the Chinaman.

—Pamphlet of California's Workingman's Party, led by Denis Kearney, an Irish immigrant, 1876

Dear husband, ever since he sojourned in a foreign land,
I've lost interest in all matters.
All day long, I stay inside the bedroom, my eyebrows knitted;
Ten thousand thoughts bring me endless remorse.
In grief, in silence,
I cannot fall asleep on my lonely pillow.

—Poem of Chinese woman left behind when her husband emigrated to the United States

"People's Natural History Embracing Living Races of Mankind," E.R. Dumont, 1902:

The physical traits of the average Chinaman may be described in a few words. The form is well built, and, though rather short to represent what we regard as perfect symmetry, is fairly proportionate. It is something between that of the lithe, supple Hindu and the muscular, fleshy European. The complexion may be described as brunette, with a strong yellowish tinge. In the south of China people are darker in tint than in the northern provinces, but their swarthiness is not so deep as that of the Portuguese.

The hair of the head is lank, black, coarse, and glossy; the beard is always black, and is very scanty; while whiskers are still more scanty or wholly wanting. Very little hair grows on the body. The eyes, distinctly typical features, are always black, narrow and apparently oblique. The latter appearance is due to the very slight degree in which the inner angles of the eyelids open, not allowing the whole iris to be seen. This Mongolian peculiarity distinguishes the races of Eastern Asia from all of the races of mankind. The cheekbones are high and the outline of the face is remarkably round; the nose is short, flat, but wide at the end; the lips are somewhat thicker than those of Europeans; while the hands are small and lower limbs of average proportions. . . .

Next to the oblique eyes, the plaited "tail" or more correctly the queue, is generally regarded as the most distinctive feature of the Chinaman. But the fashion of dressing the hair is not one of the ancient customs of the Chinese, nor was it originally practiced by them for their own gratification. The ancient Chinese wore the hair long, bound upon the top of the head in a fashion similar to that practiced by the Loochoo Islanders. They took pride in its glossy blackness, and had long distinguished themselves from other peoples as the "black haired race." But two centuries and a half ago the Manchu Tartars invaded China from the north, defeating the Chinese in successive battles. They wore their hair in the long queue with which all who have seen Chinese are now familiar, and in 1627 they issued an order that all Chinese should adopt their coiffure as a sign of allegiance on pain of death. As they overthrew the ruling dynasty at the time with ease, and the chief of the Manchus was made emperor, they en-

A Chinese garden party in China.

forced the order with such merciless rigor that the Chinese throughout the land eventually submitted. The queue was imposed on the people as a badge of such subjugation; but before the Manchu dynasty (the present rulers of China) had been 50 years established, the "tail" had the common appendage of which the Chinese were proud, and a long black queue was the subject of intense desire of every honest Chinaman.

1885 PROFILE

Bernard Schmidt's dream was simple: to own his own farm where he could work outside in the fresh air—growing tobacco—far away from the grime of any city.

Life at Home

- Thirty-eight-year-old German immigrant Bernard Schmidt was tired of the long hours making cigars.
- He'd had enough of seeing tobacco stains on his hands and living in the dirty city of Newark, New Jersey.
- His dream was to own his own tobacco farm.
- Regretfully, this dream required money; with little cash and many family obligations, Bernard saw a scant chance of making it a reality.
- Instead he was forced to live within a city growing daily, populated by eager, desperate, newly arrived immigrants.
- Bernard considered himself a native of the United States; he had emigrated to America from Bavaria when he was only two years old, and so recalled nothing of his life there.
- His only memories were of Newark and the New Jersey countryside he had visited a few times in his life.
- Bernard's father, Georg, often talked about Bavaria during long walks or around the dinner table.
- Most of these tales were about people who lived near the old family home or the traditions within Bavaria itself.
- In the end, the key lesson was that life was hard for Bernard's father Georg.
- The stories were retold in so much detail that Bernard could visualize the family home from corner to corner, and almost hear the creak from the family's front door that would not become quiet with oil.
- One of the clearest stories was about the events that led to the family's departure from Germany for America.
- To Bernard, the tale was ancient history; to his father, it occurred yesterday.
- Both Georg and his older brother Fritz were blacksmiths and shared a proud reputation in the community: Fritz as an exceptional blacksmith and Georg as a proficient toolmaker and blacksmith.

Bernard was two-years-old when he arrived in America. At 38, he was still looking for a better life.

Georg's brother and his family remained in Bavaria.

- The Grippe, or flu, had seized their father's health and he passed away when Georg and Fritz were in their early twenties in the late 1840s, a year before Georg married Anna.
- At the same time, crops failed in the region, and business slowed for the area's blacksmiths: poor farmers and struggling factories required fewer tools and often delayed shoeing horses.
- The young families of both Georg and his brother Fritz were starving; the blacksmith shop could only support one family.
- After much agonizing, a family decision was made: Fritz would keep the shop in Bavaria, and Georg, his wife Anna and two-year-old Bernard would take most of the meager savings of both families and seek their fortune in the United States.
- They did not have any family or friends in America—only hope.
- First, the family—carrying only a couple of bags of clothes—journeyed to Hamburg.
- They also took the family crucifix, which belonged to Georg's grandfather.
- They boarded the ship at Hamburg for a city called Newark, somewhere in America.
- During the journey at sea, the family survived cramped quarters and many days of nausea; young Bernard was dreadfully sick on the voyage.

- Both Anna and Georg worried and prayed to God for their son to survive the trip; he was dehydrated and listless.
- Although Bernard's health improved when they set foot on the soil of their new home, seven other passengers were less fortunate and died from a fever.
- With few options and no English language skills, Georg went to the only place he knew—the closest Catholic church.
- With the Latin he knew, he managed to communicate with Father Patrick Moran from St. John's Roman Catholic Church.
- He introduced Georg to other Germans living in the community, including a lawyer from Munich who had left to avoid the political troubles brewing in the region.
- Georg's skills helped him find a job as a blacksmith at an iron works in Newark; the family saw this opportunity as a blessing from God.
- Though he did not speak English, Georg worked closely with a few other Germans in the iron works and his family lived within a small but growing German community in Newark.
- The family's home was nothing like their place in Bavaria.
- Instead of a nice, warm cottage, the family resided in a run-down carriage house with two other German families.
- To avoid the draft from the doors, everyone slept upstairs on the wooden floor covered with some old straw.
- Georg and Anna had to live that way for several years before they could afford a proper place to rent that they didn't have to share.

The Catholic Church was a comfortable place for Georg when he first arrived in Newark NJ.

- Life in Newark was tough and filled with challenges: Georg often felt scared among immigrant-hating Americans.
- German immigrants who spoke little English and took "American" jobs were unwelcome.
- Growing up, Bernard received more than a couple of bloody noses while battling a gang of neighborhood boys who made great sport of picking on him and other German youths.
- A significant number in the native Anglo-Americans in the United States were against having immigrants in their town and even called themselves Know Nothings, based on pretending to know nothing of the crimes and acts of violence they inflicted on the immigrants.
- Many of the Know Nothings did not like seeing the city's Catholic population increase and believed the Protestant way of life was threatened.
- Catholic families named Schmidt rarely felt safe in Protestant communities, and the reaction against German immigrants was exploding.
- Crop failures and political unrest drove thousands of Germans to America.
- After that, the entire United States was hit in 1857 by a recession that threw thousands out of work.

Life at Work

- Bernard Schmidt was 10 years old when the recession of 1857 hit the nation, and working hours were suddenly limited at his father's job.
- Young Bernard had to bring income into the home, the family concluded.
- His native-born brother Charles, only four years old, was too young to work.
- Rent on the family's four-room apartment was $5 a month—a sizable portion of the family income.
- Bernard's English was strong for a child of 10 years, which delighted his parents.
- Bernard was often called upon to helped Georg and Anna with their language difficulties when shopping or getting around Newark.
- The fact that he spoke English helped Bernard find odd jobs in the neighborhood until one member of the German community hired him at his seegar (cigar) shop.
- Working in the seegar shop required a great deal of attention to detail.
- Tobacco leaves were shipped from Southern states like Virginia, and Bernard had to strip the tobacco from the midrib of the leaf.
- This demanding work earned him $0.35 per day.
- Almost immediately he decided to work his way up to a cigar maker.
- Bernard's opportunity arrived when the Civil War erupted in 1861; some of the workers in the shop enlisted and others were drafted into service.
- Bernard was not old enough to serve, but skillful enough to graduate from a tobacco stripper to a cigar maker.

Bernard began working in a cigar shop at 10-years-old, stripping the tobacco from the midrib of the leaf.

- The hours were long and tough on his hands, on which the tobacco left daily stains and imparted a strong scent that remained under his fingernails.
- But the work was steady, as cigars only grew in popularity during the war; manufacturers began competing to produce five-cent cigars.
- Demand in the 1870s increased by over 100 percent, while the population grew only 30 percent.
- To meet the demand, many cigar manufacturers hired at low wages women who spoke little to no English.

To meet the increased demand for cigars, manufacturers hired at low wages women who spoke no English.

- By 1885, the average cost to produce 1,000 cigars was roughly $43; labor cost the manufacturer $21.
- Expenses also included the cost of the tobacco and other business costs, including a $6 federal stamp tax per 1,000 cigars, so profits were small.
- To compete, manufacturers constantly fought to reduce labor costs and produce more cigars to make a reasonable profit.
- Working 10-hour days, Bernard produced just over 3,000 cigars a week, earning him $9.50 a week.
- He was also permitted to make one personal cigar a day, which he smoked while working, and provided two for his father and brother once per week.
- Bernard's cigar making job helped pay the bills, but it was not until his younger brother Charles was 12 years old that more money was earned by the family to cover additional costs.

- Bernard's father Georg found work at Hewes & Phillips Iron Works on Ogden Street, just over a mile from their current home.
- While on the job, Georg convinced the foreman to permit his son to apprentice under him while also allowing his son to translate from English to German detailed instructions that were required in the iron works.
- When Charles finished his apprenticeship, he continued to work with his father at the iron works and earned decent wages for the family.
- The two men, Georg in his early sixties and Charles in his mid-twenties, walked over a mile each day toward the Passaic River where the iron works was located.
- Bernard, being the oldest, wished he could have had the experience of working with his father and maintaining a tradition of sharing the skills Georg had acquired from his father in Germany.
- Hearing his father and brother talk shop at the dinner table made him resent the bond that his brother Charles had with his father.
- Fortunately for Georg, this father-son relationship helped keep him employed when an accident happened at Hewes & Phillips Iron Works.
- While repairing equipment, some machinery started up unexpectedly and caught Georg's hand in the gears.
- The accident crushed the fingers on his left hand; to keep his job, Georg became more dependent upon Charles at the iron works.

Georg and Bernard's brother Charles worked at an ironwork factory.

- Each day Georg and Charles arrived with the over 200 employees early in the mornings and worked nine-hour days, six days a week to manufacture Corliss engines, tubular boilers, and steam fittings.
- At the end of the week, Charles earned $8.80 and Georg $6.50.
- The elder earned less because his productivity declined after his hand was crushed.
- This did not upset Georg because he was grateful to work and to provide for his family.
- Fortunately for the family, Bernard's youngest sibling Annie started working at a tailor shop when she was 11 years old.
- She had been working at one shop for almost four years now, and managed to earn $3.75 for a 55-hour week.
- Sometimes before dinner, Charles would meet Bernard at Otto Brandt's Tavern for a drink and to socialize with some of the other Germans in the city.
- Many of the Germans in Newark were farmers who immigrated and wanted to continue farming so that they might leave factory work behind.
- Most of the plans involved saving enough money to buy farmland in the Midwestern United States where other Germans were migrating in large numbers.
- Most wanted to save enough to have a debt-free ownership of a farm of 40 acres or more.
- This typically required saving over $1,200 to purchase the land, a team of horses, a plow, seed and other feed implements.
- Most at Otto Brandt's Tavern had heard of the land speculation scandals that victimized immigrants and did not want to lose what they invested.
- All agreed it was foolish to lose now after risking everything to migrate across the Atlantic.

Bernard and Charles would often meet after work to socialize with other Germans.

- Charles and Bernard often discussed their dream of having a farm.
- Instead of farming in the Midwest, the two dreamed of traveling south to Virginia for the tobacco farming.
- There they would grow high-quality tobacco and sell it at a large profit to cigar manufacturers.
- Bernard liked the idea of working with his brother.
- It reminded him of the stories his father shared of when Georg and his brother Fritz were both blacksmiths in Germany.
- Regretfully, Bernard's father would not have any of this talk of buying a farm or growing tobacco when the family was struggling to support itself.
- Bernard realized how much his father feared starting over again, especially with the bad hand.
- Even though the family was financially secure now, his father remembered the past and feared the future.
- Family was the cornerstone within the German social structure, with the German father typically holding the dominant role.
- Even as men in their thirties eager for a future of their own choosing, both Bernard and Charles obeyed their father and heeded his demands.
- Bernard continued to make cigars with tobacco someone else had grown.
- Besides, being financially stable was one thing; having extra money was another.
- The family earned roughly $1,200 for a year's labor-with four people working—but had substantial living expenses.
- Rent alone cost $21 a month for the house they lived in at the edge of Newark's Sixth Ward.

Life in the Community: Newark, New Jersey

- To distract himself from the fatigue caused by work, Bernard made a point of being active with the German community.
- Most Germans resided in Newark's Sixth Ward and the neighborhood was full of German organizations and associations.
- One of the largest community organizations was the German Roman Catholic Central Association, or, as it was called in German, *Deutscher röm-kath. Central-Verein.*
- Besides strengthening the Catholic feeling in the area, the Association provided aid to members in the event of sickness or death.
- All of the Schmidt men were actively involved with the *Deutscher röm-kath. Central-Verein* led by Bernard's father's longstanding commitment.

Most Germans lived in Newark's sixth ward, a neighborhood filled with German associations.

The size of the German community continued to grow in Newark.

- Bernard was grateful for the community's assistance when his father was hurt and could not work for several weeks.
- He was deeply touched by the members that provided food and some money to the family during that period.
- The charity alone did not influence Bernard to be involved, because his family still maintained a strong religious tradition in the home.
- As the German immigrant community grew in Newark, so grew the size of the Catholic community.
- Although there was only one Catholic church in the area when Bernard's father first arrived, by 1885 Newark had four, including St. Mary's, St. Benedictus, St. Peter's and St. Augustine's.
- Each of the churches provided religious education to the children within the Catholic community to help them with the reading and writing skills necessary for employment, but also to provide a spiritual foundation.
- When a family was encountering a crisis in health or spiritual well-being, it was not uncommon to have a priest visit and pray with the family.
- Bernard often spent time talking with some of the local priests after Mass and, at times, expressed his concerns about his family.
- Often he felt guilty for wanting to start a life of his own outside of Newark.
- Father Adrian, a priest he knew well, understood his dreams but stressed the fact that God does not provide what you want or desire; instead he motivated Bernard to pray and determine what God asked of him.
- This did not sit well with Bernard because he wanted to leave Newark and the priest was informing him God might have other plans for him.
- Typically these priestly conversations were too much for Bernard.
- Many of the German immigrants brought with them the tradition of socializing with friends and drinking beer after the morning's religious services.
- Bernard was no exception.
- At times the discussions of politics were lively during Sunday afternoons, but one hot issue continually was discussed—that of the Freethinker movement.

Bernard desired to leave Newark and make a better life for his family.

- The movement created tension for both Protestant and Catholic Germans because it was based upon scientific thought that flourished in Germany in the 1870s and 1880s.
- For Germans like Bernard, it provided a new way of seeing the world.
- A number of German Freethinkers and others believed that science was the source of truth and that many of the ideas of Christianity were unreasonable.
- Circulating around the German community was a booklet which attacked Christianity entitled, "A Proposed Guide for Instruction in Morals from the Standpoint of a Freethinker for Adult Persons, Offered by a Dilettante."
- Bernard saw his father get rather animated over the topic and argue poorly over the role scientific thought had on religion.
- He became even more enraged when Bernard stated that he agreed with some of the points that science provided.
- When Bernard's father became upset, he talked in more German than English and often spoke so quickly it confused Bernard.
- The only thing he knew was that he was in trouble with his father and talking reasonably was impossible.
- How could Bernard explain that he could still have his faith and accept science for the truth it provides?
- It was during these discussions that Bernard realized that he lived in two different worlds: one of a younger American generation seeing the future before them and that of a German community clinging to the traditions of the world they left behind.
- It was between these two worlds that he was trapped.
- He realized he could not pursue his dream of being a tobacco farmer if the perfect opportunity arose.
- The next question was, how long would he have to wait?

HISTORICAL SNAPSHOT
1885

- A coup d'état in Eastern Rumelia led directly to a war between Serbia and Bulgaria
- John Ward and several teammates secretly formed the Brotherhood of Professional Base Ball Players, the first baseball union
- Johann Strauss' operetta, *The Gypsy Baron,* premiered in Vienna; Johannes Brahms's *4th Symphony in E* was first performed
- Tacoma, Washington vigilantes drove out Chinese residents and burned their homes and businesses
- The Canadian Pacific Railroad reached the Pacific Ocean
- Baseball set all players' salaries at $1,000-$2,000 for the 1885 season
- Pope Leo XIII published the encyclical *Immortale Dei*
- Paul Daimler, son of Gottlieb Daimler, became the first motorcyclist when he rode his father's new invention on a round trip of six miles
- The first photograph of a meteor was taken
- Dr. William W. Grant of Davenport, Iowa, performed the first appendectomy
- Bachelor Grover Cleveland entered the White House as president
- Mark Twain's *Adventures of Huckleberry Finn* was published
- The Washington Monument was dedicated
- The U.S. Post Office began offering special delivery for first-class mail
- The Eastman Film Co. of Rochester, New York, manufactured the first commercial motion picture film
- The Salvation Army was officially organized in the U.S.
- Texas was the last Confederate state readmitted to the Union
- The Congo Free State was established by King Leopold II of Belgium
- The first mass production of shoes occurred in Lynn, Massachusetts
- The Statue of Liberty arrived in New York City aboard the French ship *Isère*
- French scientist Louis Pasteur successfully tested an anti-rabies vaccine on a boy bitten by an infected dog
- Ulysses S. Grant, commander of the Union forces at the end of the Civil War and the eighteenth president of the United States, died in Mount McGregor, New York, at age 63
- Leo Daft opened America's first commercially operated electric streetcar in Baltimore
- In Rock Springs, Wyoming Territory, 28 Chinese laborers were killed and hundreds more chased out of town by striking coal miners
- The first gasoline pump was delivered to a gasoline dealer in Ft. Wayne, Indiana

German Immigration Timeline

1848

The German Revolution for "unity, justice and freedom" began.

J.J. Astor donated $400,000 for the Astor Public Library in New York City.

New York's Germania Orchestra was founded.

The Cincinnati Turnverein, a gymnastics association, was founded.

1849

The "Forty-Eighters" arrived in America after the failed democratic revolution in Germany.

The first national "Saengerfest" of the North American Singers Union performed in Cincinnati.

J. A. Sutter lost his land and his fortune in the California gold rush.

1850

Wilhelm Weitling and Hermann Kriege found the "Bund der Arbeiter" (Workers' League).

Levi Strauss produced the first jeans.

1853

Heinrich Steinweg created the Steinway piano in New York.

1854

This peak year of German immigration saw 221,253 Germans arrive in America.

1856

Mrs. Carl Schurz established the first American kindergarten in Watertown, Wisconsin.

More than 220,000 Germans arrived in America in 1854.

Timeline . . . *(continued)*

1861

Julius Sturges brought the first pretzel on the market in Lititz, Pennsylvania.

1862

The Sioux Uprising in Minnesota included an attack on the German town of New Ulm, Minnesota.

1865

Union army volunteers born in Germany numbered 5,000; 41 reached the rank of major general, while the young Count Zeppelin spent some time as a balloon observer.

1866

After Prussia's victory over its archrival, Austria was no longer a member state of the German Federation.

Adolf Pfannenschmidt from Rinteln founded Pfannenschmidtstadt—better known today as Hollywood.

1870

The U.S. Census recorded that San Antonio, Texas, was 50 percent German.

Chancellor Otto von Bismarck united the German states in the "Second Reich" (1871-1918).

1872

Beer brewers Philip Best, Valentin Blatz, Franz Falk, Frederick Miller, Jacob Obermann, Frederick Pabst, Joseph Schlitz and others made Milwaukee a leading beer exporter.

1873

Chancellor Otto van Bismarck's 14-year "Kulturkampf"—a power struggle with Catholicism over control of education, civil marriage, and church appointments—motivated Catholic emigration to America.

1878

The *New Yorker Volkszeitung* became the organ of the Socialist-Labor party.

1880

Based on census data, Wisconsin had the largest German-American population.

Twenty-five breweries were located in Cincinnati.

1882

In the largest single influx in history, 250,630 German immigrants came to America.

1883

Fifteen thousand German Mennonites from Russia settled in Kansas.

1885

The nation's 800 German-language publications represented more than 50 percent of America's foreign language press.

Selected Prices

Artificial Leg	$75.00
Carriage, Wire or Wooden Wheels	$12.35
China, 130-Piece Dinner Set	$30.00
Dental Extraction	$0.25
Dinner Knives, Silver Plated, Dozen	$3.00
Fruit, Wine, and Jelly Press	$3.00
Hotel Room, New York	$1.00
Pen, Gold	$6.25
Pocket Watch	$10.00
Violin	$5.00

Circulating Library of St. John's Church, A History of the City of Newark, New Jersey, by Frank John Urquhard, Lewis Historical Publishing Co., 1913:

To St. John's Roman Catholic Church belongs the proud distinction of giving birth to the first Circulating Library in Newark. The Newark Library Association, "for the establishment of a library with all proper conveniences and appurtenances . . . with the view to advance the interest of learning generally and better educate the youth of the city of Newark in science, literature and the arts," was only created by act of Legislature a body corporate in 1847, and opened in 1848, 13 years after St. John's Library had been put in operation. St. John's Circulating Library was founded in the year 1835, and in 1859 contained 1,300 volumes, including the best standard works on religion and morality.

"Cigar Maker Work and Income, Report on the Statistics of Wages in Manufacturing Industries," Department of the Interior, Census Office, 1886:

There appear to be some opportunities for overtime for all . . . in this industry, growing out of increased demand at times. For this overworked [employee], regular wages are paid, but it seems that the employés are in some cases allowed tobacco and cigars free for their own use.

Cigar makers are obliged to furnish a rolling-board and cutting-knife. The cost of these is quite small, however, [and] if considered would reduce the wages but a very small percent. Tobacco workers are not obliged to furnish any tools or pay out any part of their wages for help. . . .

With but one exception employés at the establishments reporting are paid in cash. . . .

It is somewhat difficult to arrive at the average hours of labor in this industry, for the reason that the men work by the piece. The general hours of work in cigar shops seem to be from 8 to 10, and in fine-cut and plug tobacco factories, 10 hours. . . .

One manufacturer states that he thinks 10 hours per day the most profitable to employers and employed. A fewer number of hours would decrease production, and would not benefit the employés either physically or morally, while longer hours would be injurious to the health of the employés and unprofitable to the employer. . . . Another employer states . . . that they tried the experiment of working two-thirds of their hands three hours overtime. This did not result in a corresponding increase in production, as the employés were tired out and unable to work well either during the regular hours or overtime.

"Machine Shop Work and Income, Report on the Statistics of Wages in Manufacturing Industries," Department of the Interior, Census Office, 1886:

Many of the works reporting state that there have been frequent opportunities for extra earnings from overtime, owing to pressing demand for the goods manufactured, and also at a number of works from repairs. . . .

In every case payments are in cash. Several establishments state that store-orders and merchandise were formerly used, but were abandoned as unsatisfactory. . . .

The usual interval of payment is weekly. . . .

Ten hours as a day's labor is almost universal in this industry at the present time. Several of the schedules note changes in the hours of labor, and the opinion is uniformly in favor of 10 hours. Neither longer nor shorter hours are favored. . . .

Quite a number of manufacturers note a change in the efficiency of labor at their works, some stating that there has been an increase in efficiency and others a decrease. The causes of increased efficiency have been a better division of labor, the depression in business causing less work and greater exertions to make the same wages as before, steadier employment, piece work, and in one instance the fact that the workmen at the present time are of a much higher grade of intelligence than formerly. . . . One manufacturer notes a decrease in the efficiency of labor, growing out of high wages leading to carelessness and disinclination to work constantly. . . .

Quite a number of establishments note the introduction of a large amount of labor-saving machinery. Where the effect of such introduction is noted, it is generally stated to be an increased output, lessened cost of production, and either no change in the number of hands employed or an actual increase.

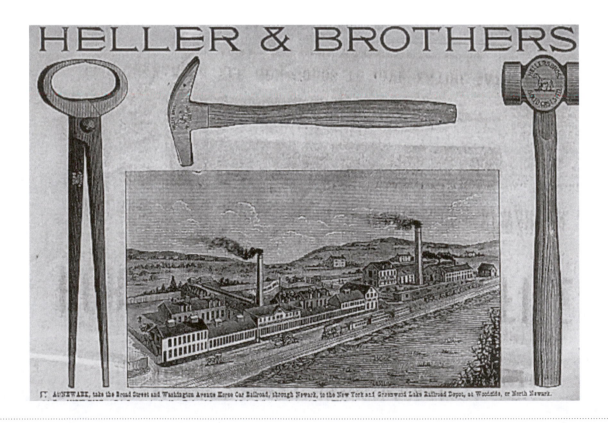

Good Cheer, A Monthly Paper Devoted to the Interest of the Home and Family, **Advertisement from a list of books for free school libraries in New Jersey, 1885:**

The Best Boys' and Girls' Paper and a Library Free

To every Public School in New Jersey, the Publisher of Good Cheer, the best and most successful Boys' and Girls' paper in the country, makes the following unexampled offer: One-half of the money received by teachers for subscriptions to Good Cheer may be retained by them and expended in the purchase of books for Free District Libraries. For example: a school subscribing for 50 copies of Good Cheer, one year, at $0.50 each, would remit one-half ($12.50) of the amount ($25), collected, and expend the remainder ($12.50), in the purchase of any desired books from the accompanying catalogue. It is believed that no offer so liberal has ever before been made, and in the manner suggested schools can find a perpetual source of increase of their libraries. Teachers and Superintendents are requested to aid in this good work for the building-up of the libraries, in the introduction of a clean, pure family paper into the homes of their people.

Best Wishes For Xmas.

1892 PROFILE

Christian Holberg, a Norwegian immigrant, has found success and prosperity in America for himself and his large extended family.

Life at Home

- The Holberg family left Norway in 1885 with more expectations than knowledge of America.
- In all, the family included 13 members comprising Christian and his wife, uncles, aunts, mother-in-law and children—all of whom had been born in Ringsanger, Norway.
- As a family they had decided to emigrate together, leaving no one behind.
- Several major crop failures and the systematic consolidation of farmland had forced the Holbergs three years before to begin discussing their future in Norway.
- After the second crop failure, America was on everyone's lips; after the third, little discussion was needed to reach consensus.
- To finance the voyage, Christian sold his farm equipment, woodworking tools, cattle, sheep, goats and a tiny strip of land that had been in the family for so many generations no one could remember its history.
- The journey, which took 57 days, was generally peaceful aboard a Norwegian ship that bucked and rolled almost continuously.
- The ship carried 181 other immigrants to North America; two passengers died on the journey, including a small three-year-old boy whose mother continued to cradle the dead child in her arms everywhere she went.
- The family had formed most of its impressions about America through reading Samuel Freeman's *The Emigrant's Handbook and Guide to Wisconsin*, one of many immigrant guidebooks published to lure Europeans.
- From this book they learned that New York City was a dangerous place, debt would get you into trouble, and life was better in Wisconsin if you were willing to work hard.
- Several people had also seen letters from America bragging about the money that could be made, the richness of the soil, and the sophistication of the farm equipment.

Christian Holberg left Norway in 1885.

- Dockage records in Québec, Canada, recorded that the 194 passengers aboard the ship brought a total of $7,200 to launch their new lives.
- To meet the baggage limitation, Christian's wife Inge wore five dresses atop each other during the trip—an exhausting experience.
- But as Christian and his family soon learned, the rigorous ocean trip to Québec was only part of the journey.
- Next was a two-day, often interrupted train ride to Detroit, Michigan, the sometimes pell-mell pace of which frightened Christian's mother-in-law more than did the giant ocean.
- The train ride was followed by a boat trip to Milwaukee, Wisconsin, aboard a cattle boat that stank of its previous occupants.
- No effort was made to clean the boat of manure or even soiled hay before loading the new arrivals for the trip to Milwaukee.
- Immigrants rarely expected first-class treatment and rarely found any.
- And in the chaos of their trip, and despite his best efforts, Christian and Inge lost two of their five children among their fellow passengers in one of the many hidden crevices of the boat.
- Both were eventually found sleeping but that did not save them from a stern spanking from Christian and his worried wife.
- The last leg of the trip was another train ride, followed by a wagon trip powered by oxen from Milwaukee to La Crosse, their new home—a place to rest, work and prosper, where they could celebrate life in America and the traditions of Norway like *Syttende Mai* (Seventeenth of May), the day in 1814 when a constitution was established by the Kingdom of Norway at the Constituent Assembly at Eidsvold, ending 400 years of Danish rule.
- In Norway, the Holbergs had always celebrated this day with parades of dressed-up children and adults carrying flags, singing and folk dancing.
- Happily, the people in La Crosse, Wisconsin, understood the old ways, including the Norwegian observance of Christmas on the evening of December 23.
- Called *"Lille Julaften"* or Little Christmas Eve, this day was when most families decorated their Christmas trees and homes.
- Trees were decked out with handmade Christmas baskets made out of red and green paper woven together and then filled with fruits, candy, and nuts.
- On Christmas Eve, the tradition called for the Holbergs to attend church, pay their respects to those who had died, and leave a bowl of porridge in the barn for the nisse, or gnome, who protected the animals.
- A special Christmas meal, which featured steamed lamb ribs called *Pinnekjøtt,* was then served toward evening.
- After the meal, gifts were distributed.
- On Christmas Day, family parties were often held and some people attended church services.

Christian farmed about 60 acres to support his growing family.

Life at Work

- For the first two years the Holberg family rented a log cabin from Swen Hansen before they were able to build a home of their own, a two-story wood frame house.
- Christian calculated that 60 acres was enough land to support his growing family and achieve his dream of being a successful farmer.

- There he taught his three boys to handle a three-yoke team of oxen from dawn to dusk, often breaking ground that had never been tilled before.
- Even his youngest son's accident, which cost the child three fingers on his left hand, did not daunt Christian's enthusiasm.
- The steel plows he bought the second spring for $8.00 each paid for themselves the same year, thanks to more acreage under cultivation.
- Working beside his boys on a farm of his own was a dream come true, especially on land so fertile.
- The grass was so tall and plentiful, often the oxen were unhitched and left to pick their own feed at night.
- Christian also cared about the future; he insisted that all the boys finish the sixth grade and acquire enough education to attain Yankee success.
- For the first several years the family spoke Norwegian almost exclusively, finding little need on the farm and in the close-knit Norwegian community to use English.
- That attitude lasted until Christian was cheated in a wheat transaction at the market by a German immigrant who knew the language.
- He demanded that his sons teach him English immediately.
- Although Norwegian was widely spoken in the community, English was taught in the schools attended by his children.
- Within two years his English skills were so admired that he became the unofficial notary of the settlement and often assisted his neighbors in writing letters or translating legal documents.
- Despite these skills, nearly all the books in the home were printed in Norwegian or German, and most of them were religious in nature.
- After arriving in America, the entire family became Lutherans, drawn to the faith by its doctrine that "the evidence of conversion must and will appear in the daily conduct of a living Christian."
- The only English language publications in the house were almanacs published free by patent medicine makers such as Ayer's, Green's and Hostetter's.
- The duties in the home were clearly divided: looking after the cows and hens and making butter were within Inge's sphere; farming the wheat was Christian's responsibility.
- He grew a tough strain of wheat, resistant to cold and drought, that was imported from Russia.

Looking after the animals were Inge's responsibility.

- Early on, the littlest children were taught to plant seed behind the plow.
- They also learned to spot wild grass fires that occasionally swept across the plains.
- Inge's signature dish was *lefse*, a type of potato flatbread that was fried until it started to bubble and was then buttered and sprinkled with cinnamon.
- Trips away were uncommon on the farm; Christian and Inge did not like leaving their animals.
- Besides, a journey of only a few miles could become an all-day affair if the ferry was out, roads turned muddy or frozen creeks had to be forged.
- So when Christian wrote to friends about life in America, all he could talk about was La Crosse, a county 40 percent foreign-born.
- Two years earlier, Christian had had to make a decision about his future: either invest money in more land or diversify by starting a grain mill.
- The final decision was made as a family once again; they would build a mill to grind flour.
- This decision allowed Christian to start a new business and leave his oldest son to take charge of the farm.
- The past two years had been frustrating and exciting; the cost of starting the mill was higher than anticipated, but when hail damaged Christian's crops the second year, grinding wheat and corn for the community supported the family very nicely.
- Because Christian's youngest son, Gunnar, hated the dusty atmosphere of the mill, he was drawn to the emerging business of dairy farming.

Life in the Community: La Crosse, Wisconsin

- Since statehood in 1830, community leaders in Wisconsin had actively recruited Europeans to the vast farmlands of the state.

Fertile lands of Wisconsin attracted many European immigrants.

- La Crosse began to grow following the completion of the La Crosse Milwaukee Railroad in 1858; for the first time people and their goods could travel without having to take a steamer connection.
- By 1870, luring new farmers to the area was a major business.
- The California gold rush had resulted in a loss of approximately 50,000 residents—almost one-third of the region's population.
- In addition, fertile prairie lands further west had begun to attract many easterners, European immigrants, and Wisconsin residents eager for the government's Homestead Act land still available there.
- By 1892 La Crosse County posted production of 596,000 pounds of butter, 24,000 pounds of cheese, and four million gallons of milk.
- The county claimed 6,000 horses, 53 mules, 79 oxen, 17,000 swine, and 70,000 chickens.
- The county's farmers produced 924,000 bushels of oats that year, 195,000 bushels of wheat, 654,000 bushels of corn, 243,000 bushels of potatoes, 77,000 bushels of barley and 5,300 pounds of tobacco.

- Lumbering also played an important role in the economy of the area; many New Englanders became rich harvesting the seemingly endless supply of pine, while thousands of new immigrants found their first jobs in the lumber yards.
- There, new arrivals could earn enough money to buy a farm; however, the work was dangerous, difficult and often resulted in accidents.
- But many Norwegians viewed emigration to the United States as temporary; the dream was to get rich in America and return home to Norway for permanent settlement.

At the turn of the century, Americans relaxed in parks and tree lined streets.

HISTORICAL SNAPSHOT
1892

- The first issue of the *Afro American* newspaper was published in Baltimore, Maryland
- Fire seriously damaged New York City's original Metropolitan Opera House
- The *Moravia*, a passenger ship arriving from Germany, brought cholera to the United States
- The first heavyweight-title boxing match fought with gloves under the rules of the Marquis of Queensbury ended when James J. Corbett, "Gentleman Jim," knocked out John L. Sullivan in the twenty-first round
- An early version of "The Pledge of Allegiance" appeared in *The Youth's Companion*
- John Philip Sousa's band made its first appearance
- The Diamond Match Co. patented book matches
- The University of Chicago opened
- The Dalton Gang, notorious for its train robberies, was practically wiped out while attempting to rob a pair of banks in Coffeyville, Kansas
- The federal government convinced the Crow Indians to give up 1.8 million acres of their reservation in the mountainous area of Montana for $0.50 per acre
- The first long-distance telephone line between Chicago and New York was formally opened
- Chicago dedicated the World's Columbian Exposition
- Former President Cleveland beat incumbent Benjamin Harrison and became the first president to win non-consecutive terms in the White House
- The pneumatic automobile tire was patented in Syracuse, New York
- The U.S. Immigration Service opened Ellis Island in New York Harbor, a new facility for processing immigrants, replacing Castle Garden, which was closed because of massive overcrowding and corruption
- In Springfield, Massachusetts, the rules of basketball were published for the first time
- Former president Abraham Lincoln's birthday was declared a national holiday
- New York State unveiled the new mechanical lever, automatic ballot voting machine
- General Electric Co., formed by the merger of the Edison Electric Light Co. and other firms, was incorporated
- The prototype of the first commercially successful American automobile was completed in Springfield, Massachusetts, by brothers Frank and Charles E. Duryea
- Congress passed the Geary Chinese Exclusion Act, which required Chinese in the United States to be registered or face deportation
- Charles Brady King of Detroit invented the pneumatic hammer
- The Sierra Club was organized in San Francisco by John Muir
- Homer Plessy was arrested after buying a railroad ticket in New Orleans and seating himself in the white-only section to test the enforcement of the 1890 Louisiana law mandating separate cars for whites and blacks
- Andrew Beard received a patent for the rotary engine

Norwegian Immigration Timeline

1825

The sloop *Restauration* sailed from Stavanger, Norway, with 52 passengers, considered the beginning of the movement of 900,000 Norwegians to North America; among countries in Europe, only Ireland had greater mass migration.

1833

Cleeng Peerson walked from Kendall township in New York State to Ohio, where he founded the first Norwegian settlement in the Midwest, in La Salle County in Illinois, southwest of Chicago.

1836

Two ships with 167 emigrants sailed from Stavanger, Norway, for the newly established Fox River settlement in Illinois.

1837

A Norwegian minister condemned "America fever" as a contagious disease.

Ole Nattestad wrote *Beskrivelse over en reise til Nordamerica* (*Description of a Journey to North America*).

1838

Ole Rynning's emigrant guide, *True Account of America*, was published.

Ole Nattestad founded the first Norwegian settlement in Wisconsin—Jefferson Prairie in Rock County.

Bishop Neumann's pastoral letter *A Word of Admonition to the Peasants in the Diocese of Bergen who Desire to Emigrate* provoked Norwegians in America.

1840

In the 1840s Wisconsin became the main region of Norwegian settlement and remained the center of Norwegian activity until the Civil War.

1841

The first book in America printed in Norwegian, *Doctor Martin Luther's Small Catechism, with Plain Introduction for Children, and Sentences from the Word of God to Strengthen the Faith of the Meek*, was published.

1842

Lay preacher Elling Eielsen built a combined dwelling and meeting house in La Salle County called a *forsamlingshus*, an assembly house, not a church.

1844

The first Norwegian Lutheran confirmation in America was conducted.

Johan R. Reiersen published *Veiviser for Norske Emigranter til De forenede Nordamerikanske Stater og Texas* (*Pathfinder for Norwegian Emigrants to the United States and Texas*).

1845

The first Norwegian church building was inaugurated in Muskego, Wisconsin.

The Muskego Manifesto, an open letter signed by 80 men, was issued in defense of the immigrants in America.

Johan R. Reiersen led a group of Norwegian peasants from Agder to land he had selected in Texas later named Normandy.

1846

The Evangelical Lutheran Church in America was founded by Elling Eielsen.

Timeline . . . *(continued)*

1847

The first Norwegian-American newspaper, *Nordlyset* (*Northern Lights*), was published in Muskego, Wisconsin.

1848

When gold was discovered in the Sacramento valley in California, many Norwegians were taken by gold fever.

1849

The repeal of the British Navigation Acts permitted Norwegian ships to transport emigrants to Québec.

1850

The first Norwegian emigrants arrived in Québec aboard Norwegian sailing ships and from there to the United States.

1851

Kirkelig Maanedstidende (*Church Monthly*) was launched.

The first Norwegian pioneers came to Minnesota.

1852

Emigranten, an important pioneer newspaper, published its first issue.

1853

The Synod of the Norwegian-Evangelical Lutheran Church in America (the Norwegian Synod) was organized.

1854

Ninety percent of the Norwegian emigrants first landed in Québec.

The first issue of *Den Norske Amerikaner* (*The Norwegian American*) was published in Madison, Wisconsin.

Norwegian settlements in Minnesota took their names from places in Norway: Vang, Toten, Eidsvold, Dovre, Sogn, and Aspelund.

1858

Minnesota became a state.

1860

About 55,000 Norwegian immigrants lived in the states of Illinois, Wisconsin, Iowa and Minnesota; 60 percent had been born in Norway.

1861

Norwegian immigrants numbering 4,100 joined the Union Army.

1862

The Homestead Act made available to every American citizen 160 acres of surveyed government land.

Dakota Indians unexpectedly attacked Norwegian settlers in the Minnesota River Valley.

1865

Emigration records showed that 77,873 Norwegians had left Norway, mainly from the fjord districts of western Norway and the mountain areas of eastern Norway.

1866

Steamships gradually replaced sailing ships, making mass emigration possible.

1868

The first illustrated periodical in Norwegian in America, *Billed-Magazin*, was published in Madison, Wisconsin.

The Norwegian Dramatic Society was established in Chicago.

Timeline . . . (continued)

1869

The first singing society, Normanna Sangerkor (Normanna Singers' Choir), was founded in La Crosse, Wisconsin.

1870

The census showed that Scandinavians were the largest foreign-born group in Minnesota.

1874

St. Olaf College was founded in Northfield, Minnesota.

1876

Skandinaven's bookstore opened in Chicago.

1879

The land boom in North Dakota was dominated by Norwegians.

1880

The Danish Thingvalla Line established the first direct passenger route by steamship between Scandinavia and the United States.

1883

Torjus and Mikkel Hemmestvedt, considered to be the best skiers of their day in Norway, became pioneer ski jumpers in America.

1884

Den norsk-amerikanske Venstreforening (The Norwegian-American Liberal Society) was formed because "our old fatherland's independence and freedom are at stake."

1885

H. A. Foss published the novel *Husmanns-Gutten* (*The Cotter's Son*).

1887

Minneapolis Tidende was one of the three most important newspapers in the Midwest.

The first statue of Leiv Eiriksson was unveiled in Boston.

1889

Dakota became a state and was divided into South and North Dakota.

1890

The United Church (Den forenede kirke) was organized with support from immigrants.

The newspaper *Western Viking* was established in Seattle.

1891

Nordisk Tidende (*Nordic Times*) was established in New York by the printer Emil Nielsen from Horten.

The Augsburg Publishing House was established by the United Norwegian Lutheran Church.

1892

Ellis Island replaced Castle Garden as a receiving and control station for immigrants.

Knute Nelson was elected governor of Minnesota.

Selected Prices

Bicycle Costume	$7.50
Candy, One Box	$0.06
Corset	$1.25
Harness, Double Buggy	$25.00
Horse Muzzle	$2.50
Shoes, Button	$1.50
Suspenders	$0.05
Ticket, Buffalo Bill's Wild West Show	$0.50
Top Coat	$10.00
Typewriter	$25.00

The Emigrant's Handbook and Guide to Wisconsin, by Samuel Freeman, 1851:

General Instructions

Having now given as clear an outline of the subject as the limits of this work will permit, and I trust fulfilled the promise made at the outset, that the emigrant should be supplied at a cheap rate, with information valuable both for present and future application, I shall draw to a conclusion by offering a few general observations to the emigrant, to guide him to this western country, and be useful to him in time to come.

New York being the principal landing place, and a large city, the emigrant is apt to be surrounded on all sides if he does not keep a sharp lookout, by a set of men who, under pretence of being his friend or his countryman, allure him among strangers, with all the snares and temptations that such a large city affords, which are calculated, in a very short time, to use up all his means before he is aware of it. I would guard him to avoid these men and shun them as he would a serpent, for their only object is to get his money and introduce him to places of resort where gaming and drinking are carried on to an endless extent; and in the end calculated to bring ruin upon himself and his family. One of the many temptations that beset the emigrant, is the numerous gambling houses there are in New York; and one of the most tempting forms of gambling is found at some of the low saloons, where raffles are constantly going on, to a great extent, either for watches, jewelry, guns, pistols, or other bogus articles; and any quantity of liquor indulged in during the intervals of the game. . . .

The emigrant's chance employment and good wages is much increased by removing from seaboard towns. New York being the principal landing place, and from the influx of strangers continually pouring in there, it is impossible for merchants, traders and others, to give employment to one-tenth that arrive here.

Under these circumstances, I strongly advise the emigrant, both mechanic and laborer, after they have spent a day or two inspecting the city, to lose no time in quitting that place whilst they have the means of doing so to assist themselves. The facilities for traveling in the United States are cheap and good. Steamboats, railroad conveyances and coaches, start daily for all parts. This you will find to be the most profitable way of laying the foundation of your future happiness. Lose no time, then, in working your way out of New York and directing your steps westward, where labor is plentiful and sure to meet with its reward. . . .

The emigrant, on landing at any port on Lake Michigan, if he has a family, had better engage a lodging for them immediately, or go into some cheap boarding house. The emigrant's next object will be, if he intends to farm, or to labor on a farm, to get into the country as soon as he can, for he will find everything there much cheaper, and have a better opportunity of becoming acquainted with the quality and the local advantages of the land. In fact, he had better hire a small farm for a season than make too hasty a purchase. By so doing he will be better able to know the quality and eligibility of land. The smallest quantity of land sold by the Government is 40 acres. This can be purchased in Wisconsin for five shillings sterling per acre. Those who have the means will find it to their advantage to purchase improved farms: they can be purchased generally for less than the improvements cost. There are two Emigration Offices in this city. Messrs. Gregory and Kickson's Office is situated in Wisconsin Street over the Post Office. Emigrants will be able at this office to select out from their maps, farms wild and improved in every part of the state. They are also Emigration Agents for Houses in New York City, and remit money to all parts of Ireland. . . .

I must also here caution emigrants, above all things, to make no purchase but what they can pay for; never run in debt with the calculation of paying the purchase money by the produce of the farm. This is undoubtedly a rock upon which many are wrecked. Many calculations are made of the expense of clearing and the cultivation of farms, with the amount and price of the produce from that cultivation, showing by the difference that it was a very profitable investment. All this looks very nice on paper, but rest assured many have found it to their sorrow, exceedingly wrong in practice. I would therefore urge to all emigrants coming to Wisconsin to buy no more land than you can comfortably pay for, and after all leave a sufficiency to purchase a few of the necessaries of life. . . .

The Emigrant's Handbook and Guide to Wisconsin . . . (continued)

Do not be downcast and disheartened after you have got here. Most of you, probably, have once been in moderate circumstances in the Old Country. You have left, probably, father, mother, brother and sister; perhaps some of you have left your wives and families behind you. You have come in search of a home in the "Far West." The industrial resources of your country refuse any longer to sustain you—and here you are come to seek the means of sustaining yourself and families—then my fellow countrymen, instead of murmuring and being disheartened, rather be thankful that God in his Providence has left an unmistakable mark on the map of the world, that guides the homeless and the destitute to a place of refuge. Therefore, I would advise, and I do it strongly, that you forbear to speak ill either of the manners or the country which you have sought refuge in. I have been a keen observer since I have been in this Western Country, and in instances without number, I have been disgusted with the Old Country people when they get here—the way they speak of America or Americans—before they know or have any means of knowing either the country or the natives. Just probably because some have not found everything to their own minds as they had it at home, or disappointment comes upon them from a false representation made to them before they started across the Atlantic; they commence raving against "Yankees" and wish themselves back again, while if they would sober down their senses, and on calm reflection they would discern the folly of the course they are pursuing.

But you, fellow-countrymen, who I am addressing, and who are perusing these pages, I hope for better things. Always bear in mind "a still tongue maketh a wise head," and instead of desponding, be thankful that your lot is cast in such pleasant places, and on your arrival in Wisconsin, turn your attention to her resources, her fertile prairies and beauteous openings. . . . This is the country you are invited to, fellow-countrymen; Americans are not a homogeneous race. Within the United States dwell representatives from every nation of Europe, and the population of Wisconsin has a large proportion of foreign-born citizens. They have brought with them their own respective languages—they are marked with the distinctive characteristics of the various States whence they came-they are unlike each other in their habits, and they differ much in sentiment. They have come to cast in their lot with a strange people—to live with them and be of them, and what does the American Government say to you? Pay attention whilst I tell you: We welcome you, for our land is broad, and we need your numbers and your aid to occupy it; we welcome you, for we know that, attracted by the fame of our country's freedom, many of you have come from oppression at home; and being free ourselves, we gladly hail you freemen and citizens. Then, instead of murmuring and being downcast when you get here, cheer up and join her glorious band. Wisconsin is one of the great company of free communities, bound together for the extension and perpetuation of civil and religious liberty, and placed in the van of all the nations of the earth, to lead the march of human progress. . . .

We, my fellow-countrymen, in this State, are indeed a favored people—none more so—and it becomes us, in a spirit of gratitude for the many blessings we enjoy, well to reflect upon, and faithfully perform the duties Heaven has allotted us—to improve to every possible extent the trust which has been confided to our care. Nations as well as individuals have missions to fulfill; and if, through design, or through heedlessness, they fail to pursue them, they may look for the righteous indignation of the Ruler above, who will hold them to a stern and fearful accountability—well remembering that whatever we may do here in Wisconsin for her glory and good, will help to swell, also, the happiness and glory of the whole Union; while the errors we may commit, or the evils we may let loose among ourselves, will be mainly ours in all the injuries or disgraces they may occasion. Finally, fellow-countrymen, let me tell you America is a country overflowing with prosperity and happiness—one which knows not the meaning of internal tumult—one which most of her citizens, with scarcely an exception, can command the necessaries of life; meat, drink, clothing and shelter from the elements in abundance—where her Members of the Congress are elected by universal suffrage—where neither game laws nor tithes exist—and where the Chief Magistrate lives with dignity in an income of L5,000 per annum.

Gunder Asmundson Bondar, Aadne Asmundson Bondar, and Kari Evensdatter. Letter to siblings in Fyrsedal, Norway. Deerfield, 17 January 1854:

Dear Sisters and Brothers:

We are firmly convinced that you have waited a long time for a writing and information from us in this, our foreign home. This step to find a way to this our farm on which we have settled was a chance course as over the ocean we went forward to take to this moral state.

We left Crag eight days after Santenhun Day and finally reached New York after eight weeks and three days of sailing. . . . We came to New York on December 1, at 6 o'clock in the morning. On the 2nd we left there at 6 o'clock in the morning and on the 3rd we were in Albany at 6 o'clock in the morning. The canal begins in the town of Albany and goes to the town of Buffalo. From there begins the long inland journey from New York to Koshkonong, it is called karskland in Norske. . . . The way has been long, about 300 Norske miles.

In the month of April we moved three miles farther west to Torge Halverson's home. There we stayed a year in his house and Hungus Holer and his wife Anne were also there. They bought for themselves 20 acres of land from Torge Halverson and then we bought 124 acres of land beside them from the government, which owns a lot of land here. Now it is all sold hereabouts. . . .

It is almost unbelievable how fortunate it has gone for us the whole time in the new world. There is no one of our ages here who have climbed upward as fast as we. Cattle is now high priced so the first thing each of us did was to sell cattle for 80 dollars each. We own four milk cows, two that are two years old, two that are one year old and one calf, five driving oxen, 10 hogs or swine, 20 chickens, two geese, and five sows. This fall we butchered four pretty big hogs.

This fall we cut so much wood that we can sell a hundred dollars' worth. We had a desirable and fruitful year. It is not often that we have this much wood and it also has a high price. There are several here who have cut a thousand bushels of wood. . . . The price per bushel is a dollar, and that is expensive.

The new railroad has just been finished to Madison, which is three Norske miles west of here. And everything is expensive here that we need to work the land. We bought a plow to work up the new ground with for $12.00. . . . A four-wheeled wagon costs $61.00. One thrashing machine for $25.00 dollars, two iron spades for $2.50. Animals or cattle are high priced. A cow costs from $15.00 to $20.00 and $25.00. For the very best is $30.00. Driving oxen are usually sold two together. It is called a team. The cost is $50.00 to $100.00, that is the very best. For a sow $1.00 to $1.50 and $2.00. For a goat $3.00 to $5.00 dollars. For a pound of the finest wheat flour $0.02 to $0.03. For one pound of pork or bacon $0.03-$0.04. For a pound of butter $0.06-$0.12. For a pound of tallow $0.10 to $0.12. For a pound of candles from $0.12 to $0.14. A pound of coffee $0.12 to $0.14. For a pound of tea $0.50 to $0.60. Clothing varies in price. Cloth that is half wool is $0.50 a yard. For the finest wool cloth $1.00 a yard. All cotton material $0.10 to $0.12 a yard. Linen 1.5 yards is $0.10 to $0.12 a yard. The best linen is $0.12 to $0.25 a yard. A pair of boots is $2.50. A pair of shoes is $1.30 to $1.50. A cap costs $0.50 to $0.60. . . .

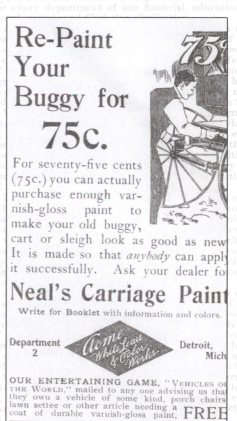

Gunder Asmundson Bondar, Aadne Asmundson Bondar, and Kari Evensdatter. Letter to siblings . . . *(continued)*

A pair of horses cost $150.00 to $200.00 dollars. There are many horses here.

All the different kind of good work tools here are so expensively made the Norske tools are like they were made by a child. All that man shall work with is made in a large factory that is usually driven by a steam engine. There are machines used to cut wood with. Some are called mower machines to cut hay with. Machines to saw wood with. Machines to thrash with. These machines are driven by horses.

Wages vary with a year's time. In the summer, wages are $15.00-$20.00 for a month. In the winter they are $10.00-$13.00 a month. . . .

Girls usually earn from $1.00 to $1.30 to $1.50 for a week. The wage is the same both summer and winter. Their work is the same as a housekeeper in Norway. They have more respect for girls here than in Norway. When an American wants to hire a maid, he comes with a horse and carriage. . . .

And here it is so that a working man will never be from the husband's or master's table to eat whether he works for a shopkeeper or others. All shall be as highly respected. Yes, Americans are friendly and high-flightedness we cannot understand. We are so used to the proud Europeans who are haughty. . . . And one never sees an American with his hands at his sides as the foreigners do.

The land's riches and fertility is impossible for us to describe. . . . The land is not flat but rolling. It is layered with hills and valleys and mountains, which are higher. These stretch for the most part north and south. . . .

Cotton does not grow. Neither does sugar. That grows south of here. Coffee and tea does not grow in the whole of North America. When you wrote about some coffee beans, it is impossible for us to obtain them. They grow in South America under sunshine and a warm and unhealthy climate. Here the climate is cold, healthy and fresh. . . .

Here the prairie has had cholera and it has ruled as in Norway. It comes to take control, and it has dominated. Cholera has been here on Koshkonong, but this fall it has not been here in these easterly places. Aadne has been sick with it two times and both times we cured him. We all have been in good health the whole time and have had better health than in Norway. I have not been this well for many years. . . . Kari also finds herself well satisfied. Now we do not want to go back even if we were the owners of the best farm in Moland. This we know you cannot believe.

My wife has had two pregnancies since we arrived here. The first was in the year 1850 the 13th of April and then she delivered twins. One was named Grumund and the other Ole. Grumund lived just 10 days and then died. Ole is doing well. The other was born August 16 in 1853 and was baptized on the 25th. That one was given the name Tone in Baptism. All of our children are in good health, growing and thriving well. We do not want to forget to thank our Father in Heaven who cares for all in his creation every day of our lives.

I would not advise any stranger or rich man to come here to this ground as those who have large estates would wonder at the beginning. But those who are good workers will go on because one has to work harder here than in the Fatherland. . . .

Here there is a great desire to go to California to look for gold. Thousands of Norske and Americans are going and coming back with hundreds of dollars in gold and money. Those who go there earn $100.00 a month. Knut Olsen Porsgrund has big thoughts about going there. I think he will. Before, money for the trip was $300.00. Now it is $100.00. Now there is a faster way to get there. The [wagon] train is now finished to California. Those who are so inclined and are able to go there are merely fortunate.

For me, Kari Evensdatter, I would like to kindly ask you who are there to greet my aged father if he is still living, and to all our sisters and brothers that we are living well and are with good health.

Gunder Asmundson Bondar, Aadne Asmundson Bondar, and Kari Evensdatter. Letter to siblings . . . *(continued)*

From your devoted brother, Aadne Asmundson, I believe that I would advise you to come here to America and that you would find it better here when you shall acquire $100.00 when you earn only $20.00 in Norway. This I am well acquainted with. I can get a large contract for steady work and get money. Otherwise do as you think, but my advice is the best.

Now we will go no further and must break off this our writing. With a diligent greeting to lovable and unforgettable sisters and brothers. And the same to all other relatives and known friends. Live well, and if we are not fortunate enough to see one another more in this world, may we all meet and go forward with gladness in the next. Write us a letter and tell of yourselves.

Koshkonong in Wisconsin the 17th of January 1854

Gunder Asmundson Bondal

Aadne Asmundson Bondal

Kari Evensdatter 1854

"Railroads and Immigrants, Westbound Passengers Must Have Clean Bills of Health," *The New York Times*, September 13, 1892:

All the railroads have refused to carry immigrants West unless each has a certificate from a surgeon in the employ the federal government. This action was due to the firm stand taken by the Illinois State Board of Health.

Last week Chairman IP Farmer of the Truck Line Commission received a circular from F. W. Reilly, Secretary of Illinois State Board of Health, saying that no Immigrants would be allowed to pass through the state or enter it over any road unless each was provided with a certificate signed by the physician of the Marine Hospital Service stating that he had been under inspection for a certain length of time, all danger of cholera had past, and there was no danger of smallpox.

The circular further stated that if the passengers of the road bringing them into the state had not such certificates, they would be quarantined, and at the expense of the road which carried them. . . .

On Saturday a large number of immigrants bound West were stopped at the Grand Central Station and the New York, Ontario and Western Station. They were sent back to Ellis Island, on Sunday were sent West over the Pennsylvania.

THE LADIES' HOME JOURNAL

FOUR SPECIAL PAGES
DEVOTED TO THE SUMMER WARDROBE FOR WOMEN AND CHILDREN

THE PRETTIEST OF THE WHITE GOWNS

By Isabel A. Mallon

ILLUSTRATIONS FROM THE JOURNAL'S OWN MODELS

THE white lawn gown shown in illustration is made over a foundation of pale heliotrope lawn separate from the skirt, except at the belt-joining. The bodice is gathered on cords, and has two rows of narrow lace of a deep écru shade gathered in with each cord. The epaulettes are edged with lace. The sleeves are corded with the lace running lengthwise, frills of it coming down over the wrists. The collar is composed of narrow ruffles of the lace, and two rows are about the edge of the skirt. The crush belt is made of the heliotrope velvet.

OF DOTTED SWISS

THE PRINCESSE EFFECT

THE fashionable materials for the white toilettes of the summer are cloth, serge, *crêpe de chine*, chiffon, piqué (always with a soft finish), duck, mull, Swiss muslin, lawn and organdy.

A dotted Swiss muslin constitutes the costume shown in illustration. The skirt is laid in lengthwise groups of fine tucks that reach quite a distance on the skirt, and then flare to give fullness, the

THE design shown in the toilette of white *crêpe de chine* in illustration consists of a skirt and bodice giving the princesse effect. The front is of guipure, while the other portions of the skirt and bodice are of *crêpe de chine*. The outline of the *crêpe de chine* is defined by rows of pale green velvet ribbon laid on in scant frills, and a sash of the same shade, but of broader velvet ribbon, is arranged in loops and long ends at the back. Narrow epaulettes are outlined with the velvet ribbon fulled on, while the sleeves are finished with rows of narrow velvet ribbon.

1896 News Feature

"Where the Immigrants Go," Editorial, *The New York Times*, January 27, 1896:

"The Immigration-Restriction League" has made an interesting and suggestive inquiry, of which it publishes results. It sent a committee to Ellis Island, in the harbor of New York, to investigate the illiteracy of immigrants, the destination of the less desirable nationalities, and the amount of money brought in by immigrants of all classes. The committee was engaged but three days, and examined only 865 immigrants, so that it is rather risky to state, as it does, that "it is believed that the results obtained are characteristic of such immigration throughout the year." For instance, among the immigrants classified in the reports there are no Irish and no Italians, nationalities which are clearly not neglectable quantities in the total of immigrants. Nevertheless, the results of the inquiry are, so far as they go, well worth considering.

The one factor that stands out more clearly than all others is that the Atlantic states, and, naturally, the largest cities in those states, get the mass of immigrants who are least desirable either as their literacy or as to nationality. They get the bulk of the illiterates of those who, coming from states least like our own, have least fitness for our form of civic life. Plus, all the Germans and Bohemians examined could read and write. Of the former, 34 percent, and of the latter, 70 percent went West of the Atlantic states. Only 10 percent of the Finns were illiterate, and 31 percent went West. But of the Russians, Hungarians, Galicians, Croats and Syrians, about 37 percent to 69 percent were illiterate and 89 percent remained in the Atlantic states. Of these, the distribution is significant. About one-half of them went to Pennsylvania, chiefly, no doubt, to the mines of that state. Of the Syrians, with 69 percent of the illiterates, 77 percent remained in New York. The information as to the money brought in by the immigrants is curious. The statistics for the fiscal year 1895 show an average of $16.34 for each immigrant and an average of $25.97 for those over 20 years of age. But of the 331 illiterates examined by the committee, only 32 percent had as much as $10 each, while 68 percent had less than that amount. This shows that the statistics are very misleading, and for all detailed reasoning are worse than useless.

It is well-known that the "Immigration-Restriction League" advocates, as an important means to its avowed end, the "exclusion of all persons between 14 and 60 years of

age who cannot read and write the English language or some other language." If this restriction were to be adopted in principle, it is probable that the advantages to be got from
it would be secured practically by the limitation of exclusion to 50 years from 60, as such
a change would lessen the hardship caused by the exclusion of parents and elder relatives
brought over by immigrants who have prospered significantly to be able to send for them.
Even in this form, however, the need of the restriction is not, in our judgment, by any
means completely established. The most serious argument generally advanced in its favor
is based on the mischief of the admission to the suffrage of unfit persons. That is very
great, beyond all question.

But this is a mischief of our own doing. The laws as they now are are quite sufficient
to prevent it if they are decently administered. The immigrant does not become a voter
unconditionally by mere length of residence. The law, on the contrary, imposes very definite conditions. Though reading and writing are not specifically included, they are implied, for the applicant for naturalization must satisfy the court, in the quaint but ex-
pressive language of the opening years of the century—the statute of 1802 still remains in
force—he is "a man of good moral character, attached to the principles of the Constitution of the United States, and well disposed to good order and happiness of the same."
Now it is perfectly plain that no honest judge really can be satisfied that a man is "attached to the principles of the Constitution of the United States" who cannot read the
Constitution, and the cases are so rare as to be of no account where a man could read the
Constitution with understanding but could not write. The disagreeable, undeniable truth
is that evils of naturalization, which have been enormous, are sorely and wholly the fruit
of the incompetency and practical corruption in our courts. For no judge in nearly a century has consented to the naturalization of an unfit applicant without betraying the trust
imposed in him. The reform we need at this point cannot be made at the entrance of our
harbors. It must be made in the bosom of every community. We must exclude ignorance
and unfitness not on the steerage of the steamships but from the benches of our courts.
This once done, the regulation of immigration with reference to other ills will be comparatively simple.

1900–1909

At the dawning of the new century, nearly one million immigrants a year were flooding to America and its promise of a better life—buoyed by their highly individuated dreams and images of these near mythic shores. In the eyes of the world, America was the land of opportunity. Millions of immigrants flooded the United States, often finding work in the new factories of the New World—many managed by men who came two generations before from countries like England, Germany or Wales. When Theodore Roosevelt proudly proclaimed in 1902, "The typical American is accumulating money more rapidly than any other man on earth," he described accurately both the joy of newcomers and the prosperity of the emerging middle class. Elevated by their education, profession, inventiveness or capital, the managerial class found numerous opportunities to flourish in the new economy. Legislation passed in 1903 and 1907 strengthened the hand of the federal government to enforce immigration laws along the Mexican border. At the time, millions also returned to their homeland to rebuild their lives based on U.S. earnings. And reform was in the air. . . .

At the beginning of the century, the 1900 U.S. population, comprising 45 states, stood at 76 million, an increase of 21 percent since 1890; 10.6 million residents were foreign-born and more were coming every day. The number of immigrants in the first decade of the twentieth century was double the number for the previous decade, exceeding one million annually in four of the 10 years, the highest level in U.S. history. Business and industry were convinced that unrestricted immigration was the fuel that drove the growth of American industry. Labor was equally certain that the influx of foreigners continually undermined the economic status of native workers and kept wages low.

The change in productivity and consumerism came with a price: the character of American life. Manufacturing plants drew people from the country into the cities. The traditional farm patterns were disrupted by the lure of urban life. Ministers complained that lifelong churchgoers who moved to the city often found less time and fewer social pressures to attend worship regularly. Between 1900 and 1920, the urban population increased by 80 percent compared to just over 12 percent for rural areas. During the same time, the non-farming workforce went from 783,000 to 2.2 million. Unlike farmers, these workers drew a regular paycheck, and spent it.

With this movement of people, technology and ideas, nationalism took on a new meaning in America. Railroad expansion in the middle of the nineteenth century had made it possible to move goods quickly and efficiently throughout the country. As a result, commerce, which had been based largely on local production of goods for local consumption, found new markets. Ambitious merchants expanded their businesses by appealing to broader markets.

In 1900, America claimed 58 businesses with more than one retail outlet called "chain stores"; by 1910, that number had more than tripled, and by 1920, the total had risen to 808. The number of clothing chains alone rose from seven to 125 during the period. Department stores such as R.H. Macy in New York and Marshall Field in Chicago offered vast arrays of merchandise along with free services and the opportunity to "shop" without purchasing. Ready-made clothing drove down prices, but also promoted fashion booms that reduced the class distinction of dress. In rural America, the mail order catalogs of Sears, Roebuck and Company reached deep into the pocket of the common man and made dreaming and consuming more feasible.

All was not well, however. A brew of labor struggles, political unrest, and tragic factory accidents demonstrated the excesses of industrial capitalism so worshipped in the Gilded Age. The labor reform movements of the 1880s and 1890s culminated in the newly formed American Federation of Labor as the chief labor advocate. By 1904, 18 years after it was founded, the AFL claimed 1.676 million of 2.07 million total union members nationwide. The reforms of the labor movement called for an eight-hour workday, child-labor regulation, and cooperatives of owners and workers. The progressive bent of the times also focused attention on factory safety, tainted food and drugs, political corruption, and unchecked economic monopolies.

1901 PROFILE

At 15 years old, Petros Bakolas arrived in America from Greece to work in a shoe factory to pay for his sisters' dowries; soon, he was not so sure he wanted to return to his homeland.

Life at Home

- When Petros Bakolas arrived at Ellis Island two years earlier, his father's first words were, "Welcome, son, it is now your turn."
- Since he was a young boy, Petros had known that he would be responsible for raising the dowries of his sisters, but that did not stop the sting of his father's words.
- Petros had come to America in the company of five young men, all from a village outside Sparta, Greece.
- All six had been recruited to work in a shoe factory in Cincinnati, Ohio, which was willing to pay the steamship fare to bring them to America.
- The entire trip over, the young Greek emigrants debated their vision of America; most believed they could make their fortune in one summer and be back in their homeland by fall.
- Petros's father had believed the same, but it took him four years to raise the money for one dowry.
- When Petros arrived, his father's comment clearly indicated that he was heading back to Greece as soon as possible.
- It was lonely enough to be a 15-year-old immigrant in America; it was twice as lonely to know that he'd soon be seeing the back of his father's shirt.
- For years Petros had dreamed about seeing his father again, feeling his rough hands upon his shoulders and sharing stories old and new.
- He had even looked forward to traveling together by train from New York to Cincinnati, where his father worked as a shoemaker since arriving in the first wave of Greeks coming to America.
- Unlike emigrants from the rest of Europe, Greek emigrants joined the flood of workers streaming into the country later than most.

At 15, Petros Bakolas arrived in America from Greece.

- And despite poverty and poor farming in their homeland, most vowed in their hearts they were only leaving their beloved Greece temporarily, just until they had enough money for their sisters' dowries, to construct a house or to buy a farm.
- The majority of Greek immigrants were young men who had left rural areas still under the oppressive rule of the Ottoman Turks.
- The people were not only poor, but their family obligations weighed very heavily upon them.
- Brothers were expected to pay their sisters' dowries before they could start their own families.
- Complicating matters, taxes were high under Turkish rule and many families carried long-standing farm debts.
- During their first meal together in America, Petros's father told him that he would not be going to Cincinnati; instead, he would be boarding a steamship the next day.
- He'd been away for four years and was eager to see his homeland.
- Then he coughed loudly, held his sides tightly and wiped some bloody spittle from his mouth.
- His advice: Only buy from Greeks; stay away from unions and American girls; avoid cold, closed buildings; and come home quickly so his younger sisters could marry.
- "Enough of America," he said in Greek as he left for the docks the next morning, "Now it is your turn."
- Arrangements had been made for Petros to work at a shoe factory in Ohio; now all he needed to do was get there.
- None of the six boys from Sparta spoke English, and none had ever ridden a train or used American money.
- Two were still dressed like Greek farmers, which attracted stares, even in New York.
- But they had jobs if they could find Ohio using the train tickets the company had provided.
- Greek immigrants were known for their excellent manual dexterity, solid work ethic and a great capacity to save money.
- This last attribute kept the workers out of bars and made them more dependable, especially on Saturdays and Mondays when hangovers were epidemic.

Petros and other arrivals from Sparta, Greece, took the train from New York to Ohio to begin work.

- Petros's mother had died in childbirth when he was nine years old.
- When his father went to America to make his fortune a few years later, Petros was raised by an aunt and uncle.
- For decades, the men of his village had been heading for other lands to make a living, but rarely were they gone for more than two years.
- So his father's letter calling for his oldest son and five other willing workers to take jobs in America caused village-wide excitement and speculation.
- Petros's village was up in the mountains where the backs of animals instead of wheels were used to carry things.
- Petros saw his first wheeled cart when he was 15 and getting ready for his journey to America.
- The trip to America also introduced him to trains, ocean-going steamships, large crowds and bananas.
- Bananas were part of a welcome basket provided by a Christian organization in New York whose gifts included several pamphlets in English, which Petros could not read, and some fruit.
- None of the six boys from Greece knew what to do with the yellow fruit until a passerby demonstrated how to peel it; Petros immediately loved the creamy exotic taste and vowed to eat bananas often.
- Once the immigrants arrived in Cincinnati aboard a train, there were people waiting for them to go directly to an apartment owned by their new employer.
- There they were treated to ice cream—another delight first enjoyed in America.

- Then the six young men were shown where they could sleep in the two-bedroom apartment and where to report for work the next day.
- Accustomed to small rooms and crowded conditions their entire lives, all six elected to sleep on the floor of one room.

Life at Work

- Petros learned quickly that the Greeks must stick together to survive in a world that spoke a different language, dressed in a different manner and seemed not to care what life was like back in Greece.
- Work quickly became an oasis of pleasure; two Greek supervisors—and friends of his father—were very willing to show Petros how to both operate the leather-sewing machinery and manage life in a new land.
- Within a week he felt capable of producing an acceptable shoe that met the standards of the company.
- And he made his first American money.
- Living with five fellow workers from Greece proved less acceptable.
- The oldest of the group, Iannis, wanted to establish all the rules and enforce them with a rigidity Petros found inappropriate.
- But following Greek tradition, he allowed the oldest to rule—until he was told he could not attend school at night to learn English.
- The YMCA down the street was offering free classes to newly arrived immigrants on how to read, write and speak English.
- Within days of his arrival, Petros had decided to learn English so he would not be hassled on the streets of Cincinnati.
- Yet the boy who had taken the role of boss said, "No."
- Iannis believed that everyone should stay together as a group; besides, he was convinced that Petros simply wanted to meet girls, not learn English.
- He said that everything in the United States was out of proportion, was too loose and free, and that going to school alone could only cause trouble.

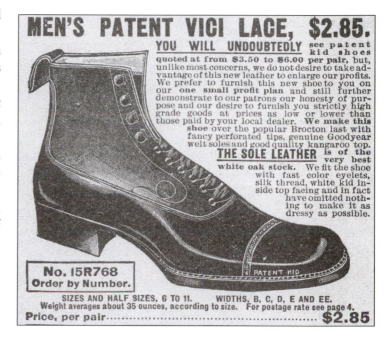

Petros quickly learned how to produce quality shoes at the shoe factory.

- Iannis said there was no YMCA in Greece, so none was necessary here.
- Petros went to the night classes anyway, only to find all the apartment doors locked when he returned.
- A major shouting match ensued and four of the six moved out so they could attend school also.
- Overnight, Petros had become the leader.
- His work started at 7 a.m. and lasted until 6 p.m. with one hour for lunch.
- He had to learn how to care for himself with no mother, no father, no uncles, no aunts or help from the community.
- In a place where all the sounds and smells were different, he had to work a full day, take care of his clothing, learn to cook and go to school at night if he wanted to be an American.
- He was paid between $4.75 and $7.50 a week, depending on his production; 10 weeks of the year he was laid off without pay when boot and shoe orders became slow.
- No sick leave was permitted, no holidays except Christmas, and no compensation if injured on the job.
- Most workers did not report on-the-job injuries for fear of losing employment; every immigrant knew that dozens of workers were willing to take his place as soon as he complained or slowed down.
- Immigrants also knew that talking to union organizers was dangerous business, especially after the major labor strikes the boot and shoemaking industry had experienced a few years earlier.
- The unions were all promising better pay, shorter hours and more breaks.

Petros learned enough English to socialize with Americans on the street.

- Within nine months Petros had learned enough English at work and at the YMCA to be willing to speak to Americans on the street.
- For the first time he understood that the ruffians in his community thought he was Italian, hated his clothes and respected his powerful shoulders.
- His YMCA classes also taught him about dangerous diseases such as tuberculosis, or TB, which was killing thousands around the world.
- Their description included the hacking cough, high fever and the bloody mouth he had seen on his arrival, and for the first time understood why his father was so eager to return to Greece: he was dying of the dread disease in a foreign land among strangers.
- On Sundays, after communion in a tiny Greek orthodox service, Petros often took the trolley outside the city so he could walk the farmlands of Ohio and dream of Greece.
- Every month he was sending money home so his two younger sisters could marry, and often shined shoes in the park on Sundays so his remittances would be larger.
- All around him he saw opportunity and often wondered whether he really wished to return to Greece when the time came.
- Now that he was learning to speak English and had acquired a passing knowledge of sums, he wondered whether he could become a merchant—an American merchant.
- Working in a factory was for animals, willing to do the same thing over and over again for the little grain the bosses chose to toss.
- Besides, he might even defy his father's advice and marry an American girl who had grown up in a brick house with heat, knew about trains and had even seen an automobile.

At 15, Petros began working in America.

Transportation by rail was especially good in Cincinnati, with more than 20 railroads within city limits.

Life in the Community: Cincinnati, Ohio

- Owing to its peculiarly eligible location, Cincinnati had long been a manufacturing center respected for its ingenuity.
- Transportation by rail and water were especially good; more than 20 railroads converged within its borders.
- Annually, the Ohio River cheaply moved abundant quantities of bituminous coal from Pennsylvania, West Virginia and Ohio to power the factories and support 500,000 people living in the city and surrounding area.
- Well-known for its whiskey distilleries, Cincinnati also boasted iron making, White Burley tobacco manufacturing, several cigar box factories and the manufacture of numerous lines of clothing, boots and shoes.
- In addition, the oldest and best-known publishing house in the West, Robert Clarke & Co., started in Cincinnati in 1857; locals liked to brag that so many schoolbook publishers existed in the city that a finished book was turned out "with every swing of the pendulum of a clock."
- The manufacture of billiard tables was one of the largest industries in Cincinnati at the turn of the twentieth century; Cincinnati was also home to Baldwin and Company, manufacturer of organs and pianos, and the famous Rookwood pottery, a high art institution of the city.

In addition to factory work, Cincinnati boasted a thriving music scene.

For many Greeks, employment as a street vendor was a first step toward a more promising career.

- Cincinnati was also proud of the well-appointed Procter & Gamble factory village, Ivorydale, created to manufacture its celebrated Ivory soap and candles.
- By contrast, ancient Greece, which had inspired one of the greatest civilizations in history of the world, scarcely showed any traces of its former glory in 1900.
- Wracked by internal conflict and conquest, Greek citizens were eager to find their fortunes elsewhere.
- For thousands, employment in American factories, mines, and as street vendors was a first step toward a more promising career.
- And once they had acquired enough capital, Greeks who elected to stay in America habitually established small shops to sell flowers, confectionery or prepared foods.
- These family-run businesses enjoyed a high degree of success, as everyone in the Greek community tended to support one another.
- So successful were the Greek restaurants, Petros was able to regularly find feta cheese, kokoresti and domathakia—reminders of home—by his second year in America.

HISTORICAL SNAPSHOT
1901

- The independent Commonwealth of Australia was proclaimed
- The New York stock exchange trading exceeded two million shares for the first time in history
- The Automobile Club of America installed directional signs on major highways
- Britain's Queen Victoria died at age 82 after presiding over her empire for nearly 64 years—the longest reign in British history
- Women Prohibitionists smashed 12 saloons in Kansas
- United States Steel Corporation was incorporated by J.P. Morgan, the biggest corporate merger of the time
- The Pan-American Exposition in Buffalo, New York, which featured the latest technologies including electricity and the baby incubator building, attracted nearly eight million people
- At the Pan-American Exposition in Buffalo, New York, deranged anarchist Leon Czolgosz shot President William McKinley who became the third American president to be assassinated
- U.S. Army soldiers led by Brig. Gen. Frederick Funston captured Emilio Aguinaldo, the leader of the Philippine Insurrection of 1899
- The Oldsmobile plant in Detroit was destroyed by fire
- New York became the first state to require automobile license plates for a fee of $1.00
- Walter Reed led the Yellow Fever Commission to Cuba to search for the cause of the disease; Cuban Dr. Carlos Finlay believed that yellow fever was spread by mosquitoes
- The Wild Bunch, led by Butch Cassidy, committed its last American robbery near Wagner, Montana, taking $65,000 from a Great Northern train
- Over 74,000 Pittsburgh steel workers went on strike
- Hubert Cecil Booth patented the vacuum cleaner
- Vice President Theodore Roosevelt offered the advice, "Speak softly and carry a big stick," in a speech at the Minnesota State Fair
- The Peace of Peking (Beijing) ended the Boxer Rebellion in China
- Theodore Roosevelt changed the name of the "Executive Mansion," to "The White House"
- Edward Elgar's "Pomp and Circumstance" march premiered in Liverpool
- Race riots across America, sparked by Booker T. Washington's visit to the White House to dine with President Theodore Roosevelt, killed 34
- The U.S. was given extensive rights by Britain for building and operating a canal through Central America
- The Army War College was established in Washington, D.C.
- King Camp Gillette, a former bottle-cap salesman, began selling safety razor blades

Selected Prices

Curtains, Muslin	$1.00
Dining Room Suite	$23.00
False Teeth, Set	$3.00
Hotel Room, Atlantic City, per Day	$3.00
Lead Paint, Pound	$0.07
Liver Pills, Bottle	$0.12
Radiator	$9.45
Rubber Teething Ring	$0.10
Tombstone, Marble	$7.65
Wedding Invitations, 100	$2.25

"Still Afraid of American Shoes," *The New York Times,* August 7, 1901:

Vienna—At a largely attended meeting of shoemakers here today it was decided, in spite of the announcement that an American firm would not open a branch in Vienna, that the shoemakers should continue the anti-American crusade, with the view of guarding against a recrudescence of "Yankee schemes." No definite decision was arrived at as to what form the next action of the shoemakers will take.

OUR ACME QUEEN PARLOR ORGAN, $27.45.

WE CHALLENGE any and all competition to produce the equal of this ELEGANT HIGH CLASS ORGAN at anything like our DIRECT FROM FACTORY PRICE.

No. 12R22 ORDER BY NUMBER

DESCRIPTION OF OUR ACME QUEEN ORGAN.

DIMENSIONS—The height is 72 inches, the length is 42 inches and the width is 23 inches. You will observe by these dimensions that it is large, full size and in this respect equal to anything your retail dealer ordinarily carries in stock.

SHIPPING WEIGHT—The weight of this organ, boxed for shipment, is about 350 pounds. We box and pack our organs with great care, paying special attention to this detail, so that the instrument may reach you in perfect condition, not marred in any way, shape or manner.

THE FREIGHT on the organ will be very little compared with what we save you. See first class freight rates as given in front of book. In most instances the freight to any point within 200 miles would be about $1.50; 500 miles, $2.25; 1,000 miles, $5.00, and so on, and when you compare the $20.00 to $30.00 saving with the small freight charges, you can readily see that there is no comparison whatever.

COMPLETE IN EVERY RESPECT.

ACTION—The action of this high grade Acme Queen Organ consists of the celebrated Newell reeds, which are used only in the highest grade instruments. This organ is fitted with Hammond's Couplers and Vox Humana, also the best Dolge felts, leather, etc.

This organ has five octaves, eleven stops, two octave couplers, one toning swell, one grand organ swell, four sets of orchestral toned resonatory high quality reeds, one set exquisitely pure and sweet Melodia reeds, 37 in all, one set of 37 charmingly brilliant Celeste reeds, one set of 24 rich, mellow, smooth, Diapason reeds, one set of 24 pleasing, soft, melodious, Principal reeds; a total of 122 reeds.

NAMES OF THE ELEVEN STOPS—Diapason, Principal, Dulciana, Melodia, Celeste, Cremona, Bass Coupler, Treble Coupler, Diapason Forte, Principal Forte and Vox Humana.

THE CASE—It is difficult from the illustration, even large as the one shown, or from a general description to give you an idea of the beauty of this case. It is one of the handsomest ever used on any organ at anything like the price. We furnish it only in solid oak, handsomely finished, beautifully carved and ornamented. It is especially constructed to develop the acoustic properties of the organ, forming a qualifying chamber, which gives a pipe like quality to the tone hitherto unattained in the finest reed organs. Special attention has been given to the seasoning of the wood of which this organ is constructed, so that it is not subject to climatic changes. It is highly finished, has a 16x14 inch French bevel plate mirror, nickel plated pedal frames and every modern improvement.

THE BELLOWS—The bellows used in this action are made of the best rubber cloth and of 3-ply bellows stock, and the finest sheepskin leather in the valves.

THE TONE—The tone is one of the most important qualities in any organ and with our Acme Queen the tone is faultless. The depth and breadth of the sounding chamber is exactly proportioned, so as to give beauty to the tone without sacrificing the sweetness. This together with the finely tempered metal used in the reeds, secures a purity of tone which can only be equaled by the soft pipe of the church organ.

We are safe in saying that in no other organ manufactured have these pipe like qualities been procured. The special feature in the action of our Acme Queen Organ will be found only in organs of this manufacture.

Do you hesitate to send cash with your order? Read what we say about cash terms on page 1.

$27.46
BUYS THE ORGAN

and we are bound to please you or the organ is shipped back to us and you get

ALL YOUR MONEY RETURNED.

25 YEARS' GUARANTEE.

FREE...

With this organ we present you FREE and ship with it, a fine **ORGAN STOOL** and a very complete and valuable **INSTRUCTION BOOK.**

SEARS, ROEBUCK & CO. ORGAN INSTRUCTOR

Acme Queen

"Flower Boys at Home," *The New York Times*, April 15, 1896:

In a rather dilapidated tenement in the rear of a building on Thirteenth Street, between Fifth and Sixth Avenues, are four rooms on the first floor that are occupied every night by 30 or 40 swarthy boys and men. They are strewn about the floor, some with mattresses and others with a single blanket between their bodies and an uncarpeted floor, but all sleeping as soundly as though stowed away in one of the rooms at the Hotel Waldorf.

In one of the rooms, there is a large ice chest, with rows of shelves, and on which stand vases of flowers divesting up so large a share of their natural bloom and fragrance that they make a sickly odor. The atmosphere of the four apartments is so deeply tainted with this odor that the visitor shrinks from entering. The occupants do not, however, seem to mind it.

A canvas cot in one room, with a rug in front of it, denotes the resting place of the master of the premises. He is known as "George the Greek." The little colony represents a large portion of the "flower boys" of New York; there the peddlers sell roses and violets along Twenty-third and Fourteenth Streets at elevated stations, along Broadway, Fifth Avenue, Park Row, and Sixth Avenue.

They are all Greeks, and they are nearly all in the employ of "George the Greek" and another enterprising Greek. They range in age from 14 to 40. They know very little English. Their monthly wages seldom amounted to $7.00, and are more frequently $4.00 and $5.00.

"George the Greek" has amassed a fortune of nearly $20,000 in the last five years. He is now able to pay $4,000 a year rent for the flower stand in front of Grand Central Station. George started in an unpretentious way. By living frugally he was enabled in a short time to buy a stand on Twenty-third Street. That was in the days when street hawkers were allowed to have stands on the sidewalk and to sell from a pushcart at one place as long as they cared to. . . .

The street trade in flowers has been usurped by the Greeks, because they are able to live on less than the Italians or Americans. The latter have consequently been driven out.

When spring comes, George wends his way to Bleecker Street and inspects the newly arrived Greek immigrants, who find temporary lodgings in that part of the city. He picks out several score of those who know the least English and the least about the value of American money, and he takes them up to his quarters, where they are instructed as to the proper way to induce pedestrians to buy flowers, the various methods of eluding police, and the way to wire flowers.

The last point is the most important. If the flowers are not wired and arranged correctly, they lose value. The process of wiring consists of thrusting a fine steel wire down through the stem every rose, violet, or any other flower that may be on the market, in such a way that it is concealed from the buyer. This enables the boys to make half a dozen flowers occupy the space in a bunch that a dozen unwired flowers would occupy.

The flowers are purchased at the Cut Flower Exchange on Thirty-fourth Street. . . . These men sell the flowers which come in every morning from Long Island, New Jersey, and New York State. The florists and big stores get the first pick. After they have taken what they want for the day, George and other street dealers get what is left, or the "dreck," according to the technical term.

A future Greek "flower boy."

continued

"Flower Boys at Home" . . . *(continued)*

Flowers are taken to the rooms on Thirteenth Street, where each boy wires his own stock for the day, and starts off to sell them. No particular districts are allotted to the boys, the object being to keep out of the clutches of the police, for, though required by law to have licenses, none of them are citizens, and, therefore cannot obtain them.

They start at about 10 o'clock in the morning and scatter through the shopping district. Toward evening they move up in the theater district. The last stand is taken along Third Ave and Twenty-third and Fourteenth Streets only. They stay out, as a rule, until they are disposed of their stock, returning shortly before midnight.

Before leaving their "home" in the morning, boys are given a breakfast of "Greek stew," the ingredients of which vary, and a weak coffee. They exist until evening on this, and a roll each is stowed away in a coat pocket and munched between sales. In the evening they are served with a meal of fruit and wine. . . .

"Risks of Modern Life," *The Youth's Companion*, February 17, 1898:

Most of the appliances of modern civilization bring risks as well as advantages. The people who lived a hundred years ago could not travel so rapidly nor communicate with each other across great distances so conveniently as we do; but on the other hand, they were strangers to some perils of which are familiar nowadays.

The journeys were slow and serious affairs; but they were in no danger of being blown up on a steamboat, tumbled over a railway embankment, or even of being run over by a trolley-car or a scorching wheelman. Their houses were not lighted by electricity or by water gas; but they were not burned out by reason of badly insulated wires or asphyxiated in their beds. They knew nothing of 15-story buildings, but they also knew nothing of elevator accidents.

Nevertheless, it is doubtful if more lives are lost by accidents of travel, in proportion of the number of people traveling, that was the case a century ago.

Hundreds of people travel by water now as one did so then; but ocean travel has been made relatively more safe as well as more swift and comfortable, by modern appliances. There are still possibilities of collision or striking a reef in the fog, but it almost never happens to modern seaworthy vessel founders through stress of weather. One steamship company which has sent steamers back and forth across the Atlantic for more than 50 years is able to boast it has never lost the life of a passenger in service.

As to the railways, in 1896 181 passengers were killed on the railways of the United States; nearly 2,900 were injured. When these figures are compared with the amount of passenger traffic, it appears that the railways carried nearly three million passengers for every one who was killed, and about 180,000 passengers for every passenger injured.

A famous humorist once compared the number of people killed in railway accidents with the number dying in their beds, and reached the conclusion it was several thousand times more risky to lie in bed than to travel on a railway. It was a playful exaggeration; but it is true that, if modern discovery and invention have resulted in new hazards to human life, they have also supplied new safeguards.

The mention of Greece fills the mind with the utmost exalted sentiments

—President James Monroe, 1822

"Fighting Tuberculosis," *The Youth's Companion*, March 18, 1909:

It has always been recognized that in warfare, knowledge of the enemy's weak points confers immense tactical advantage. This was never truer than in the tremendous crusade that mankind is banding together to wage against the dread foe, tuberculosis.

A few decades ago this particular enemy of the human race was not believed to have any vulnerable spots. It was thought by all to be invincible, and its mere touch meant death. Then it was gradually discovered that, after all, certain weapons were at hand by means of which mankind could give fight; that before sunlight, fresh air and proper food this foe would recoil like Mephistopheles before the crucifix.

Then, little by little, the fight was begun. By example and precept people were taught not to lie down and die, but to stand up and fight for themselves.

The good news was taken to the tenements and crowded parts of great cities, where sunshine and fresh air are not secured without a struggle, but where they are just as efficacious as in the haunts of wealth.

The great free exhibits given by the International Tuberculosis Exhibition are of immense value in this educational crusade; the charity that takes the form of paying car fares in order that the poor of the tenements may not miss this invaluable object lesson is a very real one. Here the mother who is trying to save her stricken child in two small rooms of the tenement district is shown those two rooms as they probably are and as they may be. In the first instance dirty, cluttered up with the useless rubbish, with every crack through which air may filter carefully stuffed with unclean rags. Then side-by-side with this picture, the same rooms cleaned and purified, with windows which will open wide and stay open, and with nothing in sight that cannot be made clean and kept clean.

The great lesson is taught in capital letters and comfort in stuffiness are not synonymous terms; that whitewash is a thousand times better than an ancient, germ-laden wallpaper, it can be applied by anyone, and as often as is desirable; that a floor that can be washed daily with soap and water feels better and looks better than the same floor covered with scraps of microbe-infested carpet; and that sanitary receptacles can be had for the asking, which make it possible to expectorate without endangering the lives of the whole family.

It would be well indeed if these exhibitions could be taken in every town and village in the country.

"Crowding Ellis Island, Record Breaking Immigration Taxes Bureau's Resources," *The New York Times*, April 13, 1902:

Within the last six weeks the quarters of the Immigration Bureau on Ellis Island have been taxed to their utmost for the first time since they were established there. The number of foreigners who arrived here in March was 59,000, or 23,000 more than the total number of immigrants to this port during the whole of last year. If the present rate of immigration continues through the year more than 300,000 people will have been accommodated on the island before next January.

The chances are that the immigration of the year will be greater than any year since 1882, and the number of newcomers will equal, if not exceed, the total number of steamship arrivals for four of the years since 1892. Last Monday night 1,498 immigrants slept on the island, more than have ever been there overnight. During six weekdays within the last fortnight the men and women accommodated were 3,000 and more each day, a one-day 6,000 passed inspection during the 12 hours succeeding 7 a.m.

1905 Profile

Deirdre Mellane, having finally made the decision to emigrate to America, settled in Boston, Massachusetts, as a servant in the home of a wealthy family.

Life at Home

- By the time Dee Mellane made her final decision to leave Ireland and journey to America, her community in County Mayo was depleted.
- So many young people had left Mayo for a better life, it was no longer a custom to stage an "American wake"—a farewell celebration to mark the passage of an Irish person to America.
- For more than 50 years, Irish men and women had been leaving the poverty of Ireland for the promise of America; most never returned.
- Dee was even forced to walk to the train station by herself since her brothers had already left for America and her sisters were angry that she was leaving, too.
- For the last decade, Irish women had been emigrating in such large numbers, more women than men were leaving Ireland, the only emigrant group in which this was the case.
- Irish women were in demand as servants, a better paying job than most men could find.
- In Ireland women had few opportunities for employment; even marriage held almost no prospects for women, since relatively few men possessed the dowry required for claiming a bride.
- Since the 1840s the Irish had been fleeing their homeland in large numbers, most with hopes of improving their condition, while retaining grateful recollections of the land they left.
- Ireland was still home to them, and held strong ties to their affection.
- Dee, at 19 years old, had come to her decision to emigrate late.
- For more than a year she had been engaged to a local farmer whose work habits and lack of luck prevented him from raising a dowry.
- Recently, against the advice of her mother and sisters, she called the wedding off and announced she was leaving for America.

Dierdre left Ireland to work for a wealthy family in Boston.

A large staff of servants was not uncommon for many upper class Boston families.

- When she was finally persuaded to stay, she received a letter from her cousin in Boston asking her emigrate and work in the home of a wealthy family.
- Then she decided to go.
- Under the proposal, her passage would be paid in advance by the family who was eager to hire another Irish girl to help tend their four children and serve meals.
- Irish servants knew their place, the letter said, and were easier to manage despite their Catholic upbringing.
- A slowing of the Irish immigration had created a tight labor market in Boston among the upper class, who typically needed half a dozen or more servants to maintain their homes.
- It wasn't the life Dee had anticipated, but she hoped to be luckier in love in America than she had been in Ireland.
- She was hired after three Welch women quit all at once and moved to New York City where salaries were higher.

Life at Work

- Dee's biggest surprise on her first day at work was not the size of the house or the sound of a water closet being flushed, but the presence of dogs inside the house.
- In Ireland dogs were used for herding, hunting and protection, and were expected to live outside.
- In America, even the dogs lived a life of luxury.
- The Vale family's three rambunctious terriers were allowed in every part of the house and were even taken for walks instead of simply being turned out when they became a nuisance.
- But that was not Dee's only surprise.
- Even the sunlight and smells of Boston seemed to be different from her native Ireland.
- At first she thought it was the burning of so much coal in the close area that created the difference, but slowly she came to realize that light, especially early morning light, was different in Boston.
- This realization was disquieting and sparked a serious case of homesickness within days of arrival.
- When she first arrived, she was provided with dresses for every occasion celebrated within the home, including toiletries in a linen handkerchief so fine she wept.
- As a live-in maid, the hours were long—17 hours—but at least she was warm and well fed.
- Her work day began at 5:30 a.m., when she cleaned the kitchen floors and heated the water.
- By 6:30 a.m., she woke the more senior staff and helped light the fires in the eight fireplaces located throughout the house.
- Next, she prepared the other servants' breakfast and delivered breakfast to the upstairs maid, who worked in the nursery.
- By 7:30 a.m., she was appropriately dressed in morning attire and assigned the responsibility of carrying jugs of water upstairs to the children; during the same trip she took away the chamber pots that had become full during the night.
- Chamber pots were emptied and replaced three or four times during the day; in addition, some of the senior servants had their own chamber pots, although most relieved themselves in an outhouse located behind the back kitchen.
- The servants' breakfast was at 7:45 a.m., followed by morning prayer services using a Protestant liturgy in the parlor with the lord and lady of the house and their four children.

Deirdre's workday began at 5:30 am when she cleaned the floors.

- The family breakfast then ensued, followed by cleanup, which could take up to an hour depending on the number of serving dishes used that day.
- Dee then took a short break to change her dress and then began to assist with the cleanup on the main floor of the house, which was covered from stem to stern with souvenirs from numerous trips along the East Coast and throughout Europe.
- In the library, a special display of seashells from around the world had been created, complete with labels that named the shells and gave their scientific designation, date of collection and location.
- Dee learned early that even commenting on a shell would evoke long, elaborate tales about where it came from and the circumstances under which it was discovered.
- At times the stories felt like extended lectures; at other times the wonderful tales of world travel made her feel like she was part of a wealthy and influential family.
- At 1 p.m., lunch was served; Dee and the other servants wore black dresses and white aprons which were always clean and well starched.
- After lunch ended at 2:30 p.m., Dee was free to nap or walk.
- Strolling through Boston listening to the sounds of a modern city excited her.
- And the prospect of romance occupied her thoughts.
- Her daydreams were often filled with a good, hard-working Irish boy picking her out of the crowd, courting her in a proper manner and proposing marriage, while her wealthy employers begged her to stay on.
- In her well-rehearsed daydream, her suitor was also handsome and articulate, with eyes that sparkled with a deep passion.
- Boston was a city endowed with many good-looking Irish boys; the question was, How would she properly entertain one when her mother and sisters were back in Ireland?
- After all, she could hardly expect to use her employer's fancy parlor for entertaining male suitors.
- Several days a week, normally when guests were in the house, the family celebrated high tea at 4:30 p.m.
- Otherwise, Dee was well occupied by 6 p.m., setting the long, custom-made mahogany table for dinner, which was normally served at 7 p.m.
- Dinner preparation included arranging the elaborately embroidered table linen, which required three servants to do properly.
- Dinner, of course, always required formal dress by the family and servants.
- During the first month she was in the home, changing clothes five times a day was exciting, but the ritual quickly lost its glitter.
- Unlike the chance to play with the children.
- In America, wealthy children were expected to play and were given dozens of toys toward that end.
- Dee was fascinated by the tiny carts, twirling tops and elaborate puzzles that the children owned, and by their willingness to share the joy of playing with them.
- Most evenings, dinner was over by 9 p.m., when she and the rest of the servants would eat their final meal of the day before retiring at 10 p.m.
- Her meals often mirrored those eaten by the family, and she was delighted to savor the sweetness of an orange on her first day at work.
- She discovered that the orange skins, when covered by a cloth, could retain their smell for weeks.
- After that, an orange symbolized all that was new and different about America, and why it might become her permanent home.

Dierdre was fascinated by the privilege enjoyed by children of wealthy families in America.

Many Irish immigrants were hardworking merchants.

Life in the Community: Boston, Massachusetts

- Anyone who knew anything about Boston told Dee that she was privileged to work on the South Side in one of its many fine homes.
- There, too, could be found the Cathedral of the Holy Cross, the largest church in New England.
- The interior was grand, she thought, divided by lines of bronzed pillars which upheld a lofty clerestory and an open timber roof.
- The chancel was very deep, and contained a rich and costly altar, and the great organ, at the other end of the church, was one of the best instruments in the country.
- The chancel's stained-glass windows depicted the Crucifixion, Nativity, and Ascension, and the transept windows, each of which covered 800 square feet, represented the Finding of the True Cross, and the Exaltation of the Cross by the Emperor Heraclius, after its recovery from the Persians.
- But Dee quickly discovered there was little in Boston of which Bostonians were more truly proud than the Common and the Public Garden.
- Other cities had larger and more elaborate public grounds, but none of them, she was repeatedly told, could boast a park of greater natural beauty.
- Everything, they said, was "of the plainest and homeliest character, the velvety greensward and the overarching foliage being the sufficient ornaments of the place."
- Dee especially enjoyed the Frog Pond with its fountain, where boys sailed their miniature ships.
- Also, on one of the little hills near the Frog Pond, was the elaborate soldiers' and sailors' monument.
- All the malls and paths were shaded by fine old trees, which formerly had their names conspicuously labeled upon them, giving an admirable opportunity for the study of grand botany.
- Near the Public Garden was the Boston Public Library, one of the most beneficent institutions that had been conceived by the public-spirited and liberal citizens of Boston.
- The immense collection constituting this library was valuable not only because of the variety and number of volumes it contained, but because of its accessibility.
- The library was open to all, and no one who made use of its offerings was charged.
- If a book not in the library was requested, it was ordered and the inquirer notified when it arrived.
- Generous donations by many wealthy and large-hearted men and women from time to time swelled the permanent fund of the institution to upwards of $100,000.
- Large additions to the general library were made yearly, and it numbered more than 450,000 volumes and over 200,000 pamphlets.
- The annual circulation amounted to about 1.3 million separate issues and thus was superior in number of volumes to the Library of Congress.

Bostonians were proud of their open space and many spent leisure time enjoying the outdoors.

Historical Snapshot
1905

- Thirty-five state Audubon organizations incorporated as the National Association of Audubon Societies for the Protection of Wild Birds and Animals

- China initiated a boycott of American goods to protest the United States' treatment of upper-class Chinese tourists

- Russian Orthodox Father George Gapon was leading a procession in St. Petersburg of 200,000 when panicked troops fired into the crowd, igniting the Russian Revolution of 1905

- Elastic rubber began replacing whalebone in women's undergarments such as corsets

- Congress granted statehood to Oklahoma; New Mexico and Arizona remained territories

- The Rotary Club was founded in Chicago by lawyer Paul Percy Harris and several friends

- President Theodore Roosevelt threatened to abolish college football by executive order if rough play was not curtailed after 18 men died and 150 were seriously injured playing the game

- American auto production topped 25,000 cars

- Congress discontinued the coinage of gold dollars

- The average American farmer cultivated 12 acres of land

- Undertaker A. B. Stroenger invented the dial telephone

- Archeologists unearthed the royal tombs of Yua and Tua in Egypt

- Rebel battle flags captured during the Civil War were returned to the South

- Berlin and Paris were linked by telephone

- A Japanese baseball team from Waseda University in Tokyo toured the West Coast for three months, playing 26 games

- Japan and Russia agreed to peace talks brokered by President Theodore Roosevelt

- The world's first theater geared exclusively for motion pictures opened in Pittsburgh

- The International Workers of the World was formed by William Haywood of the Western Federation of Miners, Daniel De Leon of the Socialist Labor Party, and Eugene V. Debs of the Socialist Party

- Race riots in Atlanta, Georgia, killed 12

- Orville Wright piloted the first flight longer than 30 minutes

- Former President Grover Cleveland wrote an article for *The Ladies' Home Journal*, saying "sensible and responsible women do not want to vote"

American auto production topped 25,000 in 1905.

Irish Immigration Timeline

1776

Men of Irish birth or descent formed between one-third to one-half of the American Revolutionary forces, including 1,492 officers and 26 generals.

1790

The first census of the United States recorded 44,000 Irish-born residents, more than half of whom lived south of Pennsylvania.

1791

Irishman James Hoban designed the White House, modeled upon Leinster House in Dublin.

1798

When a revolutionary uprising by the Society of United Irishmen was quelled by the British, many of the Society's members elected to emigrate to the United States.

1801

The Act of Union between Great Britain and Ireland abolished the Irish legislature and created the United Kingdom of Great Britain and Ireland.

1820-1830

Irish immigrants numbering 50,000 entered the United States.

1829

The Emancipation Act lifted penalties for Catholics and Presbyterians in Ireland.

1830-1840

Irish immigrants numbering 237,000 entered the United States.

1838

Poor Relief for Ireland was enacted.

1840-1850

The Great Famine forced more than one million Irish men and women to emigrate.

1840-1850

Irish immigrants numbering 800,000 entered the United States.

1846

All of Ireland was mapped for the first time.

1852

The Tenement Act provided for a uniform evaluation of property for tax purposes in Ireland.

1868

The Irish Reform Bill passed in British Parliament, which allowed a million more men the right to vote.

1870

The Irish Land Act provided protection for tenants.

Selected Prices

Adding Machine $10.00

Baking Powder, Pound $0.10

Drug, Worm Syrup, for Children $0.18

Handkerchief, Men's, White Linen $0.50

Iron Stove $19.50

Rocking Chair, Leather $9.75

Rolltop Desk $37.50

Saddle $19.90

Stockings, Women's $0.25

Tooth Cleanser, Tube $0.25

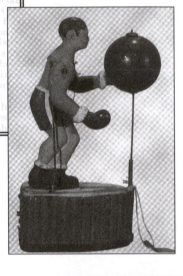

"Ireland in America," *The New York Times*, April 2, 1852:

On Sunday last, 3,000 immigrants arrived at this port. On Monday there were over 2,000. On Tuesday 5,000 arrived. On Wednesday the number was over 2,000. Thus in four days 12,000 persons were landed for the first time upon American shores. A population greater than that of some of the largest and most flourishing villages in the State, was thus added to the city of New York within 96 hours. Every setting sun has seen, thrown amongst us, men, women and children enough to constitute a town. And every year brings to our shores, from foreign lands, more than 300,000 souls. A city almost as large as Philadelphia is annually emptied from ships upon the New York docks. . . .

These are startling facts, and are well fitted to arrest attention, even in an age of startling events. The increase in American population by immigration, is now half as great as the natural increase. And everything indicates that this ratio will continue to advance, that the number of emigrants will be greater every year, for an indefinite time to come. . . .

There is no hope for Ireland, under the present state of things. Her prosperity has been sacrificed to the ambition of England. Her enforced Union to the British Empire prostrated all the barriers by which her own enterprise and industry had been encouraged, and reduced her to an unequal and ruinous competition with her conqueror. Provisions are even now as cheap in Ireland as they are with us. But there is no demand for labor at prices sufficient to pay for them. Emigration, desperate and hard as it is, seems to be the only resource of the Irish people. Transplantation to the United States is all the chance of growth that is left to them. They cannot here, of course, preserve for many generations their nationality. But they can do what is much more important for themselves and their children—they can take deep root in this soil, and grow up with the vigorous and fruitful American tree, which is soon to overshadow this portion, at least, of the planet of which we dwell. . . .

In 1847 alone, *300,000* of the Irish people perished from starvation, or from diseases incident to the lack of food. That same year, 73,000 cattle, 43,143 pigs, and 26,599 crates of eggs were sent into England from the very districts where the famine raged with most severity.

For although the Irishman had nothing for himself or his family to eat, though doomed to stand by and see his wife and children perish day by day from lack of food, he must pay his rent. The landlord must receive his due. And now, in every part of Ireland, men, women and children are turned into the open air, the roof is torn from above them, and the bare walls are leveled to the ground that they may no longer give them shelter, by the barons, or dukes, or earls, to whom the rent is due for their occupation. Is it surprising that men, when they see such inhumanities practiced in the name of order and vested rights, when they see the most heartless cruelties inflicted by grasping avarice, is it surprising that execrations against such laws should rise in the heart and to the lips of men compelled to see and to suffer such things?

The first time I saw the Statue of Liberty, all the people were rushing to the side of the boat. "Look at her, look at her," in all kinds of tongues. "There she is, there she is," like someone was greeting them.

—Elizabeth Phelps, 1920

The first man I saw on the New York pier was a black-skinned human being. He was out in front of the shed, waiting to catch a hawser from the Furnessia. The friendly sunlight dwelt on him; it was October 6, and 1901 as he stood by the bollard in his faded light blue overalls, gazing up at the rope that was being cast to him. America was his fate. It was going to be mine, so we would be having the country in common.

That was a big surprise to me, a colored man. I knew them, since one had come with a circus to Kilkenny. But here was this one, easy and free, giving a hand to us to land in his country. That was something new. It was all going to be new and different.

—Irish immigrant Francis Hackett, age 18, 1901

Make your bargain for your passage with the owner of the ship, or some well-known respectable broker ship-master. Avoid by all means those crimps that are generally found about the docks and quays where ships are taking in passengers. Be sure the ship is going to the port you contract for, as much deception has been practiced in this respect. It is important to select a well-known captain and a fast sailing ship, even at a higher rate.

—Guidebook for Irish immigrants

"Get Aboard, Children!"
Exciting fun, and a wonder as a muscle-maker — the

Irish Mail
"It's geared"

Safest, fastest, strongest, smartest hand car ever made for small boys and girls. Develops all muscles equally — over-taxes none. Rubber tired, light running, splendidly built. Write for booklet, free.

"He can't upset."

If "Irish Mail" — look for name on seat — is not on sale in your town, order from us.

THE STANDARD MANUFACTURING CO.
1453 Irish Mail Street   Anderson, Indiana

"Swelling Tide of Immigration Here, Irish the Only Nationality Showing a Falloff," *The New York Times*, October 19, 1902:

The annual report of Commissioner of Immigration Sargent was made public today. It [says] that of the 648,743 immigrants who arrived in the United States during the last fiscal year, 466,369 were males and 182,374 females. Of the entire number of arrivals, Italy supplied 178,373, an increase of 42,379 over the number for 1901; Austria-Hungary 171,989, an increase of 58,599; and Russia 107,347, an increase of 22,090. Most European countries showed an increase, but there was a falling off in arrivals from Ireland amounting to 1,423, the total from that country being 29,138. The figures concerning Asiatic immigration show a decrease from China of 810, the total being 1,649, and an increase from Japan of 9,001, the total being 14,270, or a 170 percent increase. Of the entire number arriving, 162,188 were unable to read or write, but 74,063 were under 14 years of age. Commenting upon this circumstance, Commissioner Sargent says:

"It can be roughly estimated from the foregoing figures how effective in excluding the aliens would be a reading test, such as that proposed during the recent session of Congress, which would not be applied to children under 15, adults over 50."

The total number of aliens who were refused permission to land was 4,974, or about two-thirds of 1 percent of the total arrivals. Of these, 3,944 were paupers, 709 had diseases, nine were convicts, and 275 were contract laborers.

"Immigration, a Fascinating Subject as It Is Discussed in Prescott F. Hall's Book on Its Effects in This Country," by Edward A. Bradford, *The New York Times*, March, 1906:

This current week a single immigrant ship debarked 2,000 wretched creatures, broken in spirit, weak in body, and just able to pass Inspection admitting them to our shores as not certain to become public charges. And this ship's company is no exception in either quality or number. Speaking first regarding numbers, there is an amazing contrast between the new and old volume of immigration. When single ships bring thousands, it is no wonder the single year's arrivals exceed a million, and that this year's total is at an unprecedented rate. New England's population was produced from 20,000 immigrants before 1640. Less than a generation before the Revolution, Franklin estimated the colonies at about one million descendents from an original immigration of 80,000. The first census after the Revolution, in 1790, gave a total population of four million. The records of immigration begin with 1820, and during the generation from the close of the Revolutionary War until then, immigrants numbered a quarter million, a single quarter year's arrivals now. Before this current year is so ended, the arrivals from 1820 will exceed 24 million.

There is nothing to equal it in history, and history is itself little more than a compendium of migration of races. The Tartar invasion of Europe, the Roman invasion of more than one continent, the invasion of America first by the Spaniards, later by the English, and lately all the tribes of the earth, each migrant people drifting or traveling to the west; these are the greatest facts in the development of peoples and nations. We are assisting and witnessing a racial development rivaling Burbank's experiments in plant life. Never was and never again can be such an opportunity for human stirpiculture. Yet immigration is thought dry and tedious even by those who marvel at Burbank's almost incredible results with plants, although we could if we would most powerfully mold and direct the sort of person a typical American should or will be. And indeed by merely failing to mold him for the better, we are molding him for the worse, and will yet be sorry for it.

It is bathetic to treat such a question as matter of dollars and cents, but this generation has ears for no other call. And the economic effects are stupendous. It cost $1,000 to rear a child to 14. The ages of the last million to arrive are unknown, but it is not exaggeration to say that the immigration of 1905 added a billion to the national wealth. But this is only the beginning. Millions have preceded them, and the product of their labor is authoritatively estimated $800 million annually. Paper and pencil will be needed to figure out what billions that makes her each generation. It's hardly worth mentioning that in 1904 immigrants showed at the Barge office $21 million in cash. There is an offset, of course. There are towns in Ireland and entire districts in Italy which are identifiable by the prosperity diffused by remittances from the United States. But this is rather fuel for flames than money lost to us, or

continued

"Immigration, a Fascinating Subject as It Is Discussed in Prescott F. Hall's Book on Its Effects in This Country" . . . *(continued)*

it stimulates further immigration as nothing else could do. At times it seemed that this flood of labor has created another offset nearer home, but of recent years there has been no unemployed problem except the strikers. Economically it must seem that the question whether immigration pays has been answered affirmatively. We would have developed more slowly in wealth and numbers except for foreign recruits. . . .

The high quality of early immigration needs no proof. It has proved his quality by its works. The Pilgrims, the Quakers, the Pennsylvania Dutch, German rebels, the refugees of later years, the Irish expelled by famine—these were stocks to produce a people to be proud of. Not all of them came among the earliest. They're not enough of them even so late as the Civil War, when native Americans were the stoutest in body and heart in the Army's north and south alike. In those days travel was so tedious and so costly that oceans were crossed only under the stimulus of the strongest motives. Weaklings who attempted that strenuous struggle for life succumbed and the survivors were men indeed, with women worthy of them. But those of this sort come in decreasing numbers and pitifully small totals nowadays. As travel became easier and cheaper, not love of liberty at any sacrifice, but mercenary motives animated later comers. It would have been bad enough if a worst quality of the same familiar stocks joined us as a result of state-aided immigration, meaning assisted departures of dependents, defectives and delinquents. It would be flattering to believe that recent arrivals were attracted by admiration of our institutions. The truth is to say they come by thousands for no better reason than the steamship companies advertise us like a show for the sake of earning passage money for dividends. Oceans are traversed as easily as the journey from New York to Albany was made contemporaneously with early immigration, and the cost is a tithe. Under these conditions, we no longer get the people to whom we are kin, who understand us and whom we understand. We get people of alien bloods and tongues and habits. We are developing race and class and social distinctions and hatreds such as were unknown when even Parsons worked with their hands and every man respected his neighbor. We have foreign colonies whose numbers are below the arrests of that nationality each year. We have in America crimes and criminals of outlandish names. We export as well as import anarchists. When the next depression strikes us, we shall have an unemployment problem to dwarf our Coxey Army, and perhaps to cause London to marvel even as we are marveling at London's misery.

The evils of immigration are largely temporary and local, while the benefits are permanent and national. The flow of immigration to our shores is not alone an index of our prosperity; it is also no insignificant element of the causes of that prosperity. Had an anti-foreign or Know Nothing spirit prevailed half a century ago, our great manufacturing and commercial development would have been driven to other lands.

—Oscar Straus, Secretary of the Department of Commerce and Labor, 1907

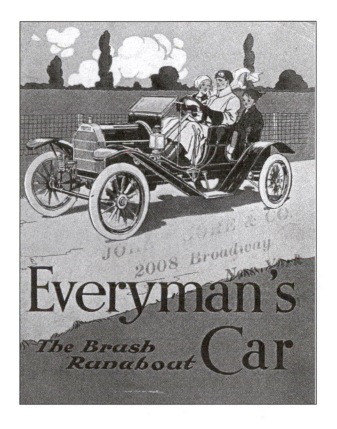

There was a custom, which must have grown up in the famine of 1848, known as the "American wake." It occurred on the eve of an Irish emigrant's departure for the United States. In those days most emigrants never returned, hence the term "wake." My relatives and neighbors gathered in the house, stood around and encouraged me. They said such things as, "Well you're going to be with your brothers, so it will be just like home." I knew that was not true, but I smiled just the same. The older people were saddened, and I had mixed emotions. I feared going to America, but I knew there was nothing left for me in Mayo. . . .

The neighbors left about midnight. Each one pressed a coin into my hand. The sum came to seven dollars in all, a tremendous amount for the poor of our parish to part with. My mother had purchased a new suit for me, tightly fitted and in keeping with the latest Irish style. It was a blue serge suit and the bottom of the jacket barely came to my hips.

The next morning my mother and sisters accompanied me on the trip to the railroad station by pony and trap. There were periods of silence when we faltered in making the best of it. At the station my sisters cried, and my mother didn't. It wasn't manly to cry, so I didn't either until the train left the station. Then I did. I felt bereft and terrified.

—Paul O'Dwyer, 1925

"They Who Never Were Brides," *The Ladies' Home Journal,* June, 1898:

A woman, unless for extraordinary reasons, rarely reaches the years of maturity without having had a chance to marry. But the chances which come into our lives are not always the opportunities which we can embrace. Chances make heralded successes of some people, of others they make silent heroines. It is not always when we turn and grasp an opportunity that we show our greatest strength: the truest character is sometimes shown when the chance comes and we stand aside and resolutely let it pass us, when it might have been ours with the simple taking. That is a quality which is rare, and yet that is a quality which is possessed by so many women who are called "old maids." It is not that these women valued any less the power of a man's love. It was not that they did not believe in it. It was not that they did not know that love was joy, and to be loved great happiness. It is not that they wish the highest gift which can come to a woman should pass through their lives instead of becoming an abiding part of them.

The consciousness of seeing her own charms reflected in a man's eyes is something which appeals to every woman. Nothing else ever makes her so proud and so happy in exactly the same way. But that consciousness is not always for expression; sometimes it is a thing for one's inner self, to be enjoyed at the time he lived over in the years to come. No; women do not willfully turn away from their own happiness. But they do sometimes darken their own lives to make brighter the lives of others who may be closer or dependent upon them. Some higher fundamental duty sometimes calls, loftier motives sometimes quiet the deepest heart longings, a God-given task sometimes points women in the opposite direction of her own instincts. There is such a thing not known to the young, albeit years bring the knowledge as a woman turning away great happiness to insure the greater comfort and happiness of others, choosing their comfort as her life-work. Men do it now and then. But women oftener do it. Memories take the place of realities, and in those memories, sweet and tender, many women are living today. They have never been brides. But they might have been. At one time in their lives the necessity of choice came to them. Prayerfully and fearfully, and yet resolutely she made the choice. Today they are not wives simply because they are heroines. And who will say which is the greater?

1909 PROFILE

The Ravage family, new to America from Romania, found help starting their lives in a new country from Jewish groups whose purpose was to follow the traditions of charity practiced in the old country.

Life at Home

- Anzia Ravage's life was centered around three things: family, home and mother.
- These unifying bonds galvanized her and her entire family against the chaos and brutality of her surroundings.
- From childhood she had been taught by her rabbi that Jews were expected to look after their own in poverty and sickness, life and death, according to the ancient traditions.
- Thus, leaving for a better life in America was not only terrifying but a betrayal of her aging mother and father.
- The one constant for 31-year-old Anzia was family.
- But her husband Aaron, desperate to leave the crushing poverty and rising political persecution of Romania, was prepared to sell all their possessions to raise money for steamship fare.
- Their goal was "di goldeneh medina" or "the golden land" in America.
- Only after a Jewish peddler was beaten to death by a hooligan gang did her father give his consent, saying, "Take my grandchildren and find them a future."
- And then he began to weep, saying, "I will never see you again."
- When her children asked, "Where is this America?" she replied, "I only know it's far away and when you get there they undress you and look you in the eyes—only then can you be an American."
- Then began the business of saying goodbye to neighbors; as a family they went house to house, sometimes spending an entire day with friends talking about the past and whispering about the future.
- Anzia saw envy in their eyes.
- The journey to America began with a train ride—the children's first—to the ocean and a physical exam required to board the ship.
- They all passed, but their nervousness didn't abate, especially when the doctor declared that a fellow Romanian emigrant woman had trachomas in her eyes and would not be allowed on the ship.

Anzia Ravage was 31-years-old when she arrived in America from Romania.

The journey to America began with a train ride to the ship.

- Her wailing hurt Anzia's ears and heart.
- Then Anzia's heart began to pound excitedly when the passengers were allowed aboard the ship and ordered downstairs to the little cages in steerage.
- There the family stayed in darkness for most of the trip.
- They were not even allowed topside to see the famous Statue of Liberty welcome them to America until the boat had docked.
- Upon arrival in New Bedford, Massachusetts, in September 1908, Anzia, Aaron and children Zalman, 9, and Rosie, 7, were shoehorned into a 435-square-foot apartment.
- To meet expenses they were forced to take in boarders, often single men who had also recently emigrated to America.
- There was always a steady stream of unmarried young men coming out of the ships.
- That meant little privacy, sleeping three or four to a room, sometimes in a single bed.
- Anzia drew up a budget that permitted her to feed and clothe the family for $0.96 a day.
- Quickly, Anzia became known in her all-immigrant neighborhood as a woman of mitzvas, of good deeds, who was also capable of making all her family's clothing and was willing to walk blocks to find the cheapest bread or meat being sold for a penny less per pound.
- To save money that first winter, she shunned coal, which was very expensive, and instead gathered old wood from crates and pallets left in the street to burn for heat.

Life at Work

- Even while the family waited at Ellis Island for admittance to America, Aaron Ravage began asking about available work.
- Supporting his new American family was his single-minded focus.
- Aaron quickly found his landsman Marcus Cohen, a friend from the same village in Romania, who agreed to help.
- Marcus had arrived in New Bedford two years earlier and knew his way around.
- Marcus knew of another landsman who had recently contracted tuberculosis so badly he was being forced to sell his Hokey Pokey cart because he could no longer work the streets.
- Like a typical greenhorn, Aaron asked, "What is this Hokey Pokey Man?"
- His new friend replied, "A Hokey Pokey Man is a peddler of ice cream and candy," to which Aaron replied, "What is ice cream?"
- When the pair met with the Hokey Pokey Man, he was so ill he could barely speak above a whisper, but still drove a hard bargain.

Anzia and her family lived in a crowded apartment in a crowded city.

- Reluctantly, he agreed to sell Aaron his cart and connections for $20.00—an immense sum for Aaron.
- "I have worked hard to establish my business and now must give it away," the Hokey Pokey Man said. "I was doing well after 15 years in that spot; only because of your landsman do I give you what I slaved for."
- But Aaron could not concentrate on the man's concerns while he pondered where he was going to find $20.00.
- As they walked away, Marcus said, "Don't worry; we are men who live off the air."
- That's when he introduced Aaron to the Gemilath Chassodim, or Hebrew Free Loan Society, which made no-interest loans to immigrants and was content with small weekly repayments.

Aaron Ravage purchased a "Hokey Pokey" cart and began peddling ice-cream and candy.

- The religious affiliation of Gemilath Chassodim helped assure proper repayments by members.
- Just as Marcus had promised, a loan for $50.00 was approved, enough to buy the Hokey Pokey cart, supplies, rent money and a small cash reserve against the possible fate of Aaron's business.
- Within a week of coming to America, Aaron had become a Hokey Pokey Man.
- Of all the unusual habits of Americans, Aaron believed that baseball was the wildest and silliest of them all.
- It made sense to teach a child dominoes or chess, but what was the point of a crazy game like baseball?
- Children could get crippled and lose their chance to be a success; maybe the newspapers were right, he thought: Irish boys wanted to be boxers and Jews wanted to be debaters.
- In matters of faith, Aaron and Anzia adopted a middle ground between strict observance and socialism, and sought to balance orthodoxy and secular humanism.
- Whenever possible they attended the synagogue, which had been dedicated only a few years before.
- Anzia was also a member of the Hebrew Ladies' Helping Hand Society, which had been organized the previous year.

Anzia was reluctant to leave her children when she worked, but the family had no choice.

- Within six months of arriving, the family realized that the income from the Hokey Pokey cart was not enough feed a family of four.
- Anzia was offered a job as a domestic in an uptown man's home, but Aaron said no; factory work offered more dignity to his wife.
- Their biggest concern was keeping the two children in school; under no circumstances would they be allowed to work and denied an education.
- Anzia had tears in her eyes when she went to work the first day as a seamstress in a small coat factory operated by a friend.
- The hours were long and Anzia's hands often bled from the work; but the pay was steady—something critical to a new immigrant family in America.

Life in the Community: New Bedford, Massachusetts

- To follow the traditions of charity practiced in the old country, immigrant Jews formed many institutions: credit unions, fraternal societies, synagogues, trade unions, political parties and educational groups.
- Most resisted any attempts to centralize or organize all Jews into a single group, preferring to adhere to a diversity of opinions.
- The Ravage family quickly found upon arrival that these organizations were critical to their ability to survive.
- As immigrants sought to balance the Old World culture with the new one in America, often their strongest advocates were people from the same neighborhood, village, or community in Europe.
- As part of that tradition, Aaron and his landsmen would gather periodically to institute a fundraiser for the sick or hungry, tell stories of the old country, play dominoes or talk about business.
- This network also allowed the establishment of a cemetery so traditional Jewish rites for burial could be practiced.
- The Hebrew Free Loan Society played a critical role in the economic life of the community, boasting thousands of customers, most of whom were born abroad.
- For greenhorn and established immigrant alike, the Gemilath Chassodim provided access to capital—often based solely on the recommendations of their landsmen.
- This would allow the owner of an established cigar store, for example, to buy supplies in larger quantities and for lower prices, thus improving profits and inventory.
- For the newly arrived, the Hebrew Free Loan Society made entrepreneurship possible through no-interest loans and flexible repayment plans that suited the cash flow of new immigrants.
- New Bedford was flooded with Romanian immigrants seeking a prosperous future.
- Since the turn of the century, this community, known for its whaling culture and participation in the Underground Railroad, was sometimes overwhelmed by the flow of new immigrants.

New Bedford was flooded with Romanian immigrants seeking a prosperous future.

HISTORICAL SNAPSHOT
1909

- Construction began on the naval base at Pearl Harbor in Hawaii
- The United States invaded Nicaragua and overthrew President Zelaya
- Glenn H. Curtiss, piloting the "Rheims Flyer," won the James Gordon Bennett cup in the first international air races, flying at an average speed of 46.5 miles an hour
- Twenty thousand members of the Ladies' Waist Makers of New York City's International Ladies' Garment Workers Union staged a three-month strike
- Color moving pictures were demonstrated at New York's Madison Square Garden
- The Wright brothers formed a million-dollar corporation for the commercial manufacture of airplanes
- The first Israeli kibbutz, Deganya Alef, a collective agricultural settlement, was founded in Palestine
- Dr. Leo H. Baekeland patented Bakelite, the first completely synthetic plastic thermosetting plastic
- The Labor Conference in Pittsburgh ended with a "declaration of war" on U.S. Steel
- U.S. socialist women rejected suffrage, denouncing it as a movement of the middle class
- The United States ended direct control over Cuba
- California law began segregating Japanese schoolchildren
- The National Association for the Advancement of Colored People (NAACP) was founded
- A government commission reported that the tobacco industry was controlled by six men operating 86 firms worth $450 million
- Pope Pius X lifted the church ban on interfaith marriages in Hungary
- Champion fox terrier Warren Remedy won best-in-show at New York City's Westminster dog show for the third year in a row
- Viennese Psychologist Sigmund Freud, accompanied by doctors Carl Gustav Jung and Sandor Ferenczi, arrived in New York City, prior to lecturing at Massachusetts' Clark University; they visited Central Park, Chinatown, the Jewish ghetto and Coney Island
- The Queensboro Bridge, the first double decker bridge, opened and linked the New York boroughs of Manhattan and Queens
- Explorers Robert E. Peary and Matthew A. Henson became the first people to reach the North Pole
- The first official evening baseball game was played in Grand Rapids, Michigan; Grand Rapids defeated Zanesville
- *Draugas*, (*The Friend*), a Lithuanian newspaper, began to be published in Chicago
- The SOS distress signal was first used by an American ship, the *Arapahoe*, off Cape Hatteras, North Carolina
- The A. J. Reach Company patented the cork-centered baseball
- The Cunard liner *Lusitania* crossed the Atlantic in four days, 15 hours and 52 minutes

Jewish-Romanian Immigration Timeline

A gradual immigration of Romanians commenced in 1880 and increased at the turn of the twentieth century, totaling 100,000 by the beginning of World War I. The majority of immigrants came from Transylvania, Banat, and Bucovina, territories under Austro-Hungarian rule, where political ethnic and religious persecution, combined with precarious social and economic conditions, forced Romanians to leave their homes in search of relief in the New World. Spread throughout the continent, the highest concentrations were in New York, New Jersey, and the cities of the Midwest, where the immigrants found employment in the factories, the mines and on the railroads.

1871

The first Yiddish and Hebrew newspaper in America was published.

1875

Isaac Mayer Wise founded Hebrew Union College, the rabbinical seminary for the reform movement in Cincinnati.

1880

The Romanian immigration movement began in earnest as immigrants sought employment in American factories, mines and railroads.

1882

A Yiddish theater production was staged in New York.

The Pittsburgh platform articulated the tenets of American Reform Judaism.

1886

A Jewish theological seminary was founded in New York.

Four hundred thirteen prominent Americans petitioned President Benjamin Harrison to support the resettlement of Russian Jews in Palestine.

1891

President Benjamin Harrison supported the resettlement of Russian Jews in Palestine.

1893

The National Council of Jewish women was founded in Chicago.

1897

The *Jewish Daily Forward* was founded in New York.

1900

The International Ladies' Garment Workers Union was founded.

1903

Oscar Strauss was appointed Secretary of Labor and Commerce, the first Jew to hold a Cabinet position.

1906

The American Newspaper, the official organ of the Union and League of Romanian Societies of America, was founded.

The American Jewish Committee was founded to safeguard Jewish rights internationally.

1907

Physicist Albert Michelson was the first American Jew to win the Nobel prize.

By the beginning of WW I, Romanian immigrants in America totaled 100,000.

Selected Prices

Camera, Kodak $50.00
Children's Woolen Hosiery, Pair $0.25
Corn Whiskey, Gallon $2.65
Horse Bit $0.50
Ice Box $16.50
Magic Lantern, 12 Colored Slides $4.98
Men's Cuffs, Pair $0.25
Petticoat $1.39
Player Piano $700.00
Snake Fight Ticket $2.00

$64^{25}

DESCRIPTION OF No. 11K1688

BODY—9 feet long by 3 feet 2 inches wide, heavily ironed and braced; drop endgate furnished with seat as shown in illustration when ordered with a top. When ordered without a top we build the seat higher. Seat has imitation leather cushion. TOP—Portable top strongly constructed; white ash bows, standards and sides; poplar slats on the roof, oil finished, covered with heavy rubber duck, colored black. GEAR—1⅛-inch axles; double gear; 15-inch short turn full malleable circle; 38-inch duplex springs, ironed, bolted and clipped; Sarven's patent wheels, 36 inches front and 40 inches rear; 1¼ by 5-16-inch steel tires riveted rims; strong shafts. PAINTING—Body blue green, striped in colors; gear, dark wine, striped with black. CAPACITY—1,500 pounds. TRACK—4 feet 8 inches or 5 feet 2 inches. State width wanted.

No. 11K1688 Price, complete with shafts, as illustrated, with top **$64.25**
No. 11K1689 Price, without top 49.95
EXTRAS. 1¼-inch axles, wheels and heavier springs, making 2,000 lbs. capacity. 3.50
Hand ratchet brake 4.90
Shipped from factory, crated 50x114 inches; weight, 900 pounds, with top.

"New Bedford's Jubilee," *The New York Times*, September 6, 1897:

Elaborate preparations are being made in this city for the coming celebration of the 50th anniversary of the city's incorporation which is to take place October 10-14, although as a matter of fact the active incorporation was accepted March 9, 1847.

The site of the city of New Bedford was purchased in 1752 from the chiefs Wasamequen and Wamsutta, father and son, the Indian name of the place being Acushnet. It was part of Dartmouth until February 1787 when it was set off and incorporated as a town. It was first named "Bedford" in honor of the Russels, early settlers to the place, and related to the Duke of Bedford. It being found that there was already a Bedford in the state, the prefix "New" was adopted.

Few cities in the United States are more cosmopolitan than is New Bedford and hence a large attendance is expected. Of the population of 55,251 as given by the census of 1895, 22,174 people were born outside the United States. There are two reasons for the settling of foreigners in New Bedford. During the period of the whale industry, many sailors, shipped in foreign ports on New Bedford whalers, were discharged here and therefore made this port their home. This is particularly true of the former subjects of Portugal, who were shipped many of them from the Western Islands. When the cotton mills were established and began to grow in number, they furnished work for skilled cotton operatives, a fact which was taken advantage of by many English men and women, particularly from the Lancashire District.

French Canadians, too, found that working New Bedford cotton mills paid better than work in the sterile farms of the provinces and flocked to New Bedford in large numbers. This accounts for three large elements of New Bedford's foreign population. Represented in the 22,174 foreigners in New Bedford are 7,340 Canadians, 5,315 from England, 3,861 from Portugal and the islands under Portuguese control, 3,314 from Ireland and 550 from Scotland, 598 from Germany, 322 from Russia, 204 from Sweden and 238 from Austria. . . .

The Duke of Bedford, in congratulating the city on its coming celebration, wrote:

"The Bedford from which you take your name has of late prospered and increased, and is now one of the most beautiful and healthy centers of education in England.

It is difficult to express its leading characteristics or to suggest a sentiment drawn from purely local considerations, but perhaps the spirit of the Midlands of England may be summed up in the word moderation, and I cannot do better than suggest to you the thought that the quiet prosperity of Bedford is due to its Midlands habit of avoiding extremes."

Jewish Daily Forward, January 17, 1906:

Do you want to meet a landsman from Lemberg, a freshly baked greenhorn who can give you the latest news about your city; or an Americanized landsman who knows how to transfer from one streetcar to the next, or whistle at the ticket copper on the elevated? Go to the northeast corner of Clinton and Rivington streets, where you can find out about a job, family scandals, landsleit parties and anything else that interests you.

I stood in a corner last week and met an old friend. He was surprised that I hadn't heard the latest. "Red—you know who I mean—has become a boss. Whenever he has to pass his corner, he stops a block before and buys a fat cigar, and watches us to make sure we see him. Once he came into our saloon and told us that we should establish a society and synagogue called Anshi Lemberg #1. To hell with him. What are we—provincials? So we got together and were going to make a Verein, a union and to spite Red we'll call it First Lemberg Ladies and Gentleman's Charity, Sick and Burial Society under the patronage of the late Australian Queen Elizabeth. A big portrait of the empress will hang over the president and we're going to give a ball and a performance. One of our members wrote a play in seven acts, with three comedians and lots of songs, in high German. You'll see Lemberger landsleit are not small-town landsleit.

Give me your tired, your poor, your huddled masses yearning to be free.

—"The New Colossus" by Emma Lazarus, composed as part of a fundraising campaign to erect the Statue of Liberty, 1883

To express loyalty with every / fiber of one's being, Land of Freedom, is the / sacred duty of every Jew.

—Opening words of Yiddish song "Land of the Free"

Every day that passes I became more and more overwhelmed at the degeneration of my fellow countrymen in this new home of theirs. Even their names had become emasculated and devoid of either character or meaning. . . . It did not seem to matter at all what one had been called at home. The first step toward Americanization was to fall into one or the other of the two great tribes of Rosies and Annies.

Cut adrift suddenly from their ancient moorings, they were floundering in a sort of moral void. Good manners and good conduct, reverence and religion, had all gone by the board, and the reason was that these things were not American. . . . The ancient racial respect for elders had completely disappeared. . . . American old-age had forfeited its claim of deference because it had thrown away its dignity. Tottering grandfathers had snipped off their white beards, laid aside their skullcaps and their snuff boxes, and paraded around the streets of a Saturday afternoon with cigarettes in their mouths, when they should've been lamenting the loss of the holy city in the study room adjoining the synagogue.

—Marcus Ravage

Hokey Pokey, a penny a lump, the more you eat, the more you jump.

—Song of immigrant ice cream vendor

"Our New York Letters,"
Statesville Landmark
(North Carolina), June 30, 1887:

Downtown on the narrow streets where the crowds press, sunstrokes happen. The ice cart is a cool thing and in some of the poorer parts of the city it is looked for as eagerly as the mail train at a country station. Little dirty-legged children run after it, gather about it when it stops and when the iceman breaks off a big lump, scramble for the chips. The small boy is never so happy as when he can steal a ride on the ice cart, unless, indeed, it is when he can buy "hokey-pokey" ice cream. Hokey-pokey ice cream is manufactured and sold by the Italians. Its composition is a mystery. It is hawked about the streets in freezers on little hand-carts bearing the legend in fantastic letters, "Hokey-Pokey Ice Cream." The small boy, by hook or by crook, obtains a cent and makes for that cart. The Italian removes the top of the freezer, dips up a dab of parti-colored ice cream with a large spoon and serves it on a bit of brown paper. The small boy takes two or three little bites at it, then licks it all up and sucks the paper.

Street vendors, including the Hokey Pokey Man, flooded the streets of many immigrant-occupied cities.

"The Origin for the Ice Cream," *The New York Times*, March 11, 1894:

The man who invented ice cream was a Negro by the name of Jackson, in the early part of the present century, and kept a small confectionery store. Cold custards, which were cooled after being made by setting them on a cake of ice, were very fashionable, and Jackson conceived the idea of freezing them, which he did by placing the ingredients in a tin bucket completely covered with ice. Each bucket contained a quart, and was sold for one dollar. It immediately became popular, and the inventor soon enlarged his store, and when he died left a considerable fortune. A good many tried to follow his example, and ice cream was hawked in the streets, being wheeled along very much as the hokey-pokey carts are now, but none of them succeeded in obtaining the flavor Jackson had in his product.

Jewish Daily Forward, February 7, 1903:

The signs on the dark, gloomy walls of the dispensary announce that patients are received at 12:30 to 2:00 p.m. It is now after 3:00 and not a single doctor is to be seen. Nobody has the courage to ask when they will come. The employees of the free dispensary all have the same cold, contemptuous stare; every gesture shouts: "You are a charity patient, so sit and wait."

The benches are filled; men, women and children hold their numbered cards. It is a sea of troubles, pain, and tragedy. You forget your own suffering.

A 40-year-old woman sits next to me. She says her husband is the sick one, not she. He works at boys' pants and earns about $7.00 a week. They have five children. "He started to cough, got pains in his back and chest. We didn't have $0.50 for the doctor, and we can't afford medicine. If he sits in the dispensaries, he will lose pay. So I go, while he works. I make believe I am the sick one, they give me the medicine, and he takes it. He feels a little better now."

The doctors began to arrive. The woman stopped talking and gave me a farewell smile.

**"The Greenhouse Cousin,"
Yiddish theatrical song:**

Once a cousin came to me
Pretty as gold was she, the greenhorn,
Her cheeks like red oranges,
Her tiny feet begging to dance.

She didn't walk, she skipped along,
She didn't talk, she sang,
Her manner was cheerful,
That's how my cousin used to be.

I found a place with my neighbor,
The one who has a millinery store,
I got a job for my cousin,
Blessed be the golden land.

Since then many years have passed.
My cousin became a wreck
For many years of collecting wages
Till nothing was left of her.

Underneath her pretty blue eyes
Black lines now are drawn,
Her cheeks once like red oranges,
Have now turned entirely green.

Today, when I meet my cousin
And I ask her: "How are you, greenhorn?"
She answers with a grimace,
"To the devil with Columbus's land."

Work Experience of Rose Cohen, 1908

About the same time that the bitter cold came, father told me one night he had found work for me in a shop where he knew the presser. I lay awake long that night. I was eager to begin life on my own responsibility, but was also afraid. We rose earlier than usual that morning for father had to take me to the shop and not be over late for his own work. I wrapped my thimble and scissors, with a piece of bread for breakfast, in a bit of newspaper, carefully stuck two needles into the lapel of my coat and we started.

The shop was on Pelem Street . . . I groped my way to the top of the stairs and, hearing the clattering noise of machines, I felt about, found a door, pushed it open and went in. A tall beardless man stood folding coats at a table. I went over to him. "Yes," he said crossly. "What do you want?"

I said, "I am the new feller hand." He looked at me from head to foot. My face felt so burning hot that I could scarcely see.

"It is more likely," he said, "that you can pull bastings than fell sleeve linings." Then turning from me he shouted over the noise of the machine: "Presser, is this the girl?" The presser put down the iron and looked at me. "I suppose so," he said, "I only know the father."

The cross man looked at me again and said, "Let's see what you can do." He kicked a chair from which the back had been broken off to the finishers table, threw a coat upon it and said raising the corner of his mouth: "Make room for the new feller hand."

One girl tittered, two men glanced at me over their shoulders and pushed their chairs apart a little. By this time I scarcely knew what I was about. I laid my coat down somewhere, and pushed my bread into the sleeve. Then I stumbled into the bit of space made for me at the table, drew in a chair and sat down. The men were so close to me at each side I felt the heat of the bodies and could not prevent myself from shrinking away. The men noticed and probably felt hurt. One made a joke, the other laughed and the girls bent their heads low over their work. All at once a thought came to me: "If I don't do this coat quickly and well he will send me away at once. I picked up the coat, threaded my needle, and began hastily repeating the lesson father impressed upon me. "Be careful not to twist the sleeve lining; make small false stitches."

My hands trembled so that I could not hold the needle properly. It took me a long while to do the coat. At last it was done. I took it over to the boss and stood at the table waiting while he was examining it. He took long, trying every stitch with his needle. Finally he put it down without looking at me and gave me two other coats. I felt very happy! When I sat down at the table I drew my knees close together and stitched as quickly as I could.

1903 News Feature

"The Tenement House Problem," by Robert W. De. Forest and Lawrence Veiller, The New York City Tenement House Commission Report of 1903:

Tenement Evils as Seen by the Tenants

The following was written by a young woman of 20, a tenement dweller all her life:

Being born and bred on the East Side, I am somewhat in a position to judge the various discomforts that exist in modern tenements. The greatest evil is the lack of light and air.

The air shaft is so narrow that the kitchen windows in two houses adjoin one another. In most houses the air shafts are the only means of light and air for at least two out of every three rooms, and the only means of lighting the staircases.

The first thing that awakens one in the morning is the loud voices of the various tenants, intermingled with the odors that arise from the kitchen windows. It is, indeed, wonderful that you can distinguish any one voice among them all. If we are to give the reason for the people's loud voices, let us first consider how difficult it is for one to make himself understood in this medley and confusion; in this congested living House of Babel, it becomes habitual for us to raise our voices.

After the children are sent to school, the various mothers commence their housecleaning, then comes the question, What is to be done with the garbage of the day? Most women solve it by throwing it into the street and air shaft. It is much easier than climbing the dark stairs and running the risk of breaking one's legs. In some cases it is almost a necessity to throw it out, the premium on space is so high in their tiny kitchens, which hold wash-tubs, water-sink, and chairs, and just enough room to turn about. In this room the cooking, the washing of clothes, and the daily ablutions of the various members of the family take place.

The cooking is generally abbreviated to one meal a day, the other meals consisting of tea or coffee, with bread and butter.

On washing and ironing days the children are sent to school with a cent to buy candy, instead of lunch.

After the principal meal of the day is over, the kitchen changes its appearance into a study room; the older children sit at the table doing their arithmetic, while the younger ones sit on the floor or any available space, with the large book on the left for a task.

The public schools are beginning to realize the East Side needs by opening their playgrounds for quiet study and play, which is a dire necessity; where every inch of space is utilized in their houses, it is a relief to get into a large, airy room.

The law forbids putting pots or pans outside of windows and fire escapes, but the rooms are not supplied with enough closet or refrigerators, hence the only means of getting rid of them.

Another step in tenement house reform would be compulsory bath-rooms and lavatories. How can the children be taught decency where male and female intermingle without the slightest regard to sex or common decency? Bathrooms would not only help to keep the people healthier, but would elevate the standard of morality.

E.B.

****

A woman who is the housekeeper of the five-story tenement house, and who for 20 years has lived in tenement houses, when asked in what way she would like them changed, exclaimed without a moment's hesitation very emphatically:

"No air shafts!" She then added, "I sweep mine every two days, but sometimes it smells so it makes me sick to my stomach. In summer I've got to sweep every day, or I can't stand it. You see it's damp down there, and the families, they throw out garbage and dirty papers and the insides of chickens, and other unmentionable filth. The housekeeper before me wasn't so particular, and I just vomited when I first cleaned up the air shaft. Then it's so hard to get into, you know. We have to crawl through the window, and in that other air shaft I have to climb down a ladder, and me with rheumatism, it aches me. That other housekeeper before me wasn't so strict. I found the cellar full of mattresses and old things when I came. Now my cellars are just as clean as my halls; my agent says it would do for Fifth Avenue. You know they call my house a flat, and the next one, just like it, a tenement. The house across the street is awful dirty, and so all kinds of people live there together, Italians and Jews and Christians, and they quarrel terrible. . . .

During the conversation the housekeeper was interrupted twice by men who wanted to see the apartment. "It's on the stoop in the rear," she explained. "Three rooms and $10 a month; two on the air shaft, and one on the back. The gas costs too much; I have to burn kerosene oil myself, and them rooms is very dark; mine's slight. The ladies that have lived in them rooms always complained of headaches and dizziness. When I used to live in dark rooms on—street I used to get headaches and get dizzy, but now I'm all right. And then when you get up on top where it's sunny, the stairs near kill you. A friend of mine has had her top floor empty three months. My husband when he was alive never could live up top. He always said it make him sick to go to the hall with the smells of so many different families. Used to say air shafts ought to have wires across the windows to keep people from throwing things out. But the noise hurts me. It comes down the air shaft so that sometimes I can't sleep all night."

****

Tenement Evils as Seen by an Inspector

I worked for the Tenement House Commission from about the middle of July until November 1, 1900, as follows: inspecting back-to-back rear tenements; inspecting existing tenants in each borough; inspecting fire- escapes in Brooklyn; inspecting a list of 64 houses declared the worst in the city in 1894 by the Board of Health.

The Water Closet

There are two kinds, with a tank and chain, or with a circular pipe around the bowl and a self-regulating pipe. The latter closet takes the place of the school sink in the Borough of Brooklyn. There are also some in Manhattan. It does not afford enough current pressure to wash out the inside of the bowl, which is usually coated, and when the pipe is itself attacked by the coating, the water supply is gradually reduced. . . . On the East Side I found things that ought to be photographed—trap-water closets heaped over the top, running over, and the stench such as to pervade the halls and homes and apartments, and to make any civilized person ill.

In many places, all over New York, patent-medicine men have a printed placard, framed, covered with glass, and fastened on a wall, ostensibly warning those who use the closet not to wet the seats, but under this warning the advertisement of medicines for private diseases of men. These are put up in family closets. One place I found five such placards.

The results of the inspections, I believe, will show about three apartments to one closet, and if we could ascertain accurately the whole number of families where there is overcrowding, the number would exceed even that. At many places there is no order about the closets, and no one knows how many families use the same closet. This tendency is when the closet is spoiled by pollution to concentrate on the cleaner ones, and abandon the others. In such cases they may have been abandoned for such a long time that the outside offal is dried and hard. I've seen all the closets and one yard so bad that the tenants in that house went across the yard to the next house to use those closets.

1910–1919

As the second decade of the century began, the economy was strong and optimism was high, especially among the newly emerging middle class—the beneficiaries of improved technology, a stable economy and the unregulated, often unsafe labor of the working class. Immigration continued at a pace of one million annually in the first four years of the decade. Between 1910 and 1913, some 11 million immigrants—an all-time record—entered the United States. The wages of unskilled workers fell, but the number of jobs expanded dramatically. Manufacturing employment rose by 3.3 million, or close to 6 percent in a year during the period. At the same time, earnings of skilled workers rose substantially and resulted in a backlash focused on protecting American workers' jobs. As a result, a series of anti-immigration laws was passed, culminating in 1917 with permanent bars to the free flow of immigrants into the United States. From the beginning of World War I until 1919, the number of immigrants fell sharply while the war effort was demanding more and more workers. As a result, wages for low-skilled work rose rapidly, forcing the managerial class—often represented by the middle class—to find new and more streamlined ways to get the jobs done, often by employing less labor or more technology. Jobs were available to everyone; America enjoyed full employment, yet hours remained long and jobs were dangerous. Child, female and immigrant exploitation remained, despite a rising level of progressive debate regarding the plight of the underclass. Women banded together for full suffrage and against alcohol. Worker-inspired unions battled for better working conditions, and minorities of various origins, colors and faiths attempted to find their voice in the midst of a dramatically changing world. Divorce was on the rise, consuming one in 12 marriages. The discovery of "salvarsan 606," the miracle treatment for syphilis, was hailed as both a life-saver and an enticement to sin. At the same time, the emerging middle class was proving that it was capable of carrying a greater load of managerial decisions, freeing factory owners and stockholders to travel, experiment and study ways to cure the ills of the poor. Millions of dollars were poured into libraries, parks and literacy classes designed to uplift the immigrant masses flooding American shores. The United States was prospering and, at the same time, the country's elite were re-evaluating America's role as an emerging world power which no longer looked to Britain for approval.

In the midst of these dynamics, the Progressive Movement, largely a product of the rising middle class, began to shape the decade, raising questions about work safety, the rights of individuals, the need for clean air and fewer work hours. It was a people's movement that grasped the immediate impact of linking the media to its cause. The results were significant and widespread. South Carolina prohibited the employment of children under 12 in mines, factories, and textile mills; Delaware began to frame employers' liability laws; the direct election of U.S. senators was approved; and nationwide, communities argued loudly over the right and ability of women to vote and the need and lawfulness of alcohol consumption.

During the decade, motorized tractors changed the lives of farmers, and electricity extended the day of urban dwellers. Powered trolley cars, vacuum cleaners, hair dryers, and electric ranges moved onto the modern scene. Wireless communications bridged San Francisco to New York and New York to Paris; in 1915, the Bell system alone operated six million telephones, which were considered essential in most middle class homes as the decade drew to a close. As the sale of parlor pianos hit a new high, more than two billion copies of sheet music were sold as ragtime neared its peak. Thousands of Bibles were placed in hotel bedrooms by the Gideon Organization of Christian Commercial Travelers, reflecting both the emerging role of the traveling "drummer" or salesman and the evangelical nature of the Progressive Movement.

Yet in the midst of blazing prosperity, the nation was changing too rapidly for many—demographically, economically and morally. Divorce was on the rise. As the technology and sophistication of silent movies improved yearly, the Missouri Christian Endeavor Society tried to ban films that included any kissing. At the same time, the rapidly expanding economy, largely without government regulation, began producing marked inequities of wealth—affluence for the few and hardship for the many. The average salary of $750 a year was rising, but not fast enough for most people.

But one of the biggest stories was America's unabashed love affair with the automobile. By 1916, the Model T cost less than half its 1908 price, and nearly everyone dreamed of owning a car. Movies were also maturing during the period, growing rapidly as an essential entertainment for the poor. Some 25 percent of the population, including many newly arrived immigrants, went weekly to the nickelodeon to marvel at the exploits of Charlie Chaplin, Mary Pickford, and Douglas Fairbanks, Sr., who each drew big salaries in the silent days of movies.

The second half of the decade was marked by the Great War, later to be known as the First World War. Worldwide, it cost more than nine million lives and swept away four empires—the German, the Austro-Hungarian, the Russian, and the Ottoman—and with them the traditional aristocratic style of leadership in Europe. It bled the treasuries of Europe dry and brought the United States forward as the richest country in the world.

When the war broke out in Europe, American exports were required to support the Allied war effort, driving the well-oiled American industrial engine into high gear. Then, when America's intervention in 1917 required the drafting of two million men, women were given their first taste of economic independence. Millions stepped forward to produce the materials needed by the nation. As a result, when the men came back from Europe, America was a changed place for both the well-traveled soldier and the newly trained female worker. Each had acquired an expanded view of the world. Yet women possessed full suffrage in only Wyoming, Colorado, Utah and Idaho.

The war forced Americans to confront one more important transformation. The United States had become a full participant in the world economy; tariffs on imported goods were reduced and exports reached all-time highs in 1919, further stimulating the American economy.

1913 Profile

Swedish-born Karin Moberg found she had to adapt to life in America very quickly after arriving in the United States to meet her father for the first time.

Life at Home

- Seven-year-old Karin Moberg was born in 1906 in the town of Karlskrona, Sweden, named for King Karl XI.
- Originally the town's name was spelled Carlskrona, as it meant Carl's crown.
- Since Karin's birth, she and her mother, Selma, lived in a one-room apartment, number 11, Ronnebygatan, the main street.
- The corner of the single room was taken up by a floor-to-ceiling white porcelain fireplace with glittery-bright brass doors.
- The home was decorated with white painted furniture made of birch.
- There was a round table flanked by chairs whose seats displayed a blue-and-white design that Karin liked enormously.
- They often took a short walk from their home to the Baltic Sea, where there were green benches by the water.
- There her mother would take out some handiwork and Karin would play in the sand, roll her hoop, or bounce a ball.
- Karin especially enjoyed running over to the inlet where the white swans swam so regally, always with an eye out for some bread that might be cast to them.
- Selma was well respected as the town seamstress and her work was much favored.
- Karin was proud of her mother.
- Years before, Selma had been trained as an apprentice to the top seamstress in southern Sweden.
- From Selma's tiny home she made dresses, men's suits, underwear, and often went to the customers' homes for fittings.
- She was also trained to knit, crochet, and embroider, as well as create beautiful cut work.

Karin Moberg was 7-years-old when she and her mother left Sweden to join her father in New York City.

Selma Moberg was a well-respected seamstress in the town of Karlskrona, Sweden.

- Often when someone needed a dress quickly, before the specified time, Selma would sew, sew, sew throughout the night, sitting at her faithful Singer trundled sewing machine until the work was done.
- Karin had been taught never, ever, to touch the materials or clothing being prepared.
- Her father Lennart Moberg was in the merchant Marines stationed in Buenos Aires, Argentina.
- She was seven years old before Lennart first saw her, and only then because of an accident on board ship.
- A highly trained ship's mechanic, Lennart was burned when a steam boiler blew up at sea.
- He was taken to the Norwegian Hospital in Brooklyn, New York, where he required an operation and a long period of recovery.
- Naturally, his ship had to continue on its schedule and he was left behind in New York City.
- That's when he made the decision to remain in the "land of opportunity" and began working several jobs, including one at an automobile plant so that he could send for his wife and the daughter he had never seen.
- Karin and her mother left the harbor of Gothenburg on the west coast of Sweden and arrived in New York City 10 days later.
- Karin was so excited about seeing her father for the first time she developed a severe nosebleed and was unable to go to the rail to look for him below in the throng.
- Instead, at the moment she had awaited her entire life, she was sitting in a deck chair with a nurse in attendance—blood covering her new, precious outfit.

Anxious arrivals to New York on the ship from Sweden.

Life at Work

- Lennart Moberg was adamant that his daughter would become as Americanized as possible—as soon as possible.
- He even considered moving somewhere other than Minnesota because Swedes were so concentrated there she might cling to the old ways.
- He told her that he would never make her work in factories like the Italian children; if she learned to be a seamstress like her mother, she might even marry an American boy.

- "It is my job to earn money; I don't want your pay from factory," he told her.
- Karin was told always to study hard and value her education; book learning was the ticket to a good life in America.
- Since the Elementary School Act of 1842, promoted by the Lutheran Church, illiteracy had become rare in Sweden.
- For decades the ability of Swedes to read and write had made them attractive to states seeking new settlers.
- As soon as Karin learned English, her father would not allow her to speak in Swedish to anyone, even at home.
- She also learned what other things not to do in America.
- All her life she had been expected to curtsy to adults when she met them on the street—a habit she continued in America—but not for long.
- Her father told her it was no longer appropriate; curtsying wasn't done in America.
- But the transition was not always easy; homesickness would overcome Karin and her mother in the strangest moments.
- One day, out of the blue, Selma asked Lennart in what direction was Sweden located, and when he showed her, she stood looking in that direction and began to weep.
- Then without a word, she dried her tears, picked up her sewing and never spoke of the incident again.
- A short time later, the family left for Minnesota to join the automobile industry in that state.
- Karin thought the idea of the six-day train ride was exciting but didn't like the way her white gloves turned black from the coal smoke or being told repeatedly not to talk to the other passengers wandering the aisles of the train.
- Mostly, it was boring.
- For more than a decade, the practical farmers of Minnesota had been tinkering in their barns with horseless carriages, Moto buggies, cycle cars, or automobiles—whichever name was in vogue.
- While living in New York, Lennart had grown intrigued by gasoline-powered internal combustion engines, especially those of the Oldsmobile, which he admired.
- Nationwide, a dizzying assortment of handmade cars and innovative technologies were being created by hundreds of manufacturers still dabbling in steam-, electricity- and gas-powered autos.
- Lennart believed that the gas-powered autos represented the future, and he wanted to be a part of it— a crucial reason to pick Minneapolis as their home.
- Innovation was rampant with no clear standards for basic vehicle architecture, body types, construction materials or controls.
- Most cars operated at a single speed using a chain drive technology, similar to a bicycle.
- Recent innovations had included an electric self-starter, independent suspension, and four-wheel brakes.
- In all, 15 different kinds of vehicles were being built in Minnesota, including the Michaelson, a fast-traveling cycle car designed for racing.

Many immigrant children worked in factories.

Skilled Swedish immigrants were welcomed employees in automobile factories.

- More than a hundred U.S. firms were producing little autos to cash in on the fad.
- The Michaelson Minneapolis Motorcycle Company was already known for its motorcycles introduced a few years earlier; building fast cars would be even more fun.
- Getting employment for skilled Swedish mechanics in Minnesota was relatively easy; making ends meet was not.
- The cost of housing, food, transportation, even the expectations of the Church, stretched the budget for the Mobergs.
- Lennart reluctantly agreed that Selma could reestablish her seamstress business—much to her delight.
- After seven years of living independently, she found that being told what she could and could not do was burdensome.
- She often felt guilty about this resentment, knowing she had often told Karin that everything would be fine once the couple was together again.

Life in the Community: Minneapolis, Minnesota

- Historically, Minnesota had been an immigration state.
- Drawn by the lure of inexpensive farmland and a growing industrial base, settlers from New England as well as immigrants from Norway, Sweden, Ireland, and Germany settled in Minnesota prior to 1850.
- By 1896, official election instructions were being issued in nine languages: English, German, Norwegian, Swedish, Finnish, French, Czech, Italian and Polish.
- The pace of immigration accelerated in Minnesota at the turn of the twentieth century.
- While the foreign-born population in the rest of the United States was approximately 15 percent in the 1890s, 40 percent of Minnesota's population was foreign-born.
- This wave of immigration to Minnesota peaked around 1910, when more than 60 percent of the immigrants came from Sweden, Norway and Germany.
- The city of Minneapolis grew up around Saint Anthony Falls, the only waterfall on the Mississippi River.
- Thanks to this water power, Minneapolis was described as "the greatest direct-drive waterpower center the world has ever seen."
- The city's importance also grew because Minneapolis was home to 34 flour mills which processed grains grown throughout the Great Plains and shipped in by rail.
- By 1905, Minneapolis delivered almost 10 percent of the country's flour and grist.
- At peak production, a single mill made enough flour for 12 million loaves of bread each day.

The first sedan-type automobile, the Hudson, was premiered at the Automobile Show in New York.

HISTORICAL SNAPSHOT
1913

- The first sedan-type automobile, a Hudson, went on display at the 13th Automobile Show in New York

- The Sixteenth Amendment to the Constitution, providing for a federal income tax, was approved

- A New York commission reported that there was widespread violation of child labor laws

- President Woodrow Wilson held the first open presidential news conference

- The Palace Theatre, the home of vaudeville, opened in New York City

- Germany announced a tax increase in order to finance the new military budget

- Suffragists marched to the Capitol in Washington, D.C.

- California passed a law excluding Japanese from owning land

- Gideon Sundback patented an all-purpose zipper

- The Seventeenth Amendment to the Constitution, providing for the election of U.S. senators by popular vote rather than selection by state legislatures, became law

- The first four-engine aircraft was built and flown by Igor Sikorsky of Russia

- The Actors' Equity Association was organized in New York City

- The Treaty of London ended the First Balkan War, and the Second Balkan War began

- The "Second Revolution" broke out in south China

- The Lincoln Highway (US 30) opened as the first paved coast-to-coast highway

- Congress authorized San Francisco the right to dam the Tuolumne River in Yosemite National Park for water-collection and power-generation

- Henry Ford created an assembly line that reduced the time it took to manufacture a car from 12 hours to 93 minutes

- The Panama Canal was completed and opened by President Woodrow Wilson, who exploded the Gamboa Dike by pressing an electric button at the White House in Washington, D.C.

- Mohandas K. Gandhi was arrested as he led a march of Indian miners in South Africa

- The first drive-in automobile service station was opened in Pittsburgh

- *The Mona Lisa,* stolen from the Louvre Museum in Paris in 1911, was recovered

- Actor Charlie Chaplin began his film career at Keystone for $150 a week

- The first crossword puzzle was published in the *New York World*

- The Federal Reserve Act was signed by President Woodrow Wilson to establish a decentralized, government-controlled banking system in the U.S.

- Charles Moyer, president of the Miners Union, was shot in the back and dragged through the streets of Chicago

Minnesota Immigration Timeline

1848

A tide of land-hungry Eastern settlers swept over the region now known as Minnesota during the first land sale.

1850

Minnesota boasted 5,354 settlers; thanks to peace, smallpox vaccinations and potato cultivation, the population of Sweden had doubled since 1750.

1858

Rapid population growth allowed the territory to gain statehood; thousands of pamphlets promoting the region's unique opportunities were issued by the Bureau of Immigration to lure Germans, Belgians, Scandinavians, French and Swiss.

1868

The growing network of railroads lured European immigrants, particularly Scandinavians and Irish, to Minnesota.

1880

The U.S. Census showed a population in Minnesota of 780,773, of which 71 percent were Europeans of the first or second generation.

Literacy among Swedes, Norwegians and Danish immigrants exceeded 70 percent.

1890

Immigration to Minnesota reached its height.

Norwegians rarely settled in areas of Swedish concentration.

Census figures showed Germany leading all nations in the numbers it was sending to Minnesota.

1900

To fill the labor needs of the packing plants, manufacturers sent agents to recruit workers in the Balkan countries as far north as Poland and Lithuania.

1910

Swedish immigrants became the largest non-native nationality in Minnesota.

Although the British Isles and Norway surpassed Sweden in the number of immigrants coming to America, in proportion to Sweden, 1.4 million Swedish first- and second-generation immigrants were listed as living in the U.S. compared to Sweden's population of 5.5 million.

Keeping Up with the Joneses ("Pop"), 1913

Bud Fisher: Mutt and Jeff toast some other famous comic characters of the period, 1913.

Mutt and Jeff *and* Keeping Up with the Jones *were popular comic strips in 1913.*

Selected Prices

Baby Walker	$2.75
Cake Turner	$0.02
Egg Incubator and Brooder	$10.00
Inlaid Linoleum, per Yard	$2.35
Phonograph Record	$0.65
Piano, Steinway Baby Grand	$2,000.00
Toilet Paper, Six Rolls	$0.27
Trunk	$16.95
Tuition, Harvard University, per Year	$150.00
Umbrella	$2.74

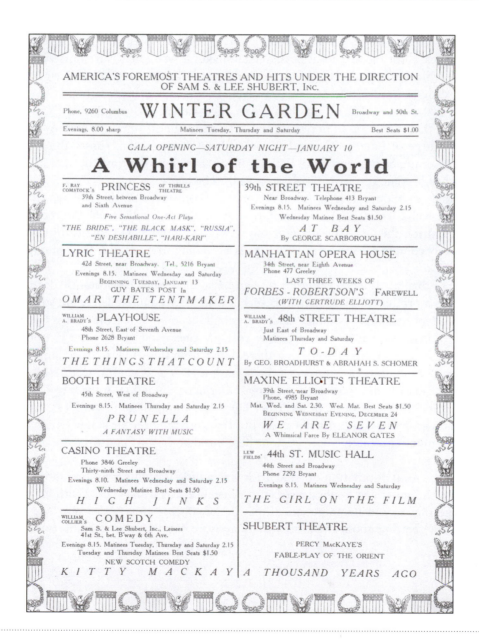

"Curious Paths Taken by the Immigrants, Interesting Peculiarities of Incoming Foreigners as Shown by Reports Just Released by the Government," *The New York Times*, February 13, 1910:

When a man gets so much money that he can lose $5 million and not know it's gone, he's got a lot of money. But this same man, if he feels wronged, can so concentrate his mind on the loss of $0.50 that he will yowl like a cat with a pinched tale. He sort of loses, for the moment, all sense of proportion, and can remember nothing except that someone has frisked him for half a dollar.

Big countries in some respects are like big men. Most of the days of the year this country does not worry much about the immigration question. We simply swallow up immigrants as fast as they come and forget they are here. But periodically we get into the frame of mind and the millionaire gentleman who was unlawfully, outrageously, and scandalously made to part with the price of a couple pounds of meat. We look about us and see nothing but Scandinavians, Mongolians, Italians, and Hungarians. We go through streets where we can understand no more what is spoken than as if we were attending a convention of parrots, blackbirds, and blue jays. And we say to ourselves just like this "this immigrant business has got to stop."

Such another period is upon us. The announcement that 957,000 foreigners took up their abode here last year has brought back all of the old uneasiness. Which makes it well to reassure ourselves with a few facts.

The fact is that this country is in about as much danger of being overrun by foreigners as the Atlantic Ocean is of being drowned out by the Mississippi River. The foreigners come here by the thousand, the tens of thousands, and the millions. They bring their wives, their babies, their stepfathers, and their mothers-in-law. They clutter up the benches in Battery Park until the native-born American citizens can hardly see over their heads to the Statue of Liberty. They fill the second-class coaches that run to the West. They settle in Chicago, Detroit, St. Paul, Sacramento, and Wahoo, Nevada. And by the time they are all at the anchor, no one can tell what has become of them. They don't seem to be here.

Contrary to public opinion, it is a statistical fact that the percentage of foreign-born citizens in American cities is becoming less and less. It isn't, of course, that immigration is falling off. On the contrary, immigration is falling on. During the last 10 years precisely 7,959,135 foreigners came to this country. Either the other countries are becoming so bad or this country is becoming so good that we can count upon an average of about a million a year.

But in the face of this fact the percentage of foreign-born inhabitants is constantly decreasing for the reason that America, as a producer of population, is such a wonderful country. There are so many millions here already that their offspring simply swamp a relatively small incoming tide from across the ocean.

Some people, for instance, hardly consider New York an American city. A recent visitor from London returned to his hometown and told the folks that there didn't seem to be many Americans in New York. The Kaiser greeted some Manhattan Germans with the remark that he was glad to welcome fellow countrymen from the city that, next to Berlin, possessed the largest German population in the world.

All of which, in its essence, is more or less true. This is a cosmopolitan town. Its size and the fact that it is the first spot that the immigrant hits make it so. But the truth requires the statement of the fact that there are not only quite a number of native-born persons here but that they are constantly increasing their relative number.

In 1870, when the total population of New York was a little less than a million, 44 percent of the population was foreign. A man going down the street, for instance, could shake dice with himself as to whether the next person he met would be an American or foreigner. But, in order to not lose money he would have had to make the betting about even, because there were 419,000 foreigners in town to only 523,000 Americans.

continued

"Curious Paths Taken by the Immigrants, Interesting Peculiarities of Incoming Foreigners as Shown by Reports Just Released by the Government" . . . *(continued)*

When the last census was taken there were 1,270,000 foreigners here. But there were also 2,167,000 native-born American persons whose names went on the list. In other words, the percentage of foreign-born residents had fallen from 44 percent in 1870 to 37 percent in 1900, notwithstanding the fact that the number of foreigners had tripled.

During the same time, the percentage of foreigners in Chicago fell from 48 to 34, Philadelphia dropped from 27 to 22, St. Louis from 36 to 19, and Baltimore from 21 to 13. Boston held its own to a decimal the percentage of foreigners in 1900, as in 1870, being 35.1. . . . Atlanta showed the smallest percentage of foreigners, only 2.8. Southern cities generally ranked exceedingly low. North Dakota has the highest percentage of foreigners and Georgia the lowest, North Dakota 35, as against 42 in 1900, and Georgia .6 as against .7.

It is an interesting, though perhaps not surprising, fact to discover that it is the American city that plays hob with the foreigner. Put him out in the country and he will do better in the matter of population than the native-born American. But in the city he is compelled to live in a manner in which no American, or at least few Americans, will consent to live. He is huddled into tenements where his children die and he himself contracts tuberculosis.

What these handicaps do to his population figures may be understood when it is explained that, in the 21 cities for which statistics have been given, there was, between 1870 and 1900, an average decrease of 14 percent in the foreign-born population. The average fell from 38 to 24. But the foreigner did much better in the country than he did in the city that the average for the United States fell only from 14.4 in 1870 to 13.7 in 1900.

All of which suggests what the foreigner might be able to do if he were enabled to compete on equal terms, if he were not forced to live where he and his children are ever menaced by death. Yet as matters stand, inexorable America is assimilating the foreigner and decreasing his relative importance as a population element.

It is interesting to note the manner in which the various states attract different nationalities. Take the Turks, for instance. It is almost necessary to get out extradition papers to induce a Turk to go to Arkansas. When the 1900 census was taken there were in the United States 9,910 countrymen of the Sudan, but the whole state of Arkansas could show but one Turk. The Turk who comes to this country is more likely to head straight for Massachusetts. Nobody knows the reason. It may be because Massachusetts is so much like Turkey, or because it is so different from Turkey; it all depends on why the Turk left home. At any rate, the old Bay State heads the list of preferred American places for Turks with an Ottoman population of 2,896. New York is the second choice with 1,915.

Arkansas is also shunned by the Portuguese. The records do not show that there are any Portuguese in the state. These little Kingdoms, like the Turks, prefer Massachusetts, which leads the list with more than 13,000. There are only 30,000 Portuguese in the whole country, with whom California and Massachusetts have almost the entire number, California with 12,000 figuring as a close second.

A Romanian, on the other hand, cannot be taken into Massachusetts unless he is sealed in a boxcar and shipped over the border before he can beat his way through the roof. There are only 128 Romanians in the state, though there are 10,000 in New York, 1,200 in Pennsylvania, and enough in other places to bring the total for the country up to 15,000. Next to Massachusetts the Romanian gives the whole wide berth to Maine, Nevada, and Vermont. In these three states there is not a single one of his nationality.

Scotchmen prefer New York, will take Pennsylvania and if they can get their first choice, and, if denied both, will turn to Massachusetts. The only states the Scotsman really fight shy of are Southern states. There are 233,000 Scotchmen In the country, but the Southern states, as a rule, have only 300 or 400 apiece, while New York has 33,000. Even Kansas has more than 4,000.

continued

"Curious Paths Taken by the Immigrants, Interesting Peculiarities of Incoming Foreigners as Shown by Reports Just Released by the Government" . . . *(continued)*

When a Dutchman comes here the only thing he can see in the country is Michigan. There are 104,000 Hollanders in the United States, of whom Michigan has 80,000. Years ago the Dutch formed a settlement west of Grand Rapids on the shore of Lake Michigan. They prospered and sent home favorable reports, and other Dutchman joined them. To this day they've retained a compact social organization, almost all of their old habits of mind. Being a deeply religious people, for instance, many of them regard life insurance as an indication of a lack of faith in the Lord's promise to provide, and, therefore as a commodity, it is very wicked to buy. Insurance agents have come out of the Dutch belt in Michigan looking more emaciated and generally rundown than Dr. Cook did when he boarded the *Hans Egede* to return from the "boreal centre." Yet the Dutch are among the best citizens in Michigan. Their eyes are always on the main chance. . . .

In the same way that the Dutch have formed the habit of going to Michigan, the Swedes have formed the habit of going to Minnesota.

Give a Swede car fare to West Virginia and he would jump off the train to walk to the late Gov. Johnson's old state. There are only 132 Swedes in all of West Virginia, while Minnesota has more than 115,000. Illinois, with 100,000, comes in second in Swedish affections.

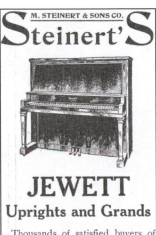
"Runaways Wed in Mid-ocean, A Romantic Marriage of Swedish Immigrants on the *Majestic*," *The New York Times*, October 25, 1906:

Passengers on the White Star liner *Majestic*, which arrived yesterday afternoon, witnessed in mid-Atlantic the wedding of two Swedish immigrants. The happy couple were Wilfred Larson and Elizabeth Wickenstrand, both natives of Broten, Sweden.

The Reverend R. C. Williams performed the ceremony last Monday morning in the purser's office. . . . After the wedding the newly wedded had a reception in the saloon and a toast to their health and future prosperity was proposed by Senator W. A. Clark of Montana and drunk by the passengers. A wedding cake had been prepared for the occasion by the ship's chief baker, C. Russell and a purse was subscribed by the saloon passengers and given to the bridegroom. . . .

What interested everybody aboard was the romance of the match. Wilfred Larson and Elizabeth Wickenstrand were sweethearts from childhood in Broten. Their parents opposed the match so they at last made up their minds to run away to America and get married. Some of their friends on board the *Majestic* suggested that there might be an order to stop them on arrival at Ellis Island, so they decided to be married at sea and land as man and wife. Captain Hayes, who has had 24 years of experience in the White Star service, said this was the first time he'd witnessed a marriage on the Atlantic. In the sailing ship days to Australia and New Zealand it was a common occurrence, but not on a short trip from Liverpool to New York.

"Auto Industry Center Is Here. Motor Car Manufacturers See New York's Approval of Their Products," *The New York Times*, January 17, 1910:

Although in actual output of motor cars, New York does not rank very high compared with some manufacturing communities, the Garden and Palace shows during the past two weeks have clearly shown that Man-hattan is the automobile center of the country. This is not only because there are probably more machines in actual use here than in any other one place, but automobile manufacturers all over the country, like those in other branches of industry, first seek metropolitan approval of their products.

The Garden show brought visitors to New York from all over the United States, and there were one or two instances of enthusiastic motorists coming here from London and Paris primarily to witness this American exhibit. These foreigners are not only impressed with the Garden show, but were surprised at the high-class exhibits in all the show rooms on both sides of the automobile row on upper Broadway, where New Yorkers may see an automobile show any time of the year.

The record of the 1909 show, which was attended during the week by 116,000, was left hopelessly in the rear. It is estimated yesterday that every day last week as many as 25,000 persons visited the show, 10,000 are in the morning and afternoon sessions and 15,000 at night. One of the show officials said yesterday that an estimate of 150,000 would be very conservative.

"My Farewell Car," advertisement, by R. E. Olds, designer:

Reo the Fifth, the car I now bring out, is considered by me as pretty close to a finality.

So close that I call it "My Farewell Car." I shall let it stand as my topmost achievement.

Embodied here are the final results of my 25 years of experience.

I have spent 18 months on Reo the Fifth. For three months I stopped the whole Reo production to devote all of our efforts to this one car.

The future is bound to bring some minor changes, folderols and fashions. But in all the essentials this car strikes my limit.

Better workmanship is impossible, better materials unthinkable. More of simplicity, silence, durability and economy can hardly be conceived.

I consider this car about as close to perfection as engineers ever will get.

This is the 24th model which I have created. My first was a steam car, built in 1887 25 years ago. My first gasoline car was built in 1895 17 years ago.

My whole life has been spent on building gasoline engines, the Olds Gas Engines, famous half the world over. My engine building successes gave first prestige to my cars. For the motor, of course, is the very heart of the car.

So it came about that tens of thousands of motorists have used cars at my designing. They have run from one to six cylinders, from 16 to 60 horsepower. They have ranged from little to big, from the primitive to the modern luxury cars. I have run the whole gamut of automobile experience.

In the process of sifting I have settled down to the 30 to 35 horse-power, four-cylinder car. That is, and will doubtlessly remain, the standard type of car.

Greater power is unnecessary; its operation expensive, weight, size and power not needed being excessive cost of upkeep. Most men who know best, and who can own good cars, are coming to this standard type. So we make for the future just one type of car.

A Tract for Autos, by Arthur Guiterman

Come, all you little Runabouts
And gather round my Knee;
I'll tell you of a touring Car
As bad as bad could be:

It worked it's Klaxton overtime
To make a Horrid Noise
And thought it Fun to mess up Hens
And little Girls and Boys.

It used to blow its Tires out
To hear its owners swear,
And loved to balk on Trolley Tracks
To give his Friends a Scare.

At last this naughty Touring Car
Got drunk on too much oil,
And went up a-boiling up the Road
As hard as it could boil,

And went a-plunging, tumbling down
A dreadful, dark Ravine;
And there it burns and burns and burns
In Smelly Gasoline!

Driving was becoming increasingly popular for both men and women.

"The Darker Side of Driving," Morrison County (Minnesota) Historical Society:

In June 1913, there were 140 automobiles in Morrison County. The newspaper published lists of car owners and the makes of the cars they owned because the automobile was such a novelty at this time.

By August 1915, there were 562 automobiles in the county and around 86,000 cars in the state.

Some driving disasters were caused by the design of vehicles and poor roads. Early cars were top heavy and had no seat belts or air bags. Roads were unpaved, bumpy and dusty, and had no shoulders or dividing lines. Just as many car catastrophes were caused by human error.

Holding political office is no guarantee of safety from automobile accidents. In May 1910, Little Falls alderman, J. F. Bastien, was struck in downtown Little Falls while crossing the street. "Due only to the fact that the car was moving at a slow rate of speed and that Mr. Bastien had presence of mind enough to cause him to clutch at the hood of the machine saved him from being severely injured."

The first auto fatality occurred in the county on April 22, 1913. Warren Farrow and Frank Kerich were on their way to Little Falls from Pierz on the Pierz Road (now Highway 27) when the accelerator stuck. In trying to free the pedal, Farrow took his eyes off the road and the car "turned turtle" over an eight-foot embankment. Kerich, the passenger, was thrown from the car and was crushed as it rolled. Farrow was thrown free of the car and became unconscious. When he awoke three hours later, he crawled to a home a half-mile away to get help. It was one o'clock in the morning by the time he reached the Mike Thommes house. News of the accident reached Coroner N. W. Chance, who brought Charles Farrow and F. P. Farrow (Warren Farrow's father) to the scene to retrieve Kerich's body and the automobile.

1913 News Feature

Immigrants Are to Be Taught on Atlantic Liners, Following 21 Trial Trips in the Steerage by Y.M.C.A. Secretaries, It Is Planned to Place a Worker on Every Ship Entering an American Port from Europe, *The New York Times,* **December 28, 1913:**

Hundreds of thousands of male immigrants are annually to begin their education in Americanism while in the steerage when plans now under way by the Young Men's Christian Association are completed. It is intended to have an association secretary in the steerage of every ship entering a United States port from Europe. Each secretary will be able to talk half a dozen or more languages, and by class teaching, by illustrated lectures, by distribution of printed matter, and by personal talks he will start the future Americans along the path which means good citizenship and industrial efficiency.

Twenty-one experimental trips have been made in the steerage by association secretaries between England and the United States and England and South America, for it is intended to extend the plan to South American immigration. Secretaries have traveled in the steerage to New York from Liverpool, London, Hamburg, Bremen, Naples, and Trieste.

It has been proved by these journeys that there is a vast field for work among immigrants on shipboard, both in extending practical assistance to individuals with various personal difficulties, and in giving suggestions and advice to the male immigrants en masse.

The opportunity open for the kind of work to be undertaken is indicated by the immigration statistics. Last year there entered the United States 1,197,000 immigrants, while 402,000 entered Canada. It is intended to have workers on ships running to Canadian ports as well as to American. Of this total immigration, about 800,000 were males between the ages of 15 and 40. About 800,000 alien immigrants also return to Europe from the United States each year, and work is likewise to be done among these people during the voyage.

The immigration section of the Industrial Department of the Y.M.C.A. International Committee now has proposals before the Cunard, White Star, and Hamburg-American steamship lines for an organization secretary to be attached regularly to each ship in the

North American trade. Negotiations with the other lines crossing the North Atlantic are also to be begun.

The Royal Mali Steamship Company asked for the services of workers for experimental trips in some of their vessels running between England and ports in South America.

Immigrants Intensely Interested

"The company was greatly pleased with the result," a *Times* reporter was told by Charles R. Towson, Secretary of the Y.M.C.A. Industrial Department in New York. "So much so that some phases of the work accomplished have just been adopted as a permanent part of the steerage organization of that line."

The most recent of all the experimental trips was made on the Cunarder *Lusitania* by John Sumner, European Emigration Secretary. He has recently sent a report to Mr. Towson of his voyage in the *Lusitania's* third cabin from Liverpool to New York. He found that intense interest was taken in his work by the immigrants, by the steamship officials, and by some of the first cabin passengers, several of the latter helping him with his activities in the third cabin.

Mr. Sumner's description of his experiences on the *Lusitania* is in part as follows:

The experimental journey was commenced when I left Liverpool with 1,042 third-class passengers.

Many aspects immediately presented themselves in regard to the short time of the voyage, huge dimensions of the third-class quarters, time of the year, and class of passengers carried.

Our passenger list was made up of approximately 400 Scandinavians, 250 British, and the balance from Central and Southern Europe. A very large percentage were returning to America after having been to the old home for a vacation. These had intimate acquaintance with the States and were well able to guide and protect their countrymen who were for the first time journeying across the ocean. In fact, the newcomer was completely swallowed up by the returning group, so that there was a striking contrast between these immigrants and those seen on steamers during the months of February, March, and April.

The steamer sailed the evening of Saturday. It was not possible to do anything that evening, for the passengers were eager to retire to their berths, having had a long and tiresome time during the period of embarkation. . . . The officials of the boat are also at this time too busy to give any cooperation. All I could do was to unpack my equipment and set it in order for the morrow. Notwithstanding the large number of passengers carried, the shore officials had generously reserved a stateroom for my use, so that I could have my equipment with me to use to the best advantage. This equipment consisted in part of portable stereopticon and four sets of slides, gramophone and 70 records, checkers and other games, song books, hymn books, illustrated magazines, letter paper and envelopes, railroad maps, and association emigration cards.

But the path of the emigration secretary is strewn with many obstacles, and my first consisted in the steamer running into a storm soon after leaving Queenstown on Sunday. This storm, the only one during the voyage, absolutely precluded any attempt to organize any association effort that day.

Monday found us settling down to the voyage, and the officials were now in a position to cooperate. Early in the day I had the gramophone on deck, provided a number of the women passengers with copies of a leading American journal, and gave the children sweets to remove the bad taste in their mouths caused by the previous day's experience. This opened the way for personal talks with the male passengers, and a distribution of our "Emigrant Guides" followed. These were eagerly accepted because of the list of association street addresses they contained.

An effort was made with the stereopticon during the evening, but a change of burners necessitated a postponement until the next evening.

Tuesday found us enjoying beautiful weather. The sea was calm and the decks crowded. Activities were resumed. The different nationalities were by this time getting acquainted and carrying out their own method of passing the time. The official vaccinating of the passengers during the afternoon put us all in such a state of excitement that nothing could be done for the men.

During the evening the stereopticon was connected in the large dining saloon and I gave a talk on "A Tour Through Ellis Island." My idea was to give the passengers some idea of what they would have to do on their arrival at the island. Those present listened intently, and it was helpful to all. Opportunity was taken also to throw on the screen copies of our emigration cards in English, German, Danish, Norwegian, and Swedish. Then I followed with a series of pictures on "A Walk Around the Ship."

This lecture caught the crows. A stereopticon talk in the mid-Atlantic, with the lantern working perfectly, was something new. Wednesday morning I was quizzed as to the extent of my equipment. One man told me that he had been in Milwaukee 27 years and knew something of the fine song services conducted in the association there by the Secretary, C.B. Willis. "All right," I said, "you find me a good pianist and we'll have a song service tonight; I have fifty hymn books and a music book."

We went on distributing a magazine here, letter paper there, pictures to others, and so forth. When the railroad maps were produced men formed little groups around them and discussed their destination. I then distributed association cards among a group of Croatians, and other cards were given men according to their nationality.

Bulletins were exhibited indicating the song service and illustrated talk to be given at 7:45 that evening. The fact that books would be provided was not omitted. I was told, "Be sure and select the most well-known old-time hymns." A most proficient pianist having been secured, this part of the programme went with a vim that would have done credit to an association on land. After 45 minutes of singing, I threw on the screen a good number of slides, showing the work of the Industrial Department, educational work, boys' work, and so forth.

Thursday found us barred from one side of the ship, this space now being rapidly filled with the mail bags and baggage brought from below. This caused endless excitement to many and much gazing for land, which was still far off. However, packing had to be done, and the immigration laws requiring the ship doctors to examine every passenger within 24 hours of landing necessitated that all of us be lined up and pass the doctor. This took all morning.

The usual concert on board ship had to be held, and I was privileged to act as Chairman. We landed early Friday morning.

Of five full days on the ship, we were interrupted on three: (1) by the storm on Sunday, (2) by vaccination on Tuesday, and (3) by medical inspection on Thursday. Notwithstanding these interruptions one was kept just as busy as he cared to be in following up activities in some part of the ship where third-class passengers were quartered. With the large number of passengers and the short period of the voyage, the best result was attained by the use of the stereopticon.

Hundreds of individuals were helped by Mr. Sumner through the giving of information about the United States and advice as to courses of action after landing.

"We have discovered beyond room for argument," said Mr. Towson to the *Times* man, "that a very large line of services can be rendered, beneficial both to the immigrants and to the steamship companies. The secretaries by sympathy and counsel will allay anxieties, give information of the utmost value about conditions in those localities to which various individual groups of immigrants are bound, will furnish advice and warnings to protect the immigrants on arrival, will teach some fundamental ideas concerning the new land of promise, will give illustrated lectures, will organize social gatherings and direct recreations, and will distribute large quantities of printed material which will be of great practical value.

"The illustrated lectures will be particularly important, and will cover such fields as American industries, agricultural activities, health protection and accident prevention."

The work in the steerage is the last to be put in operation of the five phases of service planned for the Immigration Section when it began activities in 1908. The other four kinds of services are now fully operating. These are work at port of embarkation, work at port of entry, work en route to destination, and work at destination.

In other words, the Y.M.C.A. maintains such a comprehensive system for aiding the immigrant that he is now under the eye of the organization's officials from a time before he goes on shipboard at the European port until he arrives at his final destination in the United States. After that he may or may not continue a connection with the Y.M.C.A., according to his own choice, but last year 193,000 immigrants elected to attend the lecture courses of the organization after they had reached the points where they intended to work and establish their homes.

Port secretaries are maintained at Liverpool, Bristol, Southampton, Plymouth, Glasgow, Rotterdam, Naples, Copenhagen, Antwerp, Hangö, Libau, Havre, and Gothenburg. On this continent there are port secretaries at Ellis Island, Philadelphia, Boston, Baltimore, Providence, Portland, St. John's Halifax, Quebec, and Montreal.

What Has Been Accomplished

The following table shows some of the work done for the last 12 months by these secretaries:

PORT SECRETARIAL WORK

Work	In Europe	In N. Amer.	Totals
Ships Met	889	1,014	1,903
Cards Distributed	69,047	29,297	98,344
Introductions Given	14,408	20,200	34,608
Letters Written	3,960	7,894	11,854

The table dealing with the total number of immigrants "touched" by the association's work in the last 12 months is as follows:

IMMIGRANTS "TOUCHED"

"Touched" in European ports . . . 64,047
"Touched" in North American ports . . . 29,297
Total 93,344

Organized into English classes . . . 21,914
Organized into naturalization classes . . . 1,693
Total: 23,607

Attendance at lectures: 193,339

Grand total . . . 310,290

"Our secretaries render all kinds of personal service to the immigrants at the ports of embarkation," explained Mr. Towson to the *Times* reporter. "In many of the European ports the steamship companies have huge immigrant hotels, or hostels as they are called, where the immigrants will congregate from widely scattered points a day or two before their ship sails. Our secretaries go to the hostels and the docks and introduce themselves to the immigrants. Our workers are, of course, splendid linguists.

"The secretaries offer to give the immigrants cards of introduction to the local Y.M.C.A. at the point of destination on this side of the water, and thousands of these cards are issued. The personal service includes giving advice, answering questions, helping with baggage, and protecting from grafters. Our men get the immigrants started right and with the assurance that they will meet a friend in America in the person of the organization man on this side.

"On arrival in this country the immigrant gets the same kind of personal service from the port secretary as he received at the port of embarkation. For four years we have had three secretaries at Ellis Island, who speak 28 languages between them, and who have been of prodigious aid to perplexed immigrants.

"While en route from the seaports to inland destinations the immigrants are aided by secretaries at Chicago, Pittsburgh, San Francisco, and other large centres from which the immigrants scatter. The Chicago secretary alone has served 2,700 people in one month. He aided 19 of the Volturno survivors, who arrived in Chicago without money and insufficiently clothed. When the Panama Canal is opened there will be a tide of immigration at San Francisco, and the work at Angel Island, the point of entry there as is Ellis Island here, will assume very large proportions.

"At the final destination the organization aids the immigrants by finding them employment, locating their friends, directing them to boarding places, cashing checks, introducing them to safe people, and so on. It is particularly important to bring them into contact with the right kind of associates, so that they will not get their education from the ward boss or in the saloon. One of the first great services is to give the immigrants the English language, and our classes for newly arrived foreigners have been most successful.

"In New York City an immigrant worker is maintained apart from the port secretaries, and this worker also deals with a good many second cabin passengers. . . ."

College Men Help

In various parts of the country college men are helping the association in its work of teaching the immigrants. It is stated that students from the universities of Illinois, Indiana, Iowa, and Ames are teaching foreign men and boys in railroad box cars, and that men from Cornell, Western Polytechnic Institute, McGill University, the University of California, and the University of Puget Sound are visiting the homes of immigrants and are teaching groups in boarding houses.

In the last 12 months work has been done among immigrants of 46 nationalities. The three Ellis Island secretaries between them can talk to immigrants in these tongues: Dutch, Flemish, German, French, Norwegian, Danish, Swedish, Italian, Magyar, Spanish, Portuguese, Polish, Hebrew, Bulgarian, Greek, Albanian, Russian, Turkish, English,

Romanian, Servian, Croatian, Dalmatian, Bosnian, Herzegovinian, Montenegrin, Macedonian, Wallachian.

The keynote of the immigration work is sounded in the following excerpt from Zangwill's "The Melting Pot," which the association is using in the Immigration Section circulars:

"Yes, East and West, and North and South, the palm and the pine, the pole and the equator, the crescent and the cross—how the great Alchemist melts and fuses them with his purging flame! Here shall they all unite to build the Republic of Man and the Kingdom of God. Ah, Vera, what is the glory of Rome and Jerusalem where all nations and races come to worship and look back, compared with the glory of America, where all races and nations come to labor and look forward?"

1916 PROFILE

Alexander Nodirov, whose parents had come from Kazakhstan, was ready to enter a career as a furrier, as his ancestors had done, when he saw how successful his father had become doing just that in America.

Life at Home

At 20-years-old, Alexander Nodirov was ready to enter his father's furrier business in New York City.

- Twenty-year-old Alexander Nodirov, born in New York City to Kazakh immigrants, began life in America in 1896.
- But life in the crowded tenements of the East Side of New York near 77th Street and First Avenue was hard on the health of an underfed Kazakh baby whose persistent cough kept his parents awake at night—mostly with worry.
- Alexander's father Vladimir had waited eight years to come to America, and then spent four years raising enough money to bring a 15-year-old girl from his hometown of Kyzl Orda to be his bride, but they were desperate to keep their young son alive.
- At the age of 18 months, Alexander, his father and mother Anna all returned to Kazakhstan—the only place the family could be sure his spirits would be safe and his health restored.
- Vladimir stayed two weeks in Kyzl Orda before returning to New York City and his occupation as a furrier.
- Alexander and Anna remained behind at her parents' house where local wise men openly derided the ineffectiveness of western medicine while searching for the evil spirits tainting the baby's health.
- Within weeks the cough disappeared, proving the power of Kazakh medicine.
- The two remained in their home country for another four years.
- For centuries the history of the Kazakh people was shaped by the conflicts and alliances of the Turkic and Mongol tribes.
- Historically a nomadic people, the Kazakhs understood the ways of nature, cattle and the sometimes harsh climate.
- Even after Russian settlers came south and began crowding Kazakh herders off their grazing land, the people continued to be close to the spirits that they believed ruled the natural universe.

Alexander's father was in America for four years before sending for 15-year-old Anna to be his bride.

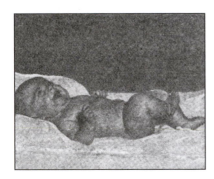

Alexander was born in New York City.

Alexander's father was a skilled textile worker.

- Alexander's father Vladimir, whose father and grandfather also had been furriers, was Kazakh to his core; he began his quest to leave the country only after the relentless onslaught of Russian settlers shifted from a trickle to a flood in the 1890s.
- Thanks to his profession and background as a skilled furrier, he was both literate and multilingual, capable of conversing with fur and clothing traders in five languages.
- He also was intensely interested in politics—a passion inherited by his son—to preserve the nomadic way of life in Kazakhstan.
- During Alexander's first six years of life, he and his mother lived in a one-room house with six other relatives in Kyzl Orda, where Kazakh was spoken by nearly everyone and the hated Russian immigrants were few.
- His most enduring memories of that time focused on the closeness of family and the presence of song.
- When he and his mother moved back to New York, he missed the richness of spontaneous song that so dominated his homeland; Kazakhs rarely missed an excuse to sing.
- His memories of his early childhood also included wintertime gatherings in which the women talked and plucked feathers to make pillows while the men made ornaments out of harness leather with carved wooden tools.
- Included in Alexander's most precious possessions was the sucala or weaver's shuttle his grandfather helped him carve during those long winter nights.
- He insisted that it be the one item besides clothing he would take back to America.
- Yet his most enduring possession was exposure to a storytelling tradition that dated back hundreds of years, honed to a fine art by a nomadic civilization.
- He particularly enjoyed tales that included werewolves and fantasy monsters; he was often fearful of the dark plains of Kazakhstan where lamp oil was expensive and rarely used frivolously to fight back the night.
- When he and his mother returned to New York, the man who met them at Ellis Island was well-dressed, plump, and excited about the future.
- During their time away, Vladimir had established his own business importing European furs and leathers, which he converted into clothing, especially finely made winter coats for the wealthy of New York City.
- Even though he had religiously sent half of all his earnings to his wife and child in Kazakhstan, the spectacular growth of New York City would have made him prosperous anyway.
  - Now he was ready to teach his young son the business; as he often said, "There is gold in the streets of New York only if you are willing to lean down and pick it up."

Life at Work

- Alexander Nodirov's first adjustment to America was learning to live around so many other people.
- The street where he lived with his parents, after he first arrived, held more people than the village in which he had been raised.
- Another adjustment was eating canned food.
- In the old country, fixing dinner meant going to the yard to catch the chicken or pluck some fruit; in New York City everything was different, including food that came in cans and did not seem to spoil the way it had in Kazakhstan.

- His other adjustment was language; Kazakh was spoken only by his mother; the children of the streets spoke Russian-English, German-English, Polish-English, but English nonetheless.
- To speed his progress in learning English, a tutor was hired for him, although early efforts were more clamorous than educational.
- For example, when he failed to understand or pronounce a word correctly, the tutor would simply say the word louder; if he made the same mistake, the correction was made even louder; if enough foibles ensued, a shouting match resulted.
- By the time he was 20 years old, speaking English was second nature, as was dealing with customers; he loved fashioning fur coats out of fine European pelts, and they were a favorite of many of his father's wealthier customers.
- It was exhilarating to talk with millionaires, but he also had to be polite to dozens of customers who were convinced he must be Russian since they had never met a Kazakh.
- These exchanges also inflamed a love for international politics and his homeland.
- Since 1914 Europe had been locked in war; most Americans assumed the Allies would win, and believed that a limited American participation was enough.
- Few were willing to unlock America's concept of isolationism and join the fight across the sea.
- Alexander's exposure to international trade made him aware of other, disturbing facts.
- By 1916, the British and French armies were reaching the last of their reserve manpower.
- Europe could be lost.
- The future of Kazakhstan was uncertain; Russia, linked with the Allies, had lost 1.7 million soldiers and was substantially weakened by the war.
- Kazakhstan could become a pawn to be negotiated away.
- German U-boats were destroying all seaborne commerce, sinking ships at the rate of 600 tons a month in an attempt to bring England to its knees.
- At the same time, German U-boats were wrecking the import/export business of Alexander and his father, who had both come to rely on high-quality European hides.
- America needed to join the fight before Germany conquered all of Europe.
- Although Americans had changed the name of the German sauerkraut to liberty cabbage and banned church services conducted in German, they seemed incapable of real action.
- Even President Woodrow Wilson's re-election campaign was based on avoiding going to war, when it was obvious to everyone that America needed to join the fight.
- Everyone, that is, with an interest in the future of Europe; many of Alexander's and Vladimir's customers, who loved wearing the latest fashions, had no interest in helping England and France at their time of need.

Alexander had to adjust to more people in America.

President Wilson's re-election campaign was based on avoiding going to war.

Alexander was interested in joining the army.

- Alexander talked to his father about joining the American army but was told he was needed more in the furrier business than he was in the trenches.
- "Save your fighting for Kazakhstan," he was told by his father repeatedly.
- After all, many of his customers were growing "war rich" supplying materials or capital to the warring nations; money was to be made from those who wanted to wear the finest fur coats in New York City.

Life in the Community: Greenwich Village, New York

- When Alexander and his mother returned from Kazakhstan, Vladimir proudly tucked into their new home in Greenwich Village—an up-and-coming section of the city.
- While The American Association of Park Superintendents was issuing "Bathing Suit Regulations" requiring that beachgoers wear proper attire, including tops for men, Greenwich Village was setting new standards in fashion and breaking new ground.
- It was clearly the place to be for a furrier focused on high-fashion coats.
- Greenwich Village, New York City, was an exciting place to operate a business focused on the trendy.
- As America's entry into the First World War loomed, the Village was being called, "The home of half the talent and half the eccentricity in the country."
- Alexander wrote to friends that within a block of his house was all the adventure in the world, within a mile every foreign country.
- The first night court in America was held in the Village, and the first theater opened devoted exclusively to films.
- The first pizza served in America was in the Village, also the first spaghetti dinner and the first ice cream soda.
- The first labor demonstration in America took place there in the 1830s, when local stonecutters protested the use of Sing Sing convicts to cut stone for the construction of New York University.
- And where else could the Unitary Household have been founded in 1859, the first free-love community in the country?
- John L. Sullivan had his first fight there and George M. Cohan made his stage debut.
- The first theatrical agency started in Greenwich Village.
- For a time Thomas Edison had his office there, as did Samuel Colt, inventor of the Colt .45 there, and Samuel F. B. Morse, inventor of the telegraph.
- Two young Village furriers, Adolph Zukor and Maurice Loew, started their dynasties at the corner of 14th Street and Sixth Avenue with Biograph Films, where Mary Pickford and the Gish sisters made their first pictures.
- Hundreds of silent movies were set in the Village.
- The buffalo nickel was designed in the Village, as were the giant balloons for the first Macy's Thanksgiving Day parade.
- John Wilkes Booth and his co-conspirators held several of their meetings in the Village.
- Among the poets, the Village was once home to Edgar Allan Poe, Walt Whitman, William Cullen Bryant, Edwin Arlington Robinson, John Masefield and Louis Untermeyer.
- Even Ezra Pound and T. S. Eliot lived in the Village for brief periods.

"I can put you up for thirty francs a day, but at that price, of course, you'll have to help dig potatoes and milk the cows."—(Le Rire, Paris.)

HISTORICAL SNAPSHOT
1916

- British authorities seized German attaché von Papen's financial records, confirming espionage activities in America
- Louis D. Brandeis was appointed to the U.S. Supreme Court, becoming its first Jewish member
- The U.S. Senate attempted to declare independence to the Philippines, effective in 1921
- Germany accepted full liability for the *Lusitania* incident and recognized the United States' right to claim indemnity
- Demonstrators protested against food shortages in Berlin
- Conscription began in Great Britain as the Military Service Act went into effect
- Jules Verne's *20,000 Leagues Under the Sea* opened in New York
- Haiti became the first U.S. protectorate
- Pancho Villa led 1,500 horsemen in a night raid on Columbus, New Mexico, that killed 17; President Woodrow Wilson ordered General John J. "Black Jack" Pershing to "pursue and disperse" the bandits
- Germany declared war on Portugal
- The first U.S. national women's swimming championships were held
- Wrigley Field in Chicago opened
- Germany agreed to limit its submarine warfare against American shipping, averting a diplomatic break with Washington
- U.S. marines invaded the Dominican Republic
- Herbert Smith designed the Sopwith Triplane in search of a plane that could climb faster, fly higher and outmaneuver its competitors
- British and German fleets fought the Battle of Skagerrak at Jutland off Denmark that killed 10,000
- The National Defense Act increased the strength of the U.S. National Guard by 450,000 men
- More than 100,000 men were killed in the first day of the Battle of the Somme
- Nathan's Famous Hot Dogs opened a stand at Brooklyn's Coney Island and held an eating contest as a publicity stunt that became an annual event
- The Boeing Company, originally known as Pacific Aero Products, was founded in Seattle by William Boeing

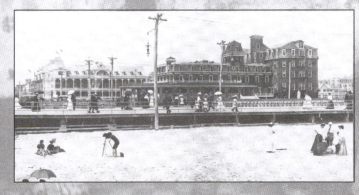

Nathan's Famous Hot Dogs opened at Brooklyn's Coney Island.

Ellis Island Timeline

1776

By the time of the American Revolution, Ellis Island was owned by Samuel Ellis, a New York merchant and owner of a small tavern.

1808

Samuel Ellis's heirs sold the island to New York State, which retained the name Ellis Island.

The federal government bought Ellis Island for $10,000.

1812

Prior to the War of 1812, a battery of 20 guns, a magazine and a barracks were constructed on the island.

1834

Ellis Island and neighboring Bedloe's Island were declared part of New York State, even though both were on the New Jersey side of the main ship channel.

1890

The States turned over control of immigration to the federal government.

The U.S. Congress appropriated $75,000 to build the first federal immigration station on Ellis Island.

1892

The first Ellis Island Immigration Station was officially opened.

The first immigrant to pass through Ellis was a "rosy-cheeked Irish girl," Annie Moore, age 15, from County Cork; she came with her two younger brothers to join their parents in New York City.

In the first year, 450,000 immigrants passed through Ellis Island.

1897

A fire destroyed most of the immigration records dating from 1855.

Since 1892, some 1.5 million immigrants had been processed.

1900

The Main Building opened, an impressive, French Renaissance structure in red brick with limestone trim, designed to process 5,000 immigrants per day.

1907

Ellis Island processed 1,004,756 immigrants in a single year.

On April 17, a total of 11,747 immigrants were processed in a single day.

1908

The Baggage and Dormitory Building was completed and the capacity of the hospital was doubled.

1916

Explosions believed to have been set by German saboteurs at nearby Black Tom Wharf in New Jersey severely damaged the Ellis Island buildings.

1917

After the U.S. entered the war in Europe, Ellis Island was used to detain crews from German merchant ships anchored in New York Harbor.

Suspected enemy aliens throughout America were rounded up and brought to Ellis Island.

During World War I immigration declined sharply as the numbers of newcomers passing through Ellis Island decreased from 178,416 in 1915, to 28,867 in 1918.

Selected Prices

Baby Shoes	$0.50
Deodorant Cream	$0.25
Men's Hat	$5.00
Milk, Quart	$0.12
Movie Ticket	$0.15
Painting, Botticelli's *Madonna and Child*	$20,000
Telephone Call, Three Minutes, New York to San Francisco	$20.70
Typewriter, Underwood	$43.85
Woman's Bracelet Watch	$7.00
Women's Bloomers	$0.90

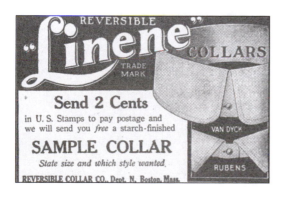

A handsome, clear-eyed Russian girl of about 20 years, the daughter of a farmer, comes in and sits down before us. She is clean and intelligent-looking. She nervously clasps and unclasps her hands and the tears are welling in her eyes. "That girl over there," says the commissioner, "is an interesting and puzzling case. Her father is a farmer in moderate circumstances. A young man with whom she grew up, the son of a neighbor, came here two years ago, and last year wrote to her father that if the girl would come over, he would marry her. So she came, alone. But the prospective bridegroom didn't show up. I wrote him—he lives somewhere in New Jersey—and last week he appeared and looked her over. Finally he said he wasn't sure whether he wanted to marry her or not. Naturally her pride was somewhat wounded, and she decided that she had doubts herself. So everything is at a standstill. The girl says she doesn't want to go back, to be laughed at; and I can't let her land. You don't know any lady who wants a servant, do you? She could work! Look at her arms. A nice girl, too. No? Well, I don't know what to do. Are you willing to marry Peter if he comes again?" The girl nods, the tears brimming over. "Well, I'll write to that fellow again and tell him he's a fool. He'll never have such a chance again."

—Recorded by Commissioner William Williams, March 1910

Ellis Island is the nation's gateway to the promised land. In a single day it has handled 7,000 immigrants. "How much you got?" shouts the inspector at the head of the long file moving up from the quay between iron rails, and, remembering, in the same breath shrieks out, "Quanto monèta?" with a gesture that brings up from the depths of Pietro's pocket a pitiful handful of paper money. Before he has half of it out, the interpreter has him by the wrist, and with a quick movement shakes the bills out upon the desk as a dice-thrower "chucks" the ivories. Ten, 20, 40 lire. He shakes his head. Not much, but—he glances at the ship's manifest-is he going to friends? "Si, si! signor," says Pietro, eagerly; his brother of the vineyard—oh, a fine vineyard! And he holds up a bundle of grapesticks as evidence. He has brought them all the way from the village at home to set them out in his brother's field. "Ugh," grunts the inspector as he stuffs the money back in the man's pocket, shoves him on, and yells, "Wie viel geld?" at a hapless German next in line. "They won't grow. They never do. Bring 'em just the same."

—Jacob A. Riis, 1903

They also questioned people on literacy. My uncle called me aside, when he came to take us off. He said, "Your mother doesn't know how to read." I said, "That's all right." For the reading you faced what they called the commissioners, like judges on a bench. I was surrounded by my aunt and uncle and another uncle who's a pharmacist—my mother was in the center. They said she would have to take a test for reading. So one man said, "She can't speak English." Another man said, "We know that. We will give her a siddur." You know what a siddur is? It's a Jewish book. The night they said this, I knew that she couldn't do that and we would be in trouble. Well, they opened the siddur. There was a certain passage they had you read. I looked at it and I saw right away what it was. I quickly studied it—I knew the whole paragraph. Then I got underneath the two of them there—I was very small—and I told her the words in Yiddish very softly. I had memorized the lines and I said them quietly and she said them louder so the commissioner could hear it. She looked at it and it sounded as if she was reading it, but I was doing the talking underneath. I was Charlie McCarthy!

—Arnold Weiss, Russian, at Ellis Island in 1921, age 13

Annihilator of Space

To be within arm's reach of distant cities it is only necessary to be within arm's reach of a Bell Telephone. It annihilates space and provides instantaneous communication, both near and far.

There can be no boundaries to a telephone system as it is now understood and demanded. Every community is a center from which people desire communication in every direction, always with contiguous territory, often with distant points. Each individual user may at any moment need the long distance lines which radiate from his local center.

An exchange which is purely local has a certain value. If, in addition to its local connections, it has connections with other contiguous localities, it has a largely increased value.

If it is universal in its connections and inter-communications, it is indispensable to all those whose social or business relations are more than purely local.

A telephone system which undertakes to meet the full requirements of the public must cover with its exchanges and connecting links the whole country.

The Bell Telephone System annihilates space for the business man to-day. It brings him and any of his far-away social or business interests together.

AMERICAN TELEPHONE AND TELEGRAPH COMPANY

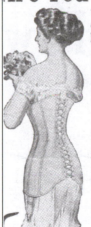

Are You Getting Stout?

You can have as good a figure as any woman if you wear one of our **Ewing Reducing Garments** and you need not diet, take drugs or tiresome exercises. We make the Ewing Hip and Abdominal Reducing Band and the Ewing Bust Reducing Garment and Corset. They are beautifully made of light materials, lined with thin rubber, ventilated, cool and comfortable to wear. No buckles, straps or steels. They will reduce you without the slightest harm or inconvenience. **We make them to your measure to reduce just the parts you wish.** Every garment guaranteed. No corset can reduce you permanently, and no other Reducing Garments are hygienic and comfortable. The Ewing Reducing Garments do not bind or distribute the flesh to other parts --- **they draw the fat completely away.**

The Ewing Hip and Abdominal Reducer weighs **only 5 oz.** Endorsed by eminent Physicians and hundreds of men and women wearers. Wear the band a few weeks before having your new gowns made. Send 2-cent stamp for illustrated booklet and measurement blanks. Don't go a week longer without knowing what we can do for you.

THE E. L. EWING COMPANY
Dept. D F, 3223 Sheffield Avenue, Chicago

"Gompers Cries for Less Immigration, Stirs National Conference to a Hot Debate," *The New York Times*, December 8, 1905:

Organized labor, speaking through the mouth of Samuel W. Gompers, president of the American Federation of Labor, had its say on the immigration question yesterday afternoon, asking issue squarely with those who would open wide the country's gates and precipitating a storm of debate that raged for the better part of the afternoon session of the National Conference on Immigration. The conference is in session in the Madison Square Garden Concert Hall. . . .

"I would like to ask this question, then: is it not strange that there are a number of gentlemen in our country who favor a system of protection for American products as against foreign-made products, and yet demand absolute free trade in the matter of American labor? Is it not inconsistent to impose a duty upon the product of the European workman when the European workman is free to come to this country and turn out the same product?"

Mr. Gompers was interrupted by an outburst of cheers which came from all parts of the hall. One delegate let out a whoop which would have done credit to a Wild West show. Mr. Gompers went on to charge that at certain stated periods workmen of a given calling were brought to this country and concentrated at a given point for the purpose of depressing labor of a certain kind. This brought out another demonstration.

"It is true now," he concluded, "as it has always been, that self-protection is the first law of nature, and it is of the utmost importance that the American workman should do all in his power to prohibit the importation of those who would still further press him down."

President Eliot of Harvard, introduced as the next speaker, proceeded without a delay to attack the doctrines promulgated by Mr. Gompers. That the sentiment was well-divided was evidenced by the generous applause with which he was interrupted.

"I question the doctrine of self-protection," he said. "It is overworked. To a certain extent it is a good thing, but if it is followed by the extent of the expense of our fellow-men it is a dangerous thing. (Cheers.) It is not the nobler, more generous attitude, and it will never commend itself to our people in regard to immigration.

"We need all the brain and sinew we can import to develop our resources. Every part of our country, North, East, West, and South, needs more labor this very minute. Keep out the criminals, the insane, and those afflicted with contagious diseases, but when it comes to excluding labor on the grounds that it has been induced to come here, we are treading on entirely different ground. There can be no reason for prohibiting sound, moral laborers from coming to our land, whether they are induced to come or not. The American people will welcome them, and will endure no legislation designed to keep them out.

continued

"Gompers Cries for Less Immigration, Stirs National Conference to a Hot Debate," . . . *(continued)*

"It is not a generous thought that American labor wants to keep out all other labor because the wages of American labor might be lowered. The mobility of capital is becoming greater and greater. It is much more mobile than the working people. The question, as it presents itself to me, is whether we prefer having more labor come here and help build up our country, or have our will go elsewhere to build up other lands.

"The industrial problem is transcending national boundaries, and we would not do well to forget that capital can always take care of itself. National greatness after all depends on the brain and the brawn of the people. . . .

The afternoon session was devoted to the subject of the selection of immigrants. There was full attendance. Congressman Gardiner of Massachusetts was the first speaker. Others heard during the afternoon included Judge Lynn Harrison of Connecticut and Herman Wolf. Mr. Wolf made an eloquent plea for the Russian Jew. The previous speaker had suggested that a good plan to keep out undesirable immigrants would be to increase the head tax on immigrants to $40. Mr. Wolf asked how such a payment would be expected from the oppressed people of the Jewish race, who were, he said, victims of the Greek Catholic Church.

"Russia to Restrict Fur Exports," *The New York Times*, August 8, 1919:

Russia has placed stringent restrictions on the shipment of furs from that country, according to advices received by the Metropolitan Fur Exchange, and as a result it is thought that the present high prices of furs will be driven even higher. Some large consignments were expected from Russia, and, if they fail to be received, the present shortage of skins will be aggravated. The exchange expects to have $1,000,000 worth of furs to offer at its auction.

"Fur Stocks Too Heavy, Manufacturer Says Overproduction Is Ruining Business," *The New York Times*, March 13, 1913:

Overproduction is the crying evil of the New York fur trade, and, according to a representative local manufacturer, until some means of preventing it are decided upon there can be little hope of the business showing real profit.

"Overproduction hurts this trade more than anything else," he said yesterday, "and until this evil is successfully combated, the trade as a whole will continue to sink from day to day. It can be stopped only by the manufacturers agreeing to run their plants seven or eight months a year, instead of trying to run them 12, as at present.

"It is because of overproduction that the buyers dominate the manufacturers to the extent they now do. Some of their actions are as non-businesslike as can be imagined. Many of them have made it a practice in the last few years to fit up their departments without expense to their respective stores. They come to the manufacturers and say 'I will buy $1,000 for the goods from you on memorandum.' And the manufacturer, always being overstocked and anxious to unload, usually gives the buyer the merchandise. Then the buyer shows his appreciation by returning, at the end of the season, all the goods bought that remained unsold on memorandum.

"What is the result, then, when the manufacturer gets back the major portion of his merchandise at the end of the season and is unable to meet his obligations? Is it any wonder under these conditions that this trade cannot get early orders, to be regularly shipped and charged, without the memorandum nuisance?

"Imagine the financial standing of this trade at the end of the 1912-1913 season, with the 13-week strike we had, and millions of dollars worth of merchandise being sold at less than $0.50 on the dollar at the season's close. It is true that the weather played a large part in a particular condition, but nothing hurt the trade to the extent it was affected by overproduction."

Charlie Chaplin's Comic Capers (E. C. Segar), 1916

S'Matter Pop? (C. M. Payne), 1916

1918 Profile

Josephine Glueck began an odyssey when she came to America from Poland and found a new family, unemployment, and the determination to establish, along with her sister Eva, her own business.

Life at Home

- Josephine Glueck grew up in the border city of Tarnow, Poland, dreaming of what it would be like to have a mother—just to talk with.
- When she was 20 months old, her mother Josie and father Samuel emigrated to America, leaving her and her sister Eva in the care of their grandmother.
- Every month their parents sent money to support their two daughters, but never the necessary immigration papers needed for them to come to America and be a family again.
- Josephine's opportunity to emigrate did not take place until she was 17 years old, and even then the journey was necessitated by the ugliness of war.
- The city of Tarnow occupied a border position in the Northern Austro-Hungary Empire when she was born at the turn of the century.
- After years of waiting to join her parents, her impetus to leave Poland was the outbreak of World War I and the intolerable persecution of civilians that resulted.
- Poland's loss of independence in the late eighteenth century had already ignited a scattering of its people throughout Europe and the United States.
- They were driven away by both the political uncertainty and the transition from an agricultural economy to an industrial society unfamiliar and unwelcome to many.
- Of the millions of Poles who emigrated to North America prior to World War I, most viewed the United States as a temporary home.
- By the outbreak of World War I in 1914, large Polish communities existed in Pittsburgh, Detroit, Buffalo, Milwaukee and Chicago.
- Chicago proudly claimed to be the third-largest Polish-populated city in the world.
- Josephine's parents had come to America believing they would stay only a short time; they were known as za chlebem, or for-bread immigrants, who planned to earn a nest egg and return home.

Josephine Glueck left Poland when she was 17-years-old to meet her parents in America.

- In Poland, Josephine's father Samuel was educated in a trade school and then opened a business for himself.
- The need for capital sparked the idea of emigration to America; a few years of earning good money would make everything possible in Poland, he told his customers before he left.
- At first he was to be the only immigrant; his wife and children would be left behind.
- But when his mother-in-law volunteered to temporarily raise the girls, he decided more money could be made by a couple who could then return to Poland sooner.
- They purposely did not wake the two daughters on the day they left; no one felt capable of surviving an emotional parting.
- Josephine awoke the morning her parents left to a weeping grandmother struggling to be brave.
- As a child, Josephine worked hard in school so she would be worthy when the invitation to visit America finally came.
- Her sister Eva's goal was to be delightfully entertaining, and she frequently succeeded.
- Eva was known as the fun one, while Josephine was the serious sister who always had her nose in a book.
- Then World War I erupted, their grandmother died, remittances from America stopped and their village became a war zone.
- First the Russian soldiers passed through the area, commandeering their home and barn.
- They were followed by Polish soldiers who took everything they could see, including the last loaf of bread the family had.
- The Polish people were caught in the crossfire of territorial hatred.
- The sisters had run out of options and patience; the time to discover America had arrived.
- They elected to leave Poland in January 1918, right after the Christmas celebration.
- Neither wanted to miss the traditional Christmas Eve dinner, or Wigila, with its 13-course Polish meal, each course representing Christ and the 12 apostles.
- Knowing it was their last holiday in Poland, the girls were careful to properly display the family paper cuttings, or wycinanki, used throughout the home to celebrate the birth of Jesus.
- Fashioned with ordinary sheep shears, the craftsmanship and shapes of the paper cutouts symbolized to the girls everything precious about Poland.
- At the last moment, Josephine decided to take one of the cutouts with her as a remembrance of the homeland she might never see again.

Josephine and her sister Eva waiting inspection on the docks.

- A few weeks later they left in the middle of the night, knowing that the authorities would come looking for them; their talents as the town bread baker's assistants made them valuable.
- In preparation for their escape, they sold an old cow, a few chickens and a wood lathe to raise money for the voyage; otherwise, they left most of their worldly possessions behind.
- They walked or rode carts for 39 days; when Josephine reached the docks, dirty and exhausted, she was terrified of undergoing the physical exam required for emigrants.
- A three-year-old farm injury to her leg had produced a pronounced limp which could make her ineligible for immigration.

- Even the presence of a vendor humorously selling pears, which he referred to as "ladies legs," could not break the tension.
- At the docks, the sisters suddenly realized that most of the other passengers had shaved their heads to demonstrate they didn't have lice; this reality made them both more uncertain and terrified.
- The medical examination itself was cursory, less personal than Josephine had been led to believe, and most of all, it was over quickly.
- Without ever looking up or acknowledging Josephine's broad smile, the ship's clerk issued an official paper that said she was headed to America after 15 years of waiting.
- The woman directly ahead of her in line was unable to demonstrate her ability to read in any language—a new requirement in America—and was rejected despite her shaved head and tearful pleas.
- Boarding the ship with an official document in her hand was the happiest moment Josephine had experienced in years.

Life at Home

- The ocean voyage was an adventure to be remembered, even in third-class accommodations, despite the determination of the gang of Spanish children to steal everything they could lay their hands on.
- Josephine was horrified when the gang snatched the brand-new Christmas doll of a terrified seven-year-old Polish girl and sent it flying over the rail, just to be mean.
- The same group of boys took a paint box set from an 11-year-old boy who plaintively cried, "My grandfather gave me that for Christmas!"
- The chaos of travel continued after landing at Ellis Island in New York Harbor.
- There the two teenage girls waited for five days to be claimed; a sponsor in America was required before they could leave.
- On the first day they were at Ellis Island, a Frenchwoman walked up and slapped Eva across the face for supposedly taking her seat; Eva wore the welt for three days.
- On the second day their suitcases full of clothes were stolen, including all their underwear embroidered with the family name.
- Josephine realized that after 15 years of waiting to see her parents again, she would have to greet them in a dirty dress.
- At night the sisters attended a beautiful theater on Ellis Island, provided for the immigrants who were still being processed.
- Josephine was dazzled to be near the stage of an opera star and witness "La Donna Mobile."
- After the concert, everyone would be lined up for Graham Crackers and milk containing Ex-Lax.
- After the second day, the sisters took the crackers and threw away the milk.
- But in the tension of waiting, conflicts were inevitable.
- On the fourth day they got into a shouting match with a German translator who was scolding them in Russian, a language they detested.
- Quickly Josephine was learning that those without the native language didn't possess a tongue.
- Never had she felt so lost, stupid and unsure about her decision to come to America.
- During the day, food was provided to the waiting immigrants; Josephine enjoyed the pickled herring and onions, but found eating hot dogs baffling.
- Nothing in her experience had prepared her for a hot dog.
- In the cafeteria, immigration officials established for Jewish immigrants a separate line and special food tables that looked very inviting.

- Josephine never had the courage to pretend she was a Jew so that she might sample the different foods.
- When her parents finally arrived, late and apologetic, she realized for the first time that she had two brothers and one sister whom she had never met or been told about.
- The reunion on Ellis Island was enthusiastic and awkward.
- Her mother spoke excitedly in Polish and English, the small children shouted at each other and yanked each other's coats, while the two girls struggled to fit into a family they didn't know existed.
- Almost immediately their father told them that they would have to work if they planned to stay in America; he had no interest in supporting loafers.
    - They were informed that he had landed both of them jobs as live-in maids and had signed a one-year commitment on their behalf.
    - Eva's only response was to cry, while Josephine remained silent.
    - Josephine's first day on the job did not go well.
    - Instead of simply doing the cleaning job she had been given, she was eager to demonstrate her skills as a baker, especially her ability to produce luscious breads.
    - This placed her on the turf of the well-established Italian staff which had no interest in learning anything from a Polish greenhorn fresh from the boat.
    - The first time she attempted to enter the kitchen, the three cooks shooed her out as though she were an errant chicken; the second time she was threatened with a broom handle.
    - The third attempt was rewarded with a bucketful of soapy water.
    - That night the mistress of the house gave her a stern lecture about the need to get along with others; because the scolding was entirely in English, Josephine understood nary a word.
    - She lasted a week before she was fired, to the outraged umbrage of her father.
    - Within a month, Eva had also lost her job.
    - Together they vowed to open a bakery and swore an allegiance to never speak of their parents again.
    - It had become obvious that their parents were ashamed of their Polish children, the Polish language and the traditional Polish ways.
- For years her parents had denied they were Polish to escape the American slur "dumb Pollack"; the appearance of the two oldest daughters straight from Poland had make them liars.
- Her father was proud of his accomplishments in America.
- Shortly after arriving 15 years earlier, with no relatives, no friends to rely on, he found work in the woods of Virginia.
- Each morning he rose at 5 o'clock to cut phenomenally tall trees from the lush woods so they could be hauled by train to sawmills near the coast.
- He often worked until 9 or 10 p.m. hauling logs in those early years, always dreaming of being his own boss again.
- One day equipment at the sawmill broke down, halting work; even though he had never worked on this type of belt-driven machinery before, he understood its mechanics.
- Within an hour he had the equipment humming again and production back underway; the next day he was taken off the logging train and assigned to equipment maintenance.

Josephine's father insisted she work as a live-in maid to support herself.

HELP WANTED
WANTED—Lumber stacker, carriage dogger, edgerman, trackmen and woodmen, logging contractors. Railroad station, Bryson, N. C. ALARKA LUMBER CO., Alarka, N. C.   (3873-3-28-7t)

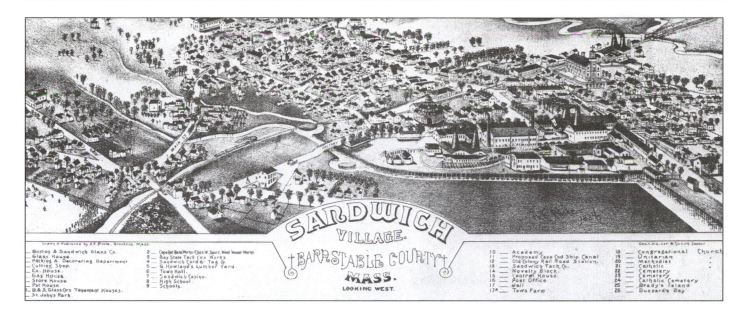

- Within weeks he was nicknamed the "Hungarian handyman" capable of fixing anything; he didn't bother to set the ethnic record straight.
- In three years he had created the reputation he needed to set up a heavy equipment business in Sandwich, Massachusetts.
- The future was to be found in America, not in Poland; the girls were better off where they were.
- His new children would be Americans, who understood American ways and didn't cling to the past.

Life in the Community: Sandwich, Massachusetts

- A decade earlier, Samuel Glueck was busy preparing a broken driveshaft when he received an offer he never expected.
- Two Sandwich, Massachusetts, businessmen offered to finance and equip a mechanical repair facility for him if he would relocate to the community in Cape Cod.
- The Sandwich community was growing steadily and needed someone to service the commercial fishing and truck farming industries that supported the economy.
- They told him they would finance the entire business and allow him to buy them out after five years.
- Their goal was to support the community, and they would charge no interest as long as he agreed to stay at least five years.
- They even offered him a two-bedroom house for rent near the shop they proposed to build to his specifications.
- Only in America, he kept telling his wife—only in America.
- Within four years he had repaid the loan, hired three additional workers, and began tithing to the Catholic Church.
- Sandwich is located in southeastern Massachusetts at the beginning of Cape Cod.
- Bordered by Cape Cod Bay, Sandwich is 57 miles southeast of Boston; 61 miles east of Providence, Rhode Island; and 238 miles from New York City.

Josephine's father found success managing a mechanical repair business.

Sandwich was a successful, happy community.

- Incorporated in 1639, Sandwich, Massachusetts, is the oldest town on Cape Cod.
- The town is well known for its beaches along Cape Cod Bay that stretch for miles and provide a wonderful view of the vessels that pass through on their way to or from the Boston area.
- Commercial fishermen and lobstermen are seen daily from the docks at the Sandwich Marina, the only harbor along the canal.
- There Samuel had a captive audience, eager for his mechanical skills and his earnestness to be successful.

Sandwich was well known for its beaches and fishermen.

HISTORICAL SNAPSHOT
1918

- Taxes were increased 250 percent to meet the cost of World War I; large incomes were taxed at a rate of 77 percent

- Mississippi was the last state in the nation to pass a mandatory school attendance law

- Daylight Saving Time was instituted to permit more work time for war production

- Camel cigarettes were a staple of a soldier's life in the trenches

- Four thousand theaters nationwide featured highly popular vaudeville acts

- Citizens of Berlin, New Hampshire, voted to rename their city

- Twelve thousand Communist supporters in Madison Square Garden were attacked by soldiers and sailors after the Reds sent greetings to the German socialists

- The pop-up toaster, three-color traffic lights, home delivery of *The New York Times*, Ripley's *Believe It or Not*, and the Raggedy Ann doll all made their first appearance

- Pitcher Babe Ruth won two World Series baseball games for the Boston Red Sox

- Popular books included *In Defense of Women* by H. L. Mencken; *In Our First Year of War* by Woodrow Wilson; *Corn Huskers* by Carl Sandburg; *The Magnificent Ambersons* by Booth Tarkington; and *Treat 'em Rough* by Ring Lardner

- Knute Rockne was named the football coach at Notre Dame

- The radio crystal oscillator was developed

- The mass spectrograph demonstrated that certain atomic elements existed in different forms with different masses

- Composer and pianist Sergei Rachmaninoff arrived in America penniless, his money and property having been confiscated by Russian revolutionaries

- Popular songs during the war included "Till We Meet Again"; "I'd Like to See the Kaiser with a Lily in his Hand"; "Oh! How I Wish I Could Sleep Until My Daddy Comes Home"; "If He Can Fight Like He Can Love"; "Good Night Germany!"; and "Rose of No Man's Land"

- Inflation numbers hit 13.5 percent and unemployment was only 1.4 percent

- The United States Supreme Court declared the 1916 Federal Child Labor Law unconstitutional

- The Sedition Act was passed, forbidding critical speeches against America or its conduct in the war

- Following the surrender of the German army to the Allies, President Woodrow Wilson announced a 14-Point Peace Plan

Child workers were frequently injured on the job.

Polish Immigration Timeline

1777

Inspired by the American colonies' battle for independence, more than 100 Poles came to America to fight in the Revolutionary War.

1854

The first permanent settlement of Poles was established at Panna Maria, Texas.

1863-1865

The "January Uprising" against the Russians resulted in the abolishment of the Kingdom of Poland and the persecution of the Catholic Church; thousands fled the country.

1872

The German language became compulsory in all schools and speaking Polish was made a crime in the Prussian-occupied zone.

A systematic attempt to uproot Polish peasants from their land sparked further immigration.

1900

Imperial repression, land shortages, and chronic unemployment encouraged the establishment of Polish communities in America, especially in the Midwest.

1905

The defeats suffered by the Russians during the Russo-Japanese War emboldened Poles to stage a wave of strikes and demonstrations demanding civil rights.

1910

The American census of 1910 found that 900,000 new immigrants spoke Polish.

1914

At the outbreak of World War I, the Poles found themselves conscripted into the armies of Germany, Austria and Russia, and forced to fight each other in a war that was not theirs; draft age men fled the country.

1915-1918

Almost all the fighting on the Eastern Front took place on Polish soil.

1918

Estimates placed more than two million Poles in America.

Selected Prices

Automobile, Franklin Runabout	$1,900.00
Boy's Suit	$2.95
Electric Radiator	$5.75
Luden's Cough Drops	$0.05
Man's Nightshirt	$1.15
Mousetrap	$0.02
Rum, Bacardi, Fifth	$3.20
Theater Ticket, including War Tax	$2.20
Woman's Hose, Artificial Silk	$0.35
Wrigley's Chewing Gum, 25 Packs	$0.73

Be "warm as toast" all winter!

Many people still dread the coming of winter, but those whose homes are radiator heated find there is more comfort, more mutual family happiness in the long winter days and evenings than in any other part of the year. No fear need mother have of chill window spaces or drafty floors, for the little folks are faithfully protected against these winter dangers, day and night, by the ever-alert, comfort-guaranteed outfits of

It was just like a dream, how my sister and I were running away from the town where we were. And I remember the bullets shooting. They were taking the straw for the cows and we were behind that, and the bullets be just like over there in the ground, we were running away and we were praying. They took us away some way out and my grandmother was sick in bed. When we got back she was dead. Dead in bed, and nobody to attend to her. It was 1914. I must've been between four and a half and five years old.

—Valeria Kozacka Demusz, 1975 interview
concerning Polish conditions in 1914

"Ousts Aid Societies from Ellis Island, Agents of Polish and Swedish Immigrants' Homes Barred by Commissioner Williams," *The New York Times*, August 11, 1909:

After consideration and numerous complaints, immigration Commissioner Williams notified yesterday the Trustees of the Saint Joseph's Home for the Protection of Polish Immigrants . . . that the privilege of having representatives at Ellis Island had been withdrawn.

In his letter to the Saint Joseph's Home the Commissioner points out that in June he requested the management to let him know what the home charged immigrants for meals and other attentions. In reply the manager stated distinctly that there were no charges made and the meals were free. Mr. Williams, however, learned a demand of $0.65 was made of each immigrant on arrival, and, upon refusal to pay, was coerced into doing so. Sometimes immigrants received meals in return and sometimes not, the commissioner declared. It was also discovered that when residents of New York applied to the home for immigrants whom they wished to employ, the agents often declined to furnish them unless a fee of $2.00 was paid for each immigrant.

"Prior to January 1909," the letter goes on to state, "one Anthony Jankowski had deposited with you in all $60. He went to Gasport, New York, and returned in August 1909, and upon demanding payment of the sum was told that the $60 had been loaned out by the home and could not be returned for a month. No interest was payable on this money, which was left for safekeeping, and returnable on-demand."

The money was finally returned after insistent demands by an inspector from Ellis Island.

The Commissioner, in commenting on the organization's claim that it tries to find relatives and friends of immigrants and to assist in reaching their destination, declares that a immigrant is seldom conducted to his destination. Mr. Williams also asserts that he is incredibly informed that there has been kept in the house a piece of rubber hose filled with some heavy substance with which blows have been inflicted on the immigrants, and that drinks were kept on the premises and consumed by the employees, who have been seen in a state of intoxication. It is also charged that immigrants have been compelled to exchange their money and improper rates of exchange, and that those who wish to return to Europe have been compelled to purchase identity slips at the rate of $2.00 each, although the agents of the home in many instances had no knowledge as to who such immigrants were.

"$2,500,000 Loan For Warsaw, Polish Textbooks Sought for Use in the Schools," *The New York Times*, August 29, 1915:

The Committee of Citizens which is discharging the functions of city government in Warsaw has voted to raise a loan of $5,000,000 rubles ($2,500,000).

The Committee on Schools has applied to the German Civil Governor for permission to obtain from Craców, Galicia, school books published in the Polish language for use in the schools here. The Russians carried away with them nearly all the valuable books and other mobile property from the public library and other institutions.

The German military and civil authorities have installed themselves in the Russian government buildings.

"Paderewski Estate Ruined, Letter to Pianist Also Tells of Starvation of Polish People," *The New York Times*, October 17, 1915:

All that remains of the estate of Ignance Paderewski in the Tarnow district of Poland are the stumps of the trees that once formed the park and forest, many of them planted by the pianist. . . . Everything else has been swept away by the war, according to a letter from a friend in Poland to Paderewski.

Mme. Paderewski said yesterday that the people of this country had little conception of what war had done to Poland.

"There are millions starving today in Poland," she said. "Whole towns have been destroyed and people without food and shelter. My husband has received a letter in which his friend says there are 2,000,000 persons living as best they can upon the site that was until a few months ago the city of Wroclawek, in Russian Poland. This multitude is without food and almost unprotected from the severity of the weather. In all of Galicia it is now hard to find a human habitation. . . . Caught between contending armies, those who had not fled were wiped out by the fighting between November and August.

"From all parts of Poland the cry is now going up for food. In the effort to stay the pangs of hunger, mothers are feeding their children a mixture of chalk and water in place of milk.

"Miss Henrietta Ely of Philadelphia, who is one of the few women allowed to enter Poland recently, has just returned to this country. She came in to see me the other day, and I cried as I listened to her. Miss Ely said that she very often could not eat because of the sight of the starving children, who gathered about to watch the visitors eat and beg food from them. Poland is desolate, and, to quote Miss Ely, beside her, Belgium is a country filled with prosperity."

Paderewski is head and organizer of the National American Committee for Polish Victims Relief Fund, and on Saturday afternoon, October 23, before his show upon recital in Carnegie Hall, he will speak on "Poland, past and present." The entire receipts will go to the relief fund.

How do you explain the fact that so many people had their names changed at Ellis Island?

They had to. They spoke very badly, were very nervous. Inspectors would say, where do you come from? And they would say Berlin. The inspector would put the name down Berliner. The name was not Berliner. That's not a name.

All the "witz's" and "ski's" got their names from their fathers. For example, Meyerson is the son of Meyer. We knew that, and changed the names here because they were spelled so badly. For instance, a Polish name would be Skyzertski, and they didn't even know how to spell it, so it would be changed to Sanda, to names like that. It was much easier that way.

Then there are names like "Vladimir." That would be Walter in American, or Willie, something like that. Vladimir was strictly a Russian name, you know; they often were very anxious to Americanize quickly.

And sometimes the children and parents would use first names; they would call the father Adam and it became Mr. Adam and that was the way they went through.

—Ellis Island Inspector Helen Barr, *Island of Hope, Island of Tears*

"Woman and the Cost of Living," Our Editorial Forum, *Christian Herald*, March 2, 1910:

Professor Patten, who fills the chair of Political Economy at the University of Pennsylvania, takes a novel view of the causes of the present high cost of living. In an article in the *Independent* he does not attribute it, as others have done, to gold overproduction, to a decrease in the value of our natural resources, or to the exploitation of the worker. He believes it arises from three causes: the bad distribution of population, the distance between consumer and producer, and the new status of women. The wife, he says, is no longer a creator of industry in the home, as she was in former days. Now, everything must be purchased outside, and what with this increased expense, false standard of living and elaborate dressing, she has become "often its chief burden." He points out that formerly a $1,000 income sufficed to keep an ordinary home in comfort, as a wife's industry in thrift made it go as far as a much larger sum. Her baking, preserving and dressmaking all saved money. The professor concludes that the "essential conditions of home life cannot be neglected without bringing prosperity to a standstill."

"'Let's Not Be Blind' Is Plea of Chairman Hayes, Chairman of Republican National Committee Issues a Statement, *The Ashville Times*, March 31, 1919:

We entered this war to vindicate American rights, interests and honor by the defeat of Hunnish hounds of hell who slaughtered innocent men, women and children; and we entered this war for an ideal, to crush a Thing and make certain forever that all which the enemy represented should no longer be on earth, and we will not stop now, for the enemy is at the knees, until both these objectives are attained.

Let us not for a moment lose sight of our own supreme nationalism. We look abroad far enough to do justice to all nations and to carry our burdens as a responsible factor in the world of today, and tomorrow we are nationalists and not internationalists. While we seek earnestly and prayerfully for methods lessening future wars, and will go far indeed in an honest effort to that end, and will accomplish very much, we'll accept no indefinite internationalism as a substitute for fervent American nationalism. We will move out and take our place in the broadest fields with the same unselfish conduct that has made America the synonym for justice the world over, but we will do it with the clear understanding that the creation of international obligations shall be in addition to, not a substitute for, the preparation for our own self-defense in a spirit of intense and disinterested American patriotism, and we will make no obligations that we cannot discharge and no contract which we do not mean to carry out. America is America for Americans first, and the preservation of its integrity in that relation is the greatest safeguard in the future, not only for the citizens of this country, but for all the peoples everywhere as the one certain Gibraltar in the world storms which may yet in the future come, and will probably come, until the millennium shall arrive

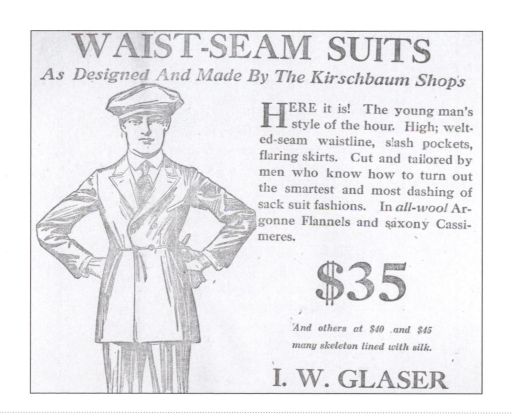

"The Submarine Issue," *The Youth's Companion,* November 16, 1916:

How shall the submarine be treated? Is it entitled to the same privileges and subject to the same restrictions as a vessel that sails on the surface, or, in the absence of any international agreement on the subject, shall it be regarded as an outlaw of the sea? That is the question that complicates and threatens to embitter, the relations between the belligerent nations and more than one of the neutral nations.

Norway has answered it by excluding all military submarines from its waters, unless they come, helpless, in search of asylum, and by ruling that submarine merchantman must only enter those waters on the surface and flying the flag of its nation.

Although that decision is less sweeping than the Allies would like, it has angered Germany. Germans insist the submarine shall have every consideration that other vessels have, besides the right to use their special advantage of invisibility whenever they choose to do so. Unable to persuade Norway to take that view, they are trying the efficacy of violence. In no other way can we account for the busy campaign the German submarines are waging against Norwegian shipping. The excuse is that the destroyed vessels were carrying contraband of war, but that does not explain why English ships, the ships of an actual enemy, shall be almost neglected while this determined destruction of neutral vessels goes on. It will be interesting to see whether the German policy induces Norway to abandon its position or goads it into open hostility to Germany.

"Immigration," Letter to the Editor, *The American Legion Weekly,* August 20, 1920:

To the Editor:

What action is to be taken on the dangerous horde of immigration that is coming in every day? We were assured during the war that certain restrictions would be thrown around immigration. Nothing has been done. The economic danger is very grave from these people, and they are being rushed here without even medical inspection. Visit Ellis Island and see the thousands of people from Poland and Russia who are coming in. These nations are urging, and even almost forcing some other people to come here. Meanwhile typhus, bubonic plague and other diseases are at our door. Washington will take no action. The people themselves must save America, for which our dear men died.

Mrs. Emma J. Arnold
New York City

This is a people's war. . . . We have made partners of women in this war; shall we admit them only to a partnership of suffering and sacrifice and toil and not to a partnership of privilege and right?

—Writer Helen Gardner

1920–1929

Unlike previous decades, national prosperity was not fueled by the cheap labor of new immigrants, but by increased factory efficiencies, innovation and more sophisticated methods of managing time and materials. Starting in the teens, the flow of new immigrants began to slow, culminating in the restrictive immigration legislation of 1924 when new workers from Europe were reduced to a trickle. The efforts were largely designed to protect the wages of American workers, many of whom were only one generation from their native land. The number of U.S. immigration visas was reduced and reallocated on the basis of national origin. That gave preference to countries whose citizens had historically emigrated to America. The act also placed an overall limitation on immigration to 150,000 persons per year beginning in 1929. As a result, wages for unskilled labor remained stable, union membership declined, and strikes, on average, decreased. American exports more than doubled during the decade and heavy imports of European goods virtually halted, a reversal of the Progressive Movement's flirtation with free trade.

The decade following the Great War was marked by a new nationalism symbolized by frenzied consumerism. By the early 1920s, urban Americans had begun to define themselves—for their neighbors and for the world—in terms of what they owned. The car was becoming ubiquitous, zooming from 4,000 registered vehicles at the dawn of the century to 1.9 million 20 years later. Radios and telephones were introduced into millions of homes and some young women felt free to dress as they pleased, wear make-up, and help select the nation's leaders, thanks to the Nineteenth Amendment allowing women's suffrage. This freedom also brought a reaction: decency societies were formed, membership in the Ku Klux Klan grew, and immigration was largely stilled. Simultaneously, aggressive new advertising methods began and were successful. Americans bought and America boomed. With expanded wages and buying power came increased leisure time for recreation, travel and even self-improvement. Although infectious disease was still a killer, an increased emphasis on sanitation, air circulation and early treatment was beginning to chase some of the most feared diseases from the nation's ghettoes.

Following the Great War, America enjoyed a period of expansion and expectation. The attitude of many Americans was expressed in President Calvin Coolidge's famous remark, "The chief business of the American people is business." The role of the federal government remained small during this period and federal expenditures actually declined following the war effort. Harry Donaldson's song "How Ya Gonna Keep 'Em Down on the Farm after They've Seen Paree?" described another basic shift in American society. The 1920 Census eported that more than 50 percent of the population—54 million people—lived in urban areas. The move to the cities was the result of changed expectations, increased industrialization, and migration of millions of Southern blacks to the urban North.

The availability of electricity expanded the universe to goods that could be manufactured and sold. The expanded use of radios, electric lights, telephones, and powered vacuum cleaners was possible for the first time, and they quickly became essential household items. Construction boomed with the rising urban population. Industry, too, benefited from the wider use of electric power. At the turn of the century, electricity ran only 5 percent of all machinery, and by 1925, 73 percent. Large-scale electric power also made possible electrolytic processes in the rapidly developing heavy chemical industry. With increasing sophistication came higher costs; wages for skilled workers continued to rise during the 1920s, putting further distance between the blue-collar worker and the emerging middle class.

Following the war years, women who had worked in men's jobs in the late teens usually remained in the workforce, although at lower wages. Women, now allowed to vote nationally, were also encouraged to consider college and options other than marriage. Average family earnings increased slightly during the first half of the period, while prices and hours worked actually declined. The 48-hour week became standard, providing more leisure time. At least 40 million people went to the movies each week, and college football became a national obsession.

These national shifts were not without powerful resistance. A bill was proposed in Utah to imprison any woman who wore her skirt higher than three inches above her ankle. Cigarette consumption reached 43 billion annually, despite smoking being illegal in 14 states and the threat of expulsion from college if caught with a cigarette. The Hays Commission, limiting sexual material in silent films, was created to prevent "loose" morals, and the Ku Klux Klan expanded to repress Catholics, Jews, open immigration, make-up on women, and the prospect of unrelenting change.

The decade ushered in Trojan contraceptives, the Pitney Bowes postage meter, the Baby Ruth candy bar, Wise potato chips, Drano, self-winding watches, State Farm Mutual auto insurance, Kleenex, and the Macy's Thanksgiving Day Parade down Central Park West in New York. Despite a growing middle class, the share of disposable income going to the top 5 percent of the population continued to increase. Fifty percent of the people, by one estimate, still lived in poverty. Coal and textile workers, Southern farmers, unorganized labor, single women, the elderly, and most blacks were excluded from the economic giddiness of the period.

In 1929, America appeared to be in an era of unending prosperity. Industrial production rose 50 percent during the decade as the concepts of mass production were refined and broadly applied. The sale of electrical appliances from radios to refrigerators skyrocketed. Consumers were able to purchase newly produced goods through the extended use of credit. Debt accumulated. By 1930, personal debt had increased to one-third of personal wealth. The nightmare on Wall Street in October 1929 brought an end to the economic festivities, setting the stage for a more proactive government and an increasingly cautious worker.

1924 Profile

Leonid Abkarian came to America to escape the Turkish slaughter of Armenians, but was determined to remain in all ways Armenian.

Life at Home

- The Armenian genocide had brought Leonid Abkarian to America; a job at Ford Motor Company in Detroit kept him in the United States for the past eight years.
- When he was reunited with his wife and children three years earlier, his American dream was to live like an Armenian.
- When he fled Armenia in 1916 his choices were these: leave or die.
- His brother and parents were already dead; safe places to hide were becoming impossible to find.
- The threat of death was so real—and near—he was forced to leave his wife and two little children behind, knowing his presence put them in greater danger.
- He prayed they would be safe in Syria until he could send for them.
- For centuries the Armenians and the Turks were at odds.
- Christian Armenians wanted independence, while the Turks envisioned a Pan-Turkic empire spreading all the way to Turkish speaking parts of Central Asia.
- The Armenian people of the Ottoman Empire were the only ethnic group in between two major pockets of Turkish speakers.
- Starting in 1894 the Turks launched a pogrom; hundreds of thousands of Armenians died in the Hamidan Massacres within a few years.
- A coup by the Young Turks in 1908 replaced the Sultan's government, but only led to more purges by Turkish nationalists who masterminded a plan to eradicate the Armenian race.
- The outbreak of World War I in 1914 gave the Turk government the cover and the excuse to carry out their plan.
- On April 24, 1915, more than 300 Armenian leaders, writers and professionals were invited to Istanbul—and then killed.

Leonid Abkarian fled Armenia in 1916.

Thousands of Armenians were killed in the streets.

The sea voyage lasted 10 days from Armenia to America.

- Over 5,000 Armenians were butchered in the streets and in their homes; thousands were marched off to concentration camps, as others were loaded onto barges that were then sunk at sea.
- The scope of the killings was so widespread that international attention was attracted by the level of centralized planning and government machinery used to implement the genocide.
- From 1915 to 1918 the Armenian people were subjected to deportation, expropriation, abduction, torture, massacre and starvation.
- The great bulk of the Armenian population was forcibly removed to Syria, where the vast majority was sent into the desert to die of thirst and hunger.
- After only a little more than a year of calm at the end of World War I, the atrocities were renewed between 1920 and 1923, and the remaining Armenians were subjected to further massacres and expulsions.
- An estimated one and a half million Armenians perished between 1915 and 1923.
- When Leonid Abkarian clambered onto an oceangoing ship to escape certain death, he knew nothing of America except that it was a place where he would be safe.
- The composition of the boat provided some comfort: many passengers were Armenian emigrants, most were farmers and few had been to America previously.
- In addition to farmers and laborers, the ship carried a cook, carpenter, druggist, watchmaker, tailor, barber, shoemaker, stonecutter and mason.
- With a flamboyant wave of his arm, one fellow emigrant shouted, "We could start a village with just those on this boat!"
- "Might be a few more women to make it a go," came the immediate answer; most of the Armenian immigrants were men who had left their wives and families behind.
- During the 10-day voyage, several men spent considerable time discussing what they would call themselves when they registered at Ellis Island.
- Some planned to take new names to accompany their new life, while others pondered how to express old family names in the New World they had elected as home.
- For centuries Armenians had used a patronymic naming system in which the surname was the father's given name followed by "ian" or "son of."
- Thus, the son of a man named Kevork Arslanian might be called Hovsep Kevorkian.
- Other Armenian surnames were based on occupation (Najarian for carpenter), geographic origin (Harpoulian for someone from Harpout), or defining characteristic (Arslanian for "like a lion").
- One man named Karnig Elmasian decided that when he landed he would become Carl Sivas, a more American-sounding name.
- Many on board already had jobs promised to them—Armenians were known to be hard workers: a third were headed to upstate New York to work in the factories; a third were bound for Illinois, and another 10 percent had jobs in the car factories in Detroit.
- Most planned to live in Armenian communities where Armenian was spoken.

- Some of the men were concerned that their journey to America would not save them from the warfare they were fleeing.
- War had made them wary.
- Leonid could not stop thinking about his wife and family; how could he be sure they were safe in Syria? How would he contact them? When would the killings stop? Could he ever return to his home?

Life at Work

- Working on the assembly line at Ford Motor Company was the toughest and easiest job Leonid Abkarian had ever had.
- Unlike backbreaking farm work that taxed the strongest man, factory work with its repetitious motions was taxing only in an active mind, Leonid felt.
- His primary job day after day, hour after hour, was to place the bumper on the right side rear of the automobile.
- At first the speed of the line was a challenge; after a few days, it was simply monotonous.
- Ford Motor Company was launched in 1903, when Henry Ford and 11 business associates invested $28,000 in cash.
- Henry Ford insisted that the company's future lay in the production of affordable cars for a mass market.
- Beginning in 1903, the company began using the first 19 letters of the alphabet to name new cars.
- In 1908, the Model T was born.

Leonid found assembly line work monotonous.

Henry Ford founded the Ford Motor Company in 1903.

- By 1924, and 15 million Model T's later, Ford Motor Company was a giant industrial complex that spanned the globe and had acquired the Lincoln Motor Company, thus branching out into luxury cars.
- This was made possible because of the invention of the moving assembly line, first implemented in 1913.
- The new technique allowed individual workers to stay in one place and perform the same task repeatedly on multiple vehicles that passed by them.
- The line proved tremendously efficient, helping the company surpass the production levels of their competitors, thereby making the vehicles more affordable.
- By the time Leonid went to work for Ford Motor Company shortly after his arrival in America, the auto industry was one of the largest industries in the nation.
- The two-decade-old industry was dominated by a handful of large companies.
- Within the factory, the auto workers were divided into three groups: white native-born workers, black native-born workers, and foreign-born workers.
- Unionization, which was already prevalent in many industries, had left the auto industry largely untouched because of its high wages.
- But by the time Leonid arrived, tensions on the shop floor were mounting.
- The increased use of efficiency engineers, line speedups and increased pressure for production were all causing discontent.

By 1924, 15 million Model Ts were produced.

- The seesaw economy in the early 1920s had precipitated long, multi-month layoffs that then alternated with demands for seven-day-a-week production shifts that often lasted 10 to 12 hours each.
- Evidence was building that lead poisoning, one of the job-related ailments, was harming the workers.
- Leonid's wife often urged him to learn English, but he would laugh and say, "What's the use? They don't allow us to talk on the line, anyway."
- He lived in a small Armenian community in Detroit, worked with fellow Armenians all day, and felt little need to speak English or become an American.

Life in the Community: Armenia
- In general, the Armenia that immigrants were leaving behind was a harsh, cold and mountainous land.
- Russia, Ukraine and Georgia were to the north; Azerbaijan to the east; Iran, Syria and Iraq to the south; and Turkey to the west.
- During its history, Armenia had been occupied and divided by Russia, Greece, Turkey and Persia.
- It was the first Christian nation completely surrounded by Muslims and nomadic tribes, a condition which influenced its people's diet, farming methods and religious beliefs.
- Lamb was the meat staple of the country for centuries; pork was never part of the diet in accordance with Biblical belief that only animals that chew their cud were to be eaten.
- Roasted vegetables such as squash, eggplant, peppers, garlic and onions were favorites.
- During the very cold winter months, Armenians looked for dried fruits, nuts, beans, rice and wheat.
- In Armenia salt was scarce and thus expensive, so lemon juice was often used as a substitute.

Typical village in Armenia.

- Another staple of the Armenian diet was mahdzoon, which Leonid learned to call yogurt in America.
- It was used as a topping or garnish for foods and rarely flavored with fruit.
- On the ship one Armenian woman was determined to bring the bacterial starter for mahdzoon through immigration, knowing it would be confiscated if found.
- First, she took clean handkerchiefs and dipped them in a bowl of mahdzoon and then hung them out to dry; after they were ready she folded and neatly stacked them with the rest of her linens so they would pass through customs without a hitch.
- Once she had arrived at her destination, she planned to put the handkerchiefs in warm milk, which would release the bacteria that formed the mahdzoon and provide her with some semblance of home.

HISTORICAL SNAPSHOT
1924

- British Egyptologist Howard Carter found the sarcophagus of Tutankhamun

- Ford Motor Company stock was valued at nearly $1 billion

- Russian revolutionary Vladimir Ilyich Lenin died, igniting a major power struggle in the Soviet Union

- The first Winter Olympic games opened in Chamonix, France

- An ice cream cone rolling machine was patented by Carl Taylor in Cleveland

- The gas chamber was used for the first time to execute a murderer, an alleged Chinese Tong member named Gee Jon at the Nevada State Prison

- George Gershwin's symphonic jazz composition *Rhapsody in Blue* premiered at Carnegie Hall

- Thomas J. Watson, general manager of Computing-Tabulating-Recording Company (CTR), renamed the firm International Business Machines (IBM)

- President Calvin Coolidge delivered the first presidential radio broadcast from the White House

- The U.S. steel industry found that an eight-hour day increased efficiency and employee relations

- The song "Happy Birthday To You" was published by Claydon Sunny

- The U.S. Supreme Court upheld a New York state law forbidding late-night work for women

- Adolf Hitler was sentenced to five years in prison for his role in the botched Nazi "Beer Hall Putsch" in the German state of Bavaria

- *The National Barn Dance* premiered on WLS radio in Chicago

- President Coolidge signed an immigration-restriction law

- Congress granted U.S. citizenship to all American Indians born in the U.S.

- J. Edgar Hoover assumed leadership of the FBI

- After an eight-year occupation, American troops left the Dominican Republic

- The comic strip *Little Orphan Annie* made its debut in the *New York Daily News*

- The first Macy's Thanksgiving Day Parade was held in New York's Herald Square

Selected Prices

Alarm Clock	$2.50
Apartment, Sacramento, Five Rooms	$70.00
Bathing Suit, Men's	$5.00
Carpet Sweeper	$5.00
Crib	$17.50
Handkerchiefs, Dozen	$1.80

Economy trips to EUROPE

DO you realize that you can make a six weeks trip to Europe for as little as $525? This price includes round trip "cabin" accommodations and all expenses except personal items.

The ships of the United States Lines are unsurpassed in the service between New York and Cobh (Queenstown), Plymouth, Southampton, Cherbourg and Bremen.

Send the Coupon

below for your Government's illustrated booklet "Economy Trips to Europe." It describes and gives complete itineraries of ten low cost trips to Europe.

United States Lines
45 Broadway   New York City
Agencies in all principal cities
Managing Operators for
UNITED STATES SHIPPING BOARD

happy legs

mean garters without metal or pads – **IVORIES**

THERE'S only one garter that does away with metal clasps and buckles—the Ivory Garter.

Ivory Garters are cool, comfortable, long-wearing—because they're just lively elastic and clean, white clasps. There are no pads—no fixed angle at which your garters must be worn. Ivory Garters fit any leg comfortably without a sign of binding.

Go to the nearest men's store and insist on Ivory Garters. Wide or standard web, single or double grip. 25c and up.

IVORY GARTER COMPANY
New Orleans, La.

Ivory Garter

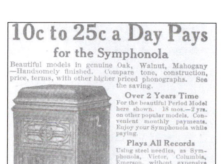

10c to 25c a Day Pays
for the Symphonola

Beautiful models in genuine Oak, Walnut, Mahogany—Handsomely finished. Compare tone, construction, price, terms, with other higher priced phonographs. See the saving.

Over 2 Years Time
For the beautiful Period Model here shown. 18 mos.—2 yrs. on other popular models. Convenient monthly payments. Enjoy your Symphonola while paying.

Plays All Records
Using steel needles, as Symphonola, Victor, Columbia, Emerson, without expensive extra attachments. Pathe or Edison Records played with sapphire or diamond point needles.

Records 70c Postpaid
Symphonola Records playable on any phonograph. Contain best of music. Get our latest Record list, and save money.

Beautiful Book FREE
Illustrates Symphonolas in natural colors. Full details, prices, terms, construction. A postal quickly brings it. Get your copy NOW—It's FREE.

Larkin Co., Inc., Desk SAW-121 BUFFALO, N. Y.

Why maids leave home

SOMETIMES it's because their rooms are cold—a fault which an American Radiator would cure at a trifling expense.

If your present old-fashioned heating plant won't provide warmth for more radiators, take it out and install an IDEAL Boiler. The one-third saving in fuel will repay the cost.

IDEAL BOILERS
COAL · OIL · GAS
and **AMERICAN RADIATORS**
save fuel

AMERICAN RADIATOR COMPANY

JELL-O

Let Clicquot Club Ginger Ale sparkle over the dry spots

Off goes the stopper, and the amber-gold Clicquot Club Ginger Ale sparkles into your glass and spills wetness all over your throat.

No wonder the educated palate likes it. No wonder everybody backs that liking by liking it also! It's the tang of ginger, the lime and lemon flavorings, the carbonated Clicquot spring water that do it!

Do you wonder why millions of bottles are spilled down happy American throats? Do you wonder that *they* all like it?

Order by the case from your grocer, druggist, or confectioner

The Clicquot Club Company
Millis, Mass., U. S. A.

Clicquot Club
Ginger Ale

Selected Prices

Hen	$25.00
Hotel Room, New York, per Day	$3.00
Poker Set, 100 Chips	$6.25
Typewriter, Remington	$60.00

"Coping with Anarchists," *The New York Times*, June 13, 1920:

Immigration was left under wartime regulations by the adjournment of Congress. Problems which the war revealed as hinging on immigration one way or another were the subject of many hearings at Immigration Committee of the House, but the shaping of an immigration policy on the lessons set forth will be a task for the next session.

Aside from the resolution extending until April 1921, the wartime control of passports, the only piece of legislation of importance bearing on the immigration question, was the passage of the bill of exclusion and expulsion of the aliens of anarchists in similar classes. Here a weakness of the old law is remedied, and is expected to facilitate getting rid of dangerous aliens.

Under the old law there were two main difficulties: one was to prove that the accused, granting that he was guilty, was a member of an organization suspected of teaching anarchy, and the other that this organization did actually advocate anarchy. As most anarchists deny that they are such, accomplishing their propaganda in secret, most of the cases when brought to trial turned on whether or not it can be established that the accused belonged to an anarchist organization. Under the law which now goes into effect, specific ways to push to establish this proof are provided to overcome the previous difficulties, and sabotage is for the first time definitely included as proof of anarchist guilt. . . .

In framing the new immigration law, the question will come up whether the United States shall provide agents to check up on immigrants before they leave Europe with the aim of weeding out anarchists there. Another question concerns the creation of some system of regulation of immigrants in the years following entry in the country. The purpose here would be not only to follow up on any dangerous aliens, but on the basis of what is learned by it, means to prevent the congregation of aliens in large undigested masses.

Representative Isaac Siegel of New York City, a member the Immigration Committee, said:

"Reports that we are to have another big incoming tide of immigration from Europe are without real foundation, and there will be a disappointment of those who have been counting on the labor shortage to be relieved in this way. I have been keeping in touch with sources of information in Europe, and it is not true that 500,000 male workers are waiting there for ship passage to come this way. European countries, especially those which were depleted in manpower by the war, need their men workers, and by the power to refuse to issue passports they have the means to keep them at home to aid in rebuilding the country. Thus the tendency would be to hold all except the undesirable.

"Wages have gone up in Europe so that they are comparable to what we pay, so this magnet in our favor is not what it once was. In the six months ended December 31 we've lost more laborers by departure to Europe than we gained, and even now the tide is not heavily in our favor. Many more are waiting for ship room to go to Europe. The Polish Consulate in New York told me he had a great many more applications than he could take care of.

"Women and children are coming in larger numbers, proportionally, than before, and men are going in larger proportions to Europe. There are in many cases relations of families in this country, and many more orphans are also arriving. The other day I heard of 30 orphan children in one group. The war, of course, has added to the number of women in Europe compared to the number of men, and it is natural to suppose that a woman can obtain a passport where a man would be refused. It is men who are needed in the work of reconstruction, primarily.

"In my opinion the old days of one million immigrants coming in a year are past; at least I think it is safe to say that in the next five years nothing like that number will be reached."

The weight of a tack in the hands of an upholsterer is insignificant, but if you have to drive eight tacks in every Ford cushion that goes by your station within a certain time, and know that if you fail to do so you're going to tie up the entire platform, and you continue to do this for four years, year after year, you're going to break under the strain.

—Ford auto worker, 1925

Ford automobile assembly line worker.

"$7,000,000 for Ford Ads," *The New York Times*, August 17, 1923:

The Ford Motor Company has decided to spend $7,000,000 in advertising on newspapers throughout the country, and has reorganized its advertising department, after five years of inactivity, with Newton P. Brotherton at its head.

The new plan apparently contemplates display advertising to be charged directly to the Ford Company itself, presumably in addition to the dealer system of publicity.

"Predicts Biggest Year In Motor Car Buying," by Edsel B. Ford, President, Ford Motor Company, *The New York Times*, January 6, 1924:

Even though 1923 exceeded all our expectations, there is every reason to believe that in 1924 business will attain to far greater proportions.

More people will buy automobiles during the coming year than ever before. Evidence of our belief in this is the extensive expansion program we are carrying out and which is aimed to effect new manufacturing economies and materially increase production. In the new year we will produce more cars and trucks and expect to sell more of them, both in the domestic and foreign fields. . . .

Today America is completely "sold" on the automobile.

Women are a greater influence in the automobile buying field than ever before and the coming year will see this influence considerably extended. It will be expressed particularly in the closed car sales. Women, through their guardianship of the family purse, are good judges of values and their knowledge in this respect extends as much to the automobile as anything else.

The manufacturer who gives the greatest value for the lowest investment must certainly enjoy the greatest share of the business. To maintain this business he must incorporate better quality in his product, for the public's motor wise transportation value is going to count most this year.

The market in the United States for foreign-built cars is slowly passing. The vast majority of Americans are forsaking European cars and turning to the homemade products.

"800,000 Armenians Counted Destroyed," *The New York Times*, October 7, 1915:

Viscount Bryce, former British Ambassador to the United States, in the House of Lords today said that such information as had reached him from many quarters showed that the figure of 800,000 Armenians destroyed since May was quite a possible number. Virtually the whole nation had been wiped out, he declared, and he did not suppose there was any case in history of a crime "so hideous and on so large a scale."

"The death of these people," said Lord Bryce, "resulted from the deliberate and premeditated policy of the gang now in possession of the Turkish Government. Orders for the massacres came in every case direct from Constantinople. In some instances local Governors, being humane, pious men, refused to carry out the orders and at least two Governors were summarily dismissed for this reason.

"The customary procedure was to round up the whole of the population of a designated town. A part of the population was thrown into prison and the remainder were marched out of town, and in the suburbs the men were separated from the women and children. The men were then taken to a convenient place and shot and bayoneted. The women and children were then put under a convoy of the lower kind of soldiers and dispatched to some distant destination.

"They were driven by the soldiers day after day. Many fell by the way and many died of hunger, for no provisions were furnished them. They were robbed of all they possessed, and in many cases the women were stripped naked and made to continue the march in that condition. Many of the women went mad and threw away their children. The caravan route was marked by a line of corpses. Comparatively few of the people ever reached their destination.

"The facts as to the slaughter in Trebizond are vouched for by the Italian Consul. Orders came for the murder of all the Armenian Christians in Trebizond. Many Mussulmans tried to save their Christian friends, but the authorities were implacable and hunted out all the Christians and then drove them down to the sea front. Then they put them aboard sail boats and carried them some distance out to sea and threw them overboard. The whole Armenian population, numbering 10,000, was thus destroyed in one afternoon." The Lord Mayor at a meeting at the Mansion House on Oct. 15, will start a fund for the aid of Armenian refugees. Among the speakers will be Lord Bryce, Cardinal Bourne and T. P. O'Connor.

Dr. Martin Niepage's Report: "The Horrors of Aleppo Seen by a German Eyewitness," 1915:

A word to Germany's Accredited Representatives by Dr. Martin Niepage, Higher Grade Teacher in the German Technical School at Aleppo

When I returned to Aleppo in September 1915 from a three months' holiday at Beirout, I heard with horror that a new phase of Armenian massacres had begun which were far more terrible than the earlier massacres under Abd-ul-Hamid, and which aimed at exterminating, root and branch, the intelligent, industrious and progressive Armenian nation, and at transferring its property to Turkish hands.

Such monstrous news left me at first incredulous. I was told that, in various quarters of Aleppo, there were lying masses of half-starved people, the survivors of so-called "deportation convoys." In order, I was told, to cover the extermination of the Armenian nation with a political cloak, military reasons were being put forward, which were said to make it necessary to drive the Armenians out of their native seats, which had been theirs for 2,500 years, and to deport them to the Arabian deserts. I was also told that individual Armenians had lent themselves to acts of espionage.

After I had informed myself about the facts and had made enquiries on all sides, I came to the conclusion that all these accusations against the Armenians were, in fact, based on trifling provocations, which were taken as an excuse for slaughtering 10,000 innocents for one guilty person, for the most savage outrages against women and children, and for a campaign of starvation against the exiles which was intended to exterminate the whole nation.

To test the conclusion derived from my information, I visited all the places in the city where there were Armenians left behind by the convoys. In dilapidated caravansaries (hans), I found quantities of dead, many corpses being half-decomposed, and others, still living, among them, who were soon to breathe their last. In other yards I found quantities of sick and starving people whom no one was looking after. In the neighborhood of the German Technical School, at which I am employed as a higher grade teacher, there were four such hans, with seven or eight hundred exiles dying of starvation. We teachers and our pupils had to pass by them every day. Every time we went out we saw through the open windows their pitiful forms, emaciated and wrapped in rags. In the mornings our school children, on their way through the narrow streets, had to push past the two-wheeled ox-carts, on which every day from eight to 10 rigid corpses, without coffin or shroud, were carried away, their arms and legs trailing out of the vehicle.

"Whole Plain Strewn by Armenian Bodies, Turks and Kurds Reported to Have Massacred Men, Women and Children," *The New York Times,* March 20, 1915:

Appalling accounts of conditions in Armenia have reached the officials in London of the Armenian Red Cross Fund and have been given out by them.

The latest recital is from an Armenian doctor named Derderian, who says that the whole plain of Alashgerd is virtually covered with the bodies of men, women and children.

When the Russian forces retreated from this district the Kurds fell upon the helpless people and shut them up in mosques. The men were killed and the women were carried away to the mountains.

The organizers of the Red Cross Fund say there are 120,000 destitute Armenians now in the Caucasus.

The death toll of our country and accidents of all kinds industrial and public last year was between 75,000 and 80,000 human lives. The total death toll as a result of our engagement in the late war, covering a period of 19 months, including deaths on the front and those resulting from wounds, everything but deaths from disease, was 56,000. In our own city last year 3,800 persons were killed by accident. Of this number 1,054 were children. The weekly average was 73 resulting in death, of which approximately 20 were children.

—Arthur Williams, President of the Safety Institute of America, 1922

1926 Profile

Reynaldo Lucero found that his dream of getting rich on the sugar plantations of Hawaii meant a betrayal to his family in the Philippines, even though he was doing it for them.

Life at Home

- When Reynaldo Lucero was 14 years old, a fire began to grow in him that urged him to leave Caoayan I Sur, the Philippines, where he had lived all his life, in order to help his family.
- Following the pattern set by his brothers and sisters, he had dropped out of school in the sixth grade, and now wanted to re-establish the family farm to make his family proud.
- Then, two years later, after he turned 16, he was spotted by the Hawaiian labor recruiter, who said he had the build of a cane worker.
- He knew that even speaking to the Hawaiian sugar cane labor recruiter was trouble, but he had to for the sake of the family.
- Since Reynaldo was a little boy, his father and grandfather had spoken bitterly about the battles they had fought in 1901 and 1902 to secure the independence of the Philippines.
- Like many, his father and grandfather had at first welcomed the American soldiers who arrived in 1899 to throw out the Spanish colonists.
- They were greeted as liberators from the Land of the Free, the only major country in the world to have avoided imperialistic colonization.
- But then the Americans decided to stay and occupy the Philippines, eventually sending 170,000 soldiers to tame their "little brown brothers" in the name of democracy.
- Reynaldo's father and grandfather had joined the insurrection after American soldiers indiscriminately killed 21 members of their village.
- During the subsequent fighting, his father lost an arm, his grandfather lost his land, and the family lost its position in Philippine society.
- Now he had to tell the same two men that he wanted to work for an American corporation in Hawaii, as though history were something that lived in the past only.

Reynaldo Lucero left the Philippines when he was 16.

Reynaldo's father and uncle joined the insurrection and fought the Americans.

- In addition, no one in his family had ever left the village to live; it was considered the most beautiful place in the world.
- Tradition dictated that every member of the family, especially the older generation, be informed about an important decision such as his emigration to Hawaii; to leave without the permission of his entire family was virtually unthinkable.
- Raised to believe that every Filipino was an uncle, aunt, cousin, grandfather, or grandmother, he understood intuitively that family was central to his very existence.
- It was not an entirely welcome tradition.
- He had seen it all before: first his grandfather would rise to his feet and make a speech about harvesting his lush fields before the coming of the Americans a quarter-century ago.
- Then his father would slowly rise, holding his amputated arm up over his head and mumble, "They did this to me; now you want to work for them."
- His uncle would shout, "Times are different now"; his mother would whisper, "What has changed?"; his grandfather would get to his feet again and his grandmother would declare it time to eat.
- After that, everyone would nurse hurt feelings until the men announced a decision; then the women would sulk and everyone would get mad again.
  - Within a week, a decision could be made; then he would know.
  - But he needed to know now.
  - Jobs were scarce, the family farm was gone, school was out of the question, and opportunity was awaiting, according to the recruiter, in the sugar cane fields of Hawaii.
  - He kept telling his mother privately that within three years, he would make enough to buy the family land and feed them all.
  - Just three years of being away could give them a lifetime of wealth.
  - With fire in her eyes, she asked, "Do they even have churches in Hawaii?"
  - "Of course," he answered, immediately realizing he did not know the real answer.
  - He could not imagine any place did not have a Catholic church, replete with statues of the Virgin Mary and the crucified Christ.
  - "What language will you speak? Do you know Hawaiian? How will a little boy like you with skinny legs cut cane as big as your arm?" she questioned.
  - The recruiter had not told him the answers to any of these questions; all he knew was that his future was in Hawaii.
  - The recruiter was even willing to waive the customary $75 upfront steamship fare normally charged to workers.
  - Reynaldo was not told of the current workers' strike on the Hawaiian plantations, or that he could be considered a strike breaker by the other workers.
  - At the time, 1,600 Filipino sugar workers were on strike, forcing the closure of 23 of the Island's 45 plantations.

Family life was very important in the Philippines.

- What he heard were the recruiter's stories detailing the consistent good fortune of Philippine workers who were praised as heroes at home after they had sent riches back to their families every month.
- His sisters quietly asked how he was going to meet his future wife in a place that had no chaperones and few proper women.
- He knew that his older sister was careful not even to touch the tips of the fingers of a man so that she would remain totally pure for her husband.
- Then, before the family meeting was held, Reynaldo's uncle told everyone in the village that his nephew had succumbed to Hawaiian Fever.
- Stories floated back to his father that he was leaving no matter what was decided.
- The entire family felt betrayed, feeling his decision had been made without proper consideration, and he was told to go without their consent.

Honolulu, Hawaii.

Life at Work

- When Reynaldo's ship arrived in Hawaii, the Filipino workers aboard received special treatment—going through fumigation but bypassing immigration—because they were American nationals and not aliens like those from China, Japan, and Korea.
- It was the first—and last—privilege he would enjoy as a Filipino.
- Reynaldo quickly learned the order of things: haoles (whites) held management positions, Spanish and Portuguese served as plantation overseers, the Japanese were given mechanical jobs and the Filipinos were the workers.
- The plantation village where he slept was also segregated: separate camps were established for the "haoles," Spanish, Japanese, and Filipinos.
- The ratio of Philippine men to women was 20 to one.
- He was told to which Hawaii Sugar Planters' Association plantation he was assigned and which job he would perform.
- Men from the same families or the same towns and provinces were intentionally separated to make them more dependent upon the plantation bosses for their needs: housing, healthcare, their food, and even recreation.
- Each sugar plantation employed 200 to 300 workers; often the Filipino crews would be told to compete against the Japanese crews, making it difficult for them ever to work together.
- Yet, he immediately felt at home when he heard the "hoy pssst-sst" call of his fellow workers, considered an informal way to get attention.
- And when he picked up a newly sharpened machete that didn't belong to him, he immediately heard a clucking sound made by the owner to show annoyance.

Filipino workers lived and worked in segregated camps.

Sugar cane plantation.

Reynaldo's sister was married in grand style.

- It, too, was a familiar sound; his disapproving grandfather made it often.
- The other sound in his head were the final words of his father: "Don't be afraid of nobody so long as you're right. Nobody."
- Initially assigned to the sugar cane fields, Reynaldo quickly changed jobs when one of the counters lost his hand in a machete accident.
- The job of recording the number of sugar cane loads that went into each railroad boxcar paid better.
- It also meant he could use his head rather than his arms, which constantly ached from the strenuous job of cutting sugar cane.
- His pay increased from $1.00 a day to $1.10 a day, six days a week; he also earned a small bonus after working for six months.
- As he had promised, almost half of the money he made was sent back home.
- But that was two years earlier, before he learned how important it was to have a drink after work with the other men.
- That was also before he learned that not all women were as prudish as his sisters, and that some women liked being with men without the benefit of marriage.
- Or that there was a lot of money to be made staging after-hours cock fights.
- The sugar cane business was hard work and men deserved their rewards.
- His letters home became less frequent.
- His older sister was married in grand style, including a night of dancing, without him present.
- His mother had stopped writing.
- Rumors circulated that he was no longer welcome to return home.
- His three-year contract with the Hawaii Sugar Planters' Association was almost over and recruiters from California were buzzing around like angry bees.
- Maybe he could earn enough in America to buy the family farm.

Life in the Community: The Hawaiian Islands

- The first successful sugar cane plantation was started at Koloa, Kauai, in 1835.
- Its first harvest in 1837 produced two tons of raw sugar, which sold for $200.
- Other pioneers, predominantly from the United States, soon began growing sugar cane on the islands of Hawaii, Maui, and Oahu.
- Early sugar planters shared many problems: shortages of water and labor, trade barriers, and the lack of markets for their sugar.
- Together with Hawaii's isolated oceanic location, these problems demanded a spirit of cooperation for survival.
- Labor shortages were eased by bringing in contract workers from Europe, North America, and Asia. Of the nearly 385,000 workers that came, many thousands stayed to become a part of Hawaii's unique ethnic mix.

- The first workers to be imported to Hawaii were the Chinese laborers starting in the 1850s; the Japanese joined the trek to Hawaii plantations in the 1880s, while the Filipinos started in 1906.
- Few brought wives with them; fewer still intermarried with non-Filipinos.
- The U.S. Territory of Hawaii boasted more than 50,000 Filipino workers when Reynaldo arrived in 1924; most of them worked in the agricultural industry dominated by American corporations.
- The first wave of Filipino workers had arrived in 1906 and were employed on the Olaa plantation on the Big Island, Hawaii.
- The Portuguese and Spanish overseers viewed the Filipinos as "country jacks" who were oversexed and quick-tempered and needed to be beaten with sticks to keep them in line.
- The Hawaiian Islands were formed entirely of the tops of volcanic mountains, some still active.
- Because of the rugged terrain and the nature of the soils, only certain low lands near coasts were tillable.
- Consequently, Hawaii's sugar companies were all located along the coastlines of the four largest islands and reached into the foothills and upward along mountain slopes.
- Pioneer sugar planters solved water shortages in dry, leeward fields by building irrigation systems that included aqueducts, artesian wells and mountain wells.
- These irrigation systems enabled the planters to grow sugar cane on more than 100,000 acres of arid land.
- The major trade barrier to Hawaii's largest market for its raw sugar was eliminated by the 1876 Treaty of Reciprocity between the United States and the Kingdom of Hawaii.
- Through the treaty, the U.S. received a coaling station at Pearl Harbor, and Hawaii's sugar planters acquired duty-free entry into U.S. markets for their sugar.
- This arrangement was solidified with the U.S. annexation of Hawaii in 1898 after the Spanish-American War.
- In that year, sugar production stood at 225,000 tons and was rapidly moving toward one million tons when Reynaldo arrived in 1924.

Filipino workers.

HISTORICAL SNAPSHOT
1926

- Violette Neatley Anderson became the first African-American woman admitted to practice before the U.S. Supreme Court
- Walt and Roy Disney moved to their new studio at 2719 Hyperion in Los Angeles
- Land at Broadway and Wall Street in New York City sold at a record $7 per square inch
- Negro History Week, originated by Carter G. Woodson, was observed for the first time
- Teaching evolution was forbidden in schools in Atlanta, Georgia
- Contract air mail service began in the United States
- President Calvin Coolidge stated his opposition to a large air force, believing it would be a menace to world peace
- The first successful trans-Atlantic radio-telephone conversation took place between New York City and London
- Rocket science pioneer Robert H. Goddard successfully tested the first liquid-fueled rocket
- A nationwide poll on Prohibition showed that people favored a modification of the Volstead Act by a margin of nine to one
- The first issue of *Amazing Stories* concerning science fiction went on sale
- The new Book of the Month Club sent out its first selection, *Lolly Willows or The Loving Huntsman,* by Sylvia Townsend Warner
- Baseball player Satchel Paige made his pitching debut in the Negro Southern League
- Sinclair Lewis declined to accept the Pulitzer Prize awarded to his book *Arrowsmith*
- Americans Richard Byrd and Floyd Bennett claimed they had made the first flight over the North Pole
- The U.S. Army Air Corps was created by Congress
- The discovery of a spear point embedded in a rock containing 10,000 year-old bones of ancient bison in New Mexico established the existence of the Folsom culture
- The Philippines government asked the United States for a plebiscite for independence
- American Olympic gold medalist, Gertrude "Trudy" Ederle became the first woman to swim the English Channel
- Warner Bros. premiered its "Vitaphone" sound-on-disc movie system in New York
- The death of 31-year-old silent film actor Rudolph Valentino caused a worldwide frenzy among his fans
- The National Broadcasting Co., NBC, was created by the Radio Corporation of America, which had originated as Marconi Wireless
- Henry Ford initiated the 8-hour, 5-day work week in his automobile factories
- The book *Winnie-the-Pooh* by Alan Alexander Milne was published

Selected Prices

Axe	$1.20
Boy's Play Suit	$0.59
Chauffeur's Outfit	$78.00
Corn Popper	$1.75
Funeral Expenses	$935.00
Girls' Camp, Virginia, Eight Weeks	$225.00
Pistol	$12.00
Ticket, Ringside, Heavyweight Title Fight	$27.50
Toaster, Pop-up	$12.50
Vacuum Cleaner, Hoover	$75.00

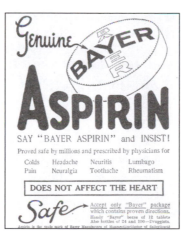

Philippine Immigration Timeline

1587

The first Filipinos in North America arrived in Morro Bay, California, on board the Manila-built galleon ship *Nuestra Señora de Esperanza* under the command of Spanish Captain Pedro de Unamuno.

1763

Filipinos from Acapulco crossed the Gulf of Mexico to Louisiana to establish seven Philippine-style fishing villages and pioneer the dried shrimp industry.

1846

Two Filipino men applied for Hawaiian citizenship from King Kalakaua.

1903

One hundred three Filipino *Pensionados* were sent to the United States to acquire an American education.

1906

Filipinos were recruited to work in the Hawaiian sugar cane plantations.

1912

Filipinos began working in California agriculture and Alaskan canning in large numbers.

"Philippines as a Dominion," Letter to the Editor by V. Martinez Del Val, *The New York Times*, January 6, 1924:

To the Editor of The New York Times:

R. Munoz Tebar in his letter to *The Times* advises the unloading of the Philippines on the Filipinos following "the example of Spain." Mr. Tebar ought not forget history so soon. Spain did not unload, she was made to download. The Filipinos did it, and the Americans did it. America was good enough to pay Spain, the vanquished, $20 million and send her soldiers back to Spain. Has the world seen a finer exhibition of international cooperation? Manly Spaniards appreciate this.

Mr. Tebar's letter contains the dynamite for its own destruction. He advises following the idea of President Roosevelt, who said that quote the time will come when it will be wise to take their own judgment [Filipinos] as to whether they wish to continue their association with America not." The present judgment of the Filipinos is to stay with America indefinitely under a dominion form of government similar to that existing between Canada and England. This, I take it, is the idea of Mr. Parr D. when he pleaded for the concession to the Philippines of what they want here; again Mr. Tebar is not au courant with history.

continued

"Philippines as a Dominion," Letter to the Editor . . . *(continued)*

Mr. Tebar speaks with patronizing spirit of delivering this country quote from future "Malayan imbroglios." If he is qualifying himself as a friend and defender of the Philippines he must have a very low conception of the good sense of the Philippine people.

A few of the reasons upheld in the wisdom of the Philippines remaining with America are:

The country is situated in the midst of an area where formidable international political plays are likely to be witnessed, and the Philippines is a small and weak country, possessing few attractions.

The Filipinos are the only Christian people in the Orient and have more advanced social and political institutions and higher standards of living than in neighboring tropical countries. The withdrawal of America from the Philippines and the impairment of the advantageous economic relations between the two countries will compel the Filipinos to compete for international economic existence with those whose living standards are below theirs, and this will mean for Philippines retrogression to a lower state of civilization.

The experience of the Filipinos of 25 years of "American Imperialism," instead of embittering them, has caused them to express their gratitude every time they speak of America. Filipinos enjoy more liberty now than a citizen in New Jersey or New York or any other state. The granting of complete local autonomy will, of course, enhance the causes of gratitude for the Filipinos.

America is not making a cent out of the Filipinos. In the exchange of commodities between the two countries under the free trade reciprocity the Philippines gain at least twice what would be collectible on American manufacturers if they were to pay duty. Total returns to American investments in the Philippines cannot offset the tariff advantage of the Filipinos after deducting the amount granted to American goods.

Other countries pay about 8 percent per annum for their bonded indebtedness. The Philippines pay only 4.75 percent. This is due to the fact that America is giving its moral backing to the Philippine bonds. The Philippine government thus saves more than $3 million a year on its indebtedness of approximately $70 million.

When speaking of the "Philippines being more attractive for outside capital," do not overlook the fact that it is the best thing we can do that can be done for Philippine farmers, industrialists and merchants. Usury in the Philippines is rampant, rates of interest are high, for there is shortage of money. If Filipinos can come to the American market for funds at lower rates, where is the fool who will deprecate the efforts to make the Philippines an attractive field for investment?

Many other reasons can be given in support of the advisability of the Philippines remaining with America a level of equality. For the present let me simply suggest to the "friends" of the Philippines who are preaching the doctrine of "scuttle" to pause and study the question more deeply and regauge their "friendship to the Filipinos" on the basis of their real welfare. Let us get down to brass tacks.

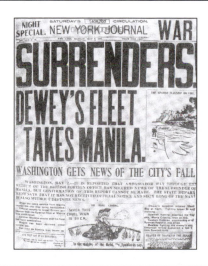

"Philippines Chafe Under Uncertainty, Both Friends and Foes of Independence Want Status Settled One Way or the Other," *The New York Times*, February 28, 1926:

The uncertain status of the relations between the United States and the Philippine Islands is considered prejudicial to America as well as to Filipino interest by leaders in political and business circles in the Philippines today. Government officials, Filipino politicians, and American, Filipino and foreign businessmen agree that the lack of a clear-cut declaration of American policy is seriously handicapping development of the islands.

Politicians want to know if the islands are to be granted independence and adjust their activities accordingly; businessmen want to know what the relations of the American government to the Islands will be in the future for purposes of investment, and Americans in the insular government service hear that the structure they have erected will be taken over and destroyed by native incompetency.

One of the principal champions of independence summed up the situation by declaring that anything is better than the present uncertainty, even announcement that the United States will remain here indefinitely.

If it is once made clear by the government in Washington that independence will not be granted for at least a generation or two, advocates of independence can turn to other issues and still retain the prestige of having been its champions.

A spokesman for American business interests in Manila recently said:

"The undeveloped resources of these islands are incredibly rich. America needs the tropical products in the Philippines. Filipinos need and want American manufactured goods and American capital for development. But so long as we do not know what the future relations of the American government to the Islands will be, we have got to move slowly. What position would we be in if, after putting in a lot of American capital, he found American control withdrawn and all our enterprises at the mercy of a capricious Filipino legislature?

"Even more concerned than the Americans is the Philippine businessman, who, if independence is granted, would be the ones to stay and have to have most to do with the politicians. They did not say anything in the open at present, but they are vitally interested in the final outcome."

The same desire for a clear-cut expression of America's intentions toward the Philippine Islands marks the conversation of the survivors of the band of American civil servants who came to the Philippines 20 to 25 years ago to devote their lives to help the Filipino people. They feel that America's work is not yet finished; they cannot believe that the American government will pull out.

An independent Filipino republic, free to call in the United States for unlimited financial aid for military and naval protection, is the substance of the public expression of most Filipino politicians. That this partnership is somewhat one-sided is recognized by those who sponsor. They say, however, that the United States being the bigger, richer and more powerful of the two partners should bear the greater share of the burden, and that by opening the Philippines and preparing the people for self-government, the United States has assumed obligations which it cannot avoid.

They have made it clear that they do not wish Americans in positions of responsibility or authority, and that those whom they may employ will have purely technical duties to perform. One of the results of the American educational system has been to confirm the younger generation of Filipinos and their opinion that they are capable of filling even the most responsible positions.

"Hold On to The Philippines But Increase Home Rule, Thompson Urges Coolidge, Sees Sovereignty Remote," *The New York Times,* December 23, 1926:

Indefinite postponement of absolute independence of the Philippines, but a gradual extension of internal autonomy, was recommended by Colonel Carmi A. Thompson of Cleveland to President Coolidge in Colonel Thompson's report on his mission to the Islands, which was made today when the President transmitted it to Congress.

The President and Colonel Thompson are in accord in holding that if the Islands are to have independence of American rule, it is a matter for consideration in the remote future.

Colonel Thompson, who spent three months in the Philippines last summer as a special representative to Mr. Coolidge, advises that the question of independence be taken up in the Islands and sufficiently developed to maintain an independent government, and that in the meantime there be granted such further freedom in the management of internal affairs as conditions may from time to time warrant. . . .

An independent government under present economic conditions would be impossible to maintain, according to Colonel Thompson. . . . Colonel Thompson declares "that no leader, either in politics or business, expects independence for a long time to come" and that he learned that with the exception of a small radical minority, "all that the Filipinos really hope for is an ultimate settlement of their relation with the United States on a basis which would eventually give them complete autonomy in internal affairs, and with the United States directing all foreign relations."

Economic conditions in the Islands he found to be very bad. Business was at a standstill and much unemployed labor was emigrating to Hawaii. Restrictive laws of the Philippines Legislature make it impossible to obtain capital for economic development, and many existing investments are regarded as unsafe. Unless there is more revenue, it is impossible for the Islands to go ahead, he reports.

It was in the year of 1916 that we migrated from the Philippines to Hawaii. . . . On the trip to Hawaii, the sea was so rough and we were all so crowded that we were forced to land in Hong Kong. We were herded into a big hall and we all slept on the floor . . . hundreds of Filipino immigrants. At the time, the epidemic of cholera was all over the Islands. I remember, as young as I was, inspectors came around and anyone that coughed or anyone who had any suspected fever of any kind was taken from the hall and we never saw them again.

—Julian Ebat

The Filipinos came at the time when all these labor sources for the plantations had been closed. . . . The planters looked at the Philippines. . . . There was a large rural population, precisely the kind of people that the sugar planters wanted, meaning people used to manual labor, and so the Hawaiian Sugar Planters' Association went to the Philippines to recruit. This was a very organized process of recruitment. The H.S.P.A. established the head office in Manila and supervised the operation of recruitment in two particular regions of the Philippines, the Visayas and Ilocos. . . . [They] wanted unskilled laborers for the plantations. They wouldn't be too unhappy to do manual work in the plantation, 10 hours a day. So, give us rural people to work on the plantation.

—Ruben Alcantara

I arrived over here February 17, 1924, the year of the big strike, in Hanapepe. They fight all the time. Two died.

—Ambrosa Balmores Marquez

[Filipinos are] little brown men about 10 years removed from a bolo and breech cloth; 15 of them will live in one room and content themselves with squatting on the floor eating rice and fish. . . . The unrestricted immigration into the State of California of natives of the Philippine Islands is viewed with alarm from a moral and sanitary standpoint while constituting a menace to white labor.

—California Justice of the Peace D. W. Rohrback, 1930

1928 News Feature

"The Church and Politics," by Dr. Gus Dyer, *Southern Agriculturist*, August 15, 1928:

The presidential campaign this year is going to be radically different from any national campaign this country has ever witnessed. Whatever may be the issues in any campaign and however vital they may be to our civilization, it is of the utmost importance that we maintain the American traditions in meeting them. The protection of American ideals is of far greater importance than any issue in the present campaign.

It is an essential part of fundamental Americanism that the Church has no proper place in any sort of political contest. Aside from other considerations, the very nature and constitution of the Churches make it grossly improper for the Church in any capacity to participate in political contest. . . .

The Church is not a product of this generation. It is an inheritance from the distant past. It is the product of the toil and prayers and sacrifices of million who have passed on. Those in charge of the Church today do not own it; they've received it as a sacred trust, and are solemnly obligated to administer to its sacred affairs in accord with the principles established generations ago. Methods may be changed, but the fundamental principles must remain.

This trust is not committed to the ministry but to the whole membership of the Church. Ministers and other Church officials are not masters but servants of the Church membership in their ministerial activities. Every church door is open to men and women of every political creed, and men of all political creeds compose the churches; Democrats, Republicans, socialists, radicals and conservatives, prohibitionists and non-prohibitionists are all in the Church on an absolutely equal footing. Together they carry its burdens and support its institutions. It is so well established by the very nature of the institution that no sort of political condition can ever be imposed on one joining the Church that would be entirely proper to write over every church door, "Equal rights to all and special privileges to none," with reference to political conviction and political affiliation. This is an essential principle of the Church. To repudiate it is to repudiate the Church as we understand it and as we have proclaimed it.

Since political convictions and political affiliations are not conditions of membership and have no power in determining the status of a member of the organization, it is grossly unfair and unjust and hence un-Christian to the Church as an organization to espouse the cause of any political creed or align itself in any way with any political question, or take any sort of stand on any question that is a political issue. . . .

Some ministers excuse themselves for discussing Prohibition from the pulpit on the grounds that Prohibition is a moral issue, and hence is not out of place as a part of the church program.

Almost every important political question involves moral questions, and political leaders give a large place to ethical considerations in discussing these questions. The free silver movement was regarded as a moral movement by the exponents of free silver. The tariff question, the farm question, the trust question, international debt question, the League of Nations issue involve morals. In one sense almost every political issue is a moral issue. . . .

The meaning of moral issue as used by those who justify making Prohibition part of the church program is that it is a contest between right and wrong. No man has any right to put Prohibition on this plane. As long as good men and intelligent men in large numbers live on both sides of the issue, no one but a narrow-minded bigot can say that the issue is between right and wrong, and hence is a moral fight.

Good men and intelligent man in large number differ fundamentally in their opinion of the effects of Prohibition. Many believe the general effects have been good, that is, the good outweighs the evil. All admit that many very serious evils have come with Prohibition, and it is a question of weighing the good effects against bad, and we have no scales that can be depended on absolutely, and no weight masters that are infallible. Many honest, intelligent people believe that Prohibition has proved itself a curse and should be modified. They believe that the lawlessness, the crimes that follow the lawless sale of liquor throughout the country outweigh the good effects that resulted from the operation of the Eighteenth Amendment. Many Americans are uncertain as to the effect. They don't know whether Prohibition should be considered good or bad, right or wrong, ethical or unethical. . . .

With so much uncertainty with reference to the moral effects of Prohibition on the part of a host of good men and intelligence, surely no intelligent person who has any regard for the truth can say this is a moral contest between right and wrong. The preacher who arbitrarily takes the position that one side is right and the other is wrong, that one side stands for morality and the other side stands for immorality is either very ignorant or very un-Christian.

Certainly the Church has no place in a contest of this nature.

1929 PROFILE

Adam Checler, a Belgian immigrant and successful lawyer, divided his time between his family in Houston, Texas, and Washington, D.C., where he lobbied against the prevailing anti-immigration mood sweeping the government.

Life at Home

- Five years earlier, Adam Checler was a 51-year-old successful lawyer, a grandfather nine times over and generally happy with his life, when he became obsessed with immigration law.
- A Belgian immigrant himself, Checler was seduced, he told friends, by the insidious nature of racist laws dressed up as economic protectionism.
- Now, five years later, he was living part-time in Washington, D.C., away from his precious children and grandchildren back in his beloved Houston, Texas, to counter the anti-immigrant mood that had swept the nation.
- Americans, he observed, loved to describe their country as a "nation of immigrants" and even rhapsodize about how their own ancestors arrived years ago, but then insist immigration today was different, more dangerous, less American and even a threat to the cause of democracy.
- Checler's parents emigrated to New York City in 1881 when his father, Jean Checler, was named head of the American branch of a Belgian bank that was heavily invested in the import and export business with the United States.
- The bank needed a United States representative who could get along with Americans, understand the shipping business and, most of all, be trusted with complicated financial transactions.
- At the urging of his wife, the elder Checler accepted the short-term assignment, quickly booked first-class passage to the United States and told friends to keep his seat warm at his downtown Brussels men's club; he would be back.
- Belgium was a growing, prosperous country in 1881 in the midst of an arts and technical explosion of innovation.
- Jean Checler was eager for the experience offered by an American assignment but had no desire to be abandoned in an American backwater for too long with so much progress under way in Europe.

Belgian immigrant Adam Checler was a successful lawyer.

Life was good for the Checler family in Houston.

- Adam was a precocious eight-year-old at the time of the move and immediately fell in love with ice skating in Central Park, speaking English to his nanny and playing with his dog.
- He named the Irish wolfhound, Hermina, after his Dutch grandmother who died the year he moved to America.
- In America, Adam's father prospered away from the encumbrances of too many rules, too much supervision, too much fear of violating the old ways of doing business.
- In the business atmosphere of New York, his father meticulously built a reputation for making solid deals that produced substantial income on both sides of the Atlantic.
- He also acquired a reputation as a knower of men, capable of remembering names and their previous transactions without extensive notes or cumbersome legal documents.
- Although an alien who spoke with a pronounced accent, Jean Checler found in the United States

Adam's father was chosen to manage the American branch of the Belgian bank he worked for.

the freedom to be successful, to experiment and to be his own man.
- The joy of resolving complex problems and the skill for remembering names were both passed along to his son.
- Adam did not fully understand his father's attachment to America until the family was ordered to return to Belgium by his firm.

- The return trip included a month-long holiday, lots of visiting and a series of secret meetings.
- Within six months the family was back in New York City, his father now president of a newly created import/export financing business; permanently returning to Belgium was never discussed again.

Adam and his family twice made the voyage from Belgium to America

Life at Work

- For the previous five years, Adam Checler had been working on ways to ameliorate the harsh impact of immigration quotas set out in the Immigration Act of 1924.
- The law was rooted in the viewpoint that the racial composition of America should not be altered by immigration.
- And the best way to insure that desire in the 1920s was to only permit immigrants in the same ratio as they had arrived in 1890.
- That way, the lawmakers said, America would maintain the proper mix of people and avoid the immigration of nationalities not interested in learning English, practicing democracy or working hard.
- During the very public debate of the immigration bill, American Nativists commonly referred to Southern and Eastern European immigrants as "undesirable races" and fought hard to continue the exclusion of Chinese and Japanese from citizenship eligibility.
- Harvard educated, Adam was drawn into the debate by legal nuance which evolved into a full-throated defense of the downtrodden newcomers in Texas.
- "To those to whom much is given, much is expected," he repeated endlessly to his wife as he planned yet another train ride to Washington to lobby Congress.
- Between 1887 and 1923, the federal courts handled 25 challenges to racial practices of citizenship, culminating in two landmark race rulings by the Supreme Court.
- In each case the Court's decision turned on whether the petitioner could be considered a white person within the meaning of the statute.
- Adam became involved in his first legal case in 1921, following the First World War.
- In that case, he was confronted by the race-based restrictions that handicapped non-whites in their effort to immigrate.
- Simply using people's presumed color to determine their nationality and eligibility for citizenship was insufficient given the "overlapping of races and gradual merging of one into another without any practical line of separation," he had argued.
- He was also unsettled by the concept that immigrants were only welcome when cheap labor was needed and then considered disposable afterward.
- Particularly offensive, he believed, were laws passed the decade before designed to drive Japanese and other Asians out of farming.
- He was aghast that the courts had ruled that the alien land laws were non-discriminatory against Japanese because the law made all aliens ineligible to citizenship, making them all equally unequal.
- To the dismay of his wife and the wonderment of his friends, Adam poured his energy into filing lawsuits and long-distance lobbying efforts against lawmakers who treated different countries unequally.
- He was appalled that elected officials believed that white America needed to be protected from Spanish, Japanese, and Mexican immigrants "bent on taking over the land."
- Experience had taught him the children and grandchildren of immigrants learned English, wanted to be Americans and uniformly were assimilated into American culture no matter their skin color.

Shifts in immigration patterns brought many workers from Mexico to America.

- The battle to control immigration had become more intense in the last few years.
- The shift in immigration patterns that brought more workers from Southern or Eastern Europe and parts of Asia and Mexico unsettled many.
- Italians, who made up 12 percent of immigrants in the early 1920s, attracted negative attention because of their darker skin.
- Groups formed around slogans such as "America for Americans."
- The rapid growth and acceptance of the Ku Klux Klan was linked to halting "the encroachment of foreigners," especially those that do not speak English or answered to "a foreign Pope as their religious authority."
- Protestant fundamentalist groups, in particular, championed anti-Catholic immigration campaigns.
- Immigrants were linked to excessive drinking by the supporters of Prohibition; the anti-communist groups preached about the potential spread of Communism by the immigrants.
- Industrialists blamed the newcomers for rising demands of labor unions, whose strikes were often branded as radical uprisings.
- But despite the popularity of the immigration legislation passed in 1924, which limited immigration into the United States to 150,000 people a year according to nation-based quotas, its implementation had been postponed several times.
- The first two reports submitted to Congress criticized Irish, German, and Scandinavian-Americans for failing to take their populations fully into account.
- Many Japanese, Chinese and other Asians were angered that they were largely excluded altogether—a continuation of American policy dating back 50 years.
- Since the mid-nineteenth century, scientific race theorists had been working to develop systems of racial classification and typology.
- Toward this end, new questions were added to the 1910 and 1920 censuses in hopes of quantifying levels of assimilation by immigrant groups.
- These questions concerned literacy, the ability to speak English, mother tongue, number of children born and living, and length of time in the United States.
- By 1928 the restrictive quotas united the Young Men's Christian Association, church congregations and the League of Women Voters, only to be opposed by the American Legion, the Grange and the Daughters of the American Revolution.
- The issues universally concerned the quota system that allotted immigration permits to countries in the same proportion that the American people traced their origins, using the 1890 Census as a base.
- The Daughters of the American Revolution and the American Legion called on Congress to stand firm against the efforts of "hyphates" who would "play politics with the nation's bloodstream."
- The law rewarded whiteness while limiting the ethnic identities of the Japanese, Chinese, Mexicans and even Filipinos.
- The act was not the first to limit "undesirables" from American shores.
- The 1917 Immigration Act, which increased the entry head tax to $8.00, also excluded "all idiots, imbeciles, feeble-minded persons, epileptics, insane persons; persons who have had one or more attacks of insanity in any time previously; persons of constitutional psychopathic inferiority; persons with chronic alcoholism, paupers, professional beggars, vagrants, persons afflicted with tuberculosis in any form or with a loathsome

or dangerous contagious disease; persons not comprehended within any of the foregoing excluded classes found to be certified by the examining surgeon as being mentally or physically defective, such physical defect being of a nature which may affect the ability of such alien to earn a living; persons who have been convicted of or admit having committed a felony or any other crime or misdemeanor involving moral turpitude; polygamists, or persons who practice polygamy or believe in the practice of polygamy; anarchists, or persons who believe in or advocate the overthrow by force or violence of the government of the United States."

- The most controversial aspect of the act was the plan to exclude all aliens over 16 years of age who could not read "the English language, or some other language or dialect, including Hebrew or Yiddish."
- Attempts at introducing literacy tests into the immigration process had been vetoed by Presidents Grover Cleveland in 1891 and William Taft in 1913.
- President Woodrow Wilson also objected to this clause in the 1917 Immigration Act, but it was approved by Congress nevertheless.
- Now Adam was faced with new arguments for the Mexican race problem emerging in the Southwest, where he was from, sparked by an all-time high Mexican immigration attracted by agricultural jobs.
- Immigration was threatening the region's current political economic structure and the pressure was on Mexico to refuse visas to all Mexican workers except those with prior residency in the United States.
- Congress was even discussing making unlawful entry into America a felony offense to halt illegal immigration from Mexico.
- Adam argued that the new wave of immigration coincided with the development of commercial agriculture that required the creation of a large migratory workforce.
- And it was unfortunate that the term "illegals" had become a synonym for "Mexican immigrant workers."
- Adam was in Texas on the day the new regulations were finally approved in 1929, surrounded by nine granddaughters more interested in riding horses than a bunch of esoteric formulas that would shape the future of immigration.

Life in the Community: Houston, Texas

- Adam Checler moved to Texas after completing law school; he believed Houston, Texas, was a wide-open canvas for a man seeking to make his fortune.
- Texas was not always viewed that way.

Adam moved to Houston, Texas after law school.

Texas oil fields employed many legal and illegal workers.

- Civil War General Sheridan was quoted as saying, "If I owned Texas and Hades, I'd rent Texas and move to the other place."
- Modern Texas was praised by *National Geographic* magazine in 1928: "Power and political experience have taught her tolerance. In her easy-going, slightly Mexican manner, she is too busy working out her own social problems and her huge economic destiny to worry over her past, sensational though it may have been."
- Texas had become so prosperous, employers found it difficult to get enough Mexican workers to pick its cotton, work its oil fields, or handle trainloads of fresh vegetables shipped annually from the lower Rio Grande.
- To meet this economic demand, workers came both lawfully through immigration offices at the border or illegally across the Rio Grande by 10,000 every year.
- Texas required a veritable army of Mexican and American labor to do its work.
- A million and a half cars of freight, mostly carrying farm products, originated in Texas every year; all told, approximately 3.5 billion cars of freight crossed the state annually.
- This activity attracted people, also.
- In the previous 20 years Texas had gained more than two million residents.
- Since 1920, more than 100,000 people had come each year to settle in Texas, mostly from the middle Western states.
- In addition to its enormous agricultural potential, more than $1 billion worth of oil was produced in Texas during the prior five years.

HISTORICAL SNAPSHOT
1929

- The United States and Canada reached an agreement on joint action to preserve Niagara Falls

- The adventure comic strip *Tarzan*, first appeared; the Popeye character was introduced in the *Thimble Theater* cartoon strip by Elzie Segar

- Frontiersman Wyatt Earp died in Los Angeles, California, after an illustrious life in the West; cowboy stars William S. Hart and Tom Mix served as pallbearers

- The U.S. Senate ratified the Kellogg-Briand anti-war pact

- Acadia National Park was established in Maine; the Grand Teton National Park opened in Wyoming

- San Francisco police took 19-year-old Frances Orlando to the police station because she was dressed in men's clothing

- In Chicago the "St. Valentine's Day Massacre" took place in a garage of the Moran gang as seven rivals of Al Capone's gang were gunned down

- The first telephone was installed in the White House

- Louie Marx introduced the yo-yo in the United States

- Harold E. Jones, director of research at the University of California Institute of Child Welfare reported that children doing poor schoolwork and those most often exhibiting objectionable traits were found to be those who attended motion picture shows frequently

- Hollywood staged an experimental publicity stunt for the movie industry that grew to become the Academy Awards extravaganza

- The first all-color talking picture, *On with the Show*, opened in New York

- Scientists at Bell Laboratories revealed a system for transmitting television pictures

- The U.S. Immigration Law of 1924 went into effect

- Transcontinental Air Transport began between New York and Los Angeles; service took 48 hours with trains for night travel at a cost of $310 a ticket

- The comedy program *Amos 'n' Andy*, starring Freeman Gosden and Charles Correll, made its network radio debut on NBC

The US and Canada worked together to preserve Niagara Falls.

GLACIER PARK HOTEL
MANY GLACIER HOTEL
PRINCE *of* WALES HOTEL

National parks were gaining popularity in the late 1920s.

Selected Prices

Ad, Full-Page, Color, in *Saturday Evening Post*	$11,000
Airplane, Single Engine	$2,000
Camera	$80.00
Handbag, Leather	$2.98
Juice Extractor	$14.95
Men's Hunting Coat	$3.50
Radio, Six Tubes	$65.00
Shaving Soap, Pound	$0.49
Suntan Lotion	$2.50
Tennis Racket	$15.00

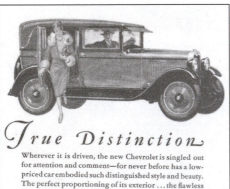

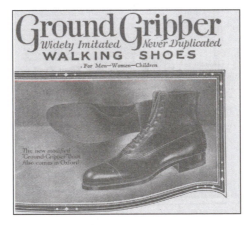

Immigration Timeline

1775

An outbreak of revolutionary violence stopped immigration from Britain.

1790

Congress passed an act requiring two years of residency in the U.S. before qualifying for citizenship and limiting citizenship to free white persons, including those who were without property.

1795

The residency period required for citizenship was raised from two years to five.

1798

The Alien and Sedition Acts were passed comprising four laws: the Naturalization Act, the Alien Act, the Alien Enemies Act, and the Sedition Act. The Naturalization Act raised the time of residency for naturalization from five to 14 years and the Alien Act allowed the president to arrest and deport any alien considered dangerous. The Alien Enemies Act allowed for the arrest and deportation of subjects of foreign powers at war with the U.S. The Sedition Act made it a criminal offense to print or publish false, malicious or scandalous statements directed against the U.S. Government, the president, or Congress, to foster opposition to the lawful acts of Congress, or to aid a foreign power in plotting against the United States.

1800

The Alien Act, one of the four Alien and Sedition acts, expired.

1802

The Naturalization Act, one of the four Alien and Sedition Acts, was repealed.

1862

Congress passed the first law restricting immigration, forbidding American vessels to transport Chinese immigrants to the U.S.

1882

The Chinese Exclusion Act was passed, freezing the number of Chinese immigrants.

1891

The Immigration and Naturalization Service (INS) was created to administer the federal laws relating to the admission, exclusion and deportation of aliens and to the naturalization of aliens lawfully residing in the U.S.

1892

The INS opened an immigration screening station at Ellis Island in New York Harbor.

1907

The U.S. and Japan signed the Gentleman's Agreement ensuring that the Japanese government would not issue passports to Japanese laborers intending to enter the U.S.

Timeline . . . *(continued)*

1917

The Immigration Act of 1917 expanded the classes of foreigners excluded from the U.S., created a geographical region covering most of eastern Asia and the Pacific islands from which no immigrants were to be admitted into the U.S., and imposed a literacy test on aliens.

1918

Congress passed the Anarchist Act of 1918 which expanded the provisions for the exclusion of subversive aliens.

1921

A quota system, detailing the maximum number of persons admitted into a nation, was first introduced.

1924

A new quota system was introduced based on the desirability of various nationalities based on the 1890 census.

Copyright, 1927, by the Philadelphia Inquirer Company

OUR LITTLE MISUNDERSTAND-
ING SEEMS TO BE PASSING AWAY

—Hanny in the Philadelphia *Inquirer.*

Comprehensive Immigration Law (1924)

By the President of the United States of America
A Proclamation

Whereas it is provided in the act of Congress approved May 26, 1924, entitled "An act to limit the immigration of aliens into the United States, and for other purposes" that "The annual quota of any nationality shall be two per centum of the number of foreign-born individuals of such nationality resident in continental United States as determined by the United States Census of 1890, but the minimum quota of any nationality shall be 100 (Sec. 11 a). . . .

"The Secretary of State, the Secretary of Commerce, and the Secretary of Labor, jointly, shall, as soon as feasible after the enactment of this act, prepare a statement showing the number of individuals of the various nationalities resident in continental United States as determined by the United States Census of 1890, which statement shall be the population basis for the purposes of subdivision (a) of section 11 (Sec. 12 b).

"Such officials shall, jointly, report annually to the President the quota of each nationality under subdivision (a) of section 11, together with the statements, estimates, and revisions provided for in this section. The President shall proclaim and make known the quotas so reported. (Sec. 12 e)

"Now, therefore I, Calvin Coolidge, President of the United States of America acting under and by virtue of the power in me vested by the aforesaid act of Congress, do hereby proclaim and make known that on and after July 1, 1924, and throughout the fiscal year 1924-1925, the quota of each nationality provided in said act shall be as follows:

COUNTRY OR AREA OF BIRTH QUOTA 1924-1925

Afghanistan: 100

Albania: 100

Andorra: 100

Arabian peninsula: 100

Armenia: 124

Australia, including Papua, Tasmania, and all islands appertaining to Australia: 121

Austria: 785

Belgium: 512

Bhutan: 100

Bulgaria: 100

Cameroon (proposed British mandate): 100

Cameroon (French mandate): 100

China: 100

Czechoslovakia: 3,073

Danzig, Free City of: 228

Denmark: 2,789

Egypt: 100

Estonia: 124

Ethiopia (Abyssinia): 100

Finland: 170

France: 3,954

Germany: 51,227

continued

Comprehensive Immigration Law (1924) . . . *(continued)*

Great Britain and Northern Ireland: 34,007

Greece: 100

Hungary: 473

Iceland: 100

India: 100

Iraq (Mesopotamia): 100

Irish Free State: 28,567

Italy, including Rhodes, Dodecanesia, and Castellorizzo: 3,845

Japan: 100

Latvia:142

Liberia: 100

Liechtenstein: 100

Lithuania: 344

Luxemburg: 100

Monaco: 100

Morocco (French and Spanish Zones and Tangier): 100

Muscat (Oman): 100

Nauru (proposed British mandate): 100

Nepal: 100

Netherlands: 1648

New Zealand (including appertaining islands: 100

Norway: 6,453

New Guinea, and other Pacific Islands under proposed Australian mandate: 100

Palestine (with Trans Jordan, proposed British mandate): 100

Persia: 100

Poland: 5,982

Portugal: 503

Ruanda and Urundi (Belgium mandate): 100

Rumania: 603

Russia, European and Asiatic: 2,248

Samoa, Western (proposed mandate of New Zealand): 100

San Marino: 100

Siam: 100

South Africa, Union of: 100

South West Africa (proposed mandate of Union of South Africa): 100

Spain: 131

Sweden: 9,561

Switzerland: 2,081

Syria and The Lebanon (French mandate): 100

Tanganyika (proposed British mandate): 100

Togoland (proposed British mandate): 100

Togoland (French mandate): 100

Turkey: 100

Yap and other Pacific islands (under Japanese mandate) (4): 100

Yugoslavia: 671

A radical departure from our national policy relating to immigrants is here presented. Heretofore we have welcomed all who come to us from other lands except those whose moral or physical condition or history threatened danger to our national welfare and safety. We have encouraged those coming from foreign countries to cast their lot with us and join in the development of our vast domain, securing in return a share in the blessings of American citizenship.

A century's stupendous growth, largely due to the assimilation and thrift of millions of sturdy and patriotic adopted citizens, attests of the success of this generous and free-handed policy which, while guarding the people's interests, exacts from our immigrants only physical and moral soundness and a willingness and ability to work.

—President Grover Cleveland, 1891, concerning the literacy requirement in the proposed Immigration Act

The passage of the Immigration Act of 1924 resulted from a mixture of passion and emotion; mixture of fears and hates, tempered by idealism and by vision, which lie behind the complex motivations of Congressional action. We were afraid of foreigners; we distrusted them; we didn't like them.

—Author Emmanuel Celler, reflecting on the 1924 Immigration Act

A race that refuses to do manual work and seeks white collar jobs is doomed through its falling birthrate to replacement by the lower races or classes. In other words, the introduction of immigrants as lowly laborers means a replacement of race.

—Madison Grant, author of *The Passing of the Great Race*, 1916

"Immigration Problems Show New Intricacies," by Arthur Cook, *The New York Times*, February 6, 1927:

At no time, perhaps, in the history of the country has the United States had less of immigration problems than at the present time. The problem of populating the country by immigration has disappeared. It gave place, following the war, to one of restricting the number of alien arrivals for residents. In the meantime restrictions upon the quality of immigrants determined by measures of health, mentality and moral fitness gradually became more drastic and enforcement more efficient. The exclusion of Orientals forestalled the arising of some of the problems which have arisen in other immigration countries. . . .

Yet the exclusion from the United States of afflicted aliens has brought criticism at times because of peculiar circumstances surrounding individual cases which have arisen. A family abroad having one or two inadmissible members is sometimes first broken by the husband and father coming to the United States and sending back from time to time for additional members; the inadmissible one remains with relatives until last and then calms over when the balance of the family is well established. If the inadmissible one is rejected, immigration officers are accused of breaking home and family ties. At such times it is not, of course, recalled that the separation took place when the admissible alien member was abandoned on the other side.

Numerical limitation, which was expressed in legislation as a permanent policy in 1924, has its special problems of administration, particularly with reference to families of residents in the United States, citizen and alien. When the head of a family leaves from abroad, and no provision is made for the issuance of quota visas for the family, it can be readily understood that when, later, the applications are filed, there may be a considerable period of waiting necessary for quota numbers before the family can be secured. The present law provides for non-quota status for wife and children under 18 years of age of American citizens, and for preference for his father and mother. The alien resident, however, no matter of how long a domicile here, must wait for the admission of his dependents until they can be reached in regular non-reference number.

The problem of keeping families together, or of uniting them at the residence of the breadwinner, is one of the major issues at this time. A remedy is suggested by the Secretary of Labor, James A. Davis, in its annual report for 1926, to solve the problem as it relates to immigrants now coming. He recommends to Congress that a provision be added to the immigration laws requiring an alien head of family seeking visa for residence in the United States to express intention regarding the future residents of the family, and in the event he expects later to have the family join him in the United States, each member of the family would be required to submit to preliminary examination to determine admissibility.

"The March of Events," *The World's Work*, December 1923:

In order properly to appreciate the immigration situation, which promises to occupy a prominent place in the discussions of the new Congress, Americans should let their minds go back 40 or 50 years, when a threatened inundation of the Pacific Coast called for dramatic remedy. At that time Chinese and other Mongolians were landing in California at a rate that, if unchecked, would make this part of the United States, in one or two generations, little better than an Asiatic domain. There was no objection to these immigrants on the ground of industry or good behavior. As a mass they were hard-working, law-abiding, in an economic sense they unquestionably possessed great value. They were found useful in building the Pacific railroads, in cultivating farms, in creating wealth in many ways. Nor were they lacking in intelligence; they were the children of a very ancient civilization, a civilization that was old when Greece and Rome were young and when the continent of Europe was the abiding place of naked savages. There was only one objection to these incomers. Mentally and physically they were absolutely alien to the races that founded the American Nation. The idea of ever incorporating them into the body politic could not be entertained. Intermarriage with Northwestern Europeans could produce only hybrid descendants, and introduce another insoluble race problem. The only possible future for these Mongolians would be existence as a people apart, a bloc of suspicious and hostile unassimilables, something which is a public evil in any nation, but which is especially hateful in a nation founded upon American principles. The statesmen of 40 years ago solved this problem in the wisest way. They abruptly stopped Asiatic immigration. There were plenty of "liberals" of that date who denounced the Chinese exclusion laws, as there are plenty subsequently who denounced the anti-Japanese measures, but the result of this foresight is now apparent. California is today a beautiful and flourishing community of Northwestern Europeans, one of the parts of the United States of which Americans are chiefly proud, instead of being, as it would have become except for the exclusion laws, a great expanse devoted largely to an Asiatic civilization.

What the country and Congress should understand is that the Atlantic Coast is now living in the shadow of a similar peril. What are the races that have poured into the great Eastern cities in the last 15 years and which are now clamoring for admission? Greeks, Armenians, Bulgars, Rumanians, Croats, Southern Italians, Eastern Jews. The folly of attempting to transform these races into American citizens, now or centuries from now, is clear to all students of history. On this point there's practically no disagreement; discussion or argument are unnecessary. Unless the flood is checked, however, and abruptly checked, the Atlantic Coast, in a few generations, will be largely peopled with this kind of human material.

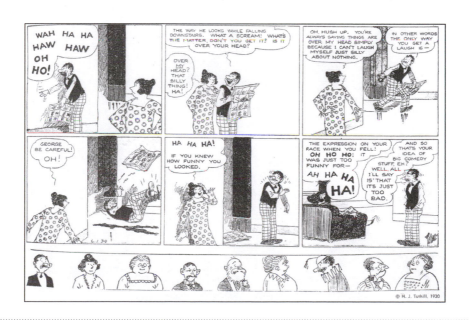

1930–1939

Few Americans escaped the devastating impact of the most severe depression in the nation's history. Economic paralysis gripped the country: banks failed, railroads became insolvent, factories closed, unemployment shot upward, and Americans took to the road looking for work, stability and something to believe in. Farmers defied court-ordered evictions, mothers desperate to feed their families staged food riots, and school attendance was back to five months. Fewer couples chose marriage, fewer still had children in this austere environment. And recent immigrants took the opportunity to return to their homeland in hopes of finding jobs. During the entire decade, the United States received a total of 528,000 immigrants, approximately the same number of immigrants who came to America annually in 1911.

By 1934, one in every four farms had been sold for taxes and 5,000 banks had closed their doors, eradicating in seconds the lifetime savings of millions of Americans, rich and poor. In some circles the American depression was viewed as the fulfillment of Marxist prophecy—the inevitable demise of capitalism. President Franklin D. Roosevelt thought otherwise. Backed by his New Deal promises and a focus on the "forgotten man," the president produced a swirl of government programs designed to lift the country out of its paralytic gloom.

Roosevelt's early social experiments were characterized by relief, recovery and reform. Believing that the expansion of the United States' economy was temporarily over, Roosevelt paid attention to better distribution of resources and planned production. The Civilian Conservation Corps (CCC), for example, put 250,000 jobless young men to work in the forests for $1.00 a day. By 1935, government deficit spending was spurring economic change. By 1937, total manufacturing output exceeded that of 1929; unfortunately, prices and wages rose too quickly and the economy dipped again in 1937, driven by inflation fears and restrictions on bank lending. Nonetheless, many roads, bridges, public buildings, dams and trees became part of the landscape, thanks to federally employed workers. The Federal Theatre Project, for example, employed 1,300 people during the period, reaching 25 million attendees with more than 1,200 productions. Despite progress, 10 million workers were still unemployed in 1938, and farm prices lagged behind manufacturing progress. Full recovery would not occur until the United States mobilized for World War II.

While the nation suffered from economic blows, the West was being whipped by nature. Gigantic billowing clouds of dust up to 10,000 feet high swept across the parched Western Plains throughout the 1930s. Sometimes the blows came with lightning and booming thunder, but often they were described as being "eerily silent, blackening everything in their path." All human activity halted. Planes were grounded. Buses and trains stalled, unable to race clouds that could move at speeds of more than 100 miles per hour. On the morning of May 9, 1934, the wind began to blow up the topsoil of Montana and Wyoming, and soon some 350 million tons were sweeping eastward. By late afternoon, 12 million tons had been deposited in Chicago. By noon the next day, Buffalo, New York, was dark with dust. Even the Atlantic Ocean was no barrier. Ships 300 miles out to sea found dust on their decks. During the remainder of 1935, there were more than 40 dust storms that reduced visibility to less than one mile. There were 68 more storms in 1936, 72 in 1937, and 61 in 1938. On the High Plains, 10,000 houses were simply abandoned, and nine million acres of farm turned back to nature. Banks offered mortgaged properties for as little as $25.00 for 160 acres and found no takers.

The people of the 1930s excelled in escape. Radio matured as a mass medium, creating stars such as Jack Benny, Bob Hope, and Fibber McGee and Molly. For a time it seemed that every child was copying the catch phrase of radio's Walter Winchell, "Good evening, Mr. and Mrs. America, and all the ships at sea," or pretending to be Jack Benny when shouting, "Now, cut that out!" Soap operas captured large followings, and sales of magazines like *Screenland* and *True Story* skyrocketed. Each edition of *True Confessions* sold 7.5 million copies. Nationwide, movie theaters prospered as 90 million Americans attended the "talkies" every week, finding comfort in the uplifting excitement of movies and movie stars. Big bands made swing the king of the decade, while jazz came into its own. And the social experiment known as Prohibition died in December 1933, when the Twenty-first Amendment swept away the restrictions against alcohol ushered in more than a decade earlier.

Attendance at professional athletic events declined during the decade, but softball became more popular than ever and golf began its drive to become a national passion as private courses went public. Millions listened to boxing on radio, especially the exploits of the "Brown Bomber," Joe Louis. As average people coped with the difficult times, they married later, had fewer children, and divorced less. Extended families often lived under one roof; opportunities for women and minorities were particularly limited. Survival, not affluence, was often the practical goal of the family. A disillusioned nation, which had worshipped the power of business, looked instead toward a more caring government.

1932 PROFILE

American-born Maria Azuela was part of the United States expulsion of Mexican-Americans that brought her, through a harrowing journey, from Los Angeles to Mexico and back to America, this time bound for Chicago.

Life at Home

- Unlike most immigrants, Maria Azuela's journey began in California, took her to Mexico, and landed her back in the United States.
- She was a 27-year-old American-born woman of Mexican descent whose husband had died suddenly, leaving behind three children.
- He died violently in a job-related accident; company officials were very sorry for her loss, but made it clear that no compensation for his death should be expected.
- As a stone mason, he worked hard and made good money.
- Their plans to buy a house were coming into focus.
- Her youngest child, three-year-old Rigo, continued to ask about his father nightly until the government officials unexpectedly banged on her door.
- After that he didn't ask anymore.
- Three weeks after the funeral, Los Angeles authorities arrived at her three-room apartment outside Los Angeles and ordered her and her American-born children to leave the country.
- The nation was in the midst of a serious Depression in 1931, he explained; unemployment was on the rise, and room must be made for U.S. workers.
- To get Americans working again, President Herbert Hoover had backed a policy to repatriate hundreds of thousands of Mexican workers.
- In public announcements, Latinos were accused of taking jobs and government services from "real Americans"; one federal official declared, "We need their jobs for needy citizens."
- The County Board of Supervisors and the Chamber of Commerce proclaimed "repatriation" of Mexicans to be a humane and utilitarian solution.

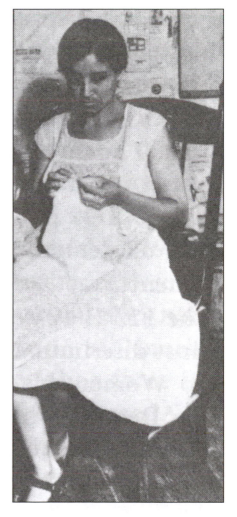

An American citizen of Mexican descent, Maria was sent back to Mexico when her husband died suddenly.

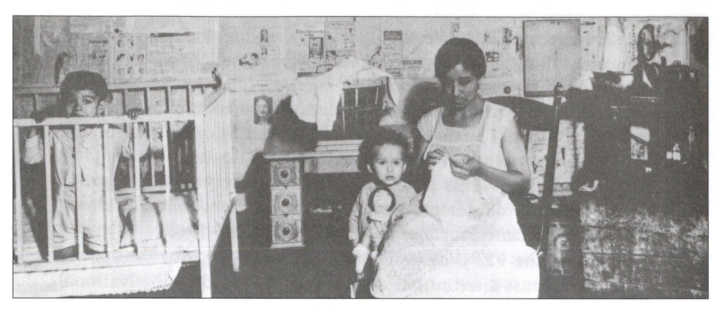

Maria was terrified to take her children from their home in America.

Maria and her children were forced to board a train to Guadalajara, Mexico.

- The Mexican government supported the purge, touting the current development of agriculture colonies and irrigation projects in Mexico that would provide work for the displaced compatriots from the north.
- In all, approximately one million people of Mexican ancestry were being relocated, more than half of whom were American citizens; 400,000 men, women and children were expelled from the state of California alone.
- As frightened as Maria was, when the officials told her she must leave, she laughed out loud.
- "I don't even speak Spanish very well," she told them, "and the children have never been to Mexico. They don't speak Spanish at all."
- He showed no interest in her American birth certificate or those of her children.
- They presented her with papers certifying that she was unemployed and thus a potential ward of the state and not welcome to return.
- Within a week she and her three children were driven to the depot and forced to board a train to Guadalajara, Mexico.
- She was one of 400 frightened people shipped south that day.
- Someone had hired a mariachi band to keep spirits high.
- The forced immigration process of this fatherless family lasted 23 hours aboard a train that stopped often but carried little food; three-year-old Rigo became dehydrated during the trip and developed a fever.
- When the train's porter finally came to check on the family, he ordered Maria to silence her son's crying—the other passengers were complaining.
- He didn't know where she could find clean drinking water and scolded her for failing to prepare more food for the long trip.
- This was only her second trip to Mexico in 27 years; the last was a decade earlier when her grandmother died.

- The Mexico of her grandmother was so foreign and desperate she refused to go back, even to visit her husband's mother.
- America was her home and she had no desire to live anywhere else.
- Later she would learn that 50,000 persons of Mexican ancestry would be expelled from Los Angeles alone during the second six months of 1931.
- For now, all she wanted was a quiet place to cry.
- Her father and pregnant mother had emigrated from near the Chihuahuan Desert in 1903, where the beauty of the land was often subtle and the environment sometimes mean.
- Revolution was in the air then, and they just wanted out.
- Her father, Raymond, had been raised on a farm and knew hard work; the farmers in America, he had been told, were desperate for pickers who would stay in the fields all day and not quit on them.
- He knew how to work from "dark to dark," and was sure he would do well.
- Seasonal crops demanded a flood of workers when the crops were ready; harvests were demanding and didn't take a holiday.
- In America, he believed, his family could find peace and prosperity.

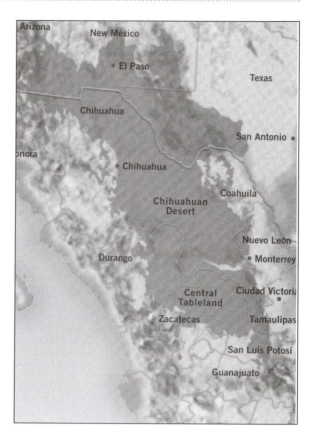

Her parents left the Chihuahuan Desert when her mother was pregnant with Maria.

Life at Work

- Maria Azuela was frozen with fear when the conductor ordered her off the train in Guadalajara.
- A month earlier she was a happily married American citizen, who spent her days raising three children and waiting for her husband to return from work at sunset.
- Her apartment was neat, fully furnished and clean; her décor echoed their Mexican past, their Catholic upbringing and love of American culture.
- Her dream life disappeared beneath an accidental rock slide at her husband's work site, her subsequent expulsion by county officials eager to keep Mexicans off the welfare rolls, a long, exhausting train ride and the persistent cough of her youngest child.
- For two days she and her children slept on the depot benches and ate scraps left by other travelers.
- She had money in her dress pocket, but was terrified to spend any and then find herself destitute.
- On the third day she was roused from sleep and ordered to leave by police officials who were highly exasperated by her inability to speak Spanish.
- Finally, they decided for her that she should be shipped by train to Chihuahua; there she wandered for two days trying to find an older, distant cousin she had met a decade earlier at her grandmother's funeral.
- Times were tough, she was told repeatedly; if she wanted to stay, her cousin told her, she would need to work raising chickens and collecting eggs.

A distant cousin in Mexico took in Maria when she arrived.

Working on her cousin's chicken farm was not easy work.

- Her primary task was guarding the free ranging chickens from hawks, foxes, dogs and ten-fingered chicken thieves.
- She immediately took two steps: ordered an English-language book on chicken farming and enrolled the children in school.
- As a result of the long Mexican Revolution, education was widely offered, even in rural regions of the country.
- Having finished the eighth grade herself, Maria knew the only path back to America was through education.
- Four months after her arrival, she learned from newly arriving refugees that everything in her apartment had been stolen two days after she left and that another family was now living in her home.
- Returning to America remained the goal, but not to Los Angeles; friends said Chicago was a friendly—albeit cold—place to raise a family.
- She also learned that keeping chickens and hawks apart was a monumental task; already her legs had been whipped twice by her cousin for losing a chicken.
- So when she decided to leave for Chicago in early March of 1932, she was told that a man she had met would get her across the border.
- After that her American birth certificate would keep her safe.

Life in the Community: Los Angeles, California

- During the early years of the twentieth century, the U.S. Immigration Service paid little attention to Mexican nationals.
- The emphasis was on turning back Chinese immigrants or persons believed to be lunatics, criminals, prostitutes, paupers and those suffering from loathsome or contagious diseases.
- Cheap Mexican labor was in demand by a host of American industries: railroads, mining and agribusiness, all of which employed agents to greet immigrants at the border to extol the rewards of working in America.
- Most Mexicans entered the United States through Arizona or Texas, with El Paso serving as the port of entry for close to 60 percent of all immigrants who eventually settled in Los Angeles.
- In El Paso, many found immediate employment; each of the city's eight railroad lines had maintenance shops that hired hundreds of Mexican workers.
- El Paso also served as a transportation hub for laborers for the mining, cattle-raising, construction and agricultural industries of the Southwest.
- Recruiters were also sent from far and wide to entice workers into signing up for work with their faraway companies, offering better wages and transportation ready for them in the form of rail cars.
- As a direct result of the chaos and violence associated with the 1910 Mexican Revolution, immigration accelerated; more than 100,000 Mexican nationals crossed the border from 1910 to 1915.
- National immigration laws were tightened in 1917 to restrict European anarchists from immigrating to America during World War 1, but enforcement of the laws were lax at the Mexican border.
- By the 1920s, opposition to Mexican labor began to grow; several national magazines, including *The Saturday Evening Post,* editorialized against the "Mexicanization" of America.

Cheap, Mexican labor was in demand.

- Between 1900 and 1930, only about 15 percent of Mexican immigrants to Los Angeles came directly to the city after crossing the border.
- Most Mexican immigrants had their initial experiences with American life elsewhere.
- Intense racial discrimination, strict segregation and low wages forced many Mexicans to migrate in large numbers to California in search of higher-paying jobs.
- So great was the exodus that employers in California tried to prevent Mexicans from purchasing automobiles and prohibit out-of-state labor recruiters in order to keep their workers both plentiful and immobile.
- The advantage of free travel offered by recruiters and railroads managed not only to add large numbers of Mexicans to the Southwest, but also to disperse workers throughout the West.
- By 1920, Mexicans formed the largest single ethnic group in the agricultural San Joaquin Valley; by 1928, 55 percent of the labor force of California's Imperial Valley was from Old-Mexico origin.
- Mexican immigrants began to cluster in Los Angeles because it already contained a large Latino community with a longstanding tradition that had experienced successive waves of immigrants from Mexico.
- Los Angeles life and culture was completely transformed in the face of rapid Mexican settlement and urbanization.
- In almost every section of Los Angeles where Mexicans lived, they "shared" neighborhoods with other ethnic groups.

Many Mexicans worked at cattle farms.

- The Plaza community was home to many different ethnic groups, the largest being Chinese in China Town and Japanese in Li'l Tokyo, Italians in Lincoln Heights, Asians in the Mission/Union Station District, Russian Molokans in Boyle Heights, Jews in Brooklyn Heights, Filipinos in the Temple Street neighborhood, Blacks in Belvedere
- The English language prevailed in the daily commerce and business world of the city, and despite the many familiarities to their homeland, Los Angeles to the many immigrants was indeed a strange new environment, in stark contrast with their rural and beloved Mexico.
- Angelinos were exceptionally mobile, and to any newcomer venturing into Los Angeles between 1900 and 1930, the burgeoning metropolis struck them as alien and inhospitable.
- Los Angeles by 1929 surpassed all other western cities in manufacturing; the city grew from a population of 50,000 in 1890 to 1.2 million by 1930, and its diversity when compared to eastern cities represented a wider range of cultures and peoples.

HISTORICAL SNAPSHOT
1932

- Mrs. Hattie W. Caraway (D-Arkansas) became the first woman elected to the U.S. Senate
- The El Salvador army killed 4,000 protesting farmers
- President Herbert Hoover pushed through a dramatic tax increase to balance the budget and restore "confidence"
- Mobster Al Capone was sent to prison in Atlanta, Georgia, for tax evasion
- George Burns and Gracie Allen debuted as regulars on the *Guy Lombardo Show*
- Irving Berlin's musical *Face the Music* premiered in New York City
- The Purple Heart award was reinstituted.
- The Glass-Steagall Act was passed, giving the Federal Reserve the right to expand credit in order to increase money circulation
- The infant son of Charles and Anne Lindbergh was kidnapped from his nursery at the family home near Princeton, New Jersey; German immigrant Bruno Richard Hauptmann was arrested and convicted for the crime
- The executive committee of the Daughters of the American Revolution voted to exclude blacks from appearing at Constitution Hall
- The Ford Motor Company unveiled its V8 engine
- Vitamin C was isolated by C. C. King at the University of Pittsburgh
- The Royal Shakespeare Theatre opened at Stratford-on-Avon; it replaced the one built in 1879 that burned down in 1926
- Ed Wynn, the Texaco fire chief, premiered on radio's *Texaco Star Theater* before a live audience
- The Pulitzer prize was awarded to Pearl S. Buck for *The Good Earth*
- The cartoon character Goofy first appeared in *Mickey's Revue* by Walt Disney
- Congress changed the name "Porto Rico" to "Puerto Rico"
- Drug Inc.; Procter & Gamble; Loew's; Nash Motors; Int'l Shoe; Int'l Business Machines; and Coca Cola were added to the Dow Jones Industrial Index
- World War I veterans marched on Washington, DC, to demand cash bonuses they weren't scheduled to receive for another 13 years
- A federal gas tax was enacted
- The United States and Canada signed a treaty to develop the St. Lawrence Seaway
- The George Washington quarter went into circulation as a 200-year commemorative of Washington's birth
- Amelia Earhart became the first woman to fly nonstop across the United States, traveling from Los Angeles to Newark, New Jersey, in just over 19 hours
- A five-day work week was established for General Motors workers

Mexican Immigration Timeline

1900–1909

Mexican immigration increased dramatically; thousands of Mexicans were recruited to work on American railroads and farms.

1910–1917

Thousands fled to the United States to escape violence brought on by the Mexican Revolution; immigrants included wealthy businessmen, poor farmers, soldiers and political refugees.

1914

World War I erupted in Europe; Mexico was accused of collaborating with Germany.

1916

In a raid led by Pancho Villa across the U.S. border, U.S. citizens were killed in Columbus, New Mexico.

1917

The Mexican Revolution ended.

Los Angeles officials, aroused by a growing anti-Mexican sentiment, sought to deport Mexican immigrants.

1918

Faced with labor shortages caused by America's entrance into WWI, labor leaders persuaded the federal government to drop the $8.00 tax and literacy test required of Mexican immigrants.

Mexicans and Mexican-Americans comprised the largest group of agricultural workers in Imperial Valley, California.

1919

More than 650,000 Mexican-Americans lived in the American Southwest.

1920–1929

A strong U.S. economy attracted nearly a half million Mexicans to migrate for work.

1924

The United States established the border patrol to stop illegal immigration from Mexico—with little success.

1925

Chicago's Mexican population topped 20,000, the largest clustering of Hispanic Americans outside the Southwest.

1929–1932

The Great Depression caused factories to close and wages to fall; one-third of all U.S. workers were unemployed.

1931

President Herbert Hoover initiated a plan to repatriate Mexicans; illegal immigrants, legal immigrants without papers and U.S. citizens of Mexican descent were all swept up in the massive effort to free up jobs for "real Americans."

Mexican desert.

Selected Prices

Baby Powder, Two Cans	$0.29
Bed Sheet	$0.65
Electric Washer	$79.85
Home Egg Hatcher	$39.95
Ice Box	$18.75
Lawn Mower	$5.49
Marshmallows, Box of 200	$0.65
Mattress	$4.65
Microphone	$1.00
Towels, Cannon, 12	$1.00

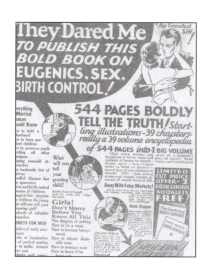

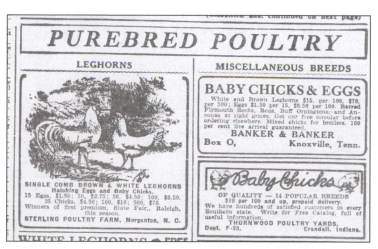

"Feeding Methods," by H.C. Knandel, *Comfort Magazine*, April 1932:

There are many methods of feeding hens for egg production. Whatever system is used, it should be so designed that maximum net returns will result. The two methods of feeding quite generally employed by poultry men are the hand and hopper method. Whichever method is adopted, it is imperative to supply the fowls with all the necessary ingredients which will not only produce a good supply of eggs but at the same time will keep the fowls in good physical condition. When the hand method is used, the mash is usually placed in hoppers so that the fowls have access to it throughout the day. The grain is fed by hand both morning and evening and is scattered in the litter. In the morning, to each 100 birds, two pounds of scratch grain are fed in the litter. At night, the birds are given all they will consume. When fowls are in heavy production, it is essential that they be fed quite heavily on scratch grain in an effort to maintain body weight so they will be able to stand up under the strain of heavy egg production.

Leghorn pullets and hens laying 50 percent or more should be fed at least 12 pounds of scratch grain per day per 100 fowls. . . .

Fowls not only require scratch grain and mash but grit, oyster shell and perhaps green food as well. Grit and oyster shell should be placed in hoppers and kept constantly before the birds. Hens, lacking teeth, must grind their food in their gizzard. Grit is the grinding machinery and should be supplied in unlimited quantities.

The Editor Looks On: Food from Everywhere," *Household Magazine*, May 1934:

Nothing shows the cosmopolitan character of the average American home more than our names for food. Hardly an important language in the world is unrepresented in the names of common articles of diet in the United States. Chocolate is Mexican Spanish; coffee from Arabic; tea from the Amoy dialect of Chinese. The word mutton has a French origin, while lamb comes from the Anglo-Saxon of our forefathers. Orange is of Persian derivation, and so is lemon. Peach goes back to classical Greek, as does cherry. Potato is one of the few English words with a Haitian origin, and the Haitians were talking of the sweet potato rather than the Irish potato. Marmalade is a slightly changed Portuguese word, but jam, to professors of language, is merely a variant of champ, which means bite and comes from a Swedish dialect. . . .

One could go on and on. The names of our foods bear witness to a variety of diet unknown in ancient or even modern times. The Venerable Bede, when about to die, gave his associates a little pepper as a prized treasure. Queen Margaret of Navarre nibbled sugar as a royal delicacy while she composed her love stories. (The sugar, appropriately enough, was unrefined.) Many persons living today can recall a time when oranges were sold only in our largest cities. Now the world is our source of food.

We left with just one trunk full of belongings. No furniture. A few metal cooking utensils. A small ceramic pitcher, because it reminded me of my mother . . . and very little clothing. We took blankets, only the very essentials.

—Emilia Castaneda, deported in 1935

The ideal farm worker is "a class of people who have not the ability to rise, who have not the initiative, who are children, who do not want to own land, who can be directed by men in the upper stratum of society.

—Texas Congressman John C. Box during a House Immigration Committee meeting on Mexican immigration

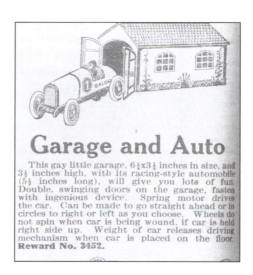

Garage and Auto

This gay little garage, 6½x3½ inches in size, and 3½ inches high, with its racing-style automobile (5½ inches long), will give you lots of fun. Double, swinging doors on the garage, fasten with ingenious device. Spring motor drives the car. Can be made to go straight ahead or in circles to right or left as you choose. Wheels do not spin when car is being wound, if car is held right side up. Weight of car releases driving mechanism when car is placed on the floor.
Reward No. 3452.

Visit the barrios of Los Angeles and you will see endless streets crowded with the shacks of the illiterate, diseased, pauperized Mexicans, taking no interest whatever in the community, living constantly on the ragged edge of starvation, bringing countless numbers of American citizens into the world with the reckless prodigality of rabbits.

—Kenneth L. Roberts, *The Saturday Evening Post*

Never again is there to be an unlimited influx of cheap alien labor; a numerical limitation of labor is here to stay, and there must be careful selection of our immigrants within the fixed limits. . . .

On the whole, immigrants from northwestern Europe furnish us the best material for American citizenship and the future of the building of the American race. They have higher living standards than the bulk of the immigrants from other lands; average higher intelligence, are better educated, more skilled, and are, on the whole, better to understand, appreciate and support our form of government. . . .

If our future population is to be prevented from deteriorating, physically and mentally, higher physical standards must be required of all immigrants. In addition, no alien should be admitted who has not an intellectual capacity superior to the American average. . . . Further, aliens whose family history indicates that they come of unsound stock should be debarred.

—Irving Fisher, professor at Yale university and chairman of the Eugenics Committee, in a statement to the Committee on Selective Immigration of the United States, January 6, 1924

1933 Profile

French Canadian Paul Lecomte did not learn much in the way of academics, but put his rowdy personality to good use, becoming a powerhouse of a fighter.

Life at Home

- Trouble followed Paul Lecomte like an angry shadow.
- His mother died only months after giving birth to him; the last of nine children, he was small as an infant and plagued by colic-inspired crying fits that only became worse when he was held.
- His older brothers and sisters had little time for the motherless boy; by the time he was two years old he had been shipped from the farm to his grandmother's sprawling mansion in the city of Quebec.
- She considered anything that came from the countryside to be low class and largely unworthy of her time, but nevertheless agreed to take in her grandson.
- There he was raised alongside the servants' children and was often relegated to the servants' dining table; his boisterous ways often upset his grandmother.
- Since the education of the unfortunate was a favorite charity, she insisted that he attend school when his time came.
- There he struggled with reading, handwriting, math and getting along with others.
- He excelled at fist-fighting, schoolyard brawling and long-distance spitting.
- His grandmother found little that was laudatory in his accomplishments.
- After he finished the sixth grade he ran away from home to work for his older brother, who was happy to have an additional hand on the farm as long as he didn't eat too much or talk back often.
- Paul did both with abandon.

Paul Lecomte was brought up by his grandmother in Quebec.

Paul's grandmother was often at odds with her boisterous grandson.

- To tame his younger brother and get some return on his food investment, Paul's brother taught him the rudiments of boxing and scheduled him every Friday night as a combatant in the area's barn fights.
- Weighing in at just 120 pounds, Paul took on all sizes of fighters during the organized brawls; he even knocked out a few, thanks to a powerful right hand and a total lack of fear.
- He quickly became a crowd favorite, especially after he spat out a broken, bloody tooth and rallied to knock out his older, bigger opponent 11 rounds later.
- At 16 he began to consider himself tiger-quality until he took on a tall thin Canadian who had enjoyed considerable military training in the high art of boxing.
- Paul lasted almost three rounds before collapsing in a pool of blood.
- He had never been whipped so completely.
- His first reaction was revenge, including thoughts of a pistol fired at close range in the dark of night.
- Then he realized he needed to know what the other man knew: punch avoidance, using his feet to avoid damage and most of all the science of counter-attacking.
- For the first time he understood the wisdom of learning from another.
- He could never ask the man who defeated him for help; but he could seek proper training, which was available in the magic land across the border in the United States.
- Recruiters from the Maine textile mills often combed French-Canada in search of willing labor.
- In 1928 America needed additional laborers—especially cheap, illegal foreign labor—after Congress imposed strict national immigration quotas and mandated literacy requirements for all immigrants.
- Paul could barely read French and certainly no English, but he figured he could haul illegal liquor boxes across the United States line and remain in America when the run was complete.
- He had made similar runs; at the risk of being arrested, this time he would acquire a bankroll and a new place to live.
- Besides, his brother's farm was in a slow death spiral; rural electrification was making farmers more prosperous in other parts of Canada, but no electrical lines had reached his farm.
- The typical Quebec farmer made $230 annually, half the income of the average farmer in Ontario.
- Within days of arriving in the United States, he had found a textile mill job, gotten in a fist fight, lost his job, received an invitation to join the Saturday night fight circuit in Maine and begun a new life.

Life at Work

- Paul Lecomte wanted to be known as the "Canadian Killer," but the locals kept referring to him as "Frenchie."
- Other fighters had great names like "Hurricane Hank" or "Perpetual Motion" or even "Kid" Lewis that brought the roaring crowd to its feet.
- In the land of liberty, they were heroes.
- His nickname of Frenchie implied that he was a foreigner and always solicited "boo" and "go back home," especially after he would knock out the hometown favorite.
- He quickly took on the villain's role.

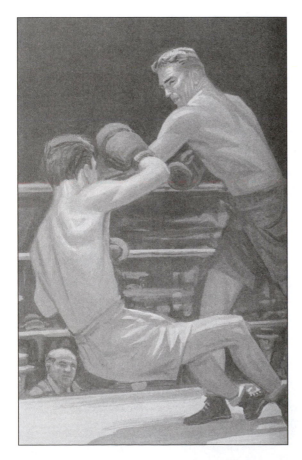

At 16-years-old, Paul was a crowd-pleasing boxer, taking on any opponent.

Paul ran away from home after sixth grade to work on his brother's farm.

- Within a few months he had built a powerful reputation for savagery; area fight fans showed up just to bet against him.
- He quickly learned how to keep the fight close and the betting lively to give everyone, especially the professional gamblers, their money's worth.
- During his first six months in Bangor, Maine, he found an Irish promoter who had married a French Canadian and spoke French who was willing to train the 160-pound boxing machine, schedule three to five fights a month and, unlike some managers, not steal all his earnings.
- Only once did money cause an argument: one night when the crowd was large and his after-fight bag lighter than usual.
- That was the night he learned how much a $100 bill can lighten the pay bag but thicken the wallet.
- Slowly he learned he could trust another man.
- Life in the United States was frustrating for him; why had no one bothered to learn French?
- After all, Americans shared a friendly border with Canada, where affluent French-speakers were important; the least Americans could do was to learn a little French.
- Paul's first fluency in English was a long string of curses and rude rebukes.
- He was not even sure they made sense, but English-speakers would invariably leave him alone.
- Luckily, Bangor's legions of tough, self-sufficient lumbermen included a crop of French Canadians whose accents brought him great comfort.
- And more than a few American girls were willing to endure his halting English to spend time with the muscular fighter from French-Quebec.

President Roosevelt's popular fireside chats fascinated Paul.

- By 1932-1933 steady paychecks were getting harder for everyone to find, including circuit riding boxers supported by gambling interests.
- A few times Paul even helped run illegal liquor across the border; Prohibition was dead—everyone knew that—and people still needed to drink their cares away while they waited for the laws to change.
- Paul kept all his money on his person, so he had little interest in the four-day bank holiday declared in March 1933, but was fascinated by President Franklin Roosevelt's "fireside chats" delivered over the radio.
- After five years in America he fully understood that the most powerful man in the country was willing to talk to him—an immigrant—personally about the future of the U.S.
- It was like having powerful friends in high places.
- The radio broadcasts were his source of information concerning the newly created Civilian Conservation Corps, or CCC, designed to employ millions of young men between the ages of 17 and 27.
- This volunteer army would work in national forests, parks and federal lands during nine-month stints and get paid.
- And young men with money loved to watch fights and gamble, Paul reasoned.
- Thus was born the idea for a traveling boxing match, touring from camp to camp, accompanied by friends willing to take a few bets.
- By October the first fights were arranged; in one night Paul would battle his sparring partner to a convincing sixth-round knockout, then take on the camp's bravest brawler.
- The bets rolled in despite the depressed economy.
- As 1933 came to a close, Paul was fighting under two different names: "Frenchie" in New England and "The Canadian Killer" in the CCC camps across the South and Midwest.

Life in the Community: Bangor, Maine

- Located in central Maine, Bangor started life as a lie.
- In the late 1500s David Ingram sailed up the Penobscot River to what is now Bangor.
- When Ingram returned to Europe, he reported finding a wealthy city whose streets were lined with gold and tall buildings with casements of silver.
- Excited at Ingram's tale, some Europeans believed Ingram had discovered Norumbega, the lost city of gold.
- In 1604, Samuel de Champlain sailed into Penobscot Bay, up the Penobscot River, and anchored at the mouth of what is now the Kenduskeag Stream.
- Champlain didn't find a wealthy city; only the Tarratines, an American Indian tribe.
- The Tarratines and Europeans found a mutual interest, not in gold, but in fur trading.
- In 1769, Jacob Buswell, his wife, and nine children from Salisbury, Massachusetts, became the first Europeans to settle at the mouth of the Kenduskeag Stream.

- The building of the first sawmill in Bangor in 1772 marked the beginning of a century of dominance by Bangor in the world lumber industry.
- In the mid 1830s, Bangor was home to more than 300 sawmills, earning the city the undisputed title "Lumber Capital of the World."
- Lumberjacks harvested the northern Maine woods and sent their logs down the Penobscot River where they were picked up by runners in Bangor.
- The Penobscot River would become swollen from shore to shore with logs; people were literally able to walk from one shore to the other.
- After the Bangor mills processed the lumber, some of the lumber was then sent farther down the Penobscot to Winterport and Belfast, where some of the world's finest schooners were built.
- Bangor's prosperity in the lumber industry began to fade in the late 1800s, as Americans began to settle farther west and harvest trees in other forest-rich states such as Minnesota and Oregon.
- The ice industry tapped another abundant commodity of the area and flourished between 1876 and 1906; every winter the Penobscot River froze and the ice was harvested.
- Penobscot River ice was considered to be the finest in the world and was shipped as far as India.
- The years of the Depression did not hit Bangor as hard as some cities: only a few shops and no banks closed.
- Between 1840 and 1930 approximately 900,000 French Canadians emigrated from Canada to the United States.
- By 1900 most French Canadians and Acadians could claim some members of their family lived in the United States, often in the New England states.
- Paul Lecomte was sure that at least three of his older brothers and sisters lived the States, but he had not had contact with them in a decade and could not be sure of their location.
- Emigration to a new land always comes at a cost—economic, emotional and cultural.
- When an individual or family leaves, assets like homes must be liquidated, often at a loss, and possessions left behind.
- To leave behind family and friends meant the loss of a support system, lifelong friendships and the ability to tell a precious inside joke developed in childhood.
- Culturally, immigrants abandon the smell of candles burning during the Easter vigil, the sound of a sling blade chopping grain or the comforting honk of geese flying overhead.
- In exchange, French Canadians journeyed to noisy factory jobs where they were forced to contend with alien languages, strange customs and offensive foods.
- The search for a better standard of living drove thousands to emigrate despite the hardships.

30's radio stars George Burns and Gracie Allen.

HISTORICAL SNAPSHOT
1933

- Congress recognized the independence of the Philippines
- An uprising of Guardia Civil in Spain left 25 dead
- The White Sands National Monument in New Mexico was established; Mount Rushmore was dedicated
- German President Paul von Hindenburg made Adolf Hitler chancellor even though Gen. Kurt von Hammerstein-Equord tried to block the appointment
- The first episode of *The Lone Ranger* radio program was broadcast on station WXYZ in Detroit

Adolf Hilter.

- The Twentieth Amendment to the Constitution was declared in effect, changing the inauguration date of members of Congress from March 4 to January 3
- President-elect Franklin Roosevelt escaped an assassination attempt in Miami by Giuseppe Zangara, an unemployed New Jersey bricklayer from Italy
- *Newsweek* magazine was first published under the title *News-Week*
- Blondie Boopadoop married Dagwood Bumstead in the comic strip *Blondie*
- Ground was broken for the Golden Gate Bridge in San Francisco
- Francis Perkins was appointed Secretary of Labor, the first woman in the Cabinet
- Hollywood premiered *King Kong* in New York featuring Fay Wray

- President Franklin D. Roosevelt ordered a four-day bank holiday in order to stop large amounts of money from being withdrawn
- George Darrow added some copyrighted art work to the board game Monopoly and began selling it commercially in Philadelphia
- President Roosevelt delivered the first of his radio "fireside chats"
- Congress authorized the Civilian Conservation Corps to relieve rampant unemployment
- Nazi Germany began persecuting Jews with a boycott of Jewish-owned businesses; 55,000 people staged a protest in New York against Hitler
- The United States went off the gold standard by presidential proclamation
- The Tennessee Valley Authority Act was created to build dams in the Tennessee Valley

- Saudi Arabia gave Standard Oil of California exclusive rights to explore for oil
- The first All-star baseball game was played
- American aviator Wiley Post completed the first solo flight around the world in seven days, 18 hours and 45 minutes
- The first issue of *Esquire* magazine was published
- Due to rising anti-Semitism and anti-intellectualism in Hitler's Germany, Albert Einstein immigrated to Princeton, New Jersey

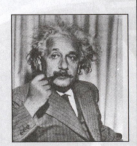

Albert Einstein.

Selected Prices

Ad in *Ladies' Home Journal,* Full-page	$12,500
Babies' Rubber Pants, Three Pairs	$0.22
Boys' Knickers	$0.77
Cedar Chest	$12.95
Cod Liver Oil, Gallon, for Livestock	$1.79
Model Airplane	$6.50
Movie Ticket, Adult	$0.25
Phonograph Records, Five	$0.29
Sanitary Napkins, Kotex, Dozen	$0.85
Silk Hosiery	$0.89

For Better Health — Mickey Mouse — MILK

Plenty of Water at the FAUCETS... with a MYERS WATER SYSTEM

WEAR HOSE WE FURNISH without cost and start cash earnings quickly. Everybody buys hose. Guaranteed to wear from 4 to 8 months without holes, snags or runs or REPLACED FREE. Big repeat sales. Doris Jensen, of Illinois, reports earnings of $11.00 in 5½ hours. Received 2 new cars as bonuses. Charles Mills of Minn., earned $120 in one week and received 2 new cars, as extra bonuses. Extra hosiery for your personal use sent with outfit, no extra cost—send size, no money. Rush name on penny postal for sample outfit, details. ACT NOW! WILKNIT HOSIERY CO. Midway C-12 Greenfield, Ohio

HOSE for your Personal Use Sent With Outfit

CAPACITY is as important as RELIABILITY in a water system. The famous old MYERS trademark assures you both. You may open one faucet at a time; or different members of the family may draw water simultaneously — in kitchen, bathroom or laundry — at outside hose taps — in barnyard and outbuildings. There will *always* be plenty of water at all faucets, when you have a precision-built MYERS Water System of adequate capacity. Quality is never sacrificed to price in MYERS products. The dependability of MYERS Water Systems is proved daily in thousands of farm and suburban homes.

RUNNING WATER — YOUR FAMILY DESERVES IT

"Pump Builders Since 1870"

Deep and shallow well models to meet all needs. For operation by electricity, gasoline engine, windmill or hand power. Write today for interesting free booklet.

The F. E. Myers & Bro. Co. 550 Orange St., Ashland, Ohio Send free Water System Booklet and name of your nearest dealer.

Please be sure to get the package with the picture of Niagara Falls and the N. B. C. Uneeda Seal.

SHREDDED WHEAT

A Product of NATIONAL BISCUIT COMPANY "Uneeda Bakers"

FORD V-8

New Touring Sedans, with Built-in Trunk

New among the Ford body styles for this year are the Tudor and Fordor Touring Sedans. Their beauty, comfort, safety, V-8 performance and economy make them popular, practical family cars. . . . The built-in trunk accents the length of these Touring Sedans and solves the luggage problem. It locks securely and is rain-proof and dust-proof. The large opening makes it easy to get luggage in and out. . . . The Ford Touring Sedans are upholstered in a choice of Bedford Cord or Wool Suede, with taupe color appointments to match. Everything is distinctively new and modern. . . . Four especially important features are the V-8 engine, Center-Poise riding comfort, all-steel body and Safety Glass throughout at no extra cost. V-8 power and smoothness mean more enjoyable motoring. These years on the road in the service of a million and a half owners have proved that the Ford V-8 is the most economical Ford ever built.

"Garden Planning Dramatic Policy Change; To End Regular Boxing, Wrestling Dates," by James P. Dawson, *The New York Times*, February 13, 1933:

The days of professional boxing and wrestling, on the comprehensive scale on which these two sports events were promoted heretofore, are numbered at Madison Square Garden.

Unless all signs fail, boxing, which, as an entertainment in the old Garden under the late Tex Rickard, was primarily responsible for the present arena, will be relegated to the status of minor importance in the future activities in the Garden.

As far as can be determined, it is proposed, commencing next fall, to eliminate the regular weekly boxing day Friday on the Garden's calendar, and the custom of semi-monthly wrestling attractions. There will be substituted only important boxing and wrestling events when, and if, they develop. Amateur boxing, it is understood, will be encouraged. . . .

Hockey, circus, rodeo, bike races, track meets and various tradeshows all give a good account of themselves, according to reliable information, but boxing and wrestling are not so profitable. Therefore, the conclusion is reached that before long many of the regular Friday night boxing and Monday night wrestling dates will be eliminated, and will be replaced by other attractions which these new improvements are making available.

"Lavelle Praises Italians of City, Americanizing of Immigrants Is Scarcely a Problem Any Longer, He Declares," *The New York Times*, October 26, 1930:

The problem of Americanizing the Italian immigrants has corrected itself to a very marked degree in the opinion of Mgr. Michael J. Lavelle, rector of St. Patrick's Cathedral. Mgr. Lavelle has been in charge of the Italian parishes in the archdiocese of New York for nearly 25 years, having been appointed to this task by the late Cardinal Farley and reappointed by Cardinal Hayes. There are now 58 parishes for Italians in the archdiocese.

"There is scarcely any Italian question today," said Mgr. Lavelle yesterday. The situation with regard to Italian immigrants is excellent. They are becoming good Americans, good Catholics and good citizens. They follow the American ways of observing the laws of the Church and are thrifty, industrious people who settle down, find homes and raise large families.

"For some time past gradual improvement has been apparent. Like every other immigrant the Italian came here to better his condition. His first need was to get work and learn the language. Elder immigrants found the language hard and were slow, in consequence, in adapting themselves to American ways and customs. They kept together a great deal in colonies and for quite a while were somewhat aloof.

"With regard to the support of the Church immigrants were somewhat perplexed. They did not understand our way of doing things, and it required much care to make them feel at home. Some of the Italian priests who came here accustomed only to the ways of the old country found it difficult to understand American customs, especially the practice of the people supporting the Church and being responsible for it. In their country the State supports the Church without taxation. It was with patience and care in building up the work with the immigrant that the problems of adjustment have been largely perfected."

It was to the women that Mgr. Lavelle gave much of the credit for what he called the improved conditions. "The earlier immigrants were mostly men and boys, largely musicians and artists," he said, and for quite a while they did not take permanent root. But once the women began to come and establish homes and raise families, the Italians settled down and became a substantial part of our population. They are supporting themselves and are becoming stronger every day. They are building their churches, beginning to build their schools and are thinking of hospitals and orphan asylums."

"Immigrants," *The New York Times*, December 24, 1932:

The Secretary of State has reported to the President of the United States the number of quota immigrants has fallen during the last fiscal year to little more than 10,000 persons (12,697), which is only 8 percent of the total annual quotas. This marked reduction is due to the restrictive policy that has been followed during the years of the Depression. The estimate is that 500,000 aliens who would normally have emigrated to the United States have been refused visas by their consular officers abroad, chiefly on the grounds that the applications are unable to give the necessary assurance that they are not likely to become public charges. Had they come they would have swollen the numbers of the unemployed. No one can question the wisdom of this policy in general.

There is also a marked decrease in the non-quota immigration, barely a fifth of what it was in 1930, the total number of visas granted to them being 24,040.

"The Blow That Hurts," Gene Tunney, *Atlantic* magazine, 1939:

A punch in the nose may seem to be an intensely personal thing, much more so, for example, than pushing the queen's rook pawn on a board of checkered squares. Yet I had been astonished to hear of the enmities and feuds in the game of chess, that epitome of abstract combat. The queen's rook's pawn seems to have occasioned a surprising lot of rancor and fury. I find it difficult to understand, but then I had been merely a boxer, a devotee of one of the most noted of all physical-contest sports. . . .

By way of contrast, take prize fighting. Few human beings have fought each other more savagely more often than Harry Greb and I. We punched and cut and bruised each other in a series of bouts, five of them. In the first, Greb gave me a ferocious beating, closed both eyes, broke my nose, chipped my teeth, and cut my lips to pieces. He did everything but knock me out. In our last fight I beat him about as badly, so badly that he was helpless in the later rounds. He seemed like a dead-game fighter, wanting to be spared the indignity of being knocked out. Pain meant nothing; he didn't want the folks back home to read of his being knocked out. From the beginning of our first to the end of our last bout, Greb and I went through the ferocious gamut of giving and taking, hitting and being hit. We were always the best of friends; never any ill will or anger. You see, we were not chess players.

There stands the city of Bangor, 50 miles up the Penobscot at the head of navigation, the principal lumber depot on this continent, like a star on the edge of night, still hewing at the forests of which it is built.

—Henry David Thoreau, upon visiting Bangor in 1846

Forest Workers Ready for New Summer Season as Congress Debates Future

BUILDING A NEW FOREST ROAD

ENROLLING RECRUITS FOR THE C

NAVY IN WAR MANEUV

New Ships, Airplanes, and S marines Tested in Pacific

ELABORATE GAMES AHE

Concentrations in Alaskan and Ha ian Waters Are Features—Fleet Return to California Stations

How Bangor got its name: /bangorinfo.com/history.html:

Accounts vary on how many settlers were at the plantation—some sources say there were as many as 576, while most others say there were between 200 and 300—but in 1791 the settlers decided to incorporate themselves as a town. Because Maine was part of Massachusetts at the time, the settlers had to petition the Massachusetts General Court to become incorporated. The Rev. Seth Noble, who had arrived in 1786 from Wakefield, Massachusetts, convinced his neighbors they should call their town Sunbury. Noble's neighbors gave him the task of going to Boston to deliver the town's petition.

While waiting to present the petition in Boston, Noble, an organist and composer, began whistling one of his favorite tunes: "Bangor," a Welsh hymn written by Tans'ur. In Welsh, "Bangor" means "high choir." In Celtic, "Bangor" means "the white choir."

When a court official asked Noble what his town wanted to be called, Noble was caught off guard. Daydreaming, perhaps, Noble thought he'd been asked the name of the tune he'd been whistling. So instead of saying "Sunbury," he said "Bangor."

And Bangor it was. On Feb. 25, 1791, the General Court approved Bangor, not Sunbury, for incorporation.

Historians don't know why Noble didn't correct the court. Perhaps he decided the name of one of his favorite tunes sounded better than Sunbury.

"Talks with Girls," by Cousin Marion, *Comfort Magazine*, January 1932:

Last spring I asked what made a girl popular, and the men fell all over themselves to tell me their ideas on the subject.

When the girls were given the same opportunity to express their ideas on what made a man popular I naturally expected to receive as many letters. . . . Weeks passed and not a single letter! I was beginning to think it was a case of women being satisfied with anything masculine and no questions asked when the letters began to straggle in. Finally there were almost as many as the men wrote, but the evident delay in writing them made me wonder if that "putting off" was responsible for the fact that men go ahead and do important things in the world while women waste their time and energy in doing the inessentials first with the result that they never do accomplish big things in life. Of course some women do, we all know that, but I wonder if it's not because some of them learned the wisdom of conserving their strength for something important instead of doing something first that could have been done later just as well or left undone entirely.

The average woman, when faced with a piece of writing, something that requires concentration and thought, is likely to put the room in which she is to work in order before sitting down to her desk; she may even put the entire house in order, stopping to wash and iron a few silk things and cleaning the refrigerator before she finally gets down to work. By that time she is too tired to think.

A man wouldn't do that. If his desk wasn't in order he'd push things back to make room for his paper and go to work. The silk things and the refrigerator, or whatever is the masculine equivalent for these things, could go unwashed and uncleaned. They would cease to exist until such time as he had finished the writing he wanted to do.

A woman would suddenly, and for no reason, decide that it was time the closets were cleaned and sprayed in case there should be a moth, or that her hair needed an oil shampoo before she had another permanent, or that she ought to find the poem Cousin Emma wanted.

After the closets were cleaned and sprayed she'd give herself an oil shampoo, and while her hair was drying she'd hunt through scrapbooks and envelopes of poems in an effort to find the particular poem Cousin Emma had mentioned.

A man wouldn't know a moth if he saw one and he'd let the barber worry about his hair, and as for Cousin Emma and her poem, he just couldn't be bothered looking for it. (Let her remember her own poems. Probably it didn't amount to anything anyway, and she'd only lose it again if she had it.)

continued

"Talks with Girls," . . . *(continued)*

If I have mentioned any of my outstanding failings in the matter of getting to work, it is because I want to make dilatory women see the error of their ways and to urge upon them the necessity of making a New Year resolution to do the important things first.

That's a fine resolution to make, short, concise and to the point. I ought to know. It's one of my favorite resolutions.

Now we'll find out what makes men popular. (I've always wondered.)

A Georgia girl writes: "I think manners and appearance should come first. Girls admire a boy with nice manners. Be a gentleman at all times. Wear neatly pressed and well-fitting clothes. Nothing is more horrible than saggy clothes. A girl wants a man for a pal and not for an affectionate flatterer. Of course a little praise now and then is appreciated, but be reasonable about it. A girl likes to be proud of the man she goes out with. He should be able to carry on a decent conversation."

Compared with a saggy chin muscle, saggy clothes are things of beauty but girl-from-Georgia is too young to know anything about saggy muscles.

A freshman from the Ohio State University expresses herself very ably. "Cleanliness and good health always help to make a man popular. I like men who are amusing, men who can talk on any and every subject. Men who are always serious are frightfully boresome. A sense of humor is a requisite. Most girls like to have their boyfriends know what to do and when to do it. They needn't follow Emily Post in every detail, but they should observe the most important rules. Few things embarrass me as much as walking with a fellow who doesn't know enough to walk along the outside of the sidewalk and gracefully keep there despite crossing streets. Being polite goes a long way with girls. There may be a few who like the cave-man type, but I think they are in the minority; however, I think fellows should have some will power. . . . When a fellow asks me for a date I like to have him know where we are going, not only so I'll know how to dress, but to save the fuss when we start of, 'Where shall we go?' 'Anywhere you say.' 'No, you decide'. . . . And there's that little something called personality. In short, it's personality combined with a sense of humor, good manners, ability to talk and be a good listener, neatness and cleanliness, and ability to plan a good time which makes a man popular with girls. Good looks? They help, but are not absolutely essential."

1936 PROFILE

Miguel Guerrero Rodriguez's life as a history professor in Spain changed dramatically when he emigrated to the United States to escape the dangers of civil war at home.

Life at Home

- Miguel Guerrero Rodriguez, born of a college professor and a woman with rumored royal lineage, was 25 years old and living in Salamanca, Spain, in 1930.
- He lived with his mother and father in a three-bedroom apartment just off Calle Rua Mayor, near the Plaza Mayor.
- Spanish children past the age of 18 living with their parents was common; apartments were expensive and housing hard to find.
- The proximity of their apartment to the Plaza Mayor meant that Miguel and his family were close to the hustle and bustle of the busy day and night life.
- Salamanca was organized literally around the Plaza Mayor and all the streets fanned out from there.
- Some of the streets leading from it were named for the direction of the next closest town; for example, Calle Zamora was in the direction of Zamora.
- He and his friends often met in the Plaza Mayor for coffee and tapas in between classes and before dinner.
- Miguel took great pride in the city's Plaza Mayor, rumored to be the most beautiful in Spain.
- Following in his father's footsteps, Miguel was a history professor at the University of Salamanca, the oldest university still in existence in Spain and one of the oldest in Europe.
- Growing up in the oldest part of town contributed to Miguel's decision to specialize in history as a professor.
- The culture of the university, as well, sparked his imagination.
- He especially admired the facade of the university that was built and designed under the direction of Queen Isabella of Castile and King Ferdinand II of Aragon.
- It was divided into columns and rows with each row increasing upward in its complexity and importance of characters.

Miguel Rodriguez was 25 when he left Spain.

The grandeur of Salamanca, Spain.

Miguel lived just off the Plaza Major.

Miguel admired the façade of the University.

- And of course, the Roman Catholic Pope was at the top.
- As a Catholic child in a Catholic country, Miguel attended Mass every Sunday in the historic New Cathedral with his parents.
- The church was a short walk from his house; he enjoyed the services more for the historic relics, architecture, and sculpture than the words being recited.
- He never debated his religion.
- He knew about other religions, but he had never had personal experience with any other since Spain was almost entirely Catholic.
- The solidarity of a single religion brought a level of togetherness, and helped establish social unity.
- Miguel also enjoyed the Spanish schedule of a very light breakfast at 9 a.m., tapas at 12, a large lunch at 2 or 3, a siesta from 2 to 5 during which no one worked, tapas at 6 or 7, and dinner at 9 or 10.
- Miguel had heard that a few shops in Madrid were staying open even during siesta, which he thought ludicrous—practically blasphemous.
- The Spanish routine guaranteed a sense of community, and personal relationships among family and friends were fostered.
- Even though the phone system had recently been improved due to ITT, an American company, winning the concession, Miguel and many other Spaniards still preferred to visit in person.

  - From his son's early years, Miguel's father stressed that being educated was one of the most powerful weapons a person could possess.
  - With it, he could defend himself against the onslaught of powerful men seeking to control the populace.
  - Also, education was an escape from the economic poverty of his fellow countrymen; two-thirds of the population worked in the agriculture sector, but only one-third of the gross domestic product was due to agriculture.
  - Essentially a farm town with a historic university situated in the middle, Salamanca owed much of its economy to the university and the students who attended.
  - By 1930 the dictatorship of General Miguel Primo de Rivera was drawing to a close and everyone was feeling the pinch of the economic bankruptcy caused by the dictator.
  - The Republic was formed in 1931.
  - Under the Republic and its new constitution, social reforms abounded: the right to divorce, freedom of speech and association, separation of Church and State, and women being granted the right to vote.
  - Although Miguel supported these changes, he felt that the Republic might have stepped too far too fast.
  - With all the new reforms, new schisms quickly formed and anarchist groups grew rapidly
  - Salamanca, being a small university town with farmland a few steps outside of the city center, was isolated from the violence associated with angry mobs in Madrid and Barcelona.
  - Miguel, however, read the newspaper reports of churches, convents, and religious buildings being burned all around Spain.
  - As a scholar of history, Miguel was deeply troubled that people could deface such historically important monuments, but said little publicly.
  - The conditions in Spain continued to deteriorate and grow more violent month by month.

- Unable to impact the world around him, Miguel taught his classes, met with friends and kept his opinions largely to himself.
- On October 7, 1934, Miguel read reports of an uprising by socialists and anarchists of the Asturias in which miners occupied the capital and killed authorities and clergymen, and burned theatres and the university.
- The next day, he signed up for a three-week intensive English class at the university and began to researching his transportation options to the United States.
- The depression in America was a concern, but he reasoned that life in the United States would be better than the worsening situation in Spain.
- He discussed his options with his mother and father and stressed the need for the entire family to leave.
- His father understood the urgency of the situation
- Miguel's mother Mercedes refused to consider leaving; she was born in Spain and would die in Spain.
- Besides, she said, she was Catholic and the heathens of the United States surely would corrupt her moral values.
- At age 29, Miguel bought a ticket for a ship that was scheduled to leave port on January 20, 1935.
- He told his students goodbye and talked extensively with them about his reasons for leaving.
- He wanted them to pay attention to the events that were happening all around them, knowing that these events would ultimately shape the future of Spain for centuries to come.
- On the 10-day trip, Miguel made several friends who were also leaving Spain for the United States.
- They talked of the building political tensions and their very uncertain future.
- Another man, Fernando Perfecto, seemed to have an idea of what life would be like in the United States.
- He had already arranged to travel to West Virginia where he heard there was a lot of work in the coal mines.
- He had heard that there were many others from Spain; besides coal mining was only temporary until he could learn enough English to find another job similar to his position in Spain as a newspaper editor.

Salamanca was a religious city, with many cathedrals and churches.

Architectural details in Miguel's hometown.

- He even heard about groups of Americans that would help immigrants.
- He said they called it "Americanizing" immigrants.
- He wasn't exactly sure what that meant, but he figured that with so many people interested in helping, things could not possibly go wrong.
- On the ship Miguel practiced the English he had learned in his class.
- He knew how to say his name, ask for the doctor, get directions to the bathroom, and a few random words.
- It was not enough, but it was all he had.

Life at Work

- Once in the United States, Fernando and Miguel took a train to Charleston, West Virginia, the capital of the state.
- From there they hitchhiked to southern West Virginia, where Fernando's cousin was already working.
- Their destination was Little Fork Valley to the headquarters of Pocahontas Fuel Company, which owned two mines there.
- The actual village was called Maybeury, a mining town built by the Pocahontas Fuel
- Company for the miners and their families.
- When Miguel and Fernando arrived in Maybeury, they saw rows of frame houses, all eerily the same, with open board fences.
- Within each fence were double red brick coal bins, two for each house.
- Poplar trees lined the fences.
- Miguel was overwhelmed.
- This was not what he had imagined.
- Where was the hustle and bustle of America that he had heard about?
- He had not explored yet, but he had a sinking suspicion that there was no Plaza Mayor.
- Over the next couple of days, Miguel was introduced to the manager of the Pocahontas Fuel Company by Fernando's cousin.
- He was shown a frame house where he could live with two other miners from Spain.
- At first, Miguel was excited that he would be living with his fellow countrymen.
- However, his delight was short-lived when he realized that although the men spoke Spanish, they had no interest in being his friends.
- The other men had been in West Virginia for over 10 years and spoke English fluently.
- They had banded together and shed their Spanish roots.
- Miguel was simply a reminder of their past.
- During the evenings, they still spoke in Spanish, but the focus was how to get what they wanted.
- They fully understood that interethnic cooperation was essential to survival.
- Other Spaniards came over and they sat around the table discussing the "rules of the game."
- Miguel was not invited for these sessions; he was not established enough, and he had nothing to offer the conversation.
- From what he understood about politics, Miguel saw their ideology as a kind of "social republicanism."
- It combined notions of social and economic reform with democratic ideals.
- Occasionally he tried to talk about Spain and the scenery, but he was always cut off.
- This was their home now; Spain was dead to them.
- At his house, the water was supplied by hydrants that were positioned at regular intervals along the street supplied by a tank that sat high up the valley side.

Pocahontas, Miguel's employer, gave vouchers to its workers.

- The house had no plumbing, but was clean and moderately comfortable.
- The Pocahontas Fuel Company demanded clean houses and imposed harsh penalties to enforce this standard.
- Sewage was dumped in the stream running nearby.
- Miguel's first day of work was a big shock.
- For most of his life, he had lived prosperously, devoid of harsh labor conditions, and he had never met a black person.
- There were many Negroes, as he learned to call them, in the mines.
- He had heard about the existence of these darker-skinned people, but Spain was fairly homogeneous.
- By the end of the day, Miguel realized that he looked just like a Negro with the dark layer of coal dust that he acquired on every exposed portion of skin.
- His first day was also full of yelling; the foreman rapidly became hostile at his slow rate of progress.

Miguel wasn't used to the hard work or black people at the coal mines.

- Fernando's cousin whispered that it was normal to be afraid on the first day; he would get used to it.
- After several weeks, indeed, Miguel did not think twice about working in the mine, until he heard about a mine explosion a couple of towns over.
- A few days later, men started arriving from that town, looking for work.
- From then on, he refused to enter a mine if he smelled gas.
- However, explosions were not the only worry.
- Miguel also heard reports of men dying from falling roofs and coal.
- These reports always made him wary.
- When he was not working, the company commissary was the social and business center of the village.
- It was no Plaza Mayor, but it would have to do.
- Here was where Miguel was paid, and the company store was where trading was done in English.
- Miguel was timid about spending time on the porch after hours, but eventually his need for a social outlet helped him overcome his bashfulness.
- He contributed very little in the beginning, not only because he was new to the town, but also because he simply did not yet understand English.
- Up until now, he had gotten along with the help of Fernando and his cousin.
- As the weeks went by, he extended his porch time and greatly improved his English.
- After three short months, he was nearly fluent.
- He could not yet read English, which pained him since he had been so educated in Spain.
- A year after Miguel had been in Maybeury, his prayers were answered.
- The people that "Americanize" immigrants came to help him.
- They consisted of teachers, settlement house workers and people who called themselves "professional patriots."
- He was walking away from the porch one day when a middle thirties aged woman approached him; her name was Susan Cranford and that she had heard that he was looking to learn to read in English.
- She explained that she was a teacher from the northern part of West Virginia and had come to help the immigrants become "adjusted" to American life.
- She explained that there was a class on Tuesday and Thursday nights in the school house for the children; English would be taught as well as "essential" American values such as "the proper way to work" and "the proper way to live."

- She made reference to Henry Ford in that the ideals that she was teaching now were ideals implemented by Henry Ford.
- Miguel was not exactly sure who Henry Ford was, but had occasionally seen a car go down the street with the name Ford on it.
- He supposed that the two were related, but wasn't sure.
- "The proper way to work" meant that Miguel was supposed to obey orders from the foreman and not to question him.
- On "the proper way to live," the teacher talked about the American schedule wherein breakfast was at 6 a.m. before work, lunch was at 12, and dinner was the largest meal of the day at 7 or 7:30.
- Until now, Miguel had tried to continue his old schedule of eating but found it difficult.
- Without the siesta, he often felt lethargic, that is, until the foreman started yelling at him.
- The new schedule seemed to make a little more sense with his work schedule.
- Yet, he still felt like he was losing a part of himself by changing.
- The teacher also talked about American holidays.
- Previously, Miguel had celebrated Christmas, but he also celebrated the coming of the Three Kings.
- In the U.S., this holiday was not that important and no break from work was granted.
- The teacher even warned that missing work on this day was grounds for layoff, as this was not an adoption of "American" views.

Life in the Community: Salamanca, Spain

- On July 17, 1936, the Spanish Civil War started.
- Miguel received word two days later and immediately felt an enormous amount of guilt.
- Although his mother and father had refused to leave, he still felt as if he should have made them come with him.
- The conflict was between the Nationalists led by Francisco Franco and the Republicans.
- Conversation in his house immediately focused on the scraps of war news they were able to find.
- Everyone still had family members living in Spain, and each new report of violence increased their worry.
- According to American reports, the Republican side was filled with intellectuals from all over the world who believed that Franco represented an end to social reforms, liberal thinking, and freedom.
- From inside Spain, the rebellion was opposed by the government and most urban workers, many of whom were members of the Communist, Socialist and anarchist groups.
- Miguel's father wrote to him and told him that he was not supportive of the rebellion, but he was also very neutral.
- He was old, he explained, and living out the rest of his days peacefully was good enough.
- In October of 1936, Miguel learned that one of his best friends, also a teacher of history at the University of Salamanca, was killed by firing squad.
- Apparently, he was teaching pro-Republic views to his students.
- In particular, his lecture about the importance of the separation of Church and State had struck the nerve of a Catholic pupil with radically conservative parents.
- The next day, the Fascist authorities entered his classroom and escorted him out.

- He was executed in the Plaza Mayor as an example to everyone of the dangers of opposing the Church and the Nationalist government.
- That day, Miguel wrote a letter to his father and told him not to say anything against the Church, to his friends or anyone.
- By 1936, Miguel was now considered one of the older immigrants and was allowed to join in the conversation.
- He found himself adopting the views of his housemates, including those of racial prejudice, especially against the black workers.
- Miguel found that in whichever immigrant circle he was in, blame and hatred was typically placed on the blacks.
- Along with acceptance in the group, Miguel acquired the coal miner's cough.
- Granted, the older, more experienced workers had a much worse cough, but Miguel knew that his health was deteriorating.
- A year earlier, his friend Fernando had died in a mining explosion that had killed five others.
- He had received word from his father that his mother was not in good health.
- Their letters had become scarce; the oppression had started to wear on his parents' health.
- Miguel did the only thing that was proactive on his end.
- He rented a typewriter and composed a letter to Columbia University seeking employment as a Spanish professor.
- And he would return to Spain as soon as he had the money, he told himself.

Historical Snapshot
1936

- In Berlin, the Nazi officials declared that their treatment of the Jews was not any of the business of the League of Nations
- *Billboard* magazine published its first music hit parade
- Baseball's Hall of Fame inducted its first members: Ty Cobb, Babe Ruth, Honus Wagner, Christy Mathewson and Walter Johnson
- Standard Oil of California found gas and oil at their initial Saudi Arabia test well The first Social Security checks were put in the mail
- Germany's Adolph Hitler announced plans to build Volkswagens
- The German press warned that all Jews who voted in the upcoming elections would be arrested
- Bruno Hauptmann, convicted for the kidnapping of the Lindbergh baby, was electrocuted in Trenton, New Jersey
- Rodgers and Hammerstein's musical *On Your Toes* premiered
- The PanAm Clipper began regular passenger flights from San Francisco to Honolulu
- *Peter and the Wolf*, a symphonic tale for children by Sergei Prokofiev, had its world premiere in Moscow
- Edward Ravenscroft patented the screw-on bottle cap with a pour lip
- Heavyweight boxing champion Joe Louis knocked out Max Schmeling of Germany
- The novel *Gone with the Wind* by Margaret Mitchell was published in New York. A 40-hour work week law was approved for federal workers
- The Triborough Bridge linking Manhattan, the Bronx and Queens opened
- The Spanish Civil War erupted after a leftist government was elected during the Second Republic; Gen. Francisco Franco led an uprising of army troops based in Spanish North Africa

- RCA broadcast the first real TV program featuring dancing, film on locomotives, a Bonwit Teller fashion show, a monologue from *Tobacco Road* and comedy
- The 11th Olympic games, dubbed "The Nazi Games," opened in Berlin with a ceremony presided over by Adolf Hitler
- The United States declared non-intervention in the Spanish Civil War
- Spanish poet Garcia Lorca was arrested in Granada and disappeared shortly thereafter
- President Franklin Roosevelt gave the FBI authority to pursue fascists and communists
- President Franklin Roosevelt dedicated Boulder Dam
- Eugene O'Neill won the Nobel Prize in Literature; his work included *A Long Day's Journey Into Night* and *The Iceman Cometh*

Selected Prices

Antifreeze, Gallon	$1.00
Baby Carriage	$12.98
Electric Coffee Mill	$9.75
Flashlight	$0.55
Fountain Pen	$1.00
Garden Tractor	$242.00
Girdle	$0.79
Lawn Mower, Power	$69.50
Motor Yacht	$26,300
Sofa and Chair	$66.85

Timeline of West Virginia Mining

1742

Coal was first discovered by John Peter Salley in the area now comprising West Virginia.

1810

The first commercial coal mine opened near Wheeling for blacksmithing and domestic use.

1843

The Baltimore and Ohio Railroad began shipping coal to Baltimore.

1863

West Virginia became a state.

1875

A bill was introduced in the West Virginia legislature to provide for better ventilation in coal mines.

1883

The first state mine inspector was hired.

1884

The state mine inspector proposed the first comprehensive mine safety laws.

1886

The first recorded mine disaster in West Virginia at Mt. Brook Mine claimed 39 victims.

United Mine Workers Association (UMWA) march.

Timeline . . . *(continued)*

1887

The Legislature passed the first significant mine safety laws.

1894

The United Mine Workers staged a strike throughout West Virginia.

1905

The West Virginia Department of Mines was created.

Six mine disasters occurred, the greatest number in any one year.

1907

A mine explosion at Monongah, the worst U.S. mine disaster, claimed 361 miners.

Mining laws were printed in the languages of the miners.

1908

Two explosions at the Lick Branch Colliery in McDowell County killed 50 and 67 miners, respectively.

1910

The first mine foreman certification examinations were established.

It was a peak year for coke production at 4,217,381 tons.

1913

A clash occurred between miners and mine guards on Paint Creek. The governor issued a Martial Law proclamation.

1914

The Eccles mine explosion killed 183.

1915

An explosion at Layland Fayette County killed 112 miners.

1917

Mine Rescue Training began.

1920

The Matewan Massacre occurred.

John L. Lewis was named president of the United Mine Workers.

1922

A nationwide strike was called by the UMWA.

1925

The highest number of mine fatalities happened for any year, a total of 686.

1931

West Virginia passed Pennsylvania as the leading producer of bituminous coal.

1935

Congress passed the National Labor Relations Act.

"All Immigrants Not Ignorant," Letter to the Editor, by Selene Ashford, *The New York Times*, March 29, 1931:

It has been my experience that the average American assumes that immigrants to these shores are naturally ignorant or simpleminded. In dealing with the foreign-born we are much of the habit of lumping them all together and prone to lose sight of backgrounds, nationality and certain points of view.

When we see them en masse or individually, they have a certain air of bewilderment. New York, the Frankenstein monster, is overwhelming with its size, noise and speed. The main feature of their bewilderment or "difference" is the language. Any English-speaking immigrant is more self-assured because he can converse in English. Yet the shy immigrant, so wide-eyed and "different," may be a well-educated person, and given a chance in his own language they prove more intelligent than the average second-generation American can realize.

A good many foreigners, particularly certain Europeans, have been used to thinking in terms of centuries. Their history, art and literature have background that has lived through ages. And this indefinable something that foreigners have—which we call the immigrants' cultural offerings—may it not be lost in the effort at standardization? It is racial traits and descent that determine nationalities. We know there are certain races that have been downtrodden and illiterate from biblical times and are glad to escape to pastures new. These are of common clay that yield more readily at the hands of the potter, asking for nothing more than three meals a day and a place to sleep. And sometimes from among these there blossoms forth a wonderful soul—a genius.

It is the second generation on which the burden must lie. The events of the past known as tradition have not always been presented in a proper light, or the methods of procedure were at fault. This usually results in abysmal ignorance of real heritage, culture and language, and the gulf widens between the two generations. We also know some immigrants are slow to make adjustments, not only with the finer factors that go to make up American life with its whims and idiosyncrasies, so they react with apathy and a little antipathy. It is their children who are the losers—the feeling of not belonging to the racial groups of their fathers for not being accepted by the land of their birth.

There are some good organizations in this country (some of them supported by the foreign-born themselves) who are carrying on a splendid crusade for the aliens here and the newly arriving immigrants. Their colossal job of understanding is an intelligent albeit sympathetic one, and should receive wider publicity and greater financial support than they are now getting.

This is a democratic country. We need not practice class distinction, but let us not lose sight of the finer sensibilities of those who are willing to choose to come along with those that are driven from their own.

Another record. Three consecutive sets of twins were born to Mrs. Henry Bates of Heber Springs, Ark. All healthy, they're said to be the only ones of their kind in the country. Here's the mother with Earl and Murrill, 4, Leola Fay and Noami Ray, 3, and the three-months-old babies, Billie Jean, a girl, and Willie Dean, a boy. The father is 42, the mother 34.
(By Wide World)

"Proud Spain She Is—Even in Turmoil," by T. R. Ybarra, *The New York Times*, March 1, 1931:

Pride, patriotism, politeness—those three basic characteristics of Spanish character flashed repeatedly from the news dispatches out of Spain during her most recent crisis, just as they flash from the most casual actions and words of Spaniards in the everyday round in their lives.

Pride inspired King Alfonso to defy the republican foes who would snatch from him his crown and from Spain the centuries-old institution of monarchy. Pride stiffened those foes in their resolution to continue defying Alfonso, despite the latest rebuff to Spanish republicanism. In this duel defiance monarch and republicans simply played true to their Spanish form.

For in Spain nobleman and tradesman, peasant and townsman, soldier and civilian, no matter how great may be their divergence in politics and principles and worldly importance, are all swayed by deep-seated, instinctive and fiery pride which influences even their most trivial doings and leads them sometimes to fantastic extremes of conduct. Spanish pride crops up in the most unexpected places at the most unexpected times—as those who've traveled to Spain know only too well. Woe foreigner who purposely or accidentally wounds it!

When a Spanish beggar is asked by a foreign visitor the way to the cathedral or post office or railway station, the beggar will, if he be a true Spaniard, immediately stop plying his trade and lead the foreigner to the place where he wishes to go—mere explanations or pointing not being enough to satisfy the requirements of the case, as interpreted in Spain. But let that foreigner beware of fumbling in his pocket for a coin to repay the man for his trouble! Logic would seem to make it perfectly clear that a beggar cannot possibly take offense at being offered money. But logic and Spanish pride have little in common.

"What? One gentleman receive money for obliging another? Never!"

And, wrapping his ragged cloak around him, he will stalk off with the carriage and gait a great star of tragedy. . . .

Patriotism is similarly strong in the average Spaniard. In flinging down the gauntlet to those who would drive him from his throne, and casting his lot with the most ardent champions of monarchism, King Alfonso, many of his fellow countrymen will tell you, is not actuated entirely by royal pride; behind his gesture is also patriotism, the belief that to maintain the power of monarchy in Spain in these critical times is the best way to serve the true interests of the country.

"Behind Spain's Conflict: The Basic Issues," *The New York Times*, October 14, 1934:

Two cities, two ages, two classes, two philosophies battle for possession of Spain. Prosperous, energetic, industrialized Barcelona is at once the general headquarters in the symbol of the struggle against somber, hungry, hierarchic Madrid, and it is a struggle which divides each of the two and every other Spanish city, town and village, within and against itself. And as a first phase of the struggle a quarrel between the national Cabinet in Madrid and the representatives of the Catalan free state in Barcelona became the pivot on which every basic political, economic and cultural problem that has anguished Spain for many years has turned heated blazing white.

Spain, in these days of what is probably the greatest crisis in her history for a century at least, is a vast battleground. Twenty-four million people each face the blood and terror of civil war, and the mighty interrogation of an unknown tomorrow.

One needs superlatives to describe the depth and the edge and the implications of this drama. It is shaped to old stuff and new stuff; and through it converge all of Spain's unresolved tragedies at all the new bitterness of twentieth-century capital and labor war. The design of 24 million lives fix the plot, and on the plot determines the way those lives will be lived.

The jurisdictional quarrel between Barcelona and Madrid, with each resultant Cabinet fall, is precisely incidental, for the greater conflicts set off by it have fed a desperate muffled roar In the inner life of the Spanish people for many years, and may mean more years of open and hidden battle before they are solved. But it is no accident that a jurisdictional quarrel between Madrid and Barcelona should have been the focus of a spreading war, for this question is like the aching vertebrae the Spanish body politic and has been from the moment when Ferdinand, King of Aragon, Count of Barcelona married Isabella, Queen of Leon and Castile. And even before that, Barcelona was already a general headquarters and symbol of blunt, rough and irreverent self-assertion in revolt.

1939 News Feature

"Unser Amerika," by S. K. Padover, *Reader's Digest*, January 1939:

America is rightfully German.

Germans played the predominant role in creating, preserving and upbuilding it; German blood predominates in a majority of its citizens; the hour is imminent when the Germans in America will take over the United States. Already they call it "Unser Amerika"—"Our America."

This is not the mere babbling of extremists; it is part of the official program of Nazi propaganda now under way in this country and in Germany on a more intensive scale than most Americans realize.

The Nazis' technique—successful in Germany, Austria and Czechoslovakia—is to stir up dissatisfaction and internal dissension, then to step in and, through the German minority they control, to dominate the chaos they have created.

It is improbable that the realistic Nazi leaders actually expect any such overwhelming triumph in the U.S. But if they can create enough dissension and enough pro-German sentiment in America to prevent us again helping Germany's enemies, they will have won victory enough.

Learned professors write that nothing except Nazism can save the United States, which is a vulgar, corrupt and basically uncultured land, owned by Jews, full of criminals, and clinging to a degenerate form of government. Worse, the Americans are neither a race nor a nation, but a sort of bastardized racial conglomeration in which the best blood, that which made the country powerful, is German.

To stir up dissatisfaction, the Nazis are attacking democracy and its institutions. Pamphlet No. 7 of the official Nazi *Instructions for Our Friends Overseas* says, "The fundamental aim must always be to discredit conditions in the United States." If Americans are ever to be free, they must destroy the Constitution, which the Nazis call "the chain that ties the whole misery of American politics." Above all, Americans are told, they must smash the Bill of Rights. As Hans Kiderlen puts it in his book, *Journey into New America*, "The Bill of Rights is the wall in which a breach must be made before America's problems can be solved."

To create dissension, the Nazis, with skill born of long practice, raise issues—issues intended to split the country socially, to undermine political institutions and instill mutual hatreds among the citizens. The chief issues which Nazi propaganda is now seeking to inflame in America are the Jewish and German problems.

The Nazis are exerting every effort to make the United States Jew-conscious. They know that nothing else splits a country wide open so thoroughly. A spokesman for the Nazi Institute for Foreign Propaganda declares that anti-Semitism in America is a vital necessity for Nazi plans.

Hence, since 1933, they have distributed thousands of pamphlets, designed to convince American farmers, workers, and lower middle class folk that the country is Jew-dominated. Repeating their time-tested formula, they trace every American ill to the Jews. They are spreading the canards that the Jews control America's money, own the American press and dominate the government. "Aryan" Americans are urged to revolt against this Jewish tyranny.

Heinrich Krieger, writing in *Die Tat*, an important official party organ, warns us sternly, "If America continues to drift along her present racial course, she must inevitably be forced to abandon calling herself a Germanic nation."

As for the Germanic issue, the Nazis claim that the United States has so much of German blood that all Hitler needs to do to control America is to arouse this "blood" to an awareness of its brotherhood.

For the basis of their claims, they go back to Pastorius, who with his Mennonites settled Germantown, Pa. The Nazis claim that they played a preponderant role in the opening of the new land. A German, Martin Waldseemüller, first named it "America" in 1507. Another German, Charles V, was king of Spain shortly after Columbus returned from his fourth voyage. This, in Nazi law, gives German title to the Western continent. (Actually, Charles V was part Austrian, part Spaniard.) Moreover, so writes a Nazi scholar, it was Martin Luther, a German, who founded Protestantism. Without Protestantism, there would have been no Protestant colonization of North America. "Thus the deepest roots of the United States go back to a German." All this, the Nazis conclude triumphantly, gives "us" as much right to claim North America is German as the British have to claim it is Anglo-Saxon.

Nor is this all. By the time of the American Revolution, a great portion of the colonists were German, or had "German blood." Large numbers of Germans fought with Washington. (The Hessians on the other side are never mentioned.) Other Germans, notably General Steuben, came over to help the colonists. When it was all over, there was a movement to make German the national tongue and to put a German king on the vacant American throne. "Some wanted a French, others a German king," according to Johannes Stoye, a popular Nazi author, but the unscrupulous Anglo-Saxon minority robbed the Germans of their victory.

In the Civil War, the Nazis tell us, every third soldier in the Northern army was a German. They quote General Robert E. Lee to the effect that "without the Germans, it would be a trifle to lick the Yankees."

Listen to the Nazis' officially endorsed propagandist, Colin Ross. Ross is the descendant of Scotch forebears who settled in Germany generations ago; he is regarded in Germany as their foremost authority on American affairs. He writes indignantly:

"We are bitterly furious at the way they treated the Germanic portion of the population from the very beginning and how thoroughly they obliterated everything that the German has done for his American fatherland."

But, the Nazis console themselves, the Germans are bound to control America by sheer numbers and "blood." They claim that from one-fourth to one-third of the population of the country is of Germanic blood. Professor Karl Haushofer, the famous geopolitical theorist, puts the number at 30 million in his *Weltpolitik*. According to Richard Nitschke, in his *Das Auslandsdeutschtum*, a public school textbook, the number may

reach 40 million. Another school textbook computes that almost half of the American population is of Germanic origin. (In a sober fact, the census of 1790 put the German population at eight percent; it may be 15 percent now.)

But whether it is 40 million or 50 million, writes Georg Timpe in his *Catholic Germans in the United States*, "German blood" is of the very essence of America. So are German words, German thought, German culture, German music, German education. "In all the veins of America's cultural body flow the German spirit, German profundity, modesty, self-sacrifice, duty, endurance, thoroughness." Herr Timpe says the hour is at hand when the "German essence" of America will reassert itself:

"The American of today would not be what he is...if no German had ever come over there. In what moment the American's German Being will again participate in world history and become a source of usefulness to the old fatherland, no one can say. But that such a moment will arrive, and that we will be compensated for the sacrifices which we have made there, is not a deceptive hope."

In the official *Handbook of Foreign Germans*, Hugo Grothe writes darkly that one-fourth of America's blood will not long be denied its rightful place. The Reich must do everything in its power to make these Americans return to their German race.

Gigantic efforts are under way to arouse this Germanic element to a feeling of solidarity with the Germany of today.

The Institute of Germans Living Abroad, at Stuttgart, is perhaps the greatest single propaganda plant in the world; its purpose, as reiterated by Hitler, Goebbels and Göring, is to bring people of "German blood" into the spiritual fold of the Reich. (Dorothy Thompson points out that it is the exact counterpart of the Communist International.)

The Institute is compiling a *German World Migration Register*; agents everywhere in Germany search family Bibles and letters to trace all persons who have emigrated during the last 100 years, and to record the names of all living descendants.

"The world-migration book," says the Stuttgart *Kurier*, official organ of the Institute, "must represent not a card index, but a German world in human beings. With each human being should be established personal connection." Here is to be the colossal list of persons to be bombarded with "blood brotherhood" propaganda.

Minister of the Interior Frick, addressing the Fifth Congress of Germans Abroad in Stuttgart in 1938, sternly reminded his hearers, "No German abroad may forget that he is always and everywhere a piece of Germany." At the same meeting Göring bluntly warned the world that Germany "is not only ready but strong enough to protect Germans all over the world."

Richard Nitschke writes in *Der Auslandsdeuschtum*, "In our position, we cannot afford to give up one-third of our people. We make no distinction between Germans at home and Germans abroad."

The Stuttgart *Kurrier* states flatly: "We desire to bring back the Germans in the United States to the racial unity and common faith of all Germans. To this end, the spiritual and intellectual reform of Americans of German extraction is necessary, in accord with the model furnished by the homeland . . . German-American influence shall then be thrown in the balance *under our leadership* for the coming struggle for America's regeneration."

Nazi propaganda in this country aims at two audiences. To the non-Germans are addressed the racial, anti-Semitic and anti-labor propaganda. More sinister is the Nazi propaganda among Americans of German descent. The Nazis, by the way, protest the term "German-Americans" and prefer the plain German word "Amerikaner," which implies "Germans in America," and, as it carries no hyphen, suggests no possible division of allegiance.

The "Amerikaner" are told that Nazism is a world movement which is bound to lead to Teutonic domination of the United States. Nazis quote Dr. Goebbels' assertion that the "German idea" must conquer the world, including the United States, for the Germans are the Chosen People, selected by destiny and history to rule the earth.

To undermine the German-Americans' belief in American ideals, the Nazis have established a network of cells, agencies, organizations and press bureaus in every population center of the country. The most powerful organization is the *Amerikadeustcher Volksbund*, under Führer Fritz Kuhn, sedulous ape of Hitler. The Bund, like its parent, the propaganda institute in Stuttgart, rejects the validity of American citizenship. "The German man is and remains our fellow national (*Volksgenosse*), regardless of the citizenship papers that he may possess."

Much of the effort of the *Volksbund* is to capture American youth of German descent. The *Volksbund* holds that "our future," meaning the future of Nazi designs in America, lies in the youth. "In our youth groups we want to build young men to be useful to the German community." Free German-language schools give "careful German training" and prepare youths from seven to 18 "to become members of American Germandom." American-German youth is told that it is not enough to speak or even to think German. "We must consciously work for the totality of the folk, and become politically active in a folk-German sense," writes *Junges Volk*, official organ of the Nazi youth in the United States. "A few of our generations have permitted themselves to be robbed of what eminent men of our blood have built up and left behind in this country. To reconquer this is our most sacred duty!"

The *Yearbook* of the Bund proclaims: "We are proud of Germany! Proud of its great Führer! Proud of our culture!" The program of the Bund is, "The union of all people of German origin in the United States."

The Bund is a tightly knit organization, along military lines. Kuhn, three regional directors and one youth leader rule no less than 56 units scattered from coast to coast. Each group has its own newspaper.

Apart from the strictly party newspapers of the Bund, there are 20 German-language newspapers in the United States that are unofficial Nazi mouthpieces, preaching anti-Semitism and ridiculing democracy.

Far more significant is a book that has escaped attention in the American press—Colin Ross's astounding *Unser Amerika*, published in Leipzig in 1936. It must be taken as semi-official, since Ross is an officer of the propaganda institute in Stuttgart and since the organ of the Nazi party *National-sozialistische Monatshefte* (June 1938) urges that his book be given "the most widespread distribution." In it, Ross recites the arguments we have already reviewed. Then he urges that the "30,000,000 Germans in the United States" should assert the rights of their blood by every and any means.

He protests strenuously against the German habit of saying "we also" contributed to America. That implies a partnership, whereas the Germans were the chief factor in America's creation.

"I believe in the German Hour of America," he writes. "The great historic events usually are prepared underground until they suddenly emerge in the open. The German rebirth in the United States is more powerful than most people think. We Germans in the old country can only watch the great revolution that is preparing over there, not altogether impartially, to be sure; for our hearts will always beat for a people whose blood is one-fourth ours. When this German portion . . . will have taken a firm hold of the destiny of its new fatherland, it will do so not for our sake, but for its sake, the sake of America.

"From amongst them [Germans in America] will arise a German Thomas Paine. . . . He will unite all of German blood. All will come as soon as they have realized the simple truth that they are not 'Americans' but 'Amerikaner,' men of German blood and American soil."

Thus the Nazis will save America from "chaos and barbarism." Ross reiterates that the Germans have a sacred duty to perform; America is "a creation of the German spirit," hence the United States must become "Unser Amerika."

The mass of German-Americans have shown themselves consistently cold to such Nazi propaganda, just as they were cold to the clumsier German propaganda of World War days. Despite enormous pressure and Nazi incitation, they have remained what they always have been, loyal Americans.

The situation in the future is, nevertheless, fraught with danger. The Nazis have the theoretical and material basis for a powerful "race and blood" campaign in this country. German plans look far into the future. Hitler has proclaimed himself again and again to be supreme lord and protector of all people of German blood on earth. It is almost certain that when the Führer is ready to strike at the two great European democracies, he will instantly intensify the "race and blood" issue here, as he did in Czechoslovakia. He may even demand autonomy for "Germans in America."

1940–1949

The all-encompassing World War II both dominated the lives of all Americans and served as a national cauldron for mixing people, attitudes and relationships. Women went to work by the millions and gained confidence in their skills. Southern blacks lived and worked outside the daily tyranny of segregation. War-battered immigrants once again found America a welcoming society, while Japanese Americans were forced into internment camps. Women were encouraged to enter college or even consider becoming doctors. The military talked about desegregating its units and labor unions sensed that power was finally within the grasp of the working man. Children and adults alike joined conservation drives, suffered when tragic telegrams arrived, and learned to eat what the ration tickets made available.

People from every social stratum either signed up for the military or went to work supplying the military machine. Even children, eager to do their share, collected scrap metal and helped plant the victory gardens that symbolized America's willingness to do anything to defeat the "bullies." In fact it was the threat of war that compelled Congress to pass the Alien Registration Act of 1940 that required all non-U.S. citizens within the United States to register with the government and receive an Alien Registration card, which was later known as the "Green Card." In addition, large amounts of money and food were sent abroad as Americans observed meatless Tuesdays, gas rationing and other shortages to help the starving children of Europe.

Business worked in partnership with government; strikes were reduced, but key New Deal labor concessions were expanded, including a 40-hour week and time and a half for overtime. As manufacturing demands increased, the labor pool shrank, and wages and union membership rose. Unemployment, which stood as high as 14 percent in 1940, all but disappeared. By 1944, the U.S. was producing twice the total war output of the Axis powers combined. The wartime demand for production workers rose more rapidly than for skilled workers, reducing the wage gap between the two to the lowest level in the twentieth century.

From 1940 to 1945, the gross national product more than doubled, from $100 billion to $211 billion, despite rationing and the unavailability of many consumer goods such as cars, gasoline and washing machines. Interest rates remained low, and the upward pressure on prices remained high, yet from 1943 to the end of the war, the cost of living rose less than 1.5 percent. Following the war, as controls were removed, inflation peaked in 1948 and union demands for high wages accelerated. Between 1945 and 1952, confident Americans—and their growing families—increased consumer credit by 800 percent.

To fight inflation, government agencies regulated wages, prices and the kinds of jobs people could take. The Office of Price Administration was entrusted with the complicated tasks of setting price ceilings for almost all consumer goods and distributing ration books for items in short supply. The Selective Service and the War Manpower Commission largely determined who would serve in the military, whose work was vital to the war effort, and when a worker could transfer from one job to another. When the war ended and regulations were lifted, workers demanded higher wages. The relations between labor and management became strained. Massive strikes and inflation followed in the closing days of the decade, and many consumer goods were easier to find on the black market than on the store shelves until America retooled for a peacetime economy.

The decade of the 1940s made America a world power and Americans more worldly. Millions served overseas; millions more listened to broadcasts concerning the war in London, Rome and Tokyo. Newsreels brought the war home to moviegoers, who numbered in the millions. The war effort also redistributed the population and the demand for labor; the Pacific Coast gained wealth and power, and the South was able to supply its people with much-needed war jobs and provide blacks with opportunities previously closed to them. Women entered the work force in unprecedented numbers, reaching 18 million. The net cash income of the American farmer soared 400 percent.

But the Second World War extracted a price. Those who experienced combat entered a nightmarish world. Countries possessed far greater firepower than ever before, and within those units actually fighting the enemy, the incidence of death was high, sometimes one in three. In all, the United States lost 405,000 men and women to combat deaths. Many suffered in the war's final year, when the American army spearheaded the assault against Germany and Japan. The cost in dollars was $350 billion. But the cost was not only in American lives. Following Germany's unconditional surrender on May 4, 1945, Japan continued fighting. To prevent the loss of thousands of American lives defeating the Japanese, President Truman dropped atomic bombs on the Japanese cities of Hiroshima and Nagasaki, ending the war and ushering in the threat of "the bomb" as a key element of the Cold War during the 1950s and 1960s.

Throughout the war, soldiers from all corners of the nation fought side by side and refined nationalism and what it meant to America through this government-imposed mixing process. The newfound identity of the American GIs was further cemented by the vivid descriptions of war correspondent Ernie Pyle, who spend considerable time talking and living with the average soldier to present a "worm's eye view" of war. Yet, despite the closeness many men and women developed toward their fellow soldiers, discrimination continued. African American servicemen were excluded from the marines, the Coast Guard and the Army Corps. The regular army accepted blacks into the military—700,000 in all—only on a segregated basis. Only in the closing years of the decade would President Harry Truman lead the way toward a more integrated America by integrating the military.

Sports attendance in the 1940s soared beyond the record levels of the 1920s; in football the T-formation came into prominence; Joe DiMaggio, Ted Williams, and Stan Musial dominated baseball before and after the war, and Jackie Robinson became the first black in organized baseball. In 1946, Dr. Benjamin Spock's work, *Common Sense Baby and Child Care,* was published to guide newcomers in the booming business of raising babies.

1944 PROFILE

Gerrit DeGraaf, having joined the Dutch resistance, moved on to Belgium, then to England, and finally to Grand Rapids, Michigan, to design new parts and applications at an airplane fusillade factory.

Life at Home

- Gerrit DeGraaf had just turned 21 when the German invasion of the Netherlands began on May 10, 1940.
- Until the day he saw the planes, he was convinced that the German army would not invade Holland; his friends had bet him otherwise.
- His father had said assuredly, "The Germans would not dare invade Holland."
- For the prior nine months, false reports of the imminent attack had echoed through the Dutch rumor mill; immediately after the outbreak of fighting between Poland and Germany, the Dutch government declared itself neutral, as it had done in World War I.
- Unlike in World War I, however, when the Netherlands was unmolested by the German assault, Holland was an early target.
- The first assault came at night.
- German paratroopers were dropped into the community before the sun came up, then bombs fell near the bridges and dikes.
- Gerrit and his father were very angry; the Germans were creating unnecessary havoc.
- The German army faced little resistance at first, although their advance was eventually slowed by the Dutch army, fighting with weaponry made before 1900.
- Then the German airplanes began strafing the villages, killing anyone who happened to be outside, and bombing the cities.
- Four days into the invasion, German planes heavily bombed Rotterdam, killing thousands; the city of Utrecht was next, the Dutch were told, unless surrender came immediately.

Gerrit DeGraaf left Holland during WW II to work in an airplane factory in Michigan.

German paratroopers invading Holland.

- Surrender took four days; the occupation lasted five years.
- During the first months after the German occupation began, the Dutch expected to be liberated quickly by the Allied armies, but the Battle of France went badly.
- The Nazis dominated most of the early battles.
- By 1941 the Netherlands understood that the Nazi occupation would not be temporary and could get worse.
- Gerrit was born in Alblasserdam and attended school in nearby Kinderdyk until he was 16; he then became an apprentice toolmaker and was continuing his schooling at night when the war arrived.
- Kinderdyk was an industrial town located at the confluence of three rivers all supporting a major shipping industry.
- In the early months of the war Gerrit continued to work, although he was required to black out the lights on his bicycle when traveling from place to place and keep his mouth shut.
- German soldiers and spies were everywhere; casual conversation could be fatal.
- Many Nazi leaders, including Joseph Goebbels, had believed the Dutch would absorb National Socialism into their culture without a fight.
- The aim of the Germans was to dissolve the Dutch nation and make it part of a greater Germanic, or Aryan, nation.

German planes heavily bombed Rotterdam.

Gerrit regularly heard German war planes overhead.

Nazi's crossed the river into the Netherlands.

- Instead, the Dutch rallied around their exiled royal family, condemned the mistreatment of the Jews, and quickly became a valuable source of intelligence for the Allies.
- These total strangers did not belong in the Netherlands, and they were certainly not the super race they claimed to be, Gerrit said only to his father.
- Early on, Gerrit's older brother Simon was picked up in the dead of night and shipped to a German-based manufacturing facility for talking back to one of the German soldiers.
- The Germans' stated plan was to expand their specialized manufacturing capability to support the war effort by using trained craftsmen as slave labor.
- Simon's fate was unknown.
- He was not the only one; others were beaten so badly they lost all their teeth.
- A few men were publicly shot and allowed to float listlessly down the river.
- Then the soldiers began rounding up the Jews of the Netherlands.
- The initial wave of arrests of Jews provoked an immediate response: solidarity strikes by non-Jewish Dutch workers.
- The Dutch were very sympathetic to the Jewish people in Holland.
- Gerrit became a self-appointed agitator, who ran from factory to factory shouting for the workers to stop work and join the strike.
- Anti-German leaflets were printed up for distribution; every action was spontaneous.
- Three of the protesters—all well known to Gerrit—were picked up by the German soldiers and shot in the head.
- As Dutch citizens said, "All they did was make up a little note telling what the Germans were doing to the Jews was wrong and we should strike; for that they were shot."
- For Gerrit, "This was the first encounter, really, where it was heart against heart, where you really said, 'Well, this is it' and joined the Dutch resistance."
- The Dutch resistance assisted Dutch Jews—especially children—to escape through organizations that specialized in hiding people and forging identity papers; it also sabotaged war equipment, disrupted factory work and distributed food to the starving.
- It was dangerous work.
- A general strike was greeted with German brutality, in which 150 people were shot.
- When a notorious collaborator was assassinated by the Dutch, 250 hostages were also shot by the Germans in retaliation.
- Despite the widespread resistance efforts, two-thirds of the 140,000 Jews living in Holland would die or disappear during the war.
- The Dutch resistance also made its mark with the collection of intelligence that could be useful to the Allies and demonstrated Dutch anger through strategic assassinations; the toughest and most visible German officers were often targeted for death.
- Gerrit was forced to go fully underground in 1942 when the Germans began rounding up everyone in his age group.
- All business was handled in the dark of night.
- Gerrit served as a runner, who was assigned jobs delivering messages or food.
- When a cow was slaughtered, for example, Gerrit was assigned the task of delivering the pieces to various addresses.

Dutch Jewish families sought to escape the destruction.

- He was always in fear of being caught; life was miserable.
- There was not enough food, not enough clothes.
- To escape the German tyranny, he went to the heavily Catholic region of Brabant, then to Belgium, and from there to England.
- There he rapidly demonstrated his extraordinary mechanical skill and was asked to temporarily move to America—in a place called Michigan—to train toolmakers.
- Within days the 24-year-old refugee toolmaker was on the way to America under a temporary visa reserved for critical professions.
- The sudden change was exhilarating—his feelings about leaving Europe to aid the war effort, extremely mixed.

Life at Work

- Life in America felt safer for Gerrit DeGraaf: the people—many of Dutch ancestry—were nice, the pay was good and the company APP appreciative of his skills.
- But Gerrit was restless: his friends were dying in Europe; his parents were still in the Netherlands and he could not stop hoarding food.
- Since he had arrived in America a year earlier he had gained weight, enjoyed the opportunity to dine in restaurants, shop in stores and feast at church suppers, but could not shake the feeling that he would never see food again.
- He kept bits of food hidden everywhere—in his work bench, on his bicycle, around his home and even behind a general mercantile store fully stocked with food.
- Even worse, he always felt guilty when he had enough to eat.
- Gerrit's food hoarding obsession was exposed at church, where he also hid food to eat between services.
- After church one Sunday, the prettiest girl in the congregation pulled a head-sized chunk of bread from beneath a cabinet and asked for all the world to hear, "Who put this here?"
- It was only one of many trials in Grand Rapids, Michigan, where 40 percent of the population claimed Dutch ancestry.
- The saving grace was work designing new parts and applications at an airplane fusillade factory fully dedicated to the war effort.

Gerrit liked working at the airplane factory.

- The factory had been converted from an automobile parts manufacturing facility in the early months of 1942 after President Franklin Roosevelt decreed that America must fully mobilize if the Nazis and Japanese were to be defeated.
- Eighteen months later the factory—drained by the military of its most innovative craftsmen—was still experiencing quality issues.
- No one wanted one of their planes to fall from the sky because of a loose bolt or an overstressed frame.
- Gerrit was proud that he could make a contribution despite the handicap of language.
- So many women in the plant traced their heritage to Holland, Gerrit was often asked to address questions of geography, language and customs.

The factory had many women workers.

- Despite his inherit shyness, Gerrit often found himself surrounded by a clutch of women workers eager to talk and very prepared to laugh at his mildest attempts at humor.
- An eligible male without a noticeable disability was a rarity in Grand Rapids.
- But the war was ever present—from the work he did, the newspapers he read, the ration stamps he carried, to the guilt he felt every time he experienced joy.
- When he walked the streets at night, older women—presumably with sons overseas—would sneer, "Why aren't you in the Army?"
- Several times he attempted to answer in Dutch, only to be accused of being a German spy, after which he used silence as his response.

Life in the Community: Grand Rapids, Michigan

- Grand Rapids, Michigan, had long been a center for Dutch life in America, beginning before the American Civil War.
- Grand Rapids and the surrounding farming communities offered ample job opportunities, the availability of Dutch-language worship services and a welcoming, well-established Dutch culture.
- A second wave of Dutch immigrants arrived in the 1870s, attracted by the city's reputation as the furniture capital of America, open to the skilled European woodworkers seeking opportunity.
- By 1900 persons of Dutch birth or ancestry made up 40 percent of the city's population—the largest proportion of Dutch in any large American city.
- As a result, Grand Rapids was the headquarters of the Christian Reformed Church.
- In the 1850s-1860s several dozen Dutch immigrants living in the city of Grand Rapids became increasingly dissatisfied with the local Dutch Reformed and True Reformed congregations with which they were affiliated.
- They longed to have the pure preaching they had savored in the Netherlands.
- The earliest suburbs in the city formed around the turn of the twentieth century, arranged along the streetcar routes, spreading homes and businesses outward from the city center.
- By the late 1940s, the automobile had clearly established the pattern of city migration, freeing residents from the necessity of living near public transportation.

Historical Snapshot
1944

- The enactment of the new GI Bill of Rights helped finance college educations for veterans and provided 4 percent home loans with no down payment

- College football was emerging as the number one sport in America, replacing professional baseball whose teams had been significantly depleted by the war

- Approximately 350,000 pounds of DDT was shipped monthly to the military to fight malaria

- The city of Boston banned the distribution of *Strange Fruit*, a novel about the love between a white man and a black woman

- DNA, the basic material of heredity, was isolated by Oswald Avery of the Rockefeller Institute

- American grocers began testing self-serve meat markets

- A New York judge ruled that the novel *Lady Chatterley's Lover* was obscene

- Horseracing was banned during the war

- Graffiti reading "Kilroy was here" was seen on buildings, on phone booths and construction fences as a symbol of the valor of American GIs

- A mechanical robot with a 50-foot panel of knobs, gears and switches was created at Harvard by Howard Aiken

- The price of gasoline averaged $0.21 per gallon

- Since the Japanese attacked Pearl Harbor in December 1941, the Army Air Corps' fleet of 10,329 planes had been expanded to 79,908 planes and 2,403,000 officers and men

- The War Refugee Board revealed for the first time the mass murders that took place in Birkenau and Auschwitz, estimating that 1.7 million people had been killed

- Half the steel, tin and paper needed for the war effort was being provided by recycling

- The war cost $250 million per day

- The U.S. Army announced the development of a jet-propelled, propless airplane

- Lt. John F. Kennedy received the Navy and Marine Corps medal for extreme heroism for rescuing two sailors after a Japanese destroyer cut his PT boat in half

Selected Prices

Bunk Bed	$10.98
Chicks, 100	$7.50
Deep Freezer	$225.00
Fountain Pen	$15.00
Hotel Chesterfield, New York, per Day	$2.50
Ouija Board	$2.00
Pressure Cooker	$10.50
Records, Four 12″	$4.72
Silk Stockings	$0.98
Whiskey, Seagram's, Fifth	$2.70

European War Timeline

1939

The Nazis took Czechoslovakia.

The Nazis signed the Pact of Steel with Italy.

Britain and Poland signed a Mutual Assistance Treaty.

The British fleet was mobilized; civilian evacuations began from London.

The Nazis invaded Poland; Britain, France, Australia and New Zealand declared war on Germany.

The United States proclaimed neutrality; the Nazis began euthanasia on the sick and disabled in Germany.

An assassination attempt on Hitler failed.

The Soviets attacked Finland.

1940

Rationing began in Britain.

The Nazis invaded France, Belgium, Luxembourg and the Netherlands.

Winston Churchill became the British Prime Minister.

The Germans bombed Paris.

Norway surrendered to the Nazis; Italy declared war on Britain and France.

The Soviets began the occupation of the Baltic States.

German U-boats attacked merchant ships in the Atlantic.

The French Vichy government broke off relations with Britain.

The Germans began bombing airfields and factories in England; Hitler established a blockade of the British Isles.

The Italians invaded Egypt.

German troops entered Romania.

Italy invaded Greece.

The British joined a western desert offensive in North Africa against the Italians.

1941

Tobruk in North Africa fell to the British and Australians.

British forces arrived in Greece.

President Roosevelt signed the Lend-Lease Act, under which the U.S. supplied the Allied nations with war material in return for the use of British military bases in Newfoundland, Bermuda and the British West Indies.

Yugoslavia surrendered to the Nazis.

Greece surrendered to the Nazis.

Heavy German bombing of London continued; the British bombed Hamburg.

The *Bismarck* sank the British ship *Hood*; the British Navy sank the *Bismarck*.

The United States froze German and Italian assets in America.

Germany attacked the Soviet Union as Operation Barbarossa began.

Nazi SS Einsatzgruppen began mass murder.

Roosevelt froze Japanese assets in the United States and suspended relations between the two countries.

Timeline . . . *(continued)*

The Nazis ordered Jews to wear yellow stars.

The first experimental use of gas chambers began at Auschwitz.

The Nazis took Kiev and murdered 33,771 Jews.

The German army advanced on Moscow.

The Japanese bombed Pearl Harbor; the United States and Britain declared war on Japan, while Germany declared war on the United States.

Hitler took complete command of the German Army.

1942

The Germans began a U-boat offensive along the East Coast of the U.S.

SS Leader Heydrich held the Wannsee Conference to coordinate the "Final Solution of the Jewish Question."

The first American forces arrived in Great Britain.

Japanese-Americans were sent to relocation centers in the U.S.

German air raids began against cathedral cities in Britain.

The mass murder of Jews by gassing began at Auschwitz.

The Germans began a drive toward Stalingrad in the USSR.

The first all-American air attack occurred in Europe.

Professor Enrico Fermi set up an atomic reactor in Chicago.

British Foreign Secretary Eden told the British House of Commons of mass executions of Jews by Nazis; the U.S. declared that those crimes would be avenged.

1943

The Germans began a withdrawal from the Caucasus.

The Soviets began an offensive against the Germans in Stalingrad.

Roosevelt announced that the war could end only with an unconditional German surrender.

Britain's Eighth Army captured Tripoli.

American bombing raids on Germany began.

The Germans surrendered at Stalingrad in the first big defeat of Hitler's armies.

Soviet troops took Kursk.

The Germans began a withdrawal from Tunisia, Africa.

The Battle of the Atlantic climaxed with 27 merchant ships sunk by German U-boats.

The Waffen SS confronted Jewish resistance in the Warsaw ghetto.

German and Italian troops surrendered in North Africa.

The Germans ordered the liquidation of all Jewish ghettos in Poland.

The Allies landed in Sicily and bombed Rome; Mussolini was arrested and the Italian Fascist government fell.

The Germans rescued Mussolini, who re-established the Fascist government in Italy.

Roosevelt, Churchill, and Stalin met at Teheran.

Timeline . . . *(continued)*

1944

Soviet troops advanced into Poland.

Leningrad was relieved after a 900-day siege.

The British dropped 3,000 tons of bombs during an air raid on Hamburg, Germany.

Soviet troops launched an offensive to liberate the Crimea, where the Germans finally surrendered.

The Germans withdrew to the Adolf Hitler Line.

The Allies entered Rome.

The D-Day landings occurred in France.

The Nazis liquidated the town of Oradour-sur-Glane in France.

The Battle of the Hedgerows was fought in Normandy; the Soviets captured Minsk.

A German assassination attempt on Hitler failed.

Soviet troops liberated the concentration camp at Majdanek.

The Polish Home Army uprising against the Nazis in Warsaw began; U.S. troops reach Avranches.

Anne Frank and her family were arrested by the Gestapo in Amsterdam, Holland.

The Allied invasion of southern France began; a resistance uprising liberated Paris.

Verdun, Dieppe, Artois, Rouen, Abbeville, Antwerp and Brussels were liberated by the Allies.

An Allied airborne assault on Holland was launched.

The Allies liberated Athens; Rommel committed suicide.

French troops drove through the Beffort Gap to reach the Rhine and capture Strasbourg.

The Battle of the Bulge in the Ardennes was launched.

"Victory, Lasting Peace, Jobs for All," Republican Keynote Address by Earl Warren, Governor of California, June 26, 1944:

We are here to do a job for the American people. And we mean business. What is your job? Ask any American. Ask the anxious American mother and father. Ask the anxious wives and sweethearts of our fighting men. They will tell you what our job is.

They will give the keynote of this convention. They will tell you out of their hearts, and what they will say will be the same—East and West, North and South—it will be the same. For now the same anxieties are on every American heart—the same hour-to-hour concern for what the day will bring forth, the same steadfast courage to sustain them, the same dreams, the same hope that that they will have a chance to make their dreams come true.

This is what is on their heart. This is our job:

To get our boys back home again—victorious and with all speed.

To open the door for all Americans—to open it, not just to jobs but to opportunity!

To make and guard the peace so wisely and so well that this time will be the last time that American homes are called to give their sons and daughters to the agony and tragedy of war.

Isn't that a plain and homely story? But is there any other story which any American would put in place of it? Is there any other thing which, in his heart, any American wants more than these? Is there any American who would not give everything he has to bring these things to pass?

The only good reason I was chosen [to make the keynote speech] was because I come from the great, hopeful, energetic West. Ours is the youngest part of America. My own state of California was a child of four years when the Republican party was born.

Growth and change and adventure are still a part of our daily life.

In the West there is little fear of failure and no fear of trying. That spirit of youth is the spirit of this convention.

Certainly, we are not here to look for a road back to some status quo. There is no status to which we could or should return. The future cannot be overtaken in reverse. Neither are we here to work out some easy-sounding scheme whereby America can stand still. We believe that America wants to get going and keep going. A forward-going America is what we are here for.

"THE OPTIMIST"

"Europe Jitters," *Pathfinder*, August 27, 1938:

Once the gay occasion for military banquets, wine drinking and beer fests, Europe's summer maneuvers have turned grim in the expectancy of war. In earnest secrecy last week, 20,000 French soldiers, 30,000 British troops and 40,000 Belgians are going through annual battle practice. Regarded with calm, the noise of these maneuvers was lost in a creak and grumble heard all over Europe. To the biggest maneuvers ever held on the continent, Adolf Hitler had summoned virtually the entire German military machine.

A month ago, newspapermen were told in European diplomatic offices: "It is coming on August 15." Spoken in low tones, *iist* in Europe means war. On the continent, there had been many of seemingly tall-tale preparations. As early as last month, it was generally known that large-scale German drills would begin to take place on August 15. Several weeks ago, 300,000 conscript laborers were put to work finishing Germany's new Siegfried line, a front of fortification which faces France. Strict orders were issued that no one without an official permit could enter military areas of Germany near the Siegfried line and near the Polish border.

Two weeks ago, Italy abruptly tightened restrictions against Frenchman. Last week, France declared that no Italian could cross her border without complying with special regulations. Pleading illness as a cause, British Prime Minister Chamberlain unexpectedly returned to London from a fishing holiday in Scotland. French diplomats outside of France were instructed to relay to Paris all the military information about Germany they get. Amid this general apprehension and confusion, with only a one-line notice in the usually verbose German press, Adolf Hitler suddenly appeared at the garrison town of Juterborg, 40 miles south of Berlin, to attend the official opening of German drills. Rushing to the scene, newspapermen found the garrison surrounded by soldiers, and were able to learn only that with Hitler were an unusual number of high Nazi officials. . . .

Near the week's end, a small batch of 100,000 troops had begun to drill in Bavaria, close to Czechoslovakia, and Nazi troops were marching toward France and Belgium. Seeking to still German anxiety, the official news bureau in Berlin assured Nazis that further rumors of war were merely "jitters" caused by summer heat.

"All Together," *Naval Firepower* Magazine, January 1945:

Victory is a matter of combined operations, not only at the front but wherever people work to help win the war. The Army and Navy must work together to make the landings and hold the beachheads when enemy territory must be taken. Within the Army, the infantry, artillery, the armed forces, and the air arm must carry out a coordinated plan. Within the Navy, the various types of ships and aircraft and ordnance must be used in such a way that each will contribute the utmost to the success of every battle.

Long before the Army and Navy can go into action, however, their chances of victory are pre-determined by the combined operations that must go forward on the home front, by the planning and the carrying out of plans to provide fighting forces with the tools they need to do their job.

That means raw materials, it means parts, it means subassemblies, it means final assemblies, it means transportation between plants, it's good workmanship all along the line, and teamwork as close and predictable as that of a championship football eleven.

The naval ordnance production team has been a powerful force in the building of the fleet that now flies the flag of the United States.

Guns are what make warships! Until the ordnance is there, ready to shoot, a war vessel is just a ship, not a battlewagon. Until they are armed, the ships of the Navy can neither defend themselves nor attack the enemy. Ordnance workers in the Navy-owned and private plants that make fighting equipment for our ships hold the key to the success of the operation of the fleet.

When men and women working in naval ordnance plants and ammunition depots keep pace with the building of new ships, those ships can go out to pursue the enemy as fast as they can be fitted out. When the pace of production falls behind, the fleet may have to wait for ships to be armed and supplied with ammunition before it can undertake operations that might speed victory.

"The Innocent Victims," Editorial, *The New York Times*, May 19, 1940:

Thousands of Dutch and Belgian women and children, without possessions, without homes or hope, have found momentary refuge in Great Britain in the last few days. They are the first tragic backwash of an invasion which, as President Roosevelt said, has shocked and angered the people of the United States. The British and French people, with grief and anxiety in their own lives, have opened their arms to these refugees as they did when another invasion struck Belgium a quarter-century ago.

But the British and French are in no position now to give adequate help to these innocent victims. In London they are being housed temporarily beneath the grandstands of the huge Wembley Stadium, where they will face discomforts and hardships, and perhaps some of the same dangers which made them leave their homes. Any month, any day, the bombing planes may appear over the British soil. The British and French are making desperate efforts to conserve their own supplies of food and clothing; they will need them in the desperate months ahead.

We in America will doubtless respond generously to the Red Cross call for $10 million for war relief. But if we are wholly consistent in our desires to help the people of Holland and Belgium, and the Allied peoples as well, we could also take some of these women and children into sanctuary here. Immigration quotas from Holland and Belgium amount to 4,450 year, and only a fraction of each has been used. It would be immeasurable relief to the British and French to be able to send at least a few hundred of these refugees from the Low Countries to us, to be cared for until their homes and countries are restored. It would be only a tithe of the debt that we, in this city of Nieuw Amsterdam, owe to Holland. It would be a renewed tribute to the people of Belgium, who endured far too much undeserved misery already.

"Germany: Problem in Subtraction," *Time*, March 3, 1941:

The arithmetic that Hitler has taught the Jews in the Third Reich has been the misery of subtraction. From all of them he has taken something: privileges, property, homes, life.

The simplest subtraction has been the decrease of the rights of the Jewish population by emigration, deportation and death.

Currently:

In Germany 500,000 Jews minus 310,000 equals 190,000.

In Austria 180,000 Jews minus 135,000 equals 45,000.

In Czecho-Slovakia 185,000 Jews minus 25,000 equals 160,000.

Within the last fortnight two sardine-packed trains left Vienna, as the Nazis applied themselves again to this problem. Aboard each were more than 1,000 Jews bound for limbo, the new barbed-wire ghetto near Lublin in Poland. Elsewhere sealed trains crossed the border with more Jews (mostly very old and very young) for the starved concentration camps of occupied France. From Vienna alone the Nazis promised to dump five to 12 more trainloads a month. Hitler's final solution to his problem in subtraction is zero, to be reached, according to the most sanguine report in Germany, in just six more weeks.

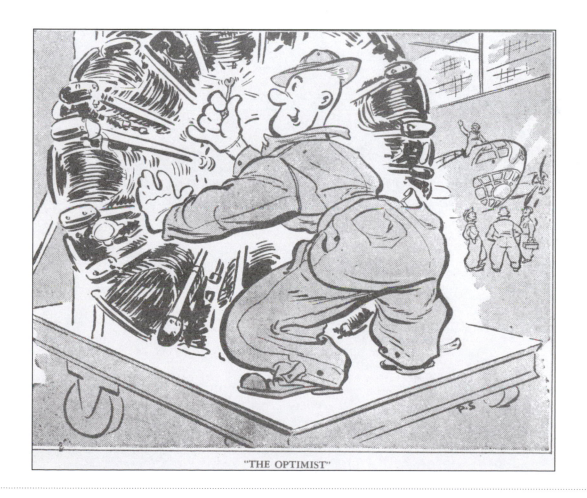

"THE OPTIMIST"

1946 Profile

After marrying her American GI husband, bubbly English city girl Eileen Andrews found herself isolated in a home in the woods of Chicopee, Massachusetts, before moving into their own home in less rural South Hadley.

Life at Home

- Eileen Andrews was the fourth-oldest of 16 children living in London, England.
- Her father earned his living as a painter, which provided barely enough to support his large family.
- When Eileen was a teenager, her father "squatted" (settled in without legal title) in a house that he was contracted to paint; he was sure no one would have the nerve to evict them.
- The house was a row house, part of what was known as council houses built as part of a welfare program.
- Situated by the docks of the Thames River, the house was surrounded by barbed wire and bomb shelters.
- There was a kitchen, living room and bedroom on the first floor with three bedrooms upstairs.
- It was a tight fit for such a large family, but they were happy to have a home.
- When the Second World War erupted in 1939, Eileen's six youngest siblings were sent off to the countryside to keep them safe from the German bombing of London; Eileen remained behind.
- As the war dragged on and America joined the fight in 1942, Eileen's friend's parents, Mr. and Mrs. Ellis, often invited American soldiers over to their house for dinner and cards, to thank them for their service to England.
- In particular, they took a special liking to Sgt. Armand Laflamme, who was an excellent cribbage player—their favorite card game.
- It was during one of his frequent visits that he and Eileen met.
- Because her parents also enjoyed spending time with Armand, the couple would spend more evenings at Eileen's house than out on the town, much to her dismay.
- Eileen was a brash, boisterous party girl who loved the city life with all the people, noise and activities.

Eileen Andrews left London after marrying an American serviceman.

261

Bombed out cathedral in London.

The Tower Bridge in London.

- She and her sisters loved learning the jive and the jitterbug from the GIs, and swinging to the Glenn Miller Band.
- These good times helped get them through the nights they spent in the air raid shelters as the bombs fell around them.
- Eileen worked as a domestic cleaning houses, and also joined the war effort as a corporal in the WAAF.
- She volunteered in the canteen waiting tables and serving as the dance hostess.
- Armand often brought luxury items to Eileen's family that were only available to American servicemen, including cigarettes, cookies, chocolate, candy and stockings.
- Eileen was swept off her feet by the handsome older American GI in his military uniform, and they were married within a few months with the permission of Armand's commanding officer.
- Bridal gown and bridesmaids' dresses were borrowed from American actresses who gave their clothes to the war effort.
- Eileen's neighborhood was a tightly knit community that pulled together to help each other, even in the midst of wartime chaos.
- They gave their saved rations to the bride's family for a wedding cake and enough food for the special occasion.
- The top layer of their wedding cake was shipped to Armand's parents in Massachusetts.
- Armand served in the army military police unit, so he was only stationed in London during his time overseas.
- Eileen's friends Kathy and Eileen Ellis also married American GIs who were Armand's friends.
- Eileen was 18 and Armand was 24 when they were married on August 12, 1944.
- Eileen continued to live with her parents while Armand remained in the army barracks.
- Their time alone was minimal but precious, especially to Eileen.
- On June 4, 1945, their first child, Ann, was born.
- When the war ended, Armand returned to the United States alone.
- Eileen and eight-month-old Ann sailed on the *Saturnia* from Southampton, England, to America.
- Except for a brief spell of seasickness, it was a pleasant voyage.
- On March 17, 1946, Eileen and Ann arrived in New York City, looking quite fashionable in clothing donated by her London neighbors.

Their Marriage Took Place In England

Sgt. Armand J. Laflamme and his bride, the former Eileen Webb, a corporal in the WAAF, are shown with their attendants following their marriage Aug. 12 in England. Sgt. Laflamme is the son of Mr. and Mrs. Noel Laflamme of Prospect St. He and his bride sent the top layer of their wedding cake to his parents and it was received this week in perfect condition.

Sgt. Laflamme is stationed at an Army Air Base in England, where he is in charge of a unit of truck drivers. He has been in the service since Aug. 5, 1942. He had his basic training in Atlantic City, N. J., after which he was stationed at Eglin Field, Fla., and later in Kearns, Utah, going overseas in June of 1943. He was associated with his father in the ice business.

News of the marriage in a local Massachusetts newspaper.

A member of the United States Army Air Force, Francis William Deane, was married at Heston Parish Church on Saturday to Miss Eileen Lilian Ellis.

Local Vet Elated by News
Wife, Daughter to Arrive

Eileen's friend also married an American GI.

- It was St. Patrick's Day and Eileen thought the celebration was in honor of the war brides arriving from England.
- The large, noisy crowd at the docks was terrifying to Eileen, but Armand and his father, both in their army uniforms, were there to greet her.
- Eileen was dismayed to discover that Armand's father only spoke French.
- Due to the housing shortage, they moved into Armand's parents' house in Chicopee, Massachusetts.
- Eileen's mother-in-law also spoke only French.
- Her in-laws were not welcoming to Eileen because they had expected Armand to marry a second cousin who lived in Canada.
- The despondent cousin became a nun when she was told that Armand had instead married a girl in England.
- In addition, even though Eileen had converted to Catholicism to marry Armand, the facts that she was English and her family was Protestant were held against her.
- Armand's brother bought a restaurant, Chateau Harmony, north of Chicopee near Granby, a small rural community.
- Since Armand still had not found work, he agreed to be the cook for the restaurant.
- The young family moved into a house on the restaurant's property, so they finally had a place to call their own.
- Eileen was somewhat apprehensive that the house was on an isolated mountaintop by the Quabbin Reservoir, but was happy to be out of her in-laws' house.
- Several months later Eileen took ill and was hospitalized for three weeks.
- Armand's parents took care of Ann.
- When Eileen was ready to bring Ann home, she was upset to discover that her baby daughter only spoke French.
- She felt that this was another attempt to shut her out of the family.
- She decided then to make sure that her children never learned French.
- Eileen missed her family and felt particularly isolated because of the language barrier with the Laflamme family.
- She made a yearly phone call to her London family at Christmas.
- An appointment had to be made with the phone company to make sure the call went through.
- In an attempt to become accepted by Armand's family, Eileen applied for citizenship as soon as she was eligible.

Eileen and daughter Ann reunite with Armand.

Armand became the cook at his brother's restaurant.

Harsh winters made it impossible to leave the house.

Life at Work

- Armand's work schedule was grueling; he cooked in the restaurant seven days a week, from 11:30 a.m. to midnight.
- Eileen's strong cockney accent was a barrier to her finding work outside the home.
- Her sole responsibility was to take care of her husband, baby and the house, and her day revolved around tending to Ann, cleaning and cooking.
- The couple did not own a washing machine, so she did all the washing by hand.
- The woods were so thick and so close to the house, Armand had to clear out an area for the clothesline.
- When Eileen hung the wash, she was constantly frightened by wild animals.
- Snakes, skunks and groundhogs were a common sight and not welcomed by a city girl.
- The closest town was Chicopee, an hour's drive, where they attended the family's French Canadian church on Sundays.
- Eileen didn't feel comfortable there.
- The restaurant where Armand worked didn't provide a social outlet, either.
- Its clientele were rich people who came for a steak dinner and not to socialize.
- Armand's weekly salary was $30.00.
- Eileen was alone on the holidays, since that was a busy time at the restaurant.
- They felt fortunate, however, to live rent-free with only the utilities to pay.
- They also took a portion of food from the restaurant's weekly delivery for their own meals.
- Armand's parents butchered their own meats, canned fruits and vegetables from their garden and even made maple syrup.
- They shared all these foodstuffs with Armand and his family.
- From the first snow until spring, there was no more traveling in the car.
- With her husband working long hours and no telephone, Eileen was often lonely and despondent during the long, cold winter.
- She looked forward to spending a few precious hours each morning playing cards with Armand.
- During their second winter, the furnace malfunctioned, spewing black soot and grease all over the house.
- This was the last straw for Eileen, who told Armand, "Either we move off this mountain or I'm going back to England."
- They bought their first home in South Hadley for $4,100.
- Now, with a mortgage to pay, Armand continued working long hours at the Chateau Harmony, which now meant longer hours away from his family.
- In 1948, Eileen joined the British War Wives Club in Holyoke, and this became a lifeline for her.
- The club provided a setting for Eileen to keep up her attachments to her homeland.
- She became best friends with Ruby, a war bride from Scotland.

- Eileen often dreamt about returning to England someday when Armand retired from the restaurant business.
- She looked forward to her family visiting, but knew that wouldn't happen for a long time.
- She didn't have the confidence to go out and make a life for herself, and relied instead on Armand for everything.
- Her parents had made it clear that if she ever returned to England, she should not expect to live with them.
- She made the decision to move to America and she had to stick by it.

Life in the Community: Chicopee, Massachusetts

- Chicopee was founded in 1848 in western Massachusetts near the Chicopee and Connecticut Rivers, and means "where the water rushes."
- It was a welcoming area for a variety of immigrants and thus has a diverse population, including French, Italian, Polish and Portuguese.
- The Holyoke hills to the north of Chicopee limited the growth of agriculture, but encouraged the establishment of dairy farms.
- The Dwight Manufacturing Company and the Chicopee Manufacturing Company owned a large number of textile mills, which employed more than 2,000 people in the late 1800s.
- Many immigrants came to work in the mills, producing firearms, foot-wear, cutlery and military equipment.
- In the mid-1900s, Chicopee had 10 Protestant churches and three Catholic churches, one of which was for a French congregation.
- War brides like Eileen came to America as part of an amazing armada carrying some 70,000 young British war brides and their babies.
- Officially known as the War Brides Operation, over five months, 20 converted warships would be in perpetual motion across the Atlantic, a floating procession of brides.
- Some 200 reporters and newsreel cameras greeted the first "petticoat pilgrims," as the British media had dubbed them.
- A special act of Congress had waived immigration quotas for the war brides, and they claimed a unique place in the country's social fabric—a mass influx of foreigners drawn here not by need but by love.
- Across America the women scattered, becoming Iowa farmwives who grew "tomahtoes" or overly polite New Yorkers who muttered "oy vey" with British accents.

Many manufacturers hired returning servicemen.

HISTORICAL SNAPSHOT
1946

- Fifty American cities banned comic books that featured crime or sex

- Postwar America experienced considerable inflation; since 1939 housing costs had doubled, clothing was up 93 percent, food was up 129 percent and rent, 12 percent

- A Gallup poll reported that 94 percent of Americans professed a belief in God

- Entertainer Jack Benny sold his NBC radio program to CBS for a reported $3 million

- Patents were acquired for the vacuum leaf raker, fountain safety razor, suction ear-muffs, and the "Adventure" bra with plastic prop-up snap-ins

- New York began a fluoridation program for 50,000 children

- Garbage disposals, non-glare headlights, heat-conducting windshields, the Land Rover, the Porsche sports car, Nestlé's Quik and Scrabble all made their first appearance

- General Dwight Eisenhower rejected Democratic efforts to draft him for president

- Peter Goldmark of CBS invented a high-fidelity, long-playing record that played up to 45 minutes of music

- The University of Chicago and seven major corporations announced plans for coop-erative atomic research for industrial use

- James Gould Cozzens won the Pulitzer Prize in fiction for his book *Guard of Honor*

- Popular books included *The Naked and the Dead* by Norman Mailer; *Crusade in Europe* by Dwight D. Eisenhower; *Sexual Behavior in the Human Male* by A. C. Kinsey; and *Other Voices, Other Rooms* by Truman Capote

- Bell Laboratories developed the transistor

- Andrew Wyeth painted *Christina's World* and Edward Hopper created *Seven A.M.*

- Congress passed the Displaced Persons Act and admitted 205,000 refugees

- Television premieres included *Candid Camera* with Allen Funk, *Toast of the Town* with Ed Sullivan, Arthur Godfrey's *Talent Scouts, The Milton Berle Show* and the *Camel Newsreel Theater,* the first nightly news show

- In professional golf, Ben Hogan won the U.S. Open and was the PGA's top money win-ner with $36,000

- President Harry Truman ordered racial equality in the Armed Forces and proposed anti-lynching legislation to Congress

- A Nevada court declared prostitution legal in Reno

- The bikini made its appearance on American beaches

The Immigration of English War Brides After World War II

- The greatest number of war brides came from England, which accounted for the largest immigrant group since the turn of the century.

- In all, there were 44,886 brides and 21,350 children.

- The marriage had to abide by U.S. Government rules: the prospective bride signed a contract agreeing not to accompany her husband out of England; the woman's background was checked for honesty; she underwent a thorough physical examination and was interviewed by the chaplain.

- After V.E. day, the American servicemen went home, leaving their brides behind.

- The GI brides were nicknamed "GI wallflowers" as many wondered if they'd ever join their husbands; they needed "evidence of support" to travel across to America.

- In December of 1945, Congress passed an act to expedite the immigration of alien wives and minor children of citizen members of the U.S. Army Forces.

- A booklet, "A Bride's Guide to USA" provided these women with vital information about their forthcoming journey across the seas and their newly adopted country.

- The booklet included facts about luggage regulations (no confiscated enemy items allowed), travel requirements for infants (two dozen diapers) and warnings that not all America was like the Hollywood movies.

- Most ships sailed from Southampton and women were often given 24 hours' notice of their departure.

- The Immigration Department fingerprinted the brides, gave them smallpox vaccinations, deloused them and took away their ration books and coupons.

- Travel arrangements were supervised by the American Red Cross, while the entire operation was under the auspices of the Department of Transportation.

- The Transatlantic Brides and Parents Association was formed to keep families connected.

- The English way of life focused on the nuclear family of the husband, wife and children.

- The church became the central focus in their lives and gave them the opportunity to get involved in the local communities.

- Several hundred words in the English vocabulary are different from American words, which made the immigrants difficult to understand. Examples are lift for elevator, crisps for chips and caravan for trailer. The brides were told "to speak American" and were treated like foreigners.

- They could apply for citizenship after five years in the country and most did in an attempt to assimilate into American society.

- English War Brides Clubs sprang up all over the country as servicemen's wives were moved from state to state.

- This gave them a place to meet and foster friendships with fellow countrywomen; for many women, this was their "family away from family."

British Wives Clubs gave women a chance to socialize with fellow countrywomen; members often organized holiday parties for children.

Selected Prices

Baby Food	$0.59
Boiled Ham, Half Pound	$0.49
Carpet Sweeper	$19.95
LP Record	$1.25
Man's Shoes	$10.95
Pepsi-Cola, One Serving Bottle	$0.05
Record Cabinet	$13.50
Sofa Bed	$79.88
Whiskey, Fifth	$3.98
Woman's Blouse, Crepe	$4.95

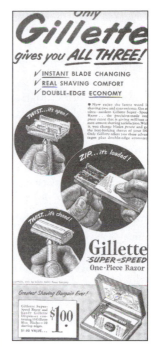

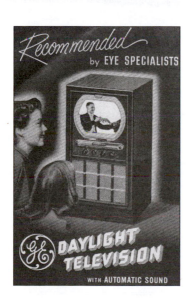

"Here Came the War Brides," by Tamara Jones,
The Washington Post, February 12, 2006:

. . . Joan Stubbs married her Walter when she was just 17. He was one of the Army Air Corps boys who played cards each night in the village cafe; she was the air-raid warden's daughter who would come remind them to draw the blackout curtains. Sometimes Walter would walk her home in the moonlight. "He liked to talk," she remembers, "and I liked to listen."

War had already torn a gaping hole in Joan's childhood. She and her older sister were among thousands of schoolchildren evacuated from the capital when the London Blitz began, sent to the countryside to live with strangers. Joan was 11. The besieged capital was 30 miles away, she guesses, and "at night you could see London burning." When Joan was 14, her father came to collect her; their house had been destroyed in a direct hit, and now her parents were fleeing the city as well. They all moved to a one-lane village called Bourne End, near the aerodrome where B-17s took off. Walter Stubbs belonged to the regiment known as Fame's Favored Few.

Joan was aboard that first love boat to America. She remembers the *Argentina* setting sail without fanfare. "We weren't allowed to have anyone see us off," she says. Families had to bid their daughters farewell at the train station. The girls then reported to processing camps, where there were mountains of forms to fill out in triplicate, thick stacks of documents to read and humiliating physicals to endure, standing naked before Army doctors who scanned their bodies with flashlights.

The U.S. military bore the cost of transportation, but the Red Cross budget to staff and supply the operation was $100,000. At the processing camps, cradles were made out of orange crates, while 20 war vessels were stocked with pureed peas, talcum powder and safety pins. Babies had to be at least three months old to travel, and women could not be more than seven months pregnant. Joan met a woman who slipped on the deck and would have lost her daughter overboard if a passing steward hadn't caught the infant. Thirteen babies who sailed from Belgium with their mothers aboard the *Zebulon Vance* were reported dead after an outbreak of diarrhea. . . .

British troops returning from years of combat would heckle and jeer at the women from the decks of their ships docking in Southampton as the brides set sail. The well-supplied American soldiers already were scorned in a popular slogan for being "oversexed, overpaid and over here." Now they were plundering the population of would-be English wives.

Joan Stubbs was oblivious to any controversy. "I think I was too young to realize the impact of what I was doing," she reflects.

Covered in ice from an overnight storm, the *Argentina* entered New York Harbor at 2:30 that February morning. Joan remembers the brides all rushing to the deck, shivering in the bitter wind to catch the first glimpse of their new homeland. "Can you imagine after four years of darkness what it was like to see the Statue of Liberty all lit up for us?" Joan's voice cracks at the memory. "It was such a beautiful sight."

THREE GI BRIDES TO REACH AREA DURING MARCH

Patrolman Dillon Awaits Colleen He Has Not Seen Since Wedding Day

Three more British brides of Western Massachusetts veterans—including the Irish colleen from whom a local GI was separated on their wedding day last June—will sail for America next month to be reunited with their husbands.

This was disclosed today by the London area transportation office of the army, which announced that one of the brides would sail from England March 4, arriving in New York city on the 11th, and the other two, together with the child of one area ex-serviceman, will leave Britain on the Saturnia March 9.

Happiest of the three husbands is Patrolman James P. Dillon of Massachusetts avenue, member of the dogwatch, who learned yesterday would soon be reunited with his Irish bride. Dillon, stationed with the field artillery in Normandy and Europe, was flown from the battlefields of Czechoslovakia to Belfast, where June 18, 1945, he and Martha Moll were married.

A few hours after the ceremony the army flew him back to his post and he has not seen her since.

Other area brides due to sail from England, both of whom will be aboard the Saturnia, include:—

Mrs Josephine R. Weld, wife of Frank Weld of 744 State street, Springfield, and Mrs Eileen LaFlamme, and Ann LaFlamme, three months, wife and daughter of Armand J. LaFlamme of Willimansett.

"If You Work and Marry, Kiss Your Social Security Goodbye," by William Laas, *McCall's*, March 1949:

Do you work? Do you pay one and one-half percent of your salary each week for OASI old-age and survivors insurance? Nice thing to have, a guaranteed pension in your old age. Only you'll never have it. Not if you get married.

The instant Dream Boy slips a gold band on your third finger, he becomes your only "Social Security." The personal contributions you have made cease to be worth a nickel. Well, maybe a nickel.

At age 65 you may claim a pension equal to half your husband's earned benefit, raised to three-fourths if he dies. Or you may claim your own earned pension if it is larger. One of the two pensions goes down the drain. Since you'd be eligible for the wife's benefit without having done a tap of work, the net benefit earned by your life's labor is merely the difference, most likely a matter of pennies, if not absolute zero.

If your husband dies while the children are less than 18 years old, you may claim a widow's pension. In exactly the same position, if you've worked and paid the identical taxes yourself, you get nothing. Neither does the family if you die.

Social Security is bargain insurance. If the pension your taxes have earned should be the smallest possible, $10 a month, it is property worth about $1,500 at current private annuity rates. The average pension is worth $3,900, no trifling gift of the U.S. Treasury on the day you marry.

Uncle Sam isn't greedy. He doesn't keep the money. He pays it out to a luckier sister who never punched the time clock in her life. A business girl who becomes a wife or widow usually receives not a dollar more than any other wife or widow who paid nothing. Sometimes less.

Great Britain, Britannica book of the year, 1944:

Of the 16 million men in Great Britain between 14 and 64 years of age, more than 15 million are either in the armed forces or in paid employment in 1943. Of the 17 million women between 14 and 64 years of age, 7,750,000 were in paid employment or in military services. Of the single women between 18 and 40 years of age, 91 percent were in paid work; and of the married women without children in the same age group, 80 percent were employed in some capacity in the war effort. More than one million men and women over 64 years of age were in paid employment.

After the outbreak of the war, 800,000 women between the ages of 40 and 60 entered industrial employment, thereby doubling the number of paid women workers in this age group.

"British Wives of GI's Score Neglect, Mistreatment in U.S.," *The New York Times*, January 8, 1947:

LONDON—Prominently headlined stories of GI "brides of despair"—British girls abandoned by their American ex-soldier husbands in New York—appeared in most London newspapers today, with purported details of neglect by United States officials and mistreatment by the American people.

The story stemmed from an interview given by Mrs. Millie Vincent when she arrived in the United States last night with a tale of "divorce by proxy" and Charles Woodrow Vincent of Birmingham, Alabama.

Mrs. Vincent, who has a 12-year-old son by a previous marriage, told the British Press Association that when she reached New York last August she was informed by an immigration official:

"You are a divorced woman. You have no right to travel here under false pretenses at the expense of the United States Government."

Until a few weeks ago, Mrs. Vincent said, she and two dozen other British women, unable to find their husbands, lived in a hotel, with government allowances of $2.00 a day for food and another $2.00 for sleeping accommodation.

"The money was only sufficient to buy breakfast," said Mrs. Vincent. "A hotel cost me $80 a week. English women were shabbily treated in New York. American women sneered at us and shop assistants kept us waiting."

In Northampton, some 55 miles northwest of London, Mrs. Vincent learned tonight that the divorce granted to her husband had been annulled. She said she did not know what to do now. . . .

The charges that hundreds of abandoned British war brides were living in squalor in New York while awaiting passage home were branded "outrageous" falsehoods by Daniel Green, Administrator of Social Service in the New York Chapter of the American Red Cross.

His denunciation of the London newspaper reports was echoed by local British officials in the English-Speaking Union, which sponsors a recreation and service program for British brides of former GIs. . . .

All the officials concerned agreed that only five percent of the Anglo-American marriages fail. Forty-three thousand British war brides have come through the port since February, Mr. Green noted, and less than 50 have been "rejected" by their husbands.

1948 Profile

After working for years in Argentina, Italian immigrant Cesare Barandoni finally came to the United States, sent for his family, and settled in New York City.

Life at Home

- Cesare Barandoni was born in Avola, a small town at the southern tip of Sicily, in 1903, the second youngest of nine children.
- His father was a farmer who worked a neighbor's land before saving enough money to buy his own plot of land.
- Farming provided a decent living for his family and instilled in his son a strong work ethic and a sense of opportunity for anyone who worked hard.
- Cesare began working in the local salt mines when he was 12 years old.
- He attended school when possible, but working always took priority over his education.
- When he was 20 and still working at the salt mines, he first met his future wife.
- Her name was Giovanna, the 14-year-old daughter of a coworker.
- One year later they were married, and soon after, they had their first child.
- Times were tough; Italy had only been a united country since 1861 and the central government based in Rome was still struggling to create a sense of national unity.
- As a result, the island of Sicily, more than 400 miles away, was often ignored when it came to issues of economic development.
- Cesare often worried about the future for his wife and newborn child.
- After the birth of his second child two years later, Cesare began to explore ways to care for his family outside Italy.
- Travelers passing through Avola told stories of a land of opportunity across the ocean in Argentina, a country hustling to attract willing workers from Europe needed by its suddenly flourishing economy.
- Cesare decided that working in Argentina would be a good way to make money, even if it meant leaving his family.
- In Argentina he could earn his way to America or his own farm in Italy.
- In 1927, at the age of 24, Cesare left Avola on a boat bound for Buenos Aires, Argentina; he was the first person in his immediate family ever to leave Sicily.

Cesare Barandoni left Italy when he was 24.

273

S.S. AUGUSTUS, 1927 Italia Line
Courtesy Steamship Historical Society Collection, Univ. of Baltimore Library

Cesare left Italy for Argentina in 1927.

- He hoped to be reunited with his wife and two children within a few years.
- In 1927, Argentina was a thriving country that was developing quickly.
- Fifty years earlier the country had been sparsely populated; an influx of immigrants from Europe vastly changed the landscape.
- Between the years 1869 and 1914, the population of the capital city of Buenos Aires grew from 180,000 inhabitants to over one million, most from Italy and Spain.
- Between 1882 and 1927, one million Italian immigrants comprised one-third of all people entering Argentina, permanently altering the ethnic demographic of the country.
- Most immigrated to work on Argentina's large wheat and cattle farms.
- Other profitable sectors included the shipping industry, where Cesare Barandoni found a job.
- Although the large Italian immigrant population made adjusting to the new country easier, Cesare found them to be poorly organized and often clustered into tight-knit groups based on their home towns in Italy.
- Italy's barely formed national identity handicapped the workers, who resisted the notion of working together and allowed employers to take advantage of them.
- This was especially true for immigrants like Cesare who hoped to stay only temporarily and save up money quickly.
- Italians who planned to put down permanent roots were usually better organized.
- When Cesare arrived in Buenos Aires, he was offered a job working on the docks of the port unloading cargo from ships.
- Although physically demanding, the work required no special training, and he was pleased to have a job.
- As part of the job, his employer provided him a place to live, and quickly carved a large piece out of his paycheck for the rent.
- As a result, even after long hours of backbreaking labor, Cesare found it difficult to save money.
- Year after year most of the money that he earned was sent to his wife and children in Sicily.
- After four years, Cesare found a warehouse job that paid better and didn't require him to live in expensive, employer-provided housing.
- He shared a room with other Italian workers in one of the poorer areas of the city to save more of his paycheck toward his goal.
- After six more years in Argentina, he had saved up enough money for the trip to America.

Cesare regularly sent money to his wife and children in Sicily.

- He left Argentina for Louisiana in 1937, a decade after he had arrived and years longer than he had expected.
- Cesare's first stop in the United States was New Orleans, Louisiana, a major port city, where he hoped to find work similar to that in Buenos Aires.
- There he found jobs scarce and the docks far less welcoming to foreigners, especially Italians, than Buenos Aires had been.
- Argentina had been far from ideal, but the size of the Italian population made day-to-day life much easier.

He set sail from Argentina for America in 1937.

- Louisiana was populated by immigrants from all over Europe, especially France.
- In addition, past episodes of violence between Italians and locals at the turn of the century, including the lynching of Sicilians, made Louisiana feel even less welcoming.
- Soon after arriving in New Orleans, Cesare followed a group of Italians to Detroit, where they had heard of job opportunities in the thriving auto industry.
- When he arrived in Detroit he met up with a distant relative, through whom he was able to secure a job working on an assembly line for the Ford Motor Company.
- He was responsible for attaching the headlights to cars.
- The American Federation of Labor, which had been founded two years earlier in 1935 to organize and protect auto workers, had made few inroads at Ford Motor Company, which was especially resistant to unionization.
- It was Cesare's first exposure to the organized labor movement.
- In Detroit, Cesare was able to earn much more money than he had in Argentina or back in Sicily and, living modestly, was able to save money for his family and his future.
- He worked for The Ford Motor Company for two years.
- In 1939 he was laid off when the company cut back the labor in the plant where he was working.
- He then decided to move to New York.
- For Cesare, like many immigrants coming to the United States, New York was seen as the center of the universe and full of opportunity.
- He also knew that New York had a prominent Italian community.
- When he arrived there in 1939, he settled into a strong Italian community on the shores of Brooklyn close to the docks.
- Most of the Italians who had come to America around the turn of the century settled in lower Manhattan's "Little Italy."
- By the end of World War I, more than half of the city's Italians were living outside of Manhattan.
- Cesare got a job as a longshoreman, unloading dry goods from ships, similar to the work in Buenos Aires.
- New York was one of the busiest ports in the world and the demand for labor was high.
- Unlike in Argentina, the longshoremen in New York were part of the International Longshoreman's Association (ILA), which had been in the city since 1908.
- The ILA had grown to be one of the most powerful unions in the city and worked to ensure fair treatment and pay for its members, in addition to creating health care and recreational facilities for the communities.
- Cesare lived alone in Brooklyn for two years, often working seven days a week, until he was finally able to send for his family.
- His wife and two children arrived in 1941.
- Giovanna was 34.
- His daughter was 17 and his son was 15.
- He hadn't seen them since he had left Sicily 14 years earlier.
- One year after his family arrived, his wife gave birth to their second son.
- Two years later their third son was born.

Cesare met up with distant relatives once in Detroit.

While Cesare saved money to send for his family, they waited in Sicily.

Cesare and Giovanna were happily reunited in New York City in 1941.

- By 1948, 21 years after Cesare left Italy, his family had adjusted to America and was enjoying their new life despite daily challenges and struggles that were part of the immigrant experience.
- In New York, Cesare and his growing family lived in a four-room apartment close to the water.
- Life in the Barandoni home in 1948 was strongly linked to the concept that the family was the most important aspect of everyone's lives.
- Everyone was expected to help out with chores and errands.
- The older children were in charge of helping to raise the younger children and making sure that they kept up at school.
- Since their parents spoke very little English, it was up to the older children to teach the younger children the language that they themselves had just recently learned in school and in the streets.
- They spoke a regional Sicilian dialect at home, often mixed with English words.
- Although the dialect was similar to standard Italian, the younger children who had never lived in Italy found that they often could not use their native tongue to communicate with their neighbors from other parts of Italy.
- Speaking little English was usually not a problem for Cesare and Giovanna because they lived in a predominantly Italian neighborhood.
- At times the children would translate for their parents.
- Even the younger boys had daily responsibilities in the family.
- Giovanna would send six-year-old Antonio to the corner store to pick up bread and other groceries.
- While Cesare had often worked seven days a week before his family arrived, in New York, he tried his best to always have Sunday off.
- Sunday was the most important day for the family.
- They were Roman Catholic, and religion was very prominent, although they usually only went to Church on major holidays such as Christmas and Easter.
- Religious holidays were celebrated with special meals, decorations and traditions at home.
- On Palm Sunday, the whole family would weave crosses out of palms and hang them around the house.

Sunday was family day for the Barandonis.

- Sunday was always a day to be spent with the family; the children knew not to make any other plans for that day.
- There was usually one large meal in the afternoon that combined both lunch and dinner, and which could last for hours.
- A typical Sunday feast would start with a large plate of pasta and homemade tomato sauce, sausage and meatballs.
- After the pasta plates were cleared, the main course would be served; often a fresh, seasonal fish prepared in the Sicilian tradition.
- With the fish or meat, there would also be a side serving of vegetables.
- Following the main course would be fresh fruit, after which the meal would end with dessert and coffee.
- Fresh bread would be a fixture throughout the meal, as would glasses of wine and water.
- After the meal, Cesare would help Giovanna clean up and then they would relax in the small garden area he maintained behind the house.
- The garden was one of Cesare's greatest passions.
- Although he didn't have much free time, he managed to maintain a dense, but very neat collection of just about everything that would grow in the Brooklyn climate.
- He grew herbs such as basil and oregano, lettuce, tomatoes and other vegetables that his wife would use for meals.
- He also had a fig tree that had special significance to him because it reminded him of his life in Sicily.
- The Brooklyn climate was much harsher than that of southern Italy, and the fig tree had to be wrapped tightly in canvas during the winter.
- The tree gave off fewer figs each year than its Italian equivalents, so Cesare treasured each one even more and would carefully share the sweet treats with his family after meals.
- Cesare's garden, typical of those of many Italian immigrants living in urban American areas, included structural pieces improvised from reused materials; vines wrapped around old pieces of pipe, tomatoes planted in recycled coffee cans, and coat hangers and pieces of string used throughout.
- Frugality was a major characteristic of the Barandoni household.
- Like the garden, Cesare's house included makeshift shelves, closets and other additions that he built so that he wouldn't have to buy them.
- He and his wife rarely spent money on themselves and never took vacations.
- A car wasn't necessary living in the city, as Cesare walked to work at the nearby docks.
- Giovanna was also known to haggle over the price of nearly everything she bought.
- While this was a commonly accepted practice in Sicily where she had spent most of her life, in America, her children were sometimes embarrassed by it.
- The family continued to save every dime.
- Now that they were united, their goal was to move out of their cramped apartment by the docks and into a house in a residential neighborhood.

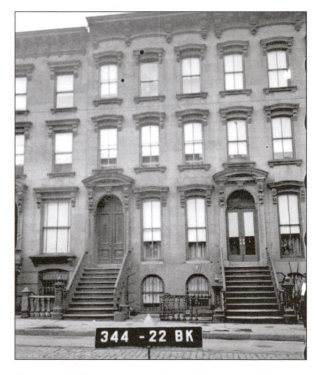

Cesare and Giovanna saved enough money to buy a brownstone in Brooklyn.

Life at Work

- Cesare Barandoni worked as a longshoreman at the Brooklyn piers.
- Although he lived close to the water, he still had to walk two miles to get to work.
- The work was very physically demanding.
- Although he no longer worked as many hours as he had before his family arrived in America, he still left the house before dawn and returned most nights just before dinner.
- Sometimes he worked late and his family ate without him.
- The work consisted of unloading dry goods such as coffee beans and salt from ships and putting them on trucks to be transported elsewhere throughout the region.
- Dry goods were moved using the traditional break bulk method.
- In this system, canvas sacks of the cargo were stacked on top of each other on wooden pallets and then transported from the ships to the docks using cranes.
- The pallets were then broken down and the cargo was unloaded by the longshoremen using short, hand-sized metal hooks with wooden handles.
- The physical difficulty of the job, which was all done outdoors, was often aggravated by the tough northeastern climate.
- Brooklyn was hot and humid during the summers, making heat exhaustion a serious danger, while regularly reaching below-freezing temperatures in the winter, presenting the risk of frostbite, among other things.
- The work was strenuous, but the protection of the union ensured job security, fair pay and safe working conditions: three things that were not guaranteed when Cesare was working the same job in Argentina.
- Another benefit of being part of the union was free health care for him and his family.
- Most of Cesare's coworkers were immigrants like him, many from Italy, and a large number did not speak English.
- Many of the workers represented by the union were not aware of the specifics of union contract deliberations and strike negotiations, but felt the positive effects of being organized.

Life in the Community: New York City

- Cesare, like many Italian immigrants of the time, rarely focused on events happening outside of his family and local community.
- Not speaking English created a significant divide between him and much of the world that he lived in, especially concerning the media and politics.
- Even though there were Italian-language newspapers published in New York, he simply didn't have the time to read them, even though America was awash in anti-Italian sentiments started during World War II because of Mussolini's alliance with Hitler.

HISTORICAL SNAPSHOT
1948

- Columbia Records introduced the long-playing 33 1/3 rpm record, which delivered 25 minutes of music per side versus the previous format that played for only four minutes

- The World Council of Churches was formed

- The Berlin Blockade was put into effect

- President Harry Truman signed the Selective Service Act, creating America's first peacetime draft

- Tito of Yugoslavia broke away from the USSR Communist Party

- Gerard Kuiper discovered Miranda, the innermost moon of Uranus

- Author William Faulkner published *Intruder in the Dust;* Norman Mailer's novel of World War II, *The Naked and the Dead,* was a major sensation; and George Orwell completed his book *1984,* originally titled *1948*

Uninterrupted music at its finest... on Columbia **long playing** records!

- The publication of Alfred C. Kinsey's *Sexual Behavior in the Human Male* ignited shock and indignation by reporting that 85 percent of married men had premarital sex

- McDonald's was franchised; the Baskin-Robbins chain began

- CBS and NBC both began nightly 15-minute television newscasts

- Cortisone was found to relieve rheumatoid arthritis

- Chrysler introduced disc brakes

- The Tony Awards, highlighting the best of theater, were introduced

- New York began a fluoridation program for 50,000 children

- Musician Leo Fender invented the electric guitar

- Western Union manufactured 50,000 Deskfax machines for fax transmission

- Patents were acquired for the vacuum leaf raker, fountain safety razor, metallic shoes and suction ear muffs

- General Dwight Eisenhower rejected efforts by the Democrats to draft him as a presidential candidate

- The Bic ballpoint pen was introduced

- The comic strip characters Charlie Brown, Lucy, and the other Peanuts began as *Li'l Folks*

- Garbage disposals, no-glare headlights, the Land Rover, car air conditioning and Nestle's Quik all made their first appearance

- European nations began to set import quotas on foreign films

Selected Prices

Adding Machine	$120.00
Antacid, Tums	$0.10
Baby's Car Seat	$1.98
Bedspread	$3.99
Child's Playsuit	$1.49
Dinette Set, Five-Piece	$89.95
Gin, Fifth	$3.12
Hairdryer	$9.95
Mink Coat	$1,650.00
Movie Ticket	$1.00

For skiing (or "she-ing") ...get a Barbasol face!

Barbasol
No brush
No lather
No rub-in

MADE WITH IMPORTED BOTANICALS

HIRAM WALKER'S GIN

This Martini makes a hit with any audience

as served on Union Pacific Dining Cars

Fine Foods · Fine Service · Fine Trains

UNION PACIFIC RAILROAD

HE WON! THE GIRL OF HIS DREAMS!

LOOK YOUNG! FEEL YOUNG! Youthful Appearance Wins!

HOLD THAT LINE! WITH THE "MANLY FORM" Supporter FEATURING THE FLAT FRONT

$1.98 POST PAID

SCIENTIFICALLY MADE FOR YOUR COMFORT

SEND NO MONEY

When you Hurry...when you Worry better take TUMS for ACID INDIGESTION Heartburn

Quick Relief for ACID INDIGESTION HEARTBURN

TUMS for the tummy

Fight tooth decay and gum troubles both— to keep your Whole Mouth Healthier!

IPANA

For healthier teeth, healthier

Oral History, Alba Fiorentino, Northampton, Massachusetts:

In 1901 my father came from Biella, Piemonte, which is in the northern part of Italy, at the foot of the Alps. They were starving. They had no land, there was no work in Italy. He had proposed marriage to my mother, Rosina Comoglio, and although she would accept, she wanted to think it over. So he came to America and he wrote letters. He made hearts and he told her how much he loved her. He hardly knew her. He kept writing to my mother to have her come over to America to get married. And finally she agreed. In 1903, she sailed from Le Havre, France, in steerage, which cost $25. The trip took one month; it was filthy. It was dirty and the food was terrible. She ate nothing but water and lemons. And there she was, knowing that she would arrive and have to get married right then and there at Ellis Island after they examined to see if she was in good health or be immediately returned to Italy.

She arrived at Ellis Island with a trunk. In the trunk, she had her trousseau, her beautiful handmade dresses, handwoven linens, all these very fine things. She must have started working on them when she was very young. As part of her trousseau, she also brought lamb's wool to make a mattress.

My mother had one passion in life: sewing. She loved to sew and would lose herself in sewing. In Italy they would sit in a little circle of people, about 10, 20 of them, the women crocheting and embroidering, in a shed where the horses furnished heat. They would sing songs; they would tell stories.

My mother embroidered her linens, towels, and other things with her initials. You must always embroider in your name, your single name, not after you're married. Because that is yours.

My parents settled in the Italian section of Northampton in Massachusetts, where only silk weavers lived, and they raised me and my sister, Rita. Our father worked in the Belding Silk Mill, 52 hours a week for five dollars. His brothers Pablo and Annibale also had jobs there. For $500, my father bought a house and 10 acres of land, which he farmed at night after working all day. He sold some of the vegetables he grew, and the chickens and rabbits. He had 350 chickens. He went hunting; we ate rabbits, squirrels, deer, and pheasants. We had good food, and we had fresh vegetables. We never suffered hunger. My mother was a gourmet cook. My father started the first cooperative in Northampton of foods imported from Italy. He would find all these things you couldn't find here. It would come in big bales, big sacks, and he would weigh it all, working as late as midnight.

My mother was also an excellent dressmaker. She made all our clothes. The fur my father obtained in the animals he stretched with nails on the board, fur side down; then he salted, and let it dry in the sun. When the hide was softened, my mother would cut it, put a small cotton underneath it, and a piece of silk over the cotton, to make fur cuffs and collars for our little coats. We were always very well-dressed.

My father had only three years of schooling, but he spoke three languages. Every night, after working his land, he would come in and clean up and show us pictures of the world he would get from the Forbes library or read us a chapter in Les Misérables. Then he would go for a walk, keeping us in suspense until the next night. He was a great storyteller. He would visit his friends, telling them stories and making them laugh, and they would pour him a glass of wine.

We were in a ghetto with our own people. We spoke the Italian dialect in our home. We spoke English when we played with other children, who did the same thing, but when we returned to the house, we spoke Italian again. My mother insisted that we learn two languages. My parents thought they would not be staying in America permanently because they didn't feel part of America. And there was great suffering at times.

We were never even counted in the census polls. We were not part of Northampton; we were down in the meadows. There must have been about 70 or 80 families all living down there. When there were floods in the spring of the Connecticut River Valley, we helped each other, and we managed. And we had good times! We had parties with singing and music and mandolin and accordion. We never mixed with anyone else. We never felt isolated, but we knew that we were not part of anything beyond the area.

"Italian Workers Here Seen Loyal," *The New York Times*, June 12, 1940:

Luigi Antonini, State chairman of the American Labor party and leader of 40,000 Italian dressmakers in this city, sent a telegram to President Roosevelt last night endorsing his attack on Premier Mussolini and condemning Italy's entry into the war as a "criminal" act against democracy.

Mr. Antonini, who is the first vice president of the International Ladies Garment Workers Union, an affiliate of the American Federation of Labor and secretary of the Italian Dressmakers Union, Local 89, assured the President that the great bulk of Italians in this country would remain "loyal and faithful" to the United States in peace or war.

He expressed the hope that the government and people of the United States would take all precaution to halt Fascist activities in this country, but that they would not stoop to "blind prejudice and discrimination against Italian immigrants who cannot be held accountable for the wrongful actions of an enraged dictator."

Mr. Antonini urged the President to remember that "the first declaration of war" was made by Mussolini in 1922 against "the Italian nation whose freedom and happiness he destroyed." Congratulating Mr. Roosevelt on his "masterly" speech at Charlottesville, Va., the Italian labor leader said:

"You said that on June 10, 1940, Mussolini's dagger stabbed a neighbor in the back. It is the same dagger which on June 10, 1924, stabbed Matteotti, the same dagger which on June 10, 1937, stabbed the brothers Carlo and Bruno Rosselli, whose only crime, as in the case of Matteotti, was to oppose fascism and fight for a free Italy."

The references in the telegram were to Giacomo Matteotti, Italian Socialist leader and member of the House of Deputies, and to the Rosselli brothers, active in the underground movement against Mussolini, who were killed near Paris. Mr. Antonini declared in an interview that the fact that both these events and the declaration of war occurred on the tenth of June was an indication that Mussolini had "a perfect criminal mind."

In a message addressed to workers in the dress factories, Mr. Antonini noted that Local 89 had always allowed a policy of undivided allegiance to the government and institutions of the United States and that it had a right to protest against any "unjustified persecution" of innocent Italian immigrants because of an action in which they had no voice.

He expressed certainty that the Italian dressmakers would not stir up ill feelings in the shops by criticizing the policies of the United States and he served notice on Fascist or Communist agitators that the union would take no steps to defend those who attempted to "sow dissension and promote disunity" in the shops.

Mr. Antonini said the Communists and Fascists were working "hand in hand" and that both groups required watching. As a means of "crystallizing" Italian loyalty to this country and of guarding against Italian "fifth columns" here, Mr. Antonini will suggest to Mayor La Guardia and Lieut. Gov. Charles Poletti the desirability of calling together a special conference of prominent Italian-Americans and of considering ways to demonstrate the feeling.

"Aid to Italians Reported, Roosevelt Said to Study Use of Immigrants' Funds," *The New York Times,* September 11, 1944:

Pietro Nenni, Socialist party secretary, said in an editorial in *Avanti* today that he was reliably informed that the White House was considering the authorization of the opening of accounts in the United States by Italian immigrants in the name of Italians in Italy.

Backed by dollars deposited in the United States, the accounts would form a guarantee for reconstruction supplies needed in Italy, Mr. Nenni said.

The Socialist leader said President Roosevelt also was considering reopening Italian exports to the United States.

Letters to *The New York Times:* "Loyalty of Italians Upheld, But Their Past Culture Is Important, Count Sforza Asserts," *The New York Times,* June 18, 1942:

To the Editor of The New York Times:

Arthur Livingston writes about my new book, *The Real Italians,* in *The Times* of June 14, for which I am grateful to him even when he disagrees with some of my interpretations: "Count Sforza . . . recommends that Italians here preserve their original cultural background. Against this notion we must courageously retort that . . . to create an Italian minority . . . would be against American national interests. Our Italian immigrants must accept American concepts of school, church and State unless they wish to become and remain an element of weakness and disintegration."

When all freedom disappeared in Italy and I began writing books in English, I always left them to their fate. They were to me action not literature. And if today for the first time I answer, it is not for the sake of my book but for something really important-the problem of Italians in the United States.

In the chapter on "Italians and America" I said: "Liberal, democratic Italy had always urged upon Italo-Americans an absolute loyalty to their new country, coupled with the maintenance of cultural and spiritual bonds with the old. In this way, free Italy contributed to the welfare of the United States by helping to form good American citizens; for you cannot make a good citizen out of a man who is intellectually and spiritually impoverished by being cut off from the only past he has had. If you do this to him, he becomes a savage, a bastard, a robot."

Letters to *The New York Times* . . . *(continued)*

Since America is at war, I have spoken intimately with numerous American citizens of Italian origin, whom I have urged to serve loyally the United States. Except the Fascisti who after Pearl Harbor became arch-Americans only in appearance, I found all most loyal American citizens.

But where have I found the most inspired, deep-rooted, almost religious devotion to this country? Among sons of Italians on whose shelves I discovered *The Divine Comedy,* the *Promessi Sposi* and some much-read pages of Mazzini. Their Americanization had not meant to them forgetting Italy, buy something much higher—the identification of themselves with a new nationality destined to give someday a new gospel to the world.

Happy and grateful to be now in this country I love, but deciding to live and die an Italian, I bowed to them, I admired them. To them, the United States are the United States of tomorrow for which they are ready to give gladly their lives. Their America is not only the country which gave a better standard of life but the country which is to them—as it is to me—the forerunner of world democracy, the most glorious hope for all who suffer, for all who hate the bestiality of fascism and Nazism.

Theirs is the purest and noblest American patriotism. Vice President Wallace spoke also for them with his admirable address at Free World. Men do not die for a better standard of life; they die only for ideas—for moral ideas.

—SFORZA
New York, June 15, 1942

1943 News Feature

Diary of Nazi Propaganda Chief Joseph Goebbels, 1943:

March 2, 1943

We are now definitely pushing the Jews out of Berlin. They were suddenly rounded up last Saturday, and are to be carted off to the East as quickly as possible. Unfortunately our better circles, especially the intellectuals, once again have failed to understand our policy about the Jews and in some cases have even taken their part. As a result our plans were tipped off prematurely, so that a lot of Jews slipped through our hands. But we will catch them yet. . . .

At 4 P.M. I drove up to [Hermann] Goering's home. His home is high up on the mountain in almost wintry quiet. Goering received me most charmingly and is very open-hearted. His dress is somewhat baroque and would, if one did not know him, strike one as somewhat funny. But that's the way he is, and one must put up with his idiosyncrasies; they sometimes even have a charm about them. . . .

Goering evidenced the greatest concern about the Fuehrer. To him, too, the Fuehrer seems to have aged 15 years during the three-and-a-half years of war. It is a tragic thing that the Fuehrer has become such a recluse and leads so unhealthy a life. He doesn't get out into the fresh air. He does not relax. He sits in his bunker, fusses and broods. If one could only transfer him to other surroundings! But he has made up his mind to conduct this war in his own Spartan manner, and I suppose nothing can be done about it.

But it is equally essential that we succeed somehow in making up for the lack of leadership in our domestic and foreign policy. One must not bother the Fuehrer with everything. The Fuehrer must be kept free for the military leadership. One can understand his present mood of sometimes being fed up with life and occasionally even saying that death holds no terrors for him; but for that very reason we must now become his strongest personal support. As was always the case during crises of the Party, the duty of the Fuehrer's closest friends in time of need consists in gathering about him and forming a solid phalanx around his person. . . .

Goering realizes perfectly what is in store for all of us if we show any weakness in this war. He has no illusions about that. On the Jewish question, especially, we

Joseph Goebbels

285

have taken a position from which there is no escape. That is a good thing. Experience teaches that a movement and a people who have burned their bridges fight with much greater determination than those who are still able to retreat.

March 7, 1943

During the night Essen suffered an exceptionally severe raid. The city of the Krupps has been hard hit. The number of dead, too, is considerable. If the English continue their raids on this scale, they will make things exceedingly difficult for us. The dangerous thing about this matter, looking at it psychologically, is the fact that the population can see no way of doing anything about it. . . .

March 9, 1943

Naturally the Fuehrer will under no circumstances let air warfare continue in a slipshod way as hitherto. One need only to think six months ahead; then we would face ruin in many cities, sustain thousands of casualties, and find the morale of our people somewhat impaired. This must not be, come what may. The Fuehrer is going to see to it under all circumstances that British terror be answered by terror on our side. . . . Moreover, the Luftwaffe command staffs must be taken out of Paris; in fact, not only these, but also other command staffs. Paris is a dangerous place. No occupation force has ever stuck it out in this city without harm to its soul. . . .

The Fuehrer fully endorses my anti-Bolshevik propaganda. That is the best horse we now have in our stable. He also approves of my tactics in letting the Bolshevik reports of victories go out into the world unchallenged. Let Europe get the creeps; all the sooner will it become sensible. . . .

March 20, 1943

It remains to be seen whether an invasion will actually be attempted or not. Should the English and the Americans actually prepare for it, they will most assuredly look for a point where we are not very strong. I don't believe that the invasion will take place in the west, but more likely in the south or southeast. But these are more conjectures without any basis of fact. . . .

I proposed to the Fuehrer in the future not to bombard slums but the residential sections of the plutocracy when making air raids on England. According to my experience this makes the deepest impression. The Fuehrer agrees with this. It doesn't pay to attack harbors or industrial cities. At present we haven't sufficient means for such attacks. . . .

The Fuehrer is happy over my report that the Jews have for the most part been evacuated from Berlin. He is right in saying that the war has made possible for us the solution of a whole series of problems that could never have been solved in normal times. The Jews will certainly be the losers in this war, come what may. . . .

April 9, 1943

A report on interrogations of American prisoners is really gruesome. These American boys are human material that can in no way stand comparison with our people. One has the impression of dealing with a herd of savages. The Americans are coming to Europe with a spiritual emptiness that really makes you shake your head. They are uneducated and don't know anything. For instance, they ask whether Bavaria belongs to Germany and similar things. One can imagine what would happen to Europe if this dilettantism could spread unchallenged. But we, after all, will have something to say about that!

April 17, 1943

A number of English papers and periodicals have been laid before me which give evidence of great respect for my person and my work. News Chronicle calls me the most dangerous member of the Nazi gang. I can be very proud of this praise. . . .

April 26, 1943

It is reported that the churches in Moscow were overcrowded [on Easter day]. The Soviets, to a certain extent, have restored freedom of religion. That's very sharp and clever tactics. It would be a good thing if we also were somewhat more elastic in these matters. . . .

May 1, 1943

The Soviets at the moment are extremely insolent and arrogant. They are quite conscious of the security of their position. They have no consideration whatever for their Anglo-Saxon allies. . . . The men in power in the Kremlin know exactly how far they can go. There is great bitterness in London and Washington about it which nobody seeks to disguise. The Anglo-Saxon camp is in a blue funk about the fact that our propaganda has succeeded in driving so deep a wedge into the enemy coalition.

May 8, 1943

The Fuehrer argued that the anti-Semitism which formerly animated the Party and was advocated by it must again become the focal point of our spiritual struggle. . . .

The Fuehrer once more traced in detail the parallel between 1932 and today. It is truly amazing and most convincing. Everything that happened then is being repeated today, and just as in 1932 we attained victory only by a stubbornness that sometimes looked like veritable madness; so, too, we shall achieve it today. . . .

The Fuehrer gave expression to his unshakable conviction that the Reich will be the master of all Europe. We shall yet have to engage in many fights, but these will undoubtedly lead to most wonderful victories. From there on the way to world domination is practically certain. . . .

In this connection we naturally cannot accept questions of right and wrong even as a basis of discussion. The loss of this war would constitute the greatest wrong to the German people, victory would give us the greatest right. After all, only the victor will have the possibility of proving to the world the moral justification for his struggle. . . .

Hitler at the War Table.

1950–1959

The consequences of World War II were everywhere in the decade of the 1950s: a population eagerly on the move, industries infused with energy and confidence, plans for interstate highways, hydroelectric dams to power America, a plethora of new national brands made for Americans. Optimism was rampant. Women tended to marry at an earlier age and bear children in their twenties. As the decade progressed, much of America's energy was focused on family and the potential of children. Television programs that educated and toys that expanded creativity were in vogue. Family travel was considered a necessity and college a definite possibility. Health insurance was common and everyone knew someone who owned a television set. America was on a roll. It manufactured half of the world's products, 57 percent of the steel, 43 percent of the electricity, and 62 percent of the oil. As a result of World War II, the economies of Europe and Asia lay in ruins, while America's industrial structure was untouched and well oiled to supply the needs of a war-weary world.

Significantly, during this time Congress established the modern-day U.S. immigration system. It created a quota system which imposed limits on a per-country basis and established a preference system that gave priority to family members and people with special skills. This was followed by the Refugee Relief Acts of 1953 and 1954 that authorized the admission of another 200,000 refugees from war-torn Europe and escapees from Communist-dominated countries. During the next 40 years of the Cold War, America would remain preoccupied with immigrants and refugees from Communist regimes. The willingness of America was tested in 1956 when Soviet forces suppressed an insurrection in Hungary in 1959 as Fidel Castro came to power in Cuba.

In addition, the war years' high employment and optimism spurred the longest sustained period of peacetime prosperity in the nation's history. A decade full of employment and pent-up material desires produced demands for all types of consumer goods. Businesses of all sizes prospered. Rapidly swelling families, new suburban homes, television, and most of all, big, powerful, shiny automobiles symbolized the hopes of the era. During the 1950s, an average of seven million cars and trucks were sold annually. By 1952, two-thirds of all families owned a television set, while home freezers and high-fidelity stereo phonographs were considered necessities. Specialized markets developed to meet the demand of consumers such as amateur photographers, pet lovers and backpackers. At the same time, shopping malls, supermarkets and credit cards emerged as important economic forces.

This prosperity also ushered in conservative politics and social conformity. Tidy lawns, "proper" suburban homes with "neat and trim" interiors were certainly "in" throughout the decade as Americans adjusted to the postwar years. Properly buttoned-down attitudes concerning sexual mores brought stern undergarments for women like bonded girdles and stiff, pointed, or padded bras to confine the body. The planned community of Levittown, New York, mandated that grass be cut at least once a week and laundry washed on specific days. A virtual revival of Victorian respectability and domesticity reigned; divorce rates and female college attendance fell while birth rates and the sales of Bibles rose. Corporate America promoted the benefits of respectable men in gray flannel suits whose wives remained at home to tend house and raise children. Suburban life included ladies' club memberships, chauffeuring children to piano and ballet classes, and lots of a newly marketed product known as tranquilizers, the sales of which were astounding.

The average wage earner benefited more from the booming industrial system than at any time in American history. The 40-hour work week became standard in manufacturing. In offices, many workers were becoming accustomed to a 35-hour week. Health benefits for workers became more common and paid vacations were standard in most industries. In 1950, 25 percent of American wives worked outside the home; by the end of the decade the number had risen to 40 percent. Communications technology, expanding roads, inexpensive airline tickets, and an unbounded spirit meant that people and commerce were no longer prisoners of distance. Unfortunately, up to one-third of the population lived below the government's poverty level, largely overlooked in the midst of this prosperity.

The Civil Rights Movement was propelled by two momentous events in the 1950s. The first was a decree on May 17, 1954, by the U.S. Supreme Court which ruled that "in the field of public education the doctrine of 'separate but equal' has no place. Separate educational facilities are inherently unequal." The message was electric but the pace was slow. Few schools would be integrated for another decade. The second event established the momentum of the Civil Rights Movement. On December 1, 1955, African American activist Rosa Parks refused to vacate the white-only front section of a Montgomery, Alabama bus, leading to her arrest and a citywide bus boycott by blacks. Their spokesman became Martin Luther King, Jr., the 26-year-old pastor of the Dexter Avenue Baptist Church. The yearlong boycott was the first step toward the passage of the Civil Rights Act of 1964.

America's youths were enchanted by the TV adventures of *Leave It to Beaver*, Westerns, and *Father Knows Best*, allowing them to accumulate more time watching television during the week (at least 27 hours) than attending school. TV dinners were invented; felt skirts with sequined poodle appliqués were the rage; Elvis Presley was worshipped, and the new phenomena of *Playboy* and Mickey Spillane fiction were created, only to be read behind closed doors. The everglowing eye of television killed the "March of Time" newsreels after 16 years at the movies. Sexual jargon such as "first base" and "home run" entered the language. Learned-When-Sleeping machines appeared, along with Smokey the Bear, Sony tape recorders, adjustable shower heads, *Mad Comics,* newspaper vending machines, Levi's faded blue denims, pocket-size transistor radios and transparent plastic bags for clothing. Ultimately, the real stars of the era were the Salk and Sabin vaccines, which vanquished the siege of polio.

1956 Profile

Because of diminishing sugar plantation jobs, Annette Martinez decided to leave Puerto Rico and, in the wake of her brothers and sister, find work in the United States.

Life at Home

- Annette Martinez was born in 1930 in Salinas, a small agricultural community on the southern coast of Puerto Rico, known for its sugar production.
- During the first half of the twentieth century, Puerto Rico was one of the leading producers of sugar for the United States and other countries.
- Annette's family made their living on the sugar plantations.
- Beginning in the 1940s, many sugar plantations were replaced by large foreign-owned industrial factories.
- This change meant a higher standard of living for some, but fewer plantation jobs for others.
- As a result of the decreasing agricultural jobs, many members of Annette's family began thinking about leaving Puerto Rico to find work.
- Emigrating to the United States was the natural first choice because Puerto Ricans had American citizenship and could work legally.
- During World War II, many American labor recruiters came to the island in search of cheap labor to replace the workers lost to the military draft.
- Annette's two older brothers were the first of her family to emigrate after being recruited by an American businessman to work in a toy factory in Baltimore, Maryland, in 1945.
- Then, a year later, in 1946, Annette's older sister Glenda left to work as a domestic servant for a wealthy family in Philadelphia.
- Although Annette wanted to follow her siblings, she didn't trust the American recruiters.
- Annette stayed in Puerto Rico, hoping that her brothers or sister could find her a stable job in America.
- In 1953, during a trip to San Juan to visit her cousins, 23-year-old Annette met an American family there on vacation.

Annette Martinez was 23-years-old when she left Puerto Rico.

Annette's family worked on sugar plantations in Puerto Rico.

Annette's parents and her brother.

Two sisters celebrate Annette's First Communion.

- The father, Mr. Santos, offered her a job working in his hotel in New York City.
- Annette trusted him because he had not come to Puerto Rico specifically to recruit workers.
- Soon after, she left Puerto Rico on a plane to New York.
- Annette was terrified to fly, but was encouraged by her sister, who told her about the views from the airplane window and the food service.
- The flight took six and a half hours and cost $44.00.
- Annette paid for the trip with money she had saved since she was 14, plus $20.00 her grandmother gave her before she died.
- With the help of Mr. Santos, Annette rented a room in one of the poorest sections of Manhattan, known as Spanish Harlem.
- She shared the apartment with two other Puerto Rican women.
- Annette had little money to live on, after sending most of her paycheck home to help support her family in Puerto Rico.
- Her neighborhood was largely made up of Puerto Ricans and immigrants from other Spanish-speaking countries.
- She found that many Puerto Rican customs and traditions were preserved in New York, and she was not as homesick as she had feared she would be.
- She found many familiar foods that she had eaten at home, such as rice and beans, pork, and beef.
- Much of her island's fresh fish and tropical fruit were harder to come by.
- Once in a while, Annette went out on the weekends dancing with her friends.
- In 1954, she met Wilfredo Rivera at a dancehall.
- Willy, as she called him, rolled cigars in his father's shop.
- After a short courtship, they were married.
- Her brothers and sister were not able to travel to New York for the wedding.
- Despite being very happy at getting married, Annette felt terribly sad that she had no family to share the happy day.
- After the wedding, Annette moved in with Willy and his family in the South Bronx.

- Their first son, Carlos, was born in 1955.
- Wilfredo's mother took care of the baby so that Annette could continue working.
- Annette continued to send money to her family in Puerto Rico every week.
- Though living with her husband's family was inexpensive and convenient, both Annette and Willy longed to be able to own their own home.
- They both saved most of what was left of their paychecks after living expenses and family obligations.
- Home ownership was considered important in Puerto Rican culture.
- Annette was content with her life, but missed her family.
- She was not able to take time off from work to visit her brothers in Baltimore or her sister in Philadelphia.
- She wrote to her parents in Puerto Rico often, but knew she would never see them again.

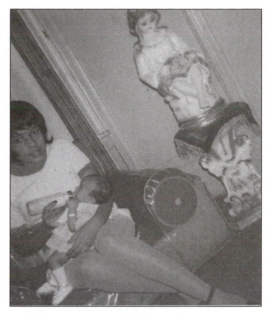

They lived with her husband's family.

Life at Work

- Annette worked as a room maid for four months at the Santos's large hotel—La Calienda Casa.
- A neighbor told Annette about an opportunity to work as a sewing machine operator in a garment factory in downtown Manhattan.
- Although she didn't mind working at the hotel, the job in the garment factory seemed like a good idea.
- The factory workers were almost entirely Puerto Ricans, giving Annette the opportunity to work and socialize with people to whom she could easily relate.
- The factory job was also unionized.
- This was important because Puerto Rican workers were easily taken advantage of.
- Unfamiliar with American work practices and unable to speak English well, they were ill equipped to argue on their own behalf.
- The factory job paid more than her job at La Calienda Casa, a result of the collective bargaining agreements of the union.
- She made $0.75 per hour and sent $12.00 to $15.00 a week to Puerto Rico.
- Once she started saving for her own house, she sent a bit less, but still had to contribute to her husband's household.
- Despite the advantages, operating a sewing machine was very grueling work.
- The hours were long and Annette had to sit at her sewing machine for eight-hour stretches with only a few brief breaks.
- The factory was overcrowded with workers; the building was often too hot during the summer and too cold in the winter.
- Once, Annette fainted from heat exhaustion.
- To supplement her factory work, Annette often mended clothes at home to make extra money.
- She was grateful that her mother-in-law was able to help care for Carlos, allowing her to devote more hours to work.
- Her dream of being able to move out of the Riveras' house was always on her mind.

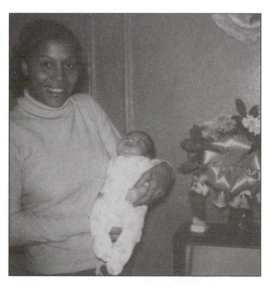

While Annette was at work, her mother-in-law took care of Carlos.

Life in the Community: New York City

- Annette was part of the group of Puerto Ricans who came to New York during the "Great Migration" of the 1940s and 1950s.
- These individuals were needed to help replenish the workforce, as many of the city's more affluent residents relocated to the suburbs.
- New York City Mayor Robert F. Wagner, Jr. was in favor of Puerto Ricans settling in the city and encouraged businesses to recruit Puerto Rican workers.
- The part of the Bronx where Annette and Willy lived was predominantly Puerto Ricans but more middle class than the impoverished Spanish Harlem section.
- Their neighborhood was full of Puerto Rican families, shops and businesses.
- Annette did grocery shopping at a nearby *Bodega* where the owners spoke only Spanish.
- She found many of the foods, including fish and produce, that she used to buy in Puerto Rico.
- Before the birth of their son, Annette and Willy would often go dancing at the same dancehall where they had first met.
- They enjoyed the music of popular Puerto Rican artists Pedro Flores and Cuarteto Victoria.
- The couple were practicing Catholics and tried to attend mass as much as possible.
- Their busy work schedules often made it difficult to do so.
- Annette considered herself very lucky to have a wonderful husband and a healthy son.
- She thanked God every day that her new family lived in a relatively safe neighborhood.
- Despite her contentment, however, tensions often ran high between Puerto Ricans and the city's other ethnic immigrant groups.
- Many resented Annette because she, like most Puerto Ricans, already had American citizenship even before arriving in the United States.
- Annette often asked herself who she was: Puerto Rican or American?
- Despite her citizenship, she was often viewed as an outsider by many of the city's longtime residents.
- Annette and Willy's family often felt pulled in opposite directions, welcomed by businesses looking for cheap labor, but shunned by residents afraid that their neighborhoods were being taken over by 'Ricans.
- Annette sometimes felt other young mothers thought their babies superior to her son.
- She secretly wondered if Carlos would ever be accepted as American.
- Oftentimes, Puerto Ricans also felt divided amongst themselves.
- Willy's parents tried to strictly preserve the culture and traditions of Puerto Rico, while Annette felt it important to integrate into American life.
- This caused some hard feelings in the Rivera household.
- Another dividing issue among Puerto Ricans was language.
- Annette spoke English as a result of the government-mandated use of English in public schools when she was growing up in Puerto Rico.
- Many Puerto Ricans, including Willy's parents, who were from the rural parts of the island, didn't have the same exposure to English.
- They struggled with the language when they came to New York, adding to their reluctance to shed their Puerto Rican traditions.
- Due to the large number of non-English-speaking immigrants, the city created services to assist the Spanish-speaking population.
- New schools, and social and civic services were established and funded by all the city's taxpayers.
- This angered longtime residents who thought that everyone should be forced to speak English.
- But this conflict was not entirely a new problem.

- Ever since Puerto Rico was ceded to the United States following the Spanish-American War of 1898, Americans struggled with what to do with a colony that was largely non-white and entirely Spanish-speaking.
- During the first 20 years of American control, two different governmental policies were established.
- In the Foraker Act of 1900, the United States modeled its governmental style after that of the British Crown Colonies.
- Islanders would be citizens of Puerto Rico but not the United States.
- Beginning in 1902, there would be no tariffs on goods between Puerto Rico and the United States.
- The U.S. president would be responsible for the appointment of the island governor and its Supreme Court.
- The U.S. Congress would retain veto power over any laws in Puerto Rico.
- There will be an 11-member Executive Council named by the governor.
- The House of Delegates (35 members) would be elected by popular vote.
- Few were pleased with the Foraker Act.
- Wealthy Americans called it undemocratic, while Puerto Ricans proclaimed it not statehood, independence, or home rule.
- After the United States acquired the Virgin Islands, President Woodrow Wilson signed the Jones Act in 1917, which provided:
  - Puerto Ricans could freely travel to the U.S. mainland;
  - Puerto Ricans were U.S. citizens;
  - Although Puerto Ricans could not vote in federal elections and were not taxed, they could be drafted during wartime;
  - The Senate and House on Puerto Rico were elected by universal male suffrage until 1929, when women's suffrage was granted;
  - The governor, Supreme Court, and top officials were to be appointed by the president.
- The Jones Act was amended in 1947, granting Puerto Ricans the right to elect their own governor, but kept the U.S. Congress as the source of Puerto Rico's rights.
- In July 1950, Public Law 600 was signed which allowed the people of Puerto Rico to draft their own constitution.
- Puerto Rico was granted commonwealth status on July 25, 1952.
- This meant that Puerto Rico was self-governing on local matters, but required to pay federal taxes.
- Though not fully independent, Puerto Ricans could receive many benefits from their association with America, including social benefits such as food stamps.

HISTORICAL SNAPSHOT
1956

- The nation boasted 7,000 drive-in theaters
- The DNA molecule was photographed for the first time
- Teen fashions for boys included crew cut haircuts known as "flaptops"
- Procter and Gamble created disposable diapers sold under the name Pampers
- Ford Motor Company went public and issued over 10 million shares which were sold to 250,000 investors
- A survey showed that 77 percent of college-educated women married and 41 percent worked part-time, 17 percent full-time
- Boston religious leaders urged the banning of rock 'n' roll
- Eleven percent of all cars sold were station wagons
- For the first time the airlines carried as many passengers as trains did
- The last Union veteran of the Civil War died; he served as a drummer boy at 17
- Broadway openings included *Waiting for Godot, Long Day's Journey into Night, My Fair Lady, Bells Are Ringing* and *Separate Tables*
- After vowing never to allow Elvis Presley's vulgarity on his TV show, Ed Sullivan paid Presley $50,000 for three appearances

- Midas Muffler Shops, Comet, Raid, Salem cigarettes, La Leche League, Imperial margarine and women ordained as ministers in the Presbyterian Church all made their first appearance
- Don Larsen of the New York Yankees pitched the first perfect game in the World Series
- John F. Kennedy won the Pulitzer Prize for his book *Profiles in Courage,* a biography; *Russia Leaves the War* by George F. Kennan won in the U.S. History category
- In the art world, a canvas purchased in Chicago for $450 was discovered to be a Leonardo valued at $1 million
- Television premieres included *As the World Turns, The Edge of Night, The Huntley-Brinkley Report, The Price Is Right* and *The Steve Allen Show*
- Soviet Premier Nikita Khrushchev assailed past President Joseph Stalin as a terrorist, egotist and murderer
- Anti-Soviet demonstrations in Hungary were violently suppressed
- American colleges began actively recruiting students from the middle classes
- Martin Luther King, Jr. said, "Nonviolence is the most potent technique for oppressed people. Unearned suffering is redemptive."
- Hit songs included "Blue Suede Shoes," "Hound Dog," "Mack the Knife," "The Party's Over" and "Friendly Persuasion"
- European autos gained in popularity, including Volkswagens, Jaguars, Ferraris, Saabs and Fiats
- Ngo Diem was elected president of South Vietnam

Puerto Rican Immigration Timeline

1493

On his second voyage, Christopher Columbus discovered the Virgin Islands and Puerto Rico.

1509

Ponce de Leon was appointed governor of Puerto Rico.

1580

Imported European diseases virtually wiped out the native Indians of Puerto Rico.

1868

The Fourteenth Amendment to the United States Constitution was adopted which declared that all people of Hispanic origin born in the United States would be U.S. citizens.

A Puerto Rican decree freed all children born of slaves.

Puerto Rican insurrectionists, fighting for independence, were defeated by the Spanish.

1870

The Spanish government freed all the slaves it owned in Cuba and Puerto Rico.

1873

All slavery was abolished in Puerto Rico.

1875

The U.S. Supreme Court ruled that the power to regulate immigration was held solely by the federal government.

1892

Revolutionary organizations focused on independence were created in both Cuba and Puerto Rico.

1897

Spain granted Puerto Rico and Cuba autonomy and home rule.

1898

Following the Spanish-American War, Spain signed the Treaty of Paris, transferring Cuba, Puerto Rico and the Philippines to the United States.

The Foraker Act established a civilian government in Puerto Rico under U.S. dominance that allowed the Islanders to elect their own House of Representatives but did not permit Puerto Rico a vote in Washington.

1917

The Jones Act was passed extending U.S. citizenship to all Puerto Ricans and created two Puerto Rican houses of legislature, elected by male suffrage.

English was declared the official language of Puerto Rico.

Congress passed the Immigration Act of 1917, imposing a literacy requirement on all immigrants.

continued

Timeline . . . *(continued)*

1921

Limits on the number of immigrants allowed in the United States in a single year were imposed for the first time in the country's history.

1926

Puerto Ricans in Harlem were attacked by non-Hispanics fearful of the growing Puerto Rican population in New York.

1930

United States interests controlled 44 percent of the cultivated land in Puerto Rico.

U.S. capitalists controlled 60 percent of the banks and public services and all the maritime lines in Puerto Rico.

1933

The Roosevelt administration reversed the policy of English as the official language of Puerto Rico.

1934

During the early years of the Depression, 20 percent of all Puerto Ricans living in the United States returned to the island.

1940

An independent union was formed as the major labor organization in Puerto Rico.

1941

The Fair Employment Practices Act was passed, designed to eliminate discrimination in employment.

1944

Operation Bootstrap, initiated by the Puerto Rican government to meet labor demands in World War II, stimulated a major wave of immigration to the United States.

1946

The first Puerto Rican Governor, Jesus T. Pinero, was appointed by President Harry Truman.

1947

Approximately 20 airlines provided air service between San Juan, Puerto Rico, and New York

1950

The United States Congress upgraded Puerto Rico's political status from protectorate to commonwealth.

1954

The U.S. Supreme Court ruled in Hernandez v. Texas that Hispanic Americans and all other racial groups had equal protection under the Fourteenth Amendment to the Constitution.

Selected Prices

Bedroom Set, Walnut $645.00
Coffee Maker, Percolator $16.88
Lipstick, Cashmere Bouquet $0.49
Mattress, Serta $79.50
Nylons $1.00
Paneling, 70 Panels $47.00
Refrigerator $259.00
Typewriter, Smith-Corona, Electric $209.35
Vacuum Cleaner, Eureka $69.95
Watch, Bulova $59.50

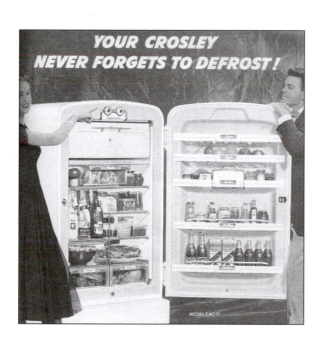

YOUR CROSLEY NEVER FORGETS TO DEFROST!

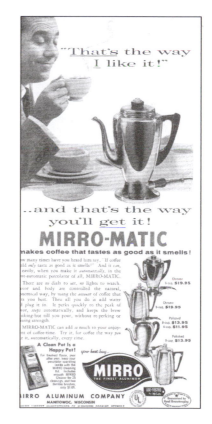

"That's the way I like it!"

...and that's the way you'll get it! MIRRO-MATIC

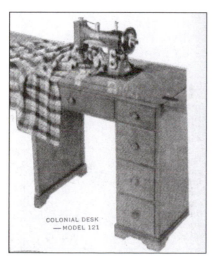

COLONIAL DESK —MODEL 121

"Find Parasite Worms in Puerto Rican Children," *Tri-State Defender* (Memphis, Tennessee), November 21, 1959:

Worm infestation diseases, which were rarely seen in the Philadelphia area, are now being found in pre-school Puerto Rican children.

In a report of research done in an overcrowded Philadelphia neighborhood, Eugene N. Myers, Roberto Negron, and Hillard Pearlstein, medical students at Temple University School of Medicine, showed that almost 70 percent of children examined, who were born in Puerto Rico, had some kind of parasitic (worm) infestation.

The most common parasite in over half the Puerto Rican-born youngsters was *Trichocephalus trichiurus*, better known as the human whipworm, a thread-like parasite about one-quarter inch long. These worms cause weakness, anemia, and stomach pains.

Tested children who were born in the U.S., but who visited Puerto Rico, had a 57 percent incidence of parasites. As a control, the medical students studied 100 children who were born in the U.S., but who had not been to Puerto Rico. Of these latter children, in contrast, only 23 percent were infected.

When housing conditions were considered as a factor, worms were found in 90 percent of those who lived in overcrowded dwellings, as compared to 10 percent in non-overcrowded dwellings.

The study, which received the second place award at the recent Student American Medical Association Scientific Forum in Chicago was reported in the current (November) issue of the *New Physician*.

"Puerto Rico Adds 50 Industries," *The New York Times*, January 3, 1950:

SAN JUAN, P.R.—"Operation Bootstrap"—Puerto Rico's program initiated under Gov. Luis Munoz Marin to free this island from dependence on its sugar industry—is now showing results.

At Carolina, a few miles from here, Beacon Textiles is completing a $1.5 million plant that will start operations late in February. Near Bayamon, a short distance to the west, private capital from the States is putting up a $500,000 rayon mill, to be finished and equipped late in the spring. Meanwhile, the last machines are being installed in the big Textron mill at Ponce, on the south coast, and the first cloth has been run off in test production there, in preparation for regular operations early in March.

At Vega Baga, in north central Puerto Rico, Crane China's factory, which cost $1.5 million, now employs nearly 500 workers and will use 200 more when the training program is completed and full production of 25,000 dozen pieces weekly is reached.

At Guayanilla, near Ponce, a site has been chosen and preliminary details ironed out for the construction of an oil refinery that may represent an investment of nearly $20 million of private capital from the mainland.

continued

"Puerto Rico Adds 50 Industries," . . . (continued)

Nearly a dozen new plants are in various stages of construction as the insular government presses its drive to industrialize this semitropical home of 2.2 million traditionally poor people.

Although there are some misgivings on the part of the operators of the sugar plants and plantations, who fear that in time the new factories will lure away too many of their workers, all admit that a new era has dawned in the midst of backward agricultural terrain.

Water power and better highways, new hotel and club facilities have come to the island as a part of the new dispensation. Most of the plants started under Government auspices to show what could be done there are working at capacity. The Government's cement plant is turning out one million barrels of cement a year, and finding a ready market for it in new housing, roads, business and factory construction.

The shoe factory at Ponce, after reaching a production of about 1,800 pairs daily to help supply a big part of the island's demand for $14 million worth of shoes a year, has been sold by the Puerto Rico Industrial Development Company to the Joyce interests of California as the first step in getting official industries into private hands.

Three bids are being considered by the development company for the Puerto Rico Clay Products plant, near here, and several offers are being weighed for the cement plant. The glass-bottle plant has made its first shipments to Central American countries. Only the paper-board plant has been listed as a failure.

The 50 new industries now operating or soon to start will give employment to about 8,000 persons, and will have an annual payroll of more than $8 million. Their output ranges from fur coats, jewelry and buttons to optical instruments and radio and television sets. The 25,000-spindle plant of Textile, perhaps the first of several planned by this company in Puerto Rico, will have a capacity of more than 10 million yards of "cotton print cloth gray goods" annually.

"Where to Go This Month," *McCall's*, February 1958:

Puerto Rico: One of the gayest of all pre-Lenten carnivals begins here on February 1 and continues through February 18. You may start out a spectator watching the passing parades of costumed celebrants, pageants, sailing regattas, coronations and other ceremonies, but before long you will probably catch the carnival spirit and don masks to join the street dancing, Battle of the Flowers, masquerade balls and parties at all the hotels.

"The World of Children," by Peter Cardozo, *Good Housekeeping*, February 1951:

Want to be a fairy princess? Small fry in Oakland, California, have discovered an exciting land of make-believe. The magic passwords? Oakland Costume Loan Service. Sponsored by the city's Recreation Department, this unique community service stocks over 10,000 costumes for holiday festivals, school pageants, amateur theatricals and any make-believe in which a girl becomes a fairy princess or a boy an Indian chief. Schools, church groups, playgrounds and other nonprofit organizations can rent costumes; a small fee covers the cost of laundering. Through the magic of colorful fabrics, needles, and thread, youngsters can be transformed into Puritan maidens, elves, Dutch folk with wooden shoes, gypsies, even knights in armor. Seven thousand costumes loaned each year!

Let's make ice cream. With miniature dairy plants set up right in the classroom, three million children will soon be "pasteurizing" milk and churning make-believe scoops of ice cream. Dairy-class Workit, a new teaching aid, includes cutout sheets of trucks and machinery the children can fold, paste together and assemble on a lithographed dairy layout. By adding the full-color background picture of the farm, a three-dimensional model of the dairy plant can actually be operated. A "textbook" tells youngsters how bottles of milk get to their doorsteps. Sponsored by the National Dairy Council, these Class Workits supplement field trips to farms, giving a realistic picture of the dairy industry at work.

continued

"The World of Children," ... *(continued)*

Like a diamond in the sky. Twinkle, twinkle, Little Star! How I wonder what you are. . ." This year in New York, children are learning the scientific answer. They attend a series of heavenly talks now being given in the Theater of the Stars, at the Hayden Planetarium. Especially adapted for eight- to 14-year-olds, the Young People's astronomy course covers such topics as the sun, the planets, the moon, and the constellations. The purpose of the course: To acquaint junior astronomers with the wonders of the heavens and make them feel at home under the night sky. Each child who sits under the Planetarium's magic domed ceiling becomes a superman. He sees in seven seconds how the sky picture changes in a whole year; he can even take a trip to the moon and back!

Paper Pianos. Without leaving their desks, children in Public School 119 in New York City are learning to play the piano. Sounds impossible, but it isn't. Taking part in a "class piano" experiment, youngsters from eight to 12 spend 40 minutes a week learning to play the piano. Each child spreads out a three-octave piano keyboard. (These are made of paper, cost only $0.25.) While the teacher plays a simple melody on a real piano, the children will "play" it on their paper keyboard, following the notes and chords written on the blackboard. They sing the melody as they play, take turns at the real piano, give a recital at the end of the year. Teachers and students find group teaching (10 pupils at the same time) as satisfactory as private lessons; the children like to learn together.

NONSENSE VERSES
BY ALFRED I. TOOKE

Seventeen of Everything

There was a young lady with seventeen cats.
She went to the city to buy them some hats.
They picked out the prettiest ones they could find,
And wore them all home with the front part behind.
Before they got back they'd walked seventeen miles,
Met seventeen people with seventeen smiles,
And seventeen times had said, "How do you do!"
And seventeen people replied, "How are you!"

Now, one was a farmer with seventeen houses,
And seventeen chickens and seventeen cowses.
Said he, "I'm a farmer who does as he pleases,"
Then, milking the cows, he made seventeen cheeses.
The cats cut a cheese into seventeen pieces,
Had supper with all of their nephews and nieces,
Then took off the hats from their seventeen heads,
And went off to sleep in their seventeen beds.

1957 PROFILE

After taking a circuitous route from Poland to Germany, Venezuela, New Orleans, Missouri, Chicago, and finally Benton Harbor, Michigan, Kira Leszczow looked and acted like a typical American teenager.

Life at Home

- When her family abandoned their Polish home in the middle of the night in January 1945, Kira Leszczow barely understood how dramatically her life was about to change.
- Her father had woken her up, put her favorite doll in her hands, and carried her into the living room.
- Kira's mother, Emilia, was throwing food and clothing into a rucksack and small valuables into her beltpouch.
- Five-year-old Kira felt as if she was about to embark on an exciting adventure.
- To her parents, however, this was a life-or-death situation.
- The Second World War had recently come to a close in the European theater, and the Russian Red Army was advancing west through Eastern Europe and the eastern provinces of Germany.
- The Soviet Communists were close; they would arrive by the next day.
- Kira's father, Afanasy Leszczow, would be killed if caught by the communist solders; he had been a Russian officer during the First World War and a Czarist supporter.
- He had fled Russia once to escape the communists; now he must abandon Poland if he wanted to live long enough to complete his religious studies.
- Emilia was not as worried for herself; she was a native-born Pole.
- With the bare essentials packed and in hand, the family walked outside; it was below freezing in Bydgoszcz, Poland, and Kira could see her breath in the air.
- Snow covered the streets, cars, and houses.

Kira Leszczow left Poland with her parents when she was five.

Kira's family fled Communist Poland with other families in the dark of night.

- Parked in front of their home was a large open-bed truck; in the back, families were huddled together for warmth.
- Kira's father stood speaking to a man in German; Kira recognized him as the German Army officer whom her father had befriended, though he was not wearing his uniform.
- Helped up by a man Kira's mother knew, Kira and Emilia climbed into the back of the truck and were soon joined by Afanasy.
- At the outskirts of town, they met up with other trucks that were also packed full of people.
- A caravan formed heading west away from the advancing Soviet army and towards Germany.
- After a couple of hours of travel, the caravan stopped.
- Kira saw a man and a woman climb out of a truck with a small bundle and walk into the forest beside the road.
- A few minutes later, the man and woman trudged solemnly out of the forest, having left the bundle behind.
- Their child had frozen to death.
- Early the next morning, the caravan stopped and everyone took shelter in a school to sleep.
- They had made it out of Poland and into Germany.
- Within a heartbeat they experienced the exhilaration of having escaped the Soviets and the sadness of leaving their homes behind, perhaps forever.
- Later that day, a local farmer arrived in a horse-drawn sled.
- The German officer with whom her father spoke earlier had arranged for Kira and her family to stay with the farmer for a little while.
- For Kira that meant saying good-bye to the refugees she had befriended to go away with this stranger.
- Once they were settled, the farmer got his horse moving and they began sliding even farther away from their old lives.
- After a stay at the farmer's home, the family journeyed with other refugees to Bitterfeld, Germany.

- They stayed there for a few years until Germany was split by the treaty in 1949; the three western zones became the Federal Republic of Germany and the Soviet eastern zone became the German Democratic Republic.
- Afanasy knew that it was time to get out of the Soviet zone.
- Their next move was to southern Germany, which was occupied by the Americans.
- There, they stayed in a DP, or displaced persons, camp.
- While staying in the DP camp, Afanasy became ordained as a Russian Orthodox priest, with dreams of going to America.
- They scraped by and eventually were sponsored by a family in the United States, the Logans, who lived on a large farm in Colony, Missouri.
- When Kira was 11 years old, she and her family left Germany on an American troop ship.
- The ship first traveled to Venezuela where it dropped off other refugees, after which it continued on to New Orleans, Louisiana.
- From there, the Leszczows traveled by train to Colony, Missouri, where they spent about a year living in a chicken coop that had been converted for their use.
- Afanasy worked on the farm milking cows, delivering calves, taking care of the animals, mending fences, and performing numerous other activities.
- Emilia cleaned house for the Logans.
- Kira went to school and played with all of the local children; she began to pick up English very rapidly, filtered through a distinct Russian accent.
- She also continued to wear her European clothes and her hair in braids down the middle of her back.
- The other families in Colony loved to spoil the exotic visitors with ice cream and chocolate, so much so that Kira eventually began to dislike the taste of some sweets.
- In August of 1951, exciting news arrived: Afanasy had been assigned to a Russian Orthodox church in Chicago.
- The Leszczows quickly decamped to Chicago, where Kira's parents were more comfortable.
- As anyone could see, they were not farming material and, in addition, they could now associate with other Russian immigrants.

Immigrant families were quickly introduced to American food.

Life at Work

- Kira's father, Afanasy Leszczow, was very proud to be the priest of the local Russian Orthodox church in Chicago; at last he could perform his life's calling.
- Afanasy's church was small and could afford to pay little, so he also worked another job.
- But, as was the tradition, the church did provide lodging for the family and paid their utility bills.
- After two years, he received his new assignment, and the family's next move was to Benton Harbor, Michigan.
- The Russian Orthodox church, on Thresher Avenue in Benton Harbor, was a two-story, square, cement-block building.
- The street level was used as the church, while the top level served as the Leszczows' apartment.
- At first, Kira was ashamed that her house was unlike those of the other children with whom she went to school.
- Secretly she was most upset that they didn't have a white picket fence like she had seen in all the American movies while living in Germany.
- To make ends meet, her father also worked full-time in a factory called Twin Cities Container Corporation.
- "He went every day in the morning with his lunch bucket to catch a ride with a neighbor, and came home in the evenings, sweaty and tired," Kira remembers.
- The family carefully saved an agreed-upon amount each week, although it wasn't very much, putting it into a savings account, only to have it embezzled by a high-level administrator at the bank.
- They were devastated.
- Afanasy was 62 in 1957, and the factory work was incredibly strenuous for a man of that age, especially with the weight of a congregation on his shoulders.
- Kira's mother, Emilia, kept their apartment in order, bought groceries daily, cooked and cleaned, and occupied herself with church meetings.
- Kira worked at Wilder's Drug Store two or three times a week after school and on Saturdays.
- Wilder's employed three pharmacists and several older women who worked the jewelry and cosmetics counters.
- Kira always worked the cash register and took great pride in the fact that her cash drawer always checked out to the penny.
- When the store wasn't busy, Kira would look through the newspaper at the advertisements; she wanted to know how she would spend her next paycheck.
- As a high school senior in 1957, her world revolved around friends and family; she was rarely distracted by the tumult of civil rights demonstrations or the Russian invasion of Hungary.
- This insular world was emphasized by her parents' continued reliance on conversing mainly in Russian.
- When her family would get together with other Russian immigrants, they sang Russian songs and ate Russian food.
- Often, the adults would cry together over the bittersweet memories.
- Kira wanted nothing to do with this.
- She wanted to be an American and, on occasion, would refuse to speak Russian to her parents.
- She did everything she could to make herself look more American; she had a ponytail, a felt skirt with a poodle on it, saddle shoes, and went to sock hops and football games.

Kira dressed to look more American.

- As a teen in Benton Harbor she learned all about spending the night at friends' houses, talking about boys half the night, going to the beach in the summer with her friends, as well as the exotic joy of eating her first slice of pizza, and first hamburger.
- At school, she took the traditional classes: English, composition, literature, history, French, math, choir, and gym.
- Kira excelled especially in French, having an extensive background in languages; she was fluent in Russian, German, Polish, and English.
- It made her feel special that her teachers would often ask her for help in pronunciation of foreign names, cities, and countries.
- Kira came to realize that, despite her best efforts, she would never be one of the popular kids—none of the immigrants would.

Michigan schools were non-segregated even before the 1954 Supreme Court decision.

- The classmates who were popular were the ones who had gone to school together since kindergarten.
- They even tried to look alike with the same hairstyles and clothes.
- Kira realized they even smelled alike; they all used Revlon's Aquamarine lotion.
- Kira did experience a wide circle of friends—Americans, fellow immigrants, whites, browns and blacks.
- Michigan was one of the 17 states that prohibited the separation of races in educational settings before the landmark decision by the United States Supreme Court in 1954, Brown v. Board of Education of Topeka.
- So, even though much of the country was in upheaval dealing with the civil rights movement and its implications to its schools, Benton Harbor remained relatively insulated from it all.
- Even the growing tension wrought by Cold War conflicts between Russia and the United States did not intrude on her American world.
- Kira's life revolved around friendships, American music and American films.
- After school, she and her friends would often stop at soda shops and sip malts, cokes, and play records on the juke box.
- The Four Freshmen, Nat King Cole, and Elvis Presley were particular favorites.
- She went to movies to see stars like Pat Boone, Rita Hayworth, John Wayne, Doris Day, Gregory Peck, and Elizabeth Taylor.
- When she went to see the movie *Miss Sadie Thompson*, in which Rita Hayworth played a tongue-in-cheek ex-prostitute, Kira asked the lady in the next seat, "What is a prostitute?"
- The woman replied that she did not know either, and promptly moved several rows away.
- Kira's family didn't own a television set, so the only time she ever watched TV was when she spent the night at a friend's house.
- There she could watch *Howdy Doody, The Ed Sullivan Show, The Hit Parade,* and *Dragnet.*
- Kira and her friends were in the school choir and always took part in the musicals and plays that Benton Harbor High School produced.
- Her senior year, she was student director of the play *Oklahoma.*
- She loved it because she was able to boss the popular kids around.

As a teenager in Benton Harbor, Kira would often spend time at Lake Michigan with her American friends.

- During the warm months, Kira would go to the beaches of Lake Michigan with her friends.
- Although her parents didn't have a car, Kira's friends almost always had access to one, so they rarely had to ride the city bus.
- Her parents were making adjustments as well; they decided to simplify their last name for American usage, changing it from Leszczow to Leschoff.
- Afanasy and Emilia considered the name change a gesture of gratefulness to the United States, which they always called their "blessed land."

Life in the Community: Benton Harbor, Michigan
- Benton Harbor is in the southwest edge of Michigan, on Lake Michigan; its sister town, St. Joseph, is just across the St. Joseph River.
- Both were resort towns, due to their locations on Lake Michigan.
- However, Benton Harbor had more industry than its sister, and a bit less affluence.
- The Heath Corporation and Voice of Music both had factories in Benton Harbor.
- Both of these companies made electronic and audio equipment.
- They also had the Twin Cities Container Corporation, where Afanasy worked.
- The surrounding areas boasted mainly fruit and vegetable farms and, because of this, Benton Harbor was home to a large fruit market located in the "flats" area of town.
- Emilia shopped there for fresh cherries, blueberries, peaches, apples, and strawberries; after the family's days in displaced persons camps, nothing tasted quite so good to them as fresh fruit.

- The Russian Orthodox community was small compared to other ethnic communities.
- Most of Afanasy's congregation had just recently immigrated and spoke little English.
- The majority of them worked at either farms or factories.
- English was learned mostly by the children of these families, since they were in American schools.
- The parents stayed home on the farms, spoke only Russian, and went to a Russian church where they communicated with other Russians.
- Their children would interpret for them when it was necessary to deal with Americans.
- Afanasy had an especially difficult time learning the new language; at his factory job he had little chance to converse with English speakers, and in his position as Russian Orthodox pastor, he dealt with parishioners that could, in most cases, only speak Russian.

Historical Snapshot
1957

- The Soviet Union launched a 180-pound satellite known as Sputnik 1 into orbit around Earth

- Ford introduced a new automotive model, the Edsel

- Bestselling books included *By Love Possessed* by James Gould Cozzens; *Peyton Place* by Grace Metalious, *Atlas Shrugged* by Ayn Rand, *Kids Say the Darndest Things* by Art Linkletter and *Please Don't Eat the Daisies* by Jean Kerr

- Hits songs included "All Shook Up," "All the Way," "A White Sport Coat and a Pink Carnation," "Chances Are," "I'm Going to Sit Right Down and Write Myself a Letter" and "Jailhouse Rock"

- A USS Thor Intercontinental Ballistic Missile (ICBM) was successfully tested

- The United Nations' Emergency Force was the first multinational peacekeeping force in history

- The painkiller Darvon was marketed for the first time

- The Massachusetts governor reversed the 1692 witchcraft convictions for six Salem women

- Allen Ginsberg's book *Howl* was seized by the police and deemed obscene

- Painter Mark Rothko completed *Red, White and Brown;* Robert Rauschenberg finished *Painting with Red Letter S;* and sculptor Alexander Calder's *125,1957* was installed in the new International Arrivals building in Idlewild Airport, New York

- The Everly Brothers' song "Wake Up Little Susie" was banned in Boston

- Asian flu, *Sputnik*, meter maid, subliminal projection, shook up and funky all entered or gained new currency in the language

- Average wages for a factory production worker were $2.08 an hour, or $82.00 a week

- Volkswagen sold 200,000 vehicles known as Beetles

- Congress passed the first civil rights legislation since 1872, despite an extended filibuster by South Carolina Senator Strom Thurmond

- Products making their first appearance included pocket-size transistor radios by Sony, cars with retractable hardtops, animal insurance and the Zysser vegetable steamer

- In professional baseball, pitcher Warren Spahn of Milwaukee won the Cy Young Award and Jackie Robinson retired

Selected Prices

Automobile, Plymouth Fury	$2,866.00
Ballet Ticket	$7.50
Crystal Chandelier	$425.00
Golf Jacket, Men's	$11.95
Jeans, Children's	$1.64
Lawn Sprinkler	$16.95
Pocket Transistor Radio	$75.00
Pop Fizz Tablets, Box of 150 Drinks	$1.00
Stereo	$129.95
Television, Zenith	$550.00

Russian Immigration Timeline

1784

The Aleutian island of Kodiak became the first Russian settlement in North America.

1864

Congress legalized the importation of contract laborers.

1867

The Russian czar sold the Alaskan territory to the U.S.; Russian cultural influences persisted long afterward.

1880–1900

A great wave of emigration from the Russian Empire erupted including Ukrainians, Belarusians, Lithuanians, and Poles who moved to the United States in the hundreds of thousands; ethnic Russians were barred from leaving the country.

1881

The assassination of Czar Alexander II prompted civil unrest and economic instability throughout Russia.

1882

Russia's May Laws severely restricted the ability of Jewish citizens to live and work in Russia.

1885

Congress banned the admission of contract laborers.

1917

The imperial government of Russia was overthrown by socialist revolutionaries called Bolsheviks.

During four years of civil war more than two million fled the communist Soviet Union; around 30,000 made their way to the United States. These immigrants were called "white" Russians because of their opposition to the "red" communist Bolsheviks.

1917–1920

During the "Red Scare," the American government cracked down on political and labor organizations, especially those involved with Russian nationals; thousands of Russians were deported without a formal trial.

1929

Congress made annual immigration quotas permanent.

1930–1940

Thousands of Russians fled the Soviet Union in the fear of another world war.

continued

Timeline . . . *(continued)*

1945

Once World War II was over in Europe, refugees from across Europe fled the chaos and depression of postwar Russia. More than 20,000 Russian refugees known as DPs, or displaced persons, successfully reached the United States.

1947–1957

The Second Red Scare occurred in the United States; anyone suspected of having communist sympathies was blacklisted, jailed, or deported.

1948

The United States admitted 205,000 refugees fleeing persecution in their native lands to enter within two years.

1952

The Immigration and Nationality Act made individuals of all races eligible for naturalization; reaffirmed the national origins quota system; limited immigration from the Eastern Hemisphere; established preferences for skilled workers and relatives of U.S. citizens and permanent resident aliens; and tightened security and screening standards and procedures.

The Soviet government slowed the rate at which its artists and scientists were decamping to America, and established strict controls over emigration; Russian immigration to the U.S. became a rare and risky undertaking.

1953

Congress amended its 1948 refugee policy to allow for the admission of 200,000 more refugees.

ALL YOU DO IS
PUSH A BUTTON
WHEN YOU START
THE WASHER!

1957 HOTPOINT

"I'm the One Who Stands Out in a Crowd," by Elinor Goulding Smith, *McCall's*, February 1958:

I am the one who stands out in a crowd. See that crowd over there at that party? Now see all those women in off-the-shoulder silk dresses? Now see that one sitting by herself and a sweater and skirt? That's me.

I'll kill myself. I think I'll cut my throat. Oh, well, life is too short to fuss over such trivialities. After all, it isn't what you wear, it's what you do that counts.

See the people at the suburban dinner party? See all the women in smart tailored suits? Now see the one on the right in a strapless emerald green satin sheath? That's me.

Why should I cut my throat? What difference does it make? In a hundred years no one will even know about it. If you're neat and well groomed that's all that matters, isn't it? Besides, gas will be neater.

Oh, this is silly. Why should I turn on the gas? No one is noticing me. It doesn't even matter what I wear. Well, why aren't they noticing me? I'm just as good as they are, aren't I? What's wrong with me, all of a sudden? I'm a human being too, you know.

Sometimes I try outguessing them. Now then, I say to myself cheerfully, let's take it easy and let's us not get in a panic. We'll just figure this thing out sensibly. Tonight, for instance. Lets see, it's just dinner at a friend's house in the suburbs. They probably won't have more than one other couple. I know they're very informal people. It's a weekday night. For sure this is a wool-dress evening, with pearls just to show it's not like marketing. All right now, wool dress. But let's take into consideration one more factor, which is that I am always wrong, and see what we come up with. That would make it a good-black-silk-and-high-heeled-sandals evening. But if I wear the silk and high heels, they'll absolutely have to be wearing sweaters. Maybe I should go in a bathroom suit and be frankly wrong? Or perhaps I should dress up as Madame Defarge or Medusa? Maybe I should stay home and go to bed. I could tell them I fell and broke my leg this afternoon.

I think I'll take poison. I finally ended up in the wool dress, and there were eight couples, all the women in bouffant taffeta and lace sheaths.

Oh, that's ridiculous. You don't kill yourself because you wore the wrong thing once. They weren't talking about you behind your back. They were probably talking about their sister-in-law or the president of the P.T.A. Why would they talk about you? Well, why shouldn't they talk about me? I'm somebody, aren't I?

Oh, how silly. They don't care what I wear. They're my friends. Why don't they care what I wear? They care what they wear, don't they? They're not savages who wear clothes just to keep out the drafts. We're supposed to be civilized, and clothes are supposed to be an adornment. Also, they're supposed to show that you have a sense of style, that you have chic, that above all, oh, dear lord, you know what's done and what isn't done on a given occasion. I'll throw myself out the window.

Now, let's be sensible. It's much more important to have a sense of value of things than a sense of style or chic or being able to tell a bath towel from a hat. Take Saturday night. Dinner for 40 people at eight o'clock. This one is easy. You can't wear a sweater and skirt to a dinner party for forty on a Saturday night. I won't dress up too much either. You don't want to overdo these things. It's more sophisticated to be a little underdressed than a little overdressed. So let's see. The blue taffeta with a low neck but long sleeves? That should do it.

See that crowd over there at the dinner party? See all those women in smart little black suits? Now see that one over there in a low-necked blue taffeta? That's me.

Attack on God, *The Red Plotters*, by Hamilton Fish, 1947:

The Soviet government encourages and supports the Union of Militant Atheists, anti-religious museums, and compulsory instruction in Marxism and hatred of God in the public schools of Russia. There is no religious freedom in Russia beyond the liberty to attend a few Sovietized churches under Soviet-approved priests. There is no freedom of religious instruction, propaganda or conversion or even freedom to maintain schools for training priests and ministers. There is no real freedom of the press or unquestioned right to issue religious newspapers and magazines, or to make religious speeches. It is specifically forbidden to conduct any form of religious teaching in any private school or institution; but atheists and blasphemous anti-God groups may propagandize to their hearts' content under the special freedom given them by the new Soviet Constitution.

All Protestants, Catholics, Greek Orthodox Christians and Jews, all who believe in God, should know what a false and deceitful meaning the words "freedom of religion" have in Soviet Russia. In America freedom of religion is a sacred and fundamental right safeguarded by the Constitution and our substantive law. They have the right to publish and read the Bible, to conduct seminaries and divinity schools for religious training, to give religious instruction to the young, to circulate Christian and non-Christian newspapers, and to preach the gospel of Christ publicly and without restraint.

Let Christians be honest with themselves and brand the type of freedom of religion provided by the Soviet Constitution as a gigantic hoax, used as a device to deceive Christians throughout the world. Even the Soviet-controlled churches are now being used to attack the Catholic Church and all other creeds which dare to tell the truth regarding the suppression of religion under the Soviet regime. The only freedom of religion in Russia is atheistic or Marxist freedom. The Bible may not be printed in the Russian language. Let us rip off the veil of Communist propaganda and expose the naked facts, so the Christians in America and Europe may understand the true intentions of Communists the world over.

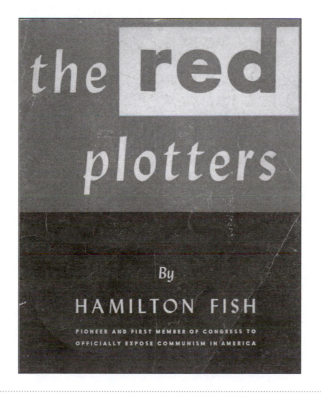

the **red** plotters

By

HAMILTON FISH

PIONEER AND FIRST MEMBER OF CONGRESS TO
OFFICIALLY EXPOSE COMMUNISM IN AMERICA

"Now the Dark Streets Shineth," by Marilyn Parks Davis, *American Home,* December 1954:

Back in the spring of 1951, in Evanston, Illinois, housewife Alice Hamm reflected upon the forthcoming Christmas. She was not pondering about her own projects, but upon the problem of how a community could recapture the spiritual significance of this holy day. What could she herself do? Could one busy mother recruit enough help make a dent in the overly commercialized observance of Christ's birthday? Not long afterward, in a meeting at the Hamm home, a room full of young married couples organized the Christian Family Christmas Committee. Their aim the first year was encouragement of public displays portraying the season's deeper meaning; their slogan: "Put Christ Back into Christmas."

They set to work immediately. By November, volunteers had given 30 talks to various groups, and 100 citizens attended the public meeting at Northwestern University. After that, all Evanston pitched in—judges businessman, housewives, churchmen, teachers, civic leaders. "Practically no one turned us down," recalls an early booster, and young people joined their elders enthusiastically in building life-size Nativity figures for outdoor displays. Lumbermen offered patterns to home craftsmen, an art studio offered free instructions in the making of creches. Pastors and priests wrote Christmastide editorials, and the local press published them. A bank ran a full-page Christ-in-Christmas ad. Buses carried slogan on cards; radio and TV joined in.

Before Christmas Eve, 60 public Nativity scenes cast their spell of love and tenderness and hope upon all who had eyes to see and hearts to receive. It was apparent to townspeople that their community had arisen to show love for Christ and his birthday. Upon out-of-towners, the impact was startling. "First," reported one woman visitor, "we stopped at the electric company to admire the beautiful creche in the window. Strains of Handel's Messiah quickened the air; we were thrilled to see the manger depicted in the windows of jewelers, bakers, and florists. Then we passed an insurance building in which a Nativity soared six stories high. Later, passing a theater we were confronted with giant letters on the marquee: 'Put Christ Back in Christmas.' The cumulative impact was impressive. We went home feeling that amid the feverish hustle of shopping, we had been warmed and nurtured by the deep, inner core of Christmas."

Excerpt, *A Brief History of the Russian Orthodox Church Outside of Russia,* composed to her 50th anniversary by Protopriest Sergii Shchukin:

Soon, Metropolitan Anastassy was to suffer through the difficult years of World War II, bringing more than a few temptations to the flock of the Church Abroad. War struck not only the Russian emigration in Europe, but forced many Russians to flee the Balkans, Poland and the Baltics and head for Central Europe. At first, before the Soviet occupation, Metropolitan Anastassy resided in Belgrade, giving succor to the morale of Russians during the bombing raids and during the German occupation. Later, moving to Austria, and then to Switzerland, Vladyka Anastassy persistently and tactfully defended the interests of the Church Abroad and her scattered flock. For example, when German forces offered to publish an appeal on his behalf to the Russian population to cooperate with the German Army, he categorically refused. In 1944 he called a conference of bishops to discuss the matter of the selection of Metropolitan Sergius as the Patriarch of Moscow. This conference determined that this appointment was uncanonical and in essence did not change the enslaved condition of the Church in the Soviet Union.

In 1946, after the war, Metropolitan Anastassy moved to Munich, where he began to organize the work of the Synod Abroad. Before him stood the daunting task of drawing together the Church Abroad, rent asunder and disorganized by the world war. The primary urgent needs of the Russian Diaspora were:

1. The spiritual nourishment of Orthodox emigrants who found themselves homeless.
2. Tending to the thousands of Orthodox refugees who flooded Germany from Poland, the Baltics and the USSR along with their bishops and clergymen.
3. The protection of the same from the possible forced repatriation into Soviet Russia and persecution by the godless state.
4. The further settlement of their lives in the emigration.

From 1946-1949, the Synod Abroad directed their efforts towards these goals. A Resettlement Committee was organized under the Synod, which worked to obtain visas for countries across the Atlantic. But while plans were being formulated for moving, the Church Abroad needed to take care of the spiritual ministry to Orthodox Russians in refugee camps in Germany, Austria and Italy.

continued

Excerpt . . . *(continued)*

Especially difficult was the situation in which Soviet "non-returners" and their families found themselves, threatened with forced repatriation to the USSR, where imprisonment in concentration camps awaited them. Clergymen and all emigré organizations were mobilized to their defense. All Russian refugees remember how Metropolitan Anastassy constantly visited refugee camps with the Miracle-working Kursk-Root Icon of the Mother of God, encouraging and supporting the Orthodox faithful. Churches were set up in the camps, along with Russian schools for children, lectures were read, theatrical and musical groups visited, spiritual and lay literature was published. Multitudes of Soviet refugees-bereft of rights and lacking the local language, frightened by Soviet propaganda-received spiritual succor and legal aid for emigrating to new lands. Thanks to these efforts, many thousands of refugees were saved from repatriation and sent across the sea, and were thus able to return to the bosom of the Orthodox Church and give their children a religious upbringing.

In 1946, the first Council of Bishops after the war convened in Munich. New bishops took part who arrived from Eastern Europe. The council made a decision: "Patriarch Alexy frequently appealed to the bishops abroad with the exhortation to enter into canonical submission to the Patriarchate, but in obedience to the directions of our pastoral consciences, we find it morally impossible to heed these calls while the Church authority in Russia is in an unnatural union with the godless state and while all of the Russian Church is deprived of true freedom." The Council also saw to the appointment of bishops to the cathedras in North and South America and Australia, where Russian refugees had gone, as well as the organization of dioceses in Europe.

At the end of 1950, when the main bulk of refugees already resettled across the ocean, Metropolitan Anastassy, together with the Miracle-working Kursk-Root Icon of the Mother of God, flew to North America, where New York became the new headquarters of the Church Abroad. That same year a Council of Bishops took place there with 11 bishops, while the others submitted written reports. A new Synod was chosen, the Council participants made a pilgrimage to Holy Trinity Monastery in Jordanville, where religious books began to be published and a seminary was opened. The Council also issued the epistle "To All Children of the Orthodox Church in the Diaspora."

1958 PROFILE

Jozsef Kertész was a 30-year-old forestry graduate student when he rushed from his classroom and into the streets to join the Hungarian Uprising against the Soviets.

Life at Home

- During the last week of October 1956, two entirely separate crises captured the attention of the world: the Battle for the Suez Canal and the spontaneous Hungarian Uprising.
- Jozsef Kertész was transformed by the latter event.
- On October 23, a group of engineering students in the Hungarian capital of Budapest decided to hold a demonstration to show their support for the oppressed people of neighboring Poland.
- Spontaneously, word spread throughout the city and people poured out of their shops, factories and homes to join the demonstration, which quickly became an anti-government, anti-Soviet revolt.
- Jozsef felt liberated by the protest; the spontaneity of the event was like a wonderful dream, an awakening from a long coma.
- As the day progressed, thousands of frustrated Hungarians joined the Uprising, creating a full-scale revolt against the Hungarian regime and its Soviet masters.
- A huge statue of former Soviet leader Joseph Stalin was toppled, Hungarian flags were displayed with holes replacing the hammer and sickle insignia. Jozsef told his friends they were witnessing a historic moment in Hungarian history.
- The euphoria was short-lived, however, for within weeks the Soviet army retook the city using military tanks and initiated an unapologetic open season on demonstrators.
- Hundreds of buildings were badly damaged or destroyed; more than 2,500 Hungarians were killed, thousands were arrested or subsequently disappeared.
- As the Soviets moved to suppress the revolt, thousands fled; more than 180,000 Hungarian refugees made their way to Austria; 20,000 headed south into Yugoslavia.

Jozsef Kertesz was 30-years-old when he fled the Soviet oppression in Hungary.

- They had one thing in their favor: the Hungarian Uprising was the first major crisis to appear simultaneously on the evening television news, the world's newspapers and movie newsreels.
- The world was shocked to see the brutality from Budapest; most were sympathetic with the forlorn refugees seen traipsing through snow-covered fields to reach Austria.
- Many in the West believed the Hungarians had risen up in response to encouragement from messages delivered by Radio Free Europe, the BBC and the Voice of America; the West had an obligation to come to Hungary's aid, especially the avalanche of refugees.
- Refugees arriving at the Austrian border initially found help from the local villagers and Austrian authorities.
- Jozsef and a friend headed to the Austrian border by oxcart, dodging police checkpoints and buying directions from a smuggler along the way.
- Jozsef was petrified: capture meant certain death or imprisonment; escape meant leaving behind everything he had known his entire life.
- When he made it to the Austrian border, his worldly possessions comprised the two layers of clothing he was wearing to protect him from the cold, his school briefcase and approximately $20.
- He knew he was safe only when he heard the villagers speak German.
- Like many Hungarian refugees, he was quickly transported to a center where he was registered before being transferred into a refugee camp, fashioned from the barracks of an abandoned military base.
- There, for the first time, he realized the world had been watching the events unfold and began to comprehend the size of the rescue effort.
- A special train from Switzerland was regularly transporting 400 refugees at a time to various cities; buses were dispatched from Sweden and trains from Belgium and the Netherlands returned with Hungarians to those countries.
- By November 28, nine European countries had taken 21,669 refugees; by December 31, a phenomenal 91,900 people had been transported out of Austria.
- In all, a total of 180,000 refugees would be distributed by trains, ships, planes and buses to 37 different countries
- Canada accepted 38,000 Hungarians with minimal screening and even relaxed its mandate concerning the resettlement of people in winter months.
- The United States passed a special law that allowed it to take people on a temporary basis, bypassing the usual, full formal process, which was known to be time-consuming.
- Initially the U.S. offered places to 6,500 refugees, the total number of visas available under the Refugee Relief Act.
- But as the magnitude of the crisis and number of refugees grew, the figure was raised several times to admit additional thousands of "parolees" with legal status as immigrants.
- Jozsef was first taken by train to Germany before setting out for the United States under the sponsorship of the International Rescue Committee, one of several major American charities working on resettlement.
- Only after he boarded an old troop carrier and was sailing past the famous White Cliffs of Dover did the momentousness of his actions hit him; Hungary was past, America was his future.
- After a rough journey through midwinter Atlantic storms, he arrived in New York in January 1957 to a hero's welcome.
- The media-magnified fight for freedom against the Communists had transformed thousands of harried, unprepared refugees into Cold War warriors in the minds of Americans.
- It seemed as though the whole world were cheering his arrival.

Life at Work

- When Jozsef Kertész arrived in New York, Hungarian translators were provided as well as immigration officials to help him establish his refugee status.
- News photographers snapped his picture, while newfound friends described a glowing future in America.
- It was a dizzying welcome.
- When asked his goals, he replied that he wanted to complete his education in forestry and find his parents, who were still in Hungary.
- His first task was finding a place to live; that, too, was provided.
- Initially he was placed at Camp Kilmer in New Jersey, a converted U.S. Army base where newcomers were sponsored by different resettlement agencies.

Jozsef lived in a converted Army camp in New Jersey.

- These agencies, representing a variety of religious, political, ethnic, and social worker groups, helped place the refugees in homes, jobs and schools nationwide.
- They also helped coordinate the huge outpouring of support emanating from American communities, including American academia.
- Numerous universities contacted the Institute of International Education in the World University Service; it was its task to coordinate scholarship offers, collect and distribute donations, and screen potential students.
- Of the 28,000 refugees admitted to the U.S. in the six months following Soviet incursion, approximately 1,200 were university students.
- Most of the students were male and most were 19 to 21 years old; a few, like Jozsef, were graduate students in their late twenties or early thirties.
- But despite their anxiousness to continue their education, most did not possess sufficient English-language skills for university-level study, and most could not be registered in time for the spring semester, already underway.
- In addition, college administrators wanted the new refugees to become more acclimated to U.S. academic life before entering school.
- Jozsef, along with 325 other Hungarian students, began his education in America at Bard College, taking a nine-week course in English.
- Even though he could scarcely stop chatting in Hungarian, he learned enough English to manage the road ahead.
- There he also learned about one of the peculiarities of his new home: the police need not always be feared or bribed as in Communist Hungary.
- When his coursework was completed, he was presented with a train ticket to Cleveland, Ohio, where distant relatives were ready to welcome him with open arms.
- A letter that accompanied the ticket—written in English and Hungarian—told him that both an apartment and a job were awaiting his arrival.
- Cleveland had long been a center of Hungarian culture and prosperity in America; many there viewed the Hungarian Uprising with enormous excitement and as their opportunity to give back to their homeland.
- When he climbed aboard the train, he had no concept of how large and prosperous America could be.
- Along the way to Ohio, he saw forests running to the horizon, manicured farms, busy cities and more cars than he could have imagined.
- In the rural sections of Hungary, oxcarts were still much in evidence, telephones rare and television unknown.

Most American universities required that Hungarian students learn English before being admitted.

Jozsef lived with distant relatives in Cleveland.

- In fact, television mesmerized him; nothing, with the exception of his first love crush at 15, had ever captured his attention so thoroughly.
- Once he settled in Cleveland, he memorized the TV schedule, learned to sing the TV theme songs in English and often laughed out loud at jokes he did not understand.
- In some ways television symbolized both the power and the mystery of America.
- His host family was distantly related to him on his mother's side and had been in America for two generations.
- While they loved talking about Hungary and the ways of the old country, Jozsef wanted only to talk about the future.
- His first job was in a prosperous sawmill; the feel of sawdust and sweat, along with hard work, felt good.
- The money was good but rarely spread as far as he anticipated.
- When school began in the fall, he was offered a scholarship to cover tuition and a job at the university to cover expenses.
- He turned them both down; the crisis in Hungary had grown worse and oppression more pronounced.
- It was his job to earn enough money to buy his parents' way into the United States and safety; completing his degree and managing the woodlands of a land so vast as America would have to wait.

Working in a sawmill was Jozsef's first job, where he enjoyed the hard work and the good pay.

Life in the Community: Cleveland, Ohio

- The Hungarian community of Cleveland, Ohio, was riveted by the Hungarian Uprising and aggressively demanded that America protect the freedom fighters from the Soviet troops.
- They viewed the Uprising as an opportunity to pull down the Iron Curtain erected by the Soviets following World War II.
- When the Uprising collapsed in the face of Soviet aggression and thousands of refugees began flooding across the Austrian border, Cleveland began organizing its support.
- The city immediately attracted national attention by sending a planeload of clothing, valued at $100,000, to the Austrian refugee camps filled with frightened Hungarians.
- Then the residents began opening up their homes.
- Following the Hungarian Uprising, about 3,000 students journeyed to Cleveland, Ohio, to start a new life.
- For more than 50 years, Cleveland had been home to a Hungarian community large enough to support two Hungarian newspapers: Magyar Katolikus Vasarnapia, or The Catholic Hungarian's Sunday, and Szabadsaq, or Liberty.
- Cleveland was a place where refugees could feel at home.
- For nearly 100 years Hungarians had been emigrating to Ohio, especially to Cleveland.
- Most Hungarians who moved to Ohio in the 1800s settled along Lake Erie, especially in Cleveland, where they found jobs in the factories or as day laborers.
- There the immigrants clustered in Hungarian communities, among people who shared similar cultural beliefs and spoke the same language they did
- By the late 1800s, Cleveland claimed six distinct Hungarian communities spread across the city.
- The more entrepreneurial immigrants established businesses to supply their fellow migrants with traditional Hungarian products.
- By 1900, the Hungarian communities had established their own Catholic church and Protestant churches and formed the Hungarian Self-Culture Society.
- This social organization allowed Hungarians to gather together and read newspapers in their home language, practice traditional beliefs, and simply socialize together.
- But they still felt conflict in the wider world; native-born residents believed that the foreigners would corrupt the morals of United States citizens, steal jobs and not adapt properly to American ways
- Some even called for laws that would either limit or ban the cultural practices of recently arrived immigrants.

HISTORICAL SNAPSHOT
1958

- For the eleventh year, Eleanor Roosevelt was first on the "Most Admired Women" list
- The paperback edition of *Lolita* sold a million copies
- Treason charges against poet Ezra Pound were dropped because he was judged "not competent" to stand trial
- College tuition had doubled since 1940 and now topped $1,300 a year
- Elvis Presley was inducted into the Army
- The Grammy award, the Chevrolet Impala, Green Giant canned beans, cocoa puffs and BankAmericard all made their first appearance

- At the movies, *Cat on a Hot Tin Roof, Gigi, Separate Tables* and *Touch of Evil* were all major hits
- An economy class round-trip ticket on Air France from New York to Paris cost $489.60; a flight from New York to Houston aboard Delta Airlines cost $66.65

- Approximately 250,000 worshippers attended a Jehovah's Witness Convention in Yankees Stadium
- Popular TV shows included *Gunsmoke, Wagon Train, Have Gun Will Travel, Maverick, The Real McCoys* and *The Legend of Wyatt Earp*
- Television premieres included the *Donna Reed Show, 77 Sunset Strip, Peter Gunn* and *Wanted: Dead or Alive*
- Stan Musial of the St. Louis Cardinals connected on his 3,000th hit; golfer Arnold Palmer was the PGA's top money winner with $42,607

- Major art sales included Van Gogh's painting *Public Gardens at Arles* for $369,600 and Renoir's *La Pensée* for $201,600
- The construction of a nuclear power plant in California was stopped by court action initiated by environmental groups
- In women's fashion the shift or sack dress gained popularity, as did nonfunctional dress decorations such as big buttons, patch pockets, bows, sashes and buckles

ENTERTAINING. *Mister Roberts,* starring Henry Fonda, William Powell and Jack Lemmon (above), premiered, as did *Oklahoma!* with Shirley Jones and Gordon MacRae (below right). And it was wunnerful when Lawrence Welk came on TV (below).

- NASA was organized to unify and develop U.S. nonmilitary space efforts; Project Mercury was its first announced project
- The first regular domestic jet service from New York to Miami began
- *Breakfast at Tiffany's* by Truman Capote and *Dr. Zhivago* by Boris Pasternak were published
- Upon Pope Pius XII's death, Pope John XXIII was elected to lead the Roman Catholic Church

Selected Prices

Candygram, Western Union, Pound	$2.95
Clearasil	$0.59
Fruit Cocktail	$0.93
Hamburger, Burger King Whopper	$0.37
Hotel Room, Ritz-Carlton, Boston	$9.00
Man's Shirt, Arrow	$5.00
Movie Projector	$89.95
Theatre Ticket, New York	$3.85
Vodka, Smirnoff, Fifth	$5.23
Woman's Suit	$17.95

Hungarian Immigration Timeline

1867

Austria and Hungary united, embracing 51 million people including 10 million Germans and nine million Hungarians, under the leadership of Emperor Franz Josef. Residents not happy with this arrangement, especially non-Catholics, were permitted to emigrate to the United States.

1848

A wave of immigration to the U.S. was sparked by the Hungarian Revolution of 1848-1849.

1873

Pest, Buda and Obuda were unified: Budapest became a European metropolis.

1880

Hungarian immigration accelerated; between 1880 and 1898 about 200,000 Hungarians traveled to America.

1918

Germany and its allies, including the Austro-Hungarian monarchy, surrendered in World War I.

1920

The Trianon Treaty reduced Hungary's land area by two-thirds.

During the previous 100 years, over 3.7 million people emigrated from the Austrian-Hungarian Empire to the United States; only Germany, Ireland and Italy recorded higher figures.

1924

New laws in Hungary limited the number of Jewish students allowed to pursue higher education in Hungary to 6 percent, sparking emigration.

1933

Hungary formed an alliance with Germany; both regimes shared an interest in revising the Trianon Peace Treaty.

1938-1940

Germany concluded treaties in Munich and Vienna, under which Southern Slovakia and Northern Transylvania were returned to Hungary.

1944

The Nazis occupied their ally Hungary; Hungarian soldiers suffered extensive losses on the Soviet front.

1945

The Soviet Army first liberated, then occupied, Hungary.

1947

The last, relatively free election was followed by Communist control; major emigration to America ensued.

1956

The Hungarian Uprising occurred; several hundred thousand Hungarians emigrated to 37 countries.

"The Firm Start of a New Life," *Life*, January 7, 1957:

With nothing in the world but their lives, their clothes and each other, the Csillags came to the U.S. in the first planeload of Hungarian refugees. Bedraggled, bewildered and more than a little afraid, they shivered at the chilling New Jersey airport. Behind them, as with those in the plane landings that followed, lay the harrowing days of their escapes to the Austrian border by truck and motorbike, then the soup kitchens, questions, refugee camps and papers. Ahead lay hope, a chance to make a place in the free world and to be what Vice President Nixon called "the kind of people who make good Americans."

For the Pal Csillag family, help came quickly and beyond believing. In Indianapolis a prosperous uncle, Joseph Singer, who had left Hungary as a boy 48 years before, offered them a new start. A brother-in-law, Alex Star (the English word for Csillag) promised to help look out for them. Two days later, dazzled and still incredulous, the Csillags found themselves rolling west aboard a fast train.

But they could not envision the new life that awaited them. They were used to a little food and less fuel. In their hometown of Csorna (population 8,957), they had known no one with flush toilets or refrigerators. Of the family only Pal, 35, had seen a telephone and that from a distance. They could only wonder if the tales they had heard would come true. . . .

Settled at last in a house, among friends, the Csillags immediately got down to the most vital business: a job for Pal and school for the girls. Both turned out to be remarkably easy. With Mrs. Star, Rose went down to see Mr. Stiebaugh, principal of P.S. 76. He told them the girls were welcome. "They're not the first to come here, strangers to the country and to English, and soon will be at home," he said.

Bill Hinkel, district manager of Anheuser-Busch, which sells baker's yeast as well as beer, read in the papers that Pal had been a baker. "I know a lot of bakers," he said. He called one. "These refugee people need help. How about giving him a job?" Pal went down to the Roselyn Bakeries and was soon at work. "Down there," Pal said, "you can drink all the coffee you want. They give it to you. It's real coffee. You can eat all the food you want free. And I am paid more than $75 a week. In Csorna I earned about $77 a month and it cost $34 for a pair of shoes." And after a week of work, Pal got another pleasant surprise. His sister and brother-in-law from Hungary, the Klopfers, were coming from the Camp Kilmer refugee center. He met them and proudly took them for a ride on the first escalator the Klopfers had ever seen.

"President Urges Wide Law Change to Aid Immigrants,"
by Anthony Lewis, *The New York Times*, February 9, 1956:

President Eisenhower today called for sweeping changes in the immigration laws.

In a special message to Congress he proposed a drastic revision of the quota system that has regulated immigration law the last 30 years. The effect would be to double the number of quota immigrants admitted in an average year and to increase sharply the proportion from Italy, Greece and other countries of southern and eastern Europe.

A private calculation showed that countries in these areas would be able to send a combined total of up to 125,000 immigrants a year to the United States under the President's proposal. They had been limited to 24,502 by the present quota.

General Eisenhower also asked Congress to do the following:

Permit a waiver of the requirement that aliens coming for temporary visits be fingerprinted before they get United States visas.

Give the Attorney General discretion to grant relief in the thousands of alien hardship cases now handled by Congress each year in private bills.

President Eisenhower

Make several administrative changes in the law to eliminate "unnecessary restrictions upon travel" and "hardships."

The message fulfills promises made by President Eisenhower in the 1952 campaign to amend the McCarran-Walter Immigration Act, which was adopted that year. The act was sponsored by the late Senator Pat McCarran, Democrat of Nevada, and Representative Francis D. Walter, Democrat of Pennsylvania. It was passed over President Truman's veto.

Although General Eisenhower had criticized the act occasionally since 1952, these were his first specific proposals for amending it. They went further than critics of the act had expected.

"The recommendations are better and more comprehensive than I expected," Senator Herbert H. Lehman, Democrat of New York and a leading proponent of more liberal immigration laws, said. "He has come a considerable way down the road I and others have been pointing out the last four years."

A statement issued for Mr. Walters, who is a power in Congress on immigration affairs, criticized the president's message. Mr. Walter had read parts of the message before leaving on a Far Eastern tour.

continued

"President Urges Wide Law Change to Aid Immigrants," . . . *(continued)*

"The President's proposals cast a threatening shadow over the basic immigration policies established by the McCarran-Walter Act," Mr. Walters said. "If, indeed, there are reasons for amending the immigration laws, they do not appear in the president's proposal, nor in the parade of politically inspired measures which had preceded them."

The far-reaching changes proposed in the quota evoked the most surprise.

The present system, virtually unchanged since 1924, allots 154,657 quota numbers annually for would-be immigrants from outside the Western Hemisphere. There are no quota restrictions on immigration from countries in this hemisphere.

The quota total is divided according to the percentages of foreign-born persons in the United States under the 1920 census. The effect is to give most of the quota numbers, 125,165, to northern and western Europe and countries where there is little desire to emigrate.

In recent years such countries as Britain and Ireland have used only fractions of their quotas, while there have been long waiting lists for quota numbers in the poor, overpopulated lands of southern Europe. In 1954, the most recent year for which figures are available, only 94,000 quota immigrants arrived. About 60,000 quota numbers went unused.

President Eisenhower said the whole concept of national origins as the method of admitting aliens "needs to be re-examined" by Congress. He proposed broad "interim measures" during the study.

First, he suggested that the quota total be raised to 220,000 a year. He said "economic growth over the next 30 years" justified the increase. He proposed that the additional 65,000 numbers be distributed according to actual sources of immigration since 1924, thus giving more weight to southern Europe.

Second, he asked that unused quota numbers be pooled and made available to aliens having special skills or relatives in the United States.

Under the first suggestion the southern European quota would rise to 45,000 and northern Europe's to 157,000. But chances are that the northern countries would use little more than their present average of about 70,000. This would leave as many as 80,000 unused numbers to be pooled each year and made available to southern Europe, raising the total immigration from that area to 125,000 a year.

The president asked that 5,000 quota numbers be set aside for admission of aliens "with special skills and cultural or technical qualifications," regardless of their national origin.

He urged the end of quota "mortgages" under the Displaced Persons Act of 1948. This provision charged off immigrant refugees against future quotas. Fifty percent of the Greek quota had just been eliminated until the year 2017.

On the fingerprinting requirement, which has brought frequent protests from abroad, the president said experience had shown that it "does not significantly contribute our national safety and security." He suggested the Attorney General and the Secretary of State be permitted to waive the regulation on a reciprocal basis with other countries.

Other recommended amendments would eliminate visa requirements for foreign travelers passing to the United States en route somewhere else; end immigration inspection of aliens coming from Hawaii or Alaska; and liberalize restrictions on obtaining citizenship by marriage or service in the Armed Forces.

"I Remember When TV Was New," *Remembrance,* May/June 2003:

When we purchased our first TV set in the '50s, a challenge arose that we hadn't expected. Our young daughters were very willing to go to bed when it was time. But if that time coincided with the commercial featuring a penguin singing out, "Smoke Kools! Smoke Kools!," we had to rush over to the set and turn down the volume. If the girls heard it, they'd be out of bed and in the living room to watch. They loved that little penguin.

—Rollin Bodin, Lake Charles, Louisiana

When my Dad bought our first TV, in 1953, we lived in Valley, Washington. At the time, KHQ-TV was broadcasting only a test pattern. Besides our family of five, there were two uncles living with us. One night we had just sat down to supper and an actual program came on the television. I think it was a Western. No one said a word. Everyone picked up their plates and went and sat in the living room.

—Betty A. T. Holloway, Valley, Washington

When television came to Des Moines, Iowa, in 1951, Donna and Floyd Webb owned a TV shop a block from where I lived. They put a TV set in their store window and installed a speaker outside along with an on/off switch. When Floyd closed the shop for the night, he turned on the TV. Kids and grownups brought chairs, snacks and drinks and watched television. Everyone had a good time; the last one to leave turned off the switch. When color came, people stopped by just to see the NBC peacock spread its tail feathers.

—Fern Darr, Federal Heights, Colorado

"You could use a haircut, young man," she said. "You're getting to look like one of these crazy Hungarians or something. . . ."

—J.D. Salinger, *Franny and Zooey*, 1955:

Solution of the problem of refugees from communism and overpopulation has become a permanent part of the foreign-policy program of the Democratic Party. We pledge continued cooperation with other free nations to solve it. We pledge continued aid to refugees from communism and the enactment of President Truman's proposals for legislation in this field. In this way we can give hope and courage to the victims of Soviet brutality and can carry on a humanitarian tradition of the Displaced Persons Act.

—The immigration plank of the 1952 Democratic Party's platform

"Hungary Rebels Still Resisting Troops of Soviets," by Elie Abel, *The New York Times*, November 7, 1956:

The Soviet re-conquest of Hungary is not yet complete.

Diehard revolutionary forces are making the Soviet army fight hard in Budapest, according to diplomatic reports received last night.

Gellert Hill, which rises steeply above the Danube, has become a battleground. This is the site of the Soviet war memorial that the revolutionaries attempted to dynamite last week.

In the narrow streets of Buda, right bank section of Budapest, women and children were reported fighting from house to house alongside the men against the Soviet Army. It seemed a hopeless struggle, but the revolutionaries would not submit, at least in this quarter of the capital and scattered points in southern and western Hungary.

A rebel-held radio station said last night that Dunapentele, an industrial town south of Budapest, was controlled by revolutionary forces.

The Budapest regime made one symbolic concession to the bitter anti-Soviet mood of the Hungarian people. It canceled celebration of the holiday today marking the Bolshevik Revolution in Russia 39 years ago. . . .

For the second day the Soviet commander Pecs, near Hungary's uranium mines, called on the civilian population to stop shielding the rebels. Heavy street fighting appeared to be in progress there.

The Pecs radio warned civilians to stay indoors because Soviet troops were "compelled to open fire" against Hungarian snipers in the windows and doorways of houses.

At the Austrian border crossing point of Hegyeshalom, Hungarian soldiers defied a Soviet ultimatum to give up their arms. Between 40 and 50 Hungarians were holding the customs house at Hegyeshalom. They have six machine guns and a number of machine pistols.

Refusing to budge when the Soviet commander telephoned them at noon to warn that his troops would open fire unless they surrender, the Hungarians were still standing firm at nightfall.

Absent-minded Prof parks wife, kisses Rambler

by Hoff

Once there was a professor who got called into the college president's office. "Is it true," said the prexy, "that last week you parked your wife and kissed your new 1959 Rambler?" "Yes, sir," said the prof, "but . . ."

"Such absent-mindedness is appalling," said the prexy. "But, sir," said the prof, "that wasn't absent-mindedness! Remember that big gas-guzzler I used to drive that didn't fit my garage and my wife couldn't park?"

"Well, I decided to trade it for a little foreign car, but my wife said, 'We have four children, dear. Remember?' 'Bless my soul,' I said, 'so we do.' Then my brightest student told me about Rambler—big car room, small car economy.

"So I got a Rambler and last week when I had to go to that conference at State U., I parked my wife at her mother's and kissed my Rambler because it's a sweetheart of a car and gets twice the mileage of my former big car," said the prof.

"That's what this string on my finger is for," said the prexy. "My wife said we're only getting five to nine miles per gallon—or is it five to nine gallons per mile—on our big car. So where is that Rambler dealer?"

1951 NEWS FEATURE

"Wetback Airlift Turns Back 28,000," by Gladwin Hill, *The New York Times,* **August 7, 1951:**

About 28,000 Mexican illegal entrants into the Southwestern part of the country have been flown back to their native land in the first two months of the new "airlift" deportation system of the United States immigration and naturalization service.

While this has cost upwards of $500,000 and has disposed of less than one-third of the total illegal entrants apprehended during the period, the system apparently is putting a considerable crimp in the annual tide of border jumping, service officers said today.

This illicit traffic has been reliably estimated upwards to one million persons a year, all attracted by the prospect of employment—albeit at substandard wages—on Southwestern fruit, vegetable and cotton ranges and in urban occupations.

For a decade, the Immigration Service, with fewer than 1,000 patrol officers for the 1,600 miles of international border between Brownsville, Texas, and San Diego has been futilely attacking this human tide with a figurative broom trundling illegals across the boundary by bus, only to have them often beat the bus back into the United States.

As a more decisive deterrence, the Immigration Service in June invoked chartered transport planes to carry the "wetbacks"—so-called because of their traffic across the Rio Grande River—so deep into Mexico they would have trouble getting back.

Daily flights to the C-16 Curtis Commando planes of the Flying Tiger Line, flying from 50 to 67 "wetbacks," were inaugurated from El Centro on California's southern border, and Brownsville to Guadalajara, 500 miles southwest of Brownsville; San Lucas Potosi, 300 southwest of Brownsville; and to Durango, 500 miles south of El Paso, Texas.

The illegal entrants were routed back to the centers nearest their known homes.

To date, more than 10,000 have flown out of Brownsville, at a rate of as many as six flights a day, and some 8,400 from El Centro.

That the system is proving of value is seen by immigration officials in the fact that, whereas the old forms of deportation had little apparent effect on the rate of influx, it has dropped sharply.

In the Los Angeles immigration district, embracing Southern California and western Arizona, although border patrol activities continue, apprehensions dropped from 21,808 in June to 9,800 in July, the lowest figure since January 1950. Similarly, in the El Paso immigration district, covering west Texas and New Mexico, apprehensions dropped from 1,051 in June to 833 in July. . . .

Apprehensions over the entire region last year totaled about 585,000. It is authoritatively estimated that for every "wetback" caught, at least one, probably more, evade capture.

Apprehensions have gone off to the point where the Brownsville airlift is being cut to an average of one flight a day, and the El Centro airlift to three a week. Part of this decline undoubtedly is due to a seasonal hiatus in agriculture in which the majority of the "wetbacks" find employment and part to the pending renewal—arranged last week—of legal intergovernmental recruiting of temporary Mexican labor for the Southwest.

One of the designated centers in Mexico for the recruiting is Guadalajara, and immigration officials indicated today this would be eliminated as an airlift terminus to avoid giving the deportees a special advantage in obtaining legal employment.

The cost of airlift transportation, borne by the Immigration Service, ranges around $10-$40 a head, depending on the termini. This is not cheap, but authoritative observers noted it aggregates only a "drop in the bucket" compared with the $28 million requested recently by President Truman for the program of legal recruitment of Mexican labor, which the deportation campaign complements.

1960–1969

The decade of the sixties made quite a reputation for itself through rebellion and protest. No aspect of American society escaped this social upheaval entirely unscathed. The decade included tragic assassinations, momentous social legislation for African Americans, remarkable space achievements, the awakening of a Native American rights movement and some of the nation's largest antiwar protests in its history. Music, hairstyles, the willingness of people to speak out would all be transformed. It was the beginning of the Beatles and the tragic end of the non-violent phase of the Civil Rights Movement. While the nation's "silent majority" slapped "Love It or Leave It" ("It" being America) bumper stickers on their cars, thousands of highly vocal, well-educated middle class citizens carried signs in the streets to loudly protest America's involvement in Vietnam. It was truly a time of wrenching conflict in search of social change.

Despite turbulence, America remained a safe haven for the politically and economically repressed refugees around the world. As an aftermath of the Cuban revolution, for example, 1,800 Cuban refugees a week were arriving in Miami in 1962; this would evolve into the formalized Cuban airlift for 3,500 refugees a month in 1965. That same year President Lyndon Johnson stood in the shadow of the Statue of Liberty and signed the new Immigration and Nationality Act of 1965 and pledged "that those who seek refuge here in America will find it. The dedication of America to our traditions as an asylum for the oppressed is going to be upheld." The final bill abolished national origin quotas and limited the Eastern Hemisphere to 170,000 immigrants a year and the Western Hemisphere to 120,000 places with no individual country limits. Significantly, the legislation dramatically increased the number of professionals flocking to America. By 1972 more than 63,000 graduates of foreign medical schools were serving as doctors in the United States.

From 1960 to 1964, the economy expanded, unemployment was low, and disposable income for music, vacations, art or simply having fun grew rapidly. Internationally, the power of the United States was immense. Congress gave the young President John F. Kennedy the defense and space-related programs Americans wanted, but few of the welfare programs he proposed. Then, inflation arrived, along with the Vietnam War. Between 1950 and 1965, inflation soared from an annual average of less than 2 percent (ranging from 6 percent to 14 percent a year) to a budget-popping average of 9.5 percent. Upper class investors, once content with the consistency and stability of banks, sought better returns in the stock market and real estate.

The Cold War became hotter during conflicts over Cuba and Berlin in the early 1960s. Fears over the international spread of Communism led to America's intervention in a foreign conflict that would become a defining event of the decade: Vietnam. Military involvement in this small Asian country grew from advisory status to full-scale war. By 1968, Vietnam had become a national obsession, leading to President Lyndon Johnson's decision not to run for another term and fueling not only debate over America's role in Vietnam, but also more inflation and division nationally. The antiwar movement grew rapidly. Antiwar marches, which had drawn but a few thousand in 1965, grew in size until millions of marchers filled the streets of New York, San Francisco, and Washington, DC, only a few years later. By spring 1970, students on 448 college campuses made ROTC voluntary or abolished it.

The struggle to bring economic equality to blacks during the period produced massive spending for school integration. By 1963, the peaceful phase of the Civil Rights movement was ending; street violence, assassinations and bombings defined the period. In 1967, 41 cities experienced major disturbances. At the same time, charismatic labor organizer Cesar Chavez's United Farm Workers led a Civil Rights-style movement for Mexican Americans, gaining national support which challenged the growers of the West with a five-year agricultural strike.

As a sign of increasing affluence and changing times, American consumers bought 73 percent fewer potatoes, 2.5 percent more fish, poultry, and meat, and 50 percent more citrus products and tomatoes than in 1940. California passed New York as the most populous state. Factory workers earned more than $100 a week, their highest wages in history. From 1960 to 1965, the amount of money spent for prescription drugs to lose weight doubled, while the per-capita consumption of processed potato chips rose from 6.3 pounds in 1958 to 14.2 pounds eight years later. In 1960, approximately 40 percent of American adult women had paying jobs; 30 years later, the number would grow to 57.5 percent. Their emergence into the workforce would transform marriage, child rearing and the economy. In 1960, women were also liberated by the FDA's approval of the birth control pill, giving both women and men a degree of control over their bodies that had never existed before.

During the decade, anti-establishment sentiments grew: men's hair was longer and wilder, beards and mustaches became popular, women's skirts rose to mid-thigh, and bras were discarded. Hippies advocated alternative lifestyles, drug use increased, especially marijuana and LSD; the Beatles, the Rolling Stones, Jimi Hendrix, and Janis Joplin became popular music figures; and college campuses became major sites for demonstrations against the war and for Civil Rights. The Supreme Court prohibited school prayer, assured legal counsel to the poor, limited censorship of sexual material, and increased the rights of the accused.

Extraordinary space achievements also marked the decade. Ten years after President Kennedy announced he would place a man on the moon, 600 million people around the world watched as Neil Armstrong gingerly lowered his left foot into the soft dust of the moon's surface. In a tumultuous time of division and conflict, the landing was one of America's greatest triumphs and an exhilarating demonstration of American genius. Its cost was $25 billion and set the stage for 10 other men to walk on the surface of the moon during the next three years.

The 1960s saw the birth of Enovid 10, the first oral contraceptive (cost $0.55 each), the start of Berry Gordy's Motown Records, felt-tip pens, Diet-Rite cola, Polaroid color film, Weight Watchers, and Automated Teller Machines. It's the decade when lyrics began appearing on record albums, Jackie and Aristotle Onassis reportedly spent $20 million during their first year together, and the Gay Liberation Front participated in the Hiroshima Day March—the first homosexual participation as a separate constituency in a peace march.

1966 Profile

When twenty-two-year-old Miguel Lopez traveled to the United States from Mexico in 1963, he also made the journey from immigrant worker to union member.

Life at Home

- Born in Monclova, a small city in the northeast Coahuila region of Mexico, Miguel Lopez grew up working alongside his parents and five younger siblings in the fields, harvesting wheat and sugarcane.
- Work was inconsistent—sometimes there would be work every day; other times there would be no work for weeks.
- A friend had a brother who had worked in the U.S. for six months and returned to Mexico with more money than Miguel could make in a year.
- Miguel had always prided himself on being a hard worker; he was physically strong, and eager for the chance to prove himself in the United States.
- He dreamed of earning money to bring back to his family in Monclova.
- On July 3, 1963, he traveled by train with a group of 15 other young men to Ciudad Juarez at the northern border of Mexico.
- He carried with him only a small satchel of clothing and a pack of cigarettes.
- The first step to employment north of the border was approval by a U.S. official after a brief face-to-face interview.
- Prospective workers were asked about their work experience and had to show the calluses on their palms to prove they did farm labor.
- Then they were searched for weapons or drugs and sprayed with DDT, a powerful insecticide.
- Of the 16 young men from Coahuila, Miguel was among the 10 that were selected to work in the U.S.
- The rest were sent back home.

Miguel Lopez was 22 when he left Mexico to harvest crops in the US.

- He was given papers to sign but, with no knowledge of English, did not know what was written on them.
- These papers were his work contract documents, outlining the terms and conditions of the Bracero Program, allowing him to work in the U.S.
- After completing the paperwork and having his picture taken for his work permit, Miguel waited in Ciudad Juarez for several days with very little food.
- Distracted by his excitement to begin work in the U.S. and his anxiety of not knowing what he would find there, he barely noticed the hunger.
- He thought about how proud his father and mother would be upon receiving the money that he would send them from America.
- Finally, the Mexican workers were instructed to board a crowded train to cross the border into El Paso, Texas.
- It would be several years before he crossed it again.

Life at Work

- Miguel Lopez's labor contract with the Bracero Program was for three months.
- The Bracero Program started in 1942 to support U.S. agriculture during World War II.
- It was controversial, as it increased competition and lowered wages for Mexican Americans already working in the agricultural industry in the United States.
- Bracero contracts for skilled agricultural workers ranged from four weeks to six months and included adequate, sanitary, free housing; low-cost meals; occupational insurance; and transportation back to Mexico.
- These terms were often not upheld by U.S. farms that employed braceros.
- Miguel was selected by a farmer in El Paso to pick cotton.
- He earned $2.20 per 100 pounds of cotton picked and was able to gather 300 pounds a day.
- Miguel was paid $35-$45 per week and most weeks, he was the top earner at the farm.
- The national minimum wage was $1.25 per hour; in Texas, migrant farm workers averaged $0.81 per hour.
- Miguel worked seven days a week from 6 a.m. to 5 p.m.
- The work was hard, but Miguel was extremely satisfied to have steady work and to be receiving good pay.
- Every Saturday after work, his boss took the workers into the town to buy food and cigarettes.
- The farmer was young and inexperienced; he inherited the farm from his father who had died in a tractor accident.
- Dealing with the Mexican workers was intimidating for the youthful, white boss, so he avoided interacting with them when possible.
- Miguel spent his money carefully, and once a month sent money home to his family.
- With his cotton crop earnings, he sent home a total of $300, and saved $20 to buy clothes for his family when he returned to Mexico.
- By late September, when Miguel's contract was almost over, he learned from other workers about opportunities in California picking grapes where the pay was even better.
- Before he left Texas, he mailed a letter home with a check for $46 and a promise to return to Mexico as soon as he could with more money.
- Miguel then boarded a train to Delano, California, and didn't look back.

Miguel consistently picked more cotton than other workers.

Bumper crops in El Paso earned Miguel $45 a week.

- The journey of nearly 950 miles took eight days.
- While he missed his family, Miguel was excited at the prospect of continuing to work and earn more money before he returned home.
- Upon arriving in Delano, the workers were transported to a grape vineyard.
- Most of the workers on the vineyard lived in the area year 'round.
- Unlike most other crops, grapes require attention for 10 months out of the year.
- Miguel's primary role was girdling, or cutting into the bark of the grapevine, disrupting the natural flow of water, thus forcing the fruit to swell.
- Though the work was tedious, it required a great deal of concentration to make cuts in the correct place.
- Miguel earned $1.10 per hour—more than he had earned in the cotton fields, but still less than the minimum wage.
- The first convention of the National Farm Workers Association (NFWA), founded by Cesar Chavez, was held on September 30, 1962—more than a year before Miguel arrived.
- Since then the NFWA had worked to organize farm workers in dozens of agricultural towns in California, concentrating on offering farm workers modest benefits and meaningful services.
- Labor unions were against the Bracero Program, as temporary laborers worked for less money in worse conditions than union workers.
- No longer a bracero, Miguel joined the NFWA in 1965 based upon promises of higher wages, better living conditions, and contract protection.
- The Delano Grape Strike began in September 1965 when the mostly Filipino American members of the Agricultural Workers Organizing Committee (AWOC) walked out against Delano-area grape growers.
- On September 16, 1965, Mexican Independence Day, Miguel joined the 1,200 members of the NFWA and voted to strike.
- The more than 200 workers at Miguel's vineyard participated in the strike.
- While he did not work for four months, Miguel was deeply moved by the passion of Chavez and the struggle for social justice.
- In early 1966 Miguel found work again in Delano with a vineyard that had signed a contract with the United Farm Workers (UFW).
- As a result of his union membership, he now earned $1.70 per hour.

Life in the Community: Delano, California

- After several years of working in America's fields, Miguel Lopez considered himself to be Mexican American, even though he was still an undocumented worker.
- If he had returned to Mexico after his three-month work permit expired in 1963, he could have applied for a permanent visa and returned to the United States legally.

The young farmer who Miguel worked for inherited the farm when his father died unexpectedly in a tractor accident.

Miguel earned more at the vineyard than picking cotton, but the work was more tedious and required more concentration.

- However, with his success in California, Miguel did not want to go home and never completed the necessary paperwork.
- At the grape vineyard where he worked and lived, workers were segregated by nationality—Puerto Ricans, Filipinos, Blacks or Anglos.
- Miguel shared a room with three other Mexicans; he had his own cot and shelves.
- Fifty-six men shared a common bathroom with four toilets, three shower stalls, and six sinks.
- The cost of room and board was $2.10 per day.
- Three meals a day were provided in the common area, usually tortillas or sandwiches with iced tea.
- The food wasn't bad, but there often was not enough.
- Once or twice a week Miguel would miss a meal because he was at the end of the food line.
- When not in the fields, Miguel played basketball or card games with other Mexican workers.

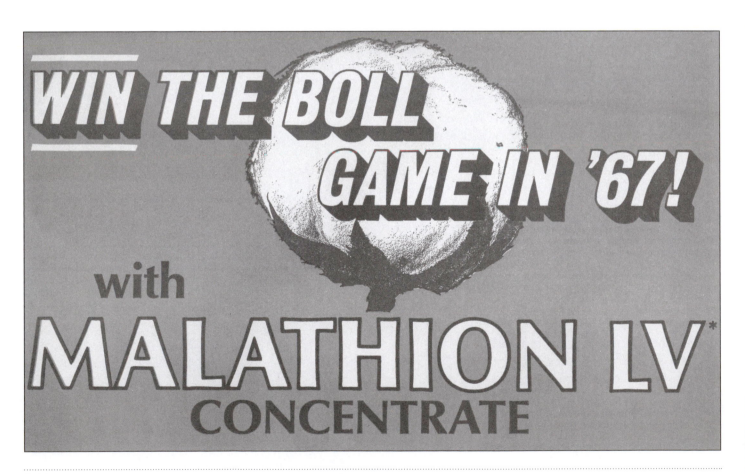

HISTORICAL SNAPSHOT
1966

- The Clean Waters Restoration Act provided funds for preventing river and air pollution
- *Time* magazine's "Man of the Year" was the 25-and-under generation
- Black Power was introduced in the Civil Rights Movement as the more militant followers of Stokely Carmichael broke with the pacifist followers of Martin Luther King
- Movie openings included *A Man for All Seasons*, *Who's Afraid of Virginia Woolf?*, *Blow-up*, *Fahrenheit 451*, and *Alfie*
- The U.S. troop strength in Vietnam reached 400,000
- A National study reported that food prices were higher in poor neighborhoods than in more affluent ones
- In professional baseball, The Major League Players Association was formed
- Cesar Chavez's National Farm Workers Union was recognized as the bargaining agent for farm workers
- Virginia Masters and William Johnson's book *Human Sexual Response* controversially asserted that women possess as much sexual energy as do men
- Frank Sinatra won a Grammy Award for his recording of "Strangers in the Night"
- Biodegradable liquid detergents were produced for the first time to reduce pollution
- Hit songs included "The Ballad of the Green Berets," "Good Vibrations," "Sunny," "Winchester Cathedral," and "The Sounds of Silence"
- Roman Catholic bishops ruled that except during Lent, American Catholics could eat meat on Friday
- The National Association of Broadcasters instructed its disc jockeys to screen all new records for hidden, obscene meanings or references to drugs
- Bestsellers included *In Cold Blood* by Truman Capote, *A Thousand Days* by Arthur Schlesinger, *Valley of the Dolls* by Jacqueline Susann and *Capable of Honor* by Allen Drury
- To meet the demands of the Vietnam War, blanket student deferments were abolished; draft calls reached 50,000 a month
- The sandwich grill toaster, tape cartridges, Bank Americard, Taster's Choice, the National Organization for Women (NOW), and the rare and endangered species list made their first appearance
- Scientists completed the deciphering of the DNA code
- Television premieres included *The Newlywed Game*, *Mission: Impossible*, *The Hollywood Squares*, *Batman*, *Star Trek*, *The Monkees*, *That Girl*, and *The Dating Game*

Mexican Immigration Timeline

1848

The Mexican-American War (1846-1848) ended with the Treaty of Guadalupe Hidalgo, in which Mexico lost 55 percent of its territory (present-day Arizona, California, New Mexico, and parts of Colorado, Nevada and Utah).

The U.S. paid Mexico $15 million for war-related damages and to ensure that existing property rights would be protected for Mexicans now living in the boundaries of the U.S.

1853–1880

Fifty-five thousand Mexican workers immigrated to the United States as agricultural laborers.

1904

The Border Patrol was established by the U.S. to stop Asian workers from entering the U.S. through Mexico.

1910

Thousands of Mexicans fled across the border when the Mexican Revolution began.

1910–1930

The total number of Mexican immigrants recorded by the U.S. Census tripled from 200,000 to 600,000.

1911

The Dillingham Commission identified Mexican laborers as the best solution to the Southwest labor shortage; Mexicans were exempted from immigrant "head taxes" set in 1903 and 1907.

1917

Prospective immigrants to the U.S. were charged an entry tax of $8 and given a literacy test as a result of the U.S. Immigration Act of 1917.

Between 1917 and 1923 more than 72,000 Mexicans entered the U.S.

1921

The U.S. Immigration Act of 1921 restricted the immigration of Southern and Eastern Europeans.

Mexican workers were formally admitted at Border Patrol stations and charged a tax upon entering.

1924

Mexican immigration reached 89,000.

Congress created a 450-man Border Patrol, shared by the Mexican and Canadian borders.

1930s

Five hundred thousand Mexicans living in the U.S. were deported back to Mexico. Around 60 percent of those deported were children born in the U.S. or legal citizens of Mexican descent.

Timeline . . . *(continued)*

1931

Mexican American parents won their case against the Lemon Grove, California School Board to prevent their children from segregation from white children.

1941

The League of United Latin American Citizens held protests against discrimination by the Southern Pacific Railroad, which refused to give skilled apprenticeships to Mexican Americans.

1942

Mexican nationals were allowed to work in the U.S. on a temporary basis, mostly in the agricultural industry, through the Bracero Program. In the first three years of the program, over 200,000 temporary workers from Mexico, the Bahamas, Canada, Barbados, and Jamaica entered the U.S.

1952

Immigration and Nationality Act, also known as the McCarran-Walter Act, gave priority to skilled workers and family members of U.S. citizens while stating that all races were eligible for naturalization.

1954

The U.S. Immigration and Naturalization Service deported over one million Mexicans during Operation Wetback in an effort to reduce illegal immigration in the southwest.

1964

The Bracero Program ended due to a surplus of agricultural workers and increased mechanization such as the mechanical corn harvester. The program had permitted temporary employment for nearly 4.5 million Mexican nationals.

Labor leaders began working toward unionizing farm workers.

1965

The Immigration and Naturalization Act of 1965 eliminated the national origin quotas of the 1920s and set annual limits of 170,000 Eastern Hemisphere European immigrants and 120,000 Western Hemisphere immigrants. For Western Hemisphere immigrants, visas were available on a first-come, first-served basis. Spouses, children and parents of U.S. citizens were exempt from the numerical limits.

Selected Prices

Crib, Portable	$22.95
Drill, Black & Decker	$10.99
Film, 35 Millimeter Color Slide	$2.49
Food Processor	$39.95
Hat, Pillbox	$4.97
Pepsi, Six-Pack	$0.59
Radio, Portable Transistor	$12.95
Socket Set, 57-Piece	$56.95
Tape Player, 8-Track	$67.95
Watch, Timex	$9.95

1899
Aspirin is first produced in quantities. It is the first effective pain remedy to be sold without prescription.

1916
A.P.C. is introduced—the best "combination of ingredients" type of product. Claimed to be somewhat more effective than aspirin.

1965
Excedrin is now available. Medical progress has made possible its extra-strength formula; special ingredients for quick, lasting relief; relief of tension; relief of depression. Tablet, 50% stronger than aspirin for headache pain. Yet enough, you need no prescription.
Excedrin, the extra-strength pain reliever. A product of today.

Pepsi-Cola cold beats any cola cold!

Getting the Nation to Pay Attention to Farm Workers, http://www.ufw.org

Roberto Bustos was an original 1965 striker and captain of the 400-mile march from Delano to Sacramento in 1966.

"I'll always remember Cesar coming into the office one day and saying, 'We are going to go to Sacramento.' I was very enthusiastic about the idea and was already loading up my car with all my things, and then he gave me the harsh news that we would be marching from Delano to Sacramento! At that moment I thought the man had lost his mind. I looked at the map and saw that the journey was 245 miles.

"I didn't think I could walk that distance, and I was right. Ultimately it came close to 400 miles since we made several stops in different towns and never went on a straight path. We stopped at Ducor, Terra Bella, Visalia and Fresno, among others.

"But the day the march started, March 17, 1966, I had no idea of the impact this journey would have. We were expecting support but never to be joined by 10,000 supporters as we arrived at the Capitol in Sacramento. It was overwhelming seeing so many people join us and support us in our struggle. When we had started on our way up we only had 70 farm workers with us. The march took a total of 25 days and finally finished on April 10, 1966.

"We walked over 15 miles a day, every day. At times I thought we wouldn't make it. In fact, had we not been given new boots by a company in Porterville, we probably wouldn't have.

"The march was very significant, and not just because it was a chance for the governor to see what we were going through. It also allowed the rest of the nation to pay attention to what was happening in Delano. Before the march we had no press coverage whatsoever. It was as if 5,000 workers were not on strike.

"Today I leave with the honor of not just being captain of the march but with the legacy and history of what the march signified: the recognition the American public gave to the farm workers' struggles.

Excerpt from the "Proclamation of the Delano Grape Workers for International Boycott Day," May 10, 1969:

We, the striking grape workers of California, join on this International Boycott Day with the consumers across the continent in planning the steps that lie ahead on the road to our liberation. As we plan, we recall the footsteps that brought us to this day and the events of this day. . . .

We have been farm workers for hundreds of years and pioneers for seven. Mexicans, Filipinos, Africans and others, our ancestors were among those who founded this land and tamed its natural wilderness. But we are still pilgrims on this land, and we are pioneers who blaze a trail out of the wilderness of hunger and deprivation that we have suffered even as our ancestors did. We are conscious today of the significance of our present quest. If this road we chart leads to the rights and reforms we demand, if it leads to just wages, humane working conditions, protection from the misuse of pesticides . . . if it changes the social order that relegates us to the bottom reaches of society, then in our wake will follow thousands of American farm workers. Our example will make them free. . . .

Grapes must remain an unenjoyed luxury for all as long as the barest human needs and basic human rights are still luxuries for farm workers. The grapes grow sweet and heavy on the vines, but they will have to wait while we reach out first for our freedom. The time is ripe for our liberation.

"Things You Should Know About Harvest Aid Chemicals," Harris H. Barnes, Jr., *Progressive Farmer*, July 1967:

Cyanamid dust is still a good defoliant if plants are mature and weather conditions are good. The best method of application is to fly on 30 pounds of the material in the still of the evening, during periods you can be certain of dews.

Chlorates work well under the same conditions as the dust. The (cotton) plants must be mature with colors greenish yellow or gold tinged with red. . . .

Some growers have added a desiccant to do the defoliant. This gives partial defoliation and partial desiccation, with mature leaves dropping and immature leaves drying up and remaining fastened to the tree plant. But growers and defoliation areas are getting away from this practice in order to cut down the amount of trash in cotton.

"California Leads the Nation in Swing to Right," Gracie Simmons, *National Guardian,* November 19, 1966:

California outstripped the rest of the nation in the November 8 swing to Republicanism. It skipped the half-step to the moderates and went straight Into the embrace of the far right. Its representative, actor Ronald Reagan, romped to victory in the race for governor over Democratic incumbent Edmund G. Brown with about a million votes to spare. . . .

The right wing was clearly on the offensive. The contest in the 29th Congressional District (Los Angeles) was marked by an attempt to whip up war hysteria. William Orozco, Republican, smeared the "peace" candidate, Rep. George E. Brown Jr., as unpatriotic. Brown won, but by a small margin, 67,857 to 64,416.

An unprecedented attack was made on state Supreme Court judges who had held unconstitutional the anti-Negro housing amendment passed by the electorate in 1964 as Proposition 14.

"Immigration and Citizenship," *The Compton Yearbook,* 1966:

The first significant change in U.S. immigration laws in 41 years was enacted by Congress in 1965. President Lyndon B. Johnson signed a new law at the base of the Statue of Liberty, in New York Harbor, on October 3. At the same time, the president announced that all refugee Cubans would be admitted immediately and that he would ask Congress for a $12.6 million appropriation to expedite the influx.

Under the 1965 law, the present quotas based on national origin will be completely eliminated by mid-1968. Replacing the quotas are overall limits on the number of immigrants to be admitted: 20,000 a year from any one country. The ceiling for Europe, Asia, and Africa combined is 170,000 annually; the Western Hemisphere, 120,000. Once the system is in full effect, all applicants, regardless of race or nationality, will be processed on a "first-come first-served" basis.

The 1965 law divides preference categories into six new classes, plus refugees from Communism. In addition to members of the "immediate family" of U.S. residents, preference is given to professional people and skilled and unskilled labor in short supply in the U.S.

"Mexico," *The Compton Yearbook*, 1966:

When Gustav Diaz Ordaz was inaugurated as its new president in December 1964, the Republic of Mexico had achieved a degree of political stability and economic growth unknown anywhere in Latin America. In the four preceding years annual construction industry output increased 127 percent and industrial production had risen 25 percent. Bulging showcases and towering skyscrapers testified to Mexico's progress.

President Diaz Ordaz knew, however, that the poverty-stricken "second economy" of the countryside had not been touched by the prosperity of the big cities. There had been no rise in income for the campesinos (peasants) and the unskilled rural workers. In January 1965, therefore, the president launched a survey of the land distribution program that began 50 years before. In September, he reported that he signed 294 bills, distributing 3,028,000 acres among 27,763 peasants.

1967 Profile

Chinese-born Peng Liu escaped the Communist regime to emigrate to America and become a medical student at the University of California, San Francisco.

Life at Home

- Peng Liu was born in 1939, 10 years before his native city of Shanghai fell under the communist control of the People's Republic of China.
- Since the late 1800s, his family had owned many successful textile factories in Shanghai that exported silk and other fabrics to the United States and Europe.
- Peng was aware at a very young age of the differences between rich and poor.
- He grew up with servants, cooks, gardeners and chauffeurs, and attended the best private schools in Shanghai with his two younger brothers.
- As in many wealthy Chinese homes, Peng was surrounded by Western influences, such as tennis courts, crystal chandeliers and Frank Sinatra music.
- He enjoyed going to school, especially when Western movies and cartoons were shown in his English classes.
- After the success of the Communist Revolution in China in 1949, English classes were no longer included in the curriculum at Peng's school.
- Instead, he was required to study the language and history of Russia.
- As a teenager, Peng was aware of the Communist regime, but did not realize the serious implications until later; he was more interested in listening to records, going out with his friends and talking to girls.
- Western influence was tolerated in the early years of Communist China, but when Peng was a teenager, he was told to hand over his record albums to be destroyed by the communists.
- When his family lost control of their factories to the communists in 1950, his father applied for a visa to travel to Hong Kong, which was under non-communist British rule.
- Eventually, he was granted a one-month travel visa in 1952 after lying to the authorities about his plans, saying he was visiting relatives in Hong Kong in order to persuade them to return to China with him.

Peng Liu was 26-years-old when he left Communist China on a student visa.

Peng's parents before the Communist takeover.

The Liu brothers had a happy childhood growing up in Shanghai.

The city of Shanghai.

- In truth, Peng's father actually wanted to relocate his family to Hong Kong to escape the tight grip of communist rule in Shanghai and possibly open another textile factory there.
- Surmising his father's intentions, the government kept a close watch on Peng's family, who remained in Shanghai.
- As the news of his father going to Hong Kong spread, Peng and his brothers were harassed in school and accused of being the sons of a Hong Kong spy.
- Thirteen-year-old Peng became isolated from his friends and classmates, whose parents feared that association with Peng might link their own families to Party dissent.
- Peng spent much of his time studying.
- As was required for all children, Peng and his brothers were part of the Pioneer Movement—an organization to teach children the principles of communism.
- His mother cried silently as she tied the red scarves on their necks each morning before school.
- She expressed disdain at how children and adults had to pretend they believed in something they didn't to avoid political persecution at the hands of the communist leaders.
- Peng's school, now run by the government, was infiltrated with anti-American propaganda.
- At the age of 14 he became part of a youth group to prepare him for Party membership.
- His mother began working as a teacher, and became increasingly frustrated with the restrictions of the Communist regime, which forced previously wealthy Chinese to work for the government.
- She communicated with his father secretly through letters written in code.
- In 1958, letters were discovered in a "routine" search of their home.
- Peng and his brothers were taken from their mother, who was arrested for disloyalty to the Communist Party.
- Peng never saw his mother again.
- The three boys were taken to separate communes in the countryside where they were assigned duties such as working in the fields and scrubbing floors.
- Three years later, in 1961, Peng's father finally located his sons and applied for a visa for 17-year-old Peng to join him in Hong Kong.
- Upon arriving in Hong Kong, Peng learned that both of his younger brothers had died, most likely of starvation or disease such as tuberculosis.
- Even though Peng's formal schooling had been interrupted in 1958, he had excelled in academics, especially math and science, so his father immediately helped him apply to schools.

- Peng was admitted to the University of Hong Kong in 1962 after passing rigorous entrance examinations.
- His father encouraged him to study medicine, and Peng maintained the highest grades in most of his courses.
- In Hong Kong, Peng's father had established another small, but very successful silk factory, but fearing future communist takeover, decided to leave Asia in search of more secure freedom in the United States.
- Through his silk export business, Peng's father had become familiar with U.S. business and knew a few Chinese and American businessmen in San Francisco.
- The Chinese Exclusion Act had banned Chinese nationals from immigrating to the United States for over 60 years.
- After fighting alongside China as allies in World War II, the U.S. passed a series of laws, including the Immigration Act of 1965, which permitted the immigration of Chinese.
- Following his graduation from the University of Hong Kong, Peng applied for a student visa to continue his studies in the United States.
- After earning a passing score on the Test of English as a Foreign Language (TOEFL) and submitting the appropriate documentation, he was admitted to the University of California in San Francisco.
- Peng arrived in San Francisco as a medical student in 1966, full of hope.

Before the Communist takeover, Peng's family lived in an expensive home with many servants.

The house in Shanghai had beautiful gardens.

Life at Work

- In America, Peng Liu was most comfortable in the classes that included chemistry and math, especially working with numeric formulas and graphs.
- The informal nature of Peng's classes surprised him.
- In China, students did not converse with teachers or ask questions in the middle of class.
- One day, his chemistry professor even admitted that he had made a mistake when writing a formula on the board.
- More surprising to Peng was that a student had pointed out the error.
- Peng could not remember any of his Chinese teachers admitting to a mistake.
- He was also surprised that students were allowed to eat and drink in class, and that some teachers walked around the classroom or sat on desks as they lectured.
- Peng enjoyed the atmosphere of the American university but struggled with using English in both academic and social situations.

When his silk factory in Shanghai was shut down, Peng's father was successful in establishing another in Hong Kong.

Peng liked living in San Francisco.

San Francisco was full of Chinese influence.

- He had difficulty interacting with the American students and was amazed at the confidence that they displayed.
- Peng often wrote down questions for his professors because they had difficulty understanding his English.
- He was frequently lost with the lectures in English and re-read all of his notes and lecture material many times after class.
- With the exception of a rare few, he felt like his American professors gave him high grades for less work as compared to his teachers in China.
- Upon graduating from medical school, Peng hoped to work as a dermatologist in the United States.
- While doctors were respected in China, he would earn a better salary in America.

Life in the Community: San Francisco, California
- Peng Liu enjoyed the environment of San Francisco during his first full year in America.
- There were a lot of trees and parks, and it was very clean compared to Shanghai or Hong Kong.
- However, Peng did not make friends easily and spent most of his time on his studies.
- He liked his apartment that had been provided by the university as part of his research assistantship through the medical school, but was very lonely.
- He felt as though he did not fit in with the other students.
- Most seemed loud, arrogant and disrespectful.
- One afternoon, after his biology class, Peng was reviewing his notes while waiting to catch the bus back to his apartment.
- It was raining, and Peng was grateful that there was a covered seating area at the bus stop.
- Suddenly, he heard the screeching of car tires and looked up to see a red Chevrolet fast approaching the bus stop just before feeling the wet splash of cool mud cover the entire front side of his body.

- As the car quickly sped away Peng heard roaring laughter as one of the students in the car mimicked his Chinese language in a sing-song voice.
- His heart sank as he wiped mud from his glasses and tried to salvage his notes, written in a combination of English and Chinese.
- The few other Chinese medical students at his university who had started the program before him seemed to have taken on the attitude of the American students.
- Moreover, they were from different cities in China, and spoke dialects of Chinese that were nearly incomprehensible to Peng.
- Although he preferred to stay within the familiarity of his small apartment and the university, Peng traveled to Chinatown each Saturday morning with David Li, a 58-year-old professor of biology who was originally from Hong Kong.
- Established in the 1850s, San Francisco's Chinatown was the largest and oldest Chinatown in the U.S.
- There, Peng came into contact with many others from Hong Kong, and also some from Shanghai.
- While he was appreciative of the opportunity to get fresh fish and vegetables, he often found the experience of Chinatown depressing.
- In contrast to the university environment, the streets of Chinatown were dirty with rats scurrying underfoot and children running in the street.
- It reminded Peng of riding into the industrial district of Shanghai as a very young child and seeing dilapidated buildings and street beggars.
- The Chinese here were struggling, working for very little money in laundries or restaurants, living in cramped quarters with several other families.
- But at least, Peng thought, it was better for them here than back in China where the oppressive Cultural Revolution was taking place.
- Mao Zedong, chairman of the Chinese Communist Party, started the Cultural Revolution in 1966 in an attempt to bring China out of an economic depression, utilizing Chinese youths as "Red Guards" to renew excitement in the Party and discourage any anti-Party intellectualism.

San Francisco's Chinatown reminded Peng of the struggling street vendors in China.

HISTORICAL SNAPSHOT
1967

- The connection between a cholesterol-lowering diet and a reduced incidence of heart disease was shown in a five-year study
- Both CBS and NBC televised the Super Bowl
- A reported 100,000 hippies lived in the San Francisco area, principally around Haight-Ashbury
- The first rock festival was held at Monterey, California, featuring the Grateful Dead and Big Brother and the Holding Company starring Janis Joplin
- Heavyweight boxer Muhammad Ali was denied conscientious objector status after refusing induction in the Army
- George Lincoln Rockwell, president of the U.S. Nazi Party, was shot to death
- The United States revealed that an anti-ballistic missile defense plan had been developed against Chinese attack
- Hit songs included *Natural Woman, Soul Man, I Never Loved a Man, Penny Lane, By The Time I Get to Phoenix,* and *Can't Take My Eyes Off You*
- Bolivia confirmed the capture and death of Che Guevara
- When Army physician Captain Harold Levy refused to train Green Berets heading to Vietnam in the treatment of skin disease, he was court-martialed and sent to Fort Leavenworth prison
- Coed dorms opened at numerous colleges across the country for the first time
- *Sgt Pepper's Lonely Hearts Club Band* by the Beatles captured a Grammy award for best album
- Jogging, Mickey Mouse watches, protest buttons and psychedelic art were all important fads
- U.S. troop levels in Vietnam reached 225,000; the U.S. death toll reached 15,997
- Thurgood Marshall became the first African American appointed to the U.S. Supreme Court
- Television premieres included *The Flying Nun, The Carol Burnett Show, Ironsides* and *The Phil Donahue Show*
- Annual beef consumption, per capita, reached 105.6 pounds, up from 99 pounds in 1960
- Black leader Rap Brown said of the ghetto riots, "Violence is as American as apple pie"
- Journalist Bernard Fall was killed in Vietnam by a landmine

1960s folk singers Joni Mitchell and Melanie.

Chinese Immigration Timeline

1848

Chinese immigration began in California with the beginning of the gold rush.

1850

The Chinese American population in the U.S. was about 4,000, out of a population of 23.2 million.

The U.S. Census reported only two Chinese, working as house servants in Los Angeles.

1854

Chinese was included on a list of racial groups not allowed to testify against whites in the California Supreme Court.

1860

The Chinese American population in the U.S. was 34,933 out of a total population of 31.4 million.

1864–1865

Central Pacific Railroad Company recruited thousands of Chinese workers to build the first transcontinental railroad.

1870

The Naturalization Act limited American citizenship to "white persons and persons of African decent," preventing Asians from gaining U.S. citizenship.

1871

Anti-Chinese violence erupted in Los Angeles and other cities across the U.S.

About 75 percent of the U.S. Chinese population was in California.

1882

Congress passed the Chinese Exclusion Act, banning further entry of Chinese nationals to the U.S.

Since 1850, approximately 250,000 Chinese had entered the U.S.

1890

The Chinese American population was recorded as 107,488 out of a total of 62.9 million.

1891

The first public telephone pay station was started in San Francisco's Chinatown, called the Chinese American Telephone Exchange.

1892

The Geary Act was introduced, extending the Chinese Exclusion Act. Chinese resident laborers were required to obtain a certificate of residence or face deportation or imprisonment.

1898

The Supreme Court ruled that anyone born in the U.S. was a citizen.

1906

A massive earthquake and fire destroyed all records in San Francisco, including immigration records.

continued

Timeline . . . *(continued)*

1910

The Chinese American population in the U.S. was 94,414 out of a total population of 92.2 million.

The Angel Island Immigration Station in California opened to process Chinese immigrants who were restricted by the Chinese Exclusion Act.

Prospective immigrants endured intense, specific questioning to weed out "paper sons," or those who had false documentation that claimed relation to a Chinese U.S. citizen.

1924

The Immigration Act of 1924 placed further restrictions on immigration using a national origins quota.

1930

The Chinese American population in the U.S. was recorded as 60,000 out of a total population of 123.2 million.

Chinese wives married to American men prior to May 1924 were allowed to enter the U.S.

1940

The Angel Island Immigration Station closed due to a fire in the administration building.

1941

The United States entered World War II after the Japanese attacked Pearl Harbor. China was an ally of the United States.

1943

Congress passed the Magnuson Act, which repealed the Chinese Exclusion Act; an annual Chinese immigration quota of 105 was established and Chinese were also granted the right to become naturalized citizens.

The Yale Institute of Far Eastern Languages was founded to teach Chinese language and culture.

1945

World War II ended when the U.S. dropped an atomic bomb on Hiroshima and Nagasaki, Japan, and Japan surrendered to the U.S. and its allies.

The War Brides Act enabled 118,000 wives and children of U.S. military men to immigrate to the U.S., including Chinese.

1949

The Chinese Civil War ended with the Communist conquest of mainland China. The Communist Party of China established the People's Republic of China.

1950

The Chinese American population in the U.S. was 150,005 out of a total population of 151,325,798.

1952

The Immigration and Nationality Act, also known as the McCarran-Walter Act, ended exclusion of immigrants based on race, but included a racial quota system.

continued

Timeline . . . *(continued)*

1953

The Refugee Relief Act authorized 214,000 non-quota immigrant visas for refugees.

1955

The Chinese Chamber of Commerce was established in Los Angeles to promote and encourage the development of the Chinese American business community.

1958

A movement in Communist China referred to as "The Great Leap Forward" began, designed to turn China into a leading industrial power and resulting in widespread famine.

1959

The U.S. Immigration and Naturalization Service began the "Confession Program" (1959-1966), which enabled Chinese immigrants who had entered the country illegally to confess their status and become eligible to be naturalized citizens.

1962

The Kennedy Emergency Immigration Act permitted 15,000 Chinese immigrants to enter the United States between 1962 and 1965 as a result of "The Great Leap Forward" and Communist oppression in the People's Republic of China.

1965

National origin quotas were eliminated as part of the Immigration Reform Act of 1965.

A quota of 170,000 immigrants, with a maximum of 20,000 per country, was established with categories of preference set for each.

This is a four-girl typing pool.

Selected Prices

Automobile, Datsun	$2,196.00
Calculator, Electric Printing	$1,495.00
Circular Saw	$27.77
Electric Shaver	$13.97
Guitar, Electric	$199.95
Ketchup, Hunt's, 14 Ounces	$0.22
Refrigerator, Frigidaire	$208.00
Rider Mower	$352.95
Router	$34.95
Whiskey, Seagram's, Fifth	$5.79

Seagram's Crown Royal is the finest Canadian whisky in the world. If it weren't, it wouldn't cost you what it does.
About nine dollars!
That's a lot to put out for a fifth of whisky. But Seagram has put a lot into Crown Royal. Smoothness you find hard to believe. And good taste that will spoil you for anything else. In a way what you're paying for is inspiration. And that doesn't grow on trees.

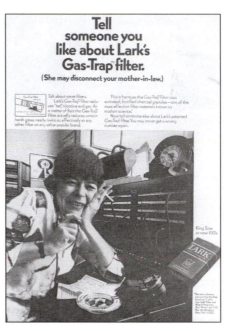

Tell someone you like about Lark's Gas-Trap filter.
(She may disconnect your mother-in-law.)

Remington introduces a smaller electric for a smaller office.

Remington realizes that not all offices are big. So we built a fully electric compact typewriter that's perfect for smaller offices.
The Remington® 713 typewriter. Priced under $300.
The new 713 is tough. Its cover is almost indestructible and its working parts are made of tempered carbon steel.
The new 713 is versatile, too. It can handle oversized typing jobs because it's got a 13-inch paper capacity. As an option the 713 has Extra-Type, to let you add special type faces for math, medical and engineering terms and foreign languages.
So whether you use the new 713 in a small office or a big office, you'll find it's simple to type on, simple to service, simple to afford. Call your Remington representative today.
From typewriters and duplicators to copiers and calculators, we're making business work simpler by making business machines simple to work.

"Chinaman's Chance," *Time*, September 8, 1967:

To sightseers tramping its cluttered avenues, San Francisco's Chinatown has always displayed a pungent blend of yang and yin. Those intertwined opposites—good and evil, sweet and sour, light and dark—describe not only Chinese philosophy but also the inner contradictions of a district whose neon signs and tourist bustle mask a swarming, sweatshop world of long hours, low pay, hard work and fear. For all its outward ambiance, the largest Chinese enclave outside Asia is one of America's most wretched slums.

Over 40,000 Chinese are jammed into the 42 blocks of Chinatown proper between Bush Street and Broadway, Kearny and Powell. About 30,000 have spilled north and west into adjacent residential districts; 10,000 more live throughout the Bay Area.

They first came by the thousands to California—Gum San, land of the Golden Mountains—when the gold fields and railroads beckoned, and in smaller streams when the U.S. set up immigration quotas and California passed its racial exclusion laws in 1892. Despite the restrictions, so many Chinese have entered the U.S. in the past seven decades that perhaps as many as half the people of Chinatown are there in violation of the immigration laws.

Since Mao Tse-tung took over the Chinese mainland, immigration via Hong Kong has swelled incrementally: more than 4,000 Chinese a year now settle in the Bay Area, creating a job shortage so severe that exploitation is the order of the day—and night. The traditional Chinese family fabric has visibly frayed. With mothers working, delinquency climbs. Tenement squalor sustains a tuberculosis rate double that of San Francisco as a whole.

Working conditions are no better. The major sources of jobs are restaurants, curio stores and the sewing shops, comprising 151 small, family-oriented contract clothing factories employing about 20 seamstresses apiece. Paid on a piecework basis, the women often labor from 8:30 a.m. until after midnight, seven days a week, fingers darting frenetically to make ends meet. Asked why she would work at least 12 hours a day for a net income of $26 a week, one mother of five said succinctly: "You have to in Chinatown."

Ever since one Chum Ming sailed east from his native Kwangtung in 1847 to grow up with the country, California's Chinese have been victimized by their language problems (even today, no more than 40 percent speak fluent English), their fear of deportation, and traditional kowtowing to fate and station. San Francisco's youngest, brightest Chinese Americans leave for the suburbs at a rate of up to 15,000 a year, and Chinatown has become a way station for immigrants and a ghetto of the old and unemployed poor.

Only recently has Chinese pride permitted a lowering of the all but impenetrable veil that shrouded their condition from the outside world. California's Labor Commission and the San Francisco Central Labor Council have heard depressing testimony from Chinatown residents about working conditions in the district. Last week, led by the International Ladies' Garment Workers Union, labor opened a campaign of pickets, sanctions and the threat of boycott against eight Chinatown sewing shops and a contracting firm. Although the goal is not immediate unionization, the 25,000-member culinary workers union is waiting in the wings, and a labor spokesman called the drive "the opening gun in a campaign we hope will eventually end substandard wages and conditions in Chinatown shops, stores, factories and bars."

"Hopes for the Second Generation of Asian Americans,"
http://www.asianamericans.com/ChineseImmigration.htm

During the 1960s to 1980s, there was a shift in Asian American demographics. Large numbers of college-bound students from Korea to Taiwan were migrating to America. Many decided to make America their home by opening their own businesses and raising a family. Now, the products of that hardworking generation are growing up. Tradition demands that the children take over their parents' small businesses; however, the change in geography and times has redefined this custom. Instead of "keeping the business in the family," parents are now encouraging their children to do what they want, even if they still would like to pass the business on.

"I would like my children to do what makes them happy. I want them to have a sense of satisfaction and growth. Whatever they choose to do, I will support them," states Angie Mao-Wong, proud parent of three. Parents are realizing that their children have ambitions other than business. Yet, all parents agree that it is mandatory for their children to go to college. Not only that, many strongly prefer their children to seek professional careers, such as in medicine or law.

Byoung Lee explains, "I don't want them to take over my gift store because I want them to be more specialized. I want them to be their own boss." Mr. Lee has three sons, two of them lawyers and one a doctor, who all received strong guidance to seek these fields. Parents want their children to be specialized because many believe it is more respectable and also less hardworking than operating a small business.

Aside from encouraging them, some parents also feel a sense of sadness when it comes to looking at their children's future. They see their children as less aware of their culture. "They have so much privilege and yet no sense of ambition," sighs Alina Chu. "I came here fluent in Chinese, Spanish and English. My kids can barely master English and they don't know any Chinese. They no longer reach to do what I wanted to do years ago. Living in United States has given little sense of our culture." Times have changed and the next generation of Asian Americans is foraging their own paths. As Scott Wang, father of two, simply put it, "I want my kids to create what they want to do, let them fulfill hopes. I mean, that's what I came here to do, isn't it?"

Making ready for the Chinese marketplace.

"Chinese Immigration to the United States,"
http://nhs.needham.k12.ma.us/cur/kane98/
kane_p3_immig/China/china.html

In many respects, the motivations for the Chinese to come to the United States are similar to those of most immigrants. Some came to "The Gold Mountain," and others came to the United States to seek better economic opportunity. Yet there were others that were compelled to leave China either as contract laborers or refugees. The Chinese brought with them their language, culture, social institutions and customs. Over time they made lasting contributions to their adopted country and tried to become an integral part of the United States population.

Chinese immigration can be divided into three periods: 1849-1882, 1882-1965, and 1965 to the present. The first period began shortly after the California Gold Rush and ended abruptly with the passage of the Chinese Exclusion Act of 1882. During this period thousands of Chinese, mostly young male peasants, left their villages in the rural countries to become laborers in the American West. They were recruited to extract metals and minerals, construct a vast railroad network, reclaim swamplands, build irrigation systems, work as migrant agricultural laborers, develop the fishing industry, and operate highly competitive manufacturing industries. At the end of the first period, the Chinese population in the United States was about 110,000.

Throughout most of the second period (1882-1965), only diplomats, merchants, and students and their dependents were allowed to travel to the United States. Otherwise, throughout this period, Chinese Americans were confined to segregated ghettos, called Chinatowns, in major cities and isolated regions in rural areas across the country. Because the Chinese were deprived of their democratic rights, they made extensive use of the courts and diplomatic channels to defend themselves. The Civil Rights movement in the 1960s, particularly the enactment of the Civil Rights Act of 1964 and the Immigration and Nationality Act of 1965, brought in a new period in Chinese American immigration. Now Chinese Americans were liberated from a structure of racial oppression. The former legislation restored many of the basic rights that were earlier denied to Chinese Americans. Under these new laws, thousands of Chinese people came to the United States each year to reunite with their families, and young Chinese Americans mobilized to demand racial equality and social justice. Equally significant are two types of Chinese immigrants that have been entering the United States since the 1970s. The first type consists of highly select and well-educated Chinese. The second type is made up of thousands of Chinese immigrants who have entered the United States to escape either political instability or repression throughout East and Southeast Asia. Others are ethnic Chinese from Vietnam and Cambodia who became poverty-stricken refugees. They have run away from such threats as "ethnic cleansing. . . ."

continued

"Chinese Immigration to the United States," . . . *(continued)*

Assimilation was never a viable choice for Chinese Americans, who were excluded and denied citizenship because they were deemed nonassimilable by the white mainstream. By congressional and judicial decisions, the Chinese immigrants were made ineligible for naturalization, which made them politically disenfranchised in a "so-called democracy" and exposing them to violations of their Constitutional rights. Legally discriminated against and politically disenfranchised, Chinese Americans established their roots in Chinatowns, fought racism through aggressive litigation and participated with active roles in economic development projects and political movements to modernize China. Assimilation was seen as an impossibility. In the nineteenth century, most Chinese immigrants saw no future in the United States for themselves. With this mentality, they developed a high degree of tolerance for hardship and racial discrimination and maintained an efficient Chinese lifestyle. This included living modestly, observing Chinese customs and festivals through family associations, sending consistent remittance to parents, wives, and children. Parents tried to drill Chinese language and culture into their children, send them to Chinese schools in the community or in China, motivate them to excel in American education, and above all arrange marriages. The Chinese also joined social organizations and family associations that represented collective interests and well-being of persons with the same family names. These organizations acted to arbitrate disputes, help find jobs and housing, establish schools and temples, and sponsor social and cultural events. Their activities brought mixed blessings to the community. At times, these organizations became too powerful and oppressive, and they also obstructed social and political progress.

1969 Profile

Bian "Betty" Scott came to America as a Vietnam War bride; she met her husband Jim while living in Saigon, and they moved to Westover, Massachusetts, with their infant son.

Life at Home

- Bian Le was born in 1951 in Bien Hoa, a small village outside of Ho Chi Minh City, then known as Saigon.
- Her biological parents were very poor and unable to care for their nine children.
- Bian and her six sisters were given away or sold to other families so that her parents could afford to send their two sons to school.
- As was common for farming families in rural South Vietnam, Bian's foster parents adopted her as cheap labor to help farm their small property.
- Her foster family owned a farm of about 10 acres that ran along the Long Tau River, growing oranges, coconuts and bananas.
- As a child Bian was forced to work 14-hour days in the fields under the hot sun.
- She often became so dehydrated that she would faint, only to be beaten by her foster father for wasting time.
- Bian's foster family had one biological son, Minh, and four other adopted daughters.
- In the spring of 1965, when Bian was 15 years old, she ran away from home with a friend to Saigon with plans to sell vegetables and earn $40 a month.
- Upon arriving in Saigon, Bian became separated from her friend.
- With no money, and nowhere else to turn, she took a job as a prostitute.
- She earned $100 a month working at a busy teahouse frequented by the U.S. military serving in the Vietnam War.
- She sent money home to her foster family every month for a year, before finding out that their neighborhood had been destroyed by the fighting underway in Vietnam.
- As a teenager struggling to survive, Bian did not identify with the Vietnam War; she only wanted the violence to end.
- As a prostitute, Bian became pregnant three times.

Bian was 17 when she met American soldier Jim Scott.

Bian's brothers were kept by her parents and sent to school; the seven girls were given away or sold.

- Her first pregnancy resulted in a miscarriage, and she gave two infants up for adoption when they were only days old.
- She met Jim Scott, a U.S. Air Force pilot, at the teahouse where she worked in the spring of 1968.
- He was stationed at the Bian Hoa Air Force Base near Saigon.
- Fascinated by Bian's dark eyes and exotic beauty, Jim became a frequent customer at the teahouse.
- Despite the respect and kindness Jim showed her, including gifts of scarves and perfume, Bian did not view him differently from any other customer.
- She had learned to guard herself against American soldiers.
- Jim was persistent in his affection toward Bian, and when she became pregnant in the fall of 1968, he begged her to return to America with him to raise their child.

Her adopted family forced Bian to work long hours in the fields under the hot sun.

- She was reluctant to leave the familiarity of Vietnam, but finally agreed to escape the ongoing violence.
- Before they left, Jim sent for first- and second-grade American readers and sat with her almost every day to help her learn as much English as she could.
- Illiterate in her own language, she did not see much use for the books.
- When Jim suddenly stopped coming to see her, Bian assumed that he had either been killed or returned to the U.S.
- She began making arrangements to give their unborn child up for adoption.
- One night, Bian was awoken by U.S. military officials who told her that Jim had been injured in a land mine explosion and was recovering in America.
- He had told the officials that she was his wife and that they had plans for her to join him in the U.S.
- Bian made a decision then that required every ounce of her strength and courage: she left the teahouse for an unknown future in the U.S.
- Bian arrived alone in the U.S. on April 20, 1969.
- Jim met her at the airport where she endured passing through customs and filling out the necessary paperwork for her to legally stay in America.
- Many of the legal ceremonies, including her marriage, involved repeating English words after a U.S. official in a small, dark office with no windows on the fourth floor of a large government building.
- Jim brought Bian home to his small house in Westover, Massachusetts, where she gave birth to their son, Adam, three months later.
- After Jim recovered from his injuries, he returned to work at the Westover Air Reserve Base.
- Bian endured dinner every Sunday with Jim's parents, who would stare at her and whisper behind her back.
- She knew that they wished she would go back to Vietnam so Jim could find a nice American wife.
- During dinner Bian kept her eyes lowered and remembered to use her fork instead of her hands as Jim had told her, but she always ate quickly.
- Jim's brother's wife, Diane, grew up in a privileged family in Boston, Massachusetts, and worked as a schoolteacher.
- Diane suggested that Bian take on a "more American name, like Betty," that would be easier for everyone to pronounce.
- Humiliated, Bian, now Betty, nodded.
- The Vietnamese meaning of Bian, is "secret" and in this strange new place she felt her former life slipping away, like a secret that no one in the U.S. would ever know or understand.
- Once, while cleaning up in the kitchen after dinner, she overheard them arguing that her marriage was a disgrace to the family.
- Her mother-in-law said that she and Jim had nothing in common and that she was just interested in his money.
- Bian would never become used to the American way of making hurtful comments.

Jim Scott was an Air Force pilot stationed near Saigon.

The ongoing violence convinced Bian to leave Vietnam.

Life at Work

- Jim's Air Force salary of $585 a month was more than enough to support his family.
- He encouraged Bian to stay home with the baby all day.
- Jim worked long hours, often not returning home until 7 or 8 p.m.
- Accustomed to working around the clock from the time she was a child, Bian quickly became lonely and restless at home.
- Learning about divorce for the first time in America, Bian also became afraid that her husband, whom she barely saw, would leave her with nothing.
- Driven by this fear and wanting something more than to care for her son, she took up a neighbor's offer to her to take a job scrubbing floors.
- Knowing that Jim would never approve, she always left their house after he went to work, taking Adam with her, and arrived home before him in the evenings.
- She hid the money that she earned under a loose floorboard in the baby's nursery.
- The work was easy; Bian/Betty was paid $0.75 an hour.
- In the first six weeks she had earned $100.
- The minimum wage was $1.30, with the average salary $6,887.
- At work, Bian/Betty spoke to no one.
- Her tall American boss shouted and gestured to tell Bian her duties each day.

While Jim worked long hours, Bian stayed at home alone with her son all day.

Life in the Community: Westover, Massachusetts

- Bian had a difficult time adjusting to living in a wealthy, foreign culture.
- After growing accustomed to the city noises of Saigon, Bian thought Westover was too quiet; the only familiar sound was the airplanes overhead.
- In the first few weeks at Jim's house, she checked the kitchen constantly, making sure that there was food for the baby.
- Bian was overcome with loneliness.
- Before she began secretly scrubbing floors, she had interacted with only Jim and Adam for days at a time.
- She did not see another Asian person; immigration from Vietnam was rare.
- With a war still underway, Jim prohibited her from communicating with her friends in Vietnam, claiming it would risk his career in the Air Force.
- In Massachusetts, Bian felt isolated from everything and everyone.
- She struggled with post-traumatic stress, and often awoke from nightmares of dead bodies in the streets or floating down the river.
- She tried to cope with depression and cried every day to return home to Vietnam.

HISTORICAL SNAPSHOT
1969

- Richard Nixon was elected the thirty-seventh president of the United States and introduced Vietnamization to reduce U.S. troops in Vietnam
- More than 500,000 U.S. troops were stationed in Vietnam; the number of American soldiers killed in action averaged 1,200 a month
- *Penthouse* magazine, Frosted Mini-Wheats, bank automated teller machines and a postage stamp depicting a living American—Neil Armstrong—all made their first appearance
- The largest national demonstration against the Vietnam War was held in Washington, DC, on November 15, when 250,000 people marched in protest
- Astronaut Neil Armstrong was the first man to set foot on the moon
- DDT usage in residential areas was banned
- ARPANET, the precursor to the Internet, was created
- The Woodstock Festival, which attracted more than 300,000 music fans, was held in White Lake, New York
- The Boeing 747 jumbo jet was introduced
- Massachusetts Senator Edward M. Kennedy pleaded guilty to leaving the scene of a fatal car accident, known as the Chappaquiddick Incident
- Followers of a cult referred to as "The Family," led by Charles Manson, murdered seven people including actress Sharon Tate
- The children's television program *Sesame Street* aired for the first time
- Bestsellers included *Portnoy's Complaint* by Philip Roth, *The Godfather* by Mario Puzo, *The Love Machine* by Jacqueline Susann, *Naked Came the Stranger* by Penelope Ash and *I Know Why the Caged Bird Sings* by Maya Angelou
- Led Zeppelin released their first album, *Led Zeppelin;* the Beatles released *Abbey Road*
- After 147 years, *The Saturday Evening Post* ceased publication
- James Earl Ray pleaded guilty to the assassination of Martin Luther King, Jr.; Sirhan Sirhan was convicted of Robert Kennedy's murder
- Hit songs included "Good Morning Starshine," "Hair," "Lay Lady Lay," "Honky Tonk Women" and "Crimson and Clover"
- The Stonewall riots in New York City marked the beginning of the gay rights movement
- President Richard Nixon appointed Warren Burger Chief Justice of the Supreme Court

1. **THE HIPPIE SCENE, Carolyn Barnes, editor.** Who are they? More than that, WHY are they? News stories on various aspects of the hippie scene, including the tragic, prize-winning Linda Fitzpatrick story. (And great photos!)
~~60¢~~ YOU PAY 50¢

2. **2001: A SPACE ODYSSEY. Arthur C. Clarke.** That wild, way-out movie, novelized by the famous science-fiction author who wrote the script. Sixteen pages of photos from the movie.
~~95¢~~ YOU PAY 75¢

Vietnam War Timeline

1954

Forty thousand Vietminh surrounded Dien Bien Phu in North Vietnam, resulting in the French Army ordering a ceasefire on May 7 after 55 days of battle.

Eight nations signed the U.S.-sponsored SEATO treaty.

1955

President Eisenhower's administration sent the first U.S. advisers to South Vietnam to train the South Vietnamese Army.

1957

The Vietcong assassinated over 400 South Vietnamese officials.

1959

A specialized North Vietnamese Army unit was formed to create a supply route from North Vietnam to Vietcong forces in South Vietnam which became known as the Ho Chi Minh Trail.

1961

President John F. Kennedy ordered 100 "special forces" troops to South Vietnam.

1962

In Operation Chopper, U.S. helicopters carried 1,000 South Vietnamese soldiers near Saigon in the first U.S. combat mission against the Vietcong.

Operation Ranch, designed to clear vegetation alongside highways, set the stage for vast tracts of forest to be sprayed with "Agent Orange."

1963

United States servicemen in Vietnam numbered 16,500.

1964

The U.S. Congress passed the Tonkin Gulf Resolution, authorizing President Johnson to take "all necessary measures" to "prevent further aggression" in Vietnam.

China, North Vietnam's neighbor and ally, successfully tested an atomic bomb.

1965

The U.S. Congress provided $2.4 billion for the Vietnam War effort.

Operation Rolling Thunder began, a continuous bombing campaign of North Vietnam that would last for three years.

1967

Secretary of Defense Robert McNamara announced that U.S. bomb raids had been ineffective.

U.S. troops in Vietnam totaled 500,000.

1968

The North Vietnamese caught the U.S. by surprise with the Tet Offensive attacks on almost all the capitals of South Vietnam's 44 provinces.

The My Lai Massacre of over 200 unarmed civilians captured national attention.

Timeline . . . *(continued)*

1954

President Johnson announced he would not seek re-election, and ordered bombing to stop over 75 percent of North Vietnam.

President Nixon was elected president, and during a policy address on Vietnam in 1969, proposed an "8-Point Peace Plan" that would include mutual withdrawal of all non-Vietnamese forces.

1969

The first U.S. troop withdrawal occurred when 800 men were sent home.

President Nixon introduced his "Vietnamization" program to prepare the South Vietnamese to take over the U.S. combat role.

Congress gave the president the authority to institute the "draft lottery" system aimed at drafting 19-year-olds before older men.

President Lyndon Johnson

Selected Prices

Air Conditioner, 8,000 btu	$189.95
Blender, Proctor	$13.49
Camera, Polaroid	$50.00
Bread, Loaf	$0.20
Gas, Gallon	$0.35
Dishwasher	$119.25
Milk, Gallon	$1.10
New House	$40,000
New York City Ballet Ticket	$4.95
Slide Projector, Kodak	$80.00

It fits your pocket, palm or purse.

That's how nice and slim the Kodak Instamatic S-10 camera is. You load it instantly and have no settings to make. And you get really good, sharp color snapshots or color slides. In a complete outfit it's less than $35.

Kodak Instamatic® S-10 camera.

Price subject to change without notice.

ugly water spots spoil your party.

Discover the Cascade look of spotlessness.

Cascade eliminates drops that spot.

No-no's. for mommies from Winnie-the-Pooh

祝

Dear America —— Congratulations!

Here in Japan, as around the world, millions were enthralled by your daring Apollo flight.

This triumphant parting of the moon's last mysterious veil is another proof of the sophistication of your technology and the dedication of your scientists.

We believe the knowledge won by this historic flight will make a significant contribution towards peace, happiness and prosperity for all people.

Since our own enterprise is inspired by these same aims, we would like to congratulate all who made the Apollo success possible. We salute them. And we say, from our hearts, thank you very much.

"A View from the Villages," *Time*, January 19, 1970:

A View from the Villages. Binh Thoi, not far from Saigon, was once a prosperous farm village with red-tiled roofs, gas lamps and fertile coconut and orange groves that stretched as far as the eye could see. U.S. troops and Viet Cong guerrillas left it a wasteland. Chu Thao, a teacher from nearby Bien Hoa, describes what happened: "Not a blade of grass survived. The surface of the earth was as flat as the forehead of a bald man. Here and there the trunks of fallen coconut palms lay on the edge of the ditches, and the dead bamboo stood with its naked stalks pointing up to the sky. The dull yellow and the ash-gray covered the earth and stretched like a mourning shawl toward the horizon."

Twice the farmers of Binh Thoi tried to raise earthworms in their scorched, chemically defoliated fields to see if anything could still grow there. Twice the creatures died—as had corn seeds, and even sturdy coconut shoots. Stubbornly convinced that the earth would revive, the farmers tried a third time. Early one morning, as soon as Regional Force troops had cleared the mines and booby traps set by the Viet Cong the night before, the village elders made their way to the small plot where the earthworms were waging their struggle to survive. Writes Chu Thao:

Saigon.

"Tu Lau asked in an anxious voice, 'What about them? Still alive?' The white-haired man replied, 'Yesterday they were.' Arriving at a piece of low, damp land near a stream, Nam Khom stooped and called to the others: 'You see? You see?' The crippled farmer let his crutches drop and sat down for a better look. On the surface of the damp earth, he saw traces of earthworms. He uttered a low cry: 'They are alive! Alive! This earth is not to be abandoned.'" The farmers' faith is described in one of 500 war vignettes recently submitted in an essay contest on nationalism sponsored by the Saigon daily *Tieng Not Dan Toe (Voice of the People)*. The competition was the idea of the paper's 29-year-old publisher, Ly Quy Chung, a member of the National Assembly's lower house and a leading supporter of a neutralist "third force" settlement of the war. The winning essays, like Chung's editorial policies, tended to be antiwar and implicitly critical of the U.S. presence. But they are not primarily political documents. Many were written by teachers; but students, soldiers and workers, almost all from rural areas, contributed, too. In language that often teeters between hope and resignation, they provide intensely human glimpses of the war as seen by the people who have known nothing else for three decades.

The Binh Thoi episode, entitled "Resuscitation of the Dead Earth," was suffused, as were several of the essays, with a reverence for the land. It won second prize in the competition. First prize (a tape recorder and encyclopedia set) went to Mrs. Tran Thi Huong, a 42-year-old schoolteacher in the Mekong Delta, for her account of a tragic refugee family. The family had moved to the author's village from a Viet Cong-infested hamlet across the river that had finally been declared a "free-fire zone" by the allies. The father, who stayed behind to tend coconut groves, was killed by a stray bullet. To support themselves, his widow and six children often crossed the river by boat to gather firewood and coconuts that could be traded for rice. On one such trip, their 12-year-old daughter was struck by a shell fragment and lost a leg.

continued

"A View from the Villages," . . . *(continued)*

Just before returning from another forage, the widow noticed a stalk of bananas hanging from a tree. "Remembering how much her children liked cooked bananas, she waded into the ditch toward the tree," wrote Tran Thi Huong. "As soon as she hit the stem with her knife, a grenade at her feet exploded. The others in the group found her lying face-down on a death-warning board [a sign placed there by the Viet Cong warning civilians of booby traps]. It had fallen down under the grass so she did not see it."

Respecting the Rights. The strange, often unhappy relations between Vietnamese peasants and their defenders are described in an essay entitled "When the Americans Came to My Village," by a schoolteacher and part-time journalist in Long An province. The Americans who occupied the village for two months, says the author, were not very different from French troops who had been there in the '50s; both included blacks and whites, and "all of them were tall and very big." The Americans, however, were richer: "At their base they had incredible numbers of radios, tape recorders, cameras, cigarettes, etc." When pilfering by children and ne'er-do-wells became a problem, the author relates, U.S. military men ordered a house-by-house search to recover some of the goods. "The searchers were both Vietnamese and Americans, but in the eyes of the villagers, it was the fault of the Americans. This incident confirmed their belief that the foreigners had never respected the rights of the Vietnamese." When the Americans left, many of the villagers who had worked for them, usually by washing clothes, fled; they feared Viet Cong reprisals.

Another sort of fear—that of abandoning the scene of one's whole life—is described by an ex-South Vietnamese soldier in "The Old Man in the Free-Fire Zone." In a village near Danang that was being evacuated by the author's company, one old man, "as thin as a dry branch," refused to leave. He was determined to guard his tiny garden, the last remnant of the property handed down by his ancestors, and to wait for the return of his grandson, a soldier who had been missing for two years. His home would be his small underground bunker, a "living grave." Fourteen months later, the author returned on another operation. He writes: "The living grave had turned into a real one. Its entrance was covered with earth, and grass had begun to grow."

Top Essays. With the financial help of political friends, including General Duong Van ("Big") Minh, publisher Chung awarded modest cash prizes to runners-up and ran the top 75 essays in his paper. Neither his pals nor his prose won him much favor with the regime of President Nguyen Van Thieu. Two weeks ago, on a charge of "promoting neutralism," Thieu's censors closed down the *Voice of the People* indefinitely. That action in itself is an eloquent essay on the war in Vietnam.

"Gift for Nixon," *World Week,* January 31, 1969:

President Nixon received an unusual housewarming gift when he moved into the White House on January 20. Just a few days earlier, Congress increased the presidential salary by 100 percent. New salary: $200,000 a year.

Congress cannot increase the salary of a president while he is in office. Just before leaving office, President Johnson asked Congress to vote a pay raise that would take effect for the new president. The presidential pay raise is only the fourth in the nation's history. President Washington earned $25,000. Later the salary was increased to $50,000 (in 1873), then $75,000 (in 1909) and $100,000 (in 1949).

Members of Congress also are in line for a pay boost from the present $30,000 to $42,500 year. The increase was recommended by President Johnson and will take effect automatically unless vetoed by Congress.

Neither the President or the Congressmen will take home all of their higher pay, however. Federal income taxes will take a big bite. The President's $200,000 may be whittled down to something like $78,000 after taxes.

"In the Round, Viet Talks Resume," *World Week*, January 31, 1969:

After 10 weeks of deadlock, delegates from the U.S., South Vietnam, Communist North Vietnam, and the Communist-led National Liberation Front (NLF) sat down for the first of their "expanded" four-party talks in Paris on January 18. The breakthrough came when all four agreed to negotiate across a round table.

The 10-week wrangle over the shape of the negotiating table gave cartoonists and humorists a field day—but the negotiators were deadly serious. They could point to historical precedents for their hassle over an apparently trivial point. In the seventeenth century, for example, negotiations to end a major war were stalled six months because French and Austrian delegates couldn't agree on who should enter the conference room first.

But there was a lot more than national pride involved in the Paris dispute over settling over seating arrangements. Since April 1968 U.S. and North Vietnamese negotiators had met regularly in Paris to try to launch meaningful peace talks. All agreed that such talks would eventually have to include the other two major combatants in the Vietnam War: the South Vietnamese government and the NLF (or Viet Cong). But how should these two be represented?

South Vietnam did not want any seating arrangements that might imply equality between itself and the NLF. In South Vietnam's view, the NLF is a guerrilla organization with no claim to be an equal to any actual government. Thus, South Vietnam wanted a table with two sides—one for the Allies (U.S. and South Vietnam) and one for the Communists.

North Vietnam and the NLF, on the other hand, wanted a table with no sides (a plain round table) or a square table with four sides. This, in their view, would emphasize equality of all four parties.

In the end, it was decided to use a round table—but with two small rectangular tables (for secretaries) set just 18 inches away on opposite sides. This allowed each side to interpret seating arrangements in its own way. The U.S. and South Vietnam pointed out that the side tables formed a symbolic separation between them and the Communists—making a two-sided table. North Vietnam and the NLF pointed out that the main table was, after all, round. Said a senior U.S. spokesman: "It looks as if this show is getting back on the road."

Halong Bay in North Vietnam.

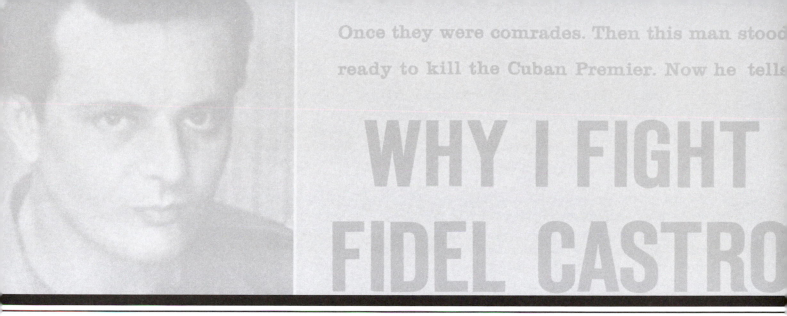

Once they were comrades. Then this man stood ready to kill the Cuban Premier. Now he tells

WHY I FIGHT FIDEL CASTRO

1960 News Feature

"Why I Fight Fidel Castro," by Pedro Luis Diaz Lanz, _Parade_, January 3, 1960:

One year ago this week, Fidel Castro triumphantly entered Havana and took over the government of Cuba. One of his first moves was to appoint me chief of the Cuban Air Force. Today, 12 short months later, I am opposing Castro's revolution with all the strength I once used to help bring it about.

For the second time in my life, I am an outlaw unable to return to my native land except at the risk of being shot. Yet I have committed no crime unless it is a crime to fight for freedom—the kind of freedom all Americans enjoy and all true Cubans long to share.

Most men become revolutionaries because of an appetite for adventure, greed for power, or a zeal for reform. A few like myself become revolutionaries by accident. Looking back, it hardly seems possible that only eight years ago I was a gay young pilot for Q airways, commuting between Cuba and Florida, without a rebellious thought in my head.

My years since have been crowded with bloodshed, death, glory, terror, and bitterness. There were escapes that still make my nerves twang like violin strings. Then came our moment of triumph. And finally I faced Fidel Castro, the man to whom I had been devoted, with a cocked pistol ready to kill him.

But I am running ahead of my story. Let me go back to early 1952 when Dr. Carlos Prio was president of Cuba. Accidentally I learned that his rival, Fulgencio Batista, planned to take over the government. I passed on this information to my father, a career government employee. And on March 10, 1952, as I had warned, Batista seized the presidency.

When, later, I met Prio, he seemed genuinely penitent about the corruption in his administration and swore he would win back freedom for the Cuban people. He was so fervent I left the interview a revolutionary dedicated to the same cause of liberty.

In those days it was common for airline pilots to smuggle nylons and scotch into Cuba—something I never did. Now, however, I started bringing in rifles. After a year, someone whispered to Batista's secret police. They tortured and humiliated my father. Then they seized me for 10 days of cross-examination.

They lacked evidence to hold me, but it was only a matter of time until they would come for me again. In a makeshift disguise, I slipped off to Camaguey, registered at a hotel under a false name, and planned my escape to Haiti with a pilot friend who was going there to dust crops. One murky morning I hid out in the grass at the end of the heavily guarded airstrip, leaped aboard the plane as it was taxiing and left my homeland behind.

Now a revolutionary, I went from Port-au-Prince to Miami. The next two years I worked as a busboy and dishwasher. In those days, Fidel Castro was only a name to me. He attacked the army barracks at Santiago de Cuba on July 26, 1953. For his pains, he was languishing in a prison cell.

When Batista granted amnesty to all political offenders in 1955, Castro was freed and I hurried home. I wanted nothing more than to resume my peaceful profession as a pilot.

But try as I might, I could not close my eyes to Batista's terror. For my own eyes witnessed Batista's police shoot down innocent victims. Personal friends were tortured and murdered. I myself was falsely accused of burning sugar cane and threatened with death. Anger boiled up inside me until I at last joined Castro's 26 of July movement and volunteered for undercover work.

My first orders were to sneak out of Cuba and ferry weapons to Castro's hideout in the Sierra Maestro Mountains. No one with my background could hope to walk into a Cuban airport and catch a flight out of the country. I had to create a new personality.

First I borrowed a passport from Carlos Bastida, a sympathetic newspaperman from Ecuador. I had never visited Ecuador, but I became an expert on that country. I even learned to talk with an Ecuadorian accent and to forge Bastida's signature. Finally, I donned the Panama hat, dark glasses and sport coat that seemed appropriate for a South American reporter. Then with Frank Fiorini, an American friend of the movement, I set out from Santiago to Camaguey. . . .

From that time on, my work for the revolution was one narrow escape after another. From Miami I went to Costa Rica, where I picked up a C-46 loaded with rifles, mortars and ammunition, and 12 recruits. . . .

I brought the big cargo plane down on a dirt road at Cianeguilla, not far from Castro's headquarters, where guerrillas were waiting to unload. Some actually wept joyful tears at the sight of ammunition arriving in the nick of time.

The road was so narrow that one prop whacked a fence post. I could neither repair the damage nor take it off again before Batista's patrols spotted the plane. Regretfully, I splashed gasoline over the C-46 and set it afire.

Then, with the rebel force, I marched into the mountains. There, on March 30, 1958, I had my first meeting with Fidel Castro. He was overflowing with excitement and hailed us as "the saviors of Cuba." At that time he had fewer than 400 men, and no ammunition except what we had brought. Castro spoke with fervor that night. If only his Tommy gun had been a staff, he might have passed for a bearded prophet crying in the wilderness. His personality had the glow of a torch.

I stayed in the mountains six weeks, fighting with the ground troops. Once I was caught in the open by a Batista F-47 fighter. Bullets kicked up dust all around me, but miraculously I wasn't even scratched. When Fidel learned I was risking myself on the ground, he sent urgent orders that I should stay out of the fighting. He had less trouble recruiting soldiers, he complained, than finding trained pilots who could fly weapons in the rugged mountains of the islands. . . .

One of my missions was to supply weapons to Calabaza where Fidel's brother Raul was in charge of the second front. From the first, he impressed me as wild and unreliable. When he grumbled that Fidel was getting most of the arms, I retorted sharply: "I'm not bringing weapons to you as an individual. I am bringing weapons to Cubans who are fighting dictatorship." Later a friend, who has my complete confidence, told me a submarine brought in a big haul of weapons. By the uniforms and language, the crew, my friend judged, was Russian. . . .

On August 24, 1958, Fidel appointed me head of the rebel Air Force. My friends had the date inscribed in a watch I still wear. Then, on New Year's Day 1959, just one year ago, came our triumph. Batista handed over the government and fled the country. I was in Costa Rica, picking up another load of weapons, when the exciting news came through. When Castro appointed me chief of the Cuban Air Force, he did so in a letter that ended with "Libertad O Muerte"—"Liberty or Death."

My faith in Castro was first jolted after his triumphant entry into Havana. Throughout the long march, adoring Catholic women had pinned holy medals on him. I overheard Che Guevara tease him about the "decorations" he was wearing. "Listen" said Fidel, "we have to go slow. Most of our people are Catholic. We cannot condemn the church right away. That is a power we cannot destroy so easily." It was the first antichurch statement I'd heard from him.

My doubts grew when I accompanied him on his official trip to Venezuela. He put on a big act of not wanting to meet Venezuela's top communist, Gustavo Machado. Yet he locked himself in the bathroom with Magado for two hours. It was the longest talk he had with anybody in Venezuela.

I complained to Fidel that his brother Raul had named communists, who hadn't fired a shot in the revolution, as army commanders. Fidel replied earnestly: "I'm going to have to dismiss Raul. I am not going to let the communists take over."

Fidel did not dismiss Raul. Instead he put him in charge of the Armed Forces and gave Che Guevara control of agrarian reform. My faith in Fidel was shaken. Having fought for free speech, I decided to put it to the test. I was wise enough to the ways of revolutions to arrange with my brother Sergio, to have a boat ready for a quick getaway. And I issued a statement that I was ready to fight any dictatorship—Batista, Trujillo, or "the worst dictatorship in the world, communism."

This was the showdown. Juan Almeida, commander of a tank regiment, came with the message that Fidel wanted to see me at his home. I strapped on my pistol, slipped in a clip of 14 bullets, and removed the safety catch. When I faced

Castro he erupted like a volcano. "Why would you make a statement against communism?" he demanded. "You will only confuse the people. You're not supposed to do anything without my consent. I'm the one who tells you what to do and when."

Angrily I asked him whether he was not becoming a dictator himself. Why should I not have freedom to express my opinions? I was against communism and I stood by my convictions, I declared. "Remember," I said, "you did not win the revolution alone. You had my help and the help of other friends."

I warned fiercely that I would not accept arrest or go to jail for saying what I believed. To silence me he would have to kill me. "You will have to carry my body on your shoulders and explain what happened," I said. "You'll have to explain to the Cuban people why I've been killed after speaking against communism."

I FIGHT CASTRO continued

My hand was on my pistol, and I was ready to use it. Castro looked at me—and at my pistol—hard for a moment. He was far from sure whether the Cuban people would support him in matching any action against his Air Force chief being anti-communist. He backed down. . . .

If I was to escape, I had to put them off balance, but only for a few hours. With an indifferent shrug I told Almeida I would write a letter of resignation. All I wanted from life, I said, was to go back to my old airline job. I said, tell Fidel I won't cause him any trouble and I don't want him to cause me any. Then I added as an afterthought: "Don't put any guards on my home or follow me around, interfering with my private life."

My ruse worked. For the next few hours I was unguarded. I got in touch with Sergio, prepared my resignation and signed it. Then, with my wife Tanya, I hurried to the dock. Fidel's men were watching airports, but apparently it never occurred to them that I might go to Miami by boat.

Yet in my heart I knew I would come back. I cannot rest until the democracy I fought to bring to Cuba has been realized.

In the U.S. I decided not to speak out immediately but to wait until events showed others that Castro was simply exchanging one form of dictatorship for another. But I was subpoenaed to testify before the Senate Internal Security Subcommittee about my knowledge of communism in Cuba. As a guest in your country, I was obliged to tell what I knew of this matter.

For the next few weeks I avoided publicity as more and more people got a glimpse behind the beard at the real Castro. Then I tried to reach my people. Because Castro had denounced me as a traitor, I wrote a reply and sent it to every Cuban newspaper. Not a single one dared print it.

This was the reason I decided to be my own mailman. I had 200,000 copies of my letter printed in range to deliver them by air. Frank Fiorini, the American who had been with me through much of the revolution, owned a B-26 that had been converted to a civilian plane. The gun openings had been permanently sealed and the bomb bay fashioned into a makeshift luggage compartment.

On the afternoon of October 21, Frank and I roared off for Havana. The winds were at peace in the sky. Except for some vibration in the left engine, nothing happened to augur the international storm our flight was to stir up. We swooped low over the country, stuffing our leaflets through the baggage opening.

I learned afterwards that Castro himself was caught in the leaflet blizzard. One copy fluttered right into his face. When he read the message, his whiskers trembled with rage. . . .

I cannot tell how I know about events inside Cuba today. There are patriots who risk their lives to keep me informed. I have a final word for you who read this newspaper, whose democratic ideals and institutions are my inspiration. Whatever I must do in the future, I will take care not to violate any of your laws or your hospitality. Thank God, freedom of expression is no crime here.

If Fidel Castro should read this, I have a word, too, for him: I demonstrated to you many times I was willing to die to restore democracy to Cuba. Be assured, I have not changed.

1970–1979

With the Vietnam War still raging, interest in the environment rising and America's troubled cities deteriorating, the turbulent legacy of the 1960s flowed into the 1970s. Racial unrest rampaged through the public schools, and books, movies, and magazines tested American mores, while protests against the Vietnam War continued. Mix in a volatile economy that caused the cost of living to climb and the result was an America stripped of its ability to dominate the world economy. A scandal-plagued president was driven from office, and another found his presidency—and the nation—held hostage by Iran. Gas prices skyrocketed when Arab oil producers declared an embargo on oil shipments to the United States, setting off shortages and gas rationing for the first time in 30 years. The sale of automobiles plummeted, unemployment and inflation nearly doubled, and the buying power of Americans fell dramatically.

While immigration patterns continued unabated, the refugee population exploded. South Vietnamese government officials, Laotian Hmong fighters and dozens of other groups all fled Southeast Asia for the United States as the Vietnam War came to a close. The rescue operation started with great fanfare when approximately 130,000 Vietnamese refugees were resettled in all states in the country in just seven months. In addition, by 1977

Jewish refugees from Soviet Russia were allowed to emigrate with 6,800 choosing the United States the first year and twice that number the second year.

The economy, handicapped by the devaluation of the dollar and inflation, did not fully recover for more than a decade, while the fast-growing economies of Japan and western Europe, especially West Germany, mounted direct competitive challenges to American manufacturers. The value of imported manufactured goods soared from 14 percent of U.S. domestic production in 1970 to 40 percent in 1979. The inflationary cycle of recession returned in 1979 to disrupt markets, throw thousands out of work and prompt massive downsizing of companies, awakening many once-secure workers to the reality of the changing economic market. A symbol of the era was the pending bankruptcy of Chrysler Corporation, whose cars were so outmoded and plants so inefficient they could not compete against Japanese imports. The federal government was forced to extend loan guarantees to the company to prevent bankruptcy and the loss of thousands of jobs.

The appointment of Paul Volcker as the chairman of the Federal Reserve Board late in the decade gave the economy the distasteful medicine it needed. To cope with inflation, Volcker slammed on the economic brakes, restricted growth of the money supply, and curbed inflation. As a result, he pushed interest rates to nearly 20 percent—their highest level since the Civil War. Almost immediately the sale of automobiles and expensive items dropped. The decade was also marred by the deep divisions caused by the Vietnam War. For more than 10 years the war had been fought on two fronts: at home and abroad. As a result, U.S. policymakers conducted the war with one eye always focused on national opinion. When U.S. involvement ended, the Vietnam War had been the longest war in American history, having cost $118 billion and resulted in 56,000 dead, 300,000 wounded, and the loss of American prestige abroad.

The decade was a time not only of movements, but also of moving. In the 1970s, the shift of manufacturing facilities to the South from New England and the Midwest accelerated. The Sunbelt became the new darling of corporate America. By the late 1970s, the South, including Texas, had gained more than a million manufacturing jobs, while the Northeast and Midwest lost nearly two million. Rural North Carolina had the highest percentage of manufacturing of any state in the nation, along with the lowest blue-collar wages and the lowest unionization rate in the country.

The largest and most striking of all the social actions of the early 1970s was the Women's Liberation Movement. It fundamentally reshaped American society. Since the 1950s, a small group of well-placed American women had attempted to convince Congress and the courts to bring about equality between the sexes. By 1972, the National Organization for Women (NOW) multiplied in size, the first issue of Ms. magazine sold out in a week, and women began demanding economic equality, the legalization of abortion, and the improvement of women's role in society. "All authority in our society is being challenged," said a Department of Health, Education and Welfare report. "Professional athletes challenge owners, journalists challenge editors, consumers challenge manufacturers . . . and young blue-collar workers, who have grown up in an environment in which equality is called for in all institutions, are demanding the same rights and expressing the same values as university graduates."

The decade also included the flowering of the National Welfare Rights Organization (NWRO), founded in 1966, which resulted in millions of urban poor demanding additional rights. The environmental movement gained recognition and momentum during the decade starting with the first Earth Day celebration in 1970 and the subsequent passage of the Federal Clean Air and Clean Water Acts. And the growing opposition to the use of nuclear power peaked after a near calamity at Three Mile Island in Pennsylvania in 1979. As the formal barriers to racial equality came down, racist attitudes became unacceptable and the black middle class began to grow. By 1972, half of all Southern black children sat in integrated classrooms, and about one-third of all black families had risen economically into the ranks of the middle class.

The changes recorded for the decade included a doubling in the amount of garbage created per capita from 2.5 pounds to five pounds. California created a no-fault divorce law, Massachusetts introduced no-fault insurance, and health food sales reached $3 billion. By mid-decade, the so-called typical nuclear family, with working father, housewife, and two children, represented only 7 percent of the population, and the family size was falling. The average family size was 3.4 persons compared with 4.3 in 1920.

1975 Profile

Jamaican Andrea Spencer emigrated to New York and, after seven years and several jobs, found an ideal position caring for two elderly sisters.

Life at Home

- Jamaica, the land of sunshine and laughter, had been hard on Andrea Spencer, even as a child.
- "All my years I been working, since I was 13."
- Seven years earlier, at age 38, she was ready for a change in a place called New York City.
- Her goal was not to leave Jamaica for America; rather, it was to exchange Jamaica for New York City where most Jamaican immigrants had settled.
- Friends who had worked there came back and said the same thing: "Twasn't bad; but 'twasn't good'; I knew it had to be better than Jamaica."
- While Andrea was still a small child, her mother died; her father left her in the care of her grandmother and disappeared.
- At 13 she left school to work as a domestic servant in a boarding school for boys.
- Her job was to clean up and feed the younger boys, some of whom were very young.
- She made $0.30 a week plus free room and board.
- Once a year she rode a bus for four hours each way to visit her grandmother in the country—"Once a year was all I could go."
- Her next job was decidedly a step up, working for "a nice, white woman" in Kingston, Jamaica.
- Next, she took a job at a wholesale dealer, where she cleaned the lobby and the shelves.
- "All my life I work for white folks and never had any trouble."
- By the time Andrea made the decision to leave, she had three children, two of whom were on their own; the youngest was left with an aunt.

Andrea Spencer left Jamaica for New York City when she was 38-years-old.

Life in Jamaica.

- Andrea was determined to come alone: "No man come with me. I like being alone, choosing my own friends. Doing what I want. I'll never marry nobody again."
- Her ticket out was a scheme that involved New York housewives, Jamaican lawyers and women like herself.
- The 1965 U.S. Immigration law included a work certificate provision that permitted individuals to enter the United States to take jobs that could not be filled from the resident workforce.
- The employer in each case had to provide evidence that he had unsuccessfully tried to find suitable workers from inside the country.
- Often employers did not try very hard, but most ran an advertisement in the local newspaper.
- Andrea paid 100 Jamaican dollars to a lawyer in Kingston; in exchange she received the work certification permit, a plane ticket, and placement as a live-in servant with a family in New York.
- She agreed to work one year at $55 per week plus room and board; the remainder of what she would have earned went to the officials who financed her trip and processed her papers.
- The agreement ended after 12 months, after which time she could negotiate her own working and living arrangements.
- The employment plan was similar to the managed service system used in the colonial era to bring employees to the Americas.
- The twentieth-century version was modified to bring a large number of domestic servants to wealthy U.S. homes in search of a maid or a cook.
- Jamaicans were particularly suited to this form of immigration; as native English speakers, they were attractive for families seeking domestic help.
- In 1968, the year Andrea emigrated, 17,000 Jamaicans entered the United States, 13,000 of whom were female; one in three of the women was a "private household worker."

Life at Work

- After seven years in New York, Andrea Spencer finally found the ideal job caring for two elderly sisters.
- The two women, both in their seventies, lived in a nice, overly decorated home, paid her well and, most important of all, treated her with respect.

- Her life in America had not begun that way.
- Andrea's first assignment upon arrival in America was caring for an upwardly mobile couple and their four children, who were accustomed to having their own way.
- The couple, who loved parties, dressing up and being seen, went out four to five times a week, leaving the children with babysitters or nannies.
- On the day Andrea arrived, the children were bold enough to lay bets in her presence on how long she would survive before quitting.
- Previously, the longest tenure of a nanny was 16 months; the shortest was 10 days.
- The two younger girls bet that Andrea would make it three to four months; the boys were determined to break their own record and see her gone in under 10 days.
- Quickly, it became clear they had overestimated the sweetness of her Jamaican accent and underestimated the strength of her Jamaican upbringing.
- When she hit the one-year mark and was free to seek other employment, the couple offered to double her pay and guaranteed one weekend a month off.
- Flattered, she accepted the raise and immediately regretted her decision; she lasted another seven months before moving on.
- Her next job was as a live-in maid to two wonderful children and their four horrid dogs.
- Every morning she awoke with eager anticipation of the children's new day and dreading the task of taking the four dogs for their walks.
- Invariably one of the little beasts would pee in the elevator on the way down from their ninth-floor apartment.
- Then at least two of the dogs would begin yapping as they walked through the marble lobby, attracting attention and humiliation.
- She tried taking the dogs out one at a time instead of as a group, but that took too much time away from the children, who were her primary responsibility.
- So she moved on and discovered that working with two elderly sisters reminded her of Jamaica, where she had spent so much time around her grandmother.
- Also, it was less painful; working with children sometimes reminded her of her own kids, whom she had not seen in years.
- The women's Manhattan apartment was very Victorian in fashion, simply jammed tight with their travel memories; at every turn were souvenirs from their many trips abroad with their husbands when they were still alive.
- Every day was an education for an impoverished girl from Jamaica.
- In addition, the two women planned their day around the civilized habit of holding high tea most afternoons at 4 o'clock.
- This quaint habit also reminded her of Jamaica and the classic culture of the former British possession, where residents liked to believe that Bach lived in every Episcopal hymn and Shakespeare was still a living force.
- Another plus was the sisters' preference that she not live in—marking the first time since she'd come to America that she had her own place.
- Andrea proudly picked Bedford-Stuyvesant, which seemed to have attracted enough West Indians to be an inland Caribbean island all by itself.
- She arrived at 7 each morning, woke the sisters, prepared a light breakfast, and settled in for the first political argument of the day.
- The older sister, Marlene, had once danced with Vice President Richard Nixon at the inaugural ball in 1957, believed that Watergate was "a big nothing," and that he was being hounded for political purposes.
- The younger sister, by two years and 11 months, was once married to a Cabinet undersecretary in the Kennedy Administration and vehemently believed that Nixon was only getting his "just desserts."

Andrea's determination and hard work afforded her a comfortable life in New York City.

Carribean Island festivals were frequently held in Andrea's neighborhood.

- From there the arguments would move to the cause of inflation, the impact of the Vietnam War and the role of women in tomorrow's America.
- Marlene was particularly proud of her granddaughters, who were focused on careers in law and medicine "if the men don't block their way."
- The younger one, Jill, would then talk about her grandchildren and how arts and motherhood were still a good combination in the twenty-first century.
- "In my day, home cooking is what kept the boys coming back," she would say and then laugh.
- Once a month the sisters hosted the Thursday Bridge Club, an event that included drinks, dinner, cigarette smoking, exuberant conversation, and cards.
- Andrea relished the exacting preparation, the elaborate meals and the carefree conversation.
- "Truly Americans have created Heaven on Earth and given it to themselves," she often thought.
- Life in Manhattan was quite a contrast to Bedford-Stuyvesant, where the music pulsed from every building, the food smells leapt from every kitchen and she thought of herself as a Jamaican.
- On any given Sunday afternoon, Jamaican teenage boys would be competing with the kids from Barbados on who could produce the best music.
- All the time the goal was to impress the girls.
- "In my day," Andrea thought to herself, "the goal was the same—to impress the girls—only I was too young to know and now I'm too old to care."

Life in the Community: New York City

- Andrea Spencer loved her apartment in the nation's second most populous black community, the Bedford-Stuyvesant section of New York City.
- Bedford-Stuyvesant was also home to the nation's largest concentration of voluntary black West Indian immigrants, a designation that included Jamaicans.
- For more than 35 years, Caribbean immigrants from Trinidad, Jamaica, Barbados, Granada, St. Vincent, and Montserrat had been congregating in Bedford-Stuyvesant's 653 square blocks.
- And for most of this time the cultural differences between West Indians and African Americans had been lost on outside observers.
- Inside Bedford-Stuyvesant, geographic distinctions and cultural habits were clearly defined and strictly noted, cultivated and respected.
- Four of the six elected officials from Bedford-Stuyvesant were West Indian, including Representative Shirley Chisholm.
- In the arts, every West Indian was openly proud of the national success of West Indian stars Harry Belafonte and Sidney Poitier.
- A quarter million Jamaicans inhabited New York City.
- Bedford-Stuyvesant was also the place to see the split between American blacks and West Indians.
- West Indians were said to work harder and succeed more than American blacks, who resented the comparisons.
- Mostly, the two groups stayed away from each other; mixing only brought trouble.

New York City was home to 250,000 Jamaicans.

HISTORICAL SNAPSHOT
1975

- A national opinion survey in the aftermath of Watergate indicated that 69 percent of the population believed that "over the last 10 years this country's leaders have consistently lied to the people"

- Former CIA Director Richard Helms divulged that the CIA had sponsored foreign assassinations, including a plan to kill Premier Fidel Castro of Cuba

- The Atomic Energy Commission was dissolved

- A whooping crane born in captivity, a hotel for dogs, the individual's right to buy gold again, an electronic watch and the awarding of the Pulitzer Prize for cartoon *Doonesbury* all made their first appearance

- To counter record low automobile sales, Chrysler introduced the concept of rebates

- Movie premieres included *One Flew Over the Cuckoo's Nest, Dog Day Afternoon, Jaws, Nashville, Monty Python* and the *Holy Grail,* and *Three Days of the Condor*

- The Brewers Society reported that Americans consumed an average of 151 pints of beer per year

- The Rolling Stones concert tour grossed $13 million

- In an effort to popularize soccer in America, the New York Cosmos soccer team signed Brazilian star Pelé to a $1 million contract

- The Khmer Rouge in Cambodia began evacuating people from its cities, which led to the intentional killing of millions

- Author Maribel Morgan declared, "A total woman caters to her man's special quirks, whether it be in salads, sex, or sports."

According to reports, Americans consumed an annual average of 151 pints of beer.

- Television premieres included *Baretta, The Jeffersons, Barney Miller, Starsky and Hutch, One Day at a Time* and *Welcome Back, Kotter*

- The Heimlich maneuver, designed to assist people who choke on food, gained government approval

- Atari of Japan introduced the first low-priced integrated circuit for TV games

- *Humboldt's Gift* by Saul Bellow won the Pulitzer Prize for fiction, while *Why Survive? Being Old in America* by Robert N. Butler won for nonfiction

- Artist Willem de Kooning completed *Whose Name Was Writ in Water*

- The so-called typical nuclear family with a working father, housewife and two children represented only 7 percent of the total American population

- Rape laws were changed in nine states, narrowing the level of collaborative evidence necessary for conviction and restricting trial questions regarding the victim's past sex life

- Bantam books paid a record $1.8 million for the paperback rights to E. L. Doctorow's *Ragtime*

- Professional golfer Jack Nicklaus won the Masters and PGA to capture his fifteenth and sixteenth major tournaments

Jamaican Immigration Timeline

1619
Twenty indentured workers from the Caribbean islands arrived in Jamestown, Virginia, where they worked as free persons.

1850s
Large numbers of Jamaicans were recruited by American and European companies to harvest sugar in Panama and Costa Rica.

1869
Jamaican workers were imported as "swallow migrants" to harvest crops in the American South after the end of slavery; most returned home when the harvest was complete.

1881-1914
A total of 90,000 Jamaicans were recruited by the United States to work on the Panama Canal.

1930
The Census Bureau reported that 100,000 documented first-generation Caribbean immigrants and their children lived in the United States.

1965
Britain restricted the number of immigrants accepted from the newly independent black majority colonies, including Jamaica.

The Immigration Reform Act opened the way for a new surge of immigrants from the Caribbean.

1966-1970
The United States legally admitted 62,700 Jamaicans.

1971-1975
The United States legally admitted 80,600 Jamaicans.

Selected Prices

Bathroom Scale	$17.99
Food Processor	$39.99
Hair Dryer	$3.88
Home, Six Rooms, Flushing, NY	$48,500
Ice Bucket	$80.00
Maternity Top	$8.00
Radio, AM	$6.99
Stereo Cassette System	$400.00
Watch, Woman's Movado	$925.00
Woman's Jumpsuit	$32.00

GIMBELS

A 6.50

Tender, smoked-sweet flavor

Smoked Hams

Cut from 14 to 16 Lb. Avg.

39¢

Shank Portion Lb.

We'd like you to test drive our car last.

Durability.

Economy.

Luxury.

Ride.

Performance

Quality.

SAAB
It's what a car should be.

Quadraphonic at its very best.

The fabulous QX-949 has everything going for it. Everything! To start it has built-in circuitry for every source of 4-channel sound reproduction — CD-4 discrete, SQ and RM matrix.

But it's a powerful 2-channel stereo receiver, too, with Pioneer's exclusive Power Boosting circuit.

In 4-channel it delivers 40 watts per channel (2-channel, 60 watts per channel) minimum continuous power, 20Hz-20,000Hz, maximum total harmonic distortion 0.3% at 8 ohms. Combined with an unbelievably wide variety of features, the QX-949 is your inevitable choice for 4-channel. $749.95, includes walnut cabinet.

U.S. Pioneer Electronics Corp., 75 Oxford Drive, Moonachie, New Jersey 07074

(ᐅ) PIONEER
when you want something better

Discover how much more you can get done in a day.

Introducing the Pocket Secretary.

LANIER

When the West Indians came here they were aware of discrimination, but they were not conditioned to accept it without making a try.

—Dr. Elliot Skinner, Trinidad-born anthropologist,
Columbia University, 1970

What this shows is that the American Southern black did not receive the incentive and certainly not the education, in most cases, to motivate him to compete. It's not that anyone is superior; we're all black, we're all the descendents of slaves. The point is that because I was born in Halfway Tree Parish in Kingston, Jamaica, I was far better equipped to cope with the American system than, say, the woman across the hall who was born in Due West, South Carolina.

—Madge Josephs, Jamaican-born city social worker, 1970

"Dialing Butterfield Hate," *Time*, February 10, 1975:

When he revealed the existence of Richard Nixon's tapes, Alexander Butterfield doomed the president. A former White House aide, Butterfield was only truthfully replying to the questions of the Senate investigators, but he incurred the enduring hatred of Nixon loyalists, who thought that he should have covered up for his old boss.

Nearly two years later, Butterfield is still being hunted down by hard-core Nixonians. Now head of the Federal Aviation Administration, which is under attack for neglecting safety standards, he has been hampered by the undercutting and sandbagging Nixon allies at the Department of Transportation, the parent body of the FAA. What is more, Butterfield has been getting midnight phone calls from old associates who berated him for coming clean about the White House tapes. One call came from Rose Mary Woods, the former president's longtime secretary, who angrily assailed Butterfield as a "son of a bitch" and charged: "You've destroyed the greatest leader this country has ever had."

But outside Washington, Butterfield has found his forthright revelation of the tapes has created quite a different reaction. On trips, Butterfield is constantly sought out by people who want to congratulate him for his honesty and candor. In Los Angeles, one woman asked him if he would shake her son's hand. "His father was killed in Vietnam," she said. "You're the kind of man he would want his son to grow up to be."

TIME

WOMEN OF THE YEAR

"Women of the Year, Great Changes, New Chances, Tough Choices," *Time,* January 5, 1976:

They have arrived like a new immigrant wave in male America. They may be cops, judges, military officers, telephone linemen, cab drivers, pipe fitters, editors, business executives or mothers and housewives, but not quite the same subordinate creatures they were before. Across the broad range of American life, from suburban tract houses to state legislatures, from church pulpits to army barracks, women's lives are profoundly changing, and with them, the traditional relationships between the sexes. Few women are unaffected, few are thinking as they did 10 years—or even a couple of years—ago. America has not entirely repealed the Code of Hammurabi (women as male property), but enough U.S. women have so deliberately taken possession of their lives that the event is the spiritual equivalent to the discovery of a new continent. Says critic Elizabeth Janeway: "The sky above us lifts, the light pours in. No maps exist for this enlarged world. We must make them as we explore."

continued

"Women of the Year, Great Changes, New Chances, Tough Choices," . . . *(continued)*

It is difficult to locate the exact moment when the psychological change occurred. A cumulative process, it owes much to the formal feminist movement of the Friedans and Steinems and Abzugs. Yet feminism has transcended the feminist movement. In 1975 the women's drive penetrated every layer of society, matured beyond ideology to a new status of general and sometimes unconscious acceptance.

Women's changing career options.

"West Indies," *Compton Yearbook*, 1976:

The Bahamas, Barbados, Grenada, Jamaica, Trinidad, and 40 other countries signed a five-year agreement with the European Economic Community in 1975. The pact called for economic aid for the less developed countries and for preferential treatment for their exports. The government of Guyana nationalized the U.S.-based Reynolds Metals Co. during the year, paying the firm $14.5 million as compensation. Guyana was a sponsor of a United Nations resolution to bar arms to South Africa, vetoed by the U.S., Great Britain, and France. Gulf Oil Corp. signed a consent decree charging the company with using the now defunct Bahamas Exploration Company to channel secret contributions to U.S. politicians.

Puerto Rico suffered from the U.S. recession in 1975 and made large cuts in its budget. It was revealed that the Federal Bureau of Investigation had in the past harassed Puerto Rican independence groups.

"Families," *Compton Yearbook*, 1976:

In 1975 the U.S. Census Bureau reported that U.S. family size has decreased to a record low in 1974 of 2.97 persons. The decrease was not an isolated event but was part of a long-term trend.

The declining birthrate was only one factor in the decrease in family size. Patterns of family living were changed; for example, fewer young people stayed home with their parents after leaving school, although many later returned for economic reasons. Also, older people tended to live alone rather than join in their children's families.

The U.S. divorce rate continued to rise, while the marriage rate, which was then rising, decreased for the first time in 16 years. About 2.2 million marriage ceremonies were performed in 1974, a decrease of 2.4 percent from 1973.

Some observers noted a trend still small but steadily increasing toward households headed by fathers only. This resulted partly from the fact that child custody was being awarded to fathers in an increasing number of divorce cases, and also from an increase in single-parent adoptions by males.

"Havana Jamboree," *Time*, January 5, 1976:

Not since the revolution of 1958 has Havana sparkled so elegantly. For two months, volunteer workers have hauled away debris, cleaned vacant lots to build parks and playgrounds, and given 38,100 houses the first coat of paint since Fidel Castro came to power. Cuban flags and bunting decorated the streets of the capital; there were even ranks of shiny new Ford Falcons, imported from Argentina, waiting at the José Marti Airport to chauffeur delegates from 87 countries to their hotels. The foreign visitors included Soviet Party ideologue Mikhail Suslov, North Viet Nam's General Vo Nguyen Giap and others who were joining 3,136 Cuban delegates for a spectacular six-day jamboree in suburban Havana's Karl Marx theater. The occasion: the first Congress of Cuba's Communist Party.

The purpose of the Congress, which ended early last week, was to "institutionalize a revolutionary process," as Castro put it in his closing address. The intention was to put the party's legal approval on the present political structure and thus ensure that whatever happens to Castro or his top lieutenants, Cuba's peculiar style of communism will survive unchanged. "Men are very fragile," said Castro, who abandoned his customary battle fatigues and appeared in a newly tailored uniform. "We disappear and go up in smoke for almost any reason."

Cuba's Fidel Castro.

1978 PROFILE

Andrei Dancescu fled in 1970 from Communist Romania to New York City, where he became a prominent photojournalist.

Life at Home

- The only child of farming parents, Andrei Dancescu was born in 1950 in a small village outside of Bucharest, Romania.
- Because Romania fell under the partial control of the Soviet Union after World War II, he grew up under Communist rule.
- From when he was very young, Andrei enjoyed drawing and sketching.
- Although it was difficult to purchase art supplies, his parents were supportive and helped him as much as they could.
- Times were hard in 1950s Romania.
- Soviet control was responsible for the exploitation of Romanian labor and resources.
- The so-called "SovRom" agreements created joint ventures between Romanian and Soviet firms that benefited the USSR almost exclusively.
- During this period, thousands of people were imprisoned by the government for political reasons.
- In 1957, when Andrei was only seven years old, his aunt (his father's sister) and her husband were among those arrested and sent to a prison camp.
- No one ever saw them again.
- Although he was young at the time, the event had a strong effect on Andrei.
- He soon began thinking about leaving the country once he got older.
- The Soviet control of Romania ended in 1958, but Communism remained in place under the rule of the new leader Nicolae Ceausescu.
- When he was 15, Andrei moved to Bucharest to attend an art institute and stayed with his mother's cousin, who lived in the city.
- In addition to studying art and design, he also began playing the guitar.

Andrei Dancescu fled Communist Romania when he was 20-years-old.

In Bucharest, Andrei enjoyed the city life and played guitar in a band.

Andrei spent time in Rome before coming to America.

His first job in America was as a line cook in a diner.

- He met a group of musicians his own age and formed a band; they became popular very quickly and wanted to play Beatles and Rolling Stones songs, but were afraid they would be considered rebellious in the eyes of the government.
- People were still afraid of the government; like many, Andrei vividly remembered the abrupt arrest of thousands, including his aunt and uncle.
- The band developed two distinct styles: traditional Romanian songs for public performances and British and American rock for underground clubs throughout the city.
- Their favorite song to play was "Twist and Shout."
- Andrei loved playing foreign rock music even though he couldn't understand the lyrics; only later in life, after he had learned English, did he fully understand the depth of his poor pronunciations.
- Andrei enjoyed city life more than his childhood in the country, but he still thought about leaving Romania; he wanted to be free to play the music he loved and not live in fear.
- Andrei left Romania in 1970, at the age of 20, and moved to Rome, Italy.
- He stayed with a family friend and enrolled in art school to sharpen his design skills; a music career seemed out of reach.
- While he developed his portfolio, he worked as a cook in a restaurant.
- There he met Samantha, the daughter of an American diplomat.
- She grew up in Rome and New York, but her father's position allowed her to travel the world.
- She had learned to speak Romanian from immigrant friends in Italy.
- Samantha and Andrei became very close and were married in Rome in 1972.
- Samantha's dream was to be a journalist in New York City; Andrei, too, secretly dreamed of living in the United States, but never thought it was possible, until he married Samantha.
- In 1973, Andrei and Samantha moved to Astoria, Queens, in New York, based on her American citizenship.
- When he first arrived in the United States, Andrei spoke practically no English; he and Samantha had always communicated in Romanian or Italian.
- Even though she was a native speaker, the only English he knew was "good day" and "thank you."

Life at Work

- Job opportunities were scarce for Andrei Dancescu because of the language barrier; his first job was as a line cook in a diner in Manhattan.
- Samantha got a job at *The New York Times* for very little money, and Andrei felt pressure to get a better job.
- Toward that end, Samantha began teaching him English after work.

- Each evening, they would read one complete page of *The New York Times* and work on the difficult parts.
- When their first child, Dan, was born, Andrei felt a deep need for his family in Romania, but couldn't afford to visit.
- His growing family motivated Andrei to work harder to find a better job.
- He soon learned enough English to get a job as an assistant at a design firm.
- He applied for a designer position, but because his portfolio was lost in the move from Italy, he had no work to show, and was hired as a guy-Friday.
- His duties included running errands and answering the phone.
- Still not confident with his English-speaking skills, he dreaded answering the phone.
- One Friday afternoon, a client called to complain about not receiving a set of sketches.
- The client described the missing sketches, and Andrei said that he would drop them off Monday morning.
- Deciding to do the sketches himself, Andrei worked all weekend and delivered them Monday morning as promised.
- When his boss learned what he had done, he was angry until the client called to say how much he liked Andrei's work.
- Andrei was then promoted and asked to contribute design work for the firm, and given a substantial raise to $8,000 per year.
- Shortly after, Andrei and Samantha took their son on vacation to Puerto Rico.
- It was a special trip, because it was the first time since they had come to America that they could afford to go on vacation.
- Andrei purchased a used Canon camera to document the trip, even though he had never seriously taken pictures before then.
- He photographed beaches, nature and the people of San Juan.
- When he got back to Queens and developed the pictures, he was so impressed and excited that he began considering a career in photography.
- Andrei started taking his camera with him everywhere.
- He walked all around the city, taking pictures of anything that caught his eye.
- He began to read books on technique; his favorite was *The Negative* by Ansel Adams.
- In 1978, Samantha got Andrei his first freelance assignment as a photojournalist covering a student protest for *The New York Times*.
- He was paid $70 for the assignment.
- More importantly, the *Times* liked his work, and his reputation grew.
- His strategy was to accept as many assignments as he could, even from small newspapers and magazines, so that his name would be seen by more people.
- Remembering the tough economic times in Romania caused him to be assertive in pursuing new assignments.

His sketches landed Andrei a promotion.

The Dancescu family on vacation in Puerto Rico.

ANSEL ADAMS: IMAGES 1923-1974. *Foreword by Wallace Stegner. 127 pages. New York Graphic Society. $65.* Magnificent examples of the reverential grandeur in Ansel Adams' photographic art, reproduced under the perfectionist eye of Adams himself. At the age of 72 he is the pre-eminent black-and-white photographer of the American West. Adams' sweeping vistas of Yosemite and the Sierras, his close-up studies of wood, rock and plants and sometimes people have been repeatedly and justly praised. The purity, directness and technical excellence of his pictures attest to Adams' belief that "a photograph is made, not taken." Yet there is also a touch of the mystic naturalist in Adams when he notes, "Sometimes, I think, I do get to places just when God is ready to have somebody click the shutter."

Photographer Ansel Adams was an inspiration to Andrei.

Taking his camera everywhere, Andrei quickly became a successful NYC photojournalist.

- If he saw photographs in a newspaper or magazine that he thought were inferior to his own, he would call and tell the editor.
- Andrei would sometimes even offer to take assignments for little or no pay in order to establish a relationship with a client.
- His aggressiveness ruffled some feathers in the competitive world of professional photographers.
- His strategy worked, however, and soon he was making as much as $300 an assignment.
- He quickly became one of the most successful photojournalists in New York.
- Andrei was determined to make sure his son had the opportunities he himself had missed growing up in Romania, and education was the first step.
- As Andrei became more successful, feuds broke out between him and other photojournalists in the city.
- Some felt that he was not fair in how he pursued assignments, while others understood that it was the nature of the business.
- Andrei was deeply hurt by some of the things that were said about him and distanced himself more and more from the photojournalism community.

Life in the Community: Queens, New York

- Andrei Dancescu's work always kept him very busy, so he didn't have much free time to spend with neighbors and friends.
- He traveled on assignment as many as 20 weeks out of each year.
- One place he never accepted assignments from was Romania, because there were things of which he did not want to be reminded.
- He would visit his family every few years when he was on assignment at a neighboring country.
- Due to his constant traveling, he became friends with the owner of the car service company that transported him to and from nearby LaGuardia Airport.
- Because of the competitive, and sometimes hostile, nature of his work, Andrei was reluctant to socialize with his colleagues in the industry.
- He had developed a love of cooking over the years and was able to find traditional Romanian ingredients in his multi-ethnic Queens neighborhood.
- He enjoyed cooking for family and close friends.
- Andrei avoided taking many pictures of friends and family, wanting to be seen with a personal, non-work side.
- He also did not want to be viewed as one of the paparazzi.
- One day, while walking around the city with his camera, he saw one of his childhood heroes, Mick Jagger.
- When Jagger saw Andrei's camera, he immediately turned and started walking in the other direction.
- The experience had a strong impact on Andrei, reminding him of the lack of personal freedom that existed in Romania when he was growing up.
- He vowed never to pry into people's lives with his photography.

New York City was full of inspiration for photographers.

HISTORICAL SNAPSHOT
1978

- The Harvard University faculty voted overwhelmingly to return to a more structured undergraduate curriculum, abandoning the "more relevant" one established in the 1960s
- Statewide limitations on indoor cigarette smoking were passed in Iowa and New Jersey
- The Karen Silkwood estate was awarded $10 million in damages by a jury that found she was poisoned by plutonium
- A study of longshoremen showed that the risk of fatal heart attack was cut in half by physical labor
- Louise Brown, the first test tube baby, was born in Oldham, England, after a fertilized egg was implanted in her mother's womb
- First Lady Betty Ford announced that she had entered a treatment program for alcohol and pill addiction
- Daniel Nathan and Hamilton Smith won the Nobel Prize for their work in restriction enzymes in molecular genetics

President Ford and wife, Betty.

- Bestselling books included *The Complete Book of Running* by James Fixx, *Mommie Dearest* by Christina Crawford, *The Memoirs of Richard Nixon* by Richard Nixon, *War and Remembrance* by Herman Wouk and *Eye of the Needle* by Ken Follett
- In horse racing, Affirmed won the Triple Crown
- The legal retirement age was raised to 70
- The Bee Gees' album *Saturday Night Fever* sold a record 12 million copies
- The exercise craze provided a new fashion statement for women: decorative T-shirts
- Sneakers comprised 50 percent of all shoe sales in America
- Nine hundred American religious cult members, under the influence of Jim Jones, committed suicide in Guyana
- Pope Paul VI died and was replaced by Pope John Paul I, who also died and replaced by Polish cardinal Pope John Paul II
- The inflation rate reached 12.4 percent, driving the prime rate to 12 percent
- Television premieres included "The Incredible Hulk," "Fantasy Island," "Dallas," "WKRP in Cincinnati," "Diff'rent Strokes," "Mork and Mindy" and "Taxi"
- The two-year American tour of the King Tutankhamen show generated $5 million for the Cairo Museum
- An original Gutenberg Bible was sold for $2.2 million
- The baseball commissioner's ban on female reporters in locker rooms was set aside by a federal judge
- Robert Penn Warren won the Pulitzer Prize for poetry for his book *Now and Then*
- Movie premieres included *The Deer Hunter, Midnight Express, An Unmarried Woman, Superman* and *National Lampoon's Animal House*

Romanian Immigration Timeline

1880s

The first wave of Romanian immigration from what is now Romania began primarily from the agricultural provinces of Transylvania, Bukovina, and Banat, which were then part of the Austro-Hungarian Empire.

1900–1910

Thirty-seven thousand Romanians emigrated to the U.S.

Overpopulation coupled with the steady consolidation of small, semi-feudal landholdings worked by peasants created a growing class of property-less laborers who sought opportunity in Europe and America.

At the height of emigration, around 94 percent of the emigrants were landless peasants and farmhands.

Romanians who came to the U.S. nearly all found homes in the industrial Northeast and Midwest; New York, Pennsylvania and Ohio absorbed more than half of the total Romanian immigration.

1911–1914

Immigration continued at a rate of about 7,000 per year until World War I.

1924

U.S. immigration restrictions limited the number of Romanian entrants to 1,000 per year.

1930–1940

Immigration statistics showed a decrease of more than 30,000 Romanians in the U.S.

1970s

Ninety percent of Romanian Americans continued to live in cities and tended to be employed as skilled factory workers and small-business entrepreneurs.

Selected Prices

Baby Carrier	$14.00
Bean Bag Chair	$37.95
Beer, Stroh's Six-Pack	$1.49
Briefcase, Leather	$35.95
CB Radio	$39.88
Circular Saw	$22.88
Coffee Maker, Norelco	$23.88
Drive-in Movie Ticket, Carload	$4.00
Turntable	$199.95
Woman's Swimsuit, Bikini	$13.00

You can't experience today's high fidelity with yesterday's record changer.

PIONEER
when you want something better

PL-71 Direct-Drive Turntable

A 100% immersible coffeemaker. Every last inch of a GE coffeemaker goes into soap and water. You get a clean pot, better tasting coffee, and a lot of people who say, "hey, great coffee."

Sesame Street is so successful, we're taking it off the air.

Sesame Street books, records and playthings.

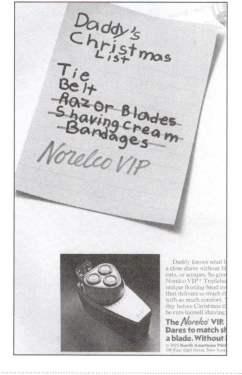

Daddy's Christmas List
Tie
Belt
Razor Blades
Shaving cream
Bandages
Norelco VIP

Daddy knows what a close shave without cuts, or scrapes. So give Norelco VIP Triplehead unique floating-head that delivers so much with so much comfort. day before Christmas he cuts himself shaving

The _Norelco_ VIP. Dares to match a blade. Without

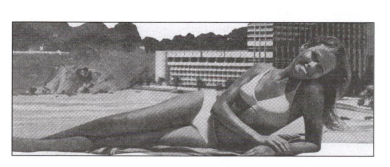

"The End of the Great Adventure," *Time*, December 18, 1972:

To see life; to see the world; to eyewitness great events . . . to see strange things, machines, armies, multitudes, shadows in this jungle and on the moon; to see man's work, his paintings, towers and discoveries; to see things thousands of miles away; things hidden beneath walks and within rooms, things dangerous to come to; the women that men love and many children; to see and to take pleasure in seeing the city and to be amazed; to see and be instructed. Thus to see, and to be shown, is now the will and new expectancy of half mankind.

Quoted countless times through the years, the prospectus written by Henry R. Luce in 1936 still expresses the beat of *LIFE*. That beat will be stilled with the year-end special issue of December 29. But its contribution to the history of journalism continues.

The announcement came after continuing losses some $30 million since 1969. In the face of soaring cost, why did *LIFE* continue to publish for four profitable years? At a valedictory staff meeting, Hedley Donovan, editor in chief of Time Inc., gave the reason: We persevered as long as we could see any realistic perspectives, within a reasonable time frame, a turnaround of *LIFE*'s economy." These prospects were extinguished this fall with melancholy prognosis for decreased circulation and advertising pages. These, coupled with postal rate increases (amounting to 170 percent over five years) made the end inevitable. At the meeting, the last of *LIFE*'s six managing editors, Ralph Graves, announced his assignment was to help place *LIFE* employees in other jobs. But he warned, "I won't pretend anyplace else is going to be like what we shared together at *LIFE*."

DAVID DOUGLAS DUNCAN PHOTOGRAPHING
AVA GARDNER (1954); MARGARET BOURKE-
WHITE ATOP CHRYSLER BUILDING (1931);
ALFRED EISENSTAEDT STRAIGHTENING
NIXON'S TIE (1960); LARRY BURROWS
IN SAIGON (1966)

The End of the Great Adventure

To see life; to see the world; to eyewiness great events...to see strange things—machines, armies, multitudes, shadows in the jungle and on the moon; to see man's work—his paintings, towers and discoveries; to see things thousands of miles away; things hidden behind walls and within rooms, things dangerous to come to; the women that men love and many children; to see and to take pleasure in seeing; to see and be amazed; to see and be instructed. Thus to see, and to be shown, is now the will and new expectancy of half mankind.

QUOTED countless times through the years, the prospectus—written by Henry R. Luce in 1936—still best expresses the beat of LIFE. That beat will be stilled with the year-end special issue of Dec. 29. But its contribution to the history of journalism remains.

The announcement came after continuing losses—some $30 million since 1969. In the face of soaring costs, why did LIFE continue to publish for four unprofitable years? At a valedictory staff meeting, Hedley Donovan, editor in chief of Time Inc., gave the reason: "We persevered as long as we could see any realistic prospects, within a reasonable time span, of a turn-around in LIFE's economy." Those prospects were extinguished this fall with melancholy prognoses for decreased circulation and advertising pages. These, coupled with postal-rate increases (amounting to 170% over five years) made the end inevitable. At the meeting, the last of LIFE's six managing editors, Ralph Graves, announced his assignment was to help place LIFE employees in other jobs. But he warned, "I won't pretend that any place else is going to be like what we shared together at LIFE."

Shared was the operative word. It applied to the LIFE staff, which was held together by an extraordinary *esprit de corps*, and it applied to the readers, who had a sense of common participation in human events that nothing else could provide—until the advent of TV. From the start, LIFE took hold of the imagination. Its editors could have been content to let it remain a national scrapbook, but at its heart there was an animal curiosity. As Photographer John Dominis said, "You worked closely with people, individual friends, for three or four weeks, perhaps sometimes three or four months, on a story. They became almost like wartime buddies."

In the weekly battle journalists became something else—students of a new medium. Each week, as they came from their mailboxes or newsstands, Americans experienced the powerful aftereffects of a new art called "photojournalism." After LIFE, the Sinclair Lewis mid-American territory of Main Street, insulated and uninformed, passed into fiction forever. Said a first-grade teacher in Cleveland last week: "I remember cutting out the photographs when I was a child and bringing them into school to my teachers. And as a teacher I brought LIFE into the classroom and had the children cut out photographs. It was a teaching tool."

Other national magazines, notably the *Saturday Evening Post*, provided entertainment and information, but LIFE brought the world home with an immediacy that made the head spin: closeups of leaders like Hitler and Stalin, Gandhi and Churchill, men who would never again be remote; color plates of modern paintings; the adventures and explorations of science and faith. And, of course, a classic parade of the world's most beautiful women. Sometimes LIFE was criticized for the shock effect of its juxtapositions: the Sistine Chapel right up against a bosomy starlet, Arnold Toynbee alongside Milton Berle. But that was part of the captivating mixture —LIFE at its most lifelike.

In 1938, when the magazine showed a sequence entitled "The Birth of a Baby," LIFE was banned in 33 American cities. A year later, the world was not so easily disturbed. The holocaust in Europe screamed in the headlines and on the radio, but it was to LIFE that millions turned for the full report. There they saw pictures that seemed to enter the collective unconscious: Robert

The Beat of LIFE

Memorable Moments from 36 Years of Photojournalism: Center: Rear view of Churchill sketching (Philippe Halsman, 1951) Clockwise from upper left: V-J day in Times Square (Alfred Eisenstaedt, 1945); Franco's Guardia Civil (W. Eugene Smith, 1951); Soldier's skull on destroyed tank (Ralph Morse, 1943); Pin-Up Queen Rita Hayworth (Bob Landry, 1941); Marine casualties at battle of Hué (John Olson, 1968); Starving Biafran child (Terence Spencer, 1970)

"Male and Female," *Time*, September 10, 1973:

Have labor-saving appliances and gadgets really freed women from household work? Joann Vanek, a sociologist at the University of Michigan, compared a series of group time new studies conducted between 1926 and 1965, and concluded that the amount of time housewives spend on housework had remained virtually the same over 40 years, despite the introduction of many labor-saving devices during that period. Accordingly, Vanek found, new appliances did save women time in specific routine tasks such as food preparation and laundry. But most of the women had apparently invented new kinds of housework to take up the slack: gourmet cooking, the direction of children's play, household management and shopping.

"Rumanians Are Seeking Contacts with Lost 4 Million in the Soviet," by David Binder, *The New York Times*, October 10, 1976:

The Rumanian Government has advised Western and independent powers with which it is friendly that it is seeking, for the first time in more than 30 years, to establish contacts with the four million ethnic Rumanians living in the Soviet Union.

American and Yugoslav officials said earlier this week that they had been told by high Rumanian authorities that this was the principal purpose of a visit last August by President Nicolae Ceausescu to the Soviet Republic of Moldavia, where most of the ethnic Rumanians live.

It was reported shortly after that visit that in talks with Leonid I. Brezhnev, the Soviet Communist Party chief, President Ceausescu had made some political concessions to the Soviet Union mainly in ideological areas. But the Rumanian authorities told American and Yugoslav officials that these concessions carried little real substance.

More important, they said, was to make clear during Mr. Ceausescu's visit that neither Rumania nor the Soviet Union had territorial designs across the long frontier between the two countries.

Specifically, Mr. Ceausescu told Mr. Brezhnev that Rumania did not dispute the post-World War II frontiers that accorded the Soviet Union control over the regions of Northern Bukovina and Bessarabia, both of which were part of Rumania before the war.

The Soviet Union forced Rumania to cede both regions in 1940, but Rumania, joining the Axis powers in 1941 when it was still a monarchy, sent armored forces into Bukovina and Bessarabia to recapture the lost territories. The Soviet Army reconquered the regions in 1944.

Since then the Soviet leadership has asserted that Soviet Moldavia, the former Bessarabia, was inhabited not by ethnic Rumanians but by Moldavians, and that Northern Bukovina was mainly inhabited by Ukrainians. Since 1965, Rumania has claimed that most of these people are Rumanians.

After the war the Soviet Union also deported more than a million Rumanians to eastern Siberia, where they form an ethnic unit to this day.

"Rumanian Decree Appears To Ease Limits on Travel," *The New York Times*, November 10, 1968:

Rumania announced a measure today that appeared to ease restrictions on travel abroad.

This would mean another step in the cautious liberalization drive that began last April.

A decree issued by the State Council and the Cabinet and published by the official press agency, Agerpres, said:

"Romanian citizens have the right to obtain passports by which they may cross the state frontier in order to travel or reside abroad."

1979 PROFILE

Vang Ghia and his Hmong family escaped from Laos into Thailand after the fall of Vietnam and emigrated to Fresno, California, where basketball became his greatest obsession.

Life at Home

- Twelve-year-old Vang Ghia was the oldest child of the Hmong clan, which followed the tradition of using the family name first, given names second.
- His mother, who believed herself to be 37, had eight other children, six of whom were still living.
- Ghia, his family and another family from the same subclan lived together in a two-bedroom apartment on the west side of Fresno, California.
- The eight members of the Vang family lived in one room, sleeping on pallets on the floor.
- The younger children, including their new-born brother, slept near the adults.
- The new baby was the first child in the family born in the United States, and the first born in a hospital.
- When he was born, the Vangs asked, through a cousin who could speak English, for the baby's placenta.
- The nurse relayed the request to the doctor, who, remembering stories he had heard of rural Asians eating their children's placentas, turned them down immediately.
- The Vangs were very upset by his refusal; in Hmong culture, the placentas of newborn children were buried with the expectation that, after the children grew up and died, they would retrace their life steps and don the placenta, the baby's first jacket, in preparation for rejoining their ancestors and eventually being born again.
- Ghia's parents were afraid that because the placenta was sent away, their child would be forced to wander naked for all of eternity after his death.
- On the third day after the birth, the family held a soul-calling ceremony to name the child; friends were invited to the house and a pig was slaughtered, an invitation for an ancestor to inhabit the child's body.

Vang Ghia escaped from Communist-occupied Laos with his family.

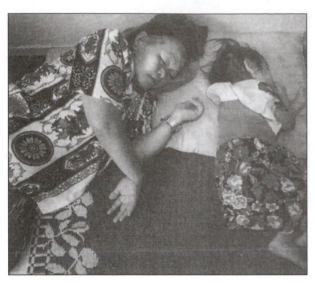

Adults and children slept on the floor.

- Eventually, the name Ger was bestowed upon the child; two chickens were then sacrificed, plucked, eviscerated and boiled.
- All in attendance were delighted to see the chicken skulls were translucent and the tongues curled backwards—signs that the soul of the ancestor was happy to reside in Ger's body and pleased with the name, even though the family had moved far away from its traditional territory and village in Laos.
- Ghia had been born in the mountains of Laos, where his family farmed, growing beans, melons, yams, corn and vegetables.
- Their most important crop was opium poppies.
- They were forced to abandon their family farm in 1976 because of the Hmong people's historic support for the United States during the Vietnam War.
- Ghia and his family fled Laos, crossing the Mekong River into Thailand to escape the wrath of the new Communist government.
- Two of Ghia's siblings and several other family members died during the arduous trek.
- In Thailand, they lived in a refugee camp, barely able to survive on the meager food supplies, but grateful to be alive.
- There, they met American missionaries who taught Ghia and his other brothers and sisters to speak English.
- In appreciation for their support during the war, Laos highland refugees, 90 percent of them Hmong, had been admitted to the United States since 1975.
- Three years after they left Laos, the family received permission to enter the United States.
- Approximately 40,000 Hmong refugees had emigrated in the past four years since the end of the Vietnam War.
- Their host family found them a place to live on the west side of Fresno, California, where a growing Hmong family was forming, including many members of the Vang clan.
- When they arrived in Fresno, Ghia's parents were not only unable to speak English, but were also labeled illiterate in their own language; the Hmong did not have an alphabet until the 1950s.
- Thanks to the missionaries in the refugee camp and hard work, the older children could read and write English, and often served as translators for their parents during the early days in the United States.

Their host family found the Vangs an apartment.

- The family initially survived with the help of public assistance checks after Ghia's father was unable to find work.
- Ghia's mother joined several other local Hmong women in sewing intricate story cloths, which told of their life in the village and exodus to Thailand.
- The ready market for story cloths helped the family meet its needs, but finding work for Ghia's father had been more difficult.
- His skills as an Asian farmer did not translate well into the highly mechanized agribusiness world of Fresno, where good knowledge of machinery, chemicals and English were necessities.
- He and several other Hmong men in the apartment complex started a large garden on a nearby vacant lot, growing a variety of fruits and vegetables for their families to eat.
- No one was certain to whom the land belonged; it was not a consideration, since the concept of private land ownership was rarely practiced by the Hmong people.

Life at School

- Vang Ghia attended the seventh grade at a public school in Fresno, California.
- When he first arrived, his skills, especially in conversational English, were far behind those of his American classmates.
- The two children from his American host family provided regular tutoring, and he worked hard to catch up.
- He understood most of what was said in class, but confusion still arose.
- At first, when his new friends would say things like, "See you later," he thought it was an invitation for another meeting.
- On several occasions, he hung around after school for anxious hours attempting to fulfill his obligation to "see you later."
- His fellow classmates were a diverse group, including African Americans, Mexicans, Chinese and a few whites.
- Ghia encountered fewer problems and less prejudice than he had expected, although the majority of his time was spent with other Hmong children, who shared his language, problems and background.
- While still in Thailand, he had learned about many aspects of American culture, including basketball, with which he had become obsessed.
- Ghia played with a middle school B team.
- Even though he rarely got to play, his family came to every home game and cheered wildly when he was on the court.
- The coach said he had natural talent and that with practice, he would catch up with the boys who'd been playing basketball their entire lives.
- Although Ghia adapted rapidly to American life, transition for his parents continued to be more difficult.
- Issues such as cars, paved streets, neon signs, traffic lights and airplanes continually upset them.
- In Laos, his father possessed great instincts about where he was in the jungle and how to return home, no matter how dense the vegetation.
- In Fresno, he rarely went more than a few blocks from home without taking a child to guide him back.
- Once the police brought him home after he had gotten lost and wandered the streets for hours.
- Afraid and unable to communicate with the police, Ghia's father showed the police the telephone number for his host family, and the police helped in the rescue mission.
- Afterward he was withdrawn and declined to talk with his family for days.
- He often sat in the community garden for hours, staring at the horizon; in Hmong culture the man was always the leader, working and providing for his family.
- The Vang family contacted a local shaman to assist in the job search; thus far, several animals had been sacrificed with no result.
- The host family was concerned he might be considering suicide.
- At Thanksgiving, when the host family held a traditional American dinner for the new Asian immigrants, everybody except Ghia's father piled into the host family's station wagon and headed across town.

Ghia worked hard at his schoolwork.

Ghia's classmates were a diverse group.

Outside of school, Ghia spent most of his time with other Hmong children.

The Vang's enjoyed their first Thanksgiving in America with their host family.

- Upon entering the home, they were struck by the strange smells of turkey, cranberry sauce and cornbread, all unknown in Laos.
- The highlight of the meal was when Ghia's mother, who was taking English classes and gaining confidence in her skills, told a story entirely in English.
- When she finished speaking, the host family was in tears.
- Ghia loved eating American food and asked for seconds of everything, especially the yams, which reminded him of home.
- To accommodate the two families, the adults and smallest children were seated at the dining room table, while Ghia and the other teens dined by themselves at fold-up card tables covered with a cloth.
- Ghia got so excited telling stories about his basketball team and his new friends that he knocked a small bowl of cranberry sauce off the table, embarrassing his mother.
- Afterward he apologized to his mother and to the host family for both his manners and his father's inability to attend this important family function.
- Before leaving, Ghia noticed that the house was filled with paintings of faraway cities or mountain ranges, or even paintings that had no point at all.
- His apartment was decorated by 8" x 10" photographs hung high on the living room wall of family members in Hmong costume and old images from Laos and the camps; and pictures of parents and grandparents, enlarged from old snapshots, who gazed out at their descendents all day long.
- In addition to practicing basketball, Ghia spent his spare time focused on learning to dance in time for his middle school's end-of-semester dance.
- Ghia had thought little about the event until Rosita, a cute Mexican girl in his class, asked him to go with her.
- After that he thought of little else.
- He asked numerous friends to teach him how to dance, got advice about what to wear, and even asked his sisters what girls liked to talk about.
- His family had neither a radio nor a television, so he went to other friends' houses just to know what music was popular.
- His mother was so excited about the dance she set aside money to buy him a new shirt to wear.
- His father's concern was that his Hmong son was going out in public with a Mexican girl.

Life in the Community: Thailand and Fresno, California

- By the late 1970s in Thailand, 21 refugee camps had been established to receive hundreds of thousands of people fleeing Vietnam, Cambodia and Laos.
- The camps were supported by the United Nations High Commissioner for Refugees and staffed by volunteers, including many missionaries.
- The Thai government was instrumental in determining official and unofficial refugee camp policies; as a result, camps were open and closed abruptly by Thai authorities, and refugees shifted about.

Ghia's large family felt comfortable in their heavily-Hmong Fresno neighborhood.

- Ban Vinai became the largest Hmong settlement, both in Thailand and in the world, containing 40,000 people in an area of less than one square mile.
- There, many were taught English and Christianity by the missionaries.
- Fresno County was one of the largest counties in California, extending across the San Joaquin Valley from the Central Coast Ranges to the crest of the Sierra Nevada.
- With a population of 175,000, Fresno, which means ash tree in Spanish, was the ninth largest city in California; when the entire county was included, the population totaled nearly 500,000.
- Ninety percent of the west side housing in Fresno was occupied by Hispanics, blacks and Asians; because of recent immigration patterns, Fresno was considered the American Hmong capital.
- Canned, frozen and dehydrated fruit and vegetable processing led all other industrial sectors in employment, accounting for one-third of all manufacturing activity.

HISTORICAL SNAPSHOT
1979

- The Broadway play *Grease* reached 3,243 performances, passing *Fiddler on the Roof* as the longest-running show
- The rate of inflation reached 13.3 percent; the prime rate was 15.75 percent
- Seven states raised the legal drinking age from 18 to 20
- The United States established diplomatic relations with China, while ties with Taiwan were severed
- An industrial accident at Three Mile Island, Pennsylvania, dramatically increased fears concerning the use of nuclear power-generated energy
- Movie openings included *Kramer vs. Kramer, Apocalypse Now, Norma Rae, The China Syndrome, Star Trek: The Motion Picture* and *10*
- The federal government approved a $1.5 billion bailout loan guarantee for the Chrysler Corporation
- *The Dukes of Hazzard, Archie Bunker's Place, Knot's Landing* and *Hart to Hart* premiered on television
- Eleven people were trampled to death while rushing for seats at a Cincinnati concert by the Who
- Hit songs included "I Will Survive," "Reunited," "Hot Stuff," "Too Much Heaven," "Money Can't Buy You Love"
- Norman Mailer's *The Executioner's Song* received the Pulitzer Prize for fiction, while Edmund Morris won the biography award for *The Rise of Theodore Roosevelt*
- Judith Krantz received a record $3.2 million advance for the paperback rights to *Princess Daisy*
- The popularity of electronic games such as Chest Challenger, Microvision, Speak and Spell and Little Professor swept the nation
- Marvel Comic, No.1 was purchased for a record $43,000
- Video digital sound discs, electronic blackboards, throwaway toothbrushes, *Drabble* cartoons and Crackerjack ice cream bars all made their first appearance

Cast of the popular TV show MASH.

Key Hmong Immigration Events

- With the withdrawal of American forces from Vietnam in 1975 and the collapse of the governments of Laos and Cambodia, over two million refugees fled from the former Indochina, fearing Communist reprisals.
- They were not welcomed by neighboring Asian countries.
- Only following negotiations with the United Nations High Commissioner for Refugees did the United States and other countries agree to accept refugees from the makeshift camps established in Thailand, Malaysia, Indonesia, the Philippines, Singapore and Hong Kong.
- The focus of these camps was on physical survival; they generally were located in remote areas and provided only the bare necessities.
- Crowded conditions, poor sanitation, minimal health care, and frequent violence were common, as were depression and boredom.
- Eventually, over 1,250,000 refugees were admitted to the United States, its largest refugee group since World War II.
- Sixty-six percent came from Vietnam, while 21 percent were from Laos, with the Hmong and other ethnic peoples from the Laotian highlands comprising slightly less than half of this group; 13 percent of the refugees were from Cambodia.
- Southeast Asian refugees and immigrants settled in every state of the Union, but more than 40 percent of them, or almost 500,000 people, made California their new home.
- Many Laotian refugees settled in California's Central Valley.
- Although the United States had a longstanding tradition of accepting people fleeing oppression in other countries, many Americans were not in favor of admitting numerous Southeast Asian refugees.
- One public opinion poll taken when Saigon fell in 1975 showed only 36 percent of the respondents in favor of Vietnamese immigration, fearing loss of jobs and increased public spending.
- President Gerald Ford strongly supported the refugees, and Congress allocated resettlement aid and passed the 1975 Indochina Migration and Refugee Act, which allowed the refugees to enter the United States under a special migration and "parole" status.
- To avoid ethnic enclaves and to lessen the impact of large numbers of refugees in one geographic area, the government initially dispersed the refugees all over the country.
- Within a few years, a significant amount of secondary migration occurred, mainly to California and Texas.
- The second-largest Southeast Asian refugee group was the Hmong from Laos.
- Independent and self-sufficient, the Hmong had migrated into Laos and neighboring countries from China, their original homeland, in the early nineteenth century.
- The transition from living in remote mountain villages and practicing slash-and-burn agriculture to industrialized American life was not easy.

Selected Prices

Bicycle	$64.99
Cigarette Case	$34.95
Computer, Apple II	$1,300.00
Hotel Room, St. Moritz, New York	$31.00
Ice Cream Machine	$24.95
Massage Shower Head	$26.95
Microwave Oven	$168.00
Organic Roast Beef, per Half-Pound	$1.99
Stroller	$24.99
Theater Ticket, *A Chorus Line*, New York	$17.50

It's gonna be a great day.

Reach for the stars. Fur.

We have enough electricity to last 200 years. But it's buried in the ground.

Progress for People.

GENERAL ELECTRIC

"I always have money with me. And I don't carry cash."
Eileen Johnston, Teacher

Letters to the Editor: "Boat People," *Life*, November 1979:

I am sick and tired of hearing about the homeless boat people (Island of Hope, September). As a veteran of 18 months in Vietnam, I will never forget that we couldn't trust most Vietnamese. The farmer by day was a fighter by night. How can the American, Australian, French and Canadian governments ascertain whether the people being accepted are communist sympathizers or not? Articles like yours are a disgrace to the millions of GIs who served in that terrible conflict. How about 11 pages on the Vietnam vet?

—Harvey Gobin, Gainesville, Florida

I was particularly struck by your account of the American official screening people, insisting that a young man must be older than 14 because he had a large Adam's apple. I could just picture my own 14-year-old son in that young man's place, trying to convince the opinionated official that he was really 14, for his voice is deeper than his father's, his Adam's apple so prominent that it looks as if he has a chicken bone stuck in his throat, and he is taller and more muscular than friends a year or two older than he. My son is a Sansei, third-generation American of Japanese descent.

Perhaps it is more difficult to tell the ages of Asians. It may not matter greatly in the long run; perhaps this young man was not destined to be an American. To have to play God is an awesome responsibility when we do not have God's ability to discern the truth when it is presented.

—Marie Honmyo, Seattle, Washington

Hmong women embroidered detailed fabric depicting their life in Laos.

Changing Lives of Refugee Hmong Women, by Nancy D. Donnelly, 1994:

"We walk 32 days from Laos to the river. All is trees. I carry one boy and one boy walk. Chue Neng carry rice. We carry one pan and knife and clothes. We carry silver, also seeds. Little Neng have four years that time, Ly more than two years. Food is not too much," Ker said.

I looked at Ker squinting into the warm spring sun, Chue Neng beside her, walking from the garden through the neighborhood of small neat houses. There was a wall of unmortared rocks beside us, well grown with cascades of alyssum. Ker pulled off a bit of green, glancing at me.

"We eat like this. What you call this? Leaves.

"We eat leaves. Everybody eat leaves. There is one leaves, I give to the younger boy and he die. Many people die from that leaves, maybe more than two hundred. We just keep going."

The Spirit Catches You and You Fall Down, "A Hmong Child, Her American Doctors and the Collision of Two Cultures," by Anne Fadiman, 1997:

If Lia Lee had been born in the highlands of northwest Laos, where her parents and 12 of her brothers and sisters were born, her mother would have squatted on the floor of the house her father had built with ax-hewn planks thatched with bamboo and grass. The floor was dirt, but it was clean. Her mother, Foua, sprinkled it regularly with water to keep the dust down and swept it every morning and evening with a broom she had made of grass and bark. . . . Even if Foua had been a less fastidious housekeeper, her newborn babies would not have gotten dirty, since she never let them actually touch the floor. She remains proud to this day she delivered each of them into her own hands, reaching between her legs to ease out the head and then letting the rest of the body slip out into her bent forearms. . . . Because Foua believed that moaning and screaming would thwart the birth, she labored in silence, with the exception of an occasional prayer to her ancestors. She was so quiet that although most of her babies were born at night, her older children slept undisturbed on a communal pallet a few feet away, and woke only when they heard the cry of their new brother or sister. . . .

When Lia was born, at 7:09 p.m. on July 19, 1982, Foua was lying on her back on a steel table, her body covered with sterile drapes, her genital area painted with a brown betaine solution, with a high wattage lamp trained on her perineum. There were no family members in the room. Gary Thueson, a family practice resident who did the delivery, noted in the chart that in order to speed up the labor, he artificially ruptured Foua's amniotic sack by poking it with a foot-long plastic "amnihook"; that no anesthesia was used; that no episiotomy, an incision to enlarge the vaginal opening, was necessary; and after birth Foua received a standard dose of Pitocin to constrict her uterus. . . . Lia was shown briefly to her mother. Then she was placed in the steel and Plexiglas warmer, where a nurse fastened a plastic identification band around her wrist and recorded her footprints by inking the soles of her feet with a stamp pad and pressing against a Newborn Identification form. . . .

Some Hmong parents have given their children American names. In addition to many standard ones, these have included Kennedy, Nixon, Pajama, Guitar, and until a nurse counseled otherwise, Baby Boy, which one mother seeing it written on her son's hospital papers assumed it was the name the doctor had already chosen for him.

"Agriculture," *California Yearbook,*
Bicentennial Edition, 1975:

Fresno County in 1974 was a leader in agricultural production in California and the nation, with an annual gross value of $967,350,000. It has been a leading county in the state for over 20 years. Field crops were the most important commodities with a gross value of $347,460,000. Cotton lint was valued at $165,456,000; cotton seed, $46,926,000; alfalfa hay, $4,250,000; barley, $28,619,000; sugar beets, $22,845,000; rice, $10,992,000. Other important field crops were wheat, corn, sorghum grain, safflower and pasture.

REFUGEE: Any person who is outside his or her country of nationality and is unable or unwilling to return to that country because of persecution or a well-founded fear of persecution that may be based on race, religion, nationality, membership in a particular social group, or political opinion.

—Adapted from the Refugee Act of 1980

We know vitamin C does a lot for them. What new discoveries lie ahead?

Like you, these youngsters can be susceptible to infection that overwhelms the body's natural immunities. Vitamin C, along with other essential nutrients, optimizes your body's natural capacity to resist illness and helps keep your tissues healthy.

Tripping and falling means cuts, scrapes, bruises or a fracture. None of these will heal properly without adequate vitamin C, along with other essential nutrients.

Vitamin C also increases the body's ability to absorb iron from foods. Iron, the most common deficiency in the diet, may be related to a loss of energy.

What about the future? A great deal of research is being directed at possible relationships of vitamin C to infections, diseases, cholesterol levels, stress, and air and chemical pollution.

The role of vitamin C is still being evaluated, but in the meantime it's still important to get enough. So eat foods rich in this essential nutrient. To be sure, you can take a vitamin C supplement. A wide selection of formulations is available. Read the label to make sure you get your vitamin C in the amount you want.

Vitamin Communications, Hoffmann-La Roche Inc., Nutley, N.J. 07110.

Vitamins. Something you can do for your health.   RCD 3389

1971 NEWS FEATURE

DEPARTMENT OF STATE
Washington, D.C. 20520

April 22, 1971

Mr. Nicholas Bageac
87-30 Justice Avenue
Apartment 5F
Elmhurst, New York 11373

Dear Mr. Bageac:

Thank you for your letter of April 2 informing me that Mr. Baciu had arrived in the United States. I was very happy to learn that the family is now reunited and that your father-in-law—for all the trouble he has lived through—remains in good health. I am sure that you will find what you describe as "small" problems ahead. However, I am equally sure that you will meet them with the same vigor and determination which successfully brought your family back together in this country. While the arrival of the sixth member of your family needs neither the assistance nor approval of the State Department, may I wish him or her the best of starts in this world.

We appreciate your comments on immigration problems. As you are well aware, our immigration law was designed to facilitate the reunification of families, but it can be effective only in helping persons to get into the United States, not in getting them out of their own countries. Through the legal process, and where applicable with assistance from the United States Refugee Program, the U.S. Government does what it can to relieve the tribulations of the refugee. We know that it sometimes takes a long time, but we hope you will urge patience on friends of yours who may undertake to come to this country.

With greetings to Mrs. Bageac and all your family,

Sincerely,

Henry W. Allen
Refugee and Migration Officer
Office of Refugee and Migration Affairs

* *

```
                    STATE – A.I.D. – USIA              DATE
                         ROUTING SLIP                  April 22, 1971
    TO:              Organ.                            Initials   Date
         Name or Title  Symbol   Room No.   Bldg.
    1.
       Mr. Charles W. Schaller  EUR/BRY  5217   NS
    2.
    3.
    4.
    5.
    Approval         X  For Your Information    Note and Return
    As Requested        Initial for Clearance   Per Conversation
    Comment             Investigate             Prepare Reply
    File                Justify                 See Me
    For Correction      Necessary Action        Signature
    REMARKS OR ADDITIONAL ROUTING
```

Attached is a letter from Romanian refugee
Nicholas Bageac of April 2, reporting the arrival
of his father-in-law, Victor Baciu, in the US.
This provides a happy ending to correspondence
between Mr. Bageac and the Department dating
back to December 1968.

```
    FROM: (Name and Org. Symbol)        ROOM NO. & BLDG.   PHONE NO.
         Henry W. Allen    S/R:ORM        2528      NS      28344
```

To DEPARTMENT OF STATE
WASHINGTON, D.C.

Nicholas Bageac
87-30 Justice Ave.
Elmhurst N Y 11373

August 20 1972

Dear Sir,

Due to the fact that I have legitimate desire and pride to vote in the presidential election this year I am asking your assistance to speed up my naturalization which has been slowly processing since March 1 when I had the first hearing with two witnesses.

The number of my file is 741768 Eastern District Brooklyn N.Y. The head of the department is Mr. Cohen and he answers at telephone no. (212) 596-3946 or 596-5165.

I called him a couple of times, and he said that more information about me is expected. I asked for an appointment offering my help to clarify any questions, but I was told that it cannot help and although I may take the trip, it is a waste of time.

Now with registration for voting closing at September 2 (yet I registered myself with the remark of naturalization underway) and the November election coming soon, I may remain out of voting if my naturalization process does not come to a conclusion. The usual time for the waiting period is three months and my case has already lapsed six months.

This is my first chance to vote freely, and besides that, being a U.S. citizen is an honor which I believe I deserve and I am deeply concerned with.

Sincerely yours,
Nicholas Bageac

* * * * * * * * * * * * * * * * * * * *

August 21 1972

Dear Mr. Allen,

I would like to write to you in personal terms as a continuation of your assistance and encouragement when a problem with my wife's parents' immigration put us in contact last year. I am sure you have hundreds of cases every month and for a quick recollection I enclosed a copy of your last and so nice letter forwarded to me in April 1971.

Since then many things changed and mostly are good news. The expected baby was what I wished the most: a wonderful girl who brought our family a lot of joy and love. My 14-year-old son achieved beautiful results in school. My father-in-law at 60 years of age got a job as a security guard in the first month he came and is extremely pleased in this country as he was born again. Me and my wife (both with degrees in engineering) we are working at the same company holding good positions. My mother-in-law takes care of the baby and household, a job for what always is hard to find labor.

We are a well-organized family, hard workers (everybody in his field), physically and morally healthy, and I see no reason why this country is not to be as pleased with us as we are (and thank God for that) with her.

We have a high income per our family of six which enables us for more and more prosperity. Within some months we will move into a new $55,000 home in Westchester, N.Y., already bought on mortgage. So we could live as well as the president of the United States and even with less tensions and headaches.

The starting point of all these achievements and future chances was in October 1966 when, having gotten a passport for Yugoslavia, I swam from Koper (Yugoslavia) to Trieste (Italy). After four to five hours of swimming over the night I reached the other side of the Iron Curtain. That was the very starting point. I had only my wet, trembling and exhausted body still alive and a pair of bathing slips. At that time I couldn't say which one was worth more. It was cold, windy and terrible dark. I was alone and yet I had a long way to go up to the destination.

I did it, and now after six years, look at us: isn't this a great performance and a complete success? Thank God we are in this country and our children are on the safe side forever.

In addition to these things which make me a pleasure to let them be known, incidentally I have another problem for what I have to address myself to the Department of State: my naturalization processing is becoming much too slow just before the presidential election of November this year. It is easy to understand my anxiety to vote and to take part in the political life of this country. Nevertheless, being an American citizen at the time I am eligible to be is a great deal of concern for me.

I came to this country not to grab some money and go to enjoy it somewhere else, but to settle forever. It is this country where my children and grandchildren will live.

I am emotionally involved in any event internal and external related to this country, and I can no longer stay aside even without the right to cast my vote. My life and behavior are an open book and it speaks for itself. Furthermore, I am the father of an American citizen and I cannot realize what is wrong with me. Friends and acquaintances who had the first hearing after me have already gotten the citizenship.

A bureaucratic interpretation of my biographical statement could destroy my pride and ambition (a legitimate ambition) and strip me of all political rights.

These are my worries right now. I am afraid that people handling my file have little or no knowledge about the Communist regime. For instance: I was in UTM = UNIUNEA TINERETULUI MUNCITOR = WORKING YOUTH UNION. It was a youth organization run by the Communist party. That happened when I was attending the university and I was registered automatically. To refuse to join it was exactly to resign from attending university. I don't believe I was somebody to graduate without being a UTM member, at least at that time (1948-1953). Usually when somebody has been excluded from UTM (and I recall many cases), it was sure and well known that in a few weeks he had to be ousted from all universities. (I was lucky I kept my membership there.) Similar happened with SINDICAT (which is the Communist party-run-only UNION) for everybody who holds a job at a state company (and all are state companies). The difference is that if they fired you from the job, they didn't exclude you first from UNION (SINDICAT). Membership is automatic, and it is out of the question not to join it.

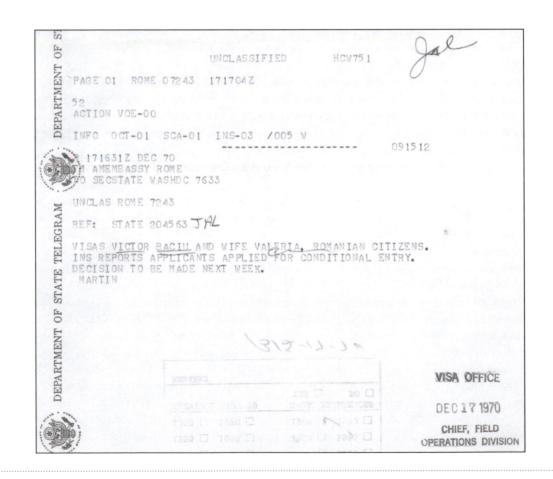

OUTGOING TELEGRAM
DEPARTMENT OF STATE

FORM DS 322-(OCR)   16 DEC 70Z 22   54   204563

ACK   204563   162254Z DEC 70   ROGERS

UNCLASSIFIED   CLASSIFICATION
                    SPECIAL CHARGES

SCA/VO:JALIVORNESE:DB   NAME
12/16/70 EXT 21915   TEL EXT.
SCA/VO - JOSEPH A. LIVORNESE NAME

        OFFICE   NAME   OFFICE   NAME

            CLEARANCES   CLEARANCES

DESIRED DISTRIBUTION

ROUTINE   ROME, NAPLES   ACTION ADDRESSES

INFO PRECEDENCE   INFO ADDRESSES

SPECIAL HANDLING   INITIALS

VISAS

VISAS THIRTEEN VICTOR BACIU AND WIFE VALERIA, ROMANIAN
CITIZENS, RESIDING AT VIA EMANUELE FILIBERTO 271, ROME.
ALSO PLEASE INCLUDE WHETHER THEY MAY BE APPLYING AS
CONDITIONAL ENTRANTS.44

DEPARTMENT OF STATE TELEGRAM

UNCLASSIFIED   HCW751

PAGE 01   ROME 07243   171704Z

52
ACTION VOE-00

INFO OCT-01 SCA-01 INS-03 /005 W
                    --------------------   091512

171631Z DEC 70
AMEMBASSY ROME
SECSTATE WASHDC 7633

UNCLAS ROME 7243

REF: STATE 204563 JAL

VISAS VICTOR BACIU AND WIFE VALERIA, ROMANIAN CITIZENS.
INS REPORTS APPLICANTS APPLIED FOR CONDITIONAL ENTRY.
DECISION TO BE MADE NEXT WEEK.
  MARTIN

VISA OFFICE

DEC 17 1970

CHIEF, FIELD
OPERATIONS DIVISION

The ones who judge my statement (which was perfectly correct) could interpret that I was like a Communist party member, which is definitely something else.

So I have many reasons to worry about. Also, I feel some explanation is necessary, but nobody asks me anything while holding my file for six months with no answer so far. More than this, I offered my help to clarify some questions, but I was told that is a waste of time.

I enclosed a letter to the Department of State, and I would be very grateful to you to forward it to the right place or to suggest to me where I should send it.

With many thanks for your goodwill,

Sincerely,
Nicholas Bageac
March 13 1973

Dear Mr. Allen,

I received your letter at the end of January and I myself don't know how I was able not to answer you so far. You have been much too good to me and a simple apology is too little for my feeling of guilt. However, later is still better than never and once again I start my letter to thank you for all your efforts in assisting me to overcome some of my major difficulties. At the present time it looks to me there are no more problems of that kind which made me appeal to you. In an order to the U.S. authority where you hold office, I believe my demands were legitimate, but I also know that it was your special attention and goodwill I have to consider and appreciate the most for the good and satisfactory results I have obtained.

Referring to the subject of my previous letter, the things went the way you supposed. Mr. Cohen of the INS office kept his promise toward you and solved my case faster than he was going to do it (but as I explained to you in my letter, still much slower than he was supposed to have it done). After you spoke to him (August 19,1972) and at the very next ceremony of naturalization in Brooklyn Court of INS Office, on October 24, I was called and granted the American citizenship. That was my most important event in my lifetime. I have received the recognition of the U.S. and I know that I belong to the U.S. by all means. It is an honor, pride and responsibility. Of course, I'll never stop loving also my native country and its people. It was only the outside imposed and maintained regime which made my life miserable there. For my son's citizenship I have already applied and as soon as my wife will be eligible, she will send the petition. The immediate satisfaction of my naturalization came on September 2 when I voted in the presidential election: first time in my life to elect from more than one candidate. The vote was possible because I registered before though I did not have papers at that time.

All in all, I am a successful immigrant and proud of my achievements. Although my English has a clear foreign accent, I still feel like I was born here. Even I don't realize how I have been able to live for so long in another part of the world. My concern for this country is not less than that of any average American, and I believe more of our problems will be solved and drastically improved in the time to come. I hope that some of the unnecessary liberties have to be trimmed to preserve the true democracy, and I believe there is a solution for all evils of our society.

As far as my family is concerned, everything is fine. We keep the same team of three breadwinners: me, my wife and my father-in-law (who was just promoted as a supervisor at a security guard company). My mother-in-law is backing up the household, my 15-year-old son (who speaks far better English than Romanian) has good results in the ninth grade of high school, and finally my two-year-old daughter is the little terrorist of the whole family. We all are in good health and good spirits. What bothers us is that the house contractor who was supposed to have finished the house in the last months is further delaying the construction; he is building a development of about 75 houses including the roads in that area and we don't know for sure when it will be ready. We still hope that in August or September we will have been moved. The house we bought (with 80 percent in mortgage) has to be built in Westchester very close to Hastings and will fit our family number and requirements, putting an end to many inconveniences we have at this time. This house is our dream, and all our future satisfaction and pleasure are related to it. More and more, the anxiety is growing, but I hope one day the dream will come true, starting a much better life.

You were very kind writing to us about your family, and it was a nice thing learning from you in such a friendly manner.

We wish you and your family all good things and good health.

Thank you again, Mr. Allen, for all you have done for me, and for your kindness and goodwill, which made me fortunate to meet you.

Gratefully yours,
Nicholas Bageac

1980–1989

The decade of the 1980s suffered an unpropitious beginning. Interest rates and the rate of inflation reached a staggering 18 percent. Unemployment was rising. America was in its deepest depression since the Great Depression of the 1930s. The two-career family became the norm; more than half of all married woman and 90 percent of female college graduates worked outside the home. This economic instability, paired with the rising number of women in the workforce, injected new energy into the movement for social change. America loudly questioned the role of nuclear weapons in world affairs, grappled with the abortion question, and furiously wrestled with the conflicting needs of the economy and Mother Nature. By the end of the decade, thanks in part to the productivity gain proved by computers and new technology, more Americans entered the rarified atmosphere of the millionaire and felt better off than they had in a decade.

In 1980 Congress approved a new refugee act that allowed as many as 50,000 homeless to the country each year—a significant increase from the 1965 law. By definition, 10 million of the world's people were eligible—including thousands from small countries largely underrepresented in decades past. Of the 21 countries responsible for the bulk of American immigration, only Greece and Italy had been traditional sources of large numbers of immigrants. Citizens of extremely poor countries such as

Bangladesh had never shown much interest in emigration. The lifting of national origin quotas in 1965 ushered in a new era of greater diversity of immigrants.

Convinced that inflation was the primary enemy of long-term economic growth, the Federal Reserve Board brought the economy to a standstill in the early days of the decade. It was a shock treatment that worked. By 1984, the tight money policies of the government, stabilizing world oil prices, and labor's declining bargaining power brought inflation to 4 percent, the lowest level since 1967. Despite the pain it caused, the plan to strangle inflation succeeded; Americans not only prospered, but many believed it was their right to be successful. The decade came to be symbolized by self-indulgence.

At the same time, defense and deficit spending roared into high gear, the economy continued to grow, and the stock market rocketed to record levels (the Dow Jones Industrial Average tripled from 1,000 in 1980 to nearly 3,000 a decade later). In the center of recovery was Mr. Optimism, President Ronald Reagan. During his presidential campaign he promised a "morning in America," and during eight years, his good nature helped transform the national mood. The Reagan era, which spanned most of the 1980s, fostered a new conservative agenda of good feeling. During the presidential election against incumbent President Jimmy Carter, Reagan joked, "A recession is when your neighbor loses his job. A depression is when you lose yours. And recovery is when Jimmy Carter loses his."

The economic wave of the 1980s was also driven by globalization, improvements in technology, and the willingness of consumers to assume higher and higher levels of personal debt. Although 42 percent of all American workers were female, their median wage was 60 percent of that of men. The rapid rise of women in the labor force, which had been accelerating since the 1960s, brought great social change, affecting married life, child rearing, family income, office culture, and the growth of the national economy.

The rising economy brought greater control of personal lives; homeownership accelerated, choices seemed limitless, debt grew, and divorce became commonplace. The collapse of Communism at the end of the 1980s brought an end to the Old World order and set the stage for a realignment of power. America was regarded as the strongest nation in the world and the only real superpower, thanks to its economic strength. As democracy swept across eastern Europe, the U.S. economy began to feel the impact of a "peace dividend" generated by a reduced military budget and a desire by corporations to participate in global markets, including Russia and China. Globalization was having another impact. At the end of World War II, the U.S. economy accounted for almost 50 percent of the global economic product; by 1987, the U.S. share was less than 25 percent as American companies moved plants offshore and countries such as Japan emerged as major competitors. This need for a global reach inspired several rounds of corporate mergers as companies searched for efficiency, market share, new products, or emerging technology to survive in the rapidly shifting business environment.

The 1980s were the age of the conservative Yuppie (Young Urban Professional). Business schools, investment banks, and Wall Street firms overflowed with eager baby boomers who placed gourmet cuisine, health clubs, supersneakers, suspenders, wine spritzers, high-performance autos, and sushi high on their agendas. Low-fat yogurt, high-fiber cereals and Jane Fonda workout videos symbolized much of the decade. As self-indulgence rose, concerns about the environment, including nuclear waste, acid rain and the greenhouse effect declined. Homelessness increased and racial tensions fostered a renewed call for a more caring government. During the decade, genetic engineering came of age, including early attempts at transplantation and gene mapping. Personal computers, which were transforming America, were still in their infancy.

The sexual revolution, undaunted by a conservative prescription of chastity, ran head-on into a powerful adversary during the 1980s with the discovery and spread of AIDS. The right of women to have an abortion, confirmed by the Supreme Court in 1973, was hotly contested during the decade as politicians fought over both the actual moment of conception and the right of a woman to control her body. Cocaine also made its reappearance, bringing drug addiction and a rapid increase in violent crime. The Center on Addiction and Substance Abuse at Columbia University found alcohol and drug abuse implicated in three-fourths of all murders, rapes, child molestations, and deaths of babies suffering from parental neglect.

For the first time in history, the Naval Academy's graduating class included women, digital clocks and cordless telephones appeared, and 24-hour-a-day news coverage captivated television viewers. Compact disks began replacing records, Smurf and E.T. paraphernalia were everywhere, New York became the first state to require seat belts, Pillsbury introduced microwave pizza, and Playtex used live lingerie models in "Cross Your Heart" bra ads. The Supreme Court ruled that states may require all-male private clubs to admit women, and 50,000 gathered at Graceland on the tenth anniversary of Elvis Presley's death.

1983 Profile

At age 23, Maggi Taylor arrived in America with her husband, Richard, who had been assigned to New York City as a foreign correspondent; years later, when Richard went back to Australia, Maggi chose to stay in America.

Life at Home

- Maggi Taylor was born in 1943 in Sydney, New South Wales, Australia; her sister Jenny was born two years later.
- Her parents split up shortly after Jenny's birth; her mother, with her two daughters, moved in with her parents.
- Her mother left for long periods of time to find work, and "Margaret" and her sister were left almost entirely in the care of their grandmother.
- Maggi was sent to boarding school at age 12, and although she came home for holidays and summer break, The Glennie School for Girls, in Toowoomba, Queensland, was her home until she graduated at age 18.
- Although she was a very bright and friendly girl, Maggi almost always felt alone.
- After graduation, and against her mother's wishes, she defiantly ran off and married Richard, a young writer she had met just a year before while on school break.
- It was 1962, and Maggi and Richard moved to New Zealand, where he had a job; she found work there on a radio station, something an inexperienced young woman could not have done in Australia.
- New Zealand needed educated workers of all kinds, and businesses were willing to hire women.
- The job away from home helped prepare her for her move to America in 1966.
- Since childhood, Maggi had been called by her given name, Margaret.

Maggi Taylor left Australia when she was 23.

Glennie School for Girls, Queensland.

Maggi and Richard in NYC.

INS gave Maggi permission to work in America.

- On her first day in New York, when asked her name, she said, "It's Maggi"; she knew right then that America was the beginning of a new life.
- As a foreigner in a foreign land, she could truly be herself—not her mother's daughter, not the lonely girl in boarding school, and not just her ambitious husband's wife.
- Twenty-three-year-old Maggi and husband Richard lived in New York, where Richard worked as a foreign correspondent from 1966 to 1968, and then both returned home to Australia.
- It wasn't until she was back in Australia, faced with the old familiar attitudes and inhibitions, that Maggi realized she wanted to return to America.
- Then in 1973, after five years away from the United States and her first taste of America, to Maggi's delight, Richard was again assigned to New York.
- As a foreign journalist, he entered the country on an H-1 visa, giving him the right to work and stay in the U.S.
- Spouses, mostly wives of H-1 workers, were technically visitors, but were given a complimentary H-2 visa, so that they would not have to exit and re-enter the country every six months to renew a visitor's visa.
- The H-2 visa was not exactly a working visa, but near enough.
- A much-Xeroxed copy of a notice from the Immigration and Naturalization Service (INS) circulated among the wives that stated that as long as the H-1 visa holder was legally employed, the INS permitted the spouse to work, too.
- Through her connections with the Australian community, Maggi got a job in the Australian Consul as a receptionist.
- She then worked at the UN for United Nations English Language Radio, which eventually led to her career as a boom operator in the film and television industry.
- When in 1980, after seven years in America, Richard returned to Australia, Maggi chose to remain behind.
- Since the late 1970s, Maggi and Richard had been navigating very rocky marital terrain.
- Maggi often worked late on a movie or television shoot or was on location for days, sometimes weeks at a time.
- As a news reporter, Richard had a schedule that was even more erratic and which included lots of out-of-town trips and lots of hotel bars.
- Richard was becoming an alcoholic, and there were other women.
- After his trips, often marked by unaccounted-for absences from his hotel room, Richard would return home contrite, affectionate, and determined to tell almost all to soothe his conscience, regardless of how much it hurt Maggi.
- She forgave him each time and they drifted back to their fractured home life.
- In the spring of 1980, Richard quit his job in order to work full-time on a novel.
- He had a publisher and a contract, but the writing wasn't going well; he said he needed to devote more time to the writing.
- He said he needed to be alone.
- Soon afterward, in June, he left for Newport, Rhode Island, where he met Joan, a visiting, well-off Australian widow.

- She was there enjoying the sunny days; it was, after all, winter in Australia, but she planned to go back to Sydney at the end of August.
- Maggi was working on a film in New Hampshire, and she and Richard talked on the phone every couple of days and even met up when she could get a day off.
- She sensed that something was wrong—more wrong than usual.
- He said the writing wasn't going very well.
- At the end of August, Richard returned to New York, but within a month he left for Australia, claiming research for his book.
- While paying the past month's phone bill, Maggi noticed an unusual number of calls to an unknown number in Australia.
- She called the number and got Joan and Richard at the other end.
- After many heart-wrenching calls back and forth, he and Maggi decided to separate; with or without Joan, he wanted to stay in Australia.
- With or without Richard, Maggi wanted to stay in America.

At United Nations English Radio.

Life at Work

- By the time Maggi and Richard Taylor decided to break up, she found that she was surprisingly relieved, and realized that she did not want him to come back.
- She had started building a career and a life, and in his absence, she realized that she had been lonelier when they were together than she was now.
- She began the long, arduous, and expensive process to get a work permit and then a Green Card so that she could stay in America on her own as a permanent legal immigrant.
- This legal journey would take many letters of inquiry, many phone calls, many forms to fill out, a second set of lawyers, a trip back to Australia, and four years of appointments and paperwork to reach her goal.
- Because of the nature of her work, there were more than the normal delays; she often had to be out of town on location for a shoot, and had to postpone appointments.
- Sometimes she spent 14 straight hours on the set, and could do nothing when she got off work but sleep.
- She never knew on the job how long a sequence would take, or how many takes it would require.
- A missed appointment could mean a long wait before another could be scheduled; government bureaucracies, she came to understand, did not operate on "show biz" time.
- She had to wait for downtime between shoots to write letters, fill out forms, and meet with lawyers or government officials.
- The process dragged on.
- To start the process, she first needed to submit an Application for Alien Employment Certification to the U.S. Department of Labor, Employment and Training Administration; this application had to identify a potential employer and describe the job to be performed.
- Maggi checked all of her film connections and The National Association of Broadcast Engineers and Technicians (NABET) bulletin board; she needed a Sound Man looking for an assistant.
- She heard through the grapevine that Joseph Neeland was looking for someone with multimedia sound experience.
- She had worked on a free-lance project with him in the past, and he was willing to be her sponsor and ready to offer her a full-time job as his assistant.
- He needed a boom person with production skills, and she fit the bill.

- Along with the application, she had to show proof that extensive recruitment efforts made by Nee-land had produced no qualified U.S. workers.
- He was required to advertise the position in a newspaper of general circulation, such as The New York Times, to run for three consecutive days (not on a Saturday).
- She also had to post the same ad on the NABET bulletin board, and had to formally apply for the job herself.
- She then had to include a copy of the ad, and all of the responses, with her application to the Department of Labor.
- The application required a full job description, work hours and salary.
- The description read: "Applicant must be responsible for correlating materials, processing and dubbing in cassette production. Responsible for supervising transfer of sound material, editing and mixing. Must be familiar will all aspects of sound recording, including studio, motion picture and video techniques, post-production, signal processing editorial procedures, boom work and equipment maintenance."
- The position paid $15,000 per year.
- Her labor certification was filed with the Department of Labor in November 1981, and she was hired by Neeland, using her complimentary H-1 visa, based on her H-2 visa, while she waited.
- She was advised that she should expect to wait another year for permanent residence status, and her application for preference status would have to be submitted to the Immigration Service and to the American Consul in Australia.
- When she was called for a visa appointment, she had to leave the U.S. and report to the American Consul in Sydney.
- She had to produce her birth certificate; the Police/Character Clearance Certificate, attesting that she did not have a police record; and a set of her Non-Criminal Fingerprints taken in New York.
- She also needed four copies of a recent photograph, 1½ x 1½ inches, and an update of her job offer, written on her employer's business stationery, and notarized.
- It was a long and costly process, involving lawyers.
- Maggi also had to have a medical examination, including X-rays and blood tests, from a physician who had been approved of in the consular district.
- When everything was in order, her papers were stamped and accepted; her health was perfect, and her past good citizenship was certified—plus, her interview went very, very well.
- She had been coached on what to say to immigration officials, advised to cover up her tattoos—she had several—and had to provide a clean police record from Australia.
- Because of the time difference between the U.S. and Australia, Maggi spent one whole night on the phone (at great expense), and finally got a promise from someone in the police department to send a fax saying that she did not have a police record.
- On the day of the interview she remembered to wear slacks and a turtleneck sweater with long sleeves, and a pleasing smile.

Maggi had a successful career as a boom operator.

- Once Maggi's application for alien labor certification was accepted, she was free to work and live in the U.S.
- Thanks to her past work in radio, and the fact that she had apprenticed on the set of *Contract on Cherry Street,* Maggi continued to get work as a boom operator while she applied for a Green Card.
- A boom operator is an assistant of the production sound mixer.
- The principal responsibility of the boom operator is microphone placement, often using a "fishpole" with a microphone attached to the end.
- Sometimes, when the situation permitted, the boom operator used a "Fischer boom," a special piece of equipment that the operator stands for more precise control of the microphone at a much greater distance away from the actors.

- The boom operator also placed wireless microphones on actors when necessary.
- The boom operator was part of the film's crew, employed during the production or photography phase for the purpose of producing a motion picture.
- Crew are distinguished from cast, consisting of the actors who appear in front of the camera or provide voices for characters in the film.
- The crew is also distinct from the production staff, consisting of producers, managers, their assistants, and those whose responsibility falls in pre-production or post-production phases, such as writers and editors.
- Communication between production and crew generally passes through the director and his/her staff.
- Medium to large crews are generally divided into departments with well-defined hierarchies and standards for interaction and cooperation among the departments.
- Other than acting, the crew handles everything in the photography phase: props and costumes, cameras, sound, lighting, sets, and special effects.
- Caterers (known in the film industry as "craft services") are usually not considered part of the crew.
- Within a short time, Maggi gained a reputation for excellence and was soon in great demand.
- *Eddie and the Cruisers,* an independent, underground hit, was one of her first feature films; she also worked on the full first season of *Law & Order.*
- Maggi had to put in long hours on various film sets, often six days a week during intensive shooting, and traveled wherever she was needed.
- In 1980 she worked on *Imposters,* directed by Mark Rappaport, which was presented at the Museum of Modern Art's New Directors/New Films series.
- She worked on TV commercials, including ones for BMW and Jumping Jack Shoes, and even an independent horror film, *You Better Watch Out,* starring Brandon Maggart and Jeffrey DeMunn.
- She worked on the American segments of foreign films, traveling to Philadelphia, Ohio and Canada.
- As a woman in a man's business, she knew it was important to establish a reputation of being not only good at her job, but also reliable and available.
- Her made-for-TV movies included *Summer,* part of the Edith Wharton Project for PBS, shot in Keene, New Hampshire, and *We're Fighting Back,* a TV movie based on the Guardian Angels with Ellen Barkin.
- Maggi traveled to Minnesota for the videotaping of a performance for television of *The Wonderful World of Oz,* which was produced by the Children's Television Theatre Company, staged at the Guthrie Center in Minneapolis.
- In 1983 she did *Over the Brooklyn Bridge,* directed by Menahem Golan and starring Elliott Gould, Margaux Hemingway, Sid Caesar and Shelley Winters.

Life in the Community: New York City
- Maggi Taylor found a small apartment in Manhattan on East 22nd Street.
- Although she kept in touch with the friends she had made in the foreign press and the Australian Consul when she had first arrived with Richard, she quickly made friends in the film industry, and spent most of her free time with them because of the odd hours they all worked.
- New York as a city was once again reinventing itself.
- In Greenwich Village, Tower Records was attracting 6,000 to 8,000 customers on an average Saturday to shop, watch MTV on 17 large video screens and learn about emerging groups like Human Sexual Response.
- The New York City Council was addressing potential birth defects by requiring liquor stores, bars and restaurants to post signs saying that pregnant women who drink alcohol were in danger of harming their babies.
- All of this while many New York 11th grade students were sitting through interdisciplinary seminars on "Nuclear Issues."

HISTORICAL SNAPSHOT
1983

- Psychologists reported increased marital stress due to computer preoccupation, which was creating computer widows and widowers
- The per-capita personal income in New York was $12,314; in Mississippi it was $7,778
- The first artificial heart recipient, Barney Clark, died after 112 days
- After four years of major losses, the automotive industry rebounded and appeared to be on the road to financial recovery
- The top movies of the year included *Terms of Endearment, The Right Stuff, The Big Chill, Silkwood, Return of the Jedi, Flashdance, Mr. Mom, The Year of Living Dangerously, Yentl,* and *Wargames*
- Actress Jennifer Beals established a new fashion trend in the movie *Flashdance* by wearing clothing with holes and tears
- Anti-drunk driver campaigns were credited with a reduction in automobile accident fatalities for the year
- Television premieres included *The A-Team, Wheel of Fortune, Night Court,* and *Webster*
- *A Chorus Line* became the longest-running show in Broadway history with a record 3,389 performances
- The Supreme Court upheld a Florida law denying high school diplomas to students who failed a literacy test
- Firsts for the year included the hatching of a California condor in captivity, fingerprinting of infants, the first black mayor of Chicago, the first woman in space and a female Secretary of Transportation
- MTV was received in 17.5 million homes and credited with reviving the record industry
- The National Basketball Association contract was the first in sports to include revenue sharing with players
- Martin Luther King, Jr. became the first person since George Washington whose birthday was declared a national holiday
- The Supreme Court reaffirmed its 1973 *Roe v. Wade* decision affirming a woman's constitutional right to an abortion
- Degas' painting *Waiting* sold for $3.7 million—a record price for an Impressionist's work, while Mary Cassatt's *Reading Le Figaro* sold for $1.1 million
- The report *A Nation at Risk* warned, "The educational foundations of our society are presently being eroded by a rising tide of mediocrity that threatens our very future as a nation and our people"
- More than 100 million people watched *The Day After,* a made-for-TV film about a nuclear attack on Lawrence, Kansas

Australian Historical Timeline

40,000 BCE

Aboriginal tribes are believed to have arrived in Australia.

1606

The Dutch ship *Duyfken,* under Captain Willem Janszoon, explored the western coast of Cape York Peninsula; it was the first recorded landfall by a European on Australian soil.

1770

Captain James Cook claimed Australia for Britain; he was the first explorer and navigator to map Newfoundland, the first European to make contact with Australia and the Hawaiian Islands, and the first to circumnavigate New Zealand.

1788

The first fleet from England arrived in Australia and founded the first European settlement and penal colony. An English settlement was founded at Norfolk Island.

1792

The first United States ship, the *Philadelphia,* entered the Australian port in Sydney.

1829

The whole of Australis was claimed as a British territory, and the settlement of Perth was founded.

1833

American merchants opened trading branches.

1836

The U.S. opened the first United States Consul in Sydney with the appointment of James Hartwell Williams, who arrived to take office in 1839.

1850

The University of Sydney was founded.

1851

Gold was discovered, and several thousand Americans arrived in Australia during the 1850s.

1891

A national Australian Convention adopted the name The Commonwealth of Australia and drafted a constitution.

1895

"Waltzing Matilda," Australia's most widely known folk song, was written by poet and nationalist Banjo Paterson.

1901

Australia became a federation free of England.

continued

Timeline . . . *(continued)*

1902

The Franchise Act guaranteed women the right to vote in federal elections, but excluded most non-European ethnic groups, including Aboriginal people.

1914

Australia entered the First World War.

1915

Surfing was introduced to Australia by Hawaiian Duke Kahanamoku, who gave an exhibition of wave riding at the Freshwater Life Saving and Surf Club.

1920

The airline Qantas was founded.

1939

Australia entered the Second World War.

1940

Scientists under Howard Florey developed penicillin.

1945

Howard Florey, Ernst Boris Chain, and Alexander Fleming shared the Nobel Prize for Medicine for the extraction of penicillin.

Australia became a founding member of the United Nations.

1950

Australian troops fought in Korea and against the communist insurgency in Malaya.

1956

Melbourne held the Summer Olympics.

1962

Indigenous Australians gained the right to vote in all states except Queensland.

Australia entered the Vietnam War.

1964

The Beatles toured Australia.

1965

Indigenous Australians gained the right to vote in Queensland.

1971

Neville Thomas Bonner was the first Indigenous Australian to be elected to the Parliament of Australia.

1973

The Sydney Opera House opened.

1983

Australia won the America's Cup, the most famous and prestigious prize in the sport of sailing, and the oldest active trophy in international sport.

Selected Prices

First-class Postage Stamp $0.15
Gas, Regular, One Gallon $1.25
Milk, One Gallon $2.16
Butter, One Pound, Land O' Lakes $1.99
Bacon, Half Pound $1.39
Aspirin, Bayer, 100 Count $1.49
Laundry Detergent, Tide, 49-Ounce Box $1.89
Sewing Machine, Kenmore $159.95
Washing Machine, Kenmore, Large $289.00
DeLorean DMC-12 Sports Car $25,000.00

"27 Spots Raided After an Inquiry on Immigration," By Lindsey Gruson, *The New York Times*, February 10, 1983:

The United States Immigration and Naturalization Service last night raided 27 Manhattan restaurants, night-clubs and massage parlors after obtaining warrants for 24 people on charges of attempting to bribe immigration officers, officials said.

Paul Shechtman, an Assistant United States Attorney for the Southern District of New York, said he could not say how many people were arrested.

Two other suspects are accused of smuggling illegal aliens into the United States through Canada, Mr. Shechtman said. Last night's actions culminated a one-and-a-half-year Immigration Service undercover investigation, dubbed Operation Handlebars, into attempts by illegal aliens to obtain permanent residency cards by bribing officials of the Immigration Service, Mr. Shechtman said. . . .

About a dozen people were taken into custody when several uniformed immigration officers raided the Sam Bok Korean Restaurant and Bar at 127 West 43rd Street, several diners said. The restaurant was one of the first businesses raided in last night's operation.

"I was sitting there waiting for someone to ask if I wanted coffee when our waiter walked by in hand-cuffs," said Geraldine Brooks, a graduate student at Columbia University who was in the restaurant at the time of the raid.

When Miss Brooks, an Australian, asked the officers whom she should pay for her dinner, one officer asked to see her visa. "Luckily I was applying for a visa to Russia this afternoon and had my papers and passport with me or I would have spent the night in jail," she said.

From The New York Times on the Web © The New York Times Company. Reprinted with Permission.

Historical Census Statistics on the Foreign-born Population of the United States Population Division, U.S. Bureau of the Census

- The 1850 census was the first in which data were collected on the birth place of the population.
- From 1850 to 1930, the foreign-born population of the United States increased from 2.2 million to 14.2 million, reflecting large-scale immigration from Europe.
- From 1930 to 1950, the foreign-born population of the United States declined from 14.2 million to 10.3 million, or from 11.6 percent to 6.9 percent of the total population.
- Immigration rose during the 1950s and 1960s, but was still low, then dropped slowly to 9.6 million in 1970, a record low of 4.7 percent of the total population.
- Since 1970, the foreign-born population of the United States has increased rapidly due to large-scale immigration, primarily from Latin America and Asia.
- The foreign-born population rose from 9.6 million in 1970 to 14.1 million in 1980.
- As a percentage of the total population, the foreign-born population increased from 4.7 percent in 1970 to 6.2 percent in 1980.

Australians Living in the United States

1960	22,209
1970	24,271
1980	36,120

Comments from Recent Immigrants

I had been in the U.S. a few days and my fiancé and I planned a dinner with some of his friends who were eager to meet me. The restaurant was rather noisy and during the course of the evening I stood up and informed them quite loudly I was going to the toilet. There was a slight pause, as all at the table looked at me in shock. I can only imagine what they must have thought; in America "going to the toilet" is like saying you are going to the dunny or the bog house.

—Cathy

I was in horror when my hubby's friend and his son, after an enjoyable evening, told us they were going to go shag. I am used to the term "go shag" meaning to go and have sex. Apparently in Texas, to "go shag" means to leave.

—Mandy

In the USA, a fanny is a rear end, and in Australia a fanny is the front end of a lady's anatomy. Try not to get the two mixed up! So, when you're in the USA, wear your fanny pack on your butt!

—Sam

I was complaining to some American colleagues about how rigid the co-op board of my apartment building is, specifically about a rule forbidding pot plants above a certain height on the balconies. They were astounded that I was allowed to have pot plants at all. After some clarification, I found that in the U.S., there's a big difference between "pot" plants and "potted" plants.

—Katherine

Australian Products Available in America

- Sheepskin and wool boots and slippers, as well as leather gore-sided boots.
- Felt hats made from a blend of rabbit and hare fur.
- Waterproof coats and hats and other outdoor all-weather clothing.
- Australian wool fleece, especially bred for hand spinning and weaving.
- Art: Aboriginal art, including bark paintings and carvings. Photographs of Aboriginal rock art.
- Artifacts: Aboriginal artifacts, including boomerangs, swords, spears, shields.
- Didgeridoos, one of the world's oldest wind instruments; all sizes of beginner to professional models available.
- Tea Tree Oils: Medicinal and cosmetic products made from *Melaleuca alternifolia* trees. Known anti-fungal and antibiotic.
- Foods: Australian foodstuffs, including lollies, Nestle Milo bars, Arnott's Biscuits (Australian cookies), Vegemite (a salty sandwich spread), Australian teas, including invigorating Australian morning tea, subtly sippable Australian afternoon tea, and more.

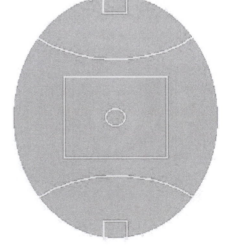

Australian football players and oval field.

Popular Music in Australia
Online: The Australian Government Culture and Recreation Portal

- Like rock music, popular, or pop music had its origins in the 1950s and 1960s, and is one of Australia's most successful musical exports.

- Australian pop music has been going strong, with stars such as Little Pattie, who made it big after she was spotted by talent scouts at the Bronte Surf Club in 1963.

- Her first hit was "He's My Blonde-Headed Stompie-Wompie Real Gone Surfer Boy." In 1966, at just 17 years of age, she was the youngest entertainer to play to Australian troops in Vietnam.

- During the 1960s other performers, such as Col Joye, the Bee Gees, Normie Rowe, and the Seekers also became well known for their tunes and (mostly) clean-cut images.

- Many of these bands or individual performers are still performing today. Helen Reddy rose to international success with her pop anthem, "I Am Woman." When she wrote the song in 1972 she tapped into the growing feminist movement.

- Like so many Australian artists of the time, and since, Helen Reddy moved to the United States before finding the fame she sought.

- The Bee Gees are an example of an Australian pop group that achieved international success as singers, songwriters, and performers. The brothers, Barry, Robin, and Maurice Gibb emigrated to Australia from Britain as children. They lived in Brisbane and recorded many of their early songs in Sydney.

- After relocating to the U.K. in 1967, they produced dozens of songs that made it to the top of the charts in the U.S., England and Australia, including their late 1970s hits "How Deep is Your Love," and "Stayin' Alive." They also wrote many hits for other successful artists.

- Two Australian pop musicians who are considered ambassadors for the Australian pop industry are John Farnham and Olivia Newton-John.

- John Farnham's first notable recording was "Sadie the Cleaning Lady" (1968). It was the largest-selling single by an Australian artist of the 1960s.

- Olivia Newton-John's first major success was in 1974 with the single "I Honestly Love You," which was a hit in the U.K. and the U.S. In the U.S., Olivia Newton-John branched off into country music.

- In 1974, she was awarded the Country Music Association's Female Vocalist of the Year. She then starred in *Grease* and *Xanadu*. In 1981, she had a number one pop hit in the U.S. with the single "Physical."

Maggi's Grandfather's Grandfather, Clancy

Poet and nationalist Banjo Paterson, who wrote Australia's most widely known folk song, "Waltzing Matilda," in 1895, also wrote "Clancy of the Overflow," a poem based on James Clarence Clancy D'Arcy Webster, Maggi's grandfather's grandfather.

Clancy of the Overflow
By Banjo Paterson

I had written him a letter which I had, for want of better
Knowledge, sent to where I met him down the Lachlan, years ago,
He was shearing when I knew him, so I sent the letter to him,
Just "on spec," addressed as follows, "Clancy, of the Overflow."
And an answer came directed in a writing unexpected,
(And I think the same was written with a thumb-nail dipped in tar)
'Twas his shearing mate who wrote it, and verbatim I will quote it:
"Clancy's gone to Queensland droving, and we don't know where he are."

In my wild erratic fancy visions come to me of Clancy
Gone a-droving "down the Cooper" where the Western drovers go;
As the stock are slowly stringing, Clancy rides behind them singing,
For the drover's life has pleasures that the townsfolk never know.

And the bush hath friends to meet him, and their kindly voices greet him
In the murmur of the breezes and the river on its bars,
And he sees the vision splendid of the sunlit plains extended,
And at night the wond'rous glory of the everlasting stars.
I am sitting in my dingy little office, where a stingy
Ray of sunlight struggles feebly down between the houses tall,
And the foetid air and gritty of the dusty, dirty city
Through the open window floating, spreads its foulness over all.

And in place of lowing cattle, I can hear the fiendish rattle
Of the tramways and the buses making hurry down the street,
And the language uninviting of the gutter children fighting,
Comes fitfully and faintly through the ceaseless tramp of feet.

And the hurrying people daunt me, and their pallid faces haunt me
As they shoulder one another in their rush and nervous haste,
With their eager eyes and greedy, and their stunted forms and weedy,
For townsfolk have no time to grow, they have no time to waste.

And I somehow rather fancy that I'd like to change with Clancy,
Like to take a turn at droving where the seasons come and go,
While he faced the round eternal of the cash-book and the journal
But I doubt he'd suit the office, Clancy, of "the Overflow."

1984 Profile

Twenty-three-year-old Rigo Garcia came to America to make enough money to build a house for himself and his fiancée in his native Costa Rica.

Life at Home

- Rigo Garcia knew in his heart he always wanted to live in Costa Rica, but to build a house, he needed money.
- The community of San Lorenzo, Costa Rica, was nurturing, warm and secure; he had spent no more than a dozen nights in his entire life away from the community of 312 people.
- His occasional trips to San Jose over Cerro de la Muerte, the Mountain of Death, which often took four to six hours by car, had taught him how treacherous the world can be.
- The activity of a city was overwhelming and exhausting.
- When on his last trip his car broke down, halfway to San Jose in the peak of the mountains, he had never felt so alone.
- At that moment, living in San Lorenzo for the rest of his days offered great appeal.
- But when his trip to San Jose was over, he was reminded once again that any man who wanted to make money must journey into the world and could not live within his mother's womb forever.
- Besides, Rigo was desperately in love with a dark-eyed beauty and broke as a Costa Rican monkey.
- Already three of his friends had journeyed to Paterson, New Jersey, and returned with tales of ready work, eager women and more riches than a Tico farm boy could imagine.
- Rigo had stopped his education at age 14 to work alongside his father on the farm, where a three-acre plot sustained the family's food needs and 10 acres of coffee plants provided ready cash every season.

Rigo Garcia left Costa Rica when he was 23-years-old.

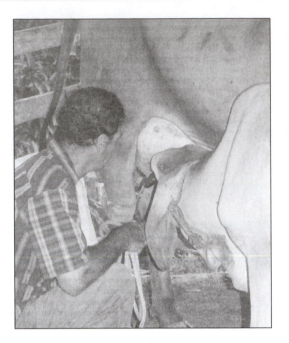

Rigo's father worked the family farm.

- Many of the neighbors also grew sugar cane, which could be crushed locally and sold in nearby San Isidro de El General, but Rigo's father never liked farming cane.
- The rough roads of mountainous San Lorenzo caused each car and truck to struggle and strain up every path and down every gully, and thus charge too much to haul away the sugar mash.
- For almost a decade, dependable electricity had energized the community; for nearly twice that time, money earned in America had been used to build the houses that everyone envied.
- Some of the houses took years to construct as local boys living in America sent dribs and drabs of money back to their parents and brothers each month for the construction of the house.
- Sometimes the money would be enough to build a single wall or construct a roof, but rarely was it enough to build the whole house at one time.
- But Rigo knew that Paterson, New Jersey, was no paradise; his best friend Renaldo had admitted that behind all the big talk and ready cash were a lot of lonely and miserable times.
- Some days work was hard to come by; some weeks there was none at all, and the landlords had no sympathy for Spanish-speaking men who did not pay their rent on time.
- Besides, no place, even America, was as friendly as San Lorenzo, where a portion of every Sunday was set aside for visiting each other's homes.
- Up the hill lived his aunts, down the hill his uncles and grandfather; across the valley lived his best friend, and his nine brothers and sisters and grandparents and half a dozen cousins all in one house.
- Even though the Catholic Church, constructed with decorative spaces in the wall shaped like crosses, was just down a hill and served as a vital anchor for the community, Sunday visiting was the buoy that allowed everyone to grow up together.
- Rigo's dream was to earn enough money so he could build an entire house with his own hands with only the help of friends and then present it to his fiancée.

- He had it all planned out: a concrete block house painted green, a red metal roof and walls outfitted with rollout jalousie windows which let in the cool air and kept out the rain.
- His house would have two couches that faced each other so his family could talk to each other every night; too much television was bad for families.
- As a special gift to his new bride, he planned to purchase beautiful green and red tile he had seen in San Isidro to cover the entire floor so the house would always look clean, bright and welcoming.
- On his last day in San Lorenzo before leaving for Mexico, Rigo watched a pair of beautiful green parrots fly across the valley near his parents' home.
- He took it as a symbol he would return soon prepared for marriage.
- To make the journey bearable, more psychologically than anything else, he took time to pick fruit from the mango trees and orange trees and then collected several sweet lemons that grew near his parents' home.
- Then he climbed into the back of his cousin's white Toyota pickup truck and rode for six days to the U.S./Mexican border.
- When they were one hour away, Rigo was instructed to crawl into a space beneath the bed of the truck for the crossing.
- There he stayed for three hours while his cousin and his wife—both U.S. legals—passed through customs and into America.
- By prior agreement, his cousin did not stop to let him go out until they were well within U.S. borders and away from suspicious eyes.
- On his first night in America, Rigo stayed with his cousin and his wife in a small apartment in Paterson, New Jersey.
- As planned, Rigo and his cousin both rose at six o'clock the next morning and headed toward a labor collection site where men congregated to get construction jobs.
- Rigo was excited by the opportunity but appalled by the smell of the urban landscape; he clearly was not in Costa Rica anymore.

The Catholic Church in San Lorenzo.

The beauty of Costa Rica.

Life at Work

- On that first day, when the man shouted, "I need a roofer," Rigo Garcia put up his hand even though he didn't have a clue what "roofer" meant in English.
- Quickly he was told to join a group Costa Ricans, Guatemalans and Mexicans—all of them standing around chatting separately, waiting for the job to start.
- Meeting fellow Ticos from Costa Rica helped settle his anxiety.
- In fact, when one of them asked him in Spanish if he really knew anything about roofing, Rigo admitted the truth and everyone laughed.
- "We will teach you," an older man said, " Ticos stick together."
- That was also the day he learned not to stand in front of the gringos who would shout at him in English and expect an answer.
- Standing in the back was always better: don't make eye contact, don't look like you know the answer, and just stand there and watch what the others do.
- Rigo discovered that he had the perfect skills to be a roofer; he was agile, sure-footed and strong.

Rigo's cousin smuggled him across the US border.

Rigo worked as a roofer in New Jersey.

- In the company of other Ticos, work was even fun, even if the foreman spent an enormous amount of energy yelling at everyone in English.
- Rigo quickly learned the construction terms and tools he needed to know by their English names; after all, doing well on the job meant returning to Costa Rica sooner.
- But clearly, some accommodations were being made for Spanish speakers; gringo foremen had learned to identify items they wanted to discard as "trash" and also in Spanish as "basura."
- At a neighborhood grocery store, signs aimed at the Spanish-speaking population read, "Esta Bud es para usted"—"This Bud's for you"—or advertised that a pesticide called Combat would spell the end of "problemas con las cucarachas"—"problems with cockroaches."
- Rigo learned to be cautious around English speakers, especially the police; since most officers in the field only spoke English, Spanish speakers would be taken to the jail to be read their rights in Spanish, and he had no desire to be close to any jail, American or Costa Rican.
- America brought several revelations.
- Never before had he seen toilets in which the waste paper was flushed away; in San Lorenzo where the sewer pipes were gravity fed and flowed into a distant field, toilet paper created too many problems when flushed and thus was placed in a trash can next to the toilet.
- He also discovered that hot water showers were truly a great invention; all his life he had taken cold showers and never thought of washing any other way.
- Non-political his entire life, Rigo became more interested in reading about American relations with Central America in the Spanish-language newspapers.
- By all appearances President Ronald Reagan was trying to get Costa Rica involved in the latest Central American squabbles even though Costa Rica had long ago dissolved its army to avoid such conflicts.
- The president also became very interested in America's immigration policies.
- Recently, immigration officials had raided job sites throughout the country in an effort to catch illegal aliens who held better-paying jobs.
- The sweeps were designed to apprehend 3,000 to 5,000 aliens, and open up jobs for citizens and legal aliens.
- Rigo was concerned that the arrests would give the impression that undocumented workers were responsible for the nation's high unemployment rate and stir up even more animosity toward Spanish-speaking immigrants.
- He was also concerned about getting caught and losing the $7-an-hour job, which paid more than twice the minimum hourly wage of $3.35.
- In the past, raids had targeted illegal aliens performing low-skilled manual labor—jobs that American citizens did not want.

Life in the Community: Paterson, New Jersey

- Paterson, New Jersey's origins date back to 1791, when Alexander Hamilton helped found the Society for the Establishment of Useful Manufactures.
- The plan was to harness energy from the Great Falls of the Passaic to secure economic independence from British manufacturers.
- French architect, engineer, and city planner Pierre L'Enfant, who developed the plans for Washington, D.C., was the first superintendent for the project.
- The industries developed in Paterson were powered by the 77-foot-high Great Falls and a system of water raceways that harnessed the power of the falls.

Factories in Paterson NJ were powered by harnessing the energy of the Great Falls.

- Dozens of mill buildings and other manufacturing structures associated with the textile industry and later, the firearms, silk, and railroad locomotive manufacturing industries, clustered around the raceways.
- In the latter half of the 1800s, silk production became the dominant industry and formed the basis of Paterson's most prosperous period, earning it the nickname "Silk City."
- The city became a Mecca for immigrant laborers who worked in its factories.
- Since its beginnings, Paterson had been a melting pot.
- Irish, Germans, Dutch and Jews settled in the city in the nineteenth century.
- Italian and Eastern European immigrants soon followed.
- As early as 1890, many Syrian and Lebanese immigrants also arrived in Paterson.
- Many second- and third-generation Puerto Ricans had been calling Paterson home since the 1950s, and recently first-generation Dominican, Peruvian, Colombian, Central American, Mexican, Bolivian, and Argentine immigrants arrived.
- Western Market Street, sometimes called Little Lima, was home to many Peruvian and other Latin American businesses.
- The Great Falls Historic District, Cianci Street, Union Avenue and 21st Avenue housed several Italian businesses.
- To the north of the Great Falls was a fast-growing Bengali population.
- Park Avenue and Market Street between Straight Street and Madison Avenue was heavily Dominican and Puerto Rican.
- Main Street was largely populated by Mexicans, with a declining Puerto Rican community.
- Costa Ricans and other Central American immigrant communities were growing in the Riverside and Peoples Park neighborhoods.
- Broadway, or Martin Luther King Jr. Way, was predominantly black, as was the Fourth Ward and parts of Eastside and Northside.
- Paterson's black community was composed of African Americans of Southern heritage and more recent Caribbean and African immigrants.
- Every summer, Patersonians enjoy an African American Day Parade, a Dominican Day Parade, a Puerto Rican Day Parade, a Peruvian Day Parade, and a Turkish American Day Parade.
- Annually, Paterson's Peruvian community celebrated "El Señor de los Milagros" or "Our Lord of Miracles" on October 18-28.

HISTORICAL SNAPSHOT
1984

- Dow and six other chemical companies settled with Agent Orange victims for $180 million
- The California Wilderness Act was passed which designated 23 new areas in 20 states
- The Supreme Court modified the Miranda ruling to say that illegally obtained evidence was admissible in court if otherwise obtainable
- Vanessa Williams, the first black Miss America, resigned after sexually explicit photographs surfaced in a national magazine
- Major movie openings included *Amadeus, The Killing Fields, Places in the Heart, Beverly Hills Cop, Ghostbusters, The Gods Must Be Crazy, The Karate Kid* and *Terminator*
- For the first time the American Cancer Society made specific dietary food recommendations endorsing whole grains and fruits and vegetables high in vitamin A and C
- Bruce Merrifield won the Nobel Prize in chemistry for developing an automated method to make proteins
- *The Bill Cosby Show* premiered on television featuring for the first time a professional upper middle class black family
- The Olympics produced a record $150 million surplus after being run as a private enterprise for the first time
- After four years of work and a cost of $55 million, the Museum of Modern Art in New York reopened twice its original size
- Androgynous rock singers such as Michael Jackson, Boy George, Prince, Duran Duran and Grace Jones captured national attention
- President Ronald Reagan proclaimed in his State of the Union speech, "America is back standing tall, looking to the eighties with courage, confidence and hope"
- The unemployment rate reached 7.5 percent; the high on the Dow Jones Stock exchange was 1,287
- Television premieres included *Miami Vice; The Bill Cosby Show; Murder, She Wrote;* and *Highway to Heaven*
- The ages of the U.S. Supreme Court justices became an issue in the national election with five of the nine justices over the age of 75
- Sheep cloning, a woman walking in space, the Apple Macintosh, a state requiring seatbelts use, male bunnies at the Playboy Club and PG-13 ratings all made their first appearance

President Ronald Reagan.

- The Reagan administration threatened to withdraw aid from nations that advocated abortion
- A study indicated that the U.S. incarcerated more people than any other western country— one out of every 529

Costa Rican Immigration Trends

- Costa Ricans who have emigrated and settled in the United States do not exhibit the same characteristics as many other Hispanic groups.

- They have not had to flee their country as refugees from political oppression or from extreme economic circumstances.

- Consequently, there have never been waves of Costa Rican emigrants.

- Costa Ricans who have decided to immigrate to the United States generally have married an American; they have been hired to work in the United States after completing a degree in an American university; or they have come to various jobs and trades in the United States.

- Less than 50,000 Costa Ricans have immigrated to the United States since 1931.

- Costa Ricans who immigrated to the United States tended to establish their residences in the states of California, Florida, Texas, and the New York City/New Jersey area.

- Since there are relatively few Costa Rican Americans in the United States, they normally do not form communities or barrios, as is usually the case with Mexican Americans, Puerto Rican Americans, and other Central American Hispanic groups.

- Costa Rican Americans tend to maintain their heritage, but also integrate into their environment quickly, especially if they want to join a church or if they have children in the public school system.

- If both parents speak Spanish, chances are that the children will be raised bilingually.

- However, if only one parent speaks Spanish, the children will usually grow up speaking only English.

- Every year in the month of December, the Costa Rican people enjoy their *fiestas cívicas*, which are similar to the state fairs in the United States.

- In addition to the varied types of food available and the usual entertainment, there are simulated bullfights in which youths try their luck "fighting" balloon-decorated *toros guacos* or mean bulls, by pulling their tails and touching their rumps.

- Costa Ricans believe in calling upon Jesus and the saints for assistance when they are in need or in danger.

- Each saint is thought to have a special mission or to be able to satisfy a particular need; Costa Ricans pray to Saint Anthony, for example, if something has been lost or misplaced.

- Colorful sayings often typify the Costa Rican attitude: "At night all cats are grey" (People can get away with things that they would not normally do in the daytime); "Between husband and wife not even a pin's head should intervene"; "When times become difficult, put on a happy face"; "An egg-eating dog will not break his habit even if one burns his mouth"; and "Skinny dogs get fleas."

Selected Prices

Apple Macintosh Computer	$2,500.00
Butter, per Pound	$1.99
China, 10-Piece Tea Set	$69.00
Coffee, per Pound	$2.19
Gas Grill	$179.99
House, Four-Bedroom, New York	$156,000
Lawn Mower, Craftsman	$299.99
Screwdrivers, Stanley Set of Four	$26.95
Shotgun, Winchester 12-Gauge	$1,200.00
Woman's Leather Bag	$49.00

"107 Immigrants Arrested As Illegal in Jersey Raid," Associated Press, August 20, 1983:

The Immigration and Nationalization Service has arrested 107 suspected illegal aliens and is holding them in custody awaiting deportation hearings as a result of a raid on a South Plainfield handbag factory, authorities reported today.

Immigration agents spent more than a day processing employees of the factory, all but three of them Haitians.

They were detained as they arrived at the Bag Bazaar factory early Thursday morning, according to the supervisory investigator, Louis Galoppo.

Mr. Galoppo said that of the 167 people detained, 60 were found to be in the country legally and were released. The others are being held at an immigration facility in Brooklyn and in county jails pending deportation hearings before an immigration judge, he said.

Officials said it was the largest round-up of suspected illegal aliens by the Immigration Service in Newark in memory.

Mr. Galoppo said the factory's owners do not face legal action because there is no law preventing employers from hiring illegal aliens.

He said that besides the Haitians, one of the persons detained was Costa Rican and two were from Panama. Officer Green said the investigation was continuing.

"Costa Rica Is Gateway for Illegal U.S. Immigrants," *The New York Times*, February 7, 1984:

Hundreds of Taiwanese and Cuban immigrants have been entering the United States using Costa Rican passports, either forged or obtained under false pretenses, according to Government officials and businessmen here.

According to the Minister of Foreign Affairs, Carlos Gutierrez, several known international terrorists have also been caught with Costa Rican passports or travel documents.

In addition, foreigners trying either to conceal political pasts or facilitate business travel have purchased legal or bogus Costa Rican passports, officials here say. These foreigners include Libyans, Iranians, mainly relatives and associates of Shah Mohammed Riza Pahlevi, and Nicaraguan supporters of the assassinated dictator, Anastasio Somoza Debayle.

"It's been too easy to obtain a Costa Rican passport, and this gives us a very bad image," Mr. Gutierrez said. "That's why we are now establishing controls."

Mr. Gutierrez said people involved in international terrorist activities who had been caught with bogus Costa Rican passports over the last few years included an Italian fascist named Freda who was deported from Costa Rica, a left-wing Basque separatist, Gregorio Jimenez, who is in jail here, and an unidentified Central American who is being held in Madrid for purported involvement with a Spanish terrorist group.

In trying to crack down on the illegal trade in passports, Costa Rican authorities recently broke up a passport counterfeiting ring and tightened procedures for issuing passports to foreigners.

Deputy Minister of Government Enrique Chacon said that a group of 10 Costa Ricans and Cubans were detained here this month after two groups of Cubans were caught in the United States with fake Costa Rican passports. The police also closed two printing presses supposedly used to doctor the passports.

Mr. Chacon said the authorities had also discovered the theft of about 200 newly printed blank passports from the national press.

According to Costa Rican sources, the illegal passport ring stole small batches of newly printed Costa Rican passports and inserted pages from passports bought from Costa Ricans holding valid United States tourist visas. The forged passports have been selling for $5,000 each.

The Deputy Minister asserted that "organized crime" was behind the racket, in which passports were sold mainly to Cubans wishing to emigrate to the United States. He said more suspects were being sought in both Costa Rica and the United States.

Costa Rican authorities have also begun revoking some of the hundreds of passports issued to foreigners and used to facilitate their entry into the United States and various European countries.

Last October Costa Rica stopped its policy of permitting foreign "retirees" who invest in the country and live here at least four months a year to obtain a Costa Rican passport valid for 10 years. A businessman who has helped foreigners obtain these passports estimates that "well over 1,000" so-called retirees have obtained Costa Rican passports. But "98 percent of them never live here," he said. He said these include about 1,000 Taiwanese, mainly businessmen and politicians, 250 Libyans, 150 Iranians and an unknown number of Nicaraguans.

"With these Costa Rican passports they can get easily into European countries and the U.S.," he said. He said many of the Taiwanese had entered the United States, usually through Los Angeles, and hired lawyers there to "fix up" their papers so they can stay permanently.

From The New York Times on the Web © The New York Times Company. Reprinted with Permission.

"Bilingual Parents Dismayed By English's Pull on Children," By Mireya Navarro, *The New York Times*, August 31, 1996:

In Marcel A. Apple's bedroom, the book "The Three Little Pigs" rests on a shelf next to "Mi primer libro de palabras en Espanol" ("My First Book of Spanish Words"). The three-year-old can sing along to both a Sesame Street song and "La Bamba," or have as much fun watching "Barney," a purple, English-speaking dinosaur, as he does "Tito," a blue, Spanish-speaking shark.

But when Marcel tired of pounding on a piano one recent afternoon and sat on the lap of his Nicaraguan nanny, it was English that he spoke.

"Estan descansando?" ("Are they resting?") Josefina Avendano asked him, pointing at a picture of a countryside in a children's book.

"No, they're eating," he answered.

"I try to put him in an environment where there's as much Spanish spoken as possible but it never seems to be enough," said Marcel's mother, Esther Perez-Apple, a Cuban American who herself is trying to recapture the Spanish she heard while growing up in her native New York. "He knows he can speak in English and people could understand him."

Last month Congress entered into a heated debate over English-only legislation, with proponents insisting that the very survival of American culture and civilization, as well as the language, was at stake. On a more down-to-earth level, the English-only drive has also been fueled by resentment against bilingual rules and other accommodation of immigrants, both old and young, who have not learned English.

But what new immigrant families across the nation are learning, as their predecessors did before them, is that the power of American culture, and particularly, the lure of television, is so strong that it is a challenge to raise a child who can speak a foreign language fluently.

Parents send their children to foreign countries for summer vacations, hire bilingual nannies and read bedtime stories in a cacophony of tongues, all in an effort to pass on the family's language, give the children a linguistic advantage for the future or simply enrich them culturally. Still, the languages, parents say, often lose out to television, schools and peer pressure.

Even in Miami, one of the country's most Hispanic areas, parents say it is hard to get their children to learn Spanish. The challenge to raise a child to be bilingual can be even greater for families speaking less-prevalent languages like German, Swedish or Japanese, parents say.

continued

"Bilingual Parents Dismayed By English's Pull on Children," . . . *(continued)*

This experience runs counter to concerns that English is in danger of being diluted. And some bilingual educators argue that anti-immigration sentiments and the English-only laws, which generally require government business to be conducted in English, only help foster a climate that plays down the importance of other languages. They say that for a child to become bilingual it is essential that he places value on speaking more than English.

"You can have a bilingual child a lot of different ways," said Barbara Z. Pearson, a linguist who is part of a University of Miami research team on bilingualism. "But what you have to make sure is that the kid hears both languages, values both languages and wants to speak to the people who speak those languages. . . ."

Many immigrant families see English as so fundamental to a better life that they allow their children to even shun their first language, researchers who have studied the subject say. Bilingual educators say English usually becomes the first and sometimes only language by the first American-born generation.

"Many teen-agers say they never spoke Spanish and their parents can't speak English," said Professor Fradd, who conducted the study for the Greater Miami Chamber of Commerce. "Something happened there trying to pass, to assimilate, not being seen as different."

1985 PROFILE

After a lifetime of dreaming, two and a half years of planning, and 18 months in America, Edwidge Dominique was no closer to being a highly recognized artist than he had been when he left Haiti.

Life at Home

- Twenty-three year-old Edwidge Dominique's anger was on the edge of bitterness.
- Since he was a small boy, Edwidge had been fascinated by the vibrant colors of Haiti's landscape and had grown adept at using paint to differentiate shadow from dimness, light from brightness.
- Color subtlety was so fascinating to Edwidge, he spent nearly a month doing six paintings of an acacia tree illuminated by different light cast at various times during the day.
- His older brothers and sisters thought the tree series was an enormous waste of time; "Pretty pictures will not feed you or get you a wife," his older sister Kaiama hissed.
- But his grandmother, the only parent he had ever known, loved his artwork and said over and over, "One day you will be famous."
- That was Edwidge's dream.
- How this fire could be quenched became clear when he met an American couple who were in Les Cayes to visit the Sisters of Charity Orphanage in the middle of the city.
- As was his habit, Edwidge was selling his latest paintings that day in the market alongside fruit vendors, woodworkers and dressmakers when the Americans stopped, admired, and then bought everything he had on display without haggling over the price.
- He trembled at the sight of US$85.00 in his hand.
- Unable as he was to understand English, only later did Edwidge learn from an old fruit dealer that the woman had said, "These will sell for five times more in America. He is very talented and should display his work in New York and Miami."
- Edwidge had never experienced such happiness; her words were burned in his soul.

Edwidge Dominique, shown here with his sisters, left Haiti to become a famous artist.

Painting by Haitian artist.

- In America, he told himself, "I can be an artist who is famous and rich."
- So for the next two and a half years, Edwidge was consumed by the idea of America, particularly Miami, where his second cousin was living and doing well enough so that every month he sent money home.
- Everyone was in agreement that he should go, especially if he planned to send money back; even his doctor, who was trained in Cuba, said, "I think you should go."
- Since the late 1970s thousands had fled Haiti with no money, using makeshift boats and totally lacking any documentation, taking only their fervent prayer "God is good" as a sign that somehow they would be admitted to the United States.
- Most were not.
- Thousands drowned during the journey; more were caught by the Coast Guard or Immigration officials and unceremoniously sent back to Haiti.
- Some made it to America and asked for asylum or at least the same privileges offered Cubans fleeing that neighboring Caribbean island.
- Terrified that an all-volunteer army of unemployed, illiterate Haitians was about to descend on America's privileged Gold Coast, Florida's residents fought back.
- Cubans should have special privileges because they were fleeing Castro's communism, they said; Haitians, they remarked, were running from poverty and would only bring more crime, AIDS, drugs and additional burdens for the area schools.
- But after a series of battles in American courts, some Haitians were given the status of "Cuban/Haitian entrant," which provided an ambiguous legal position in the United States, but did allow them to stay.
- More Haitians, most of whom could not swim, transformed themselves into "boat people" in hopes of gaining entry into the U.S.; the U.S. Coast Guard was instructed to seek them out and make sure they didn't arrive.
- Those who were captured at sea were rapidly repatriated to Haiti with the cooperation of the Haitian government and the Reagan Administration.
- By 1983, Edwidge knew that unrest was rumbling throughout Haiti and that the Duvalier family might one day be dethroned.
- Now was the time to chase his dream, he decided.
- In all, he had gathered together $480, which he gave to a well-dressed man from Port-au-Prince who promised that Edwidge would land safely in Miami "without even getting your feet wet."
- It was not the first lie Edwidge would be told.

Life at Work

- Edwidge Dominique's boat trip to America began in a rubberized raft loaded to overflowing with desperate people; 14 nervous men were jammed into a raft designed to hold eight.
- Upon hitting the first wave, the raft sagged into the sea and everyone was soaked within minutes.
- Edwidge was able to keep his spare clothing dry but the art supplies he had packed so carefully were ruined.

- The raft was then paddled very slowly into the inky night to a waiting trawler that had seen better days and soon was overwhelmed by the number of rafts that congregated at its side.
- The trawler, operating mostly at night, drifted toward Miami for more than two weeks; Edwidge's many questions went unanswered even when a group of men threatened the captain's life if land was not found soon.
- The final stage of the trip was by a small speedboat, with a faulty motor, that was intended to take the illegal immigrants to an isolated dock south of Miami near Homestead.
- Underpowered and overloaded, the boat accidentally dumped Edwidge into the water when they were just within sight of land.
- Edwidge swam for his life, guided only by lights at the dock.
- Exhausted by the long trip and the arduous swim, he offered no resistance to the police awaiting his arrival.
- Altogether the voyage had taken 18 days; the boat carried supplies for about 10 days and the trip ended in a detention facility, courtesy of the United States Government.
- For 11 months, Edwidge was held at the Krome Center in Miami while politicians and federal agencies considered whether he and nearly 15,000 other Haitian refugees should be allowed to stay in the country.
- His family did not know whether he had arrived or was lost at sea.
- No paints, no privacy and few lawyers who spoke Creole were available.
- Then, he was freed from detention without any explanation he could understand.
- He was given special permission to stay temporarily in America but denied all immigration papers that would allow him to work.
- Housing was provided until his case was settled.
- Edwidge felt listless and unable to paint; without the special light of Haiti his paintings grew dark, less vibrant and apparently unsellable.
- Every day he waited for the knock on the door that said he would be sent back; maybe it was a knock he would embrace, he repeatedly told himself.

Life in the Community: Haiti and Miami, Florida

- Even though Haiti was one of the poorest countries in the Western Hemisphere, Haitians had a rich culture and historical heritage.
- Haiti was the second-oldest republic in the Americas, established by slaves in a revolt against the French, grounded on the "rights of man" in 1804.
- Historians believe that the defeat of Napoleon's forces by the Haitian slave rebellion paved the way for the Louisiana Purchase, which doubled the size of America and dramatically reduced the holdings of the French on the continent.
- The French took possession of Santo Domingo, as colonial Haiti was known, at the end of the seventeenth century.
- By the middle of the eighteenth century, when 400,000 imported African slaves worked at the sugar cane, coffee, cotton and indigo plantations, Haiti was the most profitable colony in the world, far more valuable to the French than 13 North American colonies were to the British.
- But little of that wealth remained after the land was divided into subsistence farms and Western powers, including the United States, established punitive policies against the only country in the Americas to be established through a slave revolt.
- Situated between Spanish-speaking Cuba and the Dominican Republic, mountainous Haiti retained its distinct linguistic and cultural identity; French Creole and French remained the major languages.

- Haiti was at once the most densely populated and the most rural nation in the Caribbean region; peasant agriculture dominated the economy.
- Even in the southern seaport city of Les Cayes, with a population of 36,000, the electricity was unreliable, sometimes only working four hours a day.
- At night the entire city was dark except for a few dozen homes and businesses outfitted with solar power collectors.
- Locally made charcoal was used for heating, and clean water was a luxury; hundreds of children died yearly from waterborne diseases.
- To escape the poverty of Haiti, a growing body of Haitians, including the country's educated elite, gravitated to Miami and created the nucleus of a community that needed Creole-speaking teachers, professionals and entrepreneurs.
- Officially, 50,000 Haitians were said to live in the Miami area; Haitian community leaders put the figure closer to 75,000.
- Educated Haitians found in Miami an agreeable climate and a sense of community that had been denied them in exile elsewhere.
- Haitians who grew up in other parts of the U.S. were often ashamed of their nationality; Miami changed that, especially for professionals.
- However, the people who came by boat encountered a stream of legal and social problems in the United States, principally, the inability to gain asylum as political refugees.
- Twenty-five thousand Haitians in south Florida faced proceedings that could lead to their departure from the United States.
- The Haitian boat people were catapulted into the national spotlight in 1980 when some 15,000 began arriving in south Florida on the heels of the larger Cuban refugee boatlift.
- The United States 1980 Census found 90,000 people who said one or both parents were of Haitian ancestry, and the Immigration and Naturalization Service estimated that there were probably an equal number of Haitians in America illegally.
- A survey published by the Behavioral Science Research Institute of Coral Gables estimated that 22,800 Haitians resided in the Edison-Little River community, which included Little Haiti.
- The survey concluded that half were unemployed, half could not converse in English and two-thirds had a household income of less than $150 a week.
- Despite the high unemployment rate among Haitians, four times that of the U.S., the study noted that there was no greater dependency upon public agencies for assistance among Haitians than other groups.
- The report said this reflected the strong desire among many Haitians to be self-sufficient rather than depend on agencies for help.
- But the Haitian community had found few ways to confront the public reaction to the discovery that some victims of AIDS were Haitian.
- Of the 1,641 AIDS cases reported in the United States, 5 percent were Haitian, yet AIDS was being identified as a disease associated with homosexuals, drug users and Haitians.

HISTORICAL SNAPSHOT
1985

- A highly addictive, inexpensive cocaine derivative known as crack began appearing in America
- The Live Aid concert in Philadelphia and London was viewed by 1.6 billion people worldwide on television and grossed $70 million for famine-starved Africa
- A Nielsen study on television watching reported that young children spent more than 27 hours a week in front of the TV
- After Coca-Cola introduced a new formula known as New Coke, public reaction forced it to reintroduce the Coca-Cola Classic
- In professional baseball, Pete Rose broke Ty Cobb's record with his 4,192nd hit
- Milk cartons with photos of missing children, the Ford Taurus, a female Harlem Globetrotter, Wrestlemania and the Rock and Roll Hall of Fame all made their first appearance
- The Nobel Peace Prize went to the International Physicians for the Prevention of Nuclear War founded by two cardiologists
- The discovery of a 4.4 million-year-old anthropoid jawbone in Burma created speculation that our human ancestors may have originated in Asia and migrated to Africa
- Television premieres included *The Golden Girls, Spencer for Hire*, and *The Oprah Winfrey Show*
- Studies indicated an estimated 27 million American adults were functionally illiterate
- ABC was acquired by Capital Cities Communications for $3.43 billion
- American spy John Walker was turned in by his wife and daughter
- General Westmoreland dropped his $120 million libel suit against CBS for its documentary alleging that he deceived the public during the Vietnam War
- Movie premieres included *Out of Africa, The Color Purple, Kiss of the Spider Woman, Back to the Future, Rambo,* and *The Breakfast Club*
- Worldwide, more than 2,000 people died in plane crashes, marking it the worst year in civil air travel
- *ARTnews* magazine pressured the Austrian government to return 3,900 works seized by the Nazis during World War II
- Top albums of the year included *Born in the U.S.A.* by Bruce Springsteen, *Like a Virgin* by Madonna, *Private Dancer* by Tina Turner and *No Jacket Required* by Phil Collins
- *Lonesome Dove* by Larry McMurtry won the Pulitzer Prize for fiction; *The Flying Change* by Henry Taylor captured the prize for poetry

Selected Prices

Bicycle, Aero Urban Cowboy	$600.00
Briefcase, Leather	$565.00
Camcorder	$994.00
Coca-Cola, Two-Liter	$1.00
Doll, Playskool	$24.97
Ice Cream, Dove Bar	$1.45
Martini for Two	$1.08
Modem	$119.95
Synthesizer, Yamaha	$188.88
Walkman, Sony	$19.95

For the Yuppie Puppy

Introducing the remarkable new COMPAQ PORTABLE II

NEW LIFE NEW MOOD

What's wrong with this picture?
Nothing.
That's why it's called social drinking.
One of the good things in life.

The House of Johnnie Walker

Griswold did it.

WHY COPY ON A FLOPPY?

"Haiti's Heavenly Waters," by Patti M. Marxsen, *The Journal of Haitian Studies,* Fall 2005:

From the air, Haiti resembles a sleeping dog. The landscape is golden and angular as mountains and more mountains rest in the soft interplay of sunlight and deep fissures of rock and jungle. At an altitude of 35,000 feet, the human eye can trace the ridge line of those mountains, the silvery thread of rivers, the coastal edge of the country embroidered with blue and white beaches. Oddly, the floating world below appears to be uninhabited, stilled by heat and covered in a haze of violet shadow.

I marvel at this quiet image of Haiti. It flickers like a silent film and, like a silent film, it is sheer illusion. Down below, on the ground, this nation comprising the western third of the island of Hispaniola is far from uninhabited. It bursts at the seams with over eight million people, most of them poor and illiterate, too many of them malnourished or suffering from diseases the world knows how to cure. Any day, at any hour, Haiti's roads and villages are teeming with activity, pulsating with hope, rage, fear and anger. This human energy streams out of yards and alleys to where wild palm, hibiscus, and bougainvillea decorate village houses. The Haitian kay is made cheerful with thick coats of pink, yellow, and turquoise paint and roofed in corrugated metal. Often clustered around an outdoor cooking pavilion, these tiny houses form lakou, or small compounds, where generations of families live together. From the lakou, people move out into the countryside to haul water or to buy and sell food. Below the deceptive softness of my aerial view, this is a world in perpetual motion.

First published in the Journal of Haitian Studies.
Reprinted with permission.

Life in Haiti.

"A Helping Hand for the Haitians; Passaic Resident Is Filling the Role of Honorary Consul," by Diane Fiske, *The New York Times*, March 28, 1982:

To Jean Claude Levy, honorary consul of Haiti in New Jersey, his title is not merely decorative. Rather, Mr. Levy, who is not a Haitian, sees himself as helping the thousands of Haitian immigrants in New Jersey who live in poverty. He considers his mission as one of assisting them in settling in a school or job.

The 38-year-old Mr. Levy lives at 110 Main Street here. He runs a secretarial school in East Orange called the First School, which teaches language skills in French and Spanish as well as typing, shorthand and the use of business machines. Many of his students are Haitian or Cuban.

Mr. Levy was born in Morocco and is still a French citizen. He first saw Haiti in 1971 while on his honeymoon. "My American wife and I looked at a map of the Caribbean—and there was Haiti," he recalled. "I said, 'Let's have an adventure,' so we went to Haiti. It was love at first sight. I felt that, in many ways, Haiti is like Morocco. The climate and the people are very similar. The people are themselves and exist independently of the political climate."

Noting that Haiti is only 70 miles from Cuba, Mr. Levy said he did not think that the United States should "overlook a friendly country so close to its border."

According to Mr. Levy, his secretarial school is the only American school with branches both in the United States and Haiti. The status of many Haitians lies somewhere between immigrant and refugee, for the situation there does not present a sufficient emergency to permit them to be classified as people who have fled to avoid persecution.

Each Haitian must be granted asylum on an individual basis. "Many of these people are waiting for their standing to be determined before they register their children in American schools," Mr. Levy said. "Meanwhile, they themselves cannot find work."

Since September 1980, when he was appointed honorary consul, Mr. Levy has been working with Representative James J. Florio, Democrat of Runnemede; Representative Peter W. Rodino, Democrat of Newark, and other members of the New Jersey Congressional delegation. They have been trying to get support for legislation that would allow Cuban and Haitian immigrants to be able to convert to permanent resident alien status after two years in this country.

Mr. Levy, who said that New Jersey's Haitians—they are second in number only to those in Florida and New York City—would like to establish a Haitian civic center in East Orange.

The center would acclimate the Haitians to American life and help them decide how to earn a living. "There is a need for schools in New Jersey to accommodate these Caribbean people," Mr. Levy said. "I decided to take it upon myself in the mid-1970s to try to help educate these people, but there is much more to be done."

Mr. Levy said that he traveled to Haiti 10 to 15 times a year and had conferred with President Jean-Claude Duvalier about the schools there. "Haiti has the image of being a smiling, happy country where people are thinking poor," he said. "We are trying to change that."

"33 Haitians Drown as Boat Capsizes off Florida," by Gregory Jaynes, *The New York Times*, October 27, 1981:

Thirty-three Haitians drowned this morning in choppy waters just north of here after their jerry-built 30-foot boat capsized less than a mile from shore. Thirty-four others from the overloaded vessel swam to shore and were taken, many of them in tears, to a federal detention facility for illegal aliens.

Immigration authorities said it was the worst such accident recorded since waves of immigrants from the impoverished Caribbean country began heading for the United States 10 years ago. Gov. Bob Graham of Florida called it "a human tragedy which has been waiting to happen," and said he would press the federal government to work with Haiti to stop the flight to these shores.

Two months ago the Reagan Administration ordered the Coast Guard to interdict Haitian boats loaded with illegal aliens on the high seas and return them to Port-au-Prince, the Haitian capital. The first interdiction came last night, 123 miles northwest of Port-au-Prince, when the cutter *Chase* intercepted a leaky 30-foot boat filled with 57 passengers.

That boat, too, sank in rough seas shortly after the Haitians were transferred to the Chase. It was the first seizure of Haitians the Coast Guard had made since it began patrolling the Windward Passage off Haiti's northwest coast on Oct. 11.

In Miami, a Coast Guard spokesman said of the drownings, "It's just such a tragedy," adding, "It's what we were hoping to avoid" by intercepting vessels.

The boat apparently struck a reef and split apart in a four-foot chop before dawn today. As the lights began to go off from the expensive condominiums along Highway A1A in Hillsboro Beach, a Broward County village 10 miles north of Fort Lauderdale, the bodies began to wash ashore.

By midday, rescue workers had recovered the bodies of 19 men and 14 women, one of whom was pregnant. The surf had ripped the clothes off many of them . . . .

Residents concerned about crime and low-paid workers, fearful that job-hungry immigrants could be a threat, have been stridently vocal about stopping the tide, but this morning the word from most quarters was sympathy. "It is a human tragedy," Governor Graham emphasized, adding at one point that "probably this has already happened and went undetected."

The bodies were taken to the Broward County morgue. A spokesman for the Medical Examiner's Office there said that autopsies would be performed and that attempts would be made to identify them. "Then," said the spokesman, "the bodies will have to be disposed of in some respectable and tasteful fashion."

"6-Month Surge in AIDS Reported," UPI, August 5, 1983:

The number of cases of acquired immune deficiency syndrome that are reported weekly has more than doubled in the last six months, federal health officials said today.

The national Centers for Disease Control said the number of cases of the disease, known as AIDS, increased to a weekly average of 53 in July, as against 24 a week in January and 11 a week in July 1982. The daily average of cases reported to the centers increased to nearly eight a day from three or four a year ago.

As of Aug. 1, the federal agency said, 1,972 cases had been reported and 331, or 17 percent of the total, occurred over the last six weeks. Of all patients, 759, or 38 percent, have died.

New York City reported most of the cases, with 44 percent; San Francisco had 10 percent and Los Angeles 6 percent, the agency said in its *Morbidity and Mortality Weekly Report*.

Better Cooperation Cited

Dr. James Allen of the centers' special task force for AIDS traced the increasing number of reported AIDS cases in part to better cooperation by state health departments in reporting the disease. But he added that there was also no doubt about the rising incidence.

Seventy-one percent of the victims have been homosexuals. Other groups considered high risks for the disease are people who take narcotics intravenously, recent Haitian immigrants and hemophiliacs. There have been 117 cases that either did not fit into any of these groups, or the risk factors were not known.

Copyright UPI, August 5, 1983. Reprinted with permission of United Press International.

"Rising Immigration Tide Strains Nation's Schools," by Gene I. Maeroff, *The New York Times*, August 21, 1983:

America's classrooms, confronted by the biggest influx of immigrant students since early in the century, are once again feeling the heat that turned them into melting pots for previous generations of newcomers. The nation's face is changed by waves of fresh arrivals from Latin America, the Caribbean and Southeast Asia, as well as more traditional European sources. The impact is especially apparent in elementary and secondary schools which are struggling to absorb the immigrant young—hundreds of thousands each year.

It is pervasive transformation. In Boulder High School in Colorado, for example, students celebrate the Hmong New Year with their new classmates from Laos; at Abraham Lincoln High School in Brooklyn, new arrivals from the Soviet Union teach a few words of Russian to their fellow students; in south Florida, school districts search desperately for teachers who can speak the Creole French used by Haitian refugees. The development is also fueling a national debate over the extent to which the schools are obligated to help children preserve the Hispanic heritage that forms the background of the largest group of immigrants.

The speed with which some of the new arrivals are making their presence felt can be seen at Kinlock Park Junior High School in Miami, where Sandra and Soledad Arguelles, who arrived with their family just three years ago from Cuba not knowing any English, were graduated this year as co-valedictorians with straight-A averages. The sisters, a year apart in age but in the same grade, were part of an unexpected influx of 18,327 children from Cuba and Haiti who surged into the Dade County public schools between April 1980 and January 1982.

continued

"Rising Immigration Tide Strains Nation's Schools," . . . *(continued)*

Altogether in 1980, the United States officially received 808,000 immigrants, more than in any year since 1914, according to the Immigration and Naturalization Service. In addition, the federal government estimates that a total of 3.5 million to 6 million aliens have entered the country illegally.

Experts are not sure precisely how many school-age children are among the new arrivals, legal and illegal, but they know that the numbers are large and that the task of helping them fit into American society is falling primarily on the nation's schools. It is a responsibility that in some parts of the country, notably Florida, Texas and California, has taken on overwhelming proportions. The task has been complicated by the necessity of having to deal with large numbers of other children, mostly of Hispanic background, who are unable to pursue an education fully in English, though their families have been in the country for at least a generation.

The implications of having to absorb both immigrants and native-born students with limited English proficiency are enormous, affecting curriculum, costs, the availability of teaching jobs and educational and social philosophy. "All of this gives us tremendous diversity, but it is also one of the biggest problems facing the schools," said Robert Alioto, superintendent of the San Francisco public schools. "All that diversity requires us to render special assistance to help kids make the transition. Some of them are right out of the hills of Asia with little or no formal education. It is a great challenge to our staff."

While the situation evokes nostalgic images of the era when New York City's Lower East Side or Chicago's Maxwell Street teemed with fresh arrivals speaking a Babel of languages, there are notable differences. A major one, authorities believe, is that the effect on the schools is far greater today than in earlier immigration waves.

A larger proportion of the new arrivals are of non-European background, and if they are literate it is sometimes in a language that uses an alphabet alien to American schools. At the same time, the schools during the current tide of immigration have committed themselves to respect the culture of immigrant children and, often, to use their native language as a teaching vehicle until they become proficient in English.

Whereas many immigrant children at the turn of the century never entered school but went immediately to work at a time when child labor was accepted and menial jobs were abundant, today's new arrivals are almost certain to enroll. The schools in turn are now more likely to try to dissuade them from dropping out.

"The truth is that the immigrant children dropped out in great numbers to fall back on the customs and skills their families brought with them to America," Colin Greer wrote in *The Great School Legend*, a book challenging traditional notions about immigrants and the public schools.

An effect of this newer policy of accommodation is that group-achievement scores in schools with large numbers of new arrivals have suffered, contributing to lower overall averages in ways that are seldom acknowledged by critics who cite test scores as evidence of failure by the schools. . . .

Higher education as well has been affected by the influx of immigrants, and some colleges and universities are making allowances for gaps in the backgrounds of prospective students who have had only a portion of their earlier schooling in this country.

City College of the City University of New York had an enrollment of 13,500 last year, of which 42 percent were not born in the United States. They came from more than 80 countries, and it was necessary to offer classes in English as a second language to 1,812 of the students.

The United States and Haiti are something other than the richest and the poorest countries in the hemisphere. They are also its two oldest republics. Rarely, in fact, have two countries been as closely linked as the United States and Haiti.

—Dr. Paul Farmer, *The Uses of Haiti*

Creole is seen both as the truly Haitian form of expression and as a kind of baby talk without grammar. Creole marks a person as "stupid." On the other hand, the Creole phrase pale fwanse ("to speak French") means "to be a hypocrite" . . . Creole is not the only aspect of Haitian peasant culture that is denied legitimacy. The folk religion, vodoun, is perceived by the elite as powerful, even a necessary resort at times, but a threat to their status in Western civilization.

—*The Refugees in America in the 1990s*

News Feature

"Employing Micro-credit in the Community of Les Cayes, Haiti," by the Rev. Kenol Rock, Episcopal priest:

The first time that I had the intention to start the micro-credit was when I went to worship in one of the congregations located in the countryside named Savanette.

I met some women who told me: "Fr. Rock, how can you find some money to borrow so we may open even a small business to survive? We are helpless." I said, "Well, I can find some money to loan you and we can create an activity named micro-credit; however, the first thing that we are going to do is to gather together and learn the rules that you need to follow."

I taught them the rules which were based on honesty and trusting. Also in this gathering I motivated them that the more they managed well the loan received, the more they will have opportunity to change their life of dependency into a life of interdependency in the family. It was our first start; since then, the life of the women has been rewarded. The following ideas will give not only the impacts but also the manner to use the micro-credit for the benefit of the poorest.

After training based on honesty and trusting, I found some money from the generous partners in the USA, particularly in Kansas City. I did the distribution of the credit according to what each person listed. I realized that the best way to decrease the level of poverty was by extending this activity of economic development from below. Since the micro-credit has been started in the community of Les Cayes, remarkable progress has been made. With a small step, we can make a big step; also with the micro-credit we can make a positive difference by ameliorating gradually the poverty in the world.

The micro-credit can bring a new paradigm in the family where the wife becomes a real partner for the husband, rather than an object. For instance, since the program began, the women retrieve a certain dignity by having the opportunity to not depend totally on the husband in the house. They can even make decisions as needed, as well the men. There is, now between woman and man, a real partnership based upon mutual respect, which is a good model for the children in the house. Therefore, micro-credit is a key tool of transformation of the community of the poor into a community of justice and equity.

The women are more successful in the micro-loan activities than men, according to the experiences that I had during my period in the south part of Haiti. In the five congregations of the missions of Les Cayes, which had the opportunity to participate in such activity, there were 60 women and 40 men who were enrolled; 80 percent of the women have made success and only 15 percent of men have made success.

As a result, in the poor community the women manage money much better than men. With simple sewing they can make clothing, or they can buy a bag of rice to resell it and make a quick profit. So, there are tremendous activities that the women can make even a tiny profit in the community. We reward the women who are the best workers of the year in the micro-credit, and also we augment the rate of the loan. This is a strategy that we use to encourage them to move forward, and this is the best reason we have been successful.

1990–2007

The economy limped into the 1990s under the gloom of recession, but quickly exploded into the Era of Possibilities. This robust economy empowered and emboldened the nation's traditionally less well off. The ranks of the African American middle class swelled; women filled half of all seats at the nation's law and medical schools, and Hispanic workers immigrated in droves to chase the dream of economic prosperity in a foreign land. Predictably, this growing population Spanish-speaking workers ignited raucous rounds of debate concerning America's immigration policy—especially as it related to immigrants arriving by way of Mexico. This alarm was further exacerbated by the tragic attacks of September 11, 2001, as the government scrambled to seal its borders and protect its people from foreign terrorists. By 2005 immigration and concerns about the number of "illegal" immigrants in America was one of the most visible political issues on the landscape.

America's disabled gained new rights and more respect, and America's Christian fundamentalists found their political voice. And as wealth grew, the possibilities flourished. Colleges became overcrowded, while the buying power and media attention paid to America's youth exploded. Personal computers, fully capable of competing with television and its rapidly expanding array of specialized channels, became a fixture in millions of homes. The

1990s were characterized by steady growth, low inflation, low unemployment and dramatic gains in technology-based productivity. The resulting expansion was particularly meaningful to computer companies and the emerging concept known as the Internet—a technology that would revolutionize business, media, consumer buying and interpersonal relations in the opening years of the twenty-first century.

As the 1990s opened, America was struggling with a ballooning national debt and the economic hangover of the savings and loan industry. Media headlines were dominated by stories of rising drug use, crime, racial tensions and the increase of personal bankruptcies. Family values became a political touchstone. Guided by Federal Reserve Chair Alan Greenspan's focus on inflationary controls and a declining deficit, the U.S. economy soared, producing its best economic indicators in three decades. By the end of the 1990s the stock market was posting record returns, job creation was at a 10-year high and businesses were desperately searching for qualified workers in a technologically savvy world. As a result, the 1990s gave birth to $150 tennis shoes, condom boutiques, pre-ripped jeans, digital cameras, DVD players, and 7.7-ounce cellular telephones. The decade was also a time of debate, much of it powered by 24-hour programming on television channels and the resurgence of talk radio. Americans publicly debated limits on abortion, tougher criminal enforcement, the role of affirmative action, bilingual education, food safety and Internet child pornography.

History will record that the new century began in the United States on September 11, 2001, when four American commercial airliners were hijacked and used as weapons of terror. After the tragedies at the World Trade Center in New York; Shanksville, Pennsylvania; and the Pentagon in Washington, DC, Americans felt vulnerable to a foreign invasion for the first time in decades. America's response to the attacks was to dispatch U.S. forces around the world in a "War on Terror." The fist stop was Afghanistan, where a new brand of terrorist group known as al-Qaeda had planned and executed the attacks under the protection of the country's Taliban rulers. America's technologically superior weaponry was impressively displayed as the Afghan government was quickly overthrown, although capturing al-Qaeda leader Osama bin Laden and stabilizing a new government proved more vexing. With the shell-shocked economy in overall decline and the national debt increasing at a record pace, the United States rapidly shifted from Afghanistan to Iraq. Despite vocal opposition from traditional allies such as Germany and France, President George W. Bush launched Operation Iraqi Freedom with the goal of eliminating the regime of Saddam Hussein and his cache of weapons of mass destruction. The invasion resulted in worldwide demonstrations, including some of America's largest protest marches since the Vietnam War. As in the invasion of Afghanistan, the U.S. achieved a rapid military victory, but struggled to secure the peace. When no weapons of mass destruction were found, soldiers continued fighting while an internal, religious civil war erupted; support for the war waned and vocal protest increased.

Despite the cost of the war, the falling value of the dollar and record high oil prices, the American economy began to recover by 2004. Unemployment declined, new home purchases continued to surge, and the full potential of previous computer innovation and investment impacted businesses large and small. Men and women of all ages began to buy and sell their products on the Internet. eBay created the world's largest yard sale; Amazon demonstrated, despite sneering critics, that it could be the bookstore to the world; and we all learned to Google, whether to find the exact wording of a Shakespearian sonnet or the menu at Sarah's Pizza Parlor two blocks away. At the same time, globalization took on a new meaning and political import as jobs—thanks to computerization—moved to India, China or the Philippines, where college-educated workers were both cheap and eager. American manufacturing companies that once were the centerpiece of their community's economy closed their U.S. factories to become distributors of furniture made in China, lawn mowers made in Mexico or skirts from Peru. The resulting structural change that pitted global profits and innovation against aging textile workers unable to support their families resulted in a renewed emphasis in America on education and innovation. If the U.S. was to maintain its economic dominance, the pundits said, innovative ideas and research would lead the way.

Professional women, who for decades had struggled to rise past the glass ceiling in their companies, began to find bigger opportunities in the 2000s. Significantly, the promotion of a woman to a top slot in a Fortune 500 company ceased to make headlines. Some top female CEOs even began to boldly discuss the need for more balance in the workplace. Yet, surveys done at mid-decade showed that more Americans were working longer hours than ever before to satisfy the increasing demands of the marketplace and their own desire for more plentiful material goods. In some urban markets the average home price passed $400,000; average credit card debt continued to rise and the price of an average new car, with typical extras, passed $20,000.

1998 Profile

Emigration from India led Gashwin Gomes from a study of geology to one of theology when he settled at the University of South Carolina.

Life at Home

- Gashwin Gomes experienced a more advantageous childhood than most people in India.
- His father's occupation as an economist and his involvement in numerous business operations brought atypical opportunities, including a brief stay during Gashwin's early childhood in the United States.
- The family lived in Maryland, near where Manu Gomes, Gashwin's father, worked as an economist at the World Bank in Washington, DC.
- Some of his earliest childhood memories were of the United States—playing catch with his brother Gautam or chasing a neighbor's dog, Rusty, around in the backyard.
- When the U.S. assignment ended, his family returned to India; Gashwin was five years old.
- In his home country of India his father worked as an economic advisor for Merrill Lynch and oversaw its Indian mutual funds.
- Gashwin's mother held a position within the Indian Government's Administrative Service.
- Because Gashwin's parents both worked, a housekeeper took care of the home and watched after their two sons.
- The Gomes family grew up in a modest-sized residence: a four-bedroom condominium located in downtown Bombay.
- It was in an attractive location next to a nature sanctuary; thus, the area's beauty could be seen from the windows and balcony and would not be spoiled by the constant development in the city.
- To get around town, the family owned two Indian-made cars; one was a Fiat and the other an Ambassador.

Gashwin Gomes left India after college to further his studies in the United States.

A temple in Bombay.

- Academics were important to Gashwin's father.
- A graduate of the London School of Economics, he knew that education was imperative to success and economic stability for his children, a concept he constantly reinforced with his two sons.
- Gashwin struggled in school initially and would often cringe when bringing home scores below his father's expectations.
- He also heard a few taunts from his older brother, who did better academically.
- By high school Gashwin had discovered a strong interest in science.
- Learning about the formation of the natural world and its life fascinated him.
- He was especially interested in the physical environment; rocks and geography were his passions.
- Gashwin's bedroom shelves were covered with rocks that he discovered outside in the neighborhood or on family trips.
- His desire was to collect every known rock in the world, even the rarest forms created by volcanic activity.
- His father wished him the best of luck with this task, knowing full well that it was next to impossible.
- Education was not the only thing important to the Gomes family; religion held a special significance as well.
- Living in a Hindu household, the family made a point of practicing their beliefs, especially around the big festivals of Diwali, Dussera and Holi.
- These holy days included visits to the neighborhood temple, spending the occasions with relatives and eating wonderful family prepared meals.
- Often Gashwin and his cousins received lots of sweets from family members as part of these celebrations.
- With his success in high school, Gashwin was accepted into St. Xavier's University of Bombay, a private accredited university in Bombay administered by the Jesuits.
- It was here that he focused on his passion for geology.
- Gashwin's father retired from Merrill Lynch as soon as Gashwin received his acceptance to college.

Gashwin's large extended family gathered during holy day festivals.

- After Gashwin's parents moved to his father's hometown of Baroda, India, he remained in the family condo and attended to his university studies.
- The education system of India was strongly influenced by the British and still maintained striking similarities.
- When accepted to university, a student traditionally followed one of the three academic levels from high school—Humanities, Commerce or Science.
- The three-year program only focused on core studies based upon the program; thus, one would not traditionally see a student in the Commerce program taking a history course traditionally reserved for a Humanities student.
- However, coursework at St. Xavier's was untraditional.
- To Gashwin's surprise, he was required to take a select number of humanities courses outside of his academic tract of science.
- The experience exposed him to some history and foreign language studies; already fluent in Hindi and English, he also added the German language to his résumé.

Gashwin excelled at St. Xavier's.

- The university system in India traditionally required mostly rote memorization and less critical thinking; due to substantial government academic subsidies, the cost was approximately between US$300-$400 over the entire three years in school.
- Gashwin embraced his academic studies in geology and focused on petrology, the study of volcanic rocks.
- His scientific coursework required the least amount of mathematics and enabled him to conduct research in an outside environment.
- Socially, Gashwin spent time with friends, gathered at local dance clubs on the weekend, and watched sporting events, like soccer and cricket, on television.
- Students typically lived at home with their parents or in an apartment near school; the universities in India did not provide housing, neither dorms nor apartments, for students.
- Although like most of his friends, Gashwin was a practicing Hindu, he slowly became interested in Christianity and the teachings of Catholicism.
- This change happened gradually during his time learning from the priests at St. Xavier and becoming involved at St. Peter's Church in a suburb of Bombay.
- During his last year of university, Gashwin shared with his parents his desire to convert from Hinduism to a Christian faith.
- Though it caught his parents by surprise, they realized the decision was thought out and their son desired this conversion.
- Although bewildered at this spiritual change, they supported his decision.
- Between his academic coursework and his religious instruction at St. Peter's Church, the year was exceptionally busy for Gashwin.
- Nonetheless, he excelled in his studies.
- By April of 1993, he graduated from St. Xavier's with his degree.
- It was also during this period that he applied to a number of universities in the United States to work on his graduate education.
- His older brother Gautam acquired his doctorate of computer science at Rensselaer Polytechnic Institute in New York.
- Upon completion, he accepted a professorship at the India Institute of Technology in Delhi.
- Gashwin applied to six universities in the United States, which included the University of South Carolina and the University of Rochester in New York.

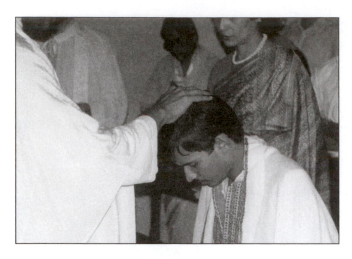

Gashwin was baptized into the Catholic faith.

With his godmother in India, before leaving for the United States.

University of Rochester.

- Both of these universities offered full scholarships in the field of geology.
- After serious contemplation and without visiting any of the options, he decided to attend the University of Rochester because his graduate advisor was receiving a grant in petrology research in India.
- It was an ideal opportunity—studying his passion and having the opportunity to return to India for research.
- Prior to his departure, Gashwin maintained strong ties with his new religious community and was baptized at St. Peter's in August.
- It was an important event and, though reluctant, his family attended the service.
- With graduation and his baptism behind him, he needed to prepare for his journey to the United States for graduate school.
- He packed two large suitcases and a few books—the sum of all he was taking with him from India.
- Outside of his belongings, his father stressed the importance of extended family.
- Family was not only the immediate relatives in India, but those he would meet and with whom he would share his life within the United States.

Life at Work

- Excitement was the initial emotion for Gashwin Gomes on his journey to the United States, but fatigue set in from the 20-hour flight on British Airways with layovers in London and Boston.
- By the time he arrived in Rochester, he was exhausted and ready for some sleep.
- Fortunately, his extended family network was already being formed.
- At the University of Rochester, the Indian Student Association sent members to greet arriving Indian students at the airport.
- Bhanu, an undergrad student, was there to meet and welcome Gashwin to Rochester and allowed him to stay at his apartment for a couple of days until he could find his own place.
- A couple of days of sleeping on a couch motivated Gashwin to find an apartment with another grad student and make contact with the Catholic community on campus.
- His father's advice on establishing an extended family was sound, Gashwin discovered, and made the transition into the United States culture less of a challenge.
- Gashwin's work-study job required him to assist his advisor with grading papers and course projects, conducting field work for research and instructing students on field assignments.

- Because his work was in geology, it was not uncommon for him to be lugging a lot of rocks around the university.
- His biggest learning curve was computers.
- Undergraduate students had no access to them in India; the only time he used his father's computer was to play video games.
- In the United States, all of his written assignments required that he fully understand Windows 3.1 and WordPerfect.
- It struck him as odd seeing everything printed using computer software on campus—flyers regarding fraternity parties, group meetings and university events.
- The university community was expressing that it was literate with software but using the technology on trivial matters—an observation he shared in handwritten letters to family and friends in India.
- His fellow graduate students were actively using a new and growing form of electronic communication, but few people in India used e-mail.
- Therefore, the number of computer messages he received was limited except for university matters such as student meetings or discovering information on the World Wide Web with Internet software GOPHER and Mosaic.

Outside his apartment in Rochester.

- His biggest concern was that his advisor "miscommunicated" the focus of his research when he recruited Gashwin to Rochester; the focus was not petrology research, but instead he had a grant to study water isotopes—a field that held no interest for Gashwin.
- With the support of the Catholic community on campus, where he developed a number of close friendships with people who were also Indians, Gashwin decided to transfer.
- He had no desire to spend four years studying in a field in which he had no interest and reporting to an uncommunicative advisor.
- He talked to his parents about the problem, but calls home were expensive and usually cost $1 per minute.
- Knowing he received a full scholarship at the University of South Carolina, he contacted the department in Columbia to see if there was an opportunity to transfer.
- After a tour and interviews with faculty, he was accepted at the beginning of the fall semester; his future advisor was able to maintain his offer of the scholarship.
- Upon his return to Rochester, Gashwin kept the exciting news quiet, telling only a small circle of friends, mostly those he knew within the Catholic community.

Life in the Community: Columbia, South Carolina

- Gashwin's ability to adapt to South Carolina was aided by his American-style accent which he had acquired early in his childhood.
- Therefore, he was more easily accepted by Americans than were his friends who had more of an "Indian English" accent.
- Upon arrival in Columbia, South Carolina, Gashwin established his extended community within the Catholic student center; he did make a few friends within the Indian community, but most Indians did not share his religious faith.
- Through an ad search he found an apartment a few blocks from the university with a master's in business student at USC.
- He quickly partook of one of the common activities during football season: tailgating outside the stadium with his girlfriend Sarah McClutchen and some of his classmates.
- He also started to define himself based upon his involvement at St. Thomas More, on the campus of USC, the Catholic student center that had become a second home.

Columbia, South Carolina

- Even though he shared Christianity with his new American friends, his view of family relationships was different from theirs.
- Most openly discussed family problems with each other, the issues of divorces or dreading family visits due to the inconvenience.
- Divorce was uncommon in India, and the extended family based upon step-parents and siblings was most unusual.
- One of his most embarrassing moments was constantly confusing Sarah's mother and stepmother on a day they both were in town visiting on Parent's Weekend.
- Sarah, a child of a divorced family, often complained about her parents.
- When her folks visited for the weekends, she mentioned the inconvenience of having family in town.
- Within Gashwin's cultural perspective, family visits were typically long and a welcomed inconvenience instead of a burden on one's individual liberty.
- While working on his master's degree in the university's Geology Department was fulfilling for Gashwin, he felt a stronger calling in another direction—the religious life.
- When he shared this news with his girlfriend Sarah, the conversation did not go well; his faith would require him to enter the priesthood, which, in the Catholic Church, required men to be unmarried and celibate.
- As Gashwin began talking extensively with those in the Catholic diocese of Charleston and changing his academic focus to Religious Studies, Sarah realized he was serious.
- At first she thought it might be a phase and he would continue in geology.
- Numerous arguments ensued between Gashwin and Sarah during the next several months when this topic was discussed; over time she came to realize that her relationship with Gashwin would not lead to marriage but would remain only as a strong friendship.

Gashwin and friends in South Carolina.

- Gashwin's decision shocked his parents.
- Converting to another faith was challenging enough to understand, but for their son never to marry was almost unfathomable.
- The idea of their son's life without a wife or children was hard to accept for them.
- During the fall of 1995, Gashwin received a fellowship at USC under the university's Chaplains Association and completed his work in the spring of 1998.
- With a degree in hand, his visa expired and required to return to India, Gashwin had some decisions to make.
- The United States was Gashwin's new home, and he could work with the diocese to acquire his legal status there.
- Under U.S. law, one may acquire documentation for permanent residency if one spends two years as a religious worker.
- To delay entering the priesthood for two years and work for the Charleston diocese was required to fulfill his dream if he wished to remain in America.
- An additional 24-month wait was required prior to any processing of a green card.
- And Gashwin was ready to move forward with his life.

HISTORICAL SNAPSHOT
1998

- Archaeologists discovered a three million-year-old skeleton said to be the missing link in human evolution
- Ku Klux Klan leader Samuel Bowers was indicted in Mississippi in the 1966 murder of civil rights leader Vernon Dahmer
- President Bill Clinton told the nation, "I did not have sexual relations with that woman, Miss Lewinsky. I never told anyone to lie, a single time."
- The movie *Titanic* was the highest-grossing film in history, earning $850 million
- Television's top-rated shows included *ER, Frasier, Friends, Veronica's Closet, Jesse, NYPD Blue,* and *Touched by an Angel*
- The IRS Reform Bill passed by Congress shifted the burden of proof from the taxpayer to the IRS
- Popular books included *The 9 Steps to Financial Freedom* by Susie Orman, *The Greatest Generation* by Tom Brokaw, *Tuesdays with Morrie* by Mitch Albom, *Slaves in the Family,* by Edward Ball and *The Death of Outrage* by William Bennett
- *Voyager 1,* launched in 1977, was still transmitting from 6.5 billion miles from Earth
- The Dow Jones Industrial Average topped 9,000 for the first time
- Undergraduate tuition including room and board at Harvard reached $30,000 a year
- Online birth, surgical glue, planets outside the solar system, a DNA database and drive-through cigar stores all made their first appearance
- The final episode of *Seinfeld* was the fourth-highest-rated show in TV history
- After Dr. Jack Kevorkian demonstrated patient-assisted suicide on the TV show *60 Minutes,* he was arrested for first-degree murder
- A peace accord was reached in Northern Ireland
- Georgia Governor Zell Miller proposed that newborns be sent home with a recording of Mozart and Bach to stimulate brain development
- As obesity rates climbed dramatically, health food and vitamin supplement mania gripped the nation
- The number of welfare recipients dropped below 4 percent, the lowest level in 25 years; unemployment, juvenile arrests and births to unwed mothers all fell to 25-year lows
- Computer giant Microsoft was accused of illegally seeking Internet control
- A consortium of tobacco companies settled state health claims for $206 billion
- Popular movies included *Shakespeare in Love, Saving Private Ryan, The Thin Red Line, There's Something about Mary,* and *Godzilla*
- The Russian debt default set off a worldwide stock market plunge

Selected Prices

Automobile, Volvo Sedan	$26,895
Bath Towel	$24.00
Breadmaker	$129.99
Cell Phone	$49.99
Computer, Apple MAC Performa	$2,699.00
Digital Camera	$800.00
Man's Belt, Italian Leather	$42.00
Palm Pilot	$369.00
Wine Bottle Holder	$150.00
Woman's Purse, Kenneth Cole	$148.50

REMOTE CONTR

PageWriter 2000 ($33
credible communicat
pocket. This compa
features a complete
board so you can re
two-way pagers, a
even Internet e-m
you happen to be s
readable screen di
27-character line
scrolling. The r
metal-hydrid
a week
ho

6
w
avai

SCRATCH RESISTANT

Ray-Ban authentic glass lenses are subjected to rigorous tests that
ensure superior scratch resistance. Perfect if you're vulnerable to scratches.

"The Streets Are Paved with PC's; Wall Street and Silicon Alley Lure a New Breed of High-Tech Immigrants," by Edward Wong, *The New York Times*, August 16, 1998:

. . . thousands of foreign workers have arrived in New York in the last three years, most carrying H-1B visas, in response to a huge growth in financial services companies and their increasing reliance on information technology. Many work as highly paid computer consultants, a far cry from the blue-collar jobs that newly arrived immigrants in New York have traditionally filled. For the most part, they are young, single and male. They often hold the equivalent of a bachelor's or master's degree from their home countries. Their tools are laptops and the latest software, and they consider languages like Visual Basic, Cobol and C++ as useful as English, which some speak with less of an accent than most native New Yorkers.

The city, particularly Wall Street and Silicon Alley, has emerged as a lucrative destination for these tech-savvy immigrants. A recent Internet survey by Janet Ruhl, a former consultant from Massachusetts and the author of *The Computer Consultant's Guide* (John Wiley & Sons, 1997), found that the median pay rate for freelance consultants in New York was $80 per hour, the highest in the country. . . .

Immigration and Naturalization Service statistics show that the largest group of immigrant consultants nationwide comes from India, which has a booming high-tech industry of its own. Many others come from China, Russia, Israel, Pakistan and the Philippines.

The foreign workers "have exceptionally strong technical skills, especially in areas of high demand in this country," said Ravi Swamy, a partner in Informatic Systems, a consulting company that has its headquarters in the Empire State Building and recruiting offices in Bombay, Dubai and Singapore. "They usually have a responsibility to support parents, sisters and brothers back home, and it makes them work harder."

"Accord Would Increase Cap on Visas for Skilled Workers," by Robert Pear, *The New York Times,* July 25, 1998:

House and Senate Republican leaders reached agreement today on a bill to increase the number of foreign computer programmers, engineers and other skilled workers who can be admitted to the United States to fill job openings at high-technology companies.

Under the agreement, the annual limit on the number of visas for such workers, now 65,000, would rise to 115,000 over three years, an increase of 77 percent.

High-tech companies and their chief executives, including William H. Gates of the Microsoft Corporation, have lobbied heavily for an increase in the quota, saying that their industry suffers from shortages of qualified employees and that they desperately need skilled foreign workers to help develop new products. . . .

Whether there is in fact a shortage of high-tech workers is a hotly debated question. An industry group, the Information Technology Association of America, says there are 346,000 openings, amounting to 10 percent of all American jobs for computer programmers, engineers and systems analysts.

But the Labor Department, the A.F.L.-C.I.O. and several groups representing American engineers say the high-tech industry, trying to hold down its labor costs by hiring from abroad, has overstated the problem.

India provides by far the largest number of skilled foreign workers under the special-visa program. Its citizens received 44 percent of the visas, known as H-1B visas, issued in the first half of the current fiscal year.

Announcements—University Classifieds, *The Gamecock,* The University of South Carolina, January 1997:

Looking for a unique educational experience? Keep life simple and live on campus. The NADA International Community pals international students with students from the United States, enabling residents to learn about different cultures as well as their own. Applications may be picked up at the Department of Housing, 1215 Blossom Street, or at the Capstone Area Office located in the lobby of Columbia Hall. The deadline for applying is Friday, February 7, 1997.

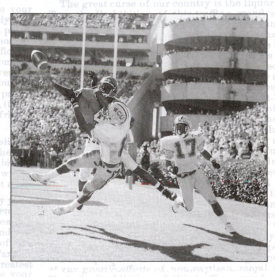

Popular USC activity.

2000 PROFILE

Stephen Teal left Japan in 1995 at the age of 15 to attend a private boarding school in Ohio and decided to stay in the United States because of the supportive community he found for pursuing his passion of painting.

Life at Home

- Stephen Teal was born in 1980 in Mito, Japan, to a Japanese mother and an American father.
- Stephen's father had come to Japan years before with his grandfather, who was a Catholic missionary.
- Stephen's father initially taught English to support himself but then returned to the United States and earned his Ph.D.
- When he returned to Japan, he got a job as a professor of English literature at a university, where he met Stephen's mother, who was working as a receptionist.
- The oldest of three children, Stephen was exposed to the English language and American culture at an early age by his father.
- At home his father would speak to him in English; Stephen would respond in Japanese.
- Life in Japan was sometimes difficult for Stephen; children of mixed-race marriages were often scorned.
- He tended to gravitate more toward American books, music and movies.
- As early as 10 years old, Stephen began thinking about attending high school in the United States.
- His parents encouraged him to enroll in a Japanese school first, but Stephen knew he wouldn't be there long.
- During his first year, he worked at a gas station to save up money for his trip to the United States.
- After one year, Stephen transferred to a private boarding school in Ohio; the plane fare to America cost $750.
- Fifteen-year-old Stephen had American Japanese dual citizenship through his father, so his entrance into America was smooth.

Stephen Teal left Japan as a teenager.

With his parents, grandmother and baby sister.

Stephen and his cousins in Japan.

Brothers and sister.

His father exposed Stephen to American culture.

- His new school had many international students but only a few Japanese.
- Stephen became close friends with the other Japanese students and would continue to keep in touch with them.
- However, he didn't feel outcast by Americans or students of other nationalities.
- He was surprised by how many American students had divorced parents.
- Overall, he found American society much more open and accepting of diversity than that of Japan.
- Stephen did well in school and particularly enjoyed literature.
- He spent much of his time reading and writing, in both Japanese and English.
- He went back to Japan to see his family once a year around New Year's Eve.
- His high school graduation was very special because it was one of the few times that both his American and Japanese family celebrated together.
- After high school, Stephen enrolled in a small, private college on Long Island, New York, that specialized in foreign-relations studies.
- He was not particularly interested in the subject, but thought it was a good choice, given his background.
- Mostly he wanted to be close to New York City, and often skipped school to spend time in Manhattan.
- As a result, his grades suffered.
- He enjoyed the openness and freedom that New York offered.
- It was during this time that he began to paint and use his art to express his feelings as a young immigrant in the U.S.
- He painted mostly self-portraits.
- After one year, he dropped out of college and went back to Japan to decide where he wanted to settle down.

High school graduation in Ohio.

- After much contemplation, he decided to pursue his art more seriously and that the United States was a better place to do that.
- As a young artist who was not formally trained, he would be seen as an outcast in Japanese society.
- In America, he found people to be less judgmental.

Life at Work

- Stephen Teal moved to Housatonic, a small town in western Massachusetts, with a college friend in 1999.
- Despite longing for the city life, he felt that a quiet New England town, with fewer distractions, would better enable him to concentrate on his painting.
- Also, the cost of living was much lower than in the city.
- He rented a one-room apartment in an old farmhouse for $350 a month.
- Stephen initially found freelance work as a translator for a heavy-machinery company; he was paid $0.07 per word.
- He translated instruction manuals from Japanese into English but did not enjoy the work very much.
- Despite being a native speaker of both English and Japanese, Stephen found translation surprisingly difficult.
- The highly specialized nature of the work meant that he often didn't know the words either in Japanese or English, and he soon began looking for other work.
- When a friend offered to get him a job in a pizza restaurant, he agreed, just wanting a job to support himself so he could paint.

Stephen painted mostly self-portraits.

Restaurant work was busy, but flexible.

- Stephen had never worked in a restaurant before, but he was a quick learner.
- He began as a prep cook.
- He started in the early morning preparing all of the ingredients for the day and then worked the lunch shift.
- He liked this schedule because he was finished by 3:00 and would go home and paint.
- When he first started working, he was making $8 per hour.
- After six months he was promoted to line cook for the dinner shift and then to assistant manager.
- He got a raise to $15 per hour.
- He liked the benefits of the job, such as free food, a relaxed environment and a flexible schedule.
- He was able to schedule his hours to work double shifts four days a week, with three days off to paint.
- His boss also let him hang his paintings in the restaurant.
- He sold several paintings this way.
- The most he ever sold a painting for was $3,000.

Life in the Community: Housatonic, Massachusetts

- Housatonic, Massachusetts, was a tourist town served by a diverse group of young people who worked in restaurants, hotels and other service-industry jobs.
- According to the 2000 census, 356 families resided in the village, which boasted a total population 1,335 people.
- Whites comprised 96.5 percent of the population, while 0.37 percent were Asian.
- The median income for a household in the village was $35,625.
- Stephen Teal didn't know any other Japanese people, but there were immigrants from other countries.
- Stephen worked with people from Mexico, Ecuador, Colombia, Venezuela and Brazil.

Stephen with his artwork.

- Some of them spoke English fluently, while others spoke it very little or not at all.
- Although Stephen didn't speak Spanish or Portuguese, it was easier to communicate with non-English speakers because of his bilingualism.
- They often talked about Americans and how they were treated by them.
- Stephen found that he faced less discrimination than immigrants from Latin America because of American stereotypes about Japanese people.
- He was expected to be very smart, a math genius and good with computers.
- People were surprised to find out that he was an artist who worked in a pizza restaurant.
- Despite these misconceptions, Stephen had no trouble getting along with Americans or other immigrants.
- He befriended a bartender who let him use a converted barn behind her house as his studio.
- He repaid her by chopping firewood and doing yard work.
- He also became friends with the owner of a coffee shop.
- After a few months of persisting, Stephen convinced her to mount a show of his artwork in the coffee shop.
- Of the 12 paintings in the show, seven were sold—one for $2,000.
- Although Housatonic had a thriving artist community, Stephen had little interest in connecting with it.
- Because of the personal nature of his paintings, Stephen felt that he could not relate to other artists, especially those with formal training.
- On his days off, Stephen would sometimes go to rock and alternative music concerts.
- He liked American bands that were similar in style to the Japanese bands he grew up hearing.
- He listened to Japanese music and followed his favorite Japanese bands through the Internet.
- His sister would also send him CDs from Japan.
- He would listen to Japanese rock during work at the restaurant, but didn't like explaining to the other employees what the lyrics meant.

HISTORICAL SNAPSHOT
2000

- Millennium celebrations were held throughout the world despite fears of major computer failures from the "Y2K" bug
- America Online was bought out by Time Warner for $162 billion in the largest-ever corporate merger
- Charles Schulz, creator of the comic strip *Peanuts,* died at the age of 77
- President Bill Clinton proposed a $2 billion program to bring Internet access to low-income houses
- The number of Internet users in China more than doubled in six months from four million to 8.9 million, most of them young, single men
- The Russian submarine K-141 *Kursk* sank in the Barents Sea, killing the 118 sailors on board
- The U.S. Supreme Court gave police broad authority to stop and question people who run from a police officer
- The International Whaling Commission turned down requests from Japan and Norway to allow expanded whaling
- The Millennium Summit among world leaders was held at the United Nations in New York
- In California, President Bill Clinton created the Giant Sequoia National Monument to protect 328,000 acres of trees from timber harvesting
- Judge Thomas Penfield Jackson ruled that Microsoft violated the Sherman Antitrust Act by tying its Internet browser to its operating system
- George W. Bush was declared the winner of the presidential race in a highly controversial election against Al Gore
- The female-oriented television cable channel Oxygen made its debut
- Carlos Santana won eight Grammy awards, including Album of the Year for *Supernatural*

Japanese Immigration Timeline

1907

The United States and Japan formed a face-saving gentleman's agreement in which Japan ended the issuance of passports to laborers and the U.S. agreed not to prohibit Japanese immigration.

1913

California's Alien Land Law stated that aliens "ineligible to citizenship" were ineligible to own agricultural property, further eroding Japanese immigrant rights.

1915

The Supreme Court ruled that first-generation Japanese were ineligible for citizenship and could not apply for naturalization.

1924

The Immigration Act of 1924 established fixed quotas based on national origin and virtually eliminated Japanese and Far East immigration.

1929

Congress made the annual immigration quotas, passed in 1924, permanent.

1941

Japan's surprise attack on Pearl Harbor, Hawaii, ignited a wave of anti-Japanese sentiment in America; more than 1,000 Japanese American community leaders were incarcerated for national security purposes.

Japanese Americans and relocation camps.

Timeline . . . *(continued)*

1942

President Franklin D. Roosevelt signed an executive order authorizing the building of relocation camps for Japanese Americans living along the Pacific Coast.

1943

Congress repealed the Chinese Exclusion Act of 1882, and established quotas for Chinese immigrants, who also became eligible for US citizenship.

1948

The U.S. Supreme Court ruled that California's alien land laws prohibiting the ownership of agricultural property violated the Constitution's Fourteenth Amendment.

A United States admitted persons fleeing persecution in their native lands, allowing 205,000 refugees to enter within two years.

1952

The Immigration and Nationality Act allowed all individuals of all races to be eligible for naturalization.

1965

The Immigration Act of 1965 established a new quota system that gave immigration preference to immediate families of immigrants and skilled workers.

1980

The Refugee Act redefined the criteria and procedures for admitting refugees.

1986

The Immigration Reform and Control Act legalized illegal aliens residing in the U.S. unlawfully since 1982.

1988

The Civil Liberties Act provided compensation of $20,000 and a presidential apology to all Japanese American survivors of the World War II internment camps.

Selected Prices

Airfare, New York to Miami, U.S Airways $257.00
Apartment, Studio, New York City $1,300.00
Automobile, Toyota Prius Hybrid $20,810
Cutlery Set, 22-Piece $19.99
Day Pack, Eddie Bauer $34.99
French Bread, Each $0.99
Reclining Sofa $1,199.00
Shotgun, 12-Gauge $189.50
Steak, Ribeye, per Pound $7.99
Treadmill $399.88

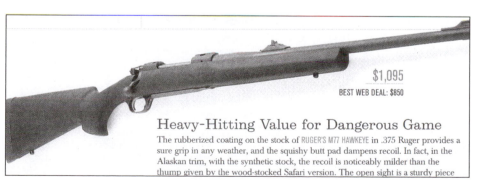

$1,095
BEST WEB DEAL: $850

Heavy-Hitting Value for Dangerous Game

The rubberized coating on the stock of RUGER'S M77 HAWKEYE in .375 Ruger provides a sure grip in any weather, and the squishy butt pad dampens recoil. In fact, in the Alaskan trim, with the synthetic stock, the recoil is noticeably milder than the thump given by the wood-stocked Safari version. The open sight is a sturdy piece

Tokyo, Japan

"Arts In America; Japanese American Gloom on Canvas, Circa '42," by Bernard Weinraub, *The New York Times*, March 28, 2001:

Several months after the attack on Pearl Harbor, Henry Sugimoto, his wife and their six-year-old daughter were interned with other Japanese Americans in California and sent to an assembly center in Fresno. Mr. Sugimoto had been a rising artist, trained in France and known as a painter of the placid fields and lush landscapes of rural California. Almost as soon as he was interned he began sketching somber portraits of the Japanese American families devastated by government policy.

"The internment experience completely transformed him, and it continued for the rest of Sugimoto's life," said Kristine Kim, associate curator at the Japanese American National Museum in downtown Los Angeles, the only museum in the nation focusing on the Japanese American experience. "He no longer looked to nature for inspiration for his art but instead depicted on canvas his personal experiences, his beliefs."

The first retrospective survey of more than 100 paintings by Mr. Sugimoto, who spent his postwar years in Manhattan, opened on Saturday at the museum in the Little Tokyo section of Los Angeles. The show offers not only a glimpse into the internment which has rarely been explored in art and, for that matter, in movies and television, but also seeks to explore the life of a relatively unknown artist whose career was cut short by his incarceration and who never regained his footing.

Lawrence M. Small, secretary of the Smithsonian Institution, which has three paintings by Mr. Sugimoto in its permanent collection, said that the artist once wrote that he was most concerned about "leaving my mark on this world." Mr. Small said that he need not have worried, adding, "Initially in secret and then openly, Sugimoto created an extensive series of paintings that powerfully capture that painful time" and "he conveys the struggles, suffering and complexity of life in a detention camp." The show runs through Sept. 16.

Mr. Sugimoto, who was born in Wakayama, Japan, and was the grandson of a samurai, moved to Hanford, Calif., when he was 19. He died at the age of 90 in 1990, living after the war in apartments on the Upper West Side and in Hamilton Heights. His daughter, Madeleine Sumile Sugimoto, who lives in New York, said her father moved there after the family was released from an internment camp in Arkansas largely because he had always yearned to experience the artistic life in the city.

"No Place Like Home, Sometimes; Children's Author Illuminates Japanese American Identity," by James Sterngold, *The New York Times,* November 22, 2000:

Allen Say never intended to become a children's book author, or any other kind of author for that matter. For years he worked as a commercial photographer in San Francisco, then did some freelance illustrations before deciding to write his own stories for children. These were truly his own stories, an immigrant's musings about a home he never quite seems to find.

In tales like "Grandfather's Journey," "Tea With Milk" and "Emma's Rug," he has produced characters who are restless misfits navigating their murky worlds like ships searching for a safe harbor, carried along by a gentle undercurrent of melancholy. Though different from traditionally upbeat children's fare, the books have won him many awards, including the prestigious Caldecott medal.

It is his vivid, slightly austere watercolors that bring his themes to life and underscore a deep connection with the Japanese American world, a fact powerfully on display at the first show of his works, at the Japanese American National Museum here, through Feb. 11.

It is a show with a poignant subtext, the confusion and complications of Japanese American identity. The museum itself is dedicated to unraveling and taking note of this complexity, and the show, "Allen Say's Journey: The Art and Words of a Children's Book Author," seems a metaphor for that experience.

His realistically detailed illustrations for what are often autobiographical tales cleverly capture the spirit of being somehow linked to two worlds Japan, where Mr. Say, 63, whose name was originally James Allen Koichi Moriwaki Seii, and America, his adopted land, but completely at home in neither. The 55 paintings in the show are often dreamlike evocations of this rootlessness, characterized by broad, empty spaces with hints of loneliness and magisterial natural settings, much like the works of one of Mr. Say's prime influences, Edward Hopper.

That influence, and Mr. Say's clever use of it, is especially apparent in his most recent book, published this fall, *The Sign Painter* (Walter Lorraine Books/Houghton Mifflin Company), in which Mr. Say borrows readily recognizable scenes from this deeply American painter and populates them with bright Asian faces, sort of a Hopperesque perspective on the new America.

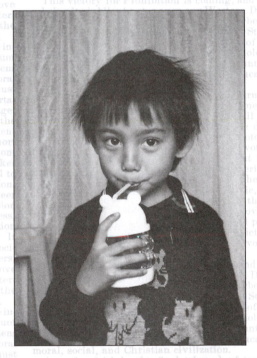

2007 NEWS FEATURE

"In Name Count, Garcias Are Catching Up to Joneses," by Sam Roberts,
***The New York Times*, November 17, 2007:**

Step aside, Moore and Taylor. Welcome, Garcia and Rodriguez.

Smith remains the most common surname in the United States, according to a new analysis released yesterday by the Census Bureau. But for the first time, two Hispanic surnames—Garcia and Rodriguez—are among the top 10 most common in the nation, and Martinez nearly edged out Wilson for 10th place.

The number of Hispanics living in the United States grew by 58 percent in the 1990s to nearly 13 percent of the total population, and cracking the list of top 10 names suggests just how pervasively the Latino migration has permeated everyday American culture.

Garcia moved to No. 8 in 2000, up from No. 18, and Rodriguez jumped to No. 9 from 22nd place. The number of Hispanic surnames among the top 25 doubled, to six.

Compiling the rankings is a cumbersome task, in part because of confidentiality and accuracy issues, according to the Census Bureau, and it is only the second time it has prepared such a list. While the historical record is sketchy, several demographers said it was probably the first time that any non-Anglo name was among the 10 most common in the nation. "It's difficult to say, but it's probably likely," said Robert A. Kominski, Assistant Chief of Social Characteristics for the Census.

Luis Padilla, 48, a banker who has lived in Miami since he arrived from Colombia 14 years ago, greeted the ascendance of Hispanic surnames enthusiastically. "It shows we're getting stronger," Mr. Padilla said. "If there's that many of us to outnumber the Anglo names, it's a great thing."

Reinaldo M. Valdes, a board member of the Miami-based Spanish American League Against Discrimination, said the milestone "gives the Hispanic community a standing within the social structure of the country."

"People of Hispanic descent who hardly speak Spanish are more eager to take their Hispanic last names," he said. "Today, kids identify more with their roots than they did before."

Demographers pointed to more than one factor in explaining the increase in Hispanic surnames.

From The New York Times on the Web © The New York Times Company. Reprinted with Permission

Generations ago, immigration officials sometimes arbitrarily Anglicized or simplified names when foreigners arrived from Europe.

"The movie studios used to demand that their employees have standard Waspy names," said Justin Kaplan, a historian and coauthor of *The Language of Names*. "Now, look at Renée Zellweger," Mr. Kaplan said.

And because recent Hispanic and Asian immigrants might consider themselves more identifiable by their physical characteristics than Europeans do, they are less likely to change their surnames, though they often choose Anglicized first names for their children.

The latest surname count also signaled the growing number of Asians in America. The surname Lee ranked No. 22, with the number of Lees about equally divided between whites and Asians. Lee is a familiar name in China and Korea and in all its variations is described as the most common surname in the world.

Altogether, the census found six million surnames in the United States. Among those, 151,000 were shared by a hundred or more Americans. Four million were held by only one person.

"The names tell us that we're a richly diverse culture," Mr. Kominski said. But the fact that about one in every 25 Americans is named Smith, Johnson, Williams, Brown, Jones, Miller or Davis "suggests that there's a durability in the family of man," Mr. Kaplan, the author, said. A million Americans share each of those seven names. An additional 268 last names are common to 10,000 or more people. Together, those 275 names account for one in four Americans.

As the population of the United States ballooned by more than 30 million in the 1990s, more Murphys and Cohens were counted when the decade ended than when it began. Smith—which would be even more common if all its variations, like Schmidt and Schmitt, were tallied—is among the names derived from occupations (Miller, which ranks No. 7, is another). Among the most famous early bearers of the name was Capt. John Smith, who helped establish the first permanent English settlement in North America at Jamestown, Va., 400 years ago. As recently as 1950, more Americans were employed as blacksmiths than as psychotherapists.

In 1984, according to the Social Security Administration, nearly 3.4 million Smiths lived in the United States. In 1990, the census counted 2.5 million. By 2000, the Smith population had declined to fewer than 2.4 million. The durability of some of the most common names in American history may also have been perpetuated because slaves either adopted or retained the surnames of their owners. About one in five Smiths is black, as is about one in three Johnsons, Browns, and Joneses and nearly half the people named Williams. The Census Bureau's analysis found that some surnames were especially associated with race and ethnicity.

More than 96 percent of Yoders, Kruegers, Muellers, Kochs, Schwartzes, Schmitts and Novaks were white. Nearly 90 percent of the Washingtons were black, as were 75 percent of the Jeffersons, 66 percent of the Bookers, 54 percent of the Banks and 53 percent of the Mosleys.

INDEX

Page numbers in italics indicate images. Bold entries indicate profile subjects.

Page numbers in italics indicate images. Bold entries indicate profile subjects.

Page numbers in italics indicate images. Bold entries indicate profile subjects.

Page numbers in italics indicate images. Bold entries indicate profile subjects.

Page numbers in italics indicate images. Bold entries indicate profile subjects.

Page numbers in italics indicate images. Bold entries indicate profile subjects.

Page numbers in italics indicate images. Bold entries indicate profile subjects.

Page numbers in italics indicate images. Bold entries indicate profile subjects.

Page numbers in italics indicate images. Bold entries indicate profile subjects.

Page numbers in italics indicate images. Bold entries indicate profile subjects.

Page numbers in italics indicate images. Bold entries indicate profile subjects.

Page numbers in italics indicate images. Bold entries indicate profile subjects.

Business Information ◆ Ratings Guides ◆ General Reference ◆ Education ◆
Statistics ◆ Demographics ◆ Health Information ◆ Canadian Information

The Directory of Business Information Resources, 2008

With 100% verification, over 1,000 new listings and more than 12,000 updates, *The Directory of Business Information Resources* is the most up-to-date source for contacts in over 98 business areas – from advertising and agriculture to utilities and wholesalers. This carefully researched volume details: the Associations representing each industry; the Newsletters that keep members current; the Magazines and Journals - with their "Special Issues" - that are important to the trade, the Conventions that are "must attends," Databases, Directories and Industry Web Sites that provide access to must-have marketing resources. Includes contact names, phone & fax numbers, web sites and e-mail addresses. This one-volume resource is a gold mine of information and would be a welcome addition to any reference collection.

"This is a most useful and easy-to-use addition to any researcher's library." –The Information Professionals Institute

Softcover ISBN 978-1-59237-193-8, 2,500 pages, $195.00 | Online Database $495.00

Nations of the World, 2007/08 A Political, Economic and Business Handbook

This completely revised edition covers all the nations of the world in an easy-to-use, single volume. Each nation is profiled in a single chapter that includes Key Facts, Political & Economic Issues, a Country Profile and Business Information. In this fast-changing world, it is extremely important to make sure that the most up-to-date information is included in your reference collection. This edition is just the answer. Each of the 200+ country chapters have been carefully reviewed by a political expert to make sure that the text reflects the most current information on Politics, Travel Advisories, Economics and more. You'll find such vital information as a Country Map, Population Characteristics, Inflation, Agricultural Production, Foreign Debt, Political History, Foreign Policy, Regional Insecurity, Economics, Trade & Tourism, Historical Profile, Political Systems, Ethnicity, Languages, Media, Climate, Hotels, Chambers of Commerce, Banking, Travel Information and more. Five Regional Chapters follow the main text and include a Regional Map, an Introductory Article, Key Indicators and Currencies for the Region. As an added bonus, an all-inclusive CD-ROM is available as a companion to the printed text. Noted for its sophisticated, up-to-date and reliable compilation of political, economic and business information, this brand new edition will be an important acquisition to any public, academic or special library reference collection.

"A useful addition to both general reference collections and business collections." –RUSQ

Softcover ISBN 978-1-59237-177-8, 1,700 pages, $155.00

The Directory of Venture Capital & Private Equity Firms, 2008

This edition has been extensively updated and broadly expanded to offer direct access to over 2,800 Domestic and International Venture Capital Firms, including address, phone & fax numbers, e-mail addresses and web sites for both primary and branch locations. Entries include details on the firm's Mission Statement, Industry Group Preferences, Geographic Preferences, Average and Minimum Investments and Investment Criteria. You'll also find details that are available nowhere else, including the Firm's Portfolio Companies and extensive information on each of the firm's Managing Partners, such as Education, Professional Background and Directorships held, along with the Partner's E-mail Address. *The Directory of Venture Capital & Private Equity Firms* offers five important indexes: Geographic Index, Executive Name Index, Portfolio Company Index, Industry Preference Index and College & University Index. With its comprehensive coverage and detailed, extensive information on each company, The Directory of Venture Capital & Private Equity Firms is an important addition to any finance collection.

"The sheer number of listings, the descriptive information and the outstanding indexing make this directory a better value than …Pratt's Guide to Venture Capital Sources. Recommended for business collections in large public, academic and business libraries." –Choice

Softcover ISBN 978-1-59237-272-0, 1,300 pages, $565/$450 Library | Online Database $889.00

The Directory of Mail Order Catalogs, 2008

Published since 1981, *The Directory of Mail Order Catalogs* is the premier source of information on the mail order catalog industry. It is the source that business professionals and librarians have come to rely on for the thousands of catalog companies in the US. Since the 2007 edition, *The Directory of Mail Order Catalogs* has been combined with its companion volume, *The Directory of Business to Business Catalogs*, to offer all 13,000 catalog companies in one easy-to-use volume. Section I: Consumer Catalogs, covers over 9,000 consumer catalog companies in 44 different product chapters from Animals to Toys & Games. Section II: Business to Business Catalogs, details 5,000 business catalogs, everything from computers to laboratory supplies, building construction and much more. Listings contain detailed contact information including mailing address, phone & fax numbers, web sites, e-mail addresses and key contacts along with important business details such as product descriptions, employee size, years in business, sales volume, catalog size, number of catalogs mailed and more. Three indexes are included for easy access to information: Catalog & Company Name Index, Geographic Index and Product Index. *The Directory of Mail Order Catalogs*, now with its expanded business to business catalogs, is the largest and most comprehensive resource covering this billion-dollar industry. It is the standard in its field. This important resource is a useful tool for entrepreneurs searching for catalogs to pick up their product, vendors looking to expand their customer base in the catalog industry, market researchers, small businesses investigating new supply vendors, along with the library patron who is exploring the available catalogs in their areas of interest.

"This is a godsend for those looking for information." –Reference Book Review

Softcover ISBN 978-1-59237-202-7, 1,700 pages, $350/$250 Library | Online Database $495.00

To preview any of our Directories Risk-Free for 30 days, call (800) 562-2139 or fax (518) 789-0556
www.greyhouse.com books@greyhouse.com

Business Information ✦ **Ratings Guides** ✦ **General Reference** ✦ **Education** ✦
Statistics ✦ **Demographics** ✦ **Health Information** ✦ **Canadian Information**

Grey House Publishing

The Encyclopedia of Emerging Industries

*Published under an exclusive license from the Gale Group, Inc.

The fifth edition of the *Encyclopedia of Emerging Industries* details the inception, emergence, and current status of nearly 120 flourishing U.S. industries and industry segments. These focused essays unearth for users a wealth of relevant, current, factual data previously accessible only through a diverse variety of sources. This volume provides broad-based, highly-readable, industry information under such headings as Industry Snapshot, Organization & Structure, Background & Development, Industry Leaders, Current Conditions, America and the World, Pioneers, and Research & Technology. Essays in this new edition, arranged alphabetically for easy use, have been completely revised, with updated statistics and the most current information on industry trends and developments. In addition, there are new essays on some of the most interesting and influential new business fields, including Application Service Providers, Concierge Services, Entrepreneurial Training, Fuel Cells, Logistics Outsourcing Services, Pharmacogenomics, and Tissue Engineering. Two indexes, General and Industry, provide immediate access to this wealth of information. Plus, two conversion tables for SIC and NAICS codes, along with Suggested Further Readings, are provided to aid the user. *The Encyclopedia of Emerging Industries* pinpoints emerging industries while they are still in the spotlight. This important resource will be an important acquisition to any business reference collection.

"This well-designed source…should become another standard business source, nicely complementing Standard & Poor's Industry Surveys. It contains more information on each industry than Hoover's Handbook of Emerging Companies, is broader in scope than The Almanac of American Employers 1998-1999, but is less expansive than the Encyclopedia of Careers & Vocational Guidance. Highly recommended for all academic libraries and specialized business collections." –Library Journal

Hardcover ISBN 978-1-59237-242-3, 1,400 pages, $325.00

Encyclopedia of American Industries

*Published under an exclusive license from the Gale Group, Inc.

The Encyclopedia of American Industries is a major business reference tool that provides detailed, comprehensive information on a wide range of industries in every realm of American business. A two volume set, Volume I provides separate coverage of nearly 500 manufacturing industries, while Volume II presents nearly 600 essays covering the vast array of services and other non-manufacturing industries in the United States. Combined, these two volumes provide individual essays on every industry recognized by the U.S. Standard Industrial Classification (SIC) system. Both volumes are arranged numerically by SIC code, for easy use. Additionally, each entry includes the corresponding NAICS code(s). The *Encyclopedia's* business coverage includes information on historical events of consequence, as well as current trends and statistics. Essays include an Industry Snapshot, Organization & Structure, Background & Development, Current Conditions, Industry Leaders, Workforce, America and the World, Research & Technology along with Suggested Further Readings. Both SIC and NAICS code conversion tables and an all-encompassing Subject Index, with cross-references, complete the text. With its detailed, comprehensive information on a wide range of industries, this resource will be an important tool for both the industry newcomer and the seasoned professional.

"Encyclopedia of American Industries contains detailed, signed essays on virtually every industry in contemporary society. … Highly recommended for all but the smallest libraries." -American Reference Books Annual

Two Volumes, Hardcover ISBN 978-1-59237-244-7, 3,000 pages, $650.00

Encyclopedia of Global Industries

*Published under an exclusive license from the Gale Group, Inc.

This fourth edition of the acclaimed *Encyclopedia of Global Industries* presents a thoroughly revised and expanded look at more than 125 business sectors of global significance. Detailed, insightful articles discuss the origins, development, trends, key statistics and current international character of the world's most lucrative, dynamic and widely researched industries – including hundreds of profiles of leading international corporations. Beginning researchers will gain from this book a solid understanding of how each industry operates and which countries and companies are significant participants, while experienced researchers will glean current and historical figures for comparison and analysis. The industries profiled in previous editions have been updated, and in some cases, expanded to reflect recent industry trends. Additionally, this edition provides both SIC and NAICS codes for all industries profiled. As in the original volumes, *The Encyclopedia of Global Industries* offers thorough studies of some of the biggest and most frequently researched industry sectors, including Aircraft, Biotechnology, Computers, Internet Services, Motor Vehicles, Pharmaceuticals, Semiconductors, Software and Telecommunications. An SIC and NAICS conversion table and an all-encompassing Subject Index, with cross-references, are provided to ensure easy access to this wealth of information. These and many others make the *Encyclopedia of Global Industries* the authoritative reference for studies of international industries.

"Provides detailed coverage of the history, development, and current status of 115 of "the world's most lucrative and high-profile industries." It far surpasses the Department of Commerce's U.S. Global Trade Outlook 1995-2000 (GPO, 1995) in scope and coverage. Recommended for comprehensive public and academic library business collections." -Booklist

Hardcover ISBN 978-1-59237-243-0, 1,400 pages, $495.00

Business Information ✦ Ratings Guides ✦ General Reference ✦ Education ✦
Statistics ✦ Demographics ✦ Health Information ✦ Canadian Information

Sports Market Place Directory, 2007

For over 20 years, this comprehensive, up-to-date directory has offered direct access to the Who, What, When & Where of the Sports Industry. With over 20,000 updates and enhancements, the *Sports Market Place Directory* is the most detailed, comprehensive and current sports business reference source available. In 1,800 information-packed pages, *Sports Market Place Directory* profiles contact information and key executives for: Single Sport Organizations, Professional Leagues, Multi-Sport Organizations, Disabled Sports, High School & Youth Sports, Military Sports, Olympic Organizations, Media, Sponsors, Sponsorship & Marketing Event Agencies, Event & Meeting Calendars, Professional Services, College Sports, Manufacturers & Retailers, Facilities and much more. The Sports Market Place Directory provides organization's contact information with detailed descriptions including: Key Contacts, physical, mailing, email and web addresses plus phone and fax numbers. *Sports Market Place Directory* provides a one-stop resources for this billion-dollar industry. This will be an important resource for large public libraries, university libraries, university athletic programs, career services or job placement organizations, and is a must for anyone doing research on or marketing to the US and Canadian sports industry.

> *"Grey House is the new publisher and has produced an excellent edition...highly recommended for public libraries and academic libraries with sports management programs or strong interest in athletics." -Booklist*

Softcover ISBN 978-1-59237-189-1, 1,800 pages, $225.00 | Online Database $479.00

Food and Beverage Market Place, 2008

Food and Beverage Market Place is bigger and better than ever with thousands of new companies, thousands of updates to existing companies and two revised and enhanced product category indexes. This comprehensive directory profiles over 18,000 Food & Beverage Manufacturers, 12,000 Equipment & Supply Companies, 2,200 Transportation & Warehouse Companies, 2,000 Brokers & Wholesalers, 8,000 Importers & Exporters, 900 Industry Resources and hundreds of Mail Order Catalogs. Listings include detailed Contact Information, Sales Volumes, Key Contacts, Brand & Product Information, Packaging Details and much more. *Food and Beverage Market Place* is available as a three-volume printed set, a subscription-based Online Database via the Internet, on CD-ROM, as well as mailing lists and a licensable database.

> *"An essential purchase for those in the food industry but will also be useful in public libraries where needed. Much of the information will be difficult and time consuming to locate without this handy three-volume ready-reference source." –ARBA*

3 Vol Set, Softcover ISBN 978-1-59237-198-3, 8,500 pages, $595 | Online Database $795 | Online Database & 3 Vol Set Combo, $995

The Grey House Performing Arts Directory, 2007

The Grey House Performing Arts Directory is the most comprehensive resource covering the Performing Arts. This important directory provides current information on over 8,500 Dance Companies, Instrumental Music Programs, Opera Companies, Choral Groups, Theater Companies, Performing Arts Series and Performing Arts Facilities. Plus, this edition now contains a brand new section on Artist Management Groups. In addition to mailing address, phone & fax numbers, e-mail addresses and web sites, dozens of other fields of available information include mission statement, key contacts, facilities, seating capacity, season, attendance and more. This directory also provides an important Information Resources section that covers hundreds of Performing Arts Associations, Magazines, Newsletters, Trade Shows, Directories, Databases and Industry Web Sites. Five indexes provide immediate access to this wealth of information: Entry Name, Executive Name, Performance Facilities, Geographic and Information Resources. *The Grey House Performing Arts Directory* pulls together thousands of Performing Arts Organizations, Facilities and Information Resources into an easy-to-use source – this kind of comprehensiveness and extensive detail is not available in any resource on the market place today.

> *"Immensely useful and user-friendly … recommended for public, academic and certain special library reference collections." –Booklist*

Softcover ISBN 978-1-59237-138-9, 1,500 pages, $185.00 | Online Database $335.00

New York State Directory, 2007/08

The New York State Directory, published annually since 1983, is a comprehensive and easy-to-use guide to accessing public officials and private sector organizations and individuals who influence public policy in the state of New York. *The New York State Directory* includes important information on all New York state legislators and congressional representatives, including biographies and key committee assignments. It also includes staff rosters for all branches of New York state government and for federal agencies and departments that impact the state policy process. Following the state government section are 25 chapters covering policy areas from agriculture through veterans' affairs. Each chapter identifies the state, local and federal agencies and officials that formulate or implement policy. In addition, each chapter contains a roster of private sector experts and advocates who influence the policy process. The directory also offers appendices that include statewide party officials; chambers of commerce; lobbying organizations; public and private universities and colleges; television, radio and print media; and local government agencies and officials.

> *"This comprehensive directory covers not only New York State government offices and key personnel but pertinent U.S. government agencies and non-governmental entities. This directory is all encompassing... recommended." -Choice*

New York State Directory - Softcover ISBN 978-1-59237-190-7, 800 pages, $145.00
New York State Directory with *Profiles of New York* – 2 Volumes, Softcover ISBN 978-1-59237-191-4, 1,600 pages, $225.00

Business Information ◆ **Ratings Guides** ◆ **General Reference** ◆ **Education** ◆
Statistics ◆ **Demographics** ◆ **Health Information** ◆ **Canadian Information**

The Grey House Homeland Security Directory, 2008

This updated edition features the latest contact information for government and private organizations involved with Homeland Security along with the latest product information and provides detailed profiles of nearly 1,000 Federal & State Organizations & Agencies and over 3,000 Officials and Key Executives involved with Homeland Security. These listings are incredibly detailed and include Mailing Address, Phone & Fax Numbers, Email Addresses & Web Sites, a complete Description of the Agency and a complete list of the Officials and Key Executives associated with the Agency. Next, *The Grey House Homeland Security Directory* provides the go-to source for Homeland Security Products & Services. This section features over 2,000 Companies that provide Consulting, Products or Services. With this Buyer's Guide at their fingertips, users can locate suppliers of everything from Training Materials to Access Controls, from Perimeter Security to BioTerrorism Countermeasures and everything in between – complete with contact information and product descriptions. A handy Product Locator Index is provided to quickly and easily locate suppliers of a particular product. This comprehensive, information-packed resource will be a welcome tool for any company or agency that is in need of Homeland Security information and will be a necessary acquisition for the reference collection of all public libraries and large school districts.

"Compiles this information in one place and is discerning in content. A useful purchase for public and academic libraries." –Booklist

Softcover ISBN 978-1-59237-196-6, 800 pages, $195.00 | Online Database $385.00

The Grey House Safety & Security Directory, 2008

The Grey House Safety & Security Directory is the most comprehensive reference tool and buyer's guide for the safety and security industry. Arranged by safety topic, each chapter begins with OSHA regulations for the topic, followed by Training Articles written by top professionals in the field and Self-Inspection Checklists. Next, each topic contains Buyer's Guide sections that feature related products and services. Topics include Administration, Insurance, Loss Control & Consulting, Protective Equipment & Apparel, Noise & Vibration, Facilities Monitoring & Maintenance, Employee Health Maintenance & Ergonomics, Retail Food Services, Machine Guards, Process Guidelines & Tool Handling, Ordinary Materials Handling, Hazardous Materials Handling, Workplace Preparation & Maintenance, Electrical Lighting & Safety, Fire & Rescue and Security. Six important indexes make finding information and product manufacturers quick and easy: Geographical Index of Manufacturers and Distributors, Company Profile Index, Brand Name Index, Product Index, Index of Web Sites and Index of Advertisers. This comprehensive, up-to-date reference will provide every tool necessary to make sure a business is in compliance with OSHA regulations and locate the products and services needed to meet those regulations.

"Presents industrial safety information for engineers, plant managers, risk managers, and construction site supervisors…" –Choice

Softcover ISBN 978-1-59237-205-8, 1,500 pages, $165.00

The Grey House Transportation Security Directory & Handbook

This is the only reference of its kind that brings together current data on Transportation Security. With information on everything from Regulatory Authorities to Security Equipment, this top-flight database brings together the relevant information necessary for creating and maintaining a security plan for a wide range of transportation facilities. With this current, comprehensive directory at the ready you'll have immediate access to: Regulatory Authorities & Legislation; Information Resources; Sample Security Plans & Checklists; Contact Data for Major Airports, Seaports, Railroads, Trucking Companies and Oil Pipelines; Security Service Providers; Recommended Equipment & Product Information and more. Using the *Grey House Transportation Security Directory & Handbook*, managers will be able to quickly and easily assess their current security plans; develop contacts to create and maintain new security procedures; and source the products and services necessary to adequately maintain a secure environment. This valuable resource is a must for all Security Managers at Airports, Seaports, Railroads, Trucking Companies and Oil Pipelines.

"Highly recommended. Library collections that support all levels of readers, including professionals/practitioners; and schools/organizations offering education and training in transportation security." -Choice

Softcover ISBN 978-1-59237-075-7, 800 pages, $195.00

The Grey House Biometric Information Directory

This edition offers a complete, current overview of biometric companies and products – one of the fastest growing industries in today's economy. Detailed profiles of manufacturers of the latest biometric technology, including Finger, Voice, Face, Hand, Signature, Iris, Vein and Palm Identification systems. Data on the companies include key executives, company size and a detailed, indexed description of their product line. Information in the directory includes: Editorial on Advancements in Biometrics; Profiles of 700+ companies listed with contact information; Organizations, Trade & Educational Associations, Publications, Conferences, Trade Shows and Expositions Worldwide; Web Site Index; Biometric & Vendors Services Index by Types of Biometrics; and a Glossary of Biometric Terms. This resource will be an important source for anyone who is considering the use of a biometric product, investing in the development of biometric technology, support existing marketing and sales efforts and will be an important acquisition for the business reference collection for large public and business libraries.

"This book should prove useful to agencies or businesses seeking companies that deal with biometric technology. Summing Up: Recommended. Specialized collections serving researchers/faculty and professionals/practitioners." -Choice

Softcover ISBN 978-1-59237-121-1, 800 pages, $225.00

To preview any of our Directories Risk-Free for 30 days, call (800) 562-2139 or fax (518) 789-0556
www.greyhouse.com books@greyhouse.com

Business Information ◆ Ratings Guides ◆ General Reference ◆ Education ◆
Statistics ◆ Demographics ◆ Health Information ◆ Canadian Information

Grey House Publishing

The Environmental Resource Handbook, 2007/08

The Environmental Resource Handbook is the most up-to-date and comprehensive source for Environmental Resources and Statistics. Section I: Resources provides detailed contact information for thousands of information sources, including Associations & Organizations, Awards & Honors, Conferences, Foundations & Grants, Environmental Health, Government Agencies, National Parks & Wildlife Refuges, Publications, Research Centers, Educational Programs, Green Product Catalogs, Consultants and much more. Section II: Statistics, provides statistics and rankings on hundreds of important topics, including Children's Environmental Index, Municipal Finances, Toxic Chemicals, Recycling, Climate, Air & Water Quality and more. This kind of up-to-date environmental data, all in one place, is not available anywhere else on the market place today. This vast compilation of resources and statistics is a must-have for all public and academic libraries as well as any organization with a primary focus on the environment.

> *"…the intrinsic value of the information make it worth consideration by libraries with environmental collections and environmentally concerned users." –Booklist*

Softcover ISBN 978-1-59237-195-2, 1,000 pages, $155.00 | Online Database $300.00

The Rauch Guide to the US Adhesives & Sealants, Cosmetics & Toiletries, Ink, Paint, Plastics, Pulp & Paper and Rubber Industries

The Rauch Guides save time and money by organizing widely scattered information and providing estimates for important business decisions, some of which are available nowhere else. Within each Guide, after a brief introduction, the ECONOMICS section provides data on industry shipments; long-term growth and forecasts; prices; company performance; employment, expenditures, and productivity; transportation and geographical patterns; packaging; foreign trade; and government regulations. Next, TECHNOLOGY & RAW MATERIALS provide market, technical, and raw material information for chemicals, equipment and related materials, including market size and leading suppliers, prices, end uses, and trends. PRODUCTS & MARKETS provide information for each major industry product, including market size and historical trends, leading suppliers, five-year forecasts, industry structure, and major end uses. Next, the COMPANY DIRECTORY profiles major industry companies, both public and private. Information includes complete contact information, web address, estimated total and domestic sales, product description, and recent mergers and acquisitions. *The Rauch Guides* will prove to be an invaluable source of market information, company data, trends and forecasts that anyone in these fast-paced industries.

> *"An invaluable and affordable publication. The comprehensive nature of the data and text offers considerable insights into the industry, market sizes, company activities, and applications of the products of the industry. The additions that have been made have certainly enhanced the value of the Guide." –Adhesives & Sealants Newsletter of the Rauch Guide to the US Adhesives & Sealants Industry*

Paint Industry: Softcover ISBN 978-1-59237-127-3 $595 | Plastics Industry: Softcover ISBN 978-1-59237-128-0 $595 | Adhesives and Sealants Industry: Softcover ISBN 978-1-59237-129-7 $595 | Ink Industry: Softcover ISBN 978-1-59237-126-6 $595 | Rubber Industry: Softcover ISBN 978-1-59237-130-3 $595 | Pulp and Paper Industry: Softcover ISBN 978-1-59237-131-0 $595 | Cosmetic & Toiletries Industry: Softcover ISBN 978-1-59237-132-7 $895

Research Services Directory: Commercial & Corporate Research Centers

This ninth edition provides access to well over 8,000 independent Commercial Research Firms, Corporate Research Centers and Laboratories offering contract services for hands-on, basic or applied research. Research Services Directory covers the thousands of types of research companies, including Biotechnology & Pharmaceutical Developers, Consumer Product Research, Defense Contractors, Electronics & Software Engineers, Think Tanks, Forensic Investigators, Independent Commercial Laboratories, Information Brokers, Market & Survey Research Companies, Medical Diagnostic Facilities, Product Research & Development Firms and more. Each entry provides the company's name, mailing address, phone & fax numbers, key contacts, web site, e-mail address, as well as a company description and research and technical fields served. Four indexes provide immediate access to this wealth of information: Research Firms Index, Geographic Index, Personnel Name Index and Subject Index.

> *"An important source for organizations in need of information about laboratories, individuals and other facilities." –ARBA*

Softcover ISBN 978-1-59237-003-0, 1,400 pages, $465.00

International Business and Trade Directories

Completely updated, the Third Edition of *International Business and Trade Directories* now contains more than 10,000 entries, over 2,000 more than the last edition, making this directory the most comprehensive resource of the worlds business and trade directories. Entries include content descriptions, price, publisher's name and address, web site and e-mail addresses, phone and fax numbers and editorial staff. Organized by industry group, and then by region, this resource puts over 10,000 industry-specific business and trade directories at the reader's fingertips. Three indexes are included for quick access to information: Geographic Index, Publisher Index and Title Index. Public, college and corporate libraries, as well as individuals and corporations seeking critical market information will want to add this directory to their marketing collection.

> *"Reasonably priced for a work of this type, this directory should appeal to larger academic, public and corporate libraries with an international focus." –Library Journal*

Softcover ISBN 978-1-930956-63-6, 1,800 pages, $225.00

To preview any of our Directories Risk-Free for 30 days, call (800) 562-2139 or fax (518) 789-0556
www.greyhouse.com books@greyhouse.com

Business Information ◆ **Ratings Guides** ◆ General Reference ◆ Education ◆
Statistics ◆ Demographics ◆ Health Information ◆ Canadian Information

TheStreet.com Ratings Guide to Health Insurers

TheStreet.com Ratings Guide to Health Insurers is the first and only source to cover the financial stability of the nation's health care system, rating the financial safety of more than 6,000 health insurance providers, health maintenance organizations (HMOs) and all of the Blue Cross Blue Shield plans – updated quarterly to ensure the most accurate information. The Guide also provides a complete listing of all the major health insurers, including all Long-Term Care and Medigap insurers. Our *Guide to Health Insurers* includes comprehensive, timely coverage on the financial stability of HMOs and health insurers; the most accurate insurance company ratings available—the same quality ratings heralded by the U.S. General Accounting Office; separate listings for those companies offering Medigap and long-term care policies; the number of serious consumer complaints filed against most HMOs so you can see who is actually providing the best (or worst) service and more. The easy-to-use layout gives you a one-line summary analysis for each company that we track, followed by an in-depth, detailed analysis of all HMOs and the largest health insurers. The guide also includes a list of TheStreet.com Ratings Recommended Companies with information on how to contact them, and the reasoning behind any rating upgrades or downgrades.

> *"With 20 years behind its insurance-advocacy research [the rating guide] continues to offer a wealth of information that helps consumers weigh their healthcare options now and in the future." -Today's Librarian*

Issues published quarterly, Softcover, 550 pages, $499.00 for four quarterly issues, $249.00 for a single issue

TheStreet.com Ratings Guide to Life & Annuity Insurers

TheStreet.com Safety Ratings are the most reliable source for evaluating an insurer's financial solvency risk. Consequently, policy-holders have come to rely on TheStreet.com's flagship publication, *TheStreet.com Ratings Guide to Life & Annuity Insurers*, to help them identify the safest companies to do business with. Each easy-to-use edition delivers TheStreet.com's independent ratings and analyses on more than 1,100 insurers, updated every quarter. Plus, your patrons will find a complete list of TheStreet.com Recommended Companies, including contact information, and the reasoning behind any rating upgrades or downgrades. This guide is perfect for those who are considering the purchase of a life insurance policy, placing money in an annuity, or advising clients about insurance and annuities. A life or health insurance policy or annuity is only as secure as the insurance company issuing it. Therefore, make sure your patrons have what they need to periodically monitor the financial condition of the companies with whom they have an investment. The TheStreet.com Ratings product line is designed to help them in their evaluations.

> *"Weiss has an excellent reputation and this title is held by hundreds of libraries. This guide is recommended for public and academic libraries." -ARBA*

Issues published quarterly, Softcover, 360 pages, $499.00 for four quarterly issues, $249.00 for a single issue

TheStreet.com Ratings Guide to Property & Casualty Insurers

TheStreet.com Ratings Guide to Property and Casualty Insurers provides the most extensive coverage of insurers writing policies, helping consumers and businesses avoid financial headaches. Updated quarterly, this easy-to-use publication delivers the independent, unbiased TheStreet.com Safety Ratings and supporting analyses on more than 2,800 U.S. insurance companies, offering auto & homeowners insurance, business insurance, worker's compensation insurance, product liability insurance, medical malpractice and other professional liability insurance. Each edition includes a list of TheStreet.com Recommended Companies by type of insurance, including a contact number, plus helpful information about the coverage provided by the State Guarantee Associations.

> *"In contrast to the other major insurance rating agencies...Weiss does not have a financial relationship worth the companies it rates. A GAO study found that Weiss identified financial vulnerability earlier than the other rating agencies." -ARBA*

Issues published quarterly, Softcover, 455 pages, $499.00 for four quarterly issues, $249.00 for a single issue

TheStreet.com Ratings Consumer Box Set

Deliver the critical information your patrons need to safeguard their personal finances with *TheStreet.com Ratings' Consumer Guide Box Set*. Each of the eight guides is packed with accurate, unbiased information and recommendations to help your patrons make sound financial decisions. TheStreet.com Ratings Consumer Guide Box Set provides your patrons with easy to understand guidance on important personal finance topics, including: *Consumer Guide to Variable Annuities, Consumer Guide to Medicare Supplement Insurance, Consumer Guide to Elder Care Choices, Consumer Guide to Automobile Insurance, Consumer Guide to Long-Term Care Insurance, Consumer Guide to Homeowners Insurance, Consumer Guide to Term Life Insurance, and Consumer Guide to Medicare Prescription Drug Coverage.* Each guide provides an easy-to-read overview of the topic, what to look out for when selecting a company or insurance plan to do business with, who are the recommended companies to work with and how to navigate through these often-times difficult decisions. Custom worksheets and step-by-step directions make these resources accessible to all types of users. Packaged in a handy custom display box, these helpful guides will prove to be a much-used addition to any reference collection.

Issues published twice per year, Softcover, 600 pages, $429.00 for two biennial issues

Business Information ♦ <u>**Ratings Guides**</u> ♦ General Reference ♦ Education ♦
Statistics ♦ Demographics ♦ Health Information ♦ Canadian Information

TheStreet.com Ratings Guide to Stock Mutual Funds

TheStreet.com Ratings Guide to Stock Mutual Funds offers ratings and analyses on more than 8,800 equity mutual funds – more than any other publication. The exclusive TheStreet.com Investment Ratings combine an objective evaluation of each fund's performance and risk to provide a single, user-friendly, composite rating, giving your patrons a better handle on a mutual fund's risk-adjusted performance. Each edition identifies the top-performing mutual funds based on risk category, type of fund, and overall risk-adjusted performance. TheStreet.com's unique investment rating system makes it easy to see exactly which stocks are on the rise and which ones should be avoided. For those investors looking to tailor their mutual fund selections based on age, income, and tolerance for risk, we've also assigned two component ratings to each fund: a performance rating and a risk rating. With these, you can identify those funds that are best suited to meet your - or your client's – individual needs and goals. Plus, we include a handy Risk Profile Quiz to help you assess your personal tolerance for risk. So whether you're an investing novice or professional, the *Guide to Stock Mutual Funds* gives you everything you need to find a mutual fund that is right for you.

> *"There is tremendous need for information such as that provided by this Weiss publication. This reasonably priced guide is recommended for public and academic libraries serving investors." -ARBA*

Issues published quarterly, Softcover, 655 pages, $499 for four quarterly issues, $249 for a single issue

TheStreet.com Ratings Guide to Exchange-Traded Funds

TheStreet.com Ratings editors analyze hundreds of mutual funds each quarter, condensing all of the available data into a single composite opinion of each fund's risk-adjusted performance. The intuitive, consumer-friendly ratings allow investors to instantly identify those funds that have historically done well and those that have under-performed the market. Each quarterly edition identifies the top-performing exchange-traded funds based on risk category, type of fund, and overall risk-adjusted performance. The rating scale, A through F, gives you a better handle on an exchange-traded fund's risk-adjusted performance. Other features include Top & Bottom 200 Exchange-Traded Funds; Performance and Risk: 100 Best and Worst Exchange- Traded Funds; Investor Profile Quiz; Performance Benchmarks and Fund Type Descriptions. With the growing popularity of mutual fund investing, consumers need a reliable source to help them track and evaluate the performance of their mutual fund holdings. Plus, they need a way of identifying and monitoring other funds as potential new investments. Unfortunately, the hundreds of performance and risk measures available, multiplied by the vast number of mutual fund investments on the market today, can make this a daunting task for even the most sophisticated investor. This Guide will serve as a useful tool for both the first-time and seasoned investor.

Editions published quarterly, Softcover, 440 pages, $499.00 for four quarterly issues, $249.00 for a single issue

TheStreet.com Ratings Guide to Bond & Money Market Mutual Funds

TheStreet.com Ratings Guide to Bond & Money Market Mutual Funds has everything your patrons need to easily identify the top-performing fixed income funds on the market today. Each quarterly edition contains TheStreet.com's independent ratings and analyses on more than 4,600 fixed income funds – more than any other publication, including corporate bond funds, high-yield bond funds, municipal bond funds, mortgage security funds, money market funds, global bond funds and government bond funds. In addition, the fund's risk rating is combined with its three-year performance rating to get an overall picture of the fund's risk-adjusted performance. The resulting TheStreet.com Investment Rating gives a single, user-friendly, objective evaluation that makes it easy to compare one fund to another and select the right fund based on the level of risk tolerance. Most investors think of fixed income mutual funds as "safe" investments. That's not always the case, however, depending on the credit risk, interest rate risk, and prepayment risk of the securities owned by the fund. TheStreet.com Ratings assesses each of these risks and assigns each fund a risk rating to help investors quickly evaluate the fund's risk component. Plus, we include a handy Risk Profile Quiz to help you assess your personal tolerance for risk. So whether you're an investing novice or professional, the *Guide to Bond and Money Market Mutual Funds* gives you everything you need to find a mutual fund that is right for you.

> *"Comprehensive... It is easy to use and consumer-oriented, and can be recommended for larger public and academic libraries." -ARBA*

Issues published quarterly, Softcover, 470 pages, $499.00 for four quarterly issues, $249.00 for a single issue

TheStreet.com Ratings Guide to Banks & Thrifts

Updated quarterly, for the most up-to-date information, *TheStreet.com Ratings Guide to Banks and Thrifts* offers accurate, intuitive safety ratings your patrons can trust; supporting ratios and analyses that show an institution's strong & weak points; identification of the TheStreet.com Recommended Companies with branches in your area; a complete list of institutions receiving upgrades/downgrades; and comprehensive coverage of every bank and thrift in the nation – more than 9,000. TheStreet.com Safety Ratings are then based on the analysts' review of publicly available information collected by the federal banking regulators. The easy-to-use layout gives you: the institution's TheStreet.com Safety Rating for the last 3 years; the five key indexes used to evaluate each institution; along with the primary ratios and statistics used in determining the company's rating. *TheStreet.com Ratings Guide to Banks & Thrifts* will be a must for individuals who are concerned about the safety of their CD or savings account; need to be sure that an existing line of credit will be there when they need it; or simply want to avoid the hassles of dealing with a failing or troubled institution.

> *"Large public and academic libraries most definitely need to acquire the work. Likewise, special libraries in large corporations will find this title indispensable." -ARBA*

Issues published quarterly, Softcover, 370 pages, $499.00 for four quarterly issues, $249.00 for a single issue

To preview any of our Directories Risk-Free for 30 days, call (800) 562-2139 or fax (518) 789-0556
www.greyhouse.com   books@greyhouse.com

Business Information ✦ **Ratings Guides** ✦ General Reference ✦ Education ✦
Statistics ✦ Demographics ✦ Health Information ✦ Canadian Information

TheStreet.com Ratings Guide to Common Stocks

TheStreet.com Ratings Guide to Common Stocks gives your patrons reliable insight into the risk-adjusted performance of common stocks listed on the NYSE, AMEX, and Nasdaq – over 5,800 stocks in all – more than any other publication. TheStreet.com's unique investment rating system makes it easy to see exactly which stocks are on the rise and which ones should be avoided. In addition, your patrons also get supporting analysis showing growth trends, profitability, debt levels, valuation levels, the top-rated stocks within each industry, and more. Plus, each stock is ranked with the easy-to-use buy-hold-sell equivalents commonly used by Wall Street. Whether they're selecting their own investments or checking up on a broker's recommendation, TheStreet.com Ratings can help them in their evaluations.

"Users... will find the information succinct and the explanations readable, easy to understand, and helpful to a novice." -Library Journal

Issues published quarterly, Softcover, 440 pages, $499.00 for four quarterly issues, $249.00 for a single issue

TheStreet.com Ratings Ultimate Guided Tour of Stock Investing

This important reference guide from TheStreet.com Ratings is just what librarians around the country have asked for: a step-by-step introduction to stock investing for the beginning to intermediate investor. This easy-to-navigate guide explores the basics of stock investing and includes the intuitive TheStreet.com Investment Rating on more than 5,800 stocks, complete with real-world investing information that can be put to use immediately with stocks that fit the concepts discussed in the guide; informative charts, graphs and worksheets; easy-to-understand explanations on topics like P/E, compound interest, marked indices, diversifications, brokers, and much more; along with financial safety ratings for every stock on the NYSE, American Stock Exchange and the Nasdaq. This consumer-friendly guide offers complete how-to information on stock investing that can be put to use right away; a friendly format complete with our "Wise Guide" who leads the reader on a safari to learn about the investing jungle; helpful charts, graphs and simple worksheets; the intuitive TheStreet.com Investment rating on over 6,000 stocks — every stock found on the NYSE, American Stock Exchange and the NASDAQ; and much more.

"Provides investors with an alternative to stock broker recommendations, which recently have been tarnished by conflicts of interest. In summary, the guide serves as a welcome addition for all public library collections." -ARBA

Issues published quarterly, Softcover, 370 pages, $499.00 for four quarterly issues, $249.00 for a single issue

TheStreet.com Ratings' Reports & Services

- Ratings Online — An on-line summary covering an individual company's TheStreet.com Financial Strength Rating or an investment's unique TheStreet.com Investment Rating with the factors contributing to that rating; available 24 hours a day by visiting www.thestreet.com/tscratings or calling (800) 289-9222.
- Unlimited Ratings Research — The ultimate research tool providing fast, easy online access to the very latest TheStreet.com Financial Strength Ratings and Investment Ratings. Price: $559 per industry.

Contact TheStreet.com for more information about Reports & Services at www.thestreet.com/tscratings or call (800) 289-9222

TheStreet.com Ratings' Custom Reports

TheStreet.com Ratings is pleased to offer two customized options for receiving ratings data. Each taps into TheStreet.com's vast data repositories and is designed to provide exactly the data you need. Choose from a variety of industries, companies, data variables, and delivery formats including print, Excel, SQL, Text or Access.
- Customized Reports - get right to the heart of your company's research and data needs with a report customized to your specifications.
- Complete Database Download – TheStreet.com will design and deliver the database; from there you can sort it, recalculate it, and format your results to suit your specific needs.

Contact TheStreet.com for more information about Custom Reports at www.thestreet.com/tscratings or call (800) 289-9222

Business Information ◆ Ratings Guides ◆ <u>General Reference</u> ◆ Education ◆
Statistics ◆ Demographics ◆ Health Information ◆ Canadian Information

The Value of a Dollar 1600-1859, The Colonial Era to The Civil War

Following the format of the widely acclaimed, *The Value of a Dollar, 1860-2004*, *The Value of a Dollar 1600-1859, The Colonial Era to The Civil War* records the actual prices of thousands of items that consumers purchased from the Colonial Era to the Civil War. Our editorial department had been flooded with requests from users of our *Value of a Dollar* for the same type of information, just from an earlier time period. This new volume is just the answer – with pricing data from 1600 to 1859. Arranged into five-year chapters, each 5-year chapter includes a Historical Snapshot, Consumer Expenditures, Investments, Selected Income, Income/Standard Jobs, Food Basket, Standard Prices and Miscellany. There is also a section on Trends. This informative section charts the change in price over time and provides added detail on the reasons prices changed within the time period, including industry developments, changes in consumer attitudes and important historical facts. This fascinating survey will serve a wide range of research needs and will be useful in all high school, public and academic library reference collections.

"The Value of a Dollar: Colonial Era to the Civil War, 1600-1865 will find a happy audience among students, researchers, and general browsers. It offers a fascinating and detailed look at early American history from the viewpoint of everyday people trying to make ends meet. This title and the earlier publication, The Value of a Dollar, 1860-2004, complement each other very well, and readers will appreciate finding them side-by-side on the shelf." -Booklist

Hardcover ISBN 978-1-59237-094-8, 600 pages, $145.00 | Ebook ISBN 978-1-59237-169-3 www.gale.com/gvrl/partners/grey.htm

The Value of a Dollar 1860-2004, Third Edition

A guide to practical economy, *The Value of a Dollar* records the actual prices of thousands of items that consumers purchased from the Civil War to the present, along with facts about investment options and income opportunities. This brand new Third Edition boasts a brand new addition to each five-year chapter, a section on Trends. This informative section charts the change in price over time and provides added detail on the reasons prices changed within the time period, including industry developments, changes in consumer attitudes and important historical facts. Plus, a brand new chapter for 2000-2004 has been added. Each 5-year chapter includes a Historical Snapshot, Consumer Expenditures, Investments, Selected Income, Income/Standard Jobs, Food Basket, Standard Prices and Miscellany. This interesting and useful publication will be widely used in any reference collection.

"Business historians, reporters, writers and students will find this source... very helpful for historical research. Libraries will want to purchase it." –ARBA

Hardcover ISBN 978-1-59237-074-0, 600 pages, $145.00 | Ebook ISBN 978-1-59237-173-0 www.gale.com/gvrl/partners/grey.htm

Working Americans 1880-1999
Volume I: The Working Class, Volume II: The Middle Class, Volume III: The Upper Class

Each of the volumes in the *Working Americans* series focuses on a particular class of Americans, The Working Class, The Middle Class and The Upper Class over the last 120 years. Chapters in each volume focus on one decade and profile three to five families. Family Profiles include real data on Income & Job Descriptions, Selected Prices of the Times, Annual Income, Annual Budgets, Family Finances, Life at Work, Life at Home, Life in the Community, Working Conditions, Cost of Living, Amusements and much more. Each chapter also contains an Economic Profile with Average Wages of other Professions, a selection of Typical Pricing, Key Events & Inventions, News Profiles, Articles from Local Media and Illustrations. The *Working Americans* series captures the lifestyles of each of the classes from the last twelve decades, covers a vast array of occupations and ethnic backgrounds and travels the entire nation. These interesting and useful compilations of portraits of the American Working, Middle and Upper Classes during the last 120 years will be an important addition to any high school, public or academic library reference collection.

"These interesting, unique compilations of economic and social facts, figures and graphs will support multiple research needs. They will engage and enlighten patrons in high school, public and academic library collections." –Booklist

Volume I: The Working Class Hardcover ISBN 978-1-891482-81-6, 558 pages, $145.00 | Volume II: The Middle Class Hardcover ISBN 978-1-891482-72-4, 591 pages, $145.00 | Volume III: The Upper Class Hardcover ISBN 978-1-930956-38-4, 567 pages, $145.00 | Ebooks www.gale.com/gvrl/partners/grey.htm

Working Americans 1880-1999 Volume IV: Their Children

This Fourth Volume in the highly successful *Working Americans* series focuses on American children, decade by decade from 1880 to 1999. This interesting and useful volume introduces the reader to three children in each decade, one from each of the Working, Middle and Upper classes. Like the first three volumes in the series, the individual profiles are created from interviews, diaries, statistical studies, biographies and news reports. Profiles cover a broad range of ethnic backgrounds, geographic area and lifestyles – everything from an orphan in Memphis in 1882, following the Yellow Fever epidemic of 1878 to an eleven-year-old nephew of a beer baron and owner of the New York Yankees in New York City in 1921. Chapters also contain important supplementary materials including News Features as well as information on everything from Schools to Parks, Infectious Diseases to Childhood Fears along with Entertainment, Family Life and much more to provide an informative overview of the lifestyles of children from each decade. This interesting account of what life was like for Children in the Working, Middle and Upper Classes will be a welcome addition to the reference collection of any high school, public or academic library.

Hardcover ISBN 978-1-930956-35-3, 600 pages, $145.00 | Ebook ISBN 978-1-59237-166-2 www.gale.com/gvrl/partners/grey.htm

Business Information ✦ Ratings Guides ✦ <u>General Reference</u> ✦ Education ✦
Statistics ✦ Demographics ✦ Health Information ✦ Canadian Information

Grey House
Publishing

Working Americans 1880-2003 Volume V: Americans At War

Working Americans 1880-2003 Volume V: Americans At War is divided into 11 chapters, each covering a decade from 1880-2003 and examines the lives of Americans during the time of war, including declared conflicts, one-time military actions, protests, and preparations for war. Each decade includes several personal profiles, whether on the battlefield or on the homefront, that tell the stories of civilians, soldiers, and officers during the decade. The profiles examine: Life at Home; Life at Work; and Life in the Community. Each decade also includes an Economic Profile with statistical comparisons, a Historical Snapshot, News Profiles, local News Articles, and Illustrations that provide a solid historical background to the decade being examined. Profiles range widely not only geographically, but also emotionally, from that of a girl whose leg was torn off in a blast during WWI, to the boredom of being stationed in the Dakotas as the Indian Wars were drawing to a close. As in previous volumes of the *Working Americans* series, information is presented in narrative form, but hard facts and real-life situations back up each story. The basis of the profiles come from diaries, private print books, personal interviews, family histories, estate documents and magazine articles. For easy reference, *Working Americans 1880-2003 Volume V: Americans At War* includes an in-depth Subject Index. The Working Americans series has become an important reference for public libraries, academic libraries and high school libraries. This fifth volume will be a welcome addition to all of these types of reference collections.

Hardcover ISBN 978-1-59237-024-5, 600 pages, $145.00 | Ebook ISBN 978-1-59237-167-9 www.gale.com/gvrl/partners/grey.htm

Working Americans 1880-2005 Volume VI: Women at Work

Unlike any other volume in the *Working Americans* series, this Sixth Volume, is the first to focus on a particular gender of Americans. *Volume VI: Women at Work*, traces what life was like for working women from the 1860's to the present time. Beginning with the life of a maid in 1890 and a store clerk in 1900 and ending with the life and times of the modern working women, this text captures the struggle, strengths and changing perception of the American woman at work. Each chapter focuses on one decade and profiles three to five women with real data on Income & Job Descriptions, Selected Prices of the Times, Annual Income, Annual Budgets, Family Finances, Life at Work, Life at Home, Life in the Community, Working Conditions, Cost of Living, Amusements and much more. For even broader access to the events, economics and attitude towards women throughout the past 130 years, each chapter is supplemented with News Profiles, Articles from Local Media, Illustrations, Economic Profiles, Typical Pricing, Key Events, Inventions and more. This important volume illustrates what life was like for working women over time and allows the reader to develop an understanding of the changing role of women at work. These interesting and useful compilations of portraits of women at work will be an important addition to any high school, public or academic library reference collection.

Hardcover ISBN 978-1-59237-063-4, 600 pages, $145.00 | Ebook ISBN 978-1-59237-168-6 www.gale.com/gvrl/partners/grey.htm

Working Americans 1880-2005 Volume VII: Social Movements

Working Americans series, Volume VII: Social Movements explores how Americans sought and fought for change from the 1880s to the present time. Following the format of previous volumes in the Working Americans series, the text examines the lives of 34 individuals who have worked -- often behind the scenes --- to bring about change. Issues include topics as diverse as the Anti-smoking movement of 1901 to efforts by Native Americans to reassert their long lost rights. Along the way, the book will profile individuals brave enough to demand suffrage for Kansas women in 1912 or demand an end to lynching during a March on Washington in 1923. Each profile is enriched with real data on Income & Job Descriptions, Selected Prices of the Times, Annual Incomes & Budgets, Life at Work, Life at Home, Life in the Community, along with News Features, Key Events, and Illustrations. The depth of information contained in each profile allow the user to explore the private, financial and public lives of these subjects, deepening our understanding of how calls for change took place in our society. A must-purchase for the reference collections of high school libraries, public libraries and academic libraries.

Hardcover ISBN 978-1-59237-101-3, 600 pages, $145.00 | Ebook ISBN 978-1-59237-174-7 www.gale.com/gvrl/partners/grey.htm

Working Americans 1880-2005 Volume VIII: Immigrants

Working Americans 1880-2007 Volume VIII: Immigrants illustrates what life was like for families leaving their homeland and creating a new life in the United States. Each chapter covers one decade and introduces the reader to three immigrant families. Family profiles cover what life was like in their homeland, in their community in the United States, their home life, working conditions and so much more. As the reader moves through these pages, the families and individuals come to life, painting a picture of why they left their homeland, their experiences in setting roots in a new country, their struggles and triumphs, stretching from the 1800s to the present time. Profiles include a seven-year-old Swedish girl who meets her father for the first time at Ellis Island; a Chinese photographer's assistant; an Armenian who flees the genocide of his country to build Ford automobiles in Detroit; a 38-year-old German bachelor cigar maker who settles in Newark NJ, but contemplates tobacco farming in Virginia; a 19-year-old Irish domestic servant who is amazed at the easy life of American dogs; a 19-year-old Filipino who came to Hawaii against his parent's wishes to farm sugar cane; a French-Canadian who finds success as a boxer in Maine and many more. As in previous volumes, information is presented in narrative form, but hard facts and real-life situations back up each story. With the topic of immigration being so hotly debated in this country, this timely resource will prove to be a useful source for students, researchers, historians and library patrons to discover the issues facing immigrants in the United States. This title will be a useful addition to reference collections of public libraries, university libraries and high schools.

Hardcover ISBN 978-1-59237-197-6, 600 pages, $145.00 | Ebook ISBN 978-1-59237-232-4 www.gale.com/gvrl/partners/grey.htm

Business Information ✦ Ratings Guides ✦ <u>General Reference</u> ✦ Education ✦
Statistics ✦ Demographics ✦ Health Information ✦ Canadian Information

Grey House Publishing

The Encyclopedia of Warrior Peoples & Fighting Groups

Many military groups throughout the world have excelled in their craft either by fortuitous circumstances, outstanding leadership, or intense training. This new second edition of *The Encyclopedia of Warrior Peoples and Fighting Groups* explores the origins and leadership of these outstanding combat forces, chronicles their conquests and accomplishments, examines the circumstances surrounding their decline or disbanding, and assesses their influence on the groups and methods of warfare that followed. Readers will encounter ferocious tribes, charismatic leaders, and daring militias, from ancient times to the present, including Amazons, Buffalo Soldiers, Green Berets, Iron Brigade, Kamikazes, Peoples of the Sea, Polish Winged Hussars, Teutonic Knights, and Texas Rangers. With over 100 alphabetical entries, numerous cross-references and illustrations, a comprehensive bibliography, and index, the *Encyclopedia of Warrior Peoples and Fighting Groups* is a valuable resource for readers seeking insight into the bold history of distinguished fighting forces.

"Especially useful for high school students, undergraduates, and general readers with an interest in military history." –Library Journal

Hardcover ISBN 978-1-59237-116-7, 660 pages, $135.00 | Ebook ISBN 978-1-59237-172-3 www.gale.com/gvrl/partners/grey.htm

The Encyclopedia of Invasions & Conquests, From the Ancient Times to the Present

This second edition of the popular *Encyclopedia of Invasions & Conquests*, a comprehensive guide to over 150 invasions, conquests, battles and occupations from ancient times to the present, takes readers on a journey that includes the Roman conquest of Britain, the Portuguese colonization of Brazil, and the Iraqi invasion of Kuwait, to name a few. New articles will explore the late 20th and 21st centuries, with a specific focus on recent conflicts in Afghanistan, Kuwait, Iraq, Yugoslavia, Grenada and Chechnya. In addition to covering the military aspects of invasions and conquests, entries cover some of the political, economic, and cultural aspects, for example, the effects of a conquest on the invade country's political and monetary system and in its language and religion. The entries on leaders – among them Sargon, Alexander the Great, William the Conqueror, and Adolf Hitler – deal with the people who sought to gain control, expand power, or exert religious or political influence over others through military means. Revised and updated for this second edition, entries are arranged alphabetically within historical periods. Each chapter provides a map to help readers locate key areas and geographical features, and bibliographical references appear at the end of each entry. Other useful features include cross-references, a cumulative bibliography and a comprehensive subject index. This authoritative, well-organized, lucidly written volume will prove invaluable for a variety of readers, including high school students, military historians, members of the armed forces, history buffs and hobbyists.

"Engaging writing, sensible organization, nice illustrations, interesting and obscure facts, and useful maps make this book a pleasure to read." –ARBA

Hardcover ISBN 978-1-59237-114-3, 598 pages, $135.00 | Ebook ISBN 978-1-59237-171-6 www.gale.com/gvrl/partners/grey.htm

Encyclopedia of Prisoners of War & Internment

This authoritative second edition provides a valuable overview of the history of prisoners of war and interned civilians, from earliest times to the present. Written by an international team of experts in the field of POW studies, this fascinating and thought-provoking volume includes entries on a wide range of subjects including the Crusades, Plains Indian Warfare, concentration camps, the two world wars, and famous POWs throughout history, as well as atrocities, escapes, and much more. Written in a clear and easily understandable style, this informative reference details over 350 entries, 30% larger than the first edition, that survey the history of prisoners of war and interned civilians from the earliest times to the present, with emphasis on the 19th and 20th centuries. Medical conditions, international law, exchanges of prisoners, organizations working on behalf of POWs, and trials associated with the treatment of captives are just some of the themes explored. Entries are arranged alphabetically, plus illustrations and maps are provided for easy reference. The text also includes an introduction, bibliography, appendix of selected documents, and end-of-entry reading suggestions. This one-of-a-kind reference will be a helpful addition to the reference collections of all public libraries, high schools, and university libraries and will prove invaluable to historians and military enthusiasts.

"Thorough and detailed yet accessible to the lay reader. Of special interest to subject specialists and historians; recommended for public and academic libraries." - Library Journal

Hardcover ISBN 978-1-59237-120-4, 676 pages, $135.00 | Ebook ISBN 978-1-59237-170-9 www.gale.com/gvrl/partners/grey.htm

The Encyclopedia of Rural America: the Land & People

History, sociology, anthropology, and public policy are combined to deliver the encyclopedia destined to become the standard reference work in American rural studies. From irrigation and marriage to games and mental health, this encyclopedia is the first to explore the contemporary landscape of rural America, placed in historical perspective. With over 300 articles prepared by leading experts from across the nation, this timely encyclopedia documents and explains the major themes, concepts, industries, concerns, and everyday life of the people and land who make up rural America. Entries range from the industrial sector and government policy to arts and humanities and social and family concerns. Articles explore every aspect of life in rural America. *Encyclopedia of Rural America*, with its broad range of coverage, will appeal to high school and college students as well as graduate students, faculty, scholars, and people whose work pertains to rural areas.

"This exemplary encyclopedia is guaranteed to educate our highly urban society about the uniqueness of rural America. Recommended for public and academic libraries." -Library Journal

Two Volumes, Hardcover, ISBN 978-1-59237-115-0, 800 pages, $195.00

To preview any of our Directories Risk-Free for 30 days, call (800) 562-2139 or fax (518) 789-0556
www.greyhouse.com books@greyhouse.com

Business Information ◆ Ratings Guides ◆ __General Reference__ ◆ Education ◆
Statistics ◆ Demographics ◆ Health Information ◆ Canadian Information

Grey House
Publishing

The Religious Right, A Reference Handbook

Timely and unbiased, this third edition updates and expands its examination of the religious right and its influence on our government, citizens, society, and politics. From the fight to outlaw the teaching of Darwin's theory of evolution to the struggle to outlaw abortion, the religious right is continually exerting an influence on public policy. This text explores the influence of religion on legislation and society, while examining the alignment of the religious right with the political right. A historical survey of the movement highlights the shift to "hands-on" approach to politics and the struggle to present a unified front. The coverage offers a critical historical survey of the religious right movement, focusing on its increased involvement in the political arena, attempts to forge coalitions, and notable successes and failures. The text offers complete coverage of biographies of the men and women who have advanced the cause and an up to date chronology illuminate the movement's goals, including their accomplishments and failures. This edition offers an extensive update to all sections along with several brand new entries. Two new sections complement this third edition, a chapter on legal issues and court decisions and a chapter on demographic statistics and electoral patterns. To aid in further research, *The Religious Right*, offers an entire section of annotated listings of print and non-print resources, as well as of organizations affiliated with the religious right, and those opposing it. Comprehensive in its scope, this work offers easy-to-read, pertinent information for those seeking to understand the religious right and its evolving role in American society. A must for libraries of all sizes, university religion departments, activists, high schools and for those interested in the evolving role of the religious right.

" Recommended for all public and academic libraries." - Library Journal

Hardcover ISBN 978-1-59237-113-6, 600 pages, $135.00 | Ebook ISBN 978-1-59237-226-3 www.gale.com/gvrl/partners/grey.htm

From Suffrage to the Senate, America's Political Women

From Suffrage to the Senate is a comprehensive and valuable compendium of biographies of leading women in U.S. politics, past and present, and an examination of the wide range of women's movements. Up to date through 2006, this dynamically illustrated reference work explores American women's path to political power and social equality from the struggle for the right to vote and the abolition of slavery to the first African American woman in the U.S. Senate and beyond. This new edition includes over 150 new entries and a brand new section on trends and demographics of women in politics. The in-depth coverage also traces the political heritage of the abolition, labor, suffrage, temperance, and reproductive rights movements. The alphabetically arranged entries include biographies of every woman from across the political spectrum who has served in the U.S. House and Senate, along with women in the Judiciary and the U.S. Cabinet and, new to this edition, biographies of activists and political consultants. Bibliographical references follow each entry. For easy reference, a handy chronology is provided detailing 150 years of women's history. This up-to-date reference will be a must-purchase for women's studies departments, high schools and public libraries and will be a handy resource for those researching the key players in women's politics, past and present.

"An engaging tool that would be useful in high school, public, and academic libraries looking for an overview of the political history of women in the US." –Booklist

Two Volumes, Hardcover ISBN 978-1-59237-117-4, 1,160 pages, $195.00 | Ebook ISBN 978-1-59237-227-0 www.gale.com/gvrl/partners/grey.htm

An African Biographical Dictionary

This landmark second edition is the only biographical dictionary to bring together, in one volume, cultural, social and political leaders – both historical and contemporary – of the sub-Saharan region. Over 800 biographical sketches of prominent Africans, as well as foreigners who have affected the continent's history, are featured, 150 more than the previous edition. The wide spectrum of leaders includes religious figures, writers, politicians, scientists, entertainers, sports personalities and more. Access to these fascinating individuals is provided in a user-friendly format. The biographies are arranged alphabetically, cross-referenced and indexed. Entries include the country or countries in which the person was significant and the commonly accepted dates of birth and death. Each biographical sketch is chronologically written; entries for cultural personalities add an evaluation of their work. This information is followed by a selection of references often found in university and public libraries, including autobiographies and principal biographical works. Appendixes list each individual by country and by field of accomplishment – rulers, musicians, explorers, missionaries, businessmen, physicists – nearly thirty categories in all. Another convenient appendix lists heads of state since independence by country. Up-to-date and representative of African societies as a whole, An African Biographical Dictionary provides a wealth of vital information for students of African culture and is an indispensable reference guide for anyone interested in African affairs.

"An unquestionable convenience to have these concise, informative biographies gathered into one source, indexed, and analyzed by appendixes listing entrants by nation and occupational field." –Wilson Library Bulletin

Hardcover ISBN 978-1-59237-112-9, 667 pages, $135.00 | Ebook ISBN 978-1-59237-229-4 www.gale.com/gvrl/partners/grey.htm

Business Information ♦ Ratings Guides ♦ **General Reference** ♦ Education ♦
Statistics ♦ Demographics ♦ Health Information ♦ Canadian Information

Grey House Publishing

American Environmental Leaders, From Colonial Times to the Present

A comprehensive and diverse award winning collection of biographies of the most important figures in American environmentalism. Few subjects arouse the passions the way the environment does. How will we feed an ever-increasing population and how can that food be made safe for consumption? Who decides how land is developed? How can environmental policies be made fair for everyone, including multiethnic groups, women, children, and the poor? *American Environmental Leaders* presents more than 350 biographies of men and women who have devoted their lives to studying, debating, and organizing these and other controversial issues over the last 200 years. In addition to the scientists who have analyzed how human actions affect nature, we are introduced to poets, landscape architects, presidents, painters, activists, even sanitation engineers, and others who have forever altered how we think about the environment. The easy to use A–Z format provides instant access to these fascinating individuals, and frequent cross references indicate others with whom individuals worked (and sometimes clashed). End of entry references provide users with a starting point for further research.

"Highly recommended for high school, academic, and public libraries needing environmental biographical information." –Library Journal/Starred Review

Two Volumes, Hardcover ISBN 978-1-59237-119-8, 900 pages $195.00 | Ebook ISBN 978-1-59237-230-0
www.gale.com/gvrl/partners/grey.htm

World Cultural Leaders of the Twentieth & Twenty-First Centuries

World Cultural Leaders of the Twentieth & Twenty-First Centuries is a window into the arts, performances, movements, and music that shaped the world's cultural development since 1900. A remarkable around-the-world look at one-hundred-plus years of cultural development through the eyes of those that set the stage and stayed to play. This second edition offers over 120 new biographies along with a complete update of existing biographies. To further aid the reader, a handy fold-out timeline traces important events in all six cultural categories from 1900 through the present time. Plus, a new section of detailed material and resources for 100 selected individuals is also new to this edition, with further data on museums, homesteads, websites, artwork and more. This remarkable compilation will answer a wide range of questions. Who was the originator of the term "documentary"? Which poet married the daughter of the famed novelist Thomas Mann in order to help her escape Nazi Germany? Which British writer served as an agent in Russia against the Bolsheviks before the 1917 revolution? A handy two-volume set that makes it easy to look up 450 worldwide cultural icons: novelists, poets, playwrights, painters, sculptors, architects, dancers, choreographers, actors, directors, filmmakers, singers, composers, and musicians. *World Cultural Leaders of the Twentieth & Twenty-First Centuries* provides entries (many of them illustrated) covering the person's works, achievements, and professional career in a thorough essay and offers interesting facts and statistics. Entries are fully cross-referenced so that readers can learn how various individuals influenced others. An index of leaders by occupation, a useful glossary and a thorough general index complete the coverage. This remarkable resource will be an important acquisition for the reference collections of public libraries, university libraries and high schools.

"Fills a need for handy, concise information on a wide array of international cultural figures."-ARBA

Two Volumes, Hardcover ISBN 978-1-59237-118-1, 900 pages, $195.00 | Ebook ISBN 978-1-59237-231-7
www.gale.com/gvrl/partners/grey.htm

Political Corruption in America: An Encyclopedia of Scandals, Power, and Greed

The complete scandal-filled history of American political corruption, focusing on the infamous people and cases, as well as society's electoral and judicial reactions. Since colonial times, there has been no shortage of politicians willing to take a bribe, skirt campaign finance laws, or act in their own interests. Corruption like the Whiskey Ring, Watergate, and Whitewater cases dominate American life, making political scandal a leading U.S. industry. From judges to senators, presidents to mayors, *Political Corruption in America* discusses the infamous people throughout history who have been accused of and implicated in crooked behavior. In this new second edition, more than 250 A–Z entries explore the people, crimes, investigations, and court cases behind 200 years of American political scandals. This unbiased volume also delves into the issues surrounding Koreagate, the Chinese campaign scandal, and other ethical lapses. Relevant statutes and terms, including the Independent Counsel Statute and impeachment as a tool of political punishment, are examined as well. Students, scholars, and other readers interested in American history, political science, and ethics will appreciate this survey of a wide range of corrupting influences. This title focuses on how politicians from all parties have fallen because of their greed and hubris, and how society has used electoral and judicial means against those who tested the accepted standards of political conduct. A full range of illustrations including political cartoons, photos of key figures such as Abe Fortas and Archibald Cox, graphs of presidential pardons, and tables showing the number of expulsions and censures in both the House and Senate round out the text. In addition, a comprehensive chronology of major political scandals in U.S. history from colonial times until the present. For further reading, an extensive bibliography lists sources including archival letters, newspapers, and private manuscript collections from the United States and Great Britain. With its comprehensive coverage of this interesting topic, *Political Corruption in America: An Encyclopedia of Scandals, Power, and Greed* will prove to be a useful addition to the reference collections of all public libraries, university libraries, history collections, political science collections and high schools.

"...this encyclopedia is a useful contribution to the field. Highly recommended." - CHOICE
"Political Corruption should be useful in most academic, high school, and public libraries." Booklist

Hardcover ISBN 978-1-59237-297-3, 500 pages, $135.00

Business Information ✦ Ratings Guides ✦ <u>General Reference</u> ✦ Education ✦ Statistics ✦ Demographics ✦ Health Information ✦ Canadian Information

Religion and Law: A Dictionary

This informative, easy-to-use reference work covers a wide range of legal issues that affect the roles of religion and law in American society. Extensive A–Z entries provide coverage of key court decisions, case studies, concepts, individuals, religious groups, organizations, and agencies shaping religion and law in today's society. This *Dictionary* focuses on topics involved with the constitutional theory and interpretation of religion and the law; terms providing a historical explanation of the ways in which America's ever increasing ethnic and religious diversity contributed to our current understanding of the mandates of the First and Fourteenth Amendments; terms and concepts describing the development of religion clause jurisprudence; an analytical examination of the distinct vocabulary used in this area of the law; the means by which American courts have attempted to balance religious liberty against other important individual and social interests in a wide variety of physical and regulatory environments, including the classroom, the workplace, the courtroom, religious group organization and structure, taxation, the clash of "secular" and "religious" values, and the relationship of the generalized idea of individual autonomy of the specific concept of religious liberty. Important legislation and legal cases affecting religion and society are thoroughly covered in this timely volume, including a detailed Table of Cases and Table of Statutes for more detailed research. A guide to further reading and an index are also included. This useful resource will be an important acquisition for the reference collections of all public libraries, university libraries, religion reference collections and high schools.

Hardcover ISBN 978-1-59237-298-0, 500 pages, $135.00

Conflict in Afghanistan: An Encyclopedia

A comprehensive A–Z study of the history of conflict in Afghanistan from 1747 to the present, which traces the evolution of conflict in Afghanistan, emphasizing the broad historical developments that have shaped current events. Rivalries, skirmishes, wars, and disputes have been part of Afghanistan's history from the formation of the country as a "unified" state in 1747 to the present. This volume considers all aspects of the history of conflict in Afghanistan during this period and thus enables the reader to fully comprehend the present situation. Conflict in Afghanistan provides the reader with a historical overview of hostilities in Afghanistan and discusses their causes, history, and impact on Afghan society and on regional and international relations. An invaluable introduction provides the reader with a clear historical overview of all aspects of conflicts in Afghanistan and their impact. A single A–Z section covers the three main eras in Afghanistan's history: the period from 1747, when Afghanistan first emerged as a "unified" state; the Soviet era (1979–1989), which saw the overthrow of the monarchy, the declaration of the Republic, and the rise of the Mujahideen; and the post-Soviet period, which brought civil war, the rise of the Taliban, and finally the events of September 11 and the War on Terrorism, both of which receive special attention. The text is complemented with over 40 illustrations, including the Buddha statues at Bamyan, Kabul; Afghanistan's difficult terrain; Taliban and Mujahideen fighters; and Soviet troops along with detailed maps, including the humanitarian situation in September 2001, provinces and major towns, ethnolinguistic groups in the area, and the border with Pakistan. Conflict in Afghanistan: An Encyclopedia provides essential background information which is of crucial importance to those wishing to gain a full understanding of the events of September 11 and the War on Terrorism. A must for all reference collections.

> *"Notable features include a lengthy historical narrative introduction, several useful maps, numerous pictures, an extensive chronology, abbreviations and acronyms, an extensive topical bibliography, websites, and a useful table of contents and index ... I recommend Conflict in Afghanistan."* - American Reference Books Annual

Hardcover ISBN 978-1-59237-296-6, 400 pages, $135.00

Human Rights in the United States: A Dictionary and Documents

This two volume set offers easy to grasp explanations of the basic concepts, laws, and case law in the field, with emphasis on human rights in the historical, political, and legal experience of the United States. Human rights is a term not fully understood by many Americans. Addressing this gap, the new second edition of *Human Rights in the United States: A Dictionary and Documents* offers a comprehensive introduction that places the history of human rights in the United States in an international context. It surveys the legal protection of human dignity in the United States, examines the sources of human rights norms, cites key legal cases, explains the role of international governmental and non-governmental organizations, and charts global, regional, and U.N. human rights measures. Over 240 dictionary entries of human rights terms are detailed—ranging from asylum and cultural relativism to hate crimes and torture. Each entry discusses the significance of the term, gives examples, and cites appropriate documents and court decisions. In addition, a Documents section is provided that contains 59 conventions, treaties, and protocols related to the most up to date international action on ethnic cleansing; freedom of expression and religion; violence against women; and much more. A bibliography, extensive glossary, and comprehensive index round out this indispensable volume. This comprehensive, timely volume is a must for large public libraries, university libraries and social science departments, along with high school libraries.

> *"...invaluable for anyone interested in human rights issues ... highly recommended for all reference collections."* - American Reference Books Annual

Two Volumes, Hardcover ISBN 978-1-59237-290-4, 750 pages, $225.00

The Comparative Guide to American Elementary & Secondary Schools, 2008

The only guide of its kind, this award winning compilation offers a snapshot profile of every public school district in the United States serving 1,500 or more students – more than 5,900 districts are covered. Organized alphabetically by district within state, each chapter begins with a Statistical Overview of the state. Each district listing includes contact information (name, address, phone number and web site) plus Grades Served, the Numbers of Students and Teachers and the Number of Regular, Special Education, Alternative and Vocational Schools in the district along with statistics on Student/Classroom Teacher Ratios, Drop Out Rates, Ethnicity, the Numbers of Librarians and Guidance Counselors and District Expenditures per student. As an added bonus, *The Comparative Guide to American Elementary and Secondary Schools* provides important ranking tables, both by state and nationally, for each data element. For easy navigation through this wealth of information, this handbook contains a useful City Index that lists all districts that operate schools within a city. These important comparative statistics are necessary for anyone considering relocation or doing comparative research on their own district and would be a perfect acquisition for any public library or school district library.

> *"This straightforward guide is an easy way to find general information.*
> *Valuable for academic and large public library collections." –ARBA*

Softcover ISBN 978-1-59237-223-2, 2,400 pages, $125.00 | Ebook ISBN 978-1-59237-238-6 www.gale.com/gvrl/partners/grey.htm

The Complete Learning Disabilities Directory, 2008

The Complete Learning Disabilities Directory is the most comprehensive database of Programs, Services, Curriculum Materials, Professional Meetings & Resources, Camps, Newsletters and Support Groups for teachers, students and families concerned with learning disabilities. This information-packed directory includes information about Associations & Organizations, Schools, Colleges & Testing Materials, Government Agencies, Legal Resources and much more. For quick, easy access to information, this directory contains four indexes: Entry Name Index, Subject Index and Geographic Index. With every passing year, the field of learning disabilities attracts more attention and the network of caring, committed and knowledgeable professionals grows every day. This directory is an invaluable research tool for these parents, students and professionals.

> *"Due to its wealth and depth of coverage, parents, teachers and others… should find this an invaluable resource." -Booklist*

Softcover ISBN 978-1-59237-207-2, 900 pages, $145.00 | Online Database $195.00 | Online Database & Directory Combo $280.00

Educators Resource Directory, 2007/08

Educators Resource Directory is a comprehensive resource that provides the educational professional with thousands of resources and statistical data for professional development. This directory saves hours of research time by providing immediate access to Associations & Organizations, Conferences & Trade Shows, Educational Research Centers, Employment Opportunities & Teaching Abroad, School Library Services, Scholarships, Financial Resources, Professional Consultants, Computer Software & Testing Resources and much more. Plus, this comprehensive directory also includes a section on Statistics and Rankings with over 100 tables, including statistics on Average Teacher Salaries, SAT/ACT scores, Revenues & Expenditures and more. These important statistics will allow the user to see how their school rates among others, make relocation decisions and so much more. For quick access to information, this directory contains four indexes: Entry & Publisher Index, Geographic Index, a Subject & Grade Index and Web Sites Index. *Educators Resource Directory* will be a well-used addition to the reference collection of any school district, education department or public library.

> *"Recommended for all collections that serve elementary and secondary school professionals." –Choice*

Softcover ISBN 978-1-59237-179-2, 800 pages, $145.00 | Online Database $195.00 | Online Database & Directory Combo $280.00

Business Information ✦ Ratings Guides ✦ General Reference ✦ Education ✦
Statistics ✦ **Demographics** ✦ Health Information ✦ Canadian Information

Grey House Publishing

Profiles of New York | Profiles of Florida | Profiles of Texas | Profiles of Illinois | Profiles of Michigan | Profiles of Ohio | Profiles of New Jersey | Profiles of Massachusetts | Profiles of Pennsylvania | Profiles of Wisconsin | Profiles of Connecticut & Rhode Island | Profiles of Indiana | Profiles of North Carolina & South Carolina | Profiles of Virginia | Profiles of California

The careful layout gives the user an easy-to-read snapshot of every single place and county in the state, from the biggest metropolis to the smallest unincorporated hamlet. The richness of each place or county profile is astounding in its depth, from history to weather, all packed in an easy-to-navigate, compact format. Each profile contains data on History, Geography, Climate, Population, Vital Statistics, Economy, Income, Taxes, Education, Housing, Health & Environment, Public Safety, Newspapers, Transportation, Presidential Election Results, Information Contacts and Chambers of Commerce. As an added bonus, there is a section on Selected Statistics, where data from the 100 largest towns and cities is arranged into easy-to-use charts. Each of 22 different data points has its own two-page spread with the cities listed in alpha order so researchers can easily compare and rank cities. A remarkable compilation that offers overviews and insights into each corner of the state, each volume goes beyond Census statistics, beyond metro area coverage, beyond the 100 best places to live. Drawn from official census information, other government statistics and original research, you will have at your fingertips data that's available nowhere else in one single source.

"The publisher claims that this is the 'most comprehensive portrait of the state of Florida ever published,' and this reviewer is inclined to believe it...Recommended. All levels." –Choice on Profiles of Florida

Each Profiles of… title ranges from 400-800 pages, priced at $149.00 each

America's Top-Rated Cities, 2007

America's Top-Rated Cities provides current, comprehensive statistical information and other essential data in one easy-to-use source on the 100 "top" cities that have been cited as the best for business and living in the U.S. This handbook allows readers to see, at a glance, a concise social, business, economic, demographic and environmental profile of each city, including brief evaluative comments. In addition to detailed data on Cost of Living, Finances, Real Estate, Education, Major Employers, Media, Crime and Climate, city reports now include Housing Vacancies, Tax Audits, Bankruptcy, Presidential Election Results and more. This outstanding source of information will be widely used in any reference collection.

"The only source of its kind that brings together all of this information into one easy-to-use source. It will be beneficial to many business and public libraries." –ARBA

Four Volumes, Softcover ISBN 978-1-59237-184-6, 2,500 pages, $195.00 | Ebook ISBN 978-1-59237-233-1
www.gale.com/gvrl/partners/grey.htm

America's Top-Rated Smaller Cities, 2006/07

A perfect companion to *America's Top-Rated Cities*, *America's Top-Rated Smaller Cities* provides current, comprehensive business and living profiles of smaller cities (population 25,000-99,999) that have been cited as the best for business and living in the United States. Sixty cities make up this 2004 edition of America's Top-Rated Smaller Cities, all are top-ranked by Population Growth, Median Income, Unemployment Rate and Crime Rate. City reports reflect the most current data available on a wide-range of statistics, including Employment & Earnings, Household Income, Unemployment Rate, Population Characteristics, Taxes, Cost of Living, Education, Health Care, Public Safety, Recreation, Media, Air & Water Quality and much more. Plus, each city report contains a Background of the City, and an Overview of the State Finances. *America's Top-Rated Smaller Cities* offers a reliable, one-stop source for statistical data that, before now, could only be found scattered in hundreds of sources. This volume is designed for a wide range of readers: individuals considering relocating a residence or business; professionals considering expanding their business or changing careers; general and market researchers; real estate consultants; human resource personnel; urban planners and investors.

"Provides current, comprehensive statistical information in one easy-to-use source… Recommended for public and academic libraries and specialized collections." –Library Journal

Two Volumes, Softcover ISBN 978-1-59237-135-8, 1,100 pages, $195.00 | Ebook ISBN 978-1-59237-234-8
www.gale.com/gvrl/partners/grey.htm

Profiles of America: Facts, Figures & Statistics for Every Populated Place in the United States

Profiles of America is the only source that pulls together, in one place, statistical, historical and descriptive information about every place in the United States in an easy-to-use format. This award winning reference set, now in its second edition, compiles statistics and data from over 20 different sources – the latest census information has been included along with more than nine brand new statistical topics. This Four-Volume Set details over 40,000 places, from the biggest metropolis to the smallest unincorporated hamlet, and provides statistical details and information on over 50 different topics including Geography, Climate, Population, Vital Statistics, Economy, Income, Taxes, Education, Housing, Health & Environment, Public Safety, Newspapers, Transportation, Presidential Election Results and Information Contacts or Chambers of Commerce. Profiles are arranged, for ease-of-use, by state and then by county. Each county begins with a County-Wide Overview and is followed by information for each Community in that particular county. The Community Profiles within the county are arranged alphabetically. *Profiles of America* is a virtual snapshot of America at your fingertips and a unique compilation of information that will be widely used in any reference collection.

A Library Journal Best Reference Book "An outstanding compilation." –Library Journal

Four Volumes, Softcover ISBN 978-1-891482-80-9, 10,000 pages, $595.00

To preview any of our Directories Risk-Free for 30 days, call (800) 562-2139 or fax (518) 789-0556
www.greyhouse.com books@greyhouse.com

Business Information ✦ Ratings Guides ✦ General Reference ✦ Education ✦
Statistics ✦ Demographics ✦ Health Information ✦ Canadian Information

The Comparative Guide to American Suburbs, 2007

The Comparative Guide to American Suburbs is a one-stop source for Statistics on the 2,000+ suburban communities surrounding the 50 largest metropolitan areas – their population characteristics, income levels, economy, school system and important data on how they compare to one another. Organized into 50 Metropolitan Area chapters, each chapter contains an overview of the Metropolitan Area, a detailed Map followed by a comprehensive Statistical Profile of each Suburban Community, including Contact Information, Physical Characteristics, Population Characteristics, Income, Economy, Unemployment Rate, Cost of Living, Education, Chambers of Commerce and more. Next, statistical data is sorted into Ranking Tables that rank the suburbs by twenty different criteria, including Population, Per Capita Income, Unemployment Rate, Crime Rate, Cost of Living and more. *The Comparative Guide to American Suburbs* is the best source for locating data on suburbs. Those looking to relocate, as well as those doing preliminary market research, will find this an invaluable timesaving resource.

> *"Public and academic libraries will find this compilation useful…The work draws together figures from many sources and will be especially helpful for job relocation decisions." – Booklist*

Softcover ISBN 978-1-59237-180-8, 1,700 pages, $130.00 | Ebook ISBN 978-1-59237-235-5 www.gale.com/gvrl/partners/grey.htm

The American Tally: Statistics & Comparative Rankings for U.S. Cities with Populations over 10,000

This important statistical handbook compiles, all in one place, comparative statistics on all U.S. cities and towns with a 10,000+ population. *The American Tally* provides statistical details on over 4,000 cities and towns and profiles how they compare with one another in Population Characteristics, Education, Language & Immigration, Income & Employment and Housing. Each section begins with an alphabetical listing of cities by state, allowing for quick access to both the statistics and relative rankings of any city. Next, the highest and lowest cities are listed in each statistic. These important, informative lists provide quick reference to which cities are at both extremes of the spectrum for each statistic. Unlike any other reference, *The American Tally* provides quick, easy access to comparative statistics – a must-have for any reference collection.

> *"A solid library reference." -Bookwatch*

Softcover ISBN 978-1-930956-29-2, 500 pages, $125.00 | Ebook ISBN 978-1-59237-241-6 www.gale.com/gvrl/partners/grey.htm

The Asian Databook: Statistics for all US Counties & Cities with Over 10,000 Population

This is the first-ever resource that compiles statistics and rankings on the US Asian population. *The Asian Databook* presents over 20 statistical data points for each city and county, arranged alphabetically by state, then alphabetically by place name. Data reported for each place includes Population, Languages Spoken at Home, Foreign-Born, Educational Attainment, Income Figures, Poverty Status, Homeownership, Home Values & Rent, and more. Next, in the Rankings Section, the top 75 places are listed for each data element. These easy-to-access ranking tables allow the user to quickly determine trends and population characteristics. This kind of comparative data can not be found elsewhere, in print or on the web, in a format that's as easy-to-use or more concise. A useful resource for those searching for demographics data, career search and relocation information and also for market research. With data ranging from Ancestry to Education, *The Asian Databook* presents a useful compilation of information that will be a much-needed resource in the reference collection of any public or academic library along with the marketing collection of any company whose primary focus in on the Asian population.

> *"This useful resource will help those searching for demographics data, and market research or relocation information… Accurate and clearly laid out, the publication is recommended for large public library and research collections." -Booklist*

Softcover ISBN 978-1-59237-044-3, 1,000 pages, $150.00

The Hispanic Databook: Statistics for all US Counties & Cities with Over 10,000 Population

Previously published by Toucan Valley Publications, this second edition has been completely updated with figures from the latest census and has been broadly expanded to include dozens of new data elements and a brand new Rankings section. The Hispanic population in the United States has increased over 42% in the last 10 years and accounts for 12.5% of the total US population. For ease-of-use, *The Hispanic Databook* presents over 20 statistical data points for each city and county, arranged alphabetically by state, then alphabetically by place name. Data reported for each place includes Population, Languages Spoken at Home, Foreign-Born, Educational Attainment, Income Figures, Poverty Status, Homeownership, Home Values & Rent, and more. Next, in the Rankings Section, the top 75 places are listed for each data element. These easy-to-access ranking tables allow the user to quickly determine trends and population characteristics. This kind of comparative data can not be found elsewhere, in print or on the web, in a format that's as easy-to-use or more concise. A useful resource for those searching for demographics data, career search and relocation information and also for market research. With data ranging from Ancestry to Education, *The Hispanic Databook* presents a useful compilation of information that will be a much-needed resource in the reference collection of any public or academic library along with the marketing collection of any company whose primary focus in on the Hispanic population.

> *"This accurate, clearly presented volume of selected Hispanic demographics is recommended for large public libraries and research collections."-Library Journal*

Softcover ISBN 978-1-59237-008-5, 1,000 pages, $150.00

Business Information ◆ Ratings Guides ◆ General Reference ◆ Education ◆
Statistics ◆ Demographics ◆ Health Information ◆ Canadian Information

Ancestry in America: A Comparative Guide to Over 200 Ethnic Backgrounds

This brand new reference work pulls together thousands of comparative statistics on the Ethnic Backgrounds of all populated places in the United States with populations over 10,000. Never before has this kind of information been reported in a single volume. Section One, Statistics by Place, is made up of a list of over 200 ancestry and race categories arranged alphabetically by each of the 5,000 different places with populations over 10,000. The population number of the ancestry group in that city or town is provided along with the percent that group represents of the total population. This informative city-by-city section allows the user to quickly and easily explore the ethnic makeup of all major population bases in the United States. Section Two, Comparative Rankings, contains three tables for each ethnicity and race. In the first table, the top 150 populated places are ranked by population number for that particular ancestry group, regardless of population. In the second table, the top 150 populated places are ranked by the percent of the total population for that ancestry group. In the third table, those top 150 populated places with 10,000 population are ranked by population number for each ancestry group. These easy-to-navigate tables allow users to see ancestry population patterns and make city-by-city comparisons as well. This brand new, information-packed resource will serve a wide-range or research requests for demographics, population characteristics, relocation information and much more. *Ancestry in America: A Comparative Guide to Over 200 Ethnic Backgrounds* will be an important acquisition to all reference collections.

"This compilation will serve a wide range of research requests for population characteristics … it offers much more detail than other sources." –Booklist

Softcover ISBN 978-1-59237-029-0, 1,500 pages, $225.00

Weather America, A Thirty-Year Summary of Statistical Weather Data and Rankings

This valuable resource provides extensive climatological data for over 4,000 National and Cooperative Weather Stations throughout the United States. Weather America begins with a new Major Storms section that details major storm events of the nation and a National Rankings section that details rankings for several data elements, such as Maximum Temperature and Precipitation. The main body of Weather America is organized into 50 state sections. Each section provides a Data Table on each Weather Station, organized alphabetically, that provides statistics on Maximum and Minimum Temperatures, Precipitation, Snowfall, Extreme Temperatures, Foggy Days, Humidity and more. State sections contain two brand new features in this edition – a City Index and a narrative Description of the climatic conditions of the state. Each section also includes a revised Map of the State that includes not only weather stations, but cities and towns.

"Best Reference Book of the Year." –Library Journal

Softcover ISBN 978-1-891482-29-8, 2,013 pages, $175.00 | Ebook ISBN 978-1-59237-237-9 www.gale.com/gvrl/partners/grey.htm

Crime in America's Top-Rated Cities

This volume includes over 20 years of crime statistics in all major crime categories: violent crimes, property crimes and total crime. *Crime in America's Top-Rated Cities* is conveniently arranged by city and covers 76 top-rated cities. Crime in America's Top-Rated Cities offers details that compare the number of crimes and crime rates for the city, suburbs and metro area along with national crime trends for violent, property and total crimes. Also, this handbook contains important information and statistics on Anti-Crime Programs, Crime Risk, Hate Crimes, Illegal Drugs, Law Enforcement, Correctional Facilities, Death Penalty Laws and much more. A much-needed resource for people who are relocating, business professionals, general researchers, the press, law enforcement officials and students of criminal justice.

"Data is easy to access and will save hours of searching." –Global Enforcement Review

Softcover ISBN 978-1-891482-84-7, 832 pages, $155.00

The Complete Directory for People with Disabilities, 2008

A wealth of information, now in one comprehensive sourcebook. Completely updated, this edition contains more information than ever before, including thousands of new entries and enhancements to existing entries and thousands of additional web sites and e-mail addresses. This up-to-date directory is the most comprehensive resource available for people with disabilities, detailing Independent Living Centers, Rehabilitation Facilities, State & Federal Agencies, Associations, Support Groups, Periodicals & Books, Assistive Devices, Employment & Education Programs, Camps and Travel Groups. Each year, more libraries, schools, colleges, hospitals, rehabilitation centers and individuals add *The Complete Directory for People with Disabilities* to their collections, making sure that this information is readily available to the families, individuals and professionals who can benefit most from the amazing wealth of resources cataloged here.

"No other reference tool exists to meet the special needs of the disabled in one convenient resource for information." –Library Journal

Softcover ISBN 978-1-59237-194-5, 1,200 pages, $165.00 | Online Database $215.00 | Online Database & Directory Combo $300.00

The Complete Learning Disabilities Directory, 2008

The Complete Learning Disabilities Directory is the most comprehensive database of Programs, Services, Curriculum Materials, Professional Meetings & Resources, Camps, Newsletters and Support Groups for teachers, students and families concerned with learning disabilities. This information-packed directory includes information about Associations & Organizations, Schools, Colleges & Testing Materials, Government Agencies, Legal Resources and much more. For quick, easy access to information, this directory contains four indexes: Entry Name Index, Subject Index and Geographic Index. With every passing year, the field of learning disabilities attracts more attention and the network of caring, committed and knowledgeable professionals grows every day. This directory is an invaluable research tool for these parents, students and professionals.

"Due to its wealth and depth of coverage, parents, teachers and others… should find this an invaluable resource." -Booklist

Softcover ISBN 978-1-59237-207-2, 900 pages, $145.00 | Online Database $195.00 | Online Database & Directory Combo $280.00

The Complete Directory for People with Chronic Illness, 2007/08

Thousands of hours of research have gone into this completely updated edition – several new chapters have been added along with thousands of new entries and enhancements to existing entries. Plus, each chronic illness chapter has been reviewed by a medical expert in the field. This widely-hailed directory is structured around the 90 most prevalent chronic illnesses – from Asthma to Cancer to Wilson's Disease – and provides a comprehensive overview of the support services and information resources available for people diagnosed with a chronic illness. Each chronic illness has its own chapter and contains a brief description in layman's language, followed by important resources for National & Local Organizations, State Agencies, Newsletters, Books & Periodicals, Libraries & Research Centers, Support Groups & Hotlines, Web Sites and much more. This directory is an important resource for health care professionals, the collections of hospital and health care libraries, as well as an invaluable tool for people with a chronic illness and their support network.

"A must purchase for all hospital and health care libraries and is strongly recommended for all public library reference departments." –ARBA

Softcover ISBN 978-1-59237-183-9, 1,200 pages, $165.00 | Online Database $215.00 | Online Database & Directory Combo $300.00

The Complete Mental Health Directory, 2008/09

This is the most comprehensive resource covering the field of behavioral health, with critical information for both the layman and the mental health professional. For the layman, this directory offers understandable descriptions of 25 Mental Health Disorders as well as detailed information on Associations, Media, Support Groups and Mental Health Facilities. For the professional, The Complete Mental Health Directory offers critical and comprehensive information on Managed Care Organizations, Information Systems, Government Agencies and Provider Organizations. This comprehensive volume of needed information will be widely used in any reference collection.

"… the strength of this directory is that it consolidates widely dispersed information into a single volume." –Booklist

Softcover ISBN 978-1-59237-285-0, 800 pages, $165.00 | Online Database $215.00 | Online & Directory Combo $300.00

To preview any of our Directories Risk-Free for 30 days, call (800) 562-2139 or fax (518) 789-0556
www.greyhouse.com books@greyhouse.com

Business Information ◆ Ratings Guides ◆ General Reference ◆ Education ◆
Statistics ◆ Demographics ◆ **Health Information** ◆ Canadian Information

Grey House Publishing

The Comparative Guide to American Hospitals, Second Edition

This new second edition compares all of the nation's hospitals by 24 measures of quality in the treatment of heart attack, heart failure, pneumonia, and, new to this edition, surgical procedures and pregnancy care. Plus, this second edition is now available in regional volumes, to make locating information about hospitals in your area quicker and easier than ever before. The Comparative Guide to American Hospitals provides a snapshot profile of each of the nations 4,200+ hospitals. These informative profiles illustrate how the hospital rates when providing 24 different treatments within four broad categories: Heart Attack Care, Heart Failure Care, Surgical Infection Prevention (NEW), and Pregnancy Care measures (NEW). Each profile includes the raw percentage for that hospital, the state average, the US average and data on the top hospital. For easy access to contact information, each profile includes the hospital's address, phone and fax numbers, email and web addresses, type and accreditation along with 5 top key administrations. These profiles will allow the user to quickly identify the quality of the hospital and have the necessary information at their fingertips to make contact with that hospital. Most importantly, *The Comparative Guide to American Hospitals* provides easy-to-use Regional State by State Statistical Summary Tables for each of the data elements to allow the user to quickly locate hospitals with the best level of service. Plus, a new 30-Day Mortality Chart, Glossary of Terms and Regional Hospital Profile Index make this a must-have source. This new, expanded edition will be a must for the reference collection at all public, medical and academic libraries.

"These data will help those with heart conditions and pneumonia make informed decisions about their healthcare and encourage hospitals to improve the quality of care they provide. Large medical, hospital, and public libraries are most likely to benefit from this weighty resource."-Library Journal

Four Volumes Softcover ISBN 978-1-59237-182-2, 3,500 pages, $325.00 | Regional Volumes $135.00 |
Ebook ISBN 978-1-59237-239-3 www.gale.com/gvrl/partners/grey.htm

Older Americans Information Directory, 2007

Completely updated for 2007, this sixth edition has been completely revised and now contains 1,000 new listings, over 8,000 updates to existing listings and over 3,000 brand new e-mail addresses and web sites. You'll find important resources for Older Americans including National, Regional, State & Local Organizations, Government Agencies, Research Centers, Libraries & Information Centers, Legal Resources, Discount Travel Information, Continuing Education Programs, Disability Aids & Assistive Devices, Health, Print Media and Electronic Media. Three indexes: Entry Index, Subject Index and Geographic Index make it easy to find just the right source of information. This comprehensive guide to resources for Older Americans will be a welcome addition to any reference collection.

"Highly recommended for academic, public, health science and consumer libraries..." –Choice

1,200 pages; Softcover ISBN 978-1-59237-136-5, $165.00 | Online Database $215.00 | Online Database & Directory Combo $300.00

The Complete Directory for Pediatric Disorders, 2008

This important directory provides parents and caregivers with information about Pediatric Conditions, Disorders, Diseases and Disabilities, including Blood Disorders, Bone & Spinal Disorders, Brain Defects & Abnormalities, Chromosomal Disorders, Congenital Heart Defects, Movement Disorders, Neuromuscular Disorders and Pediatric Tumors & Cancers. This carefully written directory offers: understandable Descriptions of 15 major bodily systems; Descriptions of more than 200 Disorders and a Resources Section, detailing National Agencies & Associations, State Associations, Online Services, Libraries & Resource Centers, Research Centers, Support Groups & Hotlines, Camps, Books and Periodicals. This resource will provide immediate access to information crucial to families and caregivers when coping with children's illnesses.

"Recommended for public and consumer health libraries." –Library Journal

Softcover ISBN 978-1-59237-150-1, 1,200 pages, $165.00 | Online Database $215.00 | Online Database & Directory Combo $300.00

The Directory of Drug & Alcohol Residential Rehabilitation Facilities

This brand new directory is the first-ever resource to bring together, all in one place, data on the thousands of drug and alcohol residential rehabilitation facilities in the United States. The Directory of Drug & Alcohol Residential Rehabilitation Facilities covers over 1,000 facilities, with detailed contact information for each one, including mailing address, phone and fax numbers, email addresses and web sites, mission statement, type of treatment programs, cost, average length of stay, numbers of residents and counselors, accreditation, insurance plans accepted, type of environment, religious affiliation, education components and much more. It also contains a helpful chapter on General Resources that provides contact information for Associations, Print & Electronic Media, Support Groups and Conferences. Multiple indexes allow the user to pinpoint the facilities that meet very specific criteria. This time-saving tool is what so many counselors, parents and medical professionals have been asking for. *The Directory of Drug & Alcohol Residential Rehabilitation Facilities* will be a helpful tool in locating the right source for treatment for a wide range of individuals. This comprehensive directory will be an important acquisition for all reference collections: public and academic libraries, case managers, social workers, state agencies and many more.

"This is an excellent, much needed directory that fills an important gap..." –Booklist

Softcover ISBN 978-1-59237-031-3, 300 pages, $135.00

To preview any of our Directories Risk-Free for 30 days, call (800) 562-2139 or fax (518) 789-0556
www.greyhouse.com books@greyhouse.com

Business Information ◆ Ratings Guides ◆ General Reference ◆ Education ◆
Statistics ◆ Demographics ◆ **Health Information** ◆ Canadian Information

The Directory of Hospital Personnel, 2008

The Directory of Hospital Personnel is the best resource you can have at your fingertips when researching or marketing a product or service to the hospital market. A "Who's Who" of the hospital universe, this directory puts you in touch with over 150,000 key decision-makers. With 100% verification of data you can rest assured that you will reach the right person with just one call. Every hospital in the U.S. is profiled, listed alphabetically by city within state. Plus, three easy-to-use, cross-referenced indexes put the facts at your fingertips faster and more easily than any other directory: Hospital Name Index, Bed Size Index and Personnel Index. *The Directory of Hospital Personnel* is the only complete source for key hospital decision-makers by name. Whether you want to define or restructure sales territories… locate hospitals with the purchasing power to accept your proposals… keep track of important contacts or colleagues… or find information on which insurance plans are accepted, *The Directory of Hospital Personnel* gives you the information you need – easily, efficiently, effectively and accurately.

"Recommended for college, university and medical libraries." -ARBA

Softcover ISBN 978-1-59237-286-7, 2,500 pages, $325.00 | Online Database $545.00 | Online Database & Directory Combo, $650.00

The Directory of Health Care Group Purchasing Organizations, 2008

This comprehensive directory provides the important data you need to get in touch with over 800 Group Purchasing Organizations. By providing in-depth information on this growing market and its members, *The Directory of Health Care Group Purchasing Organizations* fills a major need for the most accurate and comprehensive information on over 800 GPOs – Mailing Address, Phone & Fax Numbers, E-mail Addresses, Key Contacts, Purchasing Agents, Group Descriptions, Membership Categorization, Standard Vendor Proposal Requirements, Membership Fees & Terms, Expanded Services, Total Member Beds & Outpatient Visits represented and more. Five Indexes provide a number of ways to locate the right GPO: Alphabetical Index, Expanded Services Index, Organization Type Index, Geographic Index and Member Institution Index. With its comprehensive and detailed information on each purchasing organization, *The Directory of Health Care Group Purchasing Organizations* is the go-to source for anyone looking to target this market.

"The information is clearly arranged and easy to access…recommended for those needing this very specialized information." –ARBA

1,000 pages; Softcover ISBN 978-1-59237-287-4, $325.00 | Online Database, $650.00 | Online Database & Directory Combo, $750.00

The HMO/PPO Directory, 2008

The HMO/PPO Directory is a comprehensive source that provides detailed information about Health Maintenance Organizations and Preferred Provider Organizations nationwide. This comprehensive directory details more information about more managed health care organizations than ever before. Over 1,100 HMOs, PPOs, Medicare Advantage Plans and affiliated companies are listed, arranged alphabetically by state. Detailed listings include Key Contact Information, Prescription Drug Benefits, Enrollment, Geographical Areas served, Affiliated Physicians & Hospitals, Federal Qualifications, Status, Year Founded, Managed Care Partners, Employer References, Fees & Payment Information and more. Plus, five years of historical information is included related to Revenues, Net Income, Medical Loss Ratios, Membership Enrollment and Number of Patient Complaints. Five easy-to-use, cross-referenced indexes will put this vast array of information at your fingertips immediately: HMO Index, PPO Index, Other Providers Index, Personnel Index and Enrollment Index. *The HMO/PPO Directory* provides the most comprehensive data on the most companies available on the market place today.

"Helpful to individuals requesting certain HMO/PPO issues such as co-payment costs, subscription costs and patient complaints. Individuals concerned (or those with questions) about their insurance may find this text to be of use to them." -ARBA

Softcover ISBN 978-1-59237-204-1, 600 pages, $325.00 | Online Database, $495.00 | Online Database & Directory Combo, $600.00

Medical Device Register, 2008

The only one-stop resource of every medical supplier licensed to sell products in the US. This award-winning directory offers immediate access to over 13,000 companies - and more than 65,000 products – in two information-packed volumes. This comprehensive resource saves hours of time and trouble when searching for medical equipment and supplies and the manufacturers who provide them. Volume I: The Product Directory, provides essential information for purchasing or specifying medical supplies for every medical device, supply, and diagnostic available in the US. Listings provide FDA codes & Federal Procurement Eligibility, Contact information for every manufacturer of the product along with Prices and Product Specifications. Volume 2 - Supplier Profiles, offers the most complete and important data about Suppliers, Manufacturers and Distributors. Company Profiles detail the number of employees, ownership, method of distribution, sales volume, net income, key executives detailed contact information medical products the company supplies, plus the medical specialties they cover. Four indexes provide immediate access to this wealth of information: Keyword Index, Trade Name Index, Supplier Geographical Index and OEM (Original Equipment Manufacturer) Index. *Medical Device Register* is the only one-stop source for locating suppliers and products; looking for new manufacturers or hard-to-find medical devices; comparing products and companies; know who's selling what and who to buy from cost effectively. This directory has become the standard in its field and will be a welcome addition to the reference collection of any medical library, large public library, university library along with the collections that serve the medical community.

"A wealth of information on medical devices, medical device companies… and key personnel in the industry is provide in this comprehensive reference work... A valuable reference work, one of the best hardcopy compilations available." -Doody Publishing

Two Volumes, Hardcover ISBN 978-1-59237-206-5, 3,000 pages, $325.00

Business Information ◆ Ratings Guides ◆ General Reference ◆ Education ◆
Statistics ◆ Demographics ◆ Health Information ◆ **Canadian Information**

Canadian Almanac & Directory, 2008

The Canadian Almanac & Directory contains sixteen directories in one – giving you all the facts and figures you will ever need about Canada. No other single source provides users with the quality and depth of up-to-date information for all types of research. This national directory and guide gives you access to statistics, images and over 100,000 names and addresses for everything from Airlines to Zoos - updated every year. It's Ten Directories in One! Each section is a directory in itself, providing robust information on business and finance, communications, government, associations, arts and culture (museums, zoos, libraries, etc.), health, transportation, law, education, and more. Government information includes federal, provincial and territorial - and includes an easy-to-use quick index to find key information. A separate municipal government section includes every municipality in Canada, with full profiles of Canada's largest urban centers. A complete legal directory lists judges and judicial officials, court locations and law firms across the country. A wealth of general information, the *Canadian Almanac & Directory* also includes national statistics on population, employment, imports and exports, and more. National awards and honors are presented, along with forms of address, Commonwealth information and full color photos of Canadian symbols. Postal information, weights, measures, distances and other useful charts are also incorporated. Complete almanac information includes perpetual calendars, five-year holiday planners and astronomical information. Published continuously for 160 years, *The Canadian Almanac & Directory* is the best single reference source for business executives, managers and assistants; government and public affairs executives; lawyers; marketing, sales and advertising executives; researchers, editors and journalists.

Hardcover ISBN 978-1-59237-220-1, 1,600 pages, $315.00

Associations Canada, 2007

The Most Powerful Fact-Finder to Business, Trade, Professional and Consumer Organizations

Associations Canada covers Canadian organizations and international groups including industry, commercial and professional associations, registered charities, special interest and common interest organizations. This annually revised compendium provides detailed listings and abstracts for nearly 20,000 regional, national and international organizations. This popular volume provides the most comprehensive picture of Canada's non-profit sector. Detailed listings enable users to identify an organization's budget, founding date, scope of activity, licensing body, sources of funding, executive information, full address and complete contact information, just to name a few. Powerful indexes help researchers find information quickly and easily. The following indexes are included: subject, acronym, geographic, budget, executive name, conferences & conventions, mailing list, defunct and unreachable associations and registered charitable organizations. In addition to annual spending of over $1 billion on transportation and conventions alone, Canadian associations account for many millions more in pursuit of membership interests. *Associations Canada* provides complete access to this highly lucrative market. *Associations Canada* is a strong source of prospects for sales and marketing executives, tourism and convention officials, researchers, government officials - anyone who wants to locate non-profit interest groups and trade associations.

Hardcover ISBN 978-1-59237-219-5, 1,600 pages, $315.00

Financial Services Canada, 2007/08

Financial Services Canada is the only master file of current contacts and information that serves the needs of the entire financial services industry in Canada. With over 18,000 organizations and hard-to-find business information, Financial Services Canada is the most up-to-date source for names and contact numbers of industry professionals, senior executives, portfolio managers, financial advisors, agency bureaucrats and elected representatives. Financial Services Canada incorporates the latest changes in the industry to provide you with the most current details on each company, including: name, title, organization, telephone and fax numbers, e-mail and web addresses. *Financial Services Canada* also includes private company listings never before compiled, government agencies, association and consultant services - to ensure that you'll never miss a client or a contact. Current listings include: banks and branches, non-depository institutions, stock exchanges and brokers, investment management firms, insurance companies, major accounting and law firms, government agencies and financial associations. Powerful indexes assist researchers with locating the vital financial information they need. The following indexes are included: alphabetic, geographic, executive name, corporate web site/e-mail, government quick reference and subject. *Financial Services Canada* is a valuable resource for financial executives, bankers, financial planners, sales and marketing professionals, lawyers and chartered accountants, government officials, investment dealers, journalists, librarians and reference specialists.

Hardcover ISBN 978-1-59237-221-8, 900 pages, $315.00

Directory of Libraries in Canada, 2007/08

The Directory of Libraries in Canada brings together almost 7,000 listings including libraries and their branches, information resource centers, archives and library associations and learning centers. The directory offers complete and comprehensive information on Canadian libraries, resource centers, business information centers, professional associations, regional library systems, archives, library schools and library technical programs. *The Directory of Libraries in Canada* includes important features of each library and service, including library information; personnel details, including contact names and e-mail addresses; collection information; services available to users; acquisitions budgets; and computers and automated systems. Useful information on each library's electronic access is also included, such as Internet browser, connectivity and public Internet/CD-ROM/subscription database access. The directory also provides powerful indexes for subject, location, personal name and Web site/e-mail to assist researchers with locating the crucial information they need. *The Directory of Libraries in Canada* is a vital reference tool for publishers, advocacy groups, students, research institutions, computer hardware suppliers, and other diverse groups that provide products and services to this unique market.

Hardcover ISBN 978-1-59237-222-5, 850 pages, $315.00

Business Information ◆ Ratings Guides ◆ General Reference ◆ Education ◆
Statistics ◆ Demographics ◆ Health Information ◆ **Canadian Information**

Canadian Environmental Directory, 2007/08

The Canadian Environmental Directory is Canada's most complete and only national listing of environmental associations and organizations, government regulators and purchasing groups, product and service companies, special libraries, and more! The extensive Products and Services section provides detailed listings enabling users to identify the company name, address, phone, fax, e-mail, Web address, firm type, contact names (and titles), product and service information, affiliations, trade information, branch and affiliate data. The Government section gives you all the contact information you need at every government level – federal, provincial and municipal. We also include descriptions of current environmental initiatives, programs and agreements, names of environment-related acts administered by each ministry or department PLUS information and tips on who to contact and how to sell to governments in Canada. The Associations section provides complete contact information and a brief description of activities. Included are Canadian environmental organizations and international groups including industry, commercial and professional associations, registered charities, special interest and common interest organizations. All the Information you need about the Canadian environmental industry: directory of products and services, special libraries and resource, conferences, seminars and tradeshows, chronology of environmental events, law firms and major Canadian companies, *The Canadian Environmental Directory* is ideal for business, government, engineers and anyone conducting research on the environment.

Hardcover ISBN 978-1-59237-218-8, 900 pages, $315.00

Canadian Parliamentary Guide, 2008

An indispensable guide to government in Canada, the annual *Canadian Parliamentary Guide* provides information on both federal and provincial governments, courts, and their elected and appointed members. The Guide is completely bilingual, with each record appearing both in English and then in French. The Guide contains biographical sketches of members of the Governor General's Household, the Privy Council, members of Canadian legislatures (federal, including both the House of Commons and the Senate, provincial and territorial), members of the federal superior courts (Supreme, Federal, Federal Appeal, Court Martial Appeal and Tax Courts) and the senior staff for these institutions. Biographies cover personal data, political career, private career and contact information. In addition, the Guide provides descriptions of each of the institutions, including brief historical information in text and chart format and significant facts (i.e. number of members and their salaries). The Guide covers the results of all federal general elections and by-elections from Confederations to the present and the results of the most recent provincial elections. A complete name index rounds out the text, making information easy to find. No other resources presents a more up-to-date, more complete picture of Canadian government and her political leaders. A must-have resource for all Canadian reference collections.

Hardcover ISBN 978-1-59237-310-9, 800 pages, $184.00
